# TREES AND WOODLANDS OF SOUTH INDIA

## Archaeological Perspectives

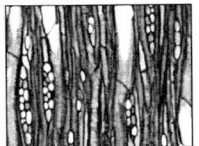

PUBLICATIONS OF THE INSTITUTE OF ARCHAEOLOGY, UNIVERSITY COLLEGE LONDON
Director of the Institute: Stephen Shennan
Founding Series Editor: Peter J. Ucko

The Institute of Archaeology of University College London is one of the oldest, largest, and most prestigious archaeology research facilities in the world. Its extensive publications programme includes the best theory, research, pedagogy, and reference materials in archaeology and cognate disciplines, through publishing exemplary work of scholars worldwide. Through its publications, the Institute brings together key areas of theoretical and substantive knowledge, improves archaeological practice, and brings archaeological findings to the general public, researchers, and practitioners. It also publishes staff research projects, site and survey reports, and conference proceedings. The publications programme, formerly developed in-house or in conjunction with UCL Press, is now produced in partnership with Left Coast Press, Inc. The Institute can be accessed online at www.ucl.ac.uk/archaeology.

*ENCOUNTERS WITH ANCIENT EGYPT Subseries, Peter J. Ucko, (ed.)*
Jean-Marcel Humbert and Clifford Price (eds.), Imhotep Today
David Jeffreys (ed.), Views of Ancient Egypt since Napoleon Bonaparte
Sally MacDonald and Michael Rice (eds.), Consuming Ancient Egypt
Roger Matthews and Cornelia Roemer (eds.), Ancient Perspectives on Egypt
David O'Connor and Andrew Reid (eds.), Ancient Egypt in Africa
John Tait (ed.), 'Never had the like occurred'
David O'Connor and Stephen Quirke (eds.), Mysterious Lands
Peter J. Ucko and Timothy Champion (eds.), The Wisdom of Egypt

*CRITICAL PERSPECTIVES ON CULTURAL HERITAGE Subseries, Beverley Butler (ed.)*
Beverley Butler, Return to Alexandria
Ferdinand de Jong and Michael Rowlands (eds.), Reclaiming Heritage
Dean Sully (ed.), Decolonizing Conservation

*OTHER TITLES*
Andrew Gardner (ed.), Agency Uncovered
Okasha El-Daly, Egyptology, The Missing Millennium
Ruth Mace, Clare J. Holden, and Stephen Shennan (eds.), Evolution of Cultural Diversity
Arkadiusz Marciniak, Placing Animals in the Neolithic
Robert Layton, Stephen Shennan, and Peter Stone (eds.), A Future for Archaeology
Joost Fontein, The Silence of Great Zimbabwe
Gabriele Puschnigg, Ceramics of the Merv Oasis
James Graham-Campbell and Gareth Williams (eds.), Silver Economy in the Viking Age
Barbara Bender, Sue Hamilton, and Chris Tilley, Stone World
Andrew Gardner, An Archaeology of Identity
Sue Hamilton, Ruth Whitehouse, and Katherine I. Wright (eds.), Archaeology and Women
Gustavo Politis, Nukak
Sue Colledge and James Conolly (eds.), The Origins and Spread of Domestic Plants in Southwest Asia and Europe
Timothy Clack and Marcus Brittain (eds.), Archaeology and the Media
Janet Picton, Stephen Quirke, and Paul C. Roberts (eds.), Living Images
Tony Waldron, Paleoepidemiology
Eleni Asouti and Dorian Q. Fuller, Trees and Woodlands of South India. Archaeological Perspectives
Russell McDougall and Iain Davidson (eds.), The Roth Family, Anthropology, and Colonial Administration
Elizabeth Pye (ed.), The Power of Touch
John Tait, Why the Egyptians Wrote Books

# TREES AND WOODLANDS OF SOUTH INDIA
## Archaeological Perspectives

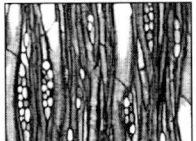

Eleni Asouti
Dorian Q. Fuller

Walnut Creek, California

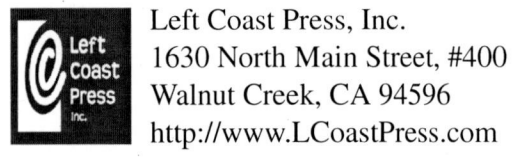
Left Coast Press, Inc.
1630 North Main Street, #400
Walnut Creek, CA 94596
http://www.LCoastPress.com

Copyright © 2008 by Left Coast Press, Inc.

*All rights reserved.* No part of this publication may be reproduced, stored in a retrieval system, or transmitted in any form or by any means, electronic, mechanical, photocopying, recording, or otherwise, without the prior permission of the publisher.

**Library of Congress Cataloging-in-Publication Data**

Asouti, Eleni.
Trees and woodlands of south India: archaeological perspectives / Eleni Asouti, Dorian Q. Fuller.
    p. cm. -- (Publications of the Institute of Archaeology, University College)
Includes bibliographical references and index.
ISBN-I3: 978-1-59874-231-2 (hardback: alk. paper)
  1. Forest plants--India. 2. Plant remains (Archaeology)--India. 3. Landscape archaeology--India. 4. Forest archaeology--India. I. Fuller, Dorian Q. II. Title.

QK358.A86 2007        578.730954--dc22        2007018758

Printed in the United States of America

♾™ The paper used in this publication meets the minimum requirements of American National Standard for Information Sciences--Permanence of Paper for Printed Library Materials, ANSI/NISO Z39.48–1992.

08 09 10 11    5 4 3 2 1

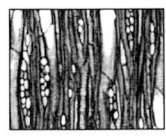

# CONTENTS

LIST OF ILLUSTRATIONS 6

ACKNOWLEDGMENTS 8

| | | |
|---|---|---|
| Chapter 1 | Producing South Indian Landscapes: The Intersection of Climate, Landforms, Economies, and Environmental History | 9 |
| Chapter 2 | Indian Forest Ecology and the Politics of Landscape Management | 15 |
| Chapter 3 | Background to Vegetation History: Climate, Geology, and Cultural History | 29 |
| Chapter 4 | South Indian Woodland Vegetation: Its Composition, Structure, and Dynamics | 45 |
| Chapter 5 | An Abridged Environmental History of South India | 71 |
| Chapter 6 | Autecology and Ethnobotany of South Indian Trees and Shrubs | 89 |
| Chapter 7 | Wood Identification and Charcoal Analysis: A Contribution to the Study of Ancient Vegetation and Past Economies in South India | 121 |
| Chapter 8 | Wood Identification Key and Anatomical Characters | 137 |
| Chapter 9 | Wood Anatomical Descriptions | 145 |

BIBLIOGRAPHY 293

LIST OF PLANT SPECIES WITH DETAILS ON BOTANICAL AUTHORITIES 309

TAXONOMIC INDEX 321

INDEX 337

ABOUT THE AUTHORS 343

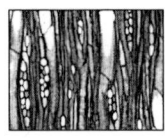

# LIST OF ILLUSTRATIONS

## Figures

| | | |
|---|---|---|
| Figure 2.1 | Generalised vegetation zones of the Indian peninsula following Champion (1936) | 18 |
| Figure 2.2 | Modern distribution of woodland vegetation in the subcontinent, including closed canopy vegetation and scrub | 21 |
| Figure 2.3 | Example of small village shrine situated within a fruit tree grove dedicated to local deities | 23 |
| Figure 2.4 | Forest shrine in Tamil Nadu | 24 |
| Figure 2.5 | Roadside tree shrine in Tamil Nadu | 24 |
| Figure 2.6 | Well-wishing tree at a roadside shrine in Tamil Nadu | 24 |
| Figure 3.1 | Topographic relief and major rivers of the Indian peninsula | 30 |
| Figure 3.2 | Topography and modern administrative boundaries in South India | 31 |
| Figure 3.3 | Average annual rainfall values in South Asia | 32 |
| Figure 3.4 | Geological zones of South India | 34 |
| Figure 3.5 | Distribution of Neolithic and Chalcolithic sites in the Indian peninsula | 37 |
| Figure 3.6 | Overview of the granite hillocks of the Kupgal area | 38 |
| Figure 3.7 | A spectacular example of the varied topography and sculpture of granite hilltops in South India | 38 |
| Figure 3.8 | Granite hills representing naturally raised and "fortified" areas | 39 |
| Figure 3.9 | Ashmounds formed through the seasonal/periodic burning of heaped cattle dung in cattle penning areas | 40 |
| Figure 4.1 | Peninsular vegetation zones | 46 |
| Figure 4.2 | Western Ghats tropical wet evergreen forest | 47 |
| Figure 4.3 | Aerial roots of *Ficus benghalensis* (Tamil Nadu) | 48 |
| Figure 4.4 | Western Ghats moist deciduous woodland dominated by *Terminalia* | 50 |
| Figure 4.5 | *Anogeissus* tree with crooked bole growing alongside teak seedlings in grassland-dominated gap inside dry deciduous woodland | 53 |
| Figure 4.6 | General view of Sandur hills dry deciduous forest | 53 |
| Figure 4.7 | *Terminalia*-dominated dry deciduous woodland | 55 |
| Figure 4.8 | Sandalwood tree in the Sandur forest | 56 |
| Figure 4.9 | Dry riverine *Acacia* woodland-savanna (Tamil Nadu) | 60 |
| Figure 4.10 | *Acacia* scrub-savanna (Tamil Nadu) | 61 |
| Figure 4.11 | "Jungle" thorn-scrub (Tamil Nadu) | 61 |
| Figure 4.12 | *Acacia* savanna grassland (Kurnool area) | 62 |
| Figure 4.13 | *Acacia* savanna grassland (Kurnool area) | 62 |
| Figure 5.1 | Map showing the geographical distribution of the palaeoecological datasets discussed in this chapter | 72 |
| Figure 5.2 | Comparison of selected pollen spectra from the Indian Ocean: MD 76135, including oxygen isotope data | 75 |
| Figure 5.3 | Selected pollen spectra from the Nilgiri and Palni hills | 77 |
| Figure 5.4 | Correlation between various palaeoclimatic proxies from northwestern South Asia | 78 |
| Figure 5.5 | Calibration model of the radiocarbon dates of the Thar desert pollen zones | 80 |
| Figure 5.6 | Didwana pollen diagram with revised calibrated radiocarbon dates | 80 |
| Figure 5.7 | Pollen spectra from the Dongar Sanbar swamp in Madhya Pradesh | 84 |

| | | |
|---|---|---|
| Figure 5.8 | Summary pollen diagram together with spore, C-13 isotope and dinoflagellate values | 85 |
| Figure 7.1 | The structure of wood: schematic three-dimensional outline of the anatomy of conifers & dicotyledons | 123 |
| Figure 7.2 | The axial and radial systems of wood tissue | 127 |
| Figure 7.3 | Detailed vegetation map of South India | 130 |
| Figure 7.4 | Scanning Electron Microscope (SEM) microphotographs of charcoals from the Southern Neolithic sites of Hallur (*Anogeissus* - top row and bottom to the left) and Sanganakallu (*Strychnos* - bottom row to the right) | 134 |
| Figure 7.5 | Scanning Electron Microscope (SEM) microphotographs of sandalwood charcoals from the site of Sanganakallu | 135 |

## Tables

| | | |
|---|---|---|
| Table 3.1 | Conventional chronological scheme for the Southern Neolithic | 36 |
| Table 3.2 | A revised chronological framework for the Southern Neolithic and subsequent periods | 41 |
| Table 4.1 | Select Western Ghats tropical wet evergreen species | 49 |
| Table 4.2 | Select tropical moist deciduous species | 51 |
| Table 4.3 | Select dry deciduous species: The *Terminalia-Anogeissus-Tectona* association | 54 |
| Table 4.4 | Select dry deciduous species: The *Anogeissus-Hardwickia* association | 55 |
| Table 4.5 | Important edible fruits of the dry deciduous zone | 57 |
| Table 4.6 | Indigenous millet cultivars of peninsular India | 58 |
| Table 4.7 | Moist deciduous riverine forest | 59 |
| Table 4.8 | Dry deciduous riverine forest | 60 |
| Table 4.9 | Dry evergreen scrub | 63 |
| Table 4.10 | Thorn savannas of the northern Deccan (*Acacia-Capparis* zone) | 64 |
| Table 4.11 | Light, shade, and drought tolerance of select South Indian tree and shrub species | 65 |
| Table 4.12 | Fire and grazing tolerance of select South Indian plant species | 66 |

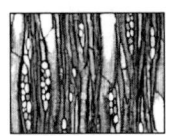

# ACKNOWLEDGMENTS

So many people became involved in the writing of this book, from the research stage to its final production, that trying to mention all of them by name is an enormous task. We would like to express our gratitude to the British Academy for supporting (through a Reckitt Travelling Fellowship) EA's first fieldwork season in South India in 2002, when much of the vegetation data presented in this volume were gathered, especially to Dr. Ken Emond for his patience and advice for the duration of the fellowship. The Leverhulme Trust has generously supported our long-term project on the origins of agriculture in South India.

In India, we owe our gratitude to our long-term collaborator, Prof. Ravi Korisettar of the Department of Archaeology, University of Karnataka, Dharwad, for his help, material and moral support, and his intellectual contribution to our research effort for many years. Our research in Tamil Nadu has been facilitated by Prof. K. Rajan of the Department of Archaeology, Tamil University, Thanjavur. EA is grateful to a number of colleagues in India for their advice and assistance during fieldwork, especially Dr. S.T. Naik, Department of Forestry Protection, Forestry College, University of Agricultural Sciences, Karnataka; Dr. S. Aruchamy, School of Earth Sciences, Bharathidasan, Tiruchirappalli; Dr. Subash C. Hiremath, Department of Botany, University of Karnataka, Dharwad; Dr. Mukund D. Kajale, Department of Archaeology, Deccan College, Pune; Dr. P. Daniel, Director of the Botanical Survey of India, Coimbatore, Tamil Nadu. EA would also like to express her thanks to three exceptional individuals without whose practical assistance, generous help, and patience very little would have been achieved in the field: Dr. Gangadhar M. Doddamani, Mr Girish N. Patil, and Mr Kalyan Malagyannavar. DF would like to thank the officers of the Botanical Survey of India, who provided assistance when he conducted a survey of the wild progenitors of the Indian pulses at the Central National Herbarium, Howrah (West Bengal), Dr. H. J. Chowdhury, and Dr. P. Venkateswara of the Western Circle Herbarium, Pune (Maharashtra), Dr. P. S. N. Rao, and Dr. Paramjit Singh of the publications office in Calcutta.

From the Institute of Archaeology, UCL, we are indebted to Prof. Stephen Shennan, Prof. David Harris, and Dr. Sue Colledge for their advice and feedback during the planning stage of the project, to Ms Sandra Bond for facilitating laboratory research and microscopy, and to Mr Stuart Laidlaw for his contribution to the preparation of the wood anatomy illustrations presented in Chapters 8 and 9. The late Prof. Peter Ucko supported our research in South India from its early stages and followed closely the production of this volume through to its publication.

We dedicate this book to all our colleagues in India and the United Kingdom who have worked over the years for the advancement of archaeological science in the subcontinent. First and foremost, however, we remain obliged to the numerous individuals of the local communities we visited and worked together in the field, without whose endurance, sense of humour, and laborious work our research would not have borne results. This volume is the product of their labour as much as ours.

*Eleni Asouti*
*Dorian Q. Fuller*

# CHAPTER 1

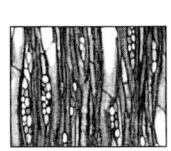

# PRODUCING SOUTH INDIAN LANDSCAPES: THE INTERSECTION OF CLIMATE, LANDFORMS, ECONOMIES AND ENVIRONMENTAL HISTORY

There are very few ecological systems in the world today where the influence of man can be disregarded; if there is no apparent influence (and this in itself is rare), there often has been in the past. Even man's activities in what we regard as the remote past may have left a mark still recognizable today . . . Archaeology in many parts of the world is contributing to a growing understanding of man's inextricable relationship to show that his evolution has been closely bound up with the environment and for much of this time has had the power to modify his habitat, though perhaps not always intentionally. (Dimbleby 1977:1)

The environment that one encounters today is largely a human artefact undergoing constant modification. It is shaped through activities of maintenance such as the planting and harvesting of crops, the channelling of watercourses and the building of terraces, the clearance and burning of woodland, and the grazing of domestic animals. It is also affected by climatic (for example, seasonally fluctuating rainfall, temperature, and daylength) and biological cycles (for instance, plant and animal reproduction and migration). The environment represents a dynamic intersection of similar processes of change occurring at variable temporal and spatial scales. Annual fluctuations in rainfall are averaged against the general climate stability that is perceived during a human generation or even an individual's lifetime. The dry evergreen tropical woodlands of Central India do not turn in the space of a single year into tundra or sand deserts. At the same time, however, while the environment might appear as a given, a backdrop to the throb of the life of human and other animal communities, in reality it is not.

Over the past few thousand years, climate has changed, followed by dramatic changes in the earth's biosphere. In the Indian peninsula, tropical rainforests have expanded and contracted, thus allowing for the migration of plant species through lengthy processes of vegetation dieback, growth, and dispersal. The traces of such changes can be still seen today in the discontinuous geographical distributions of a number of plant species between southwest and northeast India, and in the occurrence of related species in far removed areas (for example, between the Himalayas and Southeast Asia). The sand dunes of Gujarat and Rajasthan, formerly a part of arid bare deserts, today support a vegetation rich in shrubs and grasses. Human activities such as the expansion of agriculture and the extraction from the landscape of mineral and forest resources, alongside the knock-on effects of soil erosion, have further modified the environment. This dynamic history of environmental change in the subcontinent remains to this day little understood, especially regarding South India. It is a complex history of climate shifts, the variable responses of plant and animal populations, and the changing strategies, motivations, and economies of human societies. The present volume represents a small beginning in the larger enterprise of understanding the environmental and landscape history of peninsular India through the deployment of analytical tools offered by environmental archaeology and palaeoecology.

## SOUTH INDIAN ENVIRONMENTAL HISTORY: PERSPECTIVES AND ISSUES

How the environment of South India has come to be what it is today and in what ways the evolution of the local landscapes has contributed to the unfolding of the regional cultural history are issues that remain poorly documented. With regard to recent centuries, historians have contributed much detail from the investigation of written sources (Flint 1998; Mann 1999; Rangarajan 1996, 1998; Skaria 1999; Sivaramakrishnan 1999:Chapter 2; Subash Chandran 1997). For the time span corresponding to the colonial and immediately precolonial periods, written sources are few (cf. Das 1969: 105–15; Guha S. 1999). For the prehistoric and early historic periods, they are practically nonexistent. For these periods, environmental history has been written based on conjectural accounts constructed by plant ecologists and geographers and the few and of uneven quality palaeoenvironmental records provided by climatic proxies such as pollen and stable isotopes (for example, Caratini et al. 1994; Erdosy 1998:Chapter 5; Meher-Homji 1989, 2001, 2002).

The conjectural history of plant geography is subtly encoded in the classification of vegetation into different zones of so-called climax plant communities, themselves the product of climate change and human impact through deforestation, grazing, and the replacement of the natural ecosystems by managed landscapes. The potential distribution and spatial extent of natural vegetation are defined and mapped on the basis of relict vegetation patches that may persist at present as small islands in a sea of anthropogenic landscapes. However, such assumptions about the nature of vegetation change and its relationship to human impact need to be questioned and should always be assessed against the palaeoenvironmental record (Chapter 2). One issue that is particularly pertinent in this regard is the status and the distribution of grasslands. How 'natural' or anthropogenic are the savanna grasslands of peninsular India? Conventional plant geography saw Indian savannas, like grasslands elsewhere in the world, as artefacts of Neolithic and post-Neolithic economic activities in which agriculture, grazing, and the exploitation of natural resources by sedentary human communities converted forests and woodlands into grasslands or denuded deserts (for instance, Bor 1960:31–33; Meher-Homji 1989; Misra 1983; Polunin 1960:444; Puri 1960:247; Spate and Learmonth 1967:73–74; Whyte 1964). Yet, in this respect, it is equally important to question the extent to which presumed 'climax' vegetation formations (for example, the teak, sal, and mango forests) might also be a product of the dynamics of human activities rather than the inevitable outcome of climate change. To appreciate better the complex relationship among climate, soils, culture, and vegetation in the Indian peninsula, we have prefaced our discussion of vegetation ecology with a concise description of the climate, geology, and cultural history of South India (Chapter 3).

While we must be cautious not to reify our concepts and abstract categorizations of the regional landscapes, we nevertheless need a framework of operational categories in order to render ecological analysis possible. The geographical patterning of vegetation is a reality that has been observed, recorded, and classified accordingly by foresters, botanists, ecologists, and bioclimatologists. Although we argue that present-day vegetation formations represent, to varying degrees, the conflated effects of physical constraints (climate, topography, and soils) and human activities, at the same time they offer a basic framework against which we can assess new botanical data and which (when used judiciously) can assist in the interpretation of the palaeobotanical record. In addition, systems of vegetation classification can provide us with a useful starting point for making sense of the vast plant diversity encountered in South India. The established vegetation zones of South India (wet evergreen, moist deciduous and dry deciduous forest, savanna, and scrub woodland) are described in detail in Chapter 4. The chapter concludes with a brief consideration of a number of external factors that may limit and/or promote the development of individual plant species such as water and light availability and their level of resistance to fire and grazing pressures. Some understanding of species autecology is also required. Although relatively few South Indian plant species have been studied in such detail, we have compiled in Chapter 6 all the available information on the habitat preferences and the geographical distribution of individual species, as well as data on their cultural uses retrieved from sources of ethnobotanical information.

The effects of global and regional climate change on past vegetation may be reconstructed from the investigation of palaeoecological evidence such as the ancient pollen rain deposited in stratified lake sediments and deep-sea beds. The datasets from which we can obtain evidence on past climate change and its effects on the vegetation of peninsular India are synthesised in Chapter 5, with particular emphasis on the last 10,000 years corresponding to the Holocene. These datasets have their own limitations, since they often provide records of low temporal and spatial resolution, on a coarse regional scale not directly tied to the timescales of human activities and the archaeological record. Therefore, the incorporation of the material residues of people-vegetation interactions in the past, such as the remains of wood charcoal preserved from the use of wood as fuel, building, and craft material, is an essential step for achieving a more complete understanding of the environmental history of the region. It follows that archaeobotanical evidence should be seen as complementary to datasets made available through off-site pollen analysis and other palaeoclimatic proxy records. Such archaeobotanical remains include the plant residues left by human activities on ancient habitation sites and comprise mainly seeds providing information on plant foods and fodder, cultivation practices, and agricultural systems (Fuller 2002, 2003a) and, predominantly, the remains of the fuel (wood, dung) that fed the hearths used to cook food, heat homes, and provided shelter from the elements. Fuel remains constitute a prime source of information for examining how the environs of a given habitation site were used, which species of trees and shrubs grew in nearby forests and woodlands, and how human communities interfered with and managed past vegetation (Asouti and Austin 2005). Chapter 7 presents a concise account of the history, methodology, aims, and scope of the analysis of wood charcoal macroremains from archaeological sites, together with a summary of its applications in India and elsewhere in the world, and a description of the methodologies and rationale involved in the compilation of modern wood reference material to be used in archaeobotanical research of this kind. Finally, a key for the botanical identification and the detailed anatomical descriptions of selected South Indian trees and shrubs has been included in Chapters 8 and 9 respectively.

## ENVIRONMENTAL ARCHAEOLOGY AND LANDSCAPE CHANGE: TOWARDS AN INTEGRATED LANDSCAPE HISTORY

In recent years, it has become increasingly clear that archaeology has much to contribute to the study of global environmental change by providing crucial evidence about ancient human impact on the landscape and the responses of past societies to climate change (McIntosh et al. 2000; Redman 1999; van der Leeuw and Redman 2002). As environmentalist political agendas have championed policies promoting (implicitly or explicitly) a return to a 'natural' state of affairs, it has become increasingly evident from the investigation of the archaeological and palaeoecological record that we have a very limited understanding of what 'natural' (that is, devoid of extensive human influence) environments might be like, given that most terrestrial ecosystems worldwide have developed for many thousands of years in close association with human management practices (Redman 1999; Simmons 1996). Such a close interrelation between human activities and environmental processes was explicitly recognised more than fifty years ago by Carl Sauer (1947, 25), who described the proliferation of edible seed-bearing annuals, tubers, and fruit-producing trees as a 'new symbiosis between plants and men'. It becomes evident therefore that the co-determination of human economies and vegetation ecology may be more far-reaching than is usually appreciated. Consequently, the history of landscapes and environmental change can be understood only through a long-term perspective of vegetation dynamics (past and present) and the geographical distribution of vegetation communities, as well as their multiple interactions with human economies.

While collaborative research efforts between plant ecologists and archaeologists are well underway in parts of North America and Europe, a similar framework has been so far little developed in South Asia, a region that encompasses several unique vegetation and wildlife habitats that figure prominently among those most directly threatened by unregulated economic development at a global scale. It is towards the establishment of an archaeological contribution of this kind, an *environmental archaeology* of prehistoric South India, where this volume aspires to make a worthwhile contribution. Ultimately, such an archaeological and palaeoenvironmental perspective should be in a position to promote an enhanced understanding of the environmental and cultural geography of South India, thus providing a sound empirical basis for the interpretation of vegetation change (past and present) and its temporal and spatial dynamics.

Woodlands and savannas are essential to understanding the history of human economies in prehistoric South India, especially with regard to the beginnings and development of crop cultivation and later large-scale agriculture. They formed the preferred habitats for some of the annual plants (pulses, millets) collected by hunter-gatherers, which were to be transformed into domesticated crops in the Neolithic period (Fuller and Korisettar 2004; Fuller et al. 2004). Other crop species and livestock were introduced to South India from elsewhere as part of the diverse economic strategies pursued by prehistoric societies. In turn, if early cultivation practices were characterised by the production of subsistence foods over short timescales (or single growing seasons), later agricultural systems were geared toward the production of nonstaple items, such as tree fruits or plant fibres for textiles, which became important trade commodities and consumption luxuries. Their cultivation required a very different pattern of land use, extending over much longer time scales and representing true delayed-return economies with production targets being projected to years and even decades instead of the annual cycle required for the cultivation of subsistence crops. Through environmental archaeology, we can reach an empirically informed understanding of the origins and historical development of such economic practices and their relation to socioeconomic and environmental change.

At present, much of peninsular India can be described as a sea of agricultural fields interspersed with islands of scrub and woodland. Permanent human settlements, towns and villages, are distributed fairly evenly across the subcontinent. Around each habitation hotspot, routine cycles of resource exploitation involving agriculture, livestock transhumance, and the collection of forest products determine the shape and structure of the local landscapes. More distant resources are obtained through a dense network of roads that connect towns and villages. Along these communication routes and between villages are found patches of forest, woodland and scrub, with forests often being confined to hillslopes (such as most of the officially reserved and state-protected forests). Park and scrub woodlands are recurrently grazed by herds of sheep, goat, and cattle and are also heavily exploited for fuel. Other tree products such as fruits, medicinal plants, resins and honey are obtained from these forests, their exploitation often being a subsistence task reserved for the so-called tribal communities. As a result of the dense habitation network, forested areas are far more limited than cultivated fields. At the onset of the Neolithic, some 4,000 years ago, South Indian landscapes probably bore many similarities to those of the present day, albeit at a very different scale. Woodlands and grasslands were grazed mainly by wild fauna and less so by the cattle herds of early pastoralists. In the plains and on granite hilltops, smaller settlements and hamlets with cultivated fields nearby formed permanent features of the landscape. In their seasonal paths of movement, pastoralists and their cattle herds marked their passage by the periodic burning of heaped cattle dung accumulated on customary penning sites, thus resulting in the creation of ashmounds as permanent markers in the landscape. Prior to the Neolithic, South Indian landscapes would have been perhaps even more alien to present-day experience, lacking as they did the signs of sedentary human occupation and planted fields. However, they are likely to have been subjected to periodic burning by groups of hunter-gatherers, in order to attract game through enhancing grassland growth and regeneration. 'The ecological map of South Asia was strikingly different than the one we know today' (Rangarajan 2001:9). It is through environmental archaeology, the backbone of this volume, that such differences between the past and the present can begin to be reconstructed and properly appreciated in their local and regional cultural and environmental contexts.

# CHAPTER 2

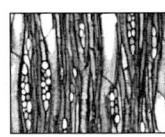

# INDIAN FOREST ECOLOGY AND THE POLITICS OF LANDSCAPE MANAGEMENT

One of the widespread misconceptions about Indian vegetation ecology is that the potential vegetation of the peninsula consists primarily of closed canopy forest. According to this popular view, India was once covered by continuous forests that in time gave way to grasslands, deserts, parklike woodlands (savannas), scrub, and swamps as a result of human impact (through woodcutting, grazing, clearance for cultivation, and so on). Such perceptions of Indian forest ecology represent a product of the history of colonial science in India and have been based mainly on two concepts, both equally problematic in defining what constitutes 'forest' and what 'climax' vegetation. In the Indian context, these concepts gained popularity arising from the fact that they expressed European tendencies of romanticising alien untamed landscapes (thus also implying early concerns about landscape conservation). Furthermore, they offered a veneer of scientific respectability to commercial forestry practices that aimed at maintaining high net productivity in timber outputs. The result of their application has been the development of a system of vegetation classification that remains to this day the principle means for describing and evaluating the arboreal vegetation of the peninsula. In this chapter, we briefly highlight the historical, scientific, and sociopolitical background of such ecological concepts in India. In so doing, we do not seek to discredit formal vegetation classification systems but instead emphasise their status primarily as heuristic devices and tools for the study of present vegetation. As such, they are open to improvement through the contributions of palaeoecology and environmental archaeology, thus contributing to the construction of a credible long-term landscape history of the Indian peninsula.

## ROMANTICISING THE FOREST, REPLACING THE JUNGLE

India was once a large subcontinental forest – or so the available ecological literature would lead us to believe. Statements to this effect are commonplace among scientists, environmentalists, historians, and archaeologists who have written on the environmental history of the subcontinent. To take one example:

> Authorities generally agree that the original vegetative cover for the subcontinent was largely arboreal . . . Because of intensive human interference in the forest lands, the floral landscape has been drastically changed over the centuries. In places all traces of the original forest have disappeared, especially in the heavily inhabited plains areas. (Fairservis 1971:16)

Among botanists we find similar opinions:

> Historically the entire Indian subcontinent should have been under the cover of woody vegetation, but today only about 20 percent of the land area is regarded as forest land, which shows the extent of forest clearing. (Pemadasa 1990:398)

Although the truth of such statements has been contradicted by palaeobotanical and other palaeoecological evidence (a point to which we shall return later on), it is interesting to examine here the ideas and the intellectual background on which such concepts have been based. We can begin with the concept of 'forest'. Many Indian ecologists have applied to their studies a quite restrictive definition of what constitutes forest vegetation, inspired mainly by ecological work performed in temperate environments:

> Forest is a group or stand of trees in a closed canopy. (Puri 1960:1)

Although such a definition may be applicable to the temperate forests of northern Europe and parts of northern America, or the rainforests of the wet tropics (including in our region tracts of eastern and northeast India as well as the Western Ghats), it cannot and should not be applied to all tree and shrub vegetation found worldwide, including peninsular India. Such an association between closed-canopy forests and the so-called primeval landscapes that predated the presumed catastrophic effects of culture owes a lot to the ecological thinking of a diverse group of authors including such intellectuals as Alexander von Humboldt and the American poet-scientist Henry David Thoreau (see Bowler 1992:205–08, 318–23; Schama 1995:226–39, 571–78; Worster 1985). Within this perspective were also included notions of the (human) loss of innocence and the degradation of the utopian, original natural Eden. Of course, such concepts were not projected exclusively onto India. As discussed in detail by Grove and Rackham (2001:8–16), a number of European writers and thinkers from the Renaissance onwards, and especially during the Enlightenment, promoted the theory of the 'ruined landscape', according to which human populations and their activities (particularly pastoralism) played the most decisive role in degrading and destroying the primeval vegetation of the continent, a process mostly evident in the Mediterranean (see also Anker 2001:218–23). Feeding into such views were also the observations of European colonial traders and travellers who, upon their visits to the tropics, especially to islands, noticed that the arrival of humans and their plant and animal domesticates had often led to local animal and plant extinctions, massive deforestation, and major hydrological changes (Grove 1995, 1998a). Closer to Europe, other examples of such thinking are the early opinions expressed by ecologists that the British Isles too had once been entirely forested, and it was only after the arrival of humans, 'the natural and inevitable enemy of the tree-communities', that 'true' forests (wildwoods) largely disappeared (Tansley 1911:66; see also Anker 2001:13–22).

The very use of the term 'forest' is not altogether free of bias. As discussed in detail by Rackham (1986:129ff.; also Pyne 1997:176), the English word 'forest' originally represented a legal term, referring to those areas of land that were reserved under the authority and protected by the ownership of the crown and other elite institutions. During the Norman period, forests were reserved for royal deer hunting. At the same time, forests did not necessarily comprise dense and continuous stands of trees and shrubs but included instead various kinds of woodland whose legal status as forests was assured by the fact that they were inaccessible to local communities. Similarly, in Germany, all oak trees growing on private and public land alike became the property of the crown as 'forest lands' in the 1850s (Schama 1995:115). In South Asia, the medieval Mughal rulers appropriated woodlands as hunting reserves. Post-Mughal states also claimed sovereignty over woodlands, especially since the commercial value of timber, particularly teak, became more and more appreciated (Grove 1995:387–99; Stebbing 1922:35).

In the context of modern India, the official use of the term 'forest' in association with 'reserved forests' or 'state forests' bears many similarities to its traditional medieval English usage, in that these forests in reality include open vegetation that is protected and centrally managed. As is the case with Mediterranean environments, 'forest' in the ecological sense (that is, a tree vegetation cover of variable structure and density) actually forms part of the 'natural' landscape (see Grove and Rackham 2001). The same holds true for much of South India, already from the time of the earliest human habitation of the peninsula (Chapters 6, 7).

Such an understanding of Indian forests as valuable yet diverse vegetation communities represents a reversal of a recurrent theme in Indian landscape history expressed in the concept of taming the 'savage' jungle. 'Jungle' is yet another English term based on the Hindi/Marathi word *jangal* that originally denoted the uncultivated wasteland but which eventually came to represent 'a forest; a thicket; a tangled wilderness' (Yule and Burnell 1886:470). In addition, 'jungles' were invariably associated with human groups who lived on the margins of society, hence representing a perceived threat to law and order. The jungle tribes became identified with the individuals or groups who inhabited the overgrown woodland wastelands and forested hills trying to escape from state officials. As discussed by Guha (1999), from the first millennium C.E. through the colonial period state authorities took an active interest in encouraging the clearance of uncultivated woodlands, in order to create new revenue from settled agriculturalists and to remove the hiding places of state enemies, rebels, criminals, and the untaxed. Overall, the available historical evidence indicates a constant interchange between periods of woodland expansion in times of political conflict and deforestation in times of peace and political stability. The British colonial attitude towards jungles was initially formed along similar lines, viewing them as untamed vegetation to be either removed or brought under management and, thus, become 'civilised' (Guha 1999:130– 49;Rangarajan 1996:10–19; Sivaramakrishnan 1999:34ff.). During the eighteenth and the early nineteenth centuries, the British colonial administration encouraged woodland clearance and the settling of farmers in forest sites. Local groups, invariably described as 'tribes' (sometimes even 'criminal tribes', see Gordon 1994:151–62), who until then lived in the forests and often followed less sedentary lifestyles (for example, practicing shifting cultivation), were regarded with a mixture of suspicion and contempt as 'savages' threatening state order and failing to contribute to the generation of revenue. Thus, when forests finally came under official state control in British India during the late nineteenth century, the event marked a watershed in patterns of land use and forest management in the peninsula and the beginning of state-enforced restrictions on the movements and subsistence activities of the indigenous groups inhabiting forest lands.

## PROGRESS, 'CLIMAX' VEGETATION AND THE EMPIRE

Another problematic but rarely questioned ecological concept is that of 'climax' vegetation. The application of this concept to the study of South Indian vegetation dates back to the first comprehensive vegetation survey of the peninsula by Harry G. Champion (see Figure 2.1). His seminal work titled 'Preliminary Survey of the Forest Types of India and Burma' (1936) mapped the potential natural vegetation of the entire peninsula, adding to and refining earlier attempts to delineate the geographical distribution of Indian vegetation (Hooker 1904; Stebbing 1922:39–58). Champion's work drew heavily on the theory of plant succession and 'climax' plant communities originally formulated by the Danish botanist Warming (1909), which was promoted in Britain by Arthur Tansley (1911) and theoretically refined by the American botanist Frederic Clements (1916). This approach drew on the continental European tradition of plant geography that began with Alexander von Humboldt at the beginning of the nineteenth century (see Bowler 1992:370–78; Rajan 1998; Worster 1985:133–35, 191–220) and on the then new science of ecology as it came to be defined through debates and scholarship at the heart of the empire, in Britain.

The scientific definition of what constitutes a 'climax' plant community needs to be viewed in the historical context of the emergence of the science of ecology, linking notions of social responsibility to the efficient economic management of the British empire. In turn, the historical roots of modern ecology can be traced back to the practices followed by British foresters and naturalists of the late eighteenth and early nineteenth centuries, and the academic development of biological sciences in British universities, especially in the early twentieth century. As detailed by Grove (1995, 1998b), during the late eighteenth and early nineteenth centuries in many of the colonies maintained by European powers amateur naturalists (frequently trained physicians) began to raise concerns about the conservation of local forests arising from their preoccupation with health issues, recurrent famines, and human-induced climate change that appeared to be linked to deforestation. In India, scientific botany and the first systematic collection of climate records, especially of rainfall and weather conditions, was similarly instigated by company surgeons. William Roxburgh, the second director

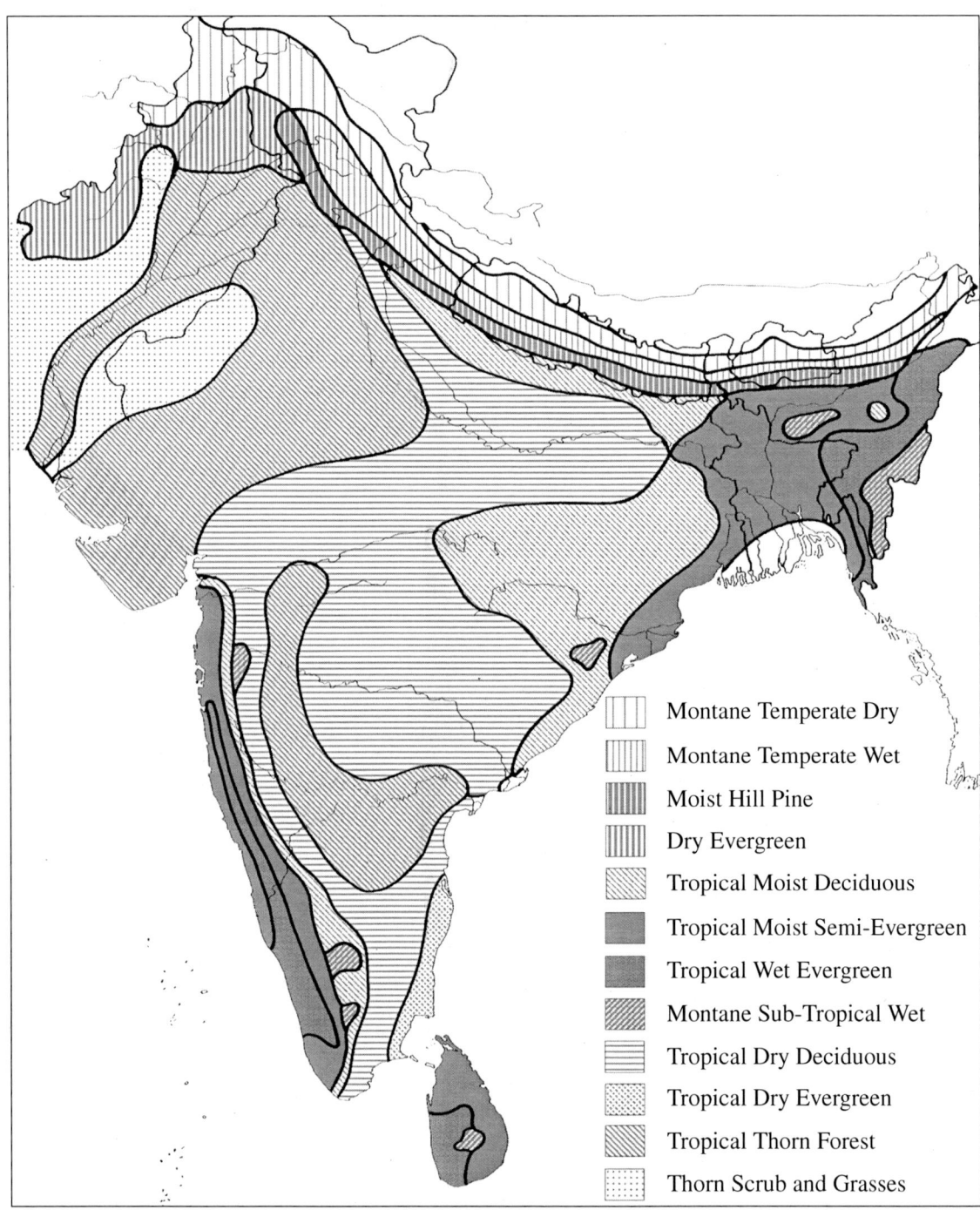

Figure 2.1. Generalised vegetation zones of the Indian peninsula following Champion (1936)

of the Botanical Gardens at Calcutta, whose posthumously published *Flora Indica* (1832) was the first systematic flora of the subcontinent, kept regular weather records and compiled detailed accounts of local famines in his attempt to demonstrate a correlation between drought years and famine events. Drawing from his studies, he argued for the need to undertake extensive tree planting in order to induce rainfall increases and thus assist the proliferation of agricultural production (Grove 1998b:128–37). Roxburgh, like Hugh Cleghorn who served as the Conservator of Madras forests between 1858 and 1867, was a typical representative of a dispersed network of colonial surgeon-naturalists who advocated intensive forest management and tree-planting as a prime imperial responsibility, aiming at securing the production of staple foods across the subcontinent.

The combination of such arguments with views about the importance of managing forests as an indispensable source of commercial timber led to the establishment by colonial administrators of official posts for foresters whose main task was the management and systematic study of local forests. Initially, Indian forestry drew heavily on the traditions and experience of continental Europe (Rajan 1998), but over time it began to build up a detailed local knowledge of Indian trees and woodland habitats (Stebbing 1922, 1923, 1926).

The other important strand in the development of formal vegetation classification systems was the emergence of ecology as a distinct scientific endeavour within British universities. This process began during the later part of the nineteenth century, at a time when biology gradually emerged as a professional rather than a personal, amateur pursuit (Bowler 1992:314). The development of university botany coincided with a vigorous interest in plant ecology, morphology and physiology. The term 'ecology' was codified in its modern form by the International Botanical Congress of 1893 (Bowler 1992:365–66). Ecological studies expanded dramatically in the early twentieth century (through the 1920s and 1930s). However, precisely what the aims of the study of plant ecology should be remained contentious, with two schools of thought prevailing in Britain. One focused on the study of plant morphology and physiology as adaptations to the environment and the other on the ordering and classification of plant communities as geographical and bioclimatic entities.

The morphological/physiological approach, generally regarded as the more conservative of the two, was initially formulated in Scotland by the eminent scientist Isaac Balfour, who espoused the Linnean tradition of systematic botany. A different approach to the study of plant communities as integrated systems was developed in London and Cambridge by the renowned botanist Arthur G. Tansley, who had been schooled in a progressive liberal social tradition that viewed science as a means to cure social ills (Anker 2001:8–13; Godwin 1977:15). Tansley's studies of plant communities gained centre stage in Britain during the 1920s, emphasising the analysis of the functions of integrated communities and drawing intellectual inspiration (at least in part) from Freudian social psychology (Anker 2001:23–31; Godwin 1977:14). Tansley eventually became professor of botany at Oxford, by that time already an important centre for the training of foresters who later worked in India. The tradition of morphological and physiological studies was carried on during the 1920s and 1930s by botanists based in South Africa under the intellectual patronage of General Jan Christian Smuts. General Smuts advocated a so-called holistic philosophy, according to which organisms acquired and subsequently adapted their biological forms in order to achieve optimal fit to their environments (Anker 2001:41–75). Both branches of ecology claimed to represent the scientific approach most appropriate to serve the interests of the British empire, and both had their followers among ecologists and botanists working in colonial India. Following 'holistic' theories, plants, animals, and humans were understood primarily as organisms adapted to the environment, the moral principle thus being that they ought to be conserved and managed through a mixture of beneficiary charitable attitude and informed practice. Such a moral compass served to justify the perception of British imperial administrators as the knowledgeable guardians and managers of woodlands and indigenous people alike. Regarding vegetation ecology, holism was consonant with Clements's notion of the 'monoclimax' (that is, the final evolutionary stage of a plant community living in equilibrium with its environment in which the different plant succession stages should eventually culminate). As a representative of the functionalist school and of a decisively different political persuasion, Tansley became increasingly critical of such concepts preferring instead to view vegetation environments as an assortment of 'climax' and non-'climax' plant communities at different succession stages that formed as a result of more or less accidental associations among species reacting individually to variable environmental conditions. Tansley's approach understood human activities as active ingredients in vegetation change and stability, in clear contrast to the Clementsian succession theories that considered human actors as wholly disruptive of the natural process (Worster 1985:239–42; also Tansley 1920, 1946: 21–26, 45–53). Tansley pursued an intellectual and political agenda asserting the role of ecological research and its practical application as an integral part of a social strategy aiming at the betterment of the human condition across the territories of the British empire (Anker 2001:80). He thus took an active interest in documenting the history of human impact on vegetation (for example, Tansley 1949), including palaeoecological evidence deriving from the then newly established field of pollen analysis, as well as the study of wood charcoal macro-remains from archaeological sites (Chapter 7).

Such differences in intellectual orientation are evident in the writings of various forest officers of that era. A number of forestry experts working in India had been trained in Oxford, where Robert Troup became director of the School of Forestry in 1920 (Anker 2001:249) after his return from India, where he had been Chief Silviculturalist at the Forest Research Institute at Dehra Dun (see Champion and Osmaston 1962: 49) and the author of the three-volume series *Silviculture of Indian Trees* (1921). As an Oxford professor he was a close associate of Tansley, promoting active forest protection and management (Anker 2001:81–82). It was within this context of intense preoccupation with issues of productive forest management and woodland conservation that studies of woodland formation and succession developed in India. The impact of such ecological thinking on botanical fieldwork can be seen, for example, in floristic studies. Earlier floras such as those authored by Roxburgh (1832), Hooker (1875–1897) and Cooke (1903–1908) provided only brief descriptions of the geographical distribution of individual species, whereas later works such as those of Talbot (1909–1912), Haines (1921–1928), Gamble (1921, 1935) and Fischer (1928), all of whom had served as colonial forest officers, included assessments of forest and species habitats, with explicit references to soil types and vegetation classifications such as the differentiation between tropical wet evergreen and moist deciduous forests.

## 'CLIMAX' AND SOCIAL EVOLUTION: THE COMPARATIVE METHOD

At the same time that the 'climax' vegetation formations of India were increasingly delineated and defined, a conjectural history of Indian vegetation and human economies was also constructed. Unlike Tansley's attempts to integrate historical records and quaternary science evidence for producing an empirically grounded ecological history of the British Isles, no such datasets were available for the Indian peninsula. Stebbing (1922:17–33) had tried to establish an historical framework for the development of human economies in parallel with environmental history (Chapter 3). For the most part, such efforts were framed by the belief in the existence of a primeval 'climax' vegetation that had gradually degraded as a result of human-induced deforestation, in a process that eventually resulted in forest destruction and its replacement by non-'climax' woodland and grassland formations. The amount of hypothetical reconstruction involved in the forest maps of Champion (1936) becomes clearer when they are compared to other maps showing the actual spatial extent of the vegetation classified as forest (Figures 2.1, 2.2). The inevitable conclusion is that the rather patchy distribution of the extant woodland vegetation (even if one allows for its greater extent during the nineteenth and early twentieth centuries) and its correlation with recent climate records for each region formed the basis for the virtual 'reforestation' of the entire subcontinent.

Within this intellectual and ecological-political context, grasslands were invariably viewed as a prime example of the destructive nature of human activities. Most grasslands worldwide, with the notable exception of the American prairies, were regarded as subclimaxes prevented from reaching an optimal wooded state by biotic (for example, grazing ungulates) and anthropogenic factors (for instance, clearance) or, alternatively, as the result of poor soil substrata (for example, Walter 1971:240). The latter were often attributed to the effects of soil erosion brought about by human activities (namely deforestation). It is under this perspective that arguments between botanists over the ecological status of grasslands in various parts of the world must be viewed, with the majority of opinion accepting very few natural grasslands (for instance, Flenley 1979:10; Netting 1974:26; Polunin 1960:444; Walter 1971:239). One such example in the peninsula is the case of the grasslands of the Nilgiri and the Palni hills (also known as *shola* grasslands), which were

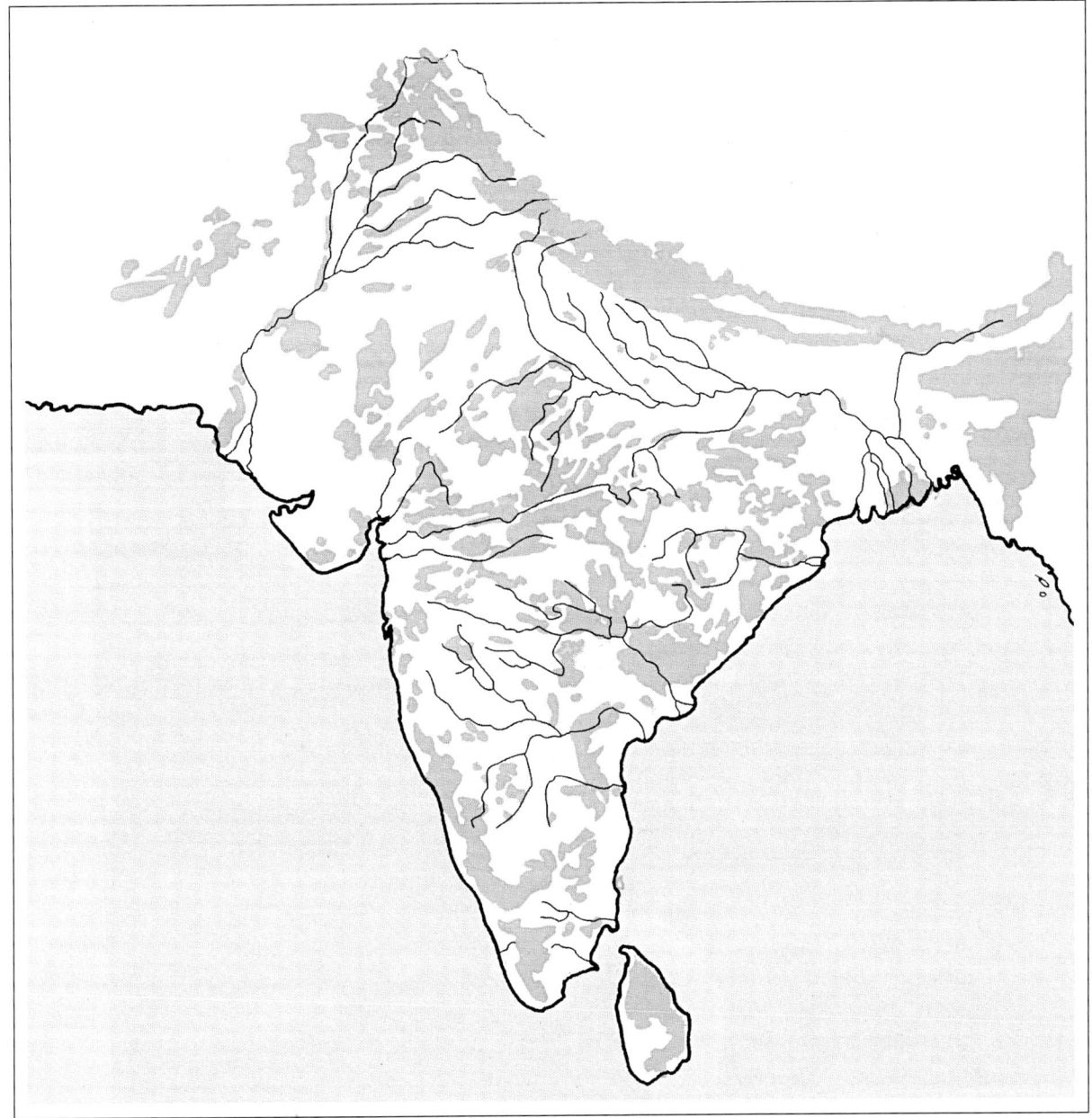

Figure 2.2. Modern distribution of woodland vegetation in the subcontinent, including closed canopy vegetation and scrub

often considered as anthropogenic. However, palynological work undertaken at the end of the 1960s established that these were in existence already from the Pleistocene and thus could not be attributed to human-induced forest degradation (Vishnu-Mittre and Sharma 1973; Chapter 5).

World vegetation maps usually depict the potential vegetation on the plains of the subcontinent as 'monsoon' or deciduous forest, while the predominant vegetation type of open woodland and/or grassland is regarded as anthropogenic. Deciduous woodland itself is considered by some authors as a degraded form of moist deciduous tropical forests (Puri 1960:198). Savannas were 'degenerated from deciduous forests by their maltreatment and anthropogenic ravages in due course of time' (Singh 1988:69). The grasslands of the peninsula were further characterised as 'inferior to the temperate grasslands and suffer considerably from the monsoon nature of the climate' (Puri 1960:271).

Such ideas were in the majority of cases not based on scientific research as such but rather on a tendency (imported from Europe) towards the idealisation of landscapes and nature at large, and overestimating the influence of climate on vegetation. In much the same way as Roxburgh in the late eighteenth century had believed that climate possesses a 'virtue' that can affect social health and moral economy (Grove 1995:399–408), the holistic ecologists of the early twentieth century believed that the development of human cultures was conditioned by the perceived ecological functions of human societies (Anker 2001:157–91). Indeed, John William Bews, who had been a student of Balfour and went on to become professor of botany in South Africa and scientific associate of General Smuts, linked explicitly human evolutionary history and plant ecology in his book *Human Ecology* (1935). In this text, he described plant succession under the dominant influence of climate as an evolutionary path towards the desired end result of a 'climax' plant community. He compared the latter to the origins of human ethnic, economic and racial differentiation as a consequence of climatic determinism and inbreeding, leading to the emergence of human communities that are optimally adapted to their environs. Conceptualising plant (and human) ecology as a gradually evolving harmonious whole eventually provided the basis for a paternalistic attitude towards nature conservation and the efficient management of physically segregated 'inferior' human groups. In effect, a conjectural (and overtly racist) history of human societies could thus be written by using virtually identical analytical tools with those employed by vegetation science and ecology.

The concept of a climatically determined 'climax' plant community has been repeatedly criticised over the years, on both theoretical and empirical grounds (for example, Blumler 1996; Connell and Slayter 1977; Flenley 1979:101ff.; Grove and Rackham 2001:15–16; McIntosh 1987; Sauer 1952; Stone and Ezrati 1996; Watt 1947). Its main weakness lies in the assumption of a timeless cycle and, at the same time, a pattern of linear direction and progress in ecological change (thus unifying the recurrent metaphors of time's arrow and cycle; see Gould 1987 for a discussion of such metaphors in the context of geology). According to the famous critique of Carl Sauer (1952:15), 'Final and stable' communities are quite exceptional in nature ... Change is in the order of nature: climax assumes an end of change'. The fundamental problem with the notion of climax plant ecosystems is therefore its innate assumption of an optimal or 'equilibrium' state that is periodically intercepted by episodes of human and/or natural disturbance. However, such theoretical positions have been in decline for sometime in ecology, owing mainly to the increasing accumulation of empirical evidence demonstrating the prevalence of non-equilibrium processes and the formulation of various models of dynamic vegetation change by theoretical ecologists (see Blumler 1996; Botkin 1990; Huggett 1995; McIntosh 1987; Sinton 1993; Stone and Ezrati 1996; Urban et al. 1987; Zimmerer 1994).

The essentially ahistorical nature of the 'climax' community concept becomes more evident when one scrutinises the methodologies used to construct such theoretical models, which parallel to some extent those adopted by evolutionary biology and anthropology. Much of the research on plant succession worked by comparing the floristic composition and structure of different patches of vegetation in the same geographical region (or those subject to the same climatic conditions), and producing abstract and largely idealised sequences of vegetation succession. The main assumption has been that vegetation zonation (for example, from grassland to scrub to woodland) in effect represents a continuum of different developmental and succession stages (Flenley 1979:101). In a similar vein, social variation across human societies was used to construct idealised stages of social development. One could argue, with some justification, that such parallels between vegetation classification and the evolution of human societies are also implicit in the choice of descriptive terms such as 'plant societies' (adopted by Clements) or again 'phytosociology' (frequently encountered in European botany; for instance, Braun-Blanquet 1932). Tansley had made abundantly clear the ways in which he used such terminology, as a kind of analogy to explain how vegetation types might be better understood:

> A human community, like a plant community, consists of separate individuals with independent powers of existence, growth and reproduction. But taken together these individuals make a new whole, a unit of higher

order, with its own structure and functions depending on the definite inter-relationships of the individuals composing it. (Tansley 1920:123)

By contrast, the 'holistic' approach of plant succession explicitly compared the evolution of vegetation communities and human societies by affirming the belief that they are affected by similar processes:

Succession has been less clearly perceived in human communities, though everywhere prevalent in prehistoric and ancient times. (Clements 1949 [1935]:9)

Another criticism often levelled against the theories of climate-induced plant succession has stemmed from empirical observations that human activities may actually be implicated in the shaping of forest types otherwise regarded by ecological orthodoxy as ancient 'climax' plant communities. In India, for example, many of the peninsular hill forests include large proportions of fruit-bearing trees. It has been proposed that this phenomenon may reflect a history of selective preservation and/or propagation of such species by human groups (Legris and Meher-Homji 1977). Indeed, pollen evidence from Rajasthan as well as Madhya Pradesh has indicated that certain economically useful species became very prominent in local vegetation only towards the end of the mid-Holocene including the *mahua* of Central India (*Madhuca indica*), and *Prosopis* and *Capparis* in Rajasthan (Chapter 5). The increased presence of these species at the expense of others that are equally well-adapted to the same habitats and climate conditions strongly suggests that human agency might have played an important role in affecting and determining woodland composition. Even for presently dominant timber species such as teak (*Tectona grandis*) and sal (*Shorea robusta*), it is increasingly recognised that they have responded positively to habitat expansion opportunities created by human activities through burning, grazing, and clearance as well as the intentional planting of seedlings in more recent times (see Flint 1998; Pyne 1994, 1997:472–74; Rangarajan 1998:587; Sivaramakrishnan 1999:211–35; Skaria 1999:49–50). The planting of fruit species has also influenced woodland composition in the wet evergreen tropical forests of the Western Ghats, particularly the ancient sacred groves in which local forest and village deities are believed to reside (Gadgil and Vartak 1976; Subash Chandran 1998; Uchiyamada 1998) (this reflects, of course, the very widespread belief in Hindu traditions that local deities inhabit woodlands and even individual trees and localities; see Figures 2.3 to 2.6). Even though the structure and floristic composition of these sacred groves are the intentional result of traditional woodland management practices (aimed at enhancing the availability of forest products such as black pepper, cinnamon, edible fruits, and flowers) they are nevertheless often cited in ecological publications as the last remaining fragments of the primeval 'climax' vegetation:

A rich network of sacred groves once covered all India, and Dietrich Brandis, the first Inspector-General of Forests, was already lamenting the destruction of much of this network under the British system of forest management by the 1880s (Brandis 1884). But remnants of this network still exist and are today *the very last representatives of the climax vegetation* in areas such as the Maharashtra Western Ghats. (Gadgil and Guha 1995:91, emphasis added)

Figure 2.3. Example of small village shrine situated within a fruit tree grove dedicated to local deities

Figure 2.4. Forest shrine in Tamil Nadu

Figure 2.5. Roadside tree shrine in Tamil Nadu

Figure 2.6. Well-wishing tree at a roadside shrine in Tamil Nadu

While no one can deny the importance of sacred groves in India from the point of view of conserving biodiversity (Gadgil and Guha 1992, 1995), their example nevertheless underlines the futility of any attempt to factor humans out of environmental and vegetation history. Indeed there have been few, if any, uninhabited forests in South Asia during prehistoric and historic times alike. Humans, among other animals, have always interacted, utilised and (to variable degrees) influenced woodland composition and structure through their activities in the landscape. Just as a credible history of human societies and social organisation needs to be approached through historical and archaeological work rather than untested ethnographically derived typologies, an empirically informed history of plant communities and their temporal changes requires the contribution of palaeobotanical and archaeobotanical evidence alongside a theoretical and analytical framework that emphasises the dynamic nature of ecological processes.

## PREDICTIVE SCIENCE, FORESTRY, AND SOCIAL CONTROL

Another reason for the initial popularity of the plant succession theories was their promise of straightforward comprehension and control of nature through human planning, a concept very much akin to that of scientific prediction:

> The plant cover on the ground is an epitome of past events and future possibilities, and the outcome of its manipulation by man, intentional or otherwise, can be predicted with much definiteness. (Clements 1949:11)

It was this promise of being able to predict accurately timber yields and make provision for the sustained exploitation of grazing lands (particularly in the context of colonial and postcolonial scientific forestry) that was mostly responsible for the wide-spread application of Clements' succession theory in Indian vegetation studies (for example, Champion 1936; Puri 1960; Whyte 1964). From the very beginning of scientific forestry in India, in the mid-nineteenth century, forest experts trained in the French and German traditions such as Brandis, the Inspector-General of forests in British India from 1865, were recruited to establish work practices aimed at maximising timber yields for the demands of commercial export, colonial naval building, and the construction of the Indian railroad system (Buchy 1998; Gadgil and Guha 1992: 118–45; Guha 1999; Rajan 1998; Rangarajan 1996:48ff.; Subash Chandran 1998; but see Grove 1995:467; Stebbing 1922, 1923). During the later part of the nineteenth century and the beginning of the twentieth, the increasing demand for timber for railway construction resulted in the formal appropriation by the colonial authorities of forested lands across India. The establishment of the Forest Department in 1865 and the passing of the Indian Forest Act in 1878 resulted in the systematic demarcation of forests into different categories of access and management. Such moves to legislate rights of access and to manage centrally these forests created renewed conflicts between the administration and local communities. Official forest management policies prevented traditional subsistence practices such as the seasonal burning of vegetation, grazing and browsing, and the collection of the so-called minor forest products, including wild fruits, gums, medicinal plants, lac, and *tasar* silk (for details on these forest products see Chapters 4, 5).

While the implementation and enforcement of such officially sanctioned rules varied across India (Rangarajan 1996; Sivaramakrishnan 1999), the overall tendency was to prevent access to forests for local communities (Buchy 1998; Flint 1998:441; Guha 1989; Guha 1999:164ff.; Rangarajan 1996; Saldanha 1998; Sivaramakrishnan 1999; Sundar 1997:41). In many areas, villagers and tribespersons were not allowed to procure fuel and fodder from the forests, and a number of subsistence practices became punishable offences (Gururani 2002). Another consequence of official forest management policies was the encouragement of the strict separation of forests from agricultural land. The result was the banishment of *kumri* cultivation, a form of long fallow shifting cultivation traditionally practised in the Western Ghats (Buchy 1998; Subash Chandran 1998). At the same time, however, there were a number of forest officials and scientists who were not entirely ill-disposed to the continuation of traditional subsistence practices and held instead the view that it was the intensive plains cultivation that was most detrimental to forest preservation. This was the case with Hugh Cleghorn, the first Inspector-General of forests in India from 1867 and earlier Conservator of the Madras forests (Grove 1995:466). Such views, however, remained a minority or at least did not figure prominently in official decision- and policy-making. In the eyes of the majority of state officials and the colonial administrative elite (including contractors, moneylenders, and those landlords who had strong commercial interests in the exploitation of cinnamon, pepper, and coffee), long-established traditional practices could be perceived only as 'destructive'. According to their views, 'primitive' people lived in the jungles and through 'primitive' forms of subsistence, such as shifting cultivation, wreaked environmental degradation, and destruction. In the words of an early twentieth-century forester, shifting cultivation was 'a pernicious system which is probably as destructive of forests as any other act of man' (Stebbing 1922:31). These negative assessments were largely incorporated into the mapping and management of vegetation by forestry experts, and in turn laid the foundations of vegetation mapping and plant ecology for the postcolonial era.

There is at present a very extensive literature on the specifics and regional manifestations of forest politics in India, present and past, dealing with nearly every aspect of the subject from the anthropological, ethnographic, and economic to the symbolic realms (for useful overviews see Guha 1999; Rangarajan 1996; Sivaramakrishnan 1999). It is impossible to deny the impact of human activities in shaping the vegetation of the peninsula. At the same time, however, it is widely recognised that deforestation has not been the culmination of a long-term cumulative process by which the masses of illiterate peasants thoughtlessly destroyed woodland vegetation. It rather represents the outcome of complex processes that weaved together sociopolitical and economic changes in their regional manifestations (including rights to forest access and use, land ownership, and the sedentarization of forest dwellers) spanning at least eight centuries and likely longer than that (Guha 1999). With regard to the present, the principal causes of the continued destruction of woodlands and forests in India are demonstrably socioeconomic ones. Yet, it has also been shown that poverty alone does not constitute a sufficient explanation for environmental degradation; instead,

> The critical and common element of these changes has been the conception, design and implementation of external interventions at the grassroots level without sufficient understanding of the ground realities, local communities' concerns, capabilities and knowledge. (Jodha 2001:276)

Furthermore, as Jodha points out, some of the more far-reaching consequences of such interventions (originating in state policies, aid agencies, and, ultimately, the global economy itself) are the disintegration of the interest of local communities in the preservation of natural resources, their disempowerment as regards resource protection and management practices, and the marginalisation of traditional knowledge and local institutions that previously ensured the continuation of such practices (Jodha 2001:276–77). It should be stressed, however, that the preceding statement does not imply that all indigenous practices of forest use are necessarily sustainable in the long-term. Indeed, as noted by Skaria in the case of the Dangs of the northern Western Ghats,

> Practices were not designed to be ecologically sustainable, nor were they based on a comprehensive knowledge of the dang [i.e., woodland] ... While Dangis and similar communities elsewhere in India know a lot about their localities -forests, trees, seasons, and produce- this knowledge remained deeply fragmented and partial, and most Dangis were aware of this. (Skaria 1999:51)

There have been over time several understandings of Indian landscapes, their vegetation environments, and how they should be approached. In this context, it should be recognised that human interventions may promote some plant species and create conditions of equilibrium or again imbalance leading to ecological change at variable temporal and spatial scales. Thus, as human activities take shape in response to economic motives and social histories, their impact on woodlands and the landscape will be influenced accordingly. This is a theoretical position that recognises the complexity of the interactions of human societies with the landscapes they inhabit, one that is far removed from simply invoking some sort of passive 'adaptive' vegetation and/or human response to climate change and resource fluctuations.

## A SOCIALLY RESPONSIBLE ARCHAEOLOGY

From an archaeological perspective, it is important to be aware of the implications of the currently promoted ecological theory and its sociopolitical ramifications with regard to the study of forest and woodland vegetation in India. This is so because such theories will form the backbone of archaeobotanical interpretations explaining plant-people interactions in the past and attempting to reconstruct their various ecological and socioeconomic contexts. One requirement of archaeological interpretation is that it rests (implicitly or explicitly) on drawing analogies with the present in order to approach the past. The same can be said about palaeoecological interpretations, particularly those relevant to the Holocene. The necessity of using ecological analogues is more acute in the case of prehistoric periods, where the researcher has no written sources and historical accounts to complement the archaeobotanical and palaeoecological record and assist in its interpretation. Even when such records are available, they constitute only *indirect* evidence of past landscapes and environmental conditions.

For this reason, the studies of inferred and/or observed vegetation succession in South India remain useful approximations for modelling the transformations of past vegetation, attributable to human impact, climate change, or both. Studies of plant succession have gathered valuable information about the dynamic effects exerted on vegetation by such processes as climate change, animal grazing, the anthropogenic burning of vegetation, and the creation/maintenance of natural and anthropogenic gaps in woodlands and forests. Descriptions of vegetation succession may therefore provide valuable heuristic categories for the interpretation of the archaeobotanical and palaeoecological data provided that they are used in a sufficiently critical way. In Chapter 4 we outline our understanding of the woodland vegetation of South India. Such descriptions constitute our starting point, a device for analysing and understanding the complexity of the regional vegetation and the possibilities and constraints that it has posed on human activities, past and present. All these are parameters that have historically produced the variable landscapes ('natural' and anthropogenic) of South India.

# CHAPTER 3

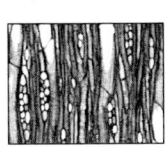

# BACKGROUND TO VEGETATION HISTORY: CLIMATE, GEOLOGY, AND CULTURE

The Indian peninsula is geologically distinct from the alluvial plains of the Indus and the Ganges occupying its western and northern flanks in that it is composed mainly of ancient metamorphic rocks with the exception of the volcanic bedrock of the northern Deccan Trap. Its southern part is characterised by high plateau areas dotted by hill ranges. To the north, the Deccan Trap forms an almost unbroken plateau dissected by river valleys. Running along the western side of the peninsula is the mountain range of the Western Ghats, consisting of a series of peaks rising like high sharp steps (hence the Indian toponym 'ghats') above the western coastal plain facing the Arabian Sea. In Maharashtra, between the Tapti river and the sources of the Krishna river, the Western Ghats are also known as the Sahyadris. In this part of the peninsula they reach elevations >1000 m a.s.l. (see Figure 3.1). They also reach high elevations at their southern end, in the high altitude Nilgiri hills near Mysore city, and the Anamalai and Palni hills further to the south. Below the east-facing slopes of the Western Ghats extends the interior plateau area, gradually dropping in altitude towards the east as indicated by the drainage of all the major rivers running through this part of the peninsula. The two largest drainage systems are those of the Godavari and Krishna rivers with their major tributaries, the Bhima in the north and the Tungabhadra in the south. Flowing from south to north into the Tungabhadra basin is the Hagari river, characterised by strongly seasonal waterflows. On the eastern half of the peninsula, south of the lower Krishna watershed, flows the Pennar river and its tributary from the north, the Kunderu river. Moving south along the east coast one encounters a number of other significant waterflows including the Palar, Ponnaiyar, Cauvery, and Chittar rivers. The location of the major rivers and hill ranges of the peninsula on the map is shown in Figure 3.1. Present-day administrative districts (superimposed on the topography) are shown in Figure 3.2.

## THE PHYSICAL BACKGROUND: CLIMATE AND GEOLOGY

The climate of India is monsoonal, characterised by prolonged periods of rainfall intermittent with more arid spells. Precipitation is therefore a very important factor controlling the rate of plant growth and the geographical distribution of woodlands and forests. In the annual cycle, the principal rain season (monsoon) extends roughly from July to September. During this time, the water content of soils is high while air and soil temperatures remain relatively low, thus encouraging plant growth and the productivity of both annual and perennial plants. The winter season lasts from October to February and is characterised by lower temperatures. As a result, the number of species decreases and ephemerals disappear. Summer extends from March to June, with high temperatures and a substantial decrease in air humidity. Aridity results in the accumulation of salts on surface soils. During this time all annuals die back, although a few trees and shrubs may give a new flush of leaves.

This general pattern varies across the subcontinent. The southwest monsoon hits the Indian peninsula in early June (peaking in July and early August), but the actual period of rains varies in different regions, with the monsoon rains starting and ending later as one moves eastward. The Malabar coast and the Western Ghats receive very high rainfall during the summer months,

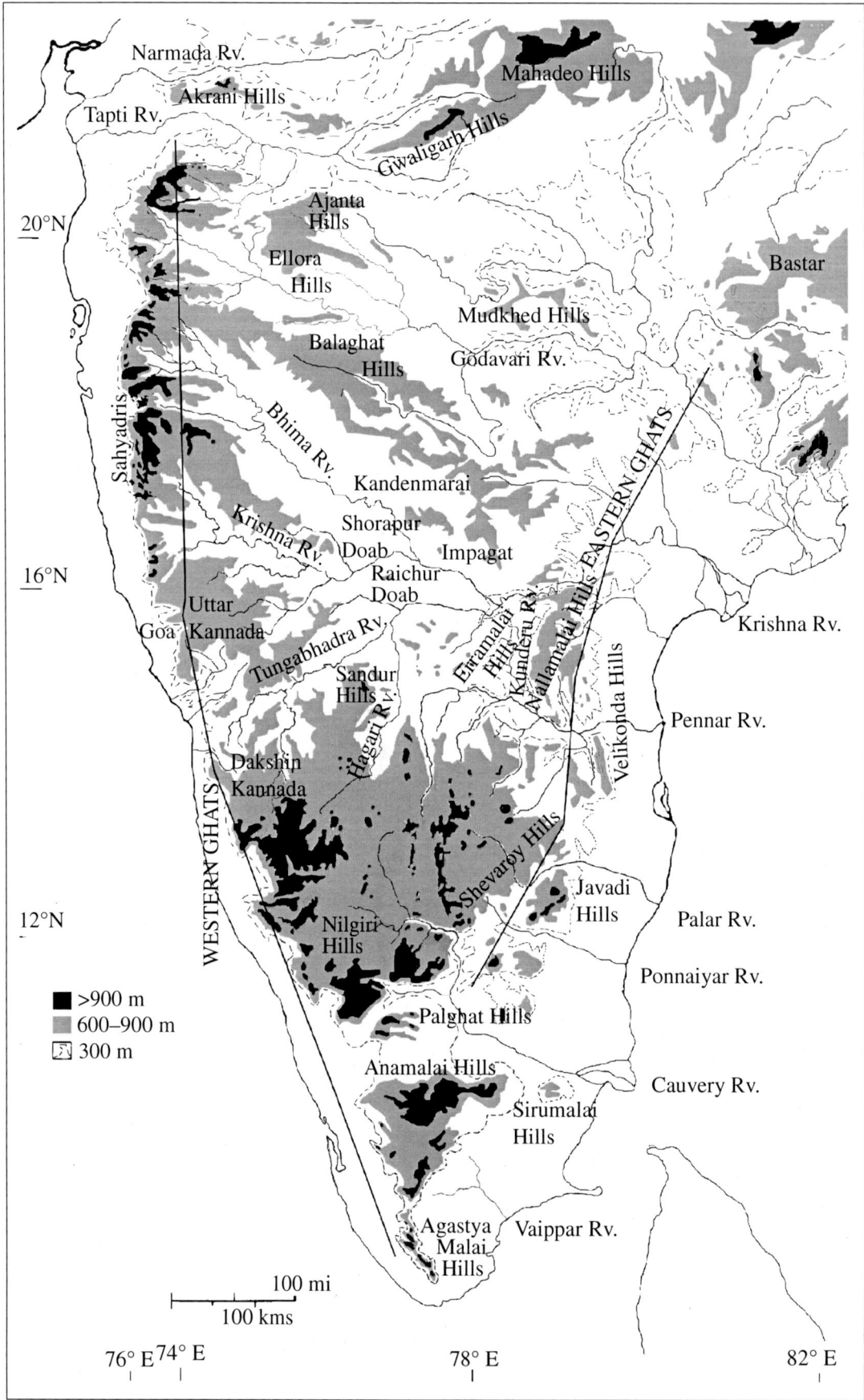

Figure 3.1. Topographic relief and major rivers of the Indian peninsula

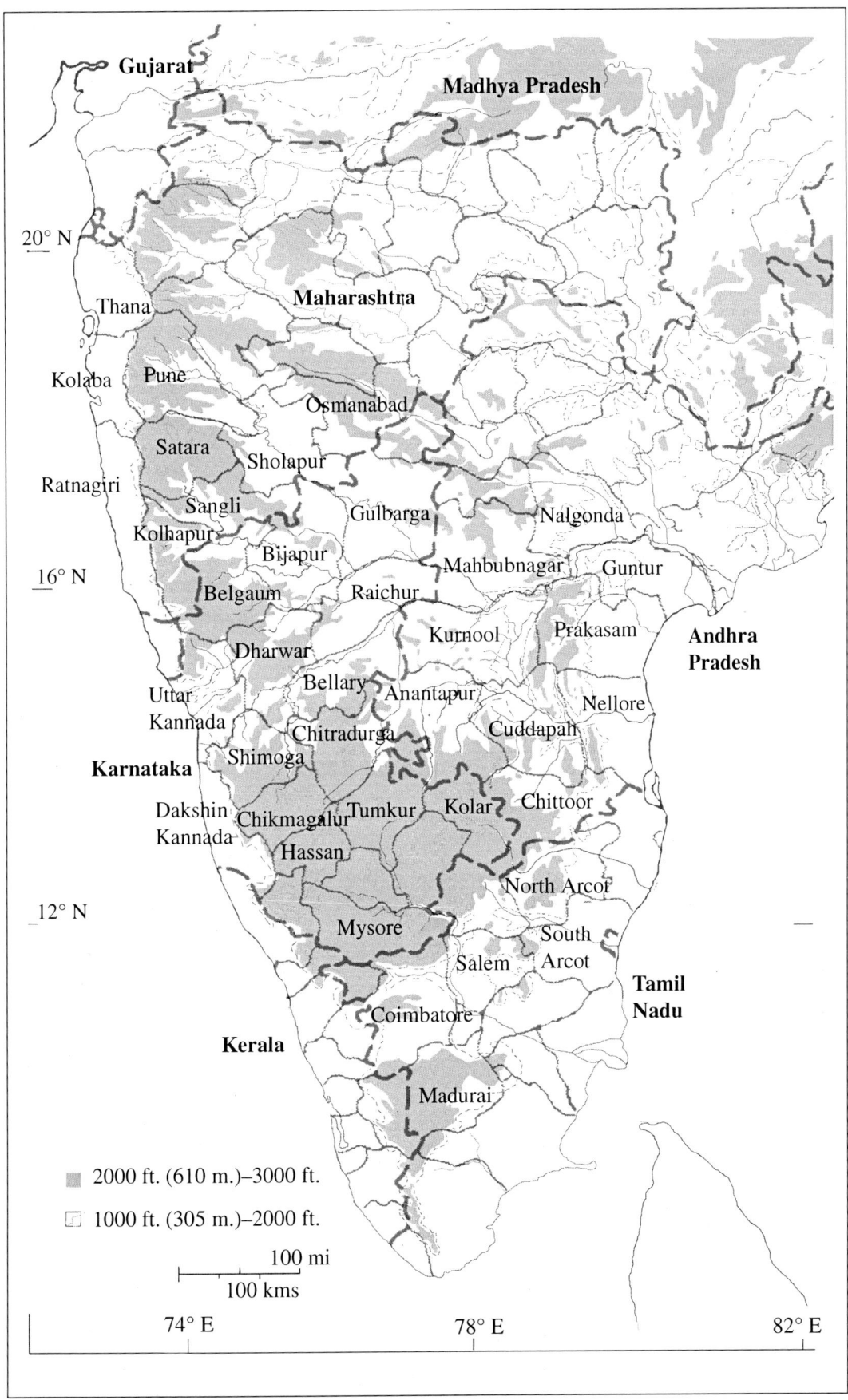

Figure 3.2. Topography and modern administrative boundaries in South India

thus creating conditions favourable to the development of tropical wet evergreen forests. On the eastern side of the Western Ghats lies an extensive rainshadow area (see Figure 3.3). It is in this part of the Indian peninsula that semi-arid savanna vegetation prevails. The rainshadow effect is more pronounced in the southern Deccan, in Karnataka where a substantial proportion of the Neolithic

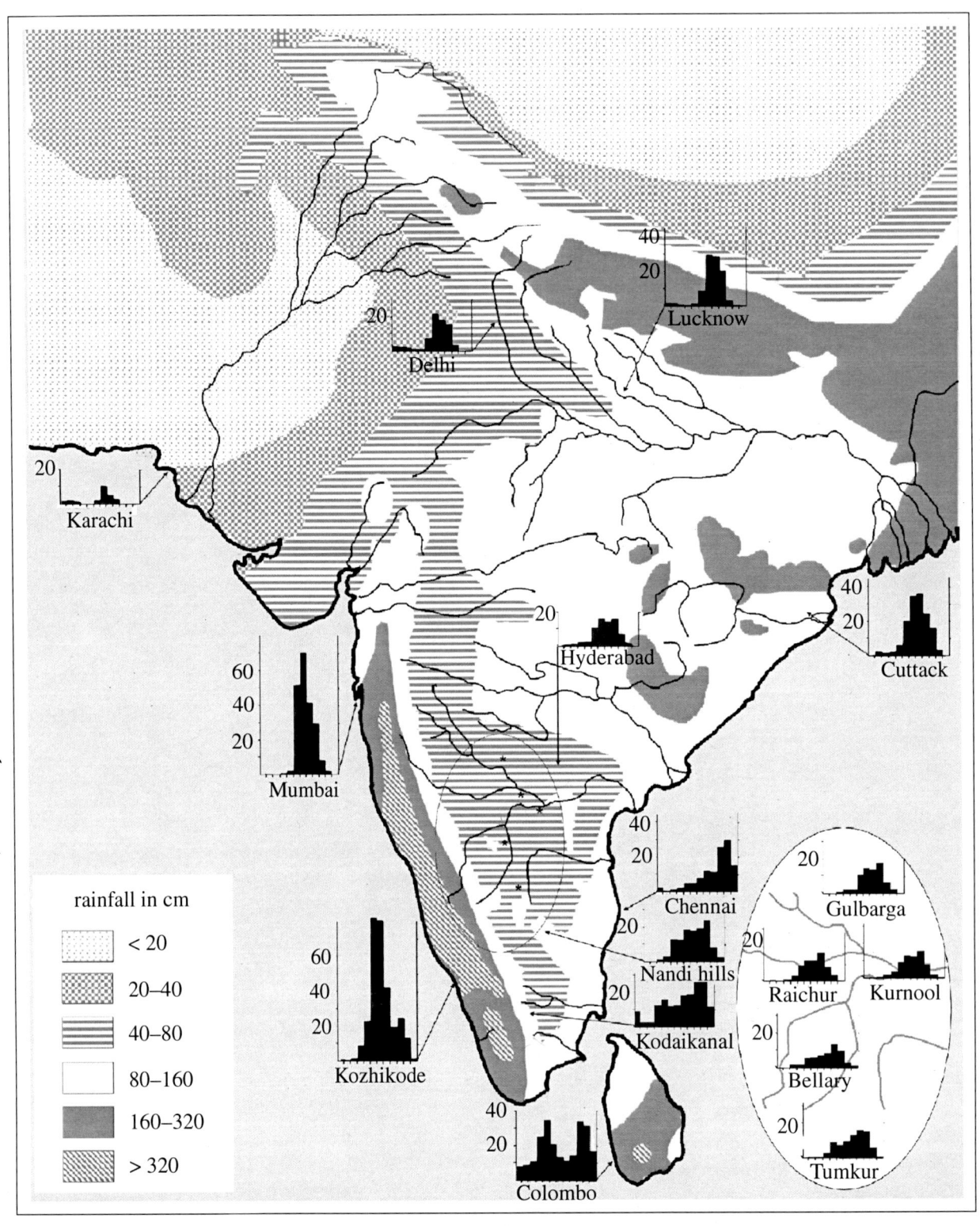

Figure 3.3. Average annual rainfall values in South Asia

hilltop and ashmound sites known from South India are located. A second major area of rainshadow is found on the eastern side of the southernmost part of the peninsula where the Palni, Anamalai, and Nilgiri hills create an extensive semi-arid tract within inland Tamil Nadu. The northeast monsoon (that is, the winter rains) affects mainly the eastern coast of the peninsula and certain parts of Central India. In Karnataka, annual rainfall reaches its minimum values in the Bellary district and adjacent Anantapur, Chitradurga, and Raichur districts (Meher-Homji 1967, 1996a). The effects of drought can be striking. Severe droughts have been calculated to occur in one to three years out of every ten (Subrahmanyam and Sastry 1971), and their effects on woodland regeneration can be devastating. Most of the trees and shrubs native to the peninsula reproduce via seed. As a result, even a single episode of drought (for example the delayed onset of the monsoon season) can bring about heavy loss of seedlings. While year-to-year variations in rainfall of comparable scale may occur in the moister parts of the peninsula as well, such as the Western Ghats, their impact in these areas is much less pronounced because there is sufficient soil moisture to compensate for periodic shortfalls in precipitation (Subrahmanyam and Sarma 1973). To the east and north of the rainshadow, precipitation values increase substantially, especially toward eastern and northeastern India.

Another key parameter, emphasised in bioclimatic vegetation classifications, is the length of the dry season and the number of months with water deficit (see Huke 1982; Meher-Homji 1967, 2001:11–31;). In the central (driest) part of the peninsula comprising the Bellary, Anantapur, and Kurnool districts, the dry season lasts for over eight months. An important aspect of aridity in this region, as well as in the rainshadow area of inland Tamil Nadu, is the particularly low level of rainfall in May and June, the hottest months of the annual cycle. It is in these areas (with combined May–June rainfall often <130 mm) where dry evergreen scrub vegetation is dominant. By contrast, deciduous woods are favoured in areas with more substantial pre-/early monsoon rainfall, in the order of c. 150–220 mm (Puri et al. 1989:307–08). As one moves toward the edges of the peninsula, the length of the dry season and total water deficit decrease. In the Western Ghats, the dry season ranges from 3–4 months on their southern tip to 5–6 months in their middle portion, and 7–8 months in the Maharashtra Sahyadris.

As the summer monsoon comes to an end over most of India, the southeast part of the peninsula and Sri Lanka prepare for fresh downpours. With the intertropical convergence zone, which drives the monsoon system shifting south of the equator over the Indian Ocean, the air currents reverse. Rainfall associated with this reversal is blocked from most of India by a massive Himalayan rainshadow, but winter rains are noticeable in southeast Andhra Pradesh (south of the Krishna river delta), coastal Tamil Nadu, and Sri Lanka. The last area has a truly bimodal distribution of rainfall, unlike much of Tamil Nadu, where the summer rains are highly depressed by the Palni-Nilgiri rainshadow. As a result of this difference in rainfall timing, many plant species display a different flowering pattern in Tamil Nadu, whereby flowering occurs in the winter rather than during the monsoon season. The transitional area between summer and winter monsoon zones covering the Nallamalai hills and much of the Cuddapah basin appears to constitute an important biogeographic boundary affecting the distribution of several woodland species. For example, Meher-Homji (1996a) notes that the red sanders tree (*Pterocarpus santalinus*) is confined to this zone of overlap between the two monsoon regimes.

Important ecological variation across the Indian peninsula is also found with regard to the underlying geology and soil types. As mentioned earlier, the peninsula is essentially a large block of various igneous and metamorphic rocks that may be broadly divided into two distinct regions (Figure 3.4). Its northern and western portions consist of the Cretaceous Deccan Trap volcanic rocks, whereas its southern and eastern parts are dominated by Archaean granites and gneisses, equivalent to the northern and southern Deccan (Bradnock 1989). The boundary between these regions lies in northern Karnataka, in the Bijapur and Gulbarga districts, and runs north-south roughly

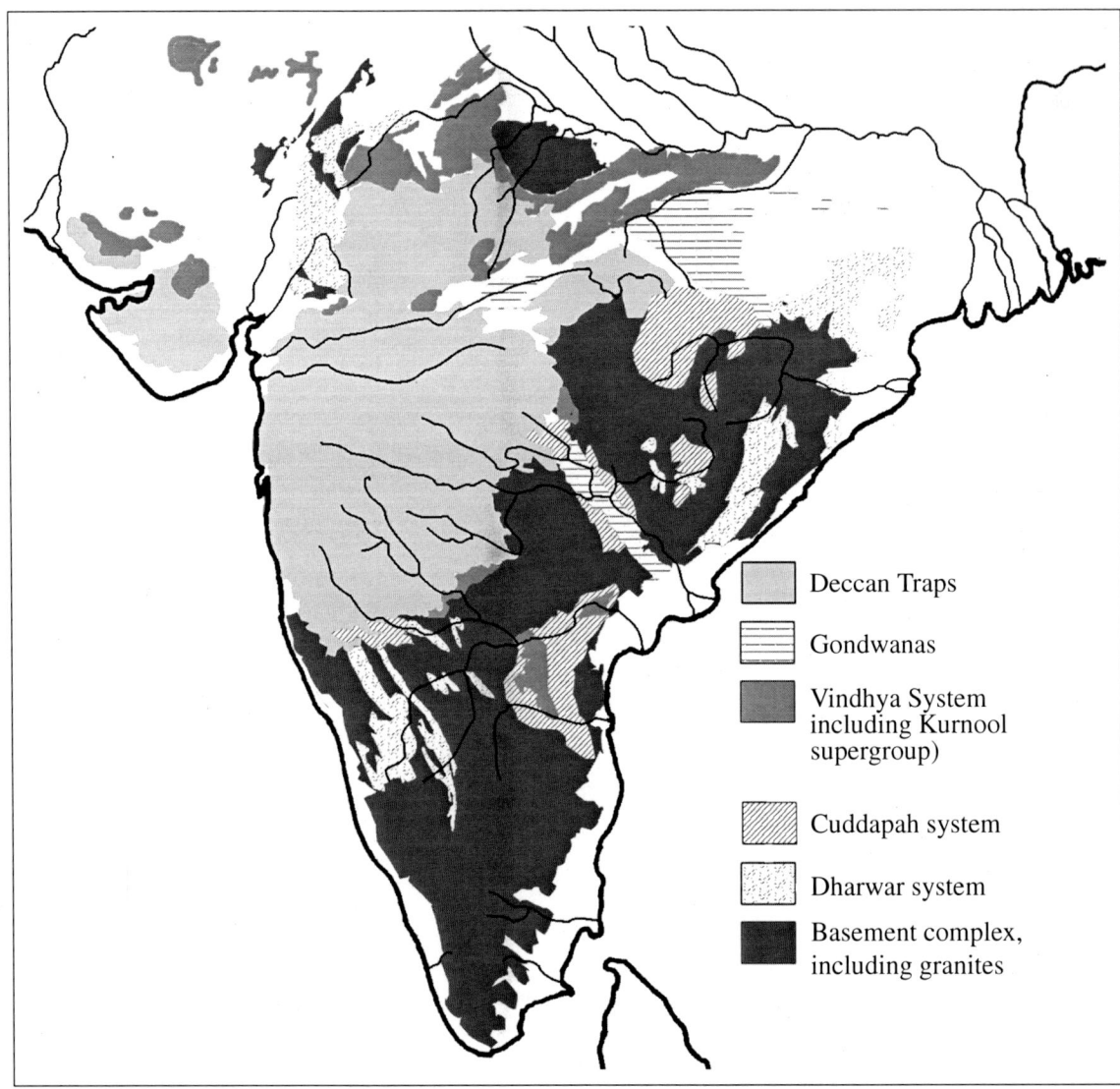

Figure 3.4. Geological zones of South India

following the western administrative boundary of the state of Andhra Pradesh (Ramam and Murty 1997) just north of the major area of Neolithic settlement. On the Deccan Trap, deep black soils (known as 'black cotton soils' or 'regurs' and technically classified as vertisols or chernozems) have developed that are highly fertile (Bradnock 1989; Radhakrishna and Vaidyanadhan 1994:242; Spate and Learmonth 1967). These soils also occur in the granite zone along the courses of the Bhima, Krishna, and Tungabahdra rivers, thus covering much of the Raichur and Shorapur Doabs. The granitic terrain, which includes the Bellary, Anantapur, and western Kurnool districts, is covered by lighter black soils (vertisols) mixed with red sandy soils that form around the granite hills (Foote 1895:189–90). The granitic region is criss-crossed by dykes of intrusive igneous rocks, such as dolerite, which served as the principal raw material source for local Neolithic ground stone industries.

The northwestern portion of the southern region (focusing on the Dharwad district) consists of the Dharwar schists (Foote 1895; Radhakrishna and Vaidyanadhan 1994) that occur as a series of north-south oriented bands. The upper Tungabhadra river, on the banks of which the Neolithic site of Hallur is located, flows through this terrain. Light reddish loam soils are found atop the schists (Foote 1895:190) forming a narrow strip of soil bordered on the west by the laterites of the Western Ghats. The Dharwar schists contain deposits of iron ores and siliceous rocks that were exploited in prehistory for the production of knapped stone industries. Other schist belts in Karnataka, such as the Hutti-Maski belt, contain occasional deposits of gold (Radhakrishna and Vaidyanadhan 1994:57–65).

Of particular relevance to early human presence in South India are the Purana basins (also known as the Gondwana formations). They consist of sedimentary rocks, especially limestone, sandstone, and shale with some quartzite and igneous intrusions. More water-retentive clays form over shale, limestone, and sand patches around quartzitic sandstones. These are the locations of a rich Palaeolithic archaeological record, probably due to the abundance of natural springs (Korisettar 2004). They are also good sources of raw materials used in the production of lithic implements, such as quartzite and limestone (lower-middle Palaeolithic) and finer siliceous materials such as chert (late Palaeolithic-Neolithic). One relatively restricted formation in this group, the Bhima subgroup, includes limestone and conglomerates. It is found along the southern border of the northern Deccan basalts and the southern granitic terrain, at the northernmost limit of the distribution of the Neolithic ashmound tradition (see below).

A similar sedimentary basin forms the Kurnool-Cuddapah geological series, a crescent-shaped area stretching from the Krishna river near Kurnool, to the south of the Pennar river east of Cuddapah city (Ramam and Murty 1997:122–36). This series is defined by three hilly scarps: the Velakonda, Nallamalai, and Erramalai hills. The geologically earlier eastern portion forms the Cuddapah group and consists mainly of alternating quartzite and shale with numerous igneous intrusions including dolerite, basalt, and some granite. Shale is rich in argillic sediments that provide parent materials for the clay-rich black cotton soils found in the Kunderu valley. To the west, the Kurnool group consists of quartzite, shale, sandstone, and limestone. The western part of this group is capped by grey-brown soils classified as red earths (Rao 1997).

## THE CULTURAL HISTORY OF SOUTH INDIA: AN ARCHAEOLOGICAL OVERVIEW

The earliest human presence in South India dates back to the lower Palaeolithic. The Palaeolithic represents a very long period that began approximately two million years ago (at least in northwest India) and about a quarter of a million years ago in the peninsula itself (Kennedy 2000; Korisettar 2001:27, 42) and ceased within the last 100,000 years (Pal 2001:78). It was characterised by low population densities and economies that are likely to have been extractive rather than transformative of the local landscapes (Allchin and Allchin 1982, 1997; Kennedy 2000). The contribution of the early groups to ancient vegetation change was probably minimal. Major shifts in the distribution of plant species are more likely to have occurred as a result of alternating glacial and interglacial climate cycles and fluctuations of shorter duration/scale that characterised the Pleistocene era as a whole (Chapter 5).

After the arrival of anatomically modern humans and the technological innovations associated with the upper Palaeolithic, human activities are likely to have had a more significant bearing on local and regional landscape dynamics. In general, global palaeoenvironmental records suggest that it was in the late Pleistocene (coinciding with the closing stages of the Palaeolithic) when humans started to use fire to modify the landscape, as indicated by the occurrence of micro-charcoal particles in sediment cores (see Bowman 1998; Haberle et al. 2001; Pyne 2001 24–36; Thevenon et al. 2004). In India, the reporting of micro-charcoal curves in the context of pollen analytical investigations of sediment cores has been rare (see Chapter 5). Nevertheless, the few available studies have indicated the likely occurrence of anthropogenic burning of the peninsular vegetation from pre-Neolithic times. The core obtained from the Sandynallah swamp in the Nilgiri hills (Sutra et al. 1997) contained micro-charcoal particles in low proportions throughout the earlier part of its sequence, which increased for the first time after c. 35,000 B.P. uncal and even more so just before 3500 B.C.E. High micro-charcoal frequencies also occur throughout playa sequences derived from the Thar desert in Rajasthan that correspond to the early Holocene (Singh et al. 1974). Recent work at the Lahuradeva and Sanai Tal lakes in the middle Ganges plain has furthermore suggested vegetation burning as early as 12,000 years ago (Sharma et al. 2004). Taken together, these datasets indicate that during the late Pleistocene and the early Holocene hunter-gatherers had already began to employ fire as a means of modifying the vegetation of the subcontinent (Chapter 5).

The first incidence of substantial changes in human-landscape interactions occurred, however, in the Neolithic. The Neolithic marked the advent of four important changes in social organisation, procurement, production, technology, and land use. These are plant cultivation, animal herding, sedentism, and pyrotechnology. Each of these changes likely entailed major impacts on the environment. Although more research is required to clarify the order and tempo of the development of the Neolithic way of life in different parts of South Asia, a broad chronological and geographical scheme pertaining to South India can be outlined here based on extant archaeological knowledge (see also Table 3.1).

The earliest archaeologically known Neolithic habitation sites in the Indian peninsula have provided evidence for an economy incorporating domesticated animals and plant cultivation (Figure 3.5). The Neolithic cultures of the peninsula are usually subdivided in two distinct traditions: that of the northern Deccan (concentrating on Maharashtra and adjacent Madhya Pradesh) known as the *Deccan Chalcolithic* (Panja 1999, 2001; Shinde 1987, 1991, 1994) and that of the southern Deccan (Karnataka, adjacent Andhra Pradesh, and northwest Tamil Nadu) labelled as the *Southern Neolithic* (Korisettar et al. 2001a). As concerns settlement pattern and cultural traditions, both seem to represent distinct regional manifestations of sedentary and/or semisedentary lifestyles. The Deccan Chalcolithic sites are mostly located on river valleys, whereas the core portion of the Southern Neolithic sites was founded away from the major rivers, often on granite hilltops (see Figures 3.6 to 3.8).

The Southern Neolithic has long attracted attention as one of the earliest indigenous food-producing village cultures in South Asia. Thanks to its distinctive ashmound sites and the pioneering fieldwork of the British geologist Bruce Foote (1887), it was the first archaeologically well-documented Neolithic culture to be discovered in India. Sites belonging to this culture have provided unequivocal evidence for the earliest known pastoralism in the peninsula (Korisettar et al. 2001a, 2001b). The ashmounds have been conclusively proven to represent accumulations of periodically

Table 3.1. Conventional chronological scheme for the Southern Neolithic, with major trends in archaeological evidence indicated (following Allchin and Allchin 1968, 1982; Korisettar et al. 2001a)

| Phase | Site Types, Representative Site Phases |
| --- | --- |
| 3000/2800 B.C.E. **Southern Neolithic Phase I** | *Mainly ashmounds.* Sites: Kodekal, Utnur, Brahmagiri IA(?), Lower Piklihal, Watgal IIA |
| 2200 B.C.E. **Southern Neolithic Phase II** | *Fewer ashmounds. Sedentary sites on hilltops.* Sites: Brahmagiri IB, Sanganakallu II.1, Tekkalakota 1, Hallur I, T. Narsipur I, Upper Piklihal, Watgal IIB |
| 1800 B.C.E. **Southern Neolithic III** | *Few/No ashmounds.* Sites: Tekkalakota II, Sanganakallu II.2, Hallur 2, Paiyampalli I, Piklihal 'intrusion', Watgal III |
| 1400/1200 B.C.E. **Neolithic/Megalithic Transition** | *Some hilltop sites abandoned, villages move onto plains. Megalithic pottery and burials begin.* Sites: Sanganakallu III, Hallur 3, Paiyampalli II |
| 800–300 B.C.E. **Megalithic (Iron Age)** | *All hilltop habitation sites abandoned. Iron-working clearly established.* |

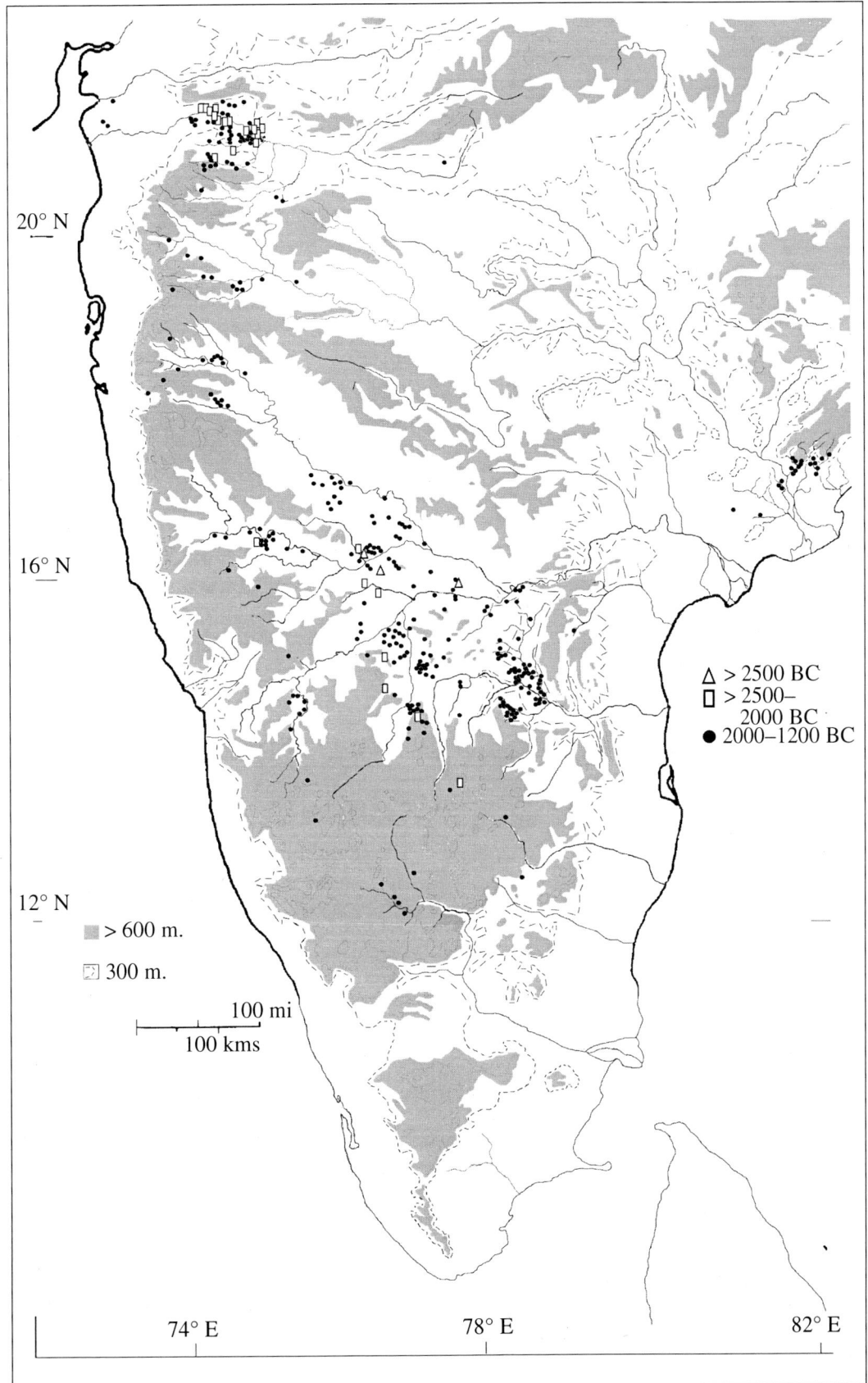

Figure 3.5. Distribution of Neolithic and Chalcolithic sites in the Indian peninsula

Figure 3.6. Overview of the granite hillocks of the Kupgal area

Figure 3.7. A spectacular example of the varied topography and sculpture of granite hilltops in South India

Figure 3.8. Granite hills representing naturally raised and "fortified" areas

burnt cattle dung at ancient penning sites (Allchin 1963; Paddayya 1998; see also Figure 3.9) thus constituting a distinct regional culture also known as the *Ashmound Tradition*. In addition, there is by now abundant archaeobotanical evidence for the existence in the Southern Neolithic of a recurrent agricultural package based on two small millets and two pulses, all domesticated from wild populations indigenous to South India (Fuller, Korisettar, and Venkatasubbaiah 2001; Fuller et al. 2004). The millets have been identified as *Brachiaria ramosa* and *Setaria verticillata*, both of which are known to be exploited on a small scale today (Kimata et al. 2000; Pandey and Chanda 1996:26). The main pulse crops are mungbean (*Vigna radiata*) and horsegram (*Macrotyloma uniflorum*) present from the earliest known Neolithic levels. Some sites have also given small quantities of wheat and barley, crops that would have required at least some irrigation during the dry winter months and that represent introductions from Northwest India. Direct radiocarbon dating of ancient crop seeds indicates that these species were introduced to South India by c. 2000–1900 B.C.E. (Fuller et al. in press). The earliest known sites of the Southern Neolithic may date back to c. 3000 B.C.E. and certainly between 2800–2500 B.C.E. Several ashmound sites that can be dated to the later part of this chronological horizon have been located in Shorapur and Raichur (see Tables 3.1, 3.2). These sites have given evidence for the herding of animal domesticates including cattle, sheep, and goats, all likely to have been introduced from the north (although cattle might have been domesticated locally in some areas) (Korisettar et al. 2001a, 2001b). They are mostly located on granitic terrain with red sands and black soils, in some of the driest parts of the central peninsula.

Further north, in the Deccan Trap zone of Maharashtra and southwest Madhya Pradesh, early village sites display a somewhat different cultural pattern, and subsistence economy. Habitation sites are found on the lower Narmada and Tapti rivers dating from 2300–2000 B.C.E. (Shinde 1998). Local archaeological cultures, such as the Kayatha, are often linked or thought to have derived from earlier Neolithic cultures in Rajasthan associated with the Ahar tradition dated from before 3000 B.C.E. at the site of Balathal (Misra and Mohanty 2001;

Figure 3.9. Ashmounds formed through the seasonal/periodic burning of heaped cattle dung in cattle penning areas

Shinde 2002; Shinde et al. 2004) and likely related to the early Harappan cultures of the greater Indus valley (Dhavalikar 1988, 2001a). Early sites with properly sampled archaeobotanical assemblages are rare. Most of the available evidence has come from assemblages dating to the later part of the second millennium B.C.E. One early site (Kaothe) that dates from the late third millennium-early second millennium B.C.E. produced a plant assemblage indicating the predominance of tropical crop species in the northern peninsula (thus rendering it comparable to subsistence patterns observed in the south) (Kajale 1990). However, owing to the site's shallow stratigraphy, concerns over the true antiquity of the plan remains are warranted until direct radiocarbon dating of the crop seeds is undertaken. The Kaothe material comprises entirely summer monsoon crops including native pulses (*Vigna mungo*) and small millets (*Setaria/Brachiaria*) alongside African pearl millet (*Pennisetum glaucum*).

In the second millennium B.C.E. Neolithic sites became much more widespread over a broader area in western Maharashtra, especially in the Malwa (1700–1500 B.C.E.) and subsequent Jorwe (1500–1200 B.C.E.) phases. Where systematic archaeobotanical sampling has taken place, the evidence for Neolithic cultivation shows a mixture of monsoon crops including native small millets (*Setaria* spp., *Brachiaria ramosa* [?], possibly *Panicum sumatrense*), mung and urd pulses (*Vigna radiata* and *V. mungo*), as well as horsegram (Fuller 2003a:372–74; Kajale 1991), together with the Southwest Asian/Harappan crop package (wheat, barley, and winter pulses such as peas, lentils, chickpeas, and grasspea). This assortment of crop species represents a significant culinary/agricultural departure from the Southern Neolithic, where only wheat and barley are present (in small quantities) from the Southwest Asian suite of plant domesticates. It follows that, with the debatable exception of Kaothe, early agriculture on the northern peninsula was strongly focused on the cultivation and consumption of winter crops that constituted the mainstay of agriculture in the Indus valley, with the likely addition of a few summer crops that were indigenous to the peninsula. Furthermore, in Chalcolithic sites of the northern peninsula copper objects are much more prominent compared to the south, thus suggesting the

**Table 3.2.** Revised chronological framework for the Southern Neolithic and subsequent periods, with major trends in archaeological evidence indicated (following Fuller, Boivin, and Korisettar In press)

| Phase | Site Type and Settlement Pattern | Geographical Location and Distribution | Subsistence Economy |
|---|---|---|---|
| 3000 B.C.E. **S Neolithic Phase I.A** | *Earliest Neolithic occupations, with ceramics. No ashmounds.* Sites: Watgal, Kodekal, Utnur. | Shorapur and Raichur. | No clear evidence of animal herding or plant economy. |
| 2500 B.C.E. **S Neolithic Phase I.B** | *Early ashmounds* Sites: Utnur, Budihal, Palavoy, Brahmagiri A(?), Kudatini(?). Early hilltop ashmounds in the Bellary District: Kurugodu, Choudammagudda(?). | Shorapur, Raichur, Bellary(?), Chitradurga, Anantapur. | Bone evidence for cattle, sheep, goats. No archaeobotanical evidence available. |
| 2200 B.C.E. **S Neolithic Phase II.A** | *Fewer ashmounds (?), habitation sites on hilltops.* Sites: Budihal Layer 3 village, Banahalli, T. Narsipur. | Beginnings of Neolithic beyond core ashmound zone, in southern Karnataka and northeast Tamil Nadu. | Animal herding. Probable cultivation based on native crops. |
| 2000 B.C.E. **S Neolithic Phase II.B** | *Early phases of hilltop sites with ashmounds that later become villages* Sites: Sannarachamma (Sanganakallu), Hiregudda. Hallur founded. Payaimpalli. | Beginnings of village sites on the Upper Tungabhadra river basin. | Abundant archaeobotanical evidence for cultivation: native crops, plus wheat and barley; abundant bone evidence. |
| 1800 B.C.E. **S Neolithic Phase III** | *Village continuity.* Sannarachamma and Hiregudda villages. Possible subdivision indicated by Tekkalakota Periods I/II. | Neolithic sites appear in the Kunderu basin and the Cuddapah District. Peak in the number and density of Neolithic sites (equivalent to the Malwa/early Jorwe periods in the northern peninsula). | Reports of chicken bone from several sites. First evidence for crops of African origin (c. 1500 BC). Possible beginnings of arboriculture, fibre crops and textile production. Copper and gold objects. |
| 1400–800 B.C.E. **Megalithic transition (Pre-Iron Megalithic)** | *Village continuity, some hilltops abandoned. Last ashmound formations cease* (e.g. Velpumagudu). *Megalithic pottery and burials begin.* | Megaliths in eastern Karnataka. By the end of the period megaliths appear in a wide region including Tamil Nadu and eastern Maharashtra. | Wheel-made ceramics. Specialised stone axe workshops. A few possible iron implements from this period (?). Possible finds of horse. |
| 800–300 B.C.E. **Classic Megalithic (Iron Age)** | *All hilltop villages abandoned.* | Megalithic burials widespread, including inland southern Tamil Nadu. | Clear attestation of iron working. Clear attestation of horses. Earliest finds of cultivated rice in South India (Veerapuram). |
| 300 BC–100 C.E. **Late Megalithic/ Early Historic** | *Settlement mounds on plains.* | Megalithic burials continue and cease during this period (?). First agricultural village sites in inland southern Tamil Nadu. | Rice cultivation becomes widespread. |

widespread occurrence of craft activities involving pyrotechnology with attendant high demands on fuel consumption.

Important social and technological changes occurred between 1400 and 800 B.C.E. This period is associated with the emergence of the Megalithic cultures and the construction of impressive stone-built burial monuments for select individuals, probably members of local elites. It was also during this period that iron metallurgy became firmly established, with its intensive demands on mineral resource extraction and the conversion of wood to charcoal. The practice of erecting Megalithic burial monuments may have emerged first in northern Karnataka and eastern Maharashtra (Vidarbha) (see Brubaker 2001; Mohanty and Selvakumar 2001). In the south there seems to be a pattern of clear continuity from the preceding Neolithic cultures, whereas in Maharashtra the Chalcolithic village sites located in the western part of the region were largely abandoned with new settlements emerging in the east. The causes of this shift in settlement location remain little understood, although Dhavalikar (1984, 1988) has put forward an explanation viewing environmental degradation as the main reason for the abandonment of the Jorwe phase villages (Chapter 5).

The gradual development of Megalithic cultures needs to be viewed in the context of the emergence of new political economies during the late Neolithic and the Chalcolithic, following an increase in craft production and long-distance exchange that might have developed alongside the cultivation of nonsubsistence crops such as cotton, flax, and tree fruits. It is at this period that we can trace the emergence of nascent local elites and the development of craft specialisation. This process is certain to have varied across the peninsula, with some regions not displaying settlement continuity from the Neolithic into the Iron Age or even through the Iron Age. Unfortunately, owing to the poor chronological resolution of the archaeological record corresponding to the Megalithic period, there is still much to be resolved concerning the local and regional trajectories of cultural change. The first unambiguous evidence for the widespread occurrence of sedentary agricultural villages in Vidarbha (eastern Maharashtra) dates from this period (Kajale 1989; Mohanty and Selvakumar 2001), and the same is the case for most of Tamil Nadu. In the later Megalithic period, from c. 300 B.C.E., when large megalithic cemeteries became widespread throughout the peninsula, sedentary agricultural villages were established throughout much of the Tamil plains and indeed over most of the peninsula. It also appears likely that, during the Megalithic, agriculture and pastoralism spread to Sri Lanka (Coningham and Allchin 1995). Overall, the late Megalithic represents a significantly higher density of agricultural settlement and population in most of the peninsula compared to earlier periods. It would seem therefore reasonable to conclude that such a settlement pattern would have increased demands on vegetation resources, including the production of charcoal for smelting, and human impact on the landscape as a result of widespread crop cultivation and the herding of livestock.

The early historic period marks the onset of historically documented (through written records) state polities, the emergence of urban centres in parts of South India, and the establishment of extensive territories for individual village communities. This period started by c. 250 B.C.E. on the northern peninsula and from the second century B.C.E. in the far south. One of its principal characteristics was the high volume of long-distance trade across the Indian Ocean toward the West, which included trading with the Roman empire. Forest products, including spices and lac, were in demand as well as cotton textiles, pearls and semiprecious stone beads (Casson 1989; Francis 2002; Gupta S. 2002; Miller 1968; Rajan 2002; Ray 1998). In later centuries, trade volume and interconnections with Southeast Asia increased, too, as suggested by the 'Indianisation' of the early polities of Malaysia and Indonesia during the first millennium C.E. (Bellwood 1997:132–36, 275ff.).

These trends of increased agricultural production geared toward craft activities and the extraction of wild forest products that were traded over long distances continued into the medieval period and, much later, into the colonial era. As historians often emphasise, throughout this period regional states tended to encourage the creation of new settlements and the conversion of forest 'jungles' into agricultural land, as indicated by records of land grants and irrigation works (such as the building of water tanks) (Nandi 2000:76–94; Stein 1980). In the later medieval period, marked by the establishment of the Delhi Sultanate of Northern India (from the thirteenth century) and the Vijayanagar centre near Hospet in central

Karnataka (from the mid-fourteenth century), urban and craft production centres grew as more efficient systems for the extraction of agricultural resources developed (mainly through taxation) alongside the more widespread use of intensive systems of agricultural production (Habib 2001; Morrison 1995). These systems paved the way for the taxation and the commercial organisation of the Mughal empire and, later, the colonial British Raj. Throughout the medieval period there is increasing textual evidence for the establishment of orchards, especially of fruit trees but also of areca palms and betel leaves (*Piper betle*) (Nandi 2000:101–05), as well as flowers (Sastri 1975:328). Such practices marked the onset of plantations being established in small areas within woodlands that were intensively managed for optimising the production of key economic arboreal species. The process of converting wildwoods into plantations was greatly accelerated during the British Raj in tandem with rising demands for cinnamon, pepper, and (later) coffee and tea (Ludden 2002:154–55; Morrison 2002; Watt 1889–1893). Subsequently, especially from the nineteenth century onwards, the conversion of woodlands to plantations was extended to include the production of commercial timber species, such as teak on the peninsula and sal in northern and eastern India. Although prior to colonial times there had been some low-level exporting of timber (especially teak) to the Arabian peninsula, it was the British colonial interest in teak and later other species as well, such as sal, that created a massive demand for the extraction of timber as a commodity (Stebbing 1926:678). This was an important transition, as timber became for the first time a highly valued economic commodity, increasingly needed for shipbuilding (the first British naval vessels built at Bombay were completed by Parsi shipwrights in 1805) (Rangarajan 1996:20) and, after the mid-nineteenth century, for railroad construction as well (Rangarajan 1996:29). It was with these new demands on timber species as crops that intensive forest management, forest ecology, and vegetation conservation emerged as distinct fields of scientific enquiry. At the same time, older traditional practices of forest exploitation were either classified as 'destructive' or relegated to the status of the exploitation of 'minor forest products'. As explained in detail in Chapter 2, it was at this stage in the ecological history of the peninsula that the composition, structure, and geographical distribution of Indian forests and woodlands began to be systematically recorded and mapped. These records have formed the basis for the outline of the arboreal vegetation of the peninsula presented in the next chapter.

# CHAPTER 4

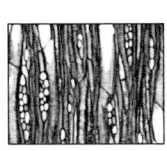

# SOUTH INDIAN WOODLAND VEGETATION: ITS COMPOSITION, STRUCTURE, AND DYNAMICS

The description of South Indian woodland vegetation presented in this chapter is largely based on the synopses of Puri (1960), Puri and colleagues (1989), and Meher-Homji (2001). The background for these more recent syntheses has been the classic study of Indian vegetation by Champion (1936). The vegetation map of the peninsula (presented in Figure 4.1) is based on the maps published by Puri and colleagues (1983) and Meher-Homji (2001), which define detailed variants of the broad vegetation types identified by earlier classification systems. We have also consulted a number of published descriptions of South Indian regional floras (Ellis 1987; Hajra et al. 1996; Singh 1988; Singh et al. 2001; Venkata Raju and Pullaiah 1995;). As discussed in Chapter 2, all the potential or 'climax' vegetation types proposed by earlier ecological work have been based on vegetation classification systems that accept the primacy of climate controls, namely rainfall and temperature, on the composition and geographical distribution of woodland vegetation. By contrast, savanna-like vegetation that is found on the drier parts of the peninsula is considered to represent a degraded version of the 'climax' forests. Puri (1960) has classified such vegetation types (dry evergreen, thorn forest, savanna, grasslands, meadows, and desert scrub) under the heading of 'biotic' (that is, anthropogenic) vegetation. Together with other edaphic 'climax' communities (beach, tidal-mangrove, fresh water swamp, riverine) Puri (1960:199) preferred to view them as fixed seral communities, that is, 'not in equilibrium but [. . .] a phase in development leading to a climax' (Tansley 1946:50). Puri contrasted these to 'true' climax vegetation types such as the tropical wet evergreen or rainforest and the semi-evergreen, moist deciduous and dry deciduous forests. Even dry deciduous woodlands were considered as likely degraded subclimax forms of the moist deciduous forests (Puri 1960:198). His vegetation classification scheme represents, therefore, an elaborate construction that attempts to categorise (and thus comprehend) in a strictly hierarchical way the multiple influences of climate, soils, and human impact on woodland composition and structure. Implicit in this argument is a conjectural history of forest exploitation and degradation leading to loss of its 'climax' status and/or preventing the process of 'natural' succession. Although this vegetation classification system has been revised, and more recent ecological work has shown that the dry deciduous and some of the dry evergreen scrub vegetation types are also determined to a large extent by rainfall and soil gradients (Meher-Homji 2001; Puri et al. 1989:267), the underlying philosophy remains the same. As we have already argued, such classification schemes should be used primarily as heuristic devices whose utility is to be tested against palaeoenvironmental evidence that can provide a historical background to the development of specific plant habitats and associations. Palaeoecology can thus contribute to the construction of an empirically grounded vegetation history and a better appreciation of the dynamic processes and historical contingencies involved in the creation and maintenance of particular vegetation types.

In the following sections, we have included tables of key representative woodland taxa for each vegetation type. The species that have been incorporated in the wood anatomical key for ancient charcoal identification (Chapter 8) have all been included in these tables. From these species, the

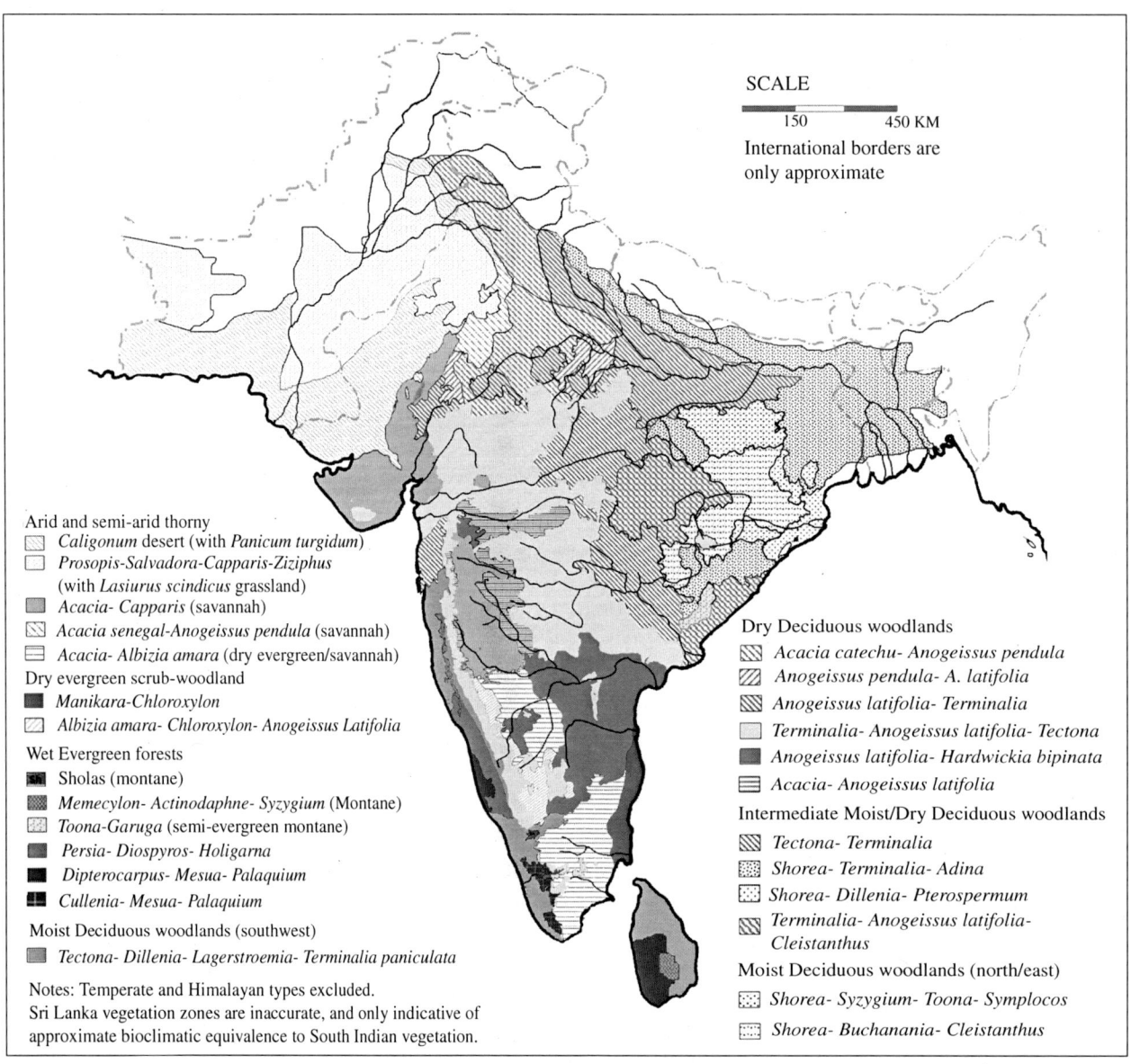

Figure 4.1. Peninsular vegetation zones

ones that have 'indicator status' (that is, they occur only in specific vegetation types) are noted in bold (note however that some of the species widely considered as indicators of dry deciduous vegetation may also occur in dry evergreen scrub savannas). The species whose wood anatomy has not been described by us have been placed in parentheses.

## TROPICAL WET EVERGREEN

Tropical wet evergreen forests (rainforests) occupy those areas receiving the highest levels of annual rainfall in the peninsula (>2500 mm) being concentrated mostly on the Western Ghats, south of Mumbai (formerly Bombay) (Arora 1963, 1966a; Legris and Meher-Homji 1977; Puri 1960; Vajravelu and Vivekananthan 1996) (see Figure 4.2). Rainforests are complex, multistoreyed (four to five storeys) forests with canopy height ranging from 30 to 50 metres. A number of fruit-producing species are found in the wet evergreen forests, although their frequency has substantially increased as a result of human intervention (Legris and Meher-Homji 1977). For example, mango trees (*Mangifera indica*) may occur among the canopy species (Puri 1960:153), although they are generally more common in the moist and (less so) in the dry deciduous forests (Saldanha 1996:206).

Figure 4.2. Western Ghats tropical wet evergreen forest

*Cinnamomum verum*, the species providing the cinnamon bark of commerce, is presently more widespread owing to its long history of selective preservation and propagation by cultivators and hunter-gatherers. Black pepper (*Piper nigrum*) also occurs in these forests as a climber. It can be found in moist deciduous vegetation as well, although there it usually appears as a cultivar and/or as feral individuals. Its native range includes the evergreen forests of Kerala, extending as far north as Uttar Kannada (Morrison 2002; Pruthi 1993:44;). Further north, in the Sahyadris of Maharashtra, its sporadic occurrence is likely to represent a case of dispersal through cultivation. Black pepper is also reported to be found occasionally in the Nallamalais (Ellis 1987; Venkata Rajau and Pullaiah 1995). Given the presence of other *Piper* species in this area, such finds may represent true relict populations despite the fact that *Piper nigrum* is widely cultivated.

On the Western Ghats, wet evergreen forests grow on laterite soils. Although laterite forms a substrate low in nutrients, under well-developed forest cover the thick humus surface layer recycles nutrients fast enough to support dense vegetation. However, once the tree and shrub cover is removed, whether by extreme climate reversals or human agency, topsoil is prone to rapid erosion by waterflows leaving exposed laterite substrata that most mature woodland species have difficulty recolonising. Thus, tropical wet evergreen forests are usually interspersed with meadows growing on exposed laterite. Such forest gaps have become more common through time as human exploitation of rainforests, especially logging, has increased.

In tropical wet evergreen forests, trees grow tall with very large buttresses, thick dark glossy leaves (pink or white-coloured when immature), and smooth trunks, forming a very dense canopy that is almost impenetrable to sunlight. Epiphytic climbers and woody lianas can be very abundant and conspicuous, as can be aerial root systems (see, for example, the likely nonnative species of *Ficus benghalensis* that may grow feral in some forests; Figure 4.3). The middle canopy includes a wide range of small trees and shrubs of the Lauraceae and Myrtaceae families. Canes and palms are also

Figure 4.3. Aerial roots of *Ficus benghalensis* (Tamil Nadu)

common, whereas bamboo thickets usually develop in forest openings. Ground vegetation is either absent or composed primarily of *Strobilanthes*, *Selaginella*, epiphytic ferns, orchids, and shrubs of the Acanthaceae and Annonaceae families. Grasses are conspicuously rare. Forest undergrowth may be particularly dense, especially near sources of water, such as springs. Some indicator species of wet evergreen forests are listed in Table 4.1.

Tropical wet evergreen forests can be subdivided into latitudinal and altitudinal variants (Legris and Meher-Homji 1977; Meher-Homji 2001:136–45; Puri et al. 1989:175–99;). As mentioned already (Chapter 3), a major influence on woodland structure and composition is the length of the dry season that increases from about three to four months at the southern tip of the peninsula up to seven months in Maharashtra. At the southern end of the Western Ghats, in Kerala and Tamil Nadu, the dry season lasts for less than four months. In this area the *Mesua-Palaquium-Cullenia* rainforest variant is dominant. Moving northward, the dry season lengthens, and some of the dominant species change accordingly. In northern Kerala and southwest Dakshina Kannada, *Dipterocarpus indicus* abounds in association with *Mesua* and *Palaquium*. Elsewhere in Dakshina Kannada the dominant species is *Hopea parviflora*, while *Palaquium* and *Mesua* are restricted to the highest ridges together with *Dipterocarpus indicus* and *Poeciloneuron indicum* (Arora 1966b). Further north, in Uttar Kannada and Goa, where the dry season lasts for up to six months, the dominant association is that of *Machilus – Holigarna – Diospyros* (Legris and Meher-Homji 1977; Meher-Homji 2001:139–40; cf. Arora 1963). The northernmost stands of *Dipterocarpus* are found on the Siddapur hills in southern Uttar Kannada. Further north, in the Belgaum district and in Maharashtra, high scarps above 700 m a.s.l. carry a distinct type of low montane wet evergreen forest (Legris and Meher-Homji 1977). These northern variants are characterised by the *Bridelia retusa – Ficus glomerata – Syzygium cumini* and *Memecylon edule – Actinodaphne – Syzygium cumini* associations. The vegetation of Mount Abu in Rajasthan includes many species of the *Bridelia retusa – Ficus glomerata – Syzygium cumini* type, alongside several moist deciduous elements; this represents the northernmost distribution of the Western Ghats wet evergreen flora.

The economic exploitation of the Western Ghats tropical wet evergreen forests has traditionally focused on plant gathering including fruit species, spices, sources of gums/resins, medicinal plants, and honey, as well as the lumbering of timber species. The main tree resins are black damar (*Canarium strictum*) and white damar (*Vateria indica*) (Drury 1873; Morris 1982:87–88). *Kamila,* the red powder traditionally used to mark the foreheads of Indian married women, is produced from the fruits of *Mallotus philippensis* (Patnaik 1993; Watt 1889–1893). Gathered fruits include jackfruit (*Artocarpus heterophylla*), gamboge (*Garcinia indica*), longan (*Dimocarpus longan*), jamoon (*Syzygium cumini*), and mango (*Mangifera indica*). Important spices are cardamon (*Elettaria*

Table 4.1. Select Western Ghats tropical wet evergreen species. Select key indicator species in bold. Taxa not included in the anatomical key in parentheses.

---

*Aglaia* spp. (Meliaceae)
*Artocarpus* spp. (Moraceae)
(*Bauhinia foveolata*) (Leguminosae-Caesalpiniaceae)
(*Bauhinia malabarica*) (Leguminosae-Caesalpinioideae)
(*Bauhinia phoenicia*) (Leguminosae-Caesalpiniaceae)
(*Bridelia retusa*) (Euphorbiaceae) prominent in the Maharashtra Sahyadris
(*Calophyllum* spp.) (Clusiaceae)
(*Canarium strictum*) (Burseraceae)
(*Capparis grandis*) (Capparaceae)
**Cinnamomum** spp. (Lauraceae)
(*Cullenia exarillata*) (Bombacaceae) frequent in the south, absent north of Kodagu (Karnataka)
*Dalbergia* spp. (Leguminosae-Papilionaceae)
(*Dimocarpus longan*) (Sapindaceae)
(*Dipterocarpus indicus*) (Dipterocarpaceae) frequent in the Karnataka Western Ghats, rare in the north
*Diospyros* spp. (Ebenaceae) (see Chapter 5)
(*Elaeocarpus* spp.) (Tiliaceae)
**Garcinia indica** (Clusiaceae)
(*Garuga gamblei*) (Burseraceae)
*Holigarna* spp. (Anacardiaceae) frequent from Karnataka northward
**Hopea** spp. (Dipterocarpaceae)
*Ixora* spp. (Rubiaceae)
(*Kingiodendron pinnatum*) (Leguminosae) in the southern Western Ghats only
(*Machilus macrantha*) (= *Persea macrantha*) (Lauraceae) from Karnataka northward
*Mallotus* spp. (Euphorbiaceae)
*Mangifera indica* (Anacardiaceae)
(*Memecylon edule*) (Melastomataceae) prominent in the Maharashtra Sahyadris
(*Mesua ferrea*) (Clusiaceae) frequent in the south, rarer in the north
(*Palaquium ellipticum*) (Sapotaceae) present in the south only
*Polyalthia fragrans* (Annonaceae)
(*Polyalthia coffeoides*) (Annonaceae)
(*Polyalthia rufescens*) (Annonaceae)
*Pterospermum* spp. (Sterculiaceae)
(*Syzygium cumini*) (= *Eugenia jambolana*) (Myrtaceae) prominent in the Maharashtra Sahyadris
(*Syzygium gardneri*) (Myrtaceae) replacing *S. cumini* from Karnataka southwards
(*Tetrameles nudiflora*) (Datiscaceae)
(*Vateria indica*) (Dipterocarpaceae), frequent in the Karnataka Western Ghats, rare in the north
*Vitex altissima* (Verbenaceae)

---

*cardamomum*), cinnamon (*Cinnamomum verum, C. iners*), pepper (*Piper nigrum*), tumeric (*Curcuma longa*), and wild ginger (*Zingiber officinale*, likely to be of anthropogenic origin) (see Dalby 2000; Fischer 1928; Watt 1889–1893). Among timber species, those that have been highly valued since the colonial period are black ebony (*Diospyros*), ironwood (*Hopea*), black wood (*Dalbergia*), wood oil tree (*Dipterocarpus*), and *Aglaia*.

Until recently, honey constituted an important trade item for many forager groups. The main production season extends from March to May, although it may also occur in December, when *Bombax malabaricum* (red cotton tree, Malayalam *ilavu*) comes into flower, and less so in October and November (Morris 1982:84–87). In the moist deciduous sal forests of northern Orissa (Simlipal hills), honey gathering takes place in the height of the dry season (March–June) and again in the post-monsoon months (October–November). Much smaller quantities are available during the rest of the annual cycle (Dash 1998:216).

## TROPICAL MOIST DECIDUOUS

Tropical moist deciduous vegetation (see Figure 4.4) occurs widely in the regions surrounding the wet evergreen zone, normally with average annual precipitation >2,000 mm, although the lower rainfall limit can be as low as 1,650 mm (in the moist deciduous teak forests of Seth and Waheed Khan; Puri et al. 1989:232). Moist deciduous species generally shed their leaves during the driest months (March and April). Most of the trees come into leaf again before the arrival of the monsoon. There are a few exceptions, such as *Dalbergia* and *Cedrela* (which come into leaf during March and April) and *Cassia fistula*, *Bombax*, and *Sterculia*, which flower before their leaves appear. Moist deciduous forests are characterised by closed canopy vegetation mixed with semideciduous species and an understorey of evergreens. On wet ground, bamboo and cane thickets may occur, while in shaded places epiphytes abound. The number of large climbers is high. Although teak often dominates these forests today, its presence is likely to have been promoted by extensive planting (Meher-Homji 2001:115). Meher-Homji (2001:112) has classified some teak forests as 'intermediate between dry and moist'. As a result, most of their constituent species are shared with adjacent vegetation zones. That moist deciduous forests were probably more widespread during the early and mid-Holocene (Chapter 7) may account for the relict formations rich in moist deciduous species that are found in parts of the Eastern Ghats (for example, the Nallamalai hills of Andhra Pradesh) (Ellis 1987:12–13; Legris and Meher-Homji 1977; Ravisankar and Hosagoudar 1995). Similarly, the semi-evergreen components of the plateau of the Sirumalai hills, otherwise covered by dry deciduous vegetation, can be considered together with moist deciduous vegetation, although they include a few true evergreen species such as *Canarium strictum* and *Elaeocarpus tuberculatus* (see Pallithanam 2001:xxii). The main species found in moist deciduous forests are listed in Table 4.2.

Honey is regularly collected in the tropical moist deciduous zone, mainly during the dry season and in early winter, alongside plants and resins such as the *kino* gum from *Pterocarpus*

Figure 4.4. Western Ghats moist deciduous woodland dominated by *Terminalia*

*marsupium*. *Schleichera oleosa*, the *kusum* tree, is important as a host of the lac insect (*Laccifer lacca* syn. *Coccus lacca*) (Watt 1889–1893). These scale insects infest the bark of some trees, especially *Butea monosperma* and *Schleichera oleosa*, and transform their sap into a hard shiny resin (known as lacquer or shellac, the latter produced by insects feeding on *Schleichera*) that can be turned into a red dye. Resinous lac is an important forest product traded from India since classical times (Casson 1989; Yule and Burnell 1886:499) and one of the commodities shipped from the Andhra coast to the Arabian peninsula during the seventeenth and eighteenth centuries (Arasaratnam 1986:104). Another dye source found in moist deciduous vegetation is *Rubia cordifolia* (Hindi *manjit*), the 'Bengal madder' (not to be confused with the other Indian madder, *Oldenlandia umbellata*, found in dry evergreen and thorn forests), the roots of which produce a red dye used on cotton textiles.

Table 4.2. Select tropical moist deciduous species. Select key indicator species in bold. Taxa not included in the anatomical key in parentheses.

| | |
|---|---|
| (*Albizia procera*) (Leguminosae-Mimosaceae) | (*Lannea coromandelica*) (Anacardiaceae) |
| *Adina cordifolia* (Rubiaceae) | (*Lantana camara*) (Verbenaceae) |
| (*Alstonia scholaris*) (Apocynaceae) | (*Leea* spp.) (Leeaceae), (*Litsea* spp.) (Lauraceae) |
| (*Bambusa arundinacea*) (Poaceae-Bambusoideae) | (*Madhuca longifolia* syn. *Bassia longifolia*) |
| (*Bauhinia malabarica*) (Leguminosae-Caesalpiniaceae) | (Sapotaceae) common in central and eastern India |
| (*Bauhinia tomentosa*) (Leguminosae-Caesalpiniaceae) | *Mallotus philippensis* (Euphorbiaceae) |
| (*Bauhinia vahlii*) (Leguminosae-Caesalpiniaceae) | (*Mallotus tetracoccus*) (Euphorbiaceae) |
| *Butea superba* (Leguminosae-Papilionaceae) | *Mangifera indica* (Anacardiaceae) |
| *Bombax ceiba*, syn. *B. malabaricum* (Bombacaceae) | (*Melia composita*) (Meliaceae) |
| *Careya arborea* (Myrtaceae) | *Mitragyna parvifolia* (Rubiaceae) |
| *Cassia fistula* (Leguminoae-Caesalpiniaceae) | (*Ougeinia dalbergioides*) (Leguminosae-Papilionaceae) |
| (*Cleistanthus collinus*) (Euphorbiaceae) | (*Petalidium barlerioides*) (Acanthaceae) |
| *Cordia dichotoma* (Ehretiaceae form. in Boraginaceae) | *Phyllanthus emblica* (Euphorbiaceae) |
| *Dalbergia latifolia* (Leguminosae-Papilionaceae) | *Pterocarpus marsupium* (Leguminosae-Papilionaceae) |
| *Dalbergia paniculata* (Leguminosae-Papilionaceae) | *Pterospermum diversifolium* (Sterculiaceae) |
| (*Dendrocalamus strictus*) (Poaceae-Bambusoideae) | *Pterospermum xylocarpum* (Sterculiaceae) |
| *Dillenia pentagyna* (Dilleniaceae) | *Schleichera oleosa* (Sapindaceae) |
| (*Dimocarpus langan*) (Sapindaceae) | (*Syzygium cumini*) (Myrtaceae) |
| (*Erythrina stricta*) (Leguminosae-Papilionaceae) | *Tectona grandis* (Verbenaceae) |
| *Ficus* spp. (Moraceae) (see Chapter 5) | *Terminalia bellerica* (Combretaceae) |
| (*Flemingia* spp., syn. *Moghania*) (Leguminosae-Papilionaceae) | (*Terminalia crenulata*) (Combretaceae) |
| | *Terminalia tomentosa* (Combretaceae) |
| (*Garuga pinnata*) (Burseraceae), *Grewia tiliaefolia* (Tiliaceae), *Grewia* spp. (Tiliaceae) | *Terminalia paniculata* (Combretaceae) |
| *Ixora* spp. (Rubiaceae) | (*Tetrameles nudiflora*) (Datiscaceae) |
| (*Kydia calycina*) (Malvaceae) | (*Trema orientalis*) (Ulmaceae) |
| *Lagerstroemia microcarpa* (Lythraceae) | *Xylia xylocarpa* (Leguminosae-Mimosaceae) |
| *Lagerstroemia parviflora* (Lythraceae) | *Vitex altissima* (Verbenaceae) |

Archaeo-botanical finds of *Rubia* seeds from the Neolithic site of Sanganakallu in the Bellary district suggest that this species was already being transported across South India, perhaps as a dye source, from as early as 1800–1400 B.C.E. (Fuller 1999).

Several fruit species are found in moist deciduous forests. These include mango (*Mangifera indica*), *Phyllanthus emblica* (the emblic myrobalan renowned for the medicinal properties of its fruit), *Cordia dichotoma* (one of the sebesten plum species), *Syzygium cumini* (Indian jambo), and the medicinal *Terminalia bellerica*, all of which have been recovered from Neolithic and Chalcolithic sites in Karnataka and Maharashtra (Kajale 1988, 1991). Most of these species may also occur in dry deciduous vegetation or can be planted there, and their fruits may be transported over long distances, so on their own they do not provide clear evidence on the ancient distribution of moist deciduous forests. The sugary flowers of *Madhuca longifolia* are traditionally gathered during the dry summer months and may be consumed raw, cooked, or fermented into an alcoholic beverage. Edible oil can also be prepared from its seeds, which is sold as cakes of 'illipe butter' (Watt 1889–1893: *Bassia longifolia*). Illipe butter forms an important component of some traditional tribal economies, such as the Gonds of the Bastar region (Grigson 1949) and the Dangs living at the northern end of the Western Ghats in Maharashtra and Gujarat (Skaria 1999:46).

Moist deciduous forests include a number of commercially important timber species. Teak (*Tectona grandis*) is the most prominent and has been under intensive management through systematic coppicing, planting, and selective propagation. Other timber species include *Dillenia, Dalbergia, Lagerstroemia, Pterocarpus marsupium, Terminalia,* and *Xylia.* Coarse fibres are processed for rope from the bark of *Bauhinia vahlii* and *Grewia tiliaefolia.*

Woodland edges and forest gaps in moist deciduous vegetation were probably among the natural habitats of the wild progenitors of mung and urd bean (Fuller 2002; Fuller et al. 2004; Fuller and Korisettar 2004). These crops are now recognised to derive from two distinct wild species, *Vigna radiata* subsp. *sublobata* and *Vigna mungo* subsp. *sylvestris* (Smart 1990), although in older published floras they were often subsumed under *Phaseolus sublobatus* or *Vigna radiata* subsp. *sublobata.* The wild progenitors of other South Indian plant domesticates are likely to have been widespread in the dry deciduous zone (see below). It follows that ecotone habitats between the moist and dry deciduous zones might have been significant in determining the geographical distribution of the wild progenitors of indigenous pulse crops and, by implication, the beginning of the cultivation of tropical millets and pulses in peninsular India (Fuller and Korisettar 2004).

## TROPICAL DRY DECIDUOUS

Dry deciduous tropical forests (Figures 4.5, 4.6) are dominated by species that remain leafless for the greater part of the dry season owing to low rainfall and/or very low levels of soil moisture. Forest canopy is uneven and relatively open. The few evergreen species that are found in these woodlands are confined to moister localities. Their undergrowth comprises a few shrubs while the ground flora is dominated by grasses that take advantage of the much higher frequency of forest fires compared to wet evergreen and moist deciduous forests. Canes and palms are absent from the flora of the dry deciduous forests while climbers, epiphytes, and ferns are few and concentrated on moister spots. In more heavily disturbed and/or arid areas, dry deciduous woodland closely resembles tropical savanna habitats (see thorn forests, below). At present, most of the areas where dry deciduous forests are considered to form the 'climax' vegetation are covered by scrub and grasslands owing to ungulate herding, burning, and intensive cultivation.

Dry deciduous forests are thought to represent the natural vegetation over most of the southern Deccan (Champion 1936:129–42; Legris and Meher-Homji 1977; Puri 1960:192–94; Puri et al. 1983; Singh 1988). The *Terminalia tomentosa – Anogeissus latifolia – Tectona grandis* association (Table 4.3) hosts a number of moist deciduous elements and occurs in better watered areas (east of the Western Ghats moist deciduous zone and on the Nallamalai hills) and further north in the east-central part of the peninsula. Relict vegetation patches are also found on the Sandur hills (Bellary district). These areas receive on average 800–1,100 mm of annual rainfall. On the northern and eastern edges of the teak distribution, dry deciduous forests have been classified as *Tectona – Terminalia,* whereas *Acacia* and *Anogeissus* dominate a transitional zone linking the *Anogeissus latifolia-Terminalia tomentosa-Tectona grandis* type to the thorny *Acacia – Capparis* savannas, especially in Maharashtra and Gujarat.

The *Anogeissus – Hardwickia* subtype is believed to represent the 'climax' vegetation of drier areas (Table 4.4) in the eastern peninsula, the southern Cuddapah district, and parts of Anantapur (to the south and east of the driest parts of the central peninsula). Annual rainfall ranges between 500 mm and 1,200 mm, with a dry season of 6–8 months. *Hardwickia* colonises successfully sandstone substrates, silica-rich black soils, and alluvium (Meher-Homji 2001:96–97). If not heavily disturbed by grazing it can form extensive stands, but it does not coppice well and reproduces poorly from seed. Because of the hardness of its wood, *Hardwickia* may persist in forest edges as other species are cut down, whereas within mixed woods it is more readily out-competed by better adapted species (Meher-Homji 2001:97). *Anogeissus – Hardwickia* vegetation occurs on hillslopes and the more water-retentive soils of central Karnataka, such as the Sandur hills west of Bellary and the Erramalai hills of Kurnool and Cuddapah. The herbaceous layer in *Hardwickia* woods is often dominated by grasses including *Aristida* spp., *Cymbopogon* spp., and *Heteropogon contortus.*

The *Acacia – Anogeissus* association constitutes a transitional vegetation type between the dry

Figure 4.5. *Anogeissus* tree with crooked bole growing alongside teak seedlings in grassland-dominated gap inside dry deciduous woodland (Sandur hills, Karnataka)

Figure 4.6. General view of the Sandur hills dry deciduous forest

Table 4.3. Select dry deciduous species: the *Terminalia-Anogeissus-Tectona* association. Select key indicator species in bold, those specific only to this variant are marked with an asterisk. Some of these species may also occur in scrub savannas. Species that overlap with the moist deciduous zone but are absent/rare in *Anogeissus-Hardwickia* vegetation are marked with a superscript 'w'. Species/Genera not included in the anatomical key in parentheses.

| | |
|---|---|
| (*Aegle marmelos**) (Rutaceae) | *Feronia limonia* (Rutaceae) more common in the southern peninsula |
| *Albizia amara* (Leguminosae-Mimosaceae) | |
| (*Albizia odoratissima*) (Leguminosae-Mimosaceae) | (*Flacourtia indica*) (Flacourtiaceae) |
| *Albizia procera* (Leguminosae-Mimosaceae) | (*Flacourtia jangomas*) (Flacourtiaceae) |
| *Acacia chundra/catechu* (Leguminosae-Mimosaceae) | *Gardenia resinifera* (Rubiaceae) |
| (*Acacia feruginea*) (Leguminosae-Mimosaceae) | (*Gardenia turgida*) (Rubiaceae) |
| (*Acacia pennata*) (Leguminosae-Mimosaceae) | *Gmelina arborea** (Verbenaceae) |
| *Anogeissus latifolia* (Combretaceae) | *Grewia tiliaefolia*$^w$ (Tiliaceae) |
| (*Atalantia monophylla*) (Rutaceae), *Azadirachta indica* (Meliaceae) | *Grewia* spp. (Tiliaceae) |
| | *Gyrocarpus americanus* (Hernandiaceae) |
| (*Balanites aegyptiaca*) (Balanitaceae) | *Holarrhena antidysenterica* (Apocynaceae) |
| *Bauhinia racemosa* (Leguminosae-Caesalpiniaceae) | (*Holoptelea integrifolia*) (Urticaceae) |
| *Bombax ceiba*, syn. *B. malabaricum* (Bombacaceae) | (*Ixora arborea*) (Rubiaceae) |
| (*Boswellia serrata*) (Burseraceae) | *Lagerstroemia parviflora* (Lythraceae) |
| *Butea monosperma** (Leguminosae-Papilionaceae) | (*Lannea coromandelica*) (Anacardiaceae) |
| (*Calycopteris floribunda*) (Combretaceae) | (*Mimosa rubicaulis*) (Leguminosae-Mimosaceae) |
| (*Capparis divaricata*) (Capparaceae) | *Maytenus (Gymnosporia) emarginata* (Celastraceae) |
| (*C. brevispina*) (Capparaceae) | (*Nyctanthes arbor-tristes*) (Oleaceae) |
| *C. sepiaria* (Capparaceae) | (*Osyris quadripartita*) (Santalaceae) |
| *C. zeylanica* (Capparidaceae) | *Phyllanthus emblica*$^w$ (Euphorbiaceae) |
| (*Carissa congesta*) (Apocynaceae) | (*Prosopis cineraria*) (Leguminosae-Mimosaceae) |
| *Cassia fistula* (Leguminosae-Caesalpiniaceae) | *Pterocarpus marsupium* (Leguminosae-Papilionaceae) |
| (*Cassia surattensis*) (Leguminosae-Caesalpiniaceae) | *Santalum album* (Santalaceae) |
| *Chloroxylon swietenia* (Rutaceae) | *Schleichera oleosa* (Sapindaceae) |
| (*Cleistanthus collinus*$^w$) (Euphorbiaceae) | (*Smilax zeylanica*) (Smilacaceae) |
| (*Combretum decandrum*) (Combretaceae) | *Soymida febrifuga* (Meliaceae) |
| *Cordia* spp. (Boraginaceae) | *Strychnos nux-vomica** (Loganiaceae) |
| *Dalbergia latifolia* (Leguminosae-Papilionaceae) | *Tamarindus indica* (Leguminosae-Caesalpiniaceae) |
| (*Dalbergia lanceolata*) (Leguminosae-Papilionaceae) | *Tectona grandis*$^w$ (Verbanaceae) |
| *Dalbergia paniculata* (Leguminosae-Papilionaceae) | *Terminalia tomentosa*$^w$ (Combretaceae) |
| (*Dalbergia sissoo*) (Leguminosae-Papilionaceae) more common in the northern peninsula | (*Terminalia elliptica*) (Combretaceae) |
| | (*Terminalia chebula*) (Combretaceae) |
| (*Dendrocalamus strictus*) (Poaceae-Bambusoideae) | *Vitex altissima* (Verbenaceae) |
| (*Diospyros melanoxylon*) (Ebenaceae) | *Wrightia tinctoria* (Apocynaceae) |
| *Diospyros montana** (Ebenaceae) | (*Wrightia tomentosa*) (Apocynaceae) |
| *Diospyros tomentosa* (Ebenaceae) | (*Xeromphis spinosa*) (Rubiaceae) |
| (*Diospyros ovalifolia*) (Ebenaceae) | *Ziziphus mauritiana* (Rhamnaceae) |
| (*Dolichandrone atrovirens*) (Bignoniaceae) | (*Ziziphus oenoplia*) (Rhamnaceae) |
| (*Dolichandrone falcata*) (Bignoniaceae) | (*Ziziphus xylopyrus*) (Rhamnaceae) |

teak forests and the thorn-scrub *Acacia – Capparis* savannas of the northern peninsula (Maharashtra). This area receives 600–800 mm of annual rainfall and shares a number of woodland species with the southern dry deciduous vegetation types with the exception of *Tectona* and *Hardwickia*. In the Deccan Trap, *Albizia amara* and *Chloroxylon swietenia* (both important components of the dry deciduous and scrub vegetation of the southern peninsula) are also absent.

*Anogeissus – Terminalia* woodlands occur beyond the northern limit of the distribution of teak in parts of the Aravalli hills, and in the Vindyan plateau and hills. Annual rainfall ranges between 700–800 mm, with 8 dry months. Teak is absent, otherwise woodland composition resembles very

Table 4.4. Select dry deciduous species: the *Anogeissus-Hardwickia* association. Select key indicator species in bold; those specific only to this variant are marked with an asterisk. Some of these species may occur in scrub savannas. Species/Genera not included in the anatomical key in parentheses.

*Albizia amara* (Leguminosae-Mimosaceae)
*Acacia chundra/catechu* (Leguminosae-Mimosaceae)
(*Acacia pennata*) (Leguminosae-Mimosaceae)
**Anogeissus latifolia** (Combretaceae)
(*Annona squamosa*) (Annonaceae) introduction from South America
*Azadirachta indica* (Meliaceae)
**Bauhinia racemosa** (Leguminosae-Caesalpiniaceae)
(*Boswellia serrata*) (Burseraceae)
(*Boswellia ovalifoliolata**) (Burseraceae)
(*Butea superba*) (Leguminosae-Papilionaceae)
(*Calycopteris floribunda*) (Combretaceae)
**Cassia auriculata*** (Leguminosae-Caesalpiniaceae)
*Cassia fistula* (Leguminosae-Caesalpiniaceae)
(*Cassia surattensis*) (Leguminosae-Caesalpiniaceae)
*Chloroxylon swietenia* (Rutaceae)
*Cordia* spp. (Ehretiaceae form. in Boraginaceae)
(*Dalbergia lanceolata*) (Leguminosae-Papilionaceae)
*Dalbergia paniculata* (Leguminosae-Papilionaceae)
(*Dendrocalamus strictus*) (Poaceae-Bambusoideae)
(*Dichrostachys cinerea*) (Leguminosae-Mimosaceae)
**Diospyros chloroxylon*** (Ebenaceae)
*Diospyros melanoxylon* (Ebenaceae)
(*Diospyros tomentosa*) (Ebenaceae)
(*Diospyros ovalifolia*) (Ebenaceae)
**Dodonaea viscosa*** (Sapindaceae)
(*Dolichandrone atrovirens*) (Bignoniaceae)
(*Erythroxylon* sp.) (Erythroxylaceae)
(*Flacourtia indica**) (Flacourtiaceae)
**Feronia limonia** (Rutaceae)
**Gardenia resinifera*** (Rubiaceae)
*Grewia* spp. (Tiliaceae)
*Gyrocarpus americanus* (Hernandiaceae)
(*Hardwickia binata**) (Leguminosae-Caesalpiniaceae)
(*Holoptelea integrifolia*) (Moraceae)
(*Ixora arborea*) (Rubiaceae)
(*Lannea coromandelica*) (Anacardiaceae)
**Maytenus (Gymnosporia) emarginata** (Celastraceae)
(*Mundulea sericea*) (Leguminosae-Papilionaceae)
(*Osyris quadripartita*) (Santalaceae)
*Pterocarpus marsupium* (Leguminosae-Papilionaceae)
(*Pterocarpus santalinus**) (Leguminosae-Papilionaceae) in and around Cuddapah basin only
*Santalum album* (Santalaceae)
*Schleichera oleosa* (Sapindaceae)
*Soymida febrifuga* (Meliaceae)
**Strychnos potatorum*** (Loganiaceae)
(*Strychnos colubrina**) (Loganiaceae)
*Tamarindus indica* (Leguminosae-Caesalpiniaceae)
*Vitex altissima* (Verbenaceae)
**Wrightia tinctoria** (Apocynaceae)
(*Xeromphis spinosa*) (Rubiaceae)
(*Ziziphus xylopyrus*) (Rhamnaceae)
(*Ziziphus oenoplia*) (Rhamnaceae)

closely that of dry deciduous teak forests (Table 4.3). The bael (*Aegle marmelos*) is a common fruit tree in this zone, as is *Madhuca longifolia*.

Towards the eastern limit of the distribution of teak (annual rainfall >1,100 mm) *Tectona – Terminalia* woodlands are dominant. These are considered transitional between the dry and the moist deciduous teak forests (Table 4.2; Figure 4.7), and they are also found in the central part of the Nallamalai hills. A variant of this mixed dry-moist deciduous forest occurs in the northern end of the Western Ghats, south of the Tapti river, where the *Tectona – Terminalia – Anogeissus* association includes *Adina cordifolia* as a codominant species.

Dry deciduous forests have always been important sources of timber, grazing, lac, and silk. Teak (*Tectona grandis*) is the most valued commercial timber species and is often coppiced.

Figure 4.7. *Terminalia*-dominated dry deciduous woodland

Other key timber species include *Anogeissus* spp., *Chloroxylon swietenia*, *Dalbergia* spp., *Diospyros melanoxylon*, *Hardwickia binata*, *Pterocarpus* spp., *Schleichera oleosa*, and *Terminalia* spp.

The *neem* tree (*Azadirachta indica*) thrives in this zone and has many uses (Chapter 6). Sandalwood (*Santalum album*) is valued for its scented wood and medicinal properties (Figure 4.8).

Other gathered tree products include dyes, tannin substances, and cordage fibres. Plants yielding dyes are *Wrightia tinctoria* (its sap for yellow and its leaves for blue dyes), *Strychnos nux-vomica* (its fruits for brown dyes), *Chloroxylon swietenia*, and *Azadirachta indica* (their resin for yellow dye). While many plant species are used as tannin sources, indigenous leather industries have traditionally focused on the extraction (by boiling) of tannins from the wood and the bark of *Cassia auriculata*, *Acacia chundra*, *Ziziphus* spp., and the fruits of *Terminalia*. Coarse fibres are procured from *Butea monosperma*, *Bauhinia vahlii*, *Acacia leucophloea*, *Soymida febrifuga*, and *Grewia* spp.

Another category of traditional forest products comprises various tree gums and lac. There are also several resins that are gathered in dry deciduous forests, including the incense resin (olibanum) from *Boswellia* (see Burseraceae, Chapter 6) and *kino* resins from *Pterocarpus marsupium* and *Butea monosperma*. The sap of *Buchanania* is used as a varnish and the gum of *Soymida febrifuga* as an adhesive. Edible gums are gathered from *Acacia chundra/catechu* and *Anogeissus latifolia*.

*Tasar* silk is made from the cocoons of a native silk moth, *Antheraea mylitta*, which feeds on native Indian trees (including *Shorea*, *Terminalia*, and *Ziziphus*) (Chatterjee 1991; Watt 1889–1893). However, the distribution of the *tasar* silk moth extends mainly north of the Godavari river, from Central India to Orissa and Bihar (Watt 1889–1893) and is thus unlikely to have been economically significant in the south. As reported from the ethnography of the Gonds of Bastar, silk moths are usually gathered during the rainy season from tall *Terminalia tomentosa* trees (Grigson 1949). This would seem to be a likely source of the silk fibres identified from Navdatoli in the Narmada basin dated to the Jorwe period (1500–1200 B.C.E.) (Gulati 1961).

There are numerous edible fruits that can be gathered from dry deciduous woodlands, mainly

Figure 4.8. Sandalwood tree in the Sandur forest

during the dry season. The edible seeds of the Cuddapah almond (*Buchanania lanzan*) have been found in Chalcolithic Inamgaon (Kajale 1988). *Ziziphus mauritiana* (ber), *Phyllanthus emblica* (the emblic myrobalan renowned for the medicinal properties of its fruit), and *Cordia myxa* (sebesten plum) have all been found in Neolithic and Chalcolithic sites in Karnataka and Maharashtra (Fuller, Korisettar, and Venkatasubbaiah 2001; Fuller, Venkakasubbaiah, and Korisettar 2001; Kajale 1988, 1991). *Syzygium cumini* is reported to occur along river courses in the dry deciduous zone (Singh 1988:67). Other important edible fruits are listed in Table 4.5.

The leaves of *Diospyros melanoxylon* are collected for wrapping the locally made *beedi* cigarettes (Ambasta et al. 1986). Saha (2002) reports that the annual burning of woodland vegetation by the Gond tribe in northeast Maharashtra is aimed at encouraging *Diospyros* leaf growth. *Diospyros melanoxylon* is a fire-tolerant species that coppices readily producing abundant foliage (Meher-Homji 2001:110; Pimpalapure 1999). It remains unclear, however, how significant *beedi* production would have been before the introduction of tobacco during colonial times (Pimpalapure 1999).

From an archaeological viewpoint, perhaps the most important aspect of the dry deciduous zone is its status as the primary habitat of the wild progenitors of several crop species cultivated in peninsular India during the Neolithic, including various millets and (likely) the pulse horsegram.

Table 4.5. Important edible fruits of the dry deciduous zone

| |
|---|
| *Aegle marmelos* (Rutaceae) |
| *Balanites aegyptiaca* (Balanitaceae) |
| *Capparis* spp. (Capparaceae) |
| *Cordia myxa* (Ehretiaceae) |
| *Diospyros* spp. (Ebenaceae) |
| *Feronia limonia* (Rutaceae) |
| *Grewia* spp. (Tiliaceae) |
| *Phyllanthus emblica* (Euphorbiaceae) |
| *Prosopis cineraria* (Leguminosae-Mimosaceae) |
| *Rhus mysorensis* (Anacardiaceae) |
| *Securinega leucopyrus* (Euphorbiaceae) |
| *Tamarindus indica* (Leguminosae-Caesalpiniaceae) |
| *Ziziphus mauritiana* (Rhamnaceae) |

There are several indigenous millet cultivars in peninsular India (Table 4.6), in addition to a number of species that have been introduced from Africa (see Fuller 2003b) and temperate Eurasia (Fuller 2002, 2003a). Native millet grasses are widespread, although they rarely form extensive and dense stands. This is the reason why they are poorly represented in studies of Indian grassland ecology, which have focused instead on the dominant perennial species deemed important for the sustenance of grazing livestock (Dabadghao and Shankarnarayan 1973; Puri et al. 1989:313–90; Whyte 1964) Furthermore, millets form only a minor part of the annual grass component of the *Sehima – Dichanthium* grasslands that dominate most of peninsular India. The available data suggest that millet grasses are presently more common in dry deciduous woodland vegetation and along watercourses. Clearings (natural or anthropogenic) in dry deciduous woodlands created by fire or other agents and in time developing into savanna pockets might have offered suitable habitats for populations of millet grasses. It was perhaps in similar settings, on the margins of dry deciduous woodlands verging into thorn-scrub savanna, that wild horsegram (*Macrotyloma uniflorum*) was cultivated for the first time, although the limited ecological information available for this species suggests that it rather favours savanna habitats.

## EDAPHIC VEGETATION TYPES: RIVERINE FORESTS

River valley habitats often support vegetation that is somewhat different from the surrounding woodlands. This is due to increased water availability, often for the greater part of the annual cycle (if not year-round), combined with the moisture-retentive properties of alluvial soils. As a consequence, these forests are often regarded by Indian ecologists as special 'climax' types determined by edaphic conditions rather than climate. Other 'edaphic' vegetation types are found along coastlines, where water and salinity are major factors shaping vegetation composition and structure. These coastal formations, including mangroves, are not discussed here because they are of little relevance to the study of prehistoric subsistence in peninsular India.

Table 4.6. Indigenous millet cultivars of peninsular India

| Species | Wild Distribution | Early Archaeological Avidence* |
|---|---|---|
| *Brachiaria ramosa* Browntop millet | Widespread throughout India, as a weed but also occurring as an annual in all grassland types. Generally favouring deciduous hill woods, or stream edges (Singh 1988; Venkataraju and Pullaiah 1995; see also Kimata et al. 2000). | Dominant crop of the Southern Neolithic, also present in Chalcolithic Maharashtra; prominent through the early historic period. Present in Neolithic/Chalcolithic Ganges/Orissa as possible rice weed(?) |
| *Echinochloa colonum* Sawa millet | Widespread throughout India in damp soils, along streams and as a weed (De Wet et al. 1983c). | Present in Neolithic/Chalcolithic Ganges/Orissa as possible rice weed(?). Occasional in Southern Neolithic, late Harappan Saurashtra. Probable crop in Early Historic Tamil Nadu. |
| *Panicum sumatrense* (= *P. miliare*) Little millet | The wild form, *P. psilopodium* is found across north and central India, Gujarat, Rajasthan and into northwest Maharashtra (e.g., Thane) and northern Andhra Pradesh (Lisboa 1896:17; Sant 1964), is rare in eastern Karnataka (Singh 1988), absent from Kurnool (Venkataraju and Pullaiah 1995), and occasionally found in Tamil Nadu (Matthew 1999) (see also De Wet et al. 1983a; Hiremath et al. 1990). | Is the dominant millet in Harappan Saurashtra, and perhaps in north Deccan. Present in Neolithic/Chalcolithic Ganges/Orissa as possible rice weed(?). Probable crop in Early Historic Tamil Nadu. |
| *Paspalum scrobiculatum* Kodo millet | Widespread throughout India in damp soils, and as a weed (De Wet et al. 1983b). Extremely rare in wild habitats of the drier areas like eastern Karnataka or Kurnool (Singh 1988; Venkataraju and Pullaiah 1995). | Occasional in Southern Neolithic, Late Harappan Saurashtra; present in Neolithic/Chalcolithic Ganges/Orissa: as possible rice weed(?). Probable crop in Iron Age/Early Historic peninsular sites from Rajasthan through to Tamil Nadu. |
| *Setaria pumila* (= *S. glauca* syn. *S. pallidfusca* Yellow foxtail millet | Common all over India, especially as a weed, and on roadsides and wastelands (Gammie 1911; De Wet et al 1979; Kimata et al. 2000). | Present in Harappan Saurashtra; present in Neolithic/Chalcolithic Ganges/Orissa: as possible rice weed(?) |
| *Setaria verticillata* Bristley foxtail millet | Found throughout the plains and hills, esepcially along streams (Gammie 1911; Venkataraju and Pullaiah 1995). | Co-dominant crop of the Southern Neolithic; present in Harappan Saurashtra. Declines after the Neolithic. |

*Note:* This archaeological summary comprises updated information since Fuller 2002, including authors' as yet unpublished data.

From an ecological viewpoint, rivers provide vegetation hotspots allowing species from moister zones to penetrate arid areas. In this section, we briefly outline some key taxa that occur in riverine habitats in the moist and dry deciduous zones. Many of the species listed for the dry deciduous zone may also occur along watercourses in the dry evergreen savanna scrub.

Tropical moist deciduous riverine forests are very similar with regard to species composition and structure to tropical moist deciduous woodlands (Table 4.7). Dominant species include *Lagerstroemia* spp. and *Terminalia tomentosa* (Puri et al. 1989:486). They occupy alluvial soils bordering perennial streams and rivers, and their ground flora is very poor in grass species. One striking characteristic of these woodlands are the masses of epiphytic orchids forming several specialised plant communities. Other specialised vegetation types include the bamboo 'breaks' of

Table 4.7. Moist deciduous riverine forest. Including some species reported from riparian settings in the Nallamalai hills (see Ellis 1987:15)

| | |
|---|---|
| *Adina cordifolia* (Rubiaceae) | *Lagerstroemia parviflora* (Lythraceae) |
| *Albizia procera* (Leguminosae-Mimosaceae) | *Mallotus philippensis* (Euphorbiaceae) |
| *Butea* spp. (Leguminosae-Papilionaceae) | *Mangifera indica* (Anacardiaceae) |
| (*Celtis cinnamomea*) (Ulmaceae) Nallamalais | *Mitragyna parvifolia* (Rubiaceae) |
| (*Cleistanthus patulus*) (Euphorbiaceae) Nallamalais | *Phyllanthus emblica* (Euphorbiaceae) |
| *Dalbergia* spp. (Leguminosae-Papilionaceae) | *Terminalia tomentosa* (Combretaceae) |
| (*Diospyros malabarica*) (Ebenaceae) | (*Oroxylum indicum*) (Bignoniaceae) Nallamalais |
| (*Flacourtia* spp.) (Flacourtiaceae) | (*Trema orientalis*) (Ulmaceae) Nallamalais |
| *Grewia* spp. (Tiliaceae) | (*Trewia* spp.) (Euphorbiaceae) |
| (*Homonoia riparia*) (Euphorbiaceae) | (*Vitex leucoxylon*) (Verbenaceae) |
| (*Ixora pavetta*) (Rubiaceae) | *Ziziphus* (Rhamnaceae) |
| (*Lagerstroemia microcarpa*) (Lythraceae) | |

Kanara (*Bambusa arundinacea*, *Dendrocalamus strictus*, *Oxytenanthera monostigma*), where *Bambusa* is the dominant species.

Tropical dry riverine forests (Figure 4.9) are distributed mainly along the raised banks of the larger rivers and/or abandoned streambeds, growing on light sandy soils that often overlay laterite hardpans and boulder beds. Owing to increased solar radiation from the exposed rock and sandy substrata, the air temperature is usually very high. Their canopy is very uneven: Trees may be of large size, forming irregular patches intermittent with varying amounts of smaller trees and shrubby undergrowth. The dominant species are *Acacia chundra*, *Tamarix* spp., and sometimes *Prosopis*, too, extending into dry evergreen savanna habitats. In dry seasonally flooded riverbeds extending into the savanna zones, recurrent species include *Acacia nilotica* and *Phoenix sylvestris*. In addition, numerous herbaceous plant families are represented in dry riverine forests, including sedges (Cyperaceae) and grasses (Poaceae). Among the grasses, millets may abound locally, including *Setaria* spp., *Brachiaria ramosa*, *Echinochloa colonum*, *Paspalum scrobiculatum*, and *Panicum sumatrense*. This group hosts the wild progenitors of most of the millet crops found in South Indian Neolithic sites (see Table 4.6). Table 4.8 lists the main tree and shrub species that are found along watercourses in the dry deciduous zone (Henry, Rathakrishnan, and Ravisankar 1996:462, 473; Pallithanam 2001; Puri 1960:217–218; Singh 1988:67).

## DRY EVERGREEN THORN FORESTS AND SAVANNAS

The driest parts of the peninsula, in the rainshadow area east of the Western Ghats, are covered by open woodlands rich in herbaceous species, especially grasses, usually referred to as thorn forests, savannas, or dry evergreen woodlands (see Figures 4.10 to 4.13). The last term was introduced by Champion (1936) for describing the vegetation growing along the southeastern coastal plain of India, where he observed that, despite the very dry climate, evergreen species were dominant. Floristic analyses (see Puri et al. 1989:297–306) indicate that most of the species found in this area are commonly met in the thorny scrub formations of south-central India (see Table 4.9; the six species restricted to the southeast coast are also indicated). An important aspect of climate in this area is the particularly low level of rainfall (< 130 mm) during May and June, the hottest months of the year just before the onset of the monsoon, resulting in the predominance of dry evergreen scrub. By contrast, deciduous woodland is widespread in areas with more substantial pre-/early monsoon rainfall (about 150–220 mm during May and June) (Puri et al. 1989:307–08).

In much of the ecological literature, these thorn forests and scrub woodlands are classified as 'biotic' forests (for example, Puri 1960) and, like savannas, are regarded as the outcome of the over-exploitation and destruction of dry deciduous vegetation. Puri's (1960) analysis of the nature

Figure 4.9. Dry riverine *Acacia* savanna (Tamil Nadu)

Table 4.8. Dry deciduous riverine forest

*Acacia chundra* (Leguminosae-Mimosaceae)
*Acacia nilotica* (Leguminosae-Mimosaceae)
(*Acacia eburnea*) (Leguminosae-Mimosaceae)
(*Alangium salvifolium*) (Alangiaceae)
*Barringtonia acutangula* (Myrtaceae)
(*Crinum defixum*) (Amaryllidaceae)
(*Crotalaria sericea*) (Leguminosae)
(*Diospyros malabarica*) (Ebenaceae)
*Diospyros melanoxylon* (Ebenaceae)
(*Ficus hispida*) (Moraceae)
(*Ficus microcarpa*) (Moraceae)
(*Ficus racemosa*) (Moraceae)
(*Holoptelea integrifolia*) (Urticaceae)
(*Homonoia retusa*) (Euphorbiaceae)
(*Ixora arborea*) (Rubiaceae)
(*Lawsonia inermis*) (Lythraceae) in drier zones, possibly anthropogenic introduction (?)
(*Ixora pavetta*) (Rubiaceae)
*Mallotus philippensis* (Euphorbiaceae)
*Mangifera indica* (Anacardiaceae)
*Mitragyna parvifolia* (Rubiaceae)
(*Phoenix sylvestris*) (Palmae)
(*Pandanus fascicularis*) (Pandanaceae)
(*Pongamia pinnata*) (Leguminosae)
(*Prosopis cineraria*) (Leguminosae-Mimosaceae) more common on the northern peninsula
(*Prosopis juliflora*) (Leguminosae-Mimosaceae) naturalized (?)
(*Rotula aquatica*) (Boraginaceae)
(*Syzygium cumini*) (Myrtaceae)
(*Syzygium heyneanum*) (Myrtaceae)
(*Tamarix ericoides*) (Tamaricaceae)
*Tamarindus indica* (Leguminosae-Caesalpiniaceae)
*Terminalia arjuna* (Combretaceae)
(*Vitex negundo*) (Verbenaceae)

Figure 4.10. *Acacia* scrub-savanna (Tamil Nadu)

Figure 4.11. "Jungle" thorn-scrub (Tamil Nadu)

Figure 4.12. *Acacia* savanna grassland (Kurnool area)

Figure 4.13. *Acacia* savanna grassland (Kurnool area)

Table 4.9. Dry evergreen scrub

| | |
|---|---|
| *Acacia chundra* (Leguminosae-Mimosaceae) | (*Euphorbia caducifolia*) (Euphorbiaceae) |
| *Acacia leucophloea* (Leguminosae-Mimosaceae) | (*Garcinia spicata*) (Clusiaceae) southeast coastal area, winter monsoon zone |
| (*Acacia horrida*, syn. *A. latronum*) (Leguminosae-Mimosaceae) | (*Gmelina asiatica*) (Verbenaceae) |
| (*Acacia eburnea*) (Leguminosae-Mimosaceae) | (*Grewia serrulata*) (Tiliaceae) |
| (*Acacia caesia*) (Leguminosae-Mimosaceae) | *Grewia* spp. (Tiliaceae) |
| (*Acacia pennata*) (Leguminosae-Mimosaceae) | (*Givotia rottleriformis*) (Euphorbiaceae) |
| *Albizia amara* (Leguminosae-Mimosaceae) | (*Gyrocarpus jacquini*) (Hernandiaceae) |
| (*Albizia lebbek*) (Leguminosae-Mimosaceae) | (*Hugonia mystax*) (Linaceae) |
| (*Atalantia monophylla*) (Rutaceae) | (*Maba buxifolia*) (Ebenaceae) |
| (*Atalantia racemosa*) (Rutaceae) | (*Manilkara hexandra*) (Sapotaceae) southeast coastal area, winter monsoon zone |
| (*Aristolochia indica*) (Aristolochiaceae) | *Maytenus* (*Gymnosporia*) *emarginata* (Celastraceae) |
| (*Blumea obliqua*) (Compositae) | (*Maytenus heyneana*) (Celastraceae) |
| *Canthium parviflorum* (Rubiaceae) | (*Memecylon umbellatum*) (Melastomataceae) southeast coastal area, winter monsoon zone |
| (*Capparis divaricata*) (Capparaceae) | (*Osyris quadripartita*) (Santalaceae) |
| (*Capparis grandis*) (Capparaceae) | (*Phoenix humilis*) (Palmae) |
| *Capparis sepiaria* (Capparaceae) | (*Plecospermum spinosum*) (Urticaceae) |
| (*Capparis zeylanica*) (Capparaceae) | (*Prosopis cineraria*) (Leguminosae-Mimosaceae) more common on the northern peninsula |
| (*Carissa spinarum*) (Apocynaceae) | (*Pterolobium hexapetalum*) (Leguminosae) |
| (*Carmona microphylla*) (Boraginaceae) southeast coastal area, winter monsoon zone | (*Pterospermum suberifolium*) (Sterculiaceae) southeast coastal area, winter monsoon zone |
| *Cassia auriculata* (Leguminosae-Caesalpiniaceae) | (*Randia malabarica*) (Rubiaceae) |
| (*Cassia montana*) (Leguminosae-Caesalpiniaceae) | (*Rivea hypocrateriformis*) (Convolvulaceae) |
| (*Cipadessa fruticosa*) (Meliaceae) | *Securinega leucopyrus* (Euphorbiaceae) |
| (*Cissus quadrangularis*) (Vitaceae) | (*Stenosiphonium* spp.) (Acanthaceae) |
| *Commiphora berryi* (Burseraceae) | (*Strychnos colubrina*) (Loganiaceae) |
| (*Cordia gharaf*) (Ehretiaceae) | *Tamarindus indica* (Leguminosae-Caesalpiniaceae) |
| *Cordia myxa* (Ehretiaceae) | (*Tarenna asiatica*) (Rubiaceae) |
| (*Cycas circinalis*) (Cycadaceae) mainly in the far south (Tamil Nadu) | (*Tylophora indica*) (Asclepiadaceae) |
| (*Dolichandrone atrovirens*) (Bignoniaceae) | (*Ziziphus glabrata*) (Rhamnaceae) |
| *Diospyros melanoxylon* (Ebenaceae) | (*Ziziphus glaberrima*) (Rhamnaceae) |
| (*Diospyros chloroxylon*) (Ebenaceae) | *Ziziphus mauritiana* (Rhamnaceae) |
| *Dodonaea viscosa* (Sapindaceae) | (*Ziziphus nummularia*) (Rhamnaceae) |
| (*Drypetes sepiaria*) (Euphorbiaceae) southeast coastal area, winter monsoon zone | (*Ziziphus oenoplia*) (Rhamnaceae) |
| (*Erythroxylon* sp.) (Erythroxylaceae) | (*Ziziphus xylopyrus*) (Rhamnaceae) |
| (*Euphorbia antiquorum*) (Euphorbiaceae) | |
| (*Euphorbia tortilis*) (Euphorbiaceae) | |

and the status of savannas in the subcontinent enumerates the following factors as responsible for their widespread presence in Central and South India: grazing, lopping, felling, and firing. He has suggested that human activities created gaps in the original forest cover that allowed the establishment of grassland 'weeds' amid forest vegetation, and further dispersal of their seeds by ungulates resulted in grasslands taking over degraded forest lands. In alluvial plains, seasonal and/or interannual flooding may also be responsible for the uprooting and killing of tree seedlings, as well as the establishment of grasses and shrubs whose seeds are transported by water. Although heavy grazing and frequent firing of vegetation can certainly promote the expansion of savanna habitats and may also contribute to their maintenance in the long term, at the same time there is no reason to doubt that such vegetation is natural in its origins and that it existed in parts of the peninsula well before the advent of Neolithic agriculture and pastoralism (Chapter 5). Given that some species are well adapted to fire, we believe that they likely evolved in environments that might have been naturally prone to periodic fires. Palaeoecological records of micro-charcoal particles from tropical regions have indicated that natural fire regimes have fluctuated in response to global climate shifts (Haberle, Hope, and Van der Kaars 2001; Haberle and David 2004; Thevenon et al. 2004). Nevertheless, it is certain that that anthropogenic burning of vegetation since the upper Palaeolithic has favoured the propagation and reproduction of fire-tolerant taxa (see Table 4.12) and thus promoted decisively the expansion of savanna environments at the expense of closed canopy woodlands and forests.

Dry evergreen woodlands and savannas include a wide range of spiny species (resistant to grazing) as well as fire-resistant and drought-tolerant taxa (see Tables 4.9, 4.11, 4.12). Although such environments are often regarded as degraded tropical dry deciduous forests, they are just as likely to have derived from heavily grazed grasslands. Heavy grazing select in favour of spiny shrubs that are least attractive to browsing animals (Sopher 1980). Savanna-like formations within dry deciduous forests are conspicuous by their small and widely spaced 'crooked' trees with characteristically short boles. Dry evergreen/thorn-scrub may thus coexist with deciduous woodland vegetation, forming a mosaic of habitats that is controlled and influenced by both climate/soil conditions and the local history of land uses.

With regard to woodland structure, savanna trees are well spaced and usually have spreading crowns. Understorey vegetation is poorly developed and consists mainly of spiny, xerophytic shrubs. Some grassland growth may appear during the short monsoon season that is browsed by wild and domestic ungulates. Grasses can survive grazing in the sheltered shaded areas near the bases of spiny shrubs and trees as well as along watercourses. Dominant trees include spiny *Acacia* spp., the cactiform succulent *Euphorbia*, *Capparis* spp., and *Ziziphus* spp. In some places (for example, the Erramalai hills) *Cordia myxa* and *Balanites aegyptiaca* are abundant, although this may reflect the preferential non-cutting of fruit species. On the southern peninsula, the dry evergreen woodlands are dominated by *Acacia horrida*, *Acacia leucophloea*, and *Albizia amara*, which define the *Acacia – Albizia* zone. *Albizia amara* does not extend north into the Deccan Trap geological zone. On the northern peninsula, in Gujarat and southern Rajasthan it is the *Acacia – Capparis* type of bush savanna that becomes dominant (Table 4.10).

One of the most important economic uses of the dry evergreen scrub is as pasture land. Fruit species are not as common as in the moist and dry deciduous zones except for *Ziziphus*, *Cordia*, *Capparis*, *Balanites*, *Maba*, and *Canthium coromandelicum*. *Grewia serrulata* may serve as a host for lac insects (Ambasta et al. 1986) although it is not as significant in this respect as the deciduous *Butea monosperma* and *Schleichera oleosa*. Also found in this zone is *Oldenlandia umbellata*, a perennial

Table 4.10. Thorn savannas of the northern Deccan

(*Acacia-Capparis* zone)
*Acacia chundra* (Leguminosae-Mimosaceae)
*Acacia leucophloea* (Leguminosae-Mimosaceae)
(*Acacia horrida*) (syn. *A. latronum*) (Leguminosae-Mimosaceae)
(*Acacia intsia*) (Leguminosae-Mimosaceae)
*Acacia nilotica* (Leguminosae-Mimosaceae)
(*Acacia pennata*) (Leguminosae-Mimosaceae)
*Azadirachta indica* (Meliaceae)
introduction from north India (?)
(*Balanites aegyptiaca*) (Balanitaceae)
*Bauhinia racemosa* (Leguminosae-Caesalpiniaceae)
(*Capparis decidua*) (Capparaceae)
(*Capparis divaricata*) (Capparaceae)
(*Cardiospermum halicacabum*) (Sapindaceae)
**Cassia auriculata** (Leguminosae-Caesalpiniaceae)
(*Cocculus hirsutus*) (Menispermaceae)
(*Dichrostachys cinerea*) (Leguminosae)
*Diospyros melanoxylon* (Ebenaceae)
(*Dolichandrone falcata*) (Bignoniaceae)
(*Euphorbia neriifolia*) (Euphorbiaceae) cactiform Euphorbia on basalt.
(*Flacourtia indica\**) (Flacourtiaceae)
*Maytenus* (*Gymnosporia*) *emarginata* (Celastraceae)
(*Phoenix sylvestris*) (Palmae)
(*Sarcostemma acidum*) (Asclepiadaceae)
*Securinega leucopyrus* (Euphorbiaceae)
(*Xerophis spinosa*) (Rubiaceae)
*Ziziphus mauritiana* (Rhamnaceae)
(*Ziziphus xylopyrus*) (Rhamnaceae)

Table 4.11. Light, shade, and drought tolerance of select South Indian tree and shrub species

| **Light-Demanding Species** | **Partial Light-Demanding Species** |
|---|---|
| *Acacia catechu* | *Albizia lebbek* |
| *A. leucophloea* | *Albizia odoratissima* |
| *Adina cordifolia* | *Bauhinia lawii* |
| *Anogeissus latifolia* | *Dalbergia latifolia* |
| *Bassia latifolia* | *Diospyros melanoxylon* |
| *Bauhinia racemosa* | *Hardwickia binata* |
| *Boswellia serrata* | *Holarrhena antidysenterica* |
| *Bombax ceiba* | *Lagerstroemia microcarpa* |
| *B. malabaricum* | *Pterocarpus marsupium* |
| *Casuarina equisetifolia* | *Ziziphus mauritiana* |
| *Chloroxylon swietenia* | |
| *Dalbergia paniculata* | |
| *Gmelina arborea* | |
| *Grewia tiliaefolia* | |
| *Lagerstroemia parviflora* | |
| *Melia indica* | |
| *Prosopis cineraria* | |
| *Santalum album* | |
| *Spondias mangifera* | |
| *Syzygium cumini* (*Eugenia jambolana*) | |
| *Terminalia tomentosa* | |
| *Tectona grandis* | |
| *Terminalia paniculata* | |
| *T. bellerica* | |

**Shade-Tolerant Species**

*Butea frondosa*
*Careya arborea*
*Garcinia indica*
*Mangifera indica*
*Soymida febrifuga*
*Strychnos* spp.
*Wrightia tinctoria*
(& all the species encountered in the wet evergreen tropical forests)

| **Very Drought-Resistant Species** | **Medium Drought-Resistant Species** | **Drought-Sensitive Species** |
|---|---|---|
| *Acacia* spp. | *Adina cordifolia* | *Anogeissus latifolia* |
| | *Albizia procera* | *Bassia latifolia* |
| | *Butea monosperma* | *Mangifera indica* |
| | *Bauhinia racemosa* | *Terminalia tomentosa* |
| | *Careya arborea* | |
| | *Carissa spinarum* | |
| | *Cassia fistula* | |
| | *Cordia myxa* | |
| | *Holarrhena antidysenterica* | |
| | *Lagerstroemia parviflora* | |
| | *Mallotus philippensis* | |
| | *Mitragyna parvifolia* | |
| | *Syzygium cumini* (*Eugenia jambolana*) | |
| | *Terminalia bellerica* | |
| | *Wrightia tomentosa* | |
| | *Ziziphus xylopyrus* | |

Table 4.12. Fire and grazing tolerance of select South Indian plant species

| Fire-Tolerant Species | Grasses in Fire-Maintained Savanna Woodlands | Grazing-Tolerant Species |
|---|---|---|
| *Acacia* spp. | *Apluda mutica* | *Acacia* spp. |
| *Bridelia retusa* | *Aristida* spp. | *Aerva javanica* |
| *Dalbergia latifolia* | *Bothriochloa pertusa* | *Barleria buxifolia* |
| *Diospyros melanoxylon* | *Chloris barbata* | *Butea monosperma* |
| *Holarrhena antidysenterica* | *Cymbopogon* spp. | *Calotropis gigantea* |
| *Miliusa tomentosa* | *Dichanthium annulatum* | *Canthium dicoccum* |
| *Phoenix humilis* | *D. caricosum* | *Canthium parvicoccum* |
| *Phyllanthus emblica* | *Heteropogon contortus* | *Carissa congesta* |
| *Tectona grandis* | *Iseilema laxum* | *Capparis divaricata* |
| *Wrightia tinctoria* | *Oplismenus burmanii* | *Cassia auriculata* |
| *Xylia xylocarpa* | *Sehima nervosum* | *Cassia fistula* |
| *Ziziphus mauritiana* | *S. sulcata* | *Cassia tora* |
| | *Setaria pumila* | *Dichrostachys cinerea* |
| | *Themeda quadrivalvis* | *Diospyros melanoxylon* |
| | *T. triandra* | *Dodonaea viscosa* |
| | | *Euphorbia antiquorum* |
| | | *Euphorbia tirucali* |
| | | *Flacourtia indica* |
| | | *Lantana camara* |
| | | *Melochia coircorifolia* |
| | | *Phoenix humilis* |
| | | *Phoenix sylvestris* |
| | | *Pterolobium hexapetalum* |
| | | *Securinga leucopyrus* |
| | | *Sida cordifolia* |
| | | *Tectona grandis* |
| | | *Tephrosia purpurea* |
| | | *Triumfetta bartramia* |
| | | *Xeromphis spinosa* |
| | | *Ziziphus xylocarpus* |

| Plants of the Dry Deciduous Zone Promoted by Moderate-Grazing | Plants Favoured by Heavy Grazing |
|---|---|
| *Eragrostis tenella* | *Aristida adscensionis* |
| *E. elongata* | *Aristida funiculata* |
| *E. interrupta* | *Brachiaria eruciformis* |
| *Iseilema anthephoroides* | *Borreria stricta* |
| *Brachiaria eruciformis* | *Bothriochloa pertusa* |
| *Themeda quadrivalvis* | *Chloris virgata* |
| | *Chrysopogon fulvus* |
| | *Dactyloctenium aegyptium* |
| | *Eleusine indica* |
| | *Eragrostis viscosa* |
| | *Heteropogon contortus* |
| | *Iseilema anthephoroides* |
| | *Microchloa indica* |
| | *Polygala chinensis* |
| | *Setaria pumila* |
| | *Urochloa panicoides* |
| | *Zornia diphylla* |

herb growing on sandy and rocky soils (mainly from Raichur southward, present only sporadically in Maharashtra). Its roots ('chay root' or 'Indian madder', not to be confused with the 'Bengal madder' produced from *Rubia cordifolia*) are gathered to make a deep red permanent dye (Singh 1988:351) used in the traditional textile industry of southeastern India (Arasaratnam 1986:101). *Oldenlandia umbellata* was cultivated in the past along the Coromandel coast (Drury 1873). Indian bdellium resin *(Commiphora wightii)*, a kind of myrrh used for the manufacture of incense, is also native to evergreen scrub woods (see Burseraceae, Chapter 6). Coarse bark fibres can be procured from the bark of *Cordia, Acacia leucophloea*, and *A. horrida*. *Lawsonia inermis,* the source of the henna dye, is also found in this zone (see Lythraceae, Chapter 6). Tanning substances include 'cutch', extracted by boiling the wood and bark of *Acacia chundra* or *Acacia catechu*. Other *Acacia* barks can be used for this purpose, as can *Ziziphus* spp. and *Cassia* spp. Some of the *Acacia* species also produce edible gums, especially *A. nilotica*.

Thorn savannas were among the primary natural habitats of the wild progenitor of horsegram (*Macrotyloma uniflorum,* syn. *Dolichos biflorus*). Horsegram is the most abundant pulse crop found in Southern Neolithic sites (Fuller et al. 2004) and is also ubiquitous in Chalcolithic sites in Maharashtra (Fuller 2002; Kajale 1991). Unfortunately, the wild distribution of this species in South Asia has been poorly documented (Fuller 2002). Ecological studies of wild horsegram populations in Africa, where this species was not domesticated, have indicated that it abounds in *Acacia* thickets in dry savanna vegetation (Jansen 1989). Relict populations have been recorded in the drier parts of India, from Rajasthan to inner Maharashtra and northeast Karnataka (data gathered by D. Fuller from the herbaria at Calcutta [CAL] and Pune [BSI]). Herbarium specimens in Pune include *M. uniflorum* from the Madhugiri State Forest in Karnataka, where it is reported to grow as a climber on *Ziziphus mauritiana* (specimen: Singh 142187 [BSI]). The facts that wild horsegram collections are rare and this species has been largely overlooked by floristic work suggest that most of their original habitats have been replaced by cultivated land and vegetation heavily modified by human impact. Unlike other taxa found in savanna habitats, wild horsegram is unlikely to recover successfully from sustained grazing or fire pressures. As noted already, the co-occurrence of savanna scrub with dry deciduous woodland habitats might provide areas of overlap between the distributions of the wild progenitors of South Indian millets and horsegram.

Grassland vegetation constitutes an important component of savanna and dry deciduous woodland habitats. The knowledge of the distribution and ecology of the wild millet grasses that gave rise to cultivated crops is of particular significance for the study of prehistoric agriculture and pastoralism. However, as already discussed (see section on dry deciduous woodlands) most of the millet grasses that are indigenous to peninsular India are slightly hydrophytic, being encountered more frequently along watercourses or in moist micro-environments within dry deciduous woodland undergrowth. There are three main types of grasslands identified in peninsular India (Dabadghao and Shankarnarayan 1973; Whyte 1964, 1968). Their distribution generally correlates with rainfall and soil gradients, and there can be extensive overlap between them, since many grass species are shared across different types. *Dichanthium – Cenchrus – Elionurus* grasslands are associated with very dry tropical conditions (annual rainfall <750 mm). At present, this type extends over Punjab, western Uttar Pradesh, and northern Rajasthan, on alluvial sands and sandy loam soils. *Phragmites – Saccharum* type grasslands occur on alluvial sands in the plains of Punjab, western Uttar Pradesh, Assam and Manipur, in low-lying and/or poorly drained areas. They include about 24 annual and 40 perennial species. *Sehima – Dichanthium* grasslands (extending over much of the Deccan) are the most diverse. They comprise about 120 different types of grasses, amounting to about 45 perennial and 75 annual species. Such high species diversity argues for a long evolutionary history of Indian tropical grasslands, which is likely to have been closely interrelated with the vegetation history and evolution of dry deciduous and savanna woodlands in peninsular India.

## SOME LIMITING FACTORS IN VEGETATION DEVELOPMENT: WATER AVAILABILITY, SHADE, FIRE, AND ANIMAL GRAZING

Vegetation responses to climate change and/or anthropogenic pressures (clearance, grazing, agriculture, burning, an so on) depend largely on the ecological preferences of individual plant species (for the ecological preferences of South Indian species see Tables 4.11, 4.12). In tropical environments, as elsewhere, parameters such as the availability of ground moisture, the degree of shade- and fire-tolerance, and vegetation succession patterns represent complex micro- to macro-scale ecological processes that invariably affect the decline or proliferation of particular plant species. At the same time, although moisture availability and sunlight are natural environmental variables tied to climate, their effect on plant communities is also conditioned by landforms and soil substrata. Woodland structure is another key variable: sunlight is far less effective in woodlands with dense canopies, consisting of old trees and variable concentrations of deadwood and overgrowth, compared to woodland openings and savanna habitats. Woodland structure thus maintains a direct effect on patterns of species competition and reproduction rates.

Grazing differentially affects species reproduction and natural availability. Plants with highly palatable leaves are adversely affected or even completely obliterated, especially if they are at the seedling stage. By contrast, less palatable species (such as teak) benefit from the removal of competition for soil moisture and nutrients (Rangarajan 1998:587). Because of the great economic interest in pastoral productivity, much research has concentrated on the impact of animal herding on different plant species and communities, in order to assess the relative value of individual species as fodder sources (for example, Dabadghao and Shankarnarayan 1973; Sant 1964; Whyte 1964, 1968).

Fire may serve the purpose of opening up vegetation to invading light-demanding species (usually grasses), but it will also have a complex effect on the survival and the reproduction of arboreal species. Some trees and shrubs may be killed off by fire. Others, however, depend on it for their reproduction. For example, seed dispersal and germination may be facilitated by fire for some plant species, whereas the seeds of others may perish completely as a result of burning. In many ecosystems, recurrent fires provide a cyclical (seasonal or interannual) process of renewal that is essential for the maintenance of certain species or plant communities (for instance, Huggett 1995:232–39; Grove and Rackam 2001:217ff.; Pyne 1997:472–74).

In savanna environments, both grazing and fire serve to check the establishment of new woody vegetation that might develop to form closed canopy woodland by encouraging the maintenance of a herbaceous ground flora layer (Kellman and Tackaberry 1997:199). Yet, heavy grazing and fire pressures can sometimes prove incompatible. In overgrazed areas, ground vegetation may be removed completely, resulting in the suppression of fires. Eventually, thorn grazing-tolerant shrubs will come to dominate local vegetation with only minimal grass growth occurring at sheltered and/or inaccessible areas at the base of spiny shrubs.

To date, little is known about the nature and dynamics of non-anthropogenic fire cycles in peninsular India. Parameters such as the total amount of dry dead vegetation and leaf litter, the density of the grass layer, climate conditions (atmospheric moisture and wind), and ignition sources such as lightning (Kellman and Tackaberry 1997:189; Roberts 2000; Stott 2000) have not been studied in detail for South Indian grasslands and savannas. Climate data indicate that thunderstorms are common at the beginning and the end of the monsoon season (Indian Council for Agricultural Research 1980;Stott 2000). Lightning-induced wild fires are most frequent from May to June, just as the monsoon gets underway but before increasing levels of soil moisture, green plant growth, and generally moister conditions inhibit ignition. Deciduous tree leaf loss and the drying up of grassland biomass begin in the winter (dry season), particularly from January onward. Dead dry biomass reaches its maximum amount by the end of March (Saha 2002; Singh and Singh 1992). Human-induced firing within the period extending from January to May would release nutrients to the soil and support new plant growth brought about by the onset of the rainy season. Firing is also reported to encourage the proliferation of new shoots and foliage for some perennial species. Indeed, a recent study of traditional woodland burning practices among the Gonds of the Bastar area found that most anthropogenic fires are started between February and March (Saha 2002). The limited evidence that is available on prehistoric burning in India (micro-charcoal analyses from pollen cores) is discussed in Chapters 3 and 6.

# CHAPTER 5

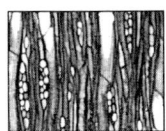

# AN ABRIDGED ENVIRONMENTAL HISTORY OF SOUTH INDIA

If vegetational history is to be factual, it must be based on fossil evidence. It is true that a study of present floras and vegetation forms is a splendid starting point for formulation of historical hypotheses but these remain untested unless fossil evidence is brought to bear. (Flenley 1979:128)

This book aims to provide the background for a new approach to the environmental history of South India; however, there is already much that is known or can be surmised about the palaeovegetation of the peninsula. Quaternary science datasets such as pollen sequences, stable carbon isotopes, and other proxy records are relatively few for South India, in contrast to many other parts of the world. They nevertheless provide some indications of its palaeoecology and periods of important changes. This chapter provides a critical review and synthesis of the available data relevant to understanding palaeoenvironmental change in South India.

Climate and seasonality in India are linked to the Indian Ocean monsoon system (Kutzbach 1987; Schott and McCreary 2001). This weather system ties the Indian peninsula to other regions bordering the Indian Ocean, such as East Africa, the southern Arabian peninsula, and Southeast Asia. Major monsoon changes during the late Pleistocene and the Holocene can be correlated in palaeoecological sequences obtained from East Africa, the Arabian Sea, and various parts of India, the Tibetan Plateau, and regions further to the east (see Hassan 1997a; Hope et al. 2004; Jung et al. 2004; Lézine et al. 1998; Naidu 1996; Sirocko 1996; Wasson 1995; Wei and Gasse 1999). In addition, recent studies have demonstrated a pattern of synchronicity between major climate cycles and events in the Indian Ocean and those of the northern hemisphere recorded in the Greenland ice cores (Sirocko 1996; Van Campo, Duplessy, and Rossignol-Strick 1982; Von Rad et al. 1999a). It follows that global climate change has affected climate change in South India with consequent effects on peninsular vegetation. In turn, such effects can be assessed by investigating the correlation of changes detected in individual South Asian datasets to interregional and global patterns of climate change. The geographical location of the regional palaeoenvironmental sequences discussed in this chapter is shown in Figure 5.1.

## LONG-TERM CLIMATE OSCILLATIONS AND PLANT MIGRATIONS

That climate change has affected the distribution and evolution of the vegetation of the Indian peninsula is indicated from observations on plant and animal biogeographic and phylogenetic patterns. South India includes a large number of disjunct species distributions across most terrestrial phyla, including plants, mammals, birds, and amphibians. Such disjunctions may occur within conventional taxonomic species as well as related species (known in biological jargon as 'vicarious ranges'; Flenley 1979:9). As argued by Karanth (2003), some caution is warranted with regard to taxonomy: documenting true biogeographic disjunctions requires that species (or populations) are phylogenetically related (that is, monophyletic) rather than representing situations of convergent evolution to similar ecological conditions from a distant common ancestor (see also Bossuyt et al. 2004). In South Asia, there clearly are true disjunctions among phylogenetically related species, even members of the same species, especially between the Western Ghats and the northeast. In turn, these disjunctions ought to be understood within the context of past environmental change, which

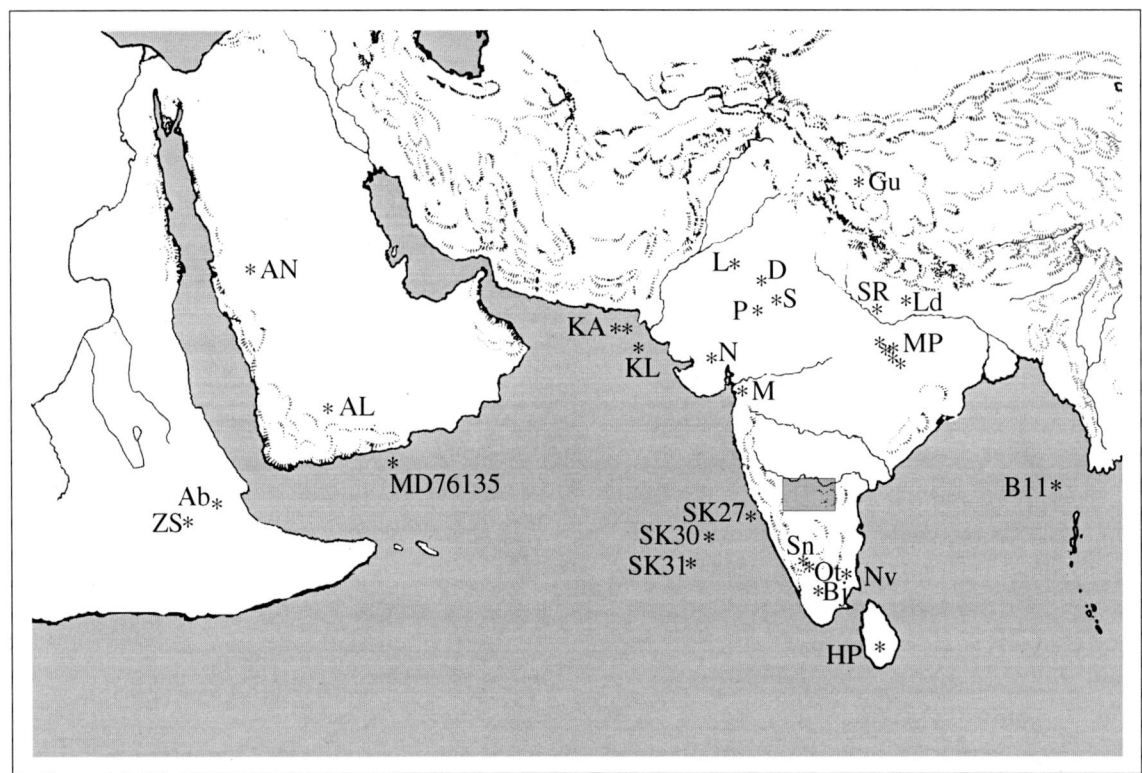

Figure 5.1. Map showing the geographical distribution of the palaeoecological datasets discussed in this chapter

might have allowed species to migrate through corridors or 'islands' of appropriate habitats (for example, the Eastern Ghats and the Satpuras; see Abdulali 1949; Biswas 1949; Hora 1949; Puri 1960:62–68) or to have had much wider and interconnected distributions in the past under particular climatic regimes (Flenley 1979:7). For example, as global climate shifted, in particular as it brought changes in glacial volume and affected sea levels, it is likely that for certain time periods Sri Lanka was connected to the Indian peninsula by land, thus rendering species migration possible. Still, a recent assessment of several animal species from these regions has demonstrated high levels of divergence between related faunas in Sri Lanka and the Western Ghats, hence suggesting that dispersal was quite restricted between the two areas. In turn, this observation highlights the importance of dry lowlands as potential barriers between moist vegetation refugia during periods of depressed sea levels (Bossuyt et al. 2004).

Among woody plants there are numerous cases of disjunct species distributions between the tropical wet evergreen ecosystems of the Western Ghats and similar environments in Northeast India and Southeast Asia. Examples of disjunct distributions were outlined by Puri (1960:33–69) together with cases of overlapping distributions between related species, which may represent more recent expansions after early episodes of separation that facilitated speciation. Examples of the former include *Xylia xylocarpa*, a common component of the tropical moist deciduous forests of the Western Ghats and the moist deciduous sal (*Shorea robusta*) forests of eastern India, and *Dillenia pentagyna,* which occurs in both types of moist deciduous forests as well as in Burma and parts of the Himalayan foothills. The wild *Vigna* pulse species that are ancestral to the mung and urd cultivars show similar disjunctions (Chapter 4). Although we do not review here all cases of discontinuous distributions, we nonetheless stress the importance of recognising their significance. Essentially, they indicate that the modern geographical distributions of plant taxa and vegetation types are not timeless. Instead, they have undergone transformations through multiple episodes of expansion and contraction. It follows that archaeobotanical and palaeobotanical evidence can contribute to evaluating past species distributions and test likely explanatory hypotheses by drawing comparisons with present-day biogeography.

Disjunctions are not limited to rainforest taxa but also include montane temperate and semi-arid savanna species. Between the montane temperate flora of the Himalayas and that of the high elevations of the Nilgiris, the Palnis, and Sri Lanka there are numerous shared species (Puri 1960:68; Sharma 2000:164–65). However, these are predominantly herbaceous species that migrate faster and more efficiently because of their shorter generation times. By contrast, shared woody taxa are very few; they include *Cotoneaster* (Rosaceae) and *Elaeagnus* (Elaeagnaceae) (Hooker 1875–1897). Also of interest in this regard is the mammalian disjunction between the Nilgiri and the Himalayan tahrs. Tahrs (genus *Hemitragus*) are goat-like caprines living in high elevations (Corbett and Hill 1992; Menon 2003:56). A pattern of past distribution in low elevations and/or migration seems likely, which may also account for the caprine fossils (*Ovis/Capra*) reported from some peninsular Pleistocene faunal assemblages (for example, Badam 1984; Badam, Sathe, and Salahuddin 1989; Pandey 1981).

Among species of drier zones there are also cases of disjunct distributions, most notable being those of anthropogenic origin. Teak (*Tectona grandis*) has a disjunct distribution among peninsular India, the dry zone of Burma, and the deciduous forests of Thailand (Flenley 1979:80; Puri 1960:46). Teak also occurs in the drier parts of eastern Indonesia (Java), where, however, it is likely to be an introduced species. Historical references before C.E. 1500 mention only Indian teak (Boomgaard 1998). It has been suggested that teak was introduced in Indonesia, probably in the tenth century C.E. (Pyne 1997:421). The dry deciduous woodlands of eastern Java are dominated by several species that suggest anthropogenic promotion and naturalised introductions including teak, silk cotton (*Bombax malabaricum*), neem (*Azadirachta indica*), palmyra palm (*Borassus flabellifer*), and the *bael* fruit (*Aegle marmelos*) (Burkill 1966; Van Balgooy 1989). A similar case of anthropogenic disjunction between South India and Java is represented by sandalwood (*Santalum album*), which might have been introduced in the other direction from Java to India (see discussion of sandalwood in Chapter 6). Disjunctions between the Indian peninsula and the semi-arid vegetation of Northeast Africa (Puri 1960:22) include mainly herbaceous species and a few woody species too, such as *Cordia myxa, Salvadora persica*, and *Capparis decidua*. These shrubs display a discontinuous distribution through the desert regions of the Middle East. The tamarind (*Tamarindus indica*) might also represent a natural disjunction of this kind, although its anthropogenic introduction from Africa to India has often been assumed (Chapter 6).

The presence of disjunctions of species adapted to wetter or drier, cooler or warmer conditions signals a past of alternating climatic regimes favouring the expansion or regression of particular species, which acted as a 'pump' for species migration and/or further speciation through subsequent episodes of disjunction (allopatry). It has been argued that in the long term such a process of fragmenting species habitats would structure the fossil record of biological evolution into pulses of speciation and extinction, both driven by climatic oscillations (the 'turnover pulse hypothesis' of Vrba 1985, 1988; see also Potts and Behrensmeyer 1992:502). This cyclical process has been in place for millions of years. At a global scale, a cooler climate, characterised by alternating periods of glacial expansion and contraction, has been in place since the Miocene intensifying in the early Pliocene c. 2.4 million years ago (Potts and Behrensmeyer 1992:425; Roberts 1992).

The origins of the Indian Ocean monsoon system (its main characteristic being the protracted summer rainfalls) are traced to the uplift of the Himalayan mountain range disrupting east-west air currents (which occurred about 8 million years ago [Valdiya 1999], although some dating evidence [Coleman and Hodges 1995] might push it back to c. 14 million years). The Himalayas attracted moisture-laden winds off the Indian Ocean, creating summer low pressures (the southwest monsoon) while blocking cool winter rains from the north, thus resulting to a marked wet-dry seasonal oscillation over the subcontinent. In this context, important shifts occurred in the regional flora from the earlier Miocene fossil assemblages dominated by wet tropical taxa (for example, Dipterocarpaceae, *Cinnamomum*) to a flora rich in deciduous taxa, such as *Terminalia* and *Bauhinia* (Valdiya 1999; cf. Sharma 2000:30–48). The process of Himalayan uplift continued through the Pliocene, with its last major phase occurring at the start of the Pleistocene resulting in a progressive increase in the strength of the dry season. Connected to this process was the invasion of the Indian subcontinent by savanna grasslands, indicated in the palaeoenvironmental record by a stable carbon isotope shift toward a higher proportion of $C_4$ plants, which include a wide range of tropical savanna grasses adapted to arid conditions. Although the emergence of savannas in Africa occurred gradually during the Miocene, starting from c. 15 million years ago, the equivalent shift in South Asia was comparatively rapid (focusing at c. 8–7 million years ago and reaching a maximum by 5 million years; see Morgan, Kingston, and Marino 1994; Jacobs, Kingston, and Jacobs 1999) with a concurrent change in fossil fauna towards more grazing species (Potts and Behrensmeyer 1992:483). From the point of view of South Indian vegetation history, the significance of this evidence is the indication that by the end of the Miocene, some 6 million years ago, the basic climate pattern of the South Asian monsoon system was in place, and a broad spectrum of vegetation ecosystems ranging from savanna grasslands to wet evergreen rainforests had been established in the subcontinent. Thereafter, the environmental history of the peninsula became subject to global climate change (for instance, glacial-interglacial cycles), which, given the relatively stable topography of peninsular India, must be viewed as the prime mover for the expansion and the contraction of specific biogeographic zones.

## GLACIAL MAXIMA, VEGETATION REFUGIA AND HOLOCENE TRANSFORMATIONS

While glaciers were established in the Miocene, the Pliocene included both a general long-term trend toward cooler global temperatures and increasing oscillations between warmer and cooler conditions. A marked downturn in global temperature has been documented from oxygen-isotope records in deep sea cores at c. 2.4 million years ago (Potts and Behrensmeyer 1992:425; Roberts 1992). It is after this time that the first early hominids (*Homo erectus*/*H. ergaster*) reached South Asia from Africa. The contrasts in temperature between warmer and cooler periods became more pronounced, with a major transition to more variable oscillations starting in the early Pleistocene by c. 900,000 years ago. From this time onward it is clear that global glacial-interglacial cycles have been driven at a fairly recurrent rate by the Milankovitch cycles linked to the variations in the earth's tilt and orbit (see Roberts 1992). During glacial periods, cooler global temperatures were linked to decreased monsoon rainfall, and sea levels dropped by up to 150 m with c. –130 m. reconstructed for the last glacial maximum c. 20,000 years ago (Yokoyama et al. 2000). During these periods, tropical wet evergreen forests became increasingly restricted to refugia, postulated for parts of Central Africa and South America, with a more extensive distribution on the exposed parts of the Sundaland shelf between Sumatra, Borneo, and Thailand (Flenley 1979:81; Hope et al. 2004). More limited refugia probably existed in other areas as well, which would account for some of the endemic species diversity, as, for example, in southwestern China, northeastern India, Sri Lanka, and the Western Ghats.

Over the last few hundred thousand years, the broad patterns of glacial-interglacial climate cycles, and attendant shifts in monsoon intensity and the proportions of wet evergreen versus deciduous and savanna elements of the regional floras, are relatively well-documented from sediment cores in the Arabian Sea (Figure 5.2). The core MD76135 on the southern side of the Arabian peninsula preserved pollen rain originating in east Africa for approximately c. 150,000 years (Van Campo, Duplessy, and Rossignol-Strick 1982), whereas the cores SK 128 A-30 and 31 off the west coast of India contained pollen from South Asia (Prabhu et al. 2004). The broad vegetation patterns reconstructed from these cores are similar (see Figure 5.2). During glacial maxima, at c. 20,000 and 60,000 years ago, drier conditions are marked by peaks in the pollen values of Chenopodiaceae/

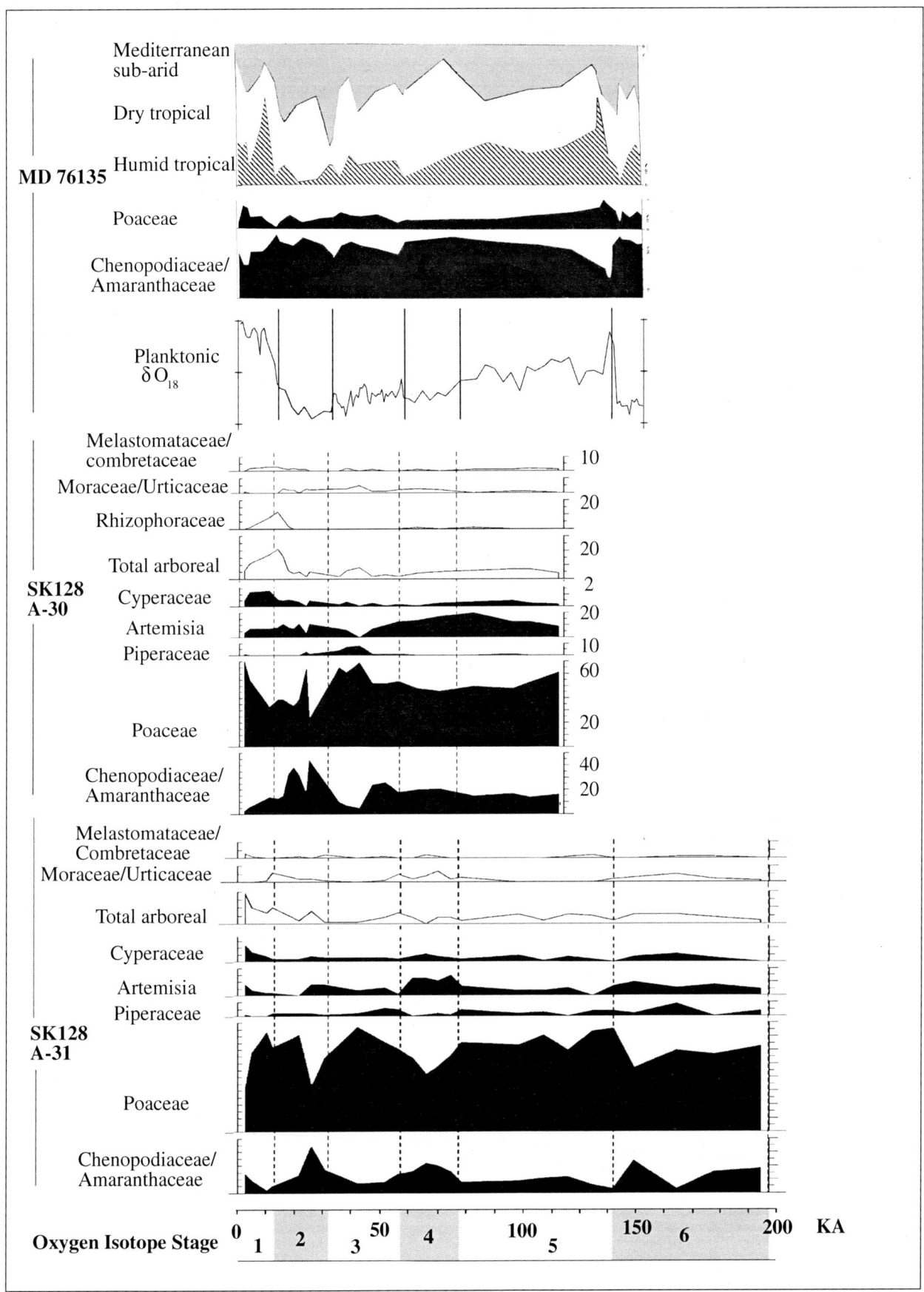

Figure 5.2. Comparison of selected pollen spectra from the Indian Ocean: MD 76135, including oxygen isotope data

Amaranthaceae, which include numerous drought and salt-tolerant desert and coastal species, although Van Campo and colleagues (1982) link them primarily to depressed sea levels and the expansion of saline marshes in coastal areas. During glacial periods grass pollen values were low, thus implying arid conditions and the restricted distribution of savanna grasslands. Wet evergreen indicators, such as the pollen of Piperaceae in the offshore Indian SK128 cores, were also low but not altogether absent. Together with the low values of Melastomataceae/Combretaceae (which include a broad range of evergreen as well as dry deciduous taxa) and Moraceae/Urticaceae (displaying their highest diversity in the wet evergreen zone), the evidence attests to the persistence of tropical rainforests forests and adjacent deciduous woodlands, presumably in more restricted refugia at higher elevations on the Western Ghats. This situation was reversed during the final Pleistocene and the early Holocene with the dramatic rise of total arboreal pollen, implying that forest cover along the western upland zone of India has been far more extensive during the last 10,000 years than it had been during earlier times.

Aspects of this pattern can be examined in more detail for the past 35,000 years in a number of sediment cores derived from high elevation peats in the Nilgiri and Palni hills (Bera, Gupta, and Farooqui 1996, 1997; Gupta 1971; Sutra, Bonnefille, and Fontugne 1997; Vishnu-Mittre and Gupta 1970). In general, these cores are dominated by grasses, sedges, and herbaceous species, with poor representation of trees (Figure 5.3). Nevertheless, there is some presence of arboreal vegetation indicators as well as herbs that are characteristic of the montane wet evergreen woodlands (the *shola* forests). Although early studies such as those of the Kakathope swamp and Rees Corner have poorly resolved chronology (only one $^{14}$C date each), they still provide a picture of more extensive grasslands during the late Pleistocene, with the expansion of shola forests taking place in the Holocene. Forest expansion is accompanied by higher values of sedge pollen, hence implying that moister early Holocene conditions probably favoured the development of marshes as well as woodland. As noted by Vishnu-Mittre and Gupta (1970), this sequence of vegetation change contradicts earlier scholarly opinion that viewed the grasslands of the hilly flanks of South India as the result of anthropogenic degradation of the primeval forests. In addition, micro-charcoal particle curves in the Sandynallah core have indicated that anthropogenic burning was probably a feature of the regional landscapes from c. 30,000 years ago and had increased substantially by c. 4000 B.C.E. (calibrated age; see Sutra, Bonnefille, and Fontugne 1997). Thus, it becomes clear that the onset of the Holocene was marked by woodland expansion in peninsular India, with conditions being warmer and moister compared to the late Pleistocene. One of the human responses to woodland expansion, at least in some parts of the subcontinent, appears to have been the increasing burning of vegetation. In turn, anthropogenic burning probably resulted in significant changes in the dynamics and geographical distribution of ancient vegetation.

## FINAL PLEISTOCENE TO MID-HOLOCENE: VEGETATION CHANGE AND MESOLITHIC HUNTER-GATHERERS

The transition from the arid and cold conditions of the Pleistocene to a warmer and moister Holocene describes the environmental context of the South Asian Mesolithic. In South India, there are few datasets that allow reconstructing palaeoenvironments for this period with the requisite chronological and spatial resolution. Some relevant sequences have come from Rajasthan, Gujarat, and eastern Madhya Pradesh. Outside the Nilgiri and Palni hill ranges there is only one deep-sea sediment core, off the west coast near Karwar, that covers the mid- to late Holocene (see below) and a few indirect proxy records derived from stable carbon isotope studies. Two such isotopic records have derived from stratified peat sequences in the Nilgiri hills (Sukumar et al. 1993) and deep confined groundwater in the Neyveli basin in eastern Tamil Nadu (Sukhija, Venkat Reddy, and Nagabhusanam 1998). Both datasets indicate increased levels of $C_3$ vegetation (including trees, shrubs, and some grasses) during the early Holocene, with a resurgence of $C_4$ vegetation (comprising savanna grasses and sedges) in the later part of the Holocene. This

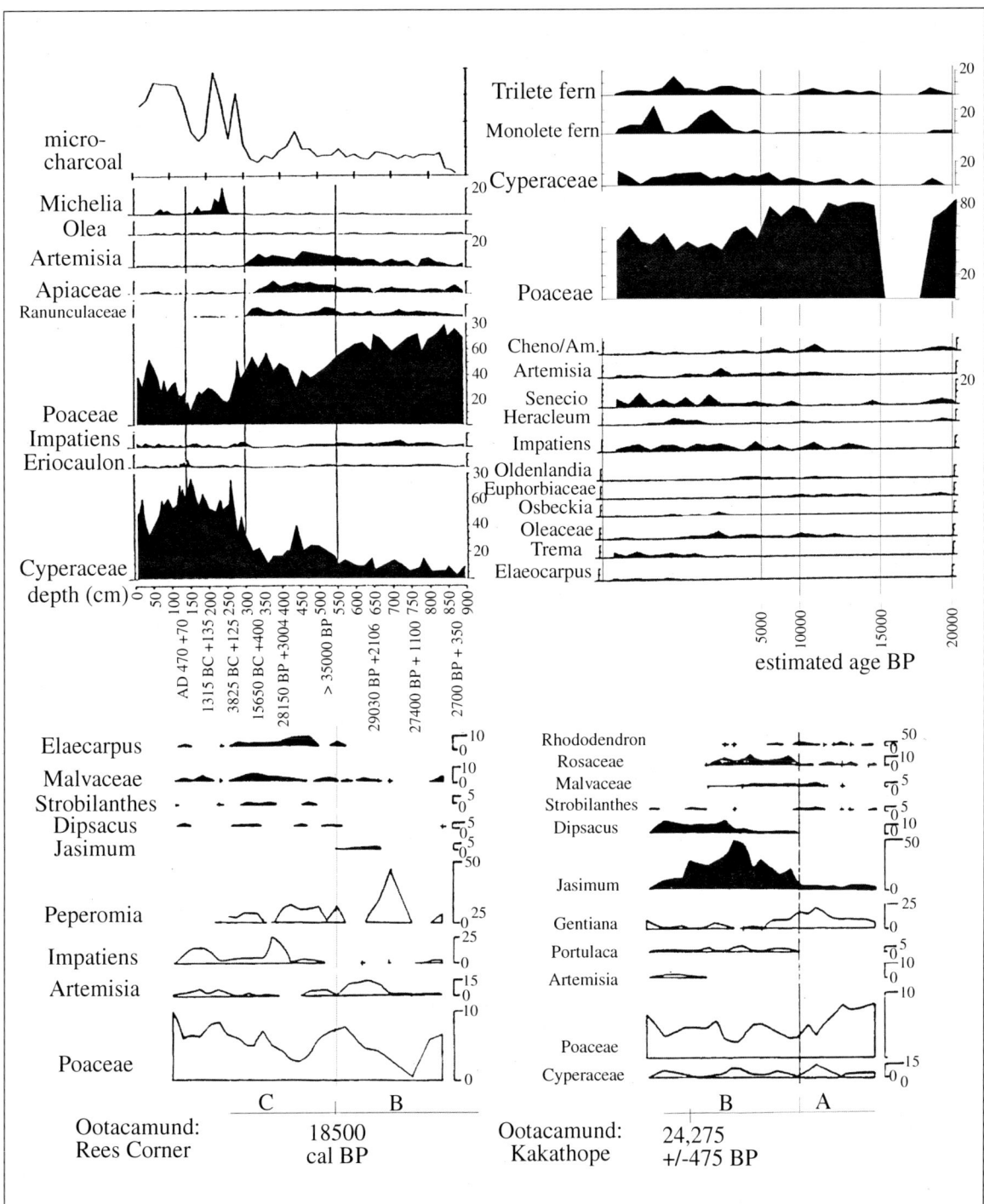

Figure 5.3. Selected pollen spectra from the Nilgiri and Palni hills

suggests a moister and perhaps more forested early to mid-Holocene, with increasing aridity and savanna expansion from the mid-Holocene onward. Drier conditions set in between 3000 B.C.E. and 2000 B.C.E.

For a general understanding of past climate change affecting the peninsular monsoon system we can refer to marine records from the Arabian Sea. Cores drilled from the continental slope off the coast of Pakistan, near the Indus river delta, preserve a finely laminated sedimentary sequence that covers much of the past 10,000 years, extending back to the previous interglacial (Jung et al. 2004; Staubwasser et al. 2002; Staubwasser and Sirocko 2001, 2002; Von Rad et al. 1999a, 1999b). For the past 13,000 years, climate trends and oscillations preserved in oxygen isotope ratios from Pakistan's continental shelf have provided evidence that can be correlated with data indicating changes in lake levels and pollen representation from the Thar desert (Figure 5.4). Changes in oxygen isotope curves are tied to global temperatures and the local influx of freshwater into the Arabian Sea from the Indus river system. Thus, higher values (that is, –2.0) imply higher Indus discharge and higher rainfall, itself linked to higher global temperatures (Staubwasser et al. 2002). This tracking of global climate is verified from the general concordance of the shape of the oxygen isotope curve with that of atmospheric methane oscillations recorded in the Greenland ice cores (see Figure 5.4). The Younger Dryas oscillation, a global cold climatic

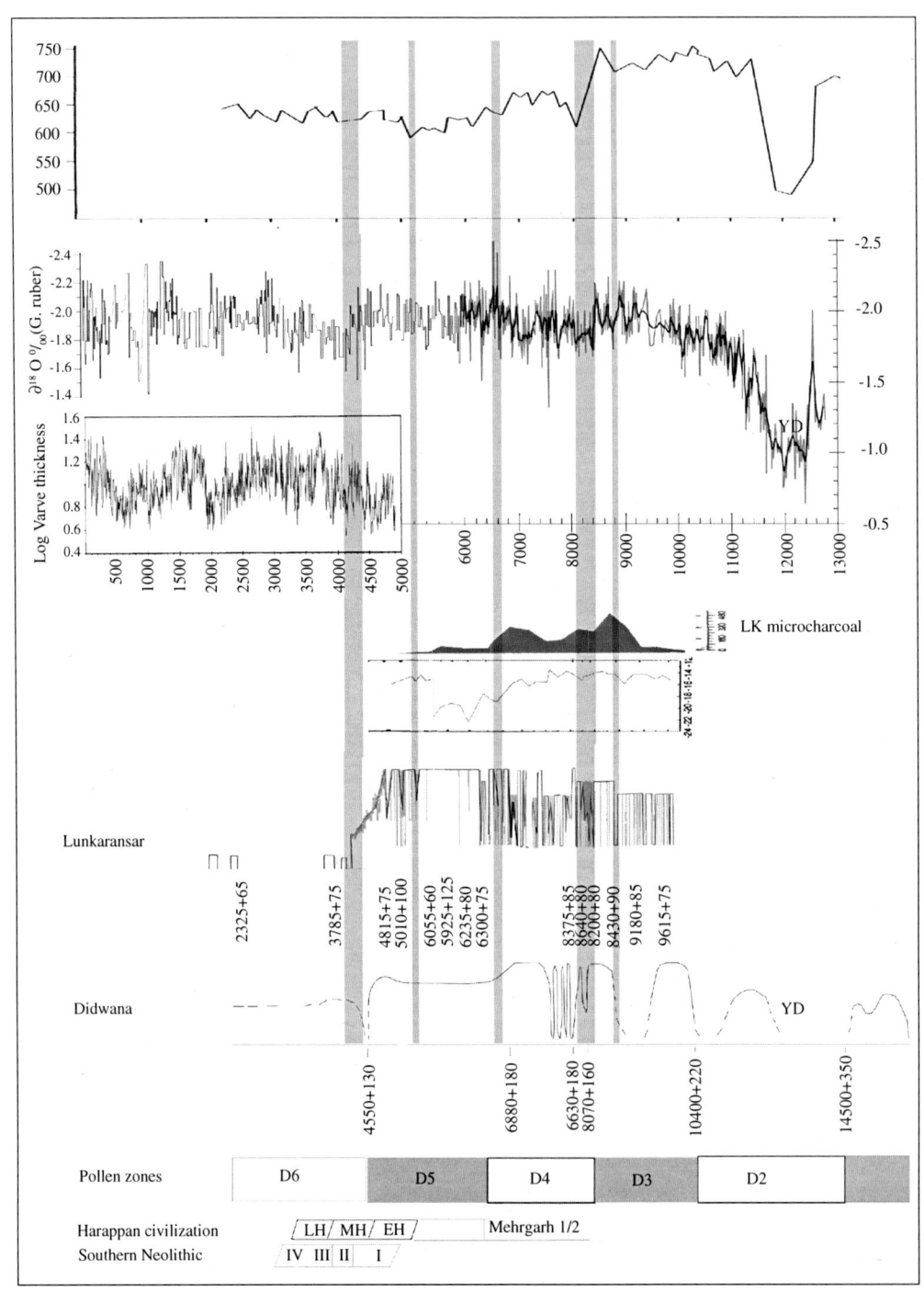

Figure 5.4. Correlation between various palaeoclimatic proxies from northwestern South Asia

episode marking the end of the Pleistocene, is evident in both datasets, followed by a reversal toward warmer and moister conditions. The same trend is evidenced in the oxygen isotope data from a core in the Bay of Bengal (Chauhan 2003; the correlation is clear when the published raw radiocarbon dates are calibrated using the marine curve of Stuiver, Reimer, and Braziunas 1998; Stuiver et al. 1998).

The Holocene begins with a markedly wet period, part of the Climatic Optimum of the current interglacial (Roberts 1998:117–23). This is reflected in terrestrial palaeoenvironmental records from the Thar desert in Rajasthan, where numerous lakes and playas acted as pollen traps preserving records dating to the late Pleistocene and the Holocene (Deotare et al. 1998; Kajale and Deotare 1997; Kajale, Deotare, and Rajaguru 2004; Singh et al. 1974, 1990). Evidence for fluctuating lake levels has been reported from the Didwana and Lunkaransar lakes (Enzel et al. 1999; Wasson, Smith, and Agrawal 1984;). The comparative palynological study of four other lake sequences by Singh and colleagues (1974) has served as the basis for reconstructing Holocene summer and winter precipitation in Rajasthan (Bryson and Swain 1981; Swain, Kutzbach, and Hastenrath 1983), although the chronological framework used in these studies was flawed, being based on a few uncalibrated radiocarbon dates (for a statistical reassessment of the radiocarbon evidence see Figure 5.5). When first published, these data were taken to indicate a period of high rainfall coinciding with the florescence of the Harappan civilisation in the Indus valley followed by a period of aridification to which the end of the Harappans was attributed (Agrawal 1982; Bryson and Swain 1981; Singh 1971). However, in light of the revised and calibrated chronology, we can clearly see that higher levels of rainfall actually predated the development of urbanism in the Indus valley (between 2600–2500 B.C.E.). Accordingly, the culmination of the aridification process (c. 2200 B.C.E.) preceded the downfall of the Harappan cities dated at c. 2000–1900 B.C.E. (Fuller and Madella 2001; Schaffer and Liechtenstein 1989).

During the early and mid-Holocene, the broad phasing of high and low lake levels appears to be well-correlated between individual lake sequences (Figure 5.4) and furthermore agrees with palynological evidence for past rainfall regimes (Figure 5.6). For earlier periods, the assemblages are rich with the pollen of grasses, sedges, Chenopodiaceae/Amaranthaceae, and *Artemisia* and are interpreted as indicating the development of grass-steppe vegetation following conditions of extreme aridity (Singh, Wasson, and Agrawal 1990; Singh et al. 1974). During cool dry glacial periods, desert habitats had expanded, and dunes had become established beyond the margins of the modern desert (Allchin, Goudie, and Hedge 1978). In pollen zone D1, which represents the period just before the Younger Dryas, *Aerva* pollen values are notably high. This species is a coloniser of sand dunes. In pollen zone D2, equated with the Younger Dryas, grass and *Artemisia* pollen decrease sharply accompanied by a peak in Chenopodiaceae/Amaranthaceae (drought and salt-tolerant desert shrubs). By contrast, the early Holocene was moister, as indicated by rises in the values of aquatic marsh plants and terrestrial (savanna) taxa (*Calligonum, Ephedra, Maytenus,* and *Capparis* alongside the occasional presence of *Oldenlandia* pollen in the Lunkaransar sequence). The gradual establishment of savanna vegetation made the Thar desert attractive to groups of Mesolithic hunter-gatherers. There is evidence for the presence of substantial quantities of early-mid Holocene microlithic, aceramic sites, often on stabilised sand dunes (Biagi and Kazi 1995; Kajale, Deotare, and Rajaguru 2004; Misra 1989, 2001; Shinde, Deshpande, and Yasuda 2004). In the Lunkaransar sequence and the early part of the Didwana profile (Singh et al. 1974), there is a dramatic increase in micro-charcoal values, dated between 7000–6600 B.C.E., suggesting higher frequency of anthropogenic burning of the savanna vegetation in Rajasthan. Since this increase predates the advent of agriculture and pastoralism in this region, one can safely conclude that burning aimed at promoting new plant growth in order to attract wild game.

This early Holocene moist phase was punctuated by brief arid spells indicated by the presence of numerous gypsum evaporite layers in Lunkaransar Zone 1 (Enzel et al. 1999) and the

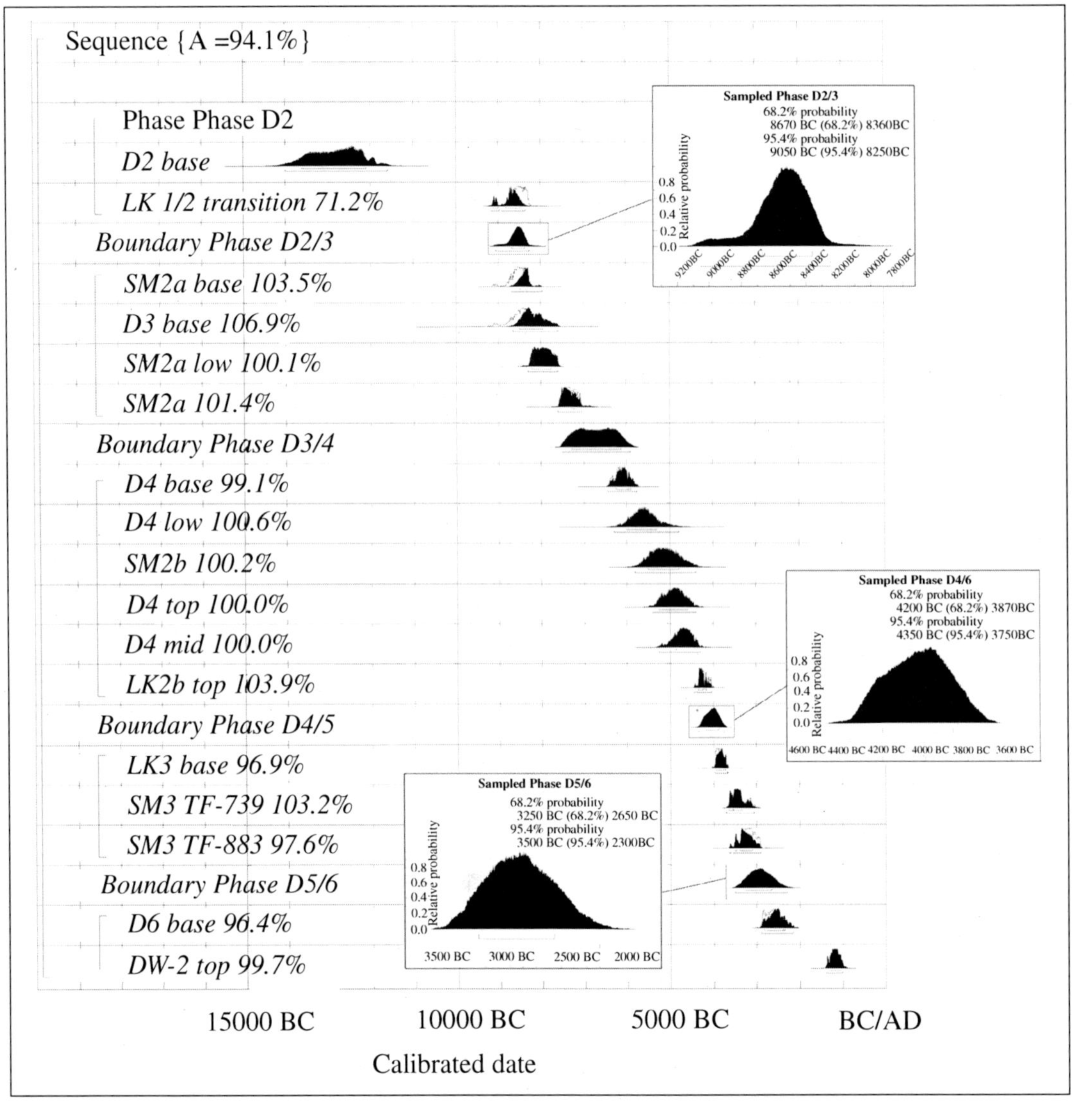

Figure 5.5. Calibration model of the radiocarbon dates of the Thar desert pollen zones

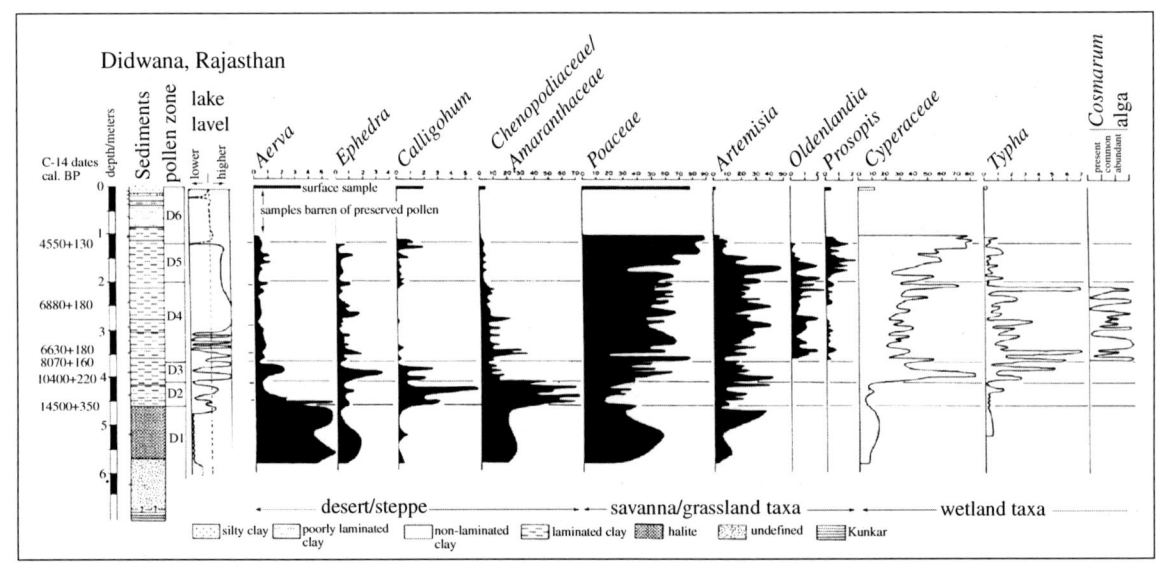

Figure 5.6. Didwana pollen diagram with revised calibrated radiocarbon dates

fluctuating curves of several plant taxa, including sedges, arid to semi-arid shrub taxa (*Calligonum, Maytenus, Ephedra*), and the sand-dune coloniser *Aerva*, most clearly observed in the Didwana sequence. These short-term fluctuations cannot be dated precisely. Yet the general trend bears similarities to the oxygen isotope record from the Arabian Sea, in which fluctuations recur on a c. 220-year cycle, likely to be driven by fluctuations in solar irradiance (Staubwasser et al. 2002). The transition from the early to mid-Holocene was marked by another arid episode lasting for approximately three centuries. This transition is not well resolved in the Rajasthan pollen chronology but appears to fall within the millennium between 7000–6000 B.C.E. (likely between 6400–6050 B.C.E. culminating at c. 6200 B.C.E.). This is a global climatic event, correlated with an oxygen isotope shift (seen also in the Pakistani offshore sequences) and a decrease in atmospheric methane recorded in the Greenland ice cores (Alley et al. 1997; Blunier et al. 1995; Gasse 2000; Staubwasser et al. 2002). The same event has been widely recognised in Africa (Gasse, 2000; also Grove 1993; Hassan 1997a; Muzzolini 1993). Yet, although this dry event correlates reasonably well with the decline in lake levels in the Arabian peninsula (Lézine et al. 1998; McClure 1976), it is not so clearly discernible in the Tibetan records (Wei and Gasse 1999) or in the Bay of Bengal core studied by Chauhan (2003). In Rajasthan, it is indicated by the occurrence of several closely spaced low lake levels at Didwana and Lunkaransar dated at c. 6200 B.C.E. The absence of this event from other regional records raises questions as to what extent this aridification affected all parts of peninsular India.

The mid-Holocene in peninsular India can be divided into two main stages. The first started with sharp fluctuations in lake levels at Rajasthan; record high levels were reached at Lunkaransar, and a continuously high level was maintained at Didwana after c. 5500 B.C.E. This moist phase appears to have been more pronounced than the early Holocene climatic optimum (at least in Rajasthan). It is likely that high lake levels were maintained owing to increased winter precipitation from the northwest (Bryson and Swain 1981:137; Swain, Kutzbach, and Hastenrath 1983). Evidence for a mid-Holocene moist phase (5000–4000 cal. B.C.E.) is largely absent from palaeolakes in the Arabian peninsula, with the exception of dated sequences from the northwest Arabian lakes of the An-Nafud region, which are thought to be connected to higher winter rainfall inputs from the Mediterranean (Lézine et al. 1998:298). This pattern suggests that the summer rainfall of the Indian Ocean monsoon system peaked in the early Holocene, whereas during the mid-Holocene winter rains from the northwest supplemented the monsoon rainfall in parts of Northwest India (such as Rajasthan) and the northern Arabian peninsula.

Pollen data also document a mid-Holocene wet phase. High values are recorded for *Oldenlandia*, a genus of herbs common in the dry evergreen and savanna vegetation of the peninsula and the Himalayan foothills, although today it is much rarer and is largely confined along watercourses in the dry northwestern peninsula (Cooke 1903–1908; Hooker 1875–1897). This period of increased winter rainfall could have also affected parts of central India. Recent pollen evidence from eastern Madhya Pradesh (Chahuan 1996, 2000, 2002) indicates that during the mid-Holocene winter rainfall was also higher in the east. The high values of *Artemisia* and grass pollen in these sequences are reminiscent of the Iranian steppe and western India (Rajasthan), and they declined only as monsoon deciduous forests became established in the second half of the third millennium B.C.E.

In the late mid-Holocene, after 4000 B.C.E., wet conditions appear to have continued in Rajasthan, while a long-term trend towards increasing aridity set in. Just before this phase, there occurred maximum lake levels at Lunkaransar and a marked decline in carbon isotope ratios (suggesting increased input from shrubs, herbs, and aquatic plants instead of savanna grasses), dated between 4300–4000 B.C.E. The same period witnessed a decline in micro-charcoal values and anthropogenic burning. After 4000 B.C.E., agriculture became established in Rajasthan and Gujarat, including sites with evidence for animal domesticates and ceramics (by 3500 B.C.E. and perhaps earlier) (Ajithprasad 2001, 2004; Shinde,

Deshpande, and Yasuda 2004). Sedentary agricultural sites of the Ahar culture, such as Balathal and other sites in the Udaipur area, were probably founded during this period (Misra and Mohanty 2001; Shinde 2002; Shinde, Deshpande, and Yasuda 2004). This likely marked the beginning of the dispersal of livestock and plant crops east of the Indus area (Fuller 2003a; Fuller and Madella 2001). By c. 3000 B.C.E., agricultural settlements were established on the Saurashtra peninsula (Ajithaprasad 2001, 2004). In the Didwana pollen sequence there is a clear decline in *Oldenlandia*, whereas shrubs such as *Prosopis* and *Capparis* increased. Although *Prosopis* is a drought-tolerant taxon, it is interestingly absent or present with very low values in earlier phases, whereas *Capparis* is less common (comparable to the Sambhar pollen core; see Singh et al. 1974: Figure 4). This suggests that human activities might have promoted these woody species that inciden-tally have edible fruits and a broad range of uses (Chapter 6).

To summarise, the available evidence suggests increased temperatures and rainfall levels during the early to mid-Holocene, followed by increasing aridity from the mid-Holocene onward. In the early Holocene, from c. 9500 B.C.E. to c. 6500 B.C.E., high lake levels have been reported with a subsequent regression from 6000 to 3000 B.C.E. in east and sub-Saharan Africa (Gasse 2000; Hassan 1997a; Jolly et al. 1998) and the Arabian peninsula (Lézine et al. 1998; McClure 1976). Archaeological evidence (including botanical and animal bone data) has also indicated higher levels of rainfall in Sahel and southern Sahara, with the contraction of the Sahara desert and the expansion of savanna vegetation to the north (for example, Hassan 1997a; Neumann 1989; Wendorf and Schild 1994). A similar sequence is reconstructed for Tibet (Thompson et al. 1997; Wei and Gasse 1999) and the Bay of Bengal (Chauhan 2003) from oxygen isotope data. The mid-Holocene wet phase is well documented in datasets from Africa and Tibet and appears to peak in most areas between 5000 and 4000 B.C.E. The offshore oxygen isotope record has indicated that the amplitude of the fluctuations (approximating a bicentennial scale) is often greater and more erratic compared to the early Holocene (see Staubwasser et al. 2002). After 4000 B.C.E. and continuing up to c. 2000 B.C.E. there is abundant evidence for a decline in total precipitation, albeit some regional datasets show discrepancies in the precise timing of arid episodes.

Returning to South India, we can postulate that broadly the same stages occurred in this region as well. Warmer and moister conditions in the early and mid-Holocene were probably punctuated by arid spells lasting for a century or two. Deciduous woodlands, especially their moister components, likely expanded while the spatial extent of savannas was probably determined (at least in part) by anthropogenic burning of vegetation. However, the empirical demonstration of the preceding patterns has been hampered by the absence of detailed palaeoenvironmental sequences and archaeological assemblages. In recent years, numerous hunter-gatherer rock shelters, many decorated with rock art, have been discovered in the Kurnool and Bellary districts, and it may be possible in the near future to establish well-dated cultural and archaeobotanical sequences from these sites. Similar rock shelters are known from central Madhya Pradesh in the Bhimbetka area (Kennedy 2000:206–08; Misra 2001) and from northwestern Orissa (Pradhan 2001). Further investigation of such sites will offer an improved understanding of human-environment interactions in peninsular India during the early and mid-Holocene.

## MID- TO LATE HOLOCENE: NEOLITHIC AGRICULTURAL COMMUNITIES AND THEIR IMPACT ON PENINSULAR LANDSCAPES

As noted above, the higher rainfall of the mid-Holocene gave way to drier conditions through a gradual process punctuated by brief spells of aridity. This general trend is evident in the declining levels of atmospheric methane from 7,000 to 5,000 years ago, with a parallel negative trend in the Arabian Sea isotope records that reached a minimum around 4,000 years ago. In the better dated Rajasthan pollen sequences, increasing aridity culminated before 2000 B.C.E.. Didwana lake dried up at c. 2500 B.C.E., and Lunkaransar underwent a protracted decline in water levels from c. 2800 to 2200 B.C.E.. Since then it has remained largely dry until the present day except for brief periods of silt deposition. The same trend is also seen in pollen indicators from the Sambhar lake sequence, where a decrease in *Artemisia* and *Oldenlandia* began before 3000 B.C.E. (Singh et al. 1974:zone SM3a).

Additional evidence for aridity has come from lakes in Gujarat. These include Nal Sarovar near the southern periphery of the Thar desert, which has been the object of palynological investigations (Vishnu-Mittre 1979; Vishnu-Mittre and Sharma 1979 ) and a more recent geochemical study (Prasad, Kusumgar, and Gupta 1997) and the Malwan lake in southeast Gujarat, where a short sequence was investigated in conjunction with excavations at a nearby Chalcolithic site (Vishnu-Mittre and Savithri 1990; Vishnu-Mittre and Sharma 1978). Both pollen datasets have indicated that, for the period corresponding to the mid-Holocene wet phase, grassland-chenopod savanna was predominant alongside dry deciduous riverine forest. The Gujarat vegetation data suggest that winter-spring precipitation from the northwest had a minimal impact in this region, and the major source of precipitation remained the summer monsoon. From the mid-Holocene onward there is a gradual decline of rainfall with a concomitant regression of the dry deciduous forest, which disappeared after 2400 B.C.E.. The chemical indicators from Nal have also pointed to declining lake levels, although this process was not completed until the second millennium B.C.E. (Prasad, Kusumgar, and Gupta 1997). The indication of low lake levels in the fifth millennium B.C.E. might represent a local signal of the dry event centred on 4600 B.C.E., especially in this part of India, where the effect of winter rains was much less pronounced than further north.

During the late Holocene, two arid episodes stand out at 3200 B.C.E. and 2200 B.C.E.. The latter in particular has received much attention in recent years as a possible prime mover in the collapse of the Harappan civilisation as well as Mesopotamian cities in the Middle East (De Menocal 2001; Dhavalikar 2001b; Hassan 1997b; Perry and Hsu 2000; Staubwasser et al. 2003; Staubwasser and Weiss 2006; Von Rad et al. 1999b; Weiss et al. 1993). As discussed, the 2200 B.C.E. event predates the extrapolated date of aridification suggested by earlier authors (for example, Allchin and Allchin 1997; Bryson and Swain 1981; Singh 1971) and the demise of the urban centres of the Indus valley (2000–1900 B.C.E.) (Enzel et al. 1999; Fuller and Madella 2001; Madella and Fuller 2006). The current evidence supports instead the contention of other scholars that Harappan urbanism occurred during a period of declining rainfall (Fuller and Madella 2001; Madella and Fuller 2006; Schaffer and Liechtenstein 1989; Vishnu-Mittre 1979;). What is noticeable about the period between the 3200 B.C.E. and 2200 B.C.E. arid episodes is the markedly wide amplitude of century-scale climate fluctuations. In this regard, it is worth considering what role the emergence of more complex urban societies in the greater Indus region might have played in the establishment of agricultural systems that were adapted to similar weather patterns. During the late Harappan period (from c. 2200 B.C.E.) and through the post-urban period (2000–1700 B.C.E.), there is increasing evidence for the cultivation of drought-tolerant monsoon crops, including indigenous millets and pulses (Fuller and Madella 2001; Weber 2003). At the same time, there was a general settlement shift toward the eastern, more monsoonal parts of the Harappan distribution (Possehl 1997a). Furthermore, there is some evidence suggesting a more localised organisation of agricultural production at the household scale (Fuller 2001; cf. Weber 1999, 2001, 2003). As argued elsewhere (Madella and Fuller 2006), these lines of evidence indicate that successful adaptations to the increasingly dry conditions of the late third millennium B.C.E. were probably based on the deployment of risk-buffering strategies through increasing reliance on the dry-cropping of millets and pulses, and the transfer of the control of agricultural surpluses and decision making from regional (urban) to local centres.

Evidence for the promotion of anthropogenic vegetation ecosystems has derived from central Madhya Pradesh. In this region, the first sedentary village sites (the Kayatha Chalcolithic culture) date from the end of the third millennium B.C.E. (c. 2300–2000 B.C.E.) (Allchin and Allchin 1982;

Possehl and Rissman 1992; Sharma and Misra 2003). Palynological data from eastern Madhya Pradesh have suggested that modern 'climax' vegetation formations emerged in this region in the context of changing woodland exploitation patterns alongside climate shifts. Evidence from five sites in eastern Madhya Pradesh (Chahuan 1996, 2000, 2002; sites shown in Figure 5.1; selected pollen spectra in Figure 5.7) has indicated that the modern 'climax' vegetation of dry-deciduous sal (*Shorea robusta*) forests and savanna grasslands took shape after the mid-third millennium B.C.E. Although archaeobotanical datasets from this area are few, there is sufficient evidence to demonstrate that winter monsoonal crops spread in the northern peninsula by the Chalcolithic (Fuller 2002, 2003b). Interestingly, large grass pollen (which could include cereals) and likely winter crop weeds (for example, *Justicia*, *Polygonum*) appeared in these pollen sequences shortly before c. 2500 B.C.E.

Although the chronological resolution of these sequences is poor, a date of 3970 bp (c. 2400 cal. B.C.E.) from the Dongar-Sarbar swamp core marks the start of the continuous occurrence and subsequent increase of *Shorea* (sal) together with increasing values for *Madhuca indica* and fern spores (Chahuan 2002). The same pattern occurs in other cores in this area (pollen zones DS-IV, BS-V, JS-III, and JS-IV, Chahuan 1996, 2000). These important deciduous forest indicators are notably absent from earlier pollen zones. Data on historical vegetation ecology have indicated that open environments, such as those generated by swidden cultivation, are ideal for the successful reproduction of *Shorea* through vegetative propagation and the facilitation of seedling establishment *en masse* in abandoned swidden fields (Flint 1998: 435; Rangarajan 1998:587; Sivaramakrishnan 1999:211–35). Likewise, Puri and colleagues (1989) regard many sal forests as products of similar processes of secondary succession (see also discussion by Flint 1998). Such a hypothesis for the role of clearance activities in promoting the expansion of sal forests is further supported by the high values of fern spores and other environmental indicators such as *Artemisia* and Caryophyllaceae in the Dongar-Sarbar core. In addition, sal forests have been traditionally maintained by burning, and the suppression of forest fires and grazing of woodland undergrowth in the late nineteenth century led to repeated failure of sal woodland to reproduce (Pyne 1997:472–73; Sivaramakrishnan 1999:211–35). In the light of such historical accounts, the correlation of the emergence of agriculture and the rise to dominance of *Shorea* in arboreal pollen spectra acquires a distinct significance. It seems likely

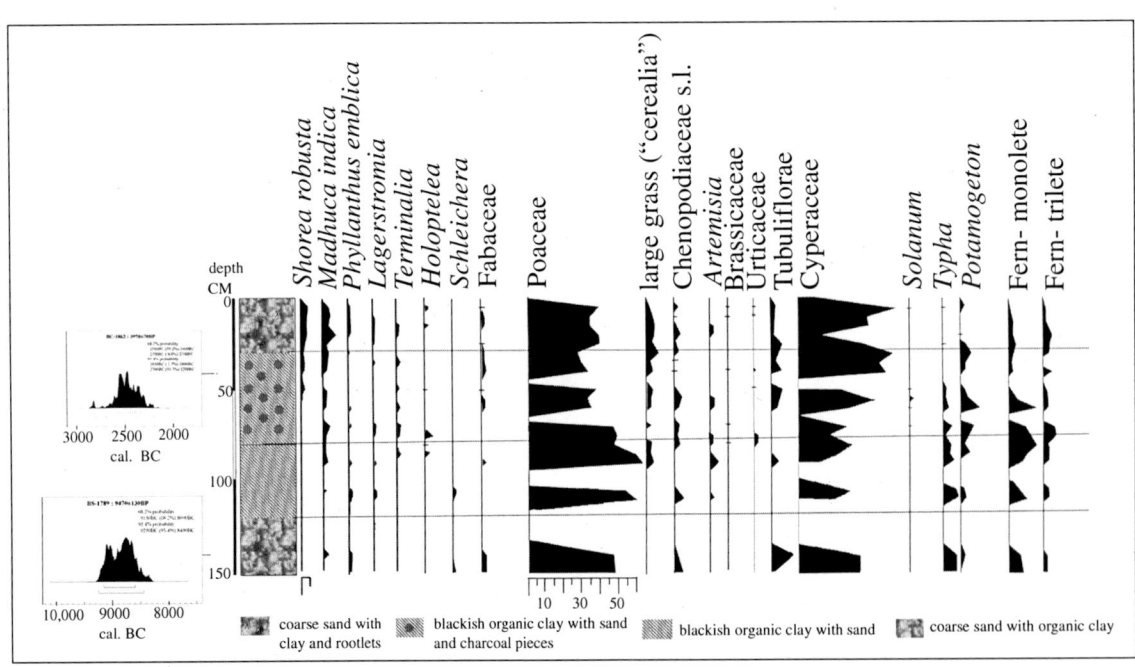

Figure 5.7. Pollen spectra from the Dongar Sanbar swamp in Madhya Pradesh

that the expansion of sal forests, interspersed with pockets of cultivation, was controlled by human practices that emerged in tandem with the gradual aridification of climate during the third millennium B.C.E.

It is only from this period, after c. 2500 B.C.E., that some direct botanical evidence becomes available again for South India. This includes archaeological wood charcoal assemblages that are currently under investigation by the authors (see Chapter 7) and a single offshore sediment core collected from the Uttar Kannada coast near Karwar that has provided pollen, dinoflagellate, and isotope data (see Figure 5.8; Bentaleb et al. 1997; Caratini et al. 1994). The datasets from this core have been the subject of conflicting interpretations (Meher-Homji 1994a, 1994b, 1996a, 1996b; Subash Chandran 1997). The pollen evidence was compiled into vegetation types by Caratini and colleagues including the wet evergreen and moist deciduous forests, the mangrove vegetation, and Cyperaceae and Poaceae (the last two taken to represent savanna vegetation) (Caratini et al. 1994). From the earliest dated part of the sequence, at c. 2500 B.C.E., there is a marked decline in the evergreen forest pollen values, which continues into the next phase (c. 1500 B.C.E.– C.E. 100). Over the same period, deciduous taxa also show a slightly declining trend, while there is a simultaneous rise in grass pollen values. Furthermore, mangroves appear to decline, too, but more precipitously from c. 1500 B.C.E. onward. Caratini and colleagues (1994) interpreted these trends as indicators of climate change, with the fairly abrupt reduction in tree pollen at c. 1500 B.C.E. attributed to the effects of rapid aridification.

An alternative reading of the same pollen evidence sees many of these changes as anthropogenic owing to forest clearance for cultivation (Fuller and Korisettar 2004; Meher-Homji 1994a, 1994b, 1996a, 1996b; Subash Chandran 1997). As noted by Mehjer-Homji (1994a, 1994b, 1996b), if the scenario of climate change was correct, one would expect decreasing rainfall to lead to the replacement of the wet evergreen forests by moist and/or dry deciduous vegetation, but no such inverse relationship is manifested in the pollen diagram. Alternatively, the conversion of forest to grassland

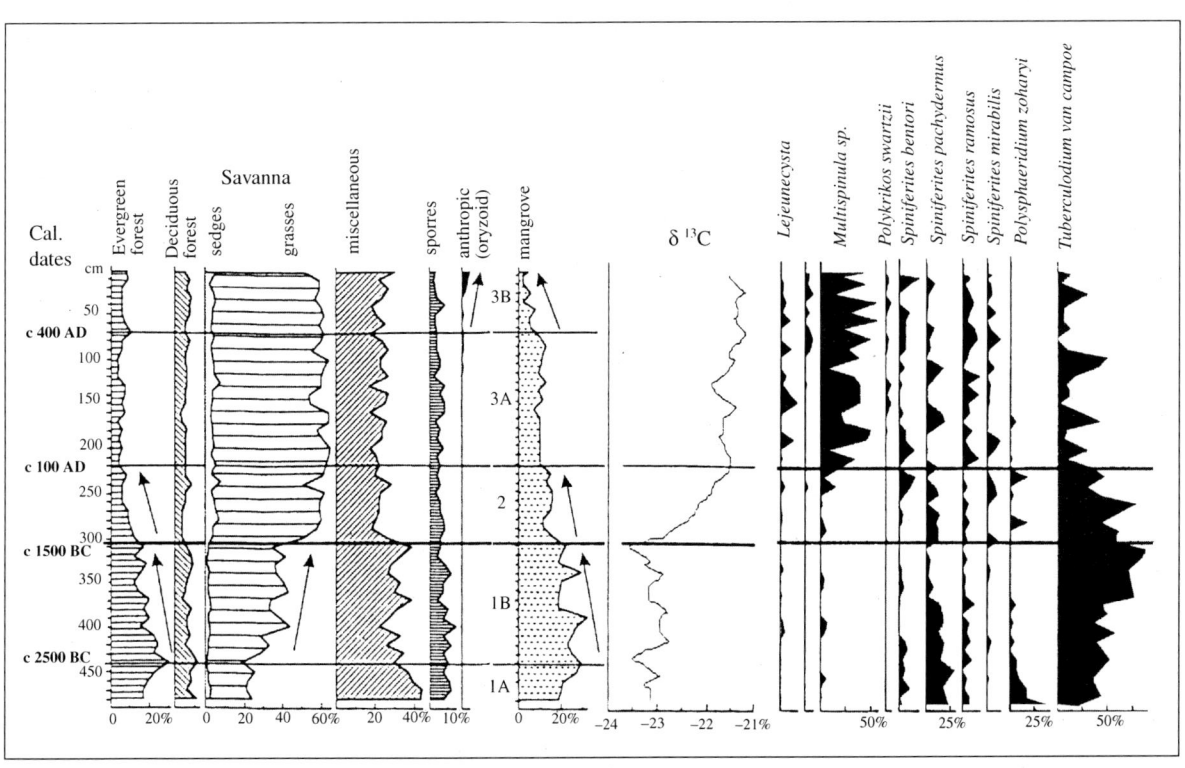

Figure 5.8. Summary pollen diagram together with spore, C-13 isotope and dinoflagellate values

could be attributed to the effects of agricultural expansion. The apparent increase in sedimentation rates from c. 1500 B.C.E. could also indicate accelerated erosion brought about by clearance for cultivation.

A reconsideration of the evidence suggests that a combination of climatic variables and anthropogenic influences on vegetation is more likely to explain adequately the patterns observed in the pollen record. One of the assumptions of the climate-based interpretation has been that cultivation was not initiated in this region until c. 1000 B.C.E. with the introduction of iron (Caratini et al. 1994:377). This assumption can now be decidedly ruled out, since the case for the onset of plant cultivation in the Deccan by the end of the third millennium B.C.E. is now well established (Fuller 2003a:Chapter 7; Kajale 1991). The fact that the most rapid vegetation changes are evident around c. 1500 B.C.E. correlates well with the available archaeological evidence, especially the Malwa-early Jorwe transition in the northern Deccan, for which the greatest number of agricultural village sites have been documented in this area. The later phases of the Southern Neolithic have also provided some indications for the cultivation of a more diverse range of crops and possibly more intensive agricultural practices, too, such as irrigation, from a number of sites (Fuller, Korisettar, and Venkatasubbaiah 2001;, Fuller et al. 2004). The evidence as a whole suggests increasing (albeit variable in its spatial extent) density of agricultural settlement between 1800 and 1200 B.C.E.

The archaeology of the late second millennium B.C.E. has often been discussed in relation to climate change, with the suggestion that aridity set in at c. 900–1200 B.C.E., leading to the collapse of the Chalcolithic cultures of the northern peninsula (Dhavalikar 1984, 1988:71–72, 2001b; Shinde 1998:34–35). This model posits that a period of increasing aridity led to declining agricultural productivity, as a result of which communities were forced to take up a nomadic lifestyle based on sheep and goat pastoralism, and has never been very convincingly argued with regard to evidence demonstrating the alleged climate fluctuation and the archaeology of the inferred socioeconomic changes. Recently, many scholars have criticised this model (Paddayya 1994; Panja 1999, 2001). Nonetheless, it remains a fact that the great majority of Malwa and Jorwe sites dating from the mid-second millennium B.C.E. were no longer inhabited during the Iron Age. Furthermore, high resolution data available from the Indus palaeoenvironmental records have indicated a period of marked fluctuations with arid spells focusing on c. 1200 B.C.E. and 900 B.C.E. While a simple correlation of climate and social change is obviously not feasible, the question remains as to how the patterns of socioeconomic change that were already underway during the second millennium B.C.E. towards more specialist craft production, nonsubsistence cultivation, long-distance trade, and the emergence of social hierarchies would have interacted with recurrent climate and associated environmental change. The answer to this question undoubtedly requires undertaking further archaeological and palaeoenvironmental research in these areas.

## TOWARDS AN ENVIRONMENTAL ARCHAEOLOGY OF SOUTH INDIA

The environment of South Asia has undergone profound changes during prehistoric and historic periods. This observation has important implications for archaeological research in the Indian peninsula. While some scholars have argued for essentially stable climatic conditions over the past 6000–7000 years (for example, Raikes 1984:118; Possehl 1997b, 1999:257–68), it becomes clear from the evidence reviewed in this chapter that this assumption is largely unfounded. In addition, it was demonstrated that environmental change played an important role in cultural developments; neither the Neolithic regional cultures nor the Harappan urban civilisation can be fully understood without some consideration of their environmental contexts and associated patterns of climate change. This statement is not meant to advocate environmental determinism. Indeed, the available evidence implies the existence of both cultural adjustments that overcame environmental constraints and substantial human impact on past vegetation that deserve further problem-oriented investigation.

Although the climate of South India was probably moister at the beginning of the Neolithic (c. 3000 B.C.E.), the area around the Bellary district (one of the habitation hotspots of the Southern Neolithic) would still have received less rainfall compared to other areas further to the west and the east. This area has also less water-retentive soils; therefore, it is more likely to have been dominated by dry evergreen *Acacia – Albizia* savanna vegetation. It is worth noting here that the potential distribution of the *Acacia – Albizia* vegetation overlaps significantly with the distribution of the archaeological sites identified with the Ashmound Tradition, perhaps reflecting the importance of cattle pastoralism in the savanna and grassland habitats of inner south Deccan. The *Acacia – Albizia* zone represents the natural habitat of the wild progenitor of horsegram.

Compared to the present day, significant differences would have existed in the distribution of moister vegetation zones, including the habitats of the wild progenitors of the *Vigna* pulse crops (especially mungbean). Wet evergreen forests most likely remained confined to the Western Ghats corridor, with some latitudinal shifts in their composition (Chapter 4). Moist deciduous forests and the transitional dry deciduous *Terminalia – Anogeissus – Tectona* woodlands probably extended only marginally further to the east and are likely to have advanced into the Deccan along hill ranges. Dry deciduous variants, including teak and some moist deciduous elements, were probably more widespread at lower elevations around the Nallamalai hills and possibly extended further to the southwest in the Eastern Ghats (Chapter 4). Overall, dry deciduous forests are likely to have been more continuous than at present, being punctuated by smaller and more dispersed grassland clearings and meadows. Yet, it is the likely association of savanna habitats with dry deciduous forests (possibly further promoted by anthropogenic burning of vegetation) that would have offered an optimal habitat for the co-occurrence of all the wild progenitors of Southern Neolithic crops in close proximity to one another.

The environmental history of South India is inextricably linked to the history and the transformations of the human societies inhabiting this region. Perceiving and portraying human societies in isolation from the environment or in the context of a strictly antagonistic relationship with it, may deprive historical and archaeological research from critical perspectives of past human ecologies and, more specifically, the complex and historically informative interplay among social norms, ecological variables, and economic production. The importance of the interplay of human and environmental history was captured by Sumit Guha when he wrote that

> social differentiation . . . had both political and economic aspects – forests, seasonal pastures, cultivated fields all provided resources exploitable by specialists, and the various communities constituted by their specialisations . . . Lands were cleared for agriculture – but lands also became covered with jungle; trade routes were opened but routes were also abandoned; cities were founded but cities vanished. The archaeological record at many sites has sterile layers, indicating periods when the location was abandoned before being reoccupied . . . Herdsmen settled to till or tax the tillers, cultivators shifted to herding; swidden farmers took to the plough [and] ploughmen fled to the forests. Certain habitats and habituses persisted through time – but their geographical locations and human occupants were in recurrent flux. (Guha 1999:28–29)

It remains the task and, at the same time, the social obligation of archaeology to recover traces of the prehistory of such human-environment entanglements and present them in an accessible and meaningful way for the benefit of ecological and historical knowledge at large.

# CHAPTER 6

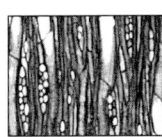

# AUTECOLOGY AND ETHNOBOTANY OF SOUTH INDIAN TREES

In evaluating the distribution of trees in the landscape and their likely occurrence in archaeological sites, one must consider them individually. Each species has its own ecological preferences and tolerances. Each offers potential for human use by providing fuel, food, medicinal substances, as well as construction and craft materials. This chapter provides a synthesis of the information available on the geographical distribution, autecology, and ethnobotany of South Indian trees and shrubs, which has been assembled from a wide range of sources in addition to our own observations in the field. The species descriptions are organised alphabetically by family and within families by genus, following the same order as the wood anatomical descriptions presented in Chapter 9. A number of species for which wood anatomical descriptions and microphotographs are not provided in Chapter 9 (mainly because of the unavailability of modern comparative specimens from South India) have still been included in the ethnobotanical and ecological descriptions. Species belonging to the same genus are discussed together.

For the sake of brevity, the number of bibliographical citations has been kept to a minimum. The following general sources were consulted for all species: Cooke (1903–1908), Drury (1873), Ellis (1987), Gamble (1902, 1921, 1935), Hooker (1875–1897), Matthew (1995), Pallithanam (2001), Saldanha (1984, 1996), Sharma et al. (1984), Singh (1988), Singh et al. (2001), Talbot (1909–1912), Venkata Raju and Pullaiah (1995). For ethnobotanical information, recurrent citations are presented in the form of numbers, which refer to the following list:

1. Drury 1873
2. Watt G. 1889–1893
3. Gamble 1902
4. Talbot 1909–1912
5. Roxburgh 1832
6. Ambasta et al. 1986
7. Maheshwari and Singh 1965
8. Chandra 1997

Other sources of ethnobotanical data are cited in full. For some species, the notes include comments on historical linguistics, which build on the evidence for cognate words across languages, language phylogeny, and archaeological correlations (Fuller 2003b; 2007; Southworth 1988; 2005). Dravidian linguistic roots follow the *Dravidian Etymological Dictionary, Revised edition* (Burrow and Emeneau 1984), referenced in the species descriptions by the standard abbreviation DEDR followed by their entry number. For ease of reading, the authorities for species names have been largely omitted from this chapter. The authorities for all species have been included in the botanical index.

## ANACARDIACEAE

This family includes 10 native genera, which are found predominantly in the Western Ghats tropical wet evergreen forests. Among these we have selected for anatomical description the fruit-producing genus *Mangifera* (often cultivated) and *Holigarna* (very common in South India) as representative of the family. Other important members of this family in deciduous forests are *Buchanania lanzan* and *B. axillaris* (Cuddapah almonds), as well as *Spondias mangifera* (the so-called Indian hogplum, also cultivated). *Lannea coromandelica* is another dry deciduous forest tree, whereas the shrubby *Rhus mysorensis* occurs in the dry savanna vegetation of central Deccan.

## Buchanania

*Buchanania lanzan* (syn. *B. latifolia*) is the almondette tree or cheronjee, whereas the closely related *B. axillaris* (syn. *B. angustifolia*) is the true cuddapah almond, or Buchnan's mango (6).

**Ecological Notes** *B. lanzan* is a tree of dry and moist deciduous forests, common in the Western Ghats and the hillslopes of interior west Karnataka. It is rarely found on the Eastern Ghats, at elevations >900 m a.s.l. on the Nallamalai and Sirumalai hills. *B. axillaris* favours drier localities. On the Eastern Ghats it is more common than *B. lanzan* (especially on slopes below 1000 m a.s.l.) and extends into the scrub forests of inner Karnataka (Pallithanam 2001; Saldanha 1996; Singh 1988; Venkata Raju and Pulaiah 1995). *B. lanzan* has a widespread distribution in India, whereas *B. axillaris* is restricted to South India.

**Ethnobotany** Both species have wood of similar properties, but that of *B. lanzan* is also reported to be resistant to termite attack (6). They produce small fruits that turn from pinkish green to black at maturity. Their kernels are edible and are used in the preparation of snacks or as confectionary (1, 2, 6).

Archaeobotanical finds of *Buchanania* fruits have been reported from Inamgaon (Kajale 1988). There is linguistic evidence of a shared root among the central and south-central Dravidian subfamilies (DEDR 2628), but it remains to be confirmed whether or not it is cognate with words in south Dravidian languages (Fuller 2003b:201).

## Holigarna

There are 5 species of *Holigarna* in South Asia, including 4 in the southern peninsula. All represent large evergreen trees. *H. beddomei* is restricted to the Anamallai hills, while the others occur in the Western Ghats, from the Konkan southward (*H. grahamii*, *H. ferruginea* and *H. arnottiana*).

**Ecological Notes** Large evergreen trees common in tropical wet evergreen forests.

**Ethnobotany** Its wood (light and soft) is reported to be used for boat and (occasionally) house building (1, 3, 4). It also provides a very acrid black sap that is used as a varnish (1, 2, 3, 5, 6). The juice of the fruit is used as a mordant in dyeing (1).

## Mangifera

There are 3 species of mango in South Asia, but only one, *M. indica*, occurs naturally in South India. A much wider range of *Mangifera* species are found in Southeast Asia (Bompard and Schnell 1997).

**Ecological Notes** Large evergreen tree (occurring naturally in valleys and in the Western Ghats forests; elsewhere cultivated). It is common in the moist deciduous forests but may also occur in the wet evergreen zone and at damper places in the dry deciduous zone. In a natural state, mango trees occur as scattered individuals in lowland forests growing on well-drained soils (Bompard and Schnell 1997). However, vegetation surveys often describe *Mangifera* as a dominant species (for example, Puri 1960), thus raising the question of whether such abundance is the result of human selection and management (Legris and Meher-Homji 1977). It is therefore likely that its distribution outside the limits of moist deciduous zone is anthropogenic. Today, mangos are widespread throughout India and elsewhere in the tropics, owing to their extensive planting and cultivation.

**Ethnobotany** Mango is one of the most important cultivated fruit species of the subcontinent. It reproduces best if raised from layers and grafts (1, 2, 5). In dry localities, seedlings and young plants require irrigation for long periods of time (until they reach a height of approximately 10–15 ft) (3).

Its fruits are eaten fresh or pickled, and its cotyledons are also used as a famine food (6). Its wood, however, is generally regarded of inferior quality for construction and craft purposes (6). The bark exudes a gum used in medicine, and the gallic acid contained in its seeds serves similar purposes (6). Mango is a symbolically and ritually important tree in a number of Hindu ceremonies. In South India, it constitutes a sacred triad of trees together with pipal (*Ficus religiosa*) and *neem* (*Azadirachta indica*) (Simoons 1998:65).

The sweet mango fruits of commerce are generally regarded as indigenous to the sub-Himalayan zone, from Garhwal and Kumoan through to Northeast India and Myanmar (Bompard and Schnell 1997). *Mangifera* is also regarded as indigenous to the Western Ghats, the Satpura hills, Chotanagpur, Orissa, and the Nallamalais (Ellis 1987; Gamble 1935; Haines 1921–1925; Hooker 1875–1897).

Mango cultivation was established in North India during the later part of the second millennium B.C.E., that is, the late Chalcolithic. The evidence consists of wood charcoal finds (dated after c. 1300 B.C.E.) from the sites of Narhan and Senuwar in the middle Ganges plain (Saraswat 2004; Saraswat, Sharma, and Saini 1994). *Mangifera* charcoal and fragments of kernel endocarps have been provisionally identified by the present authors from late Neolithic levels at Hallur, near the Western Ghats. Mangos might have occurred naturally in moist deciduous riverine forest habitats nearby the site. By contrast, its postulated presence at Sanganakallu, in the arid Bellary district, may indicate its introduction into the drier parts of South India from as early as the late second millennium B.C.E. (Chapter 7). By medieval times, mango cultivation had become widespread, including the semiarid northwest (Sind), as reported by Arab writers such as Ibn Hawqal (tenth century) and Al-Istakhri (twelfth century) (Watson 1983:181).

The English common name 'mango' has derived from Portuguese and more distantly from the Tamil word *mankay* (also the source of mango's Malaysian and Thai common names) (Burkill 1966; Yule and Burnell 1886). There appear to be three distinct roots for 'mango' in Dravidian languages (DEDR 4782, 4772, 2943) relating to the three main subfamily branches: north, central, and south/south-central. This suggests that mango cultivars dispersed in the peninsula after the three Dravidian languages had diverged (Fuller 2007:427; Southworth 2005:215). This is a pattern identical to that of the distribution of chicken, which very likely diffused throughout the Indian peninsula during the late Neolithic/Chalcolithic (mid-second millennium B.C.E.) (Fuller 2003b) and is notably different from that of several dry deciduous fruit trees (for example, *Butea monosperma, Terminalia* spp., *Diospyros melanoxylon, Gmelina arborea, Tectona grandis, Phyllanthus emblica, Pterocarpus marsupium, Schleichera oleosa, Syzygium cumini*). In Persian, Arabic, and Chinese, common names for 'mango' are borrowings of the Sanskrit word *âmra* (Laufer 1919:552). Finally, mango is known to have been cultivated in Cambodia from at least the seventh century according to Chinese sources (Laufer 1919:552; Watson 1983:181).

## Rhus

In South India this genus is exclusively represented by the shrub *Rhus mysorensis* (syn. *Rhus sinuata*), whereas in North India the Himalayas host numerous *Rhus* species.

**Ecological Notes** A thorny shrub of dry scrub vegetation and rocky areas in savanna-scrub areas in eastern Karnataka where it co-occurs with *Acacia horrida* and the succulent *Euphorbia antiquorum*.

**Ethnobotany** *Rhus* spp. have fruits with edible and oily seeds that are eaten roasted (6).

## ANNONACEAE

This family includes some 15 genera of trees and shrubs indigenous to South India, almost all of which are restricted to the wet evergreen forests of the Western Ghats, although a few extend into the Deccan (*Polyalthia* spp.) and the Eastern Ghats (for example, *Gonothalamus, Miliusa* in the Shevaroy hills, and *Alphonsea*). We have selected for anatomical description the diverse and widespread genus *Polyalthia* as representative of the family, and the introduced genus *Annona* because archaeobotanical evidence might assist elucidating the controversy surrounding the antiquity of this taxon in India.

## Annona

**Taxonomic, Ethnobotanical and Ecological Notes** The genus *Annona* is indigenous to the New World tropics (a single species occurs in west Africa) (De Candolle 1885). Many species, all of tropical American origin, produce delectable fruits. *Annona reticulata* and *A. squamosa* are both widely known by the English common name 'custard apple'. *A. squamosa* is the main custard apple of India, also known as sugar apple or sweetsop (the soursop is *A. muricata*). All three are cultivated, often as garden trees, for their fruits in north-central and peninsular India with the largest production of *A. squamosa* occurring in Andhra Pradesh and Uttar Pradesh (Bose and Mitra 1990). *A. squamosa* is the *sitaphal* or *sita pandu* fruit of South India, known as *ate* or *sharifa* in North India. De Candolle (1885) traced its origin to the West Indies. *A. cherimola*, the *cherimoya*, native to the uplands of Equador and Peru (Piperno and Pearsall 1998; Smith 1976) prefers a less tropical climate but may be found under cultivation in the drier interiors of the Deccan (Telengana) (Bose and Mitra 1990). Cultivated *atemoya* fruits derive from the hybridisation of *A. squamosa* and *A. cherimola*. *A. reticulata* (the bullock's heart or *ramphal*) is a deciduous tree, possibly native to the Antilles, which thrives in South India. *A. muricata* (the soursop) is a tropical evergreen species native to the lowlands of tropical America (Central America through to Peru) and is also cultivated in peninsular India (1, 2).

## Excursus: The Problem of *Annona* Introductions

Controversy surrounds the antiquity of custard apples, particularly *A. squamosa*, in India. Reputed artistic representations of and textual references to *Annona* trees predating European voyages to America or India (Achaya 1994, 1998; Singh R. 1992) are at odds with the botanical evidence suggesting their American origins (see De Candolle 1885:169ff.; Morton 1987; Piperno and Pearsall 1998:156; Smith 1976; Watt 1889–1893). Recent archaeobotanical evidence (Saraswat and Pokharia 1999) has compounded the argument.

The introduction of *Annona* to South and Southeast Asia from the West Indies and/or via Mexico represents the orthodox view. That this is likely to have occurred during colonial times is indicated by several lines of linguistic evidence.

Its common names in Southeast Asia indicate European introductions, with names for *A. muricata* having either Dutch or Spanish derivations (Burkill 1966). Southeast Asian names for *A. reticulata* derive from West Indian names. The appellation *ate* for *A. squamosa* is a Mexican common name of the early sixteenth century (Burkill 1966; Yule and Burnell 1886). The speed with which this species became established in the subcontinent led some early Dutch travellers to hypothesise that it was a Chinese introduction. However, in Chinese the custard apple is known as *fan-li-chi*, meaning foreign lychee (*Litchi chinensis*) (Yule and Burnell 1886).

Many Indian common names of *Annona* derive from honorific associations with deities such as the fruit of ram (*rāmphal*), the fruit of sita (*sītāphal*), and the fruit of hanuman (*hanumānphal*, applied to *A. cherimola*) (Achaya 1994:235). The word *sharīfā* means noble fruit. Therefore, these names provide no evidence as to the antiquity of *Annona* in the peninsula. Although the word *sadāphal* occurs in the *Ain-i-Akbari* (c. 1590 C.E.), it is clear that this term was used for a range of perennial fruits, including *Aegle marmelos* (Achaya 1994:235; Yule and Burnell 1886). Custard apples are not among the fruits catalogued by Baber at c. 1530 C.E. (Yule and Burnell 1886). They are also absent from late-sixteenth and early-seventeenth century Portuguese sources describing Indian plants (Chowdhury, Saraswat, and Buth 1977; Kajale 1991:181).

The arguments in favour of a much earlier introduction of *Annona* go back to Cunningham (1879:47), who claimed to have identified this fruit in sculptures at Bharut (dated to the second century B.C.E.) (Sitholey 1976:22). Cunningham supported his identification with observations that *Annona* grew wild in India, although many introduced species have become naturalised over time. Watt (1889–1893) had suggested that they could represent stylised representations of jackfruits or the flowers of *Anthocephalus*, regarded as a sacred plant. More recently, charred fragments from Sanghol, a Kushana period early historic site in northern India, have been botanically identified as deriving from the rind of an *Annona* fruit

(Saraswat and Pokharia 1998, 1999). However, despite some resemblances in form, no morphological or anatomical details have been published in support of this identification, and the one illustration published by the same authors remains unconvincing. It seems implausible that the fleshy and moist outer portion of these fruits could have survived charring intact. By contrast, archaeobotanical remains of *Annona* fruits are well attested in prehistoric tropical Americas, including finds on the Peruvian coast by c. 1000 B.C.E. and in coastal Ecuador (the latter perhaps as early as 3500 B.C.E.) (Bonavia et al. 2004; Piperno and Pearsall 1998:249, 274).

## Polyalthia

This genus includes trees and shrubs, with 6 species being reported as native to South India. The Sri Lankan *Polyalthia longifolia* is widely planted in villages and gardens.

**Ecological Notes** *Polyalthia fragrans* is a common evergreen tree widespread in the Western Ghats, whereas *P. coffeoides* is a rare evergreen species of the Western Ghats in south Karnataka being relatively more common in Kerala. *P. rufescens* is another rare evergreen species of the southern Western Ghats.

Three other species favour drier conditions (Gamble 1935). *P. cerasoides* is an evergreen tree found in drier habitats including the undergrowth of dry deciduous forests in the Deccan, the dry evergreen forests of Tamil Nadu (around Salem), and the moist-dry deciduous ecotones along the lower Godavari river in Andhra Pradesh and Orissa (Drury 1873; Gamble 1935; Haines 1921–1925; Pallithanam 2001; Saldanha 1984; Venkata Raju and Pullaiah 1995). Less common are the shrubby *P. korinthi* and *P. suberosa* that occur sporadically in dry forests from Coimbatore and Mysore northward along the Eastern Ghats (Gamble 1935). *P. suberosa* extends as far north as Orissa (Haines 1921–1925).

**Ethnobotany** *Polyalthia fragrans* wood has been used for manufacturing masts, matches, packing cases, and other light articles (1, 3, 6). *P. cerasoides* and *P. suberosa* were used during the colonial period in naval ship building, especially for masts, and in carpentry. Both have edible fruits (single-seeded red berries) (6). *P. coffeoides* has a fibrous bark used in rope-making (6).

## APOCYNACEAE

This family includes trees, shrubs, and some herbs, comprising some 20 genera native to peninsular India. Of these, the rare *Alstonia* is found in moist and dry deciduous forests. There are also several species of climbers in the wet evergreen forests, undershrubs and small trees in moist deciduous forests, spiny shrubs in the Deccan savannas (*Carissa* spp.), and a number of twining climbers in the dry Deccan scrub. We have chosen to describe anatomically the more widespread genera *Holarrhena* and *Wrightia*, both occurring in the dry deciduous vegetation of the Deccan.

## Holarrhena

The species described is *H. antidysenterica*.

**Ecological Notes** *H. antidysenterica* is a small deciduous tree. A pioneer coloniser of grasslands and wastelands, it is resistant to grazing (its leaves are avoided by goats and cattle) and cutting pressures. It flowers regularly, even as a coppiced shrub, and thus produces abundant seed that is often not released until the very end of the fire season. It also produces shoots that grow very strong and fast, even from burnt stools.

**Ethnobotany** The bitterly astringent bark of *H. antidysenterica* is used in traditional medicine to treat dysentery, and its seeds are also used medicinally for the treatment of similar ailments. It was imported to Europe during the early colonial period under the name of *Conessi bark, Codaga pala, Corte de pala,* or *Tellicherry bark* (1).

## Wrightia

This genus is represented by 2 species in South India, *Wrightia tinctoria* with a distribution focused on the Deccan woodlands and *W. arborea* (syn. *W. tomentosa*), which is more common in the area of the Western Ghats and the Nallamalais (Venkata Raju and Pullaiah 1995).

**Ecological Notes** *Wrightia* comprises small deciduous trees or shrubs found in deciduous woodlands. *W. tinctoria* occurs in dry deciduous vegetation and is a common component of scrub jungles, whereas *W. arborea* has a more restricted distribution in dry deciduous forests, especially of the *Terminalia tomentosa – Anogeissus latifolia – Tectona grandis* variant.

## Ethnobotany

*Wrightia* wood (white, close-grained, resembling ivory) is considered suitable for carving and turning (3). *W. tinctoria* leaves are used in dyeing, producing a blue dye (1, 3), whereas a yellow dye is extracted from its sap (3). Its leaves are also used as wrappers for the local *beedi* cigarettes (Singh 1988:404), although *Diospyros melanoxylon* leaves are much more widely used for this purpose. *Wrightia* seeds are often confused with those of *Holarrhena antidysenterica*, which have medicinal properties (Drury 1873: 245).

# BORAGINACEAE

See Ehretiaceae, below

# BURSERACEAE

This family includes 5 genera found in South India, represented by one or two species each. *Canarium strictum* and *Garuga gamblei* are trees of the tropical evergreen forests, whereas *Protium serratum* is an evergreen tree found in ravines and along streams in the Eastern Ghats, north of the Krishna river. *Garuga pinnata* occurs in the dry deciduous forests of the Eastern Ghats southward to Coimbatore, and in the southern Western Ghats. *Boswellia serrata* (syn. *B. glabra*, *B. thurifera*) is found throughout the Deccan (occasionally in the Western Ghats as well) as a component of dry deciduous woodlands in association with *Sterculia urens* (see Sterculiaceae) and *Chloroxylon swietenia* (see Rutaceae) on rocky slopes with poor and shallow soils (Ellis 1987:15; Singh 1988: 63). *Commiphora* shrubs occur in drier areas.

# COMMIPHORA

**Ecological Notes** The genus *Commiphora* comprises a number of spiny shrubs (*C. caudata* develops spines only on old wood). This species, together with *C. wightii* (syn. *C. mukul*, *Balsamodendron mukul*) and *C. berryi,* is reported from the dry evergreen scrub zones of peninsular India. *C. wightii* is found in the northwest through Gujarat and Sind.

## Ethnobotanical Notes

The incense myrrh (produced from gum resin) is derived from several species of *Commiphora*, but principally those native to the southern Arabian peninsula (especially Yemen) and Ethiopia (2; Dalby 2000:117–20). Incense from South Asia, known as bdellium, has been traded since antiquity (Miller 1968:69–70; Yule and Burnell 1886) from the ports of Barygaza and Barbaricon in southeast Gujarat, mentioned in the *Periplus Maris Erythraei* (Periplus of the Erythraean Sea) and from further west in the Indus region and Makran (Casson 1989:16–17). Incense myrrh was known to the Assyrians and the Israelites in the early first millennium B.C.E. (Miller 1968: 69). In South India, gum resin is reported to be collected from all species of *Commiphora* to be used for incense and medicinally (2, 4, 6, 7), although *C. wightii*, the Indian bdellium tree (Hindi *gugul*), is the favoured incense species. The fruits of *C. caudata* are edible (usually pickled) (6, 7).

Another species used for the production of aromatic resins is *Boswellia serrata*, the Indian olibanum tree (Hindi *salai*), related to the *Boswellia* that provided the classical frankincense and the main olibanum source of commerce (*Boswellia sacra*, found in Ethiopia and southern Arabia) (2; Dalby 2000:114–16). The Indian *Boswellia serrata* produces a fragrant gum resin that is widely used as incense and for medicinal purposes (1, 6, 7).

# CAPPARACEAE

This family is mostly represented by a range of shrubs and/or woody climbers belonging to the genus *Capparis*. *Niebuhria apetala* is a small tree found in the dry woodlands of Rayalaseema, and *Cadaba fruticosa* is an erect shrub of dry deciduous forests and scrub jungles. *Maerua arenaria* is a woody climber. *Crataeva religiosa* is a widely planted small tree that may also occur on river banks.

## *Capparis*

**Ecological and Taxonomic Notes** There are 19 species reported from South India, including the moister zones of the Western Ghats (for example, *C. grandis*), whereas others (*C. divaricata*, *C. brevispina*, *C. zeylanica* (syn. *C. horrida*) and *C. sepiaria*) are known from drier areas and open forests. *C. sepiaria* is most common in scrub, and *C. zeylanica* is frequent in hedges. *C. decidua* (syn. *C. aphylla*) is a desert shrub of the Sahara and the West Asian deserts extending into Sind, Rajasthan, and Gujarat. It has also been reported from the semi-desertic parts of the Deccan as far south as the Bhima river (Cooke 1903; Talbot 1912).

**Ethnobotany** Edible fruits are collected from *C. zeylanica* (2; 4; 6) as well as *C. brevispina* (6). The leaves and bark of *C. zeylanica* are also used medicinally (2, 4, 6). *C. decidua* produces edible fruits that have traditional medicinal uses in northwest South Asia (1). *C. grandis* has similar uses (6). The wood of *C. grandis* and *C. decidua* is renowned for its durability and white colour (1, 2, 4).

## CELASTRACEAE

Several members of the Celastraceae family are encountered in moist deciduous and wet evergreen vegetation zones. *Pleurostylia opposita* favours laterite soils along the west coast, with a disjunct distribution through the northern Eastern Ghats (north of the Krishna river). Deciduous taxa include *Microtropis* (7 species) occurring throughout the Western Ghats and *Euonymus* (6 species) found sporadically in the southern parts of the Eastern Ghats (Sirumalai hills: *E. crenulatus*). *Celastrus paniculatus* is a small straggler with a similar distribution in the Western Ghats as well as parts of the Eastern Ghats, including the Nallamalai and Sirumalai Hills. *Lophopetalum wightianum* and *Kurrimia indica* are tropical evergreen trees, whereas *Gliptopetalum* comprises moist forest shrubs (3 species).

The genus *Cassine* (syn. *Elaeodendron*) includes dry deciduous forest species. *C. paniculata* is found in woodlands on the leeward side of the Western Ghats, and *C. glauca* is more frequent in the dry deciduous woods of inner Karnataka and in the Eastern Ghats. For anatomical description we have focused on the genus *Maytenus* (syn. *Gymnosporia*), a prominent component of savanna woodlands.

## *Maytenus* (syn. *Gymnosporia*)

**Ecological Notes**

*Maytenus emarginata* (syn. *Gymnosporia montana*, *Celastrus emarginatus*) is a common shrub, often spiny, of the Deccan scrub and dry forests. *M. heyneana* is common in the Erramalai hills. *M. rothiana* is an occasional understorey tree in the moist deciduous forests of the Western Ghats, whereas *M. puberula* is a rare endemic shrub of the central Western Ghats wet evergreen vegetation.

**Ethnobotany** *Maytenus emarginata* leaves are used as fodder and its branches as roofing material (3).

## CLUSIACEAE (SYN. GUTTIFERAE)

This family includes *Garcinia* (in India the most diverse genus of the family), *Hypericum* spp., *Calophyllum* spp., *Mesua* spp., *Poeciloneuron indicum*, and *Mammea suriga* in the wet evergreen forests of the Western Ghats and the Konkan coast.

## *Garcinia*

**Ecological Notes** Most *Garcinia* species are at home in the wet evergreen tropical forests of western India, including the widespread *G. indica* and *G. morella*.

**Ethnobotanical Notes** *Garcinia indica*, known in India as gamboge (Hindi *kokam*, Kannada *murgala*) has a purple fruit (the size of a small orange) that is sweet and fragrant (2, 3, 4, 6). The fruit can be dried, and its rind is added to curries in the coastal areas of southern Maharashtra (2). The seed is pressed to extract an oil (known as *kokam butter*) used in cuisine and as a medicinal substance (3, 4, 6). It is also widely cultivated for its fruit in the Western Ghats. Several other species of the genus *Garcinia* have edible fruits (6, 7).

## COMBRETACEAE

This is an important tree family in peninsular India, including the major dry deciduous species of *Anogeissus* and *Terminalia*. *Combretum* is a genus of woody vines including species in wet evergreen (for example, *C. latifolium*) and dry deciduous forests (for instance, *C. ovalifolium*). *Calycopteris floribunda* is another liane of the moist deciduous and wet evergreen zones. (*Gyrocarpus* is segregated from this family, in the Hernandiaceae.)

### Anogeissus

Although some authors have subdivided *Anogeissus latifolia* into different subspecies (*glabra, villosa,* and *parviflora*), other authors have argued that these botanical subdivisions cannot be accepted (Ellis 1987:179).

**Ecological Notes** *Anogeissus* is a common dry deciduous forest species found throughout northern India and the peninsula. To the northwest, through Rajasthan and Gujarat, *A. latifolia* is replaced by *A. sericea* and *A. pendula*. To the northeast, it gives way to *A. acuminata*, which occurs in the northern Eastern Ghats, north of the Godavari river basin.

*A. latifolia* reproduces readily from seed. Its seeds are fire intolerant.

**Ethnobotany** *Anogeissus* is renowned for its strong wood, especially *A. pendula* (3, 5, 6). It makes excellent fuel both as dry wood and charcoal. Its leaves are used in tanning (3).

### Terminalia

This genus consists of some 10 species that are native to South India.

### Ecological Notes

The genus *Terminalia* comprises deciduous trees, found mainly in dry deciduous woodlands and in riverine forests (the latter especially favoured by *T. arjuna*). They are among the dominant canopy trees in dry deciduous vegetation (especially *T. elliptica* [syn. *T. tomentosa, T. coriacea*]) and abound in moist deciduous woodlands as well (particularly on the eastern slopes of the Western Ghats). *T. chebula* grows to a large tree in deep nutrient-rich soils but remains a stunted shrub in drier rocky places. *T. travancorensis* differs from the rest of the family in being part of the Western Ghats tropical evergreen forest flora. These species propagate readily from seed and take about 30 years to attain full size. *T. catappa* (the Indian almond) is a species originating in Indonesia and Malaya and is widely cultivated (Burkill 1966).

**Ethnobotany** Two *Terminalia* species form part of the group of medicinal trees known as myrobalans (Achaya 1998:4; Patnaik 1993). Known as *triphala* ('three fruits'), they are associated with prosperity and the goddess Lakshmi, and they include *Phyllanthus emblica* (emblic myrobalan), *Terminalia chebula* (chebulic myrobalan, Hindi *harra*), and *Terminalia bellerica* (belleric myrobalan, Hindi *bahera*). The fruits of the last two species, however, are not eaten. They are rich in tannins and have laxative and purgative properties (1, 2, 6). The seeds of *T. bellerica* are reported to be eaten despite the fact that they can be slightly toxic (2). *T. arjuna, T. chebula,* and *T. bellerica* are often planted in towns and villages as ornamental plants and sources of medicinal substances. *T. arjuna* also has medicinal uses (2). *T. catappa*, the so-called Indian almond, is an introduced cultivar with edible seeds (4, 6). Its galls are used in the manufacture of ink (1). *T. elliptica* provides durable timber used in cattle-cart wheels (1) and makes an excellent fuel both as dry wood and charcoal (3).

Archaeological finds of belleric have derived from Iron Age sites on the Indian peninsula, such as Veerapruam and Bhagimohari, and from Chalcolithic Daimabad (Kajale 1989, 1991). *T. chebula* fruit remains have been reported from Harappan Balu (2600–2000 B.C.E.) in Haryana (Saraswat 2002). Fruits of the same species were among the charred remains recovered from a fire altar dated to the Kushana period (50–250 C.E.) at

Sanghol in Punjab (Saraswat and Pokharia 1999). The *triphala* medicinal mixture was exported to China during early historic times (by c. 300 C.E.).

With the exception of the north Dravidian subfamily, the other three recognised subfamilies (see Fuller 2003b, 2007; Southworth 1988; 2005:220) share cognate terms for *Terminalia chebula* (Tamil *katu*, Telugu *karaka*, DEDR 1134), *T. bellerica* (Tamil *tānri*, Telugu *tāndra*, DEDR 3198), and *T. elliptica* (Tamil *marutu*, Telugu *matti*, DEDR 4718). Common names for *T. arjuna* appear to be composites of these names, for example, *billi-matti* (Kannada), *erra-matti* (Telugu) (see Saldanha 1996; Watt 1889–1893).

## DILLENIACEAE

This family is represented in South India mainly by 4 species of *Dillenia*. *Tetracera laevis* is a climbing shrub of the coastal forests of Kerala.

### Dillenia

**Ecological Notes** *D. pentagyna* is a common component of the moist deciduous vegetation but is also found occasionally in the Nallamalais. Its saplings grow very fast and have straight, white fleshy stems that render them capable of withstanding forest fires. *D. indica* is an evergreen tree that is more common in North India but also abounds in moist valleys in the Eastern Ghats north of the Krishna river, and in the southern Western Ghats. It is also widely planted as an ornamental tree. *D. bracteata* is a rare evergreen tree found in the dry woodlands of the Western Ghats from the Nilgiris southward. *D. retusa* is distributed from the Anamallai hills southward to Sri Lanka.

**Ethnobotany** The timber of *D. pentagyna* is considered durable but is liable to warping and splitting. It is used for house posts, boats, and occasionally furniture as well (2, 3, 6). Its flower buds and fruits are edible and have a pleasant acid flavour (2, 3, 6). *D. indica* has edible fruits, too (2, 5, 6). The leaves of *Dillenia* (the largest after teak) are used as plates and in Poona as bedding material for thatched roofs (2, 3). Its wood is reported to make good charcoal (3).

## DIPTEROCARPACEAE

An important family of tropical hardwoods. The genus *Dipterocarpus* is represented by only two species with disjunct distributions in South India, whereas the genus *Hopea* comprises species that are fairly frequent in the wet evergreen zone. Dipterocarpaceae also include a number of less common wet evergreen forest species found in the Western Ghats: *Balanocarpus* (2 species), *Vatica chinensis* (especially on the coastal plains), *Vateria indica*, *Shorea talura*, and *S. tumbuggaia*. The related *Shorea robusta* is an important timber species abounding in northern and eastern India, known by the common name of *sal*, derived from Old Indo-Aryan *śāla* and the root *\*car-* common to Central and South-Central Dravidian languages (Southworth 2005:220).

### Dipterocarpus

This genus is a major constituent of the rain forests of Southeast Asia. In South Asia it is found mainly in Sri Lanka and Northeast India (Hooker 1875–1897). In the wet evergreen forests of the southern Western Ghats, two species occur, *D. bourdilloni* (restricted to lower elevations in Kerala) and *D. indicus* (found in southern Karnataka and Kerala at higher elevations, up to 1,000 m a.s.l.) (Gamble 1935).

**Ecological Notes** Large evergreen trees of the Western Ghats wet evergreen forests.

**Ethnobotany** *Dipterocarpus* provides general purpose timber. *D. bourdilloni* is reported to be used for canoes, and *D. indicus* in shipbuilding for masts (6).

### Hopea

The genus *Hopea* comprises large evergreen trees of which three species occur in the Western Ghats: *H. parviflora*, *H. racophloea*, and *H. wightiana*. Numerous other species occur in northeastern India and in parts of Southeast Asia.

**Ecological Notes** Large evergreen trees of wet evergreen and moist deciduous forests. It is shade-tolerant and prefers rich and deep soils, growing best on river banks and in moist valleys. Reproduces from seed.

**Ethnobotany** *Hopea* provides heavy and durable brown timber that is resistant to insect attacks (3, 6). In south Karnataka, its wood is valued for building temples (3) but is also used in carts and boats. The bark of *H. parviflora* is considered a good tannin source (6).

## EBENACEAE

The ebony family is represented by numerous *Diospyros* spp. Some authors segregate a number of shrubs into the genus *Maba*.

## Diospyros

**Ecological Notes** *Diospyros* can be divided on ecological grounds into four groups, among which the wet evergreen to semi-evergreen species predominate:

1. Wet evergreen and moist deciduous trees. *D. affinis, D. assimilis, D. angustifolia* (syn. *Maba nigrescens*), *D. barberi, D. bourdilloni, D. buxifolia* (syn. *D. microphylla*), *D. candolleana, D. crumenata, D. ebenum* (this is the highly prized ebony tree also reported to occur in dry evergreen woodland in Tamil Nadu northward to Kurnool district, and in evergreen forests in Karnataka; its distribution may have been influenced by anthropogenic dispersal), *D. foliosa, D. humilis, D. insignis, D. nilagirica* (above 1,000 m a.s.l. in shola forests), *D. oocarpa, D. pruriens, D. paniculata, D. sulcata, D. sylvatica, D. toposia*.
2. Dry deciduous forests. *D. exsculpta* (syn. *D. tomentosa*) (generally more common in North India but also found in Maharashtra), *D. montana* (syn. *D. cordifolia*), *D. ovalifolia*.
3. Dry rocky hills and scrub. *D. melanoxylon, D. chloroxylon, M. buxifolia*.
4. Riparian forests, along hill streams. *D. malabarica* (syn. *D. embryopteris, D. peregrina*) is an evergreen tree growing in moist localities and next to streams. It is also characteristic of swamp habitats in many parts of India but is absent from the driest parts of the interior Deccan (Singh 1988; Venkata Raju and Pullaiah 1995).

The dry deciduous *D. montana* and the riparian *D. embryopteris* have been selected for wood anatomical description.

**Ethnobotany** Most of *Diospyros* species are valued sources of hard and close-grained timber. Several species produce the well-known black ebony wood. The true black ebony of colonial commerce is generally thought to derive from *Diospyros ebenum*, which earlier botanists regarded as originating in Sri Lanka (1, 5). If this is indeed the case, then it has by now become widely naturalised in South India. During the early colonial period (before 1600), most of the ebony derived from mainland Southeast Asia (Boomgaard 1998:385). Other species that are reported to produce kinds of ebony wood are *D. cordifolia, D. chloroxylon* (1, 2, 3), *D. melanoxylon, D. montana, D. oocarpa* (2, 6), *D. crumenata, D. assimilis* (2, 4), and *D. exsculpta* ('Nepal ebony'). *D. montana* wood is commonly used for agricultural implements. The wood of *D. malabarica* is little used (3), and the same is the case with *D. buxifolia*, which is reported to rot easily (4).

Early exports of ebony are recorded in the *Periplus Maris Erythraei* (c. 50 C.E.) together with teak and sissoo or blackwood (see *Dalbergia*, Leguminosae – Papilionaceae, below) from Barygaza (Broach, at the Narmada river mouth) to the Persian coast (Casson 1989:18, 73). Much earlier evidence of exports comes from Akkadian texts of the late third millennium B.C.E. that list a 'black wood' (thought by many scholars to be ebony) as an import from Harappan Meluhha (Ratnagar 2004:131, 139; but see also entry for *Dalbergia latifolia*). In favour of the ebony identification is the distribution of *Diospyros montana* in the Himalayas, from the upper Ravi river eastward. However, if 'black wood' came via Harappan Gujarat, either identification is possible (*Dalbergia* or *Diospyros*). *D. montana* has been identified among wood charcoals from Harappan Banawali (Saraswat 2002).

The fruit pulp of *D. malabarica* is used in tanning and dyeing, and oil extracted from its seeds is used in indigenous medicine (2, 3, 4). *D. melanoxylon* fruits are also used in tanning (2, 7).

Edible berries include those of *D. chloroxylon* (2, 4, 7), *D. ebenum* (7), *D. malabarica* (7), *D. melanoxylon* (2 4), *D. tomentosa* (7), and *Maba buxifolia* (1, 5, 7). *D. montana* is reported as edible in some areas but as bitter and poisonous in others (2). The leaves of *D. melanoxylon* are the most common wrapping material for locally made *beedi* cigarettes (6; Pimpalapure 1999:Chapter 4).

Linguistically, a common root can be identified for *Diospyros melanoxylon* across the south, south-central, and central Dravidian language subfamilies that is related to Tamil *tumpi*, Kannada *tumaki* or *tumari* (DEDR 3329; Fuller 2007:424; see also vernacular names in Gamble 1921; Saldanha 1984).

## EHRETIACEAE (FORM. INCLUDED IN THE BORAGINACEAE)

This family includes 4 woody genera. *Cordia* spp. (discussed below) and *Ehretia* spp., occur in dry deciduous vegetation (*E. aspera* is found in the drier central peninsula). *Carmona retusa* and *Rotula aquatica* are small shrubs found in scrub jungles on riverbanks and rocky areas, respectively.

## Cordia

There are 10 species of *Cordia* native to South India. In many published floras *C. dichotoma* and *C. obliqua* have been subsumed under *C. myxa* (Johnston 1951).

**Ecological Notes** The genus *Cordia* comprises mainly moderately sized deciduous trees and shrubs abounding in dry deciduous vegetation. *C. macleodii* is a canopy species in moist deciduous forests (the *Terminalia-Anogeissus-Tectona* woodlands of the Western Ghats) and in the Nallamalais. *C. domestica* and *C. wallichii* occur in moister localities in the Western Ghats often in association with teak (*Tectona*). *C. dichotoma* may be encountered in the same zone, although some sources suggest that *C. dichotoma* is mainly an extra-peninsular species. It may be encountered in some of the hill ranges of eastern India and on the southern Vindyan plateau (Mudgal et al. 1997). Further afield, it is found throughout Southeast Asia, South China, the sub-Himalayan tracts of Kashmir, and in Pakistan (Baquar 1995; Nasir 1989; Zhu et al. 1995).

Other species are found in drier zones. *C. gharaf* (syn. *C. rothii*) and *C. myxa* (not always equivalent to the *C. myxa* species determination used by many authors) are more common in the Deccan plains, including those parts covered by dry scrub. *C. myxa* is distributed throughout western India and from southern Pakistan to eastern Iran (Nasir 1989). *C. evolutior*, *C. monoica*, and *C. octandra* abound on hillslopes. *C. perrottetii* was reported growing on black cotton soils in the Bellary district by Gamble (1921–1935), but it has not been possible to verify its presence in the same areas during more recent explorations (Singh 1988).

**Ethnobotany** *Cordia* wood is relatively soft and strong (albeit susceptible to insect attacks). It seasons well and has been used in boat building, the manufacture of agricultural implements, and so on It makes an excellent fuel (3). *Cordia* wood has also been favoured for fire-making by friction (1; Thurston 1907). The bark is used for making ropes and other fibrous materials (2, 3). Numerous *Cordia* species produce small edible drupes (2, 8). *Cordia dichotoma* and *C. obliqua* (*C. myxa*) are the two most widely used species and are sometimes cultivated for their edible fruits. In the past, they were exported to Europe for medicinal purposes under the common name *sebesten* (1, 2).

Archaeological evidence has indicated that *Cordia* fruits were fairly common in prehistoric South India. *Cordia myxa*, or *Cordia* sp. seeds have been reported from several Neolithic sites as, for example, Budihal (2300–1700 B.C.E.) and sporadically in Imamgaon throughout the Malwa and Jorwe phases (1700–900 B.C.E.) (Kajale 1988). *Cordia dichotoma* seeds are reported from Kunal, a Harappan site in Haryana (Saraswat and Pokharia 2003). Linguistically, cognate names are found in South & South-Central Dravidian languages (DEDR 3627, 5408; Fuller 2003b:201).

## EUPHORBIACEAE

This is a large and highly diverse family with species ranging from small herbs to trees. Prominent in the more arid parts of the Deccan are the spiny succulent shrub *Euphorbia antiquorum* (the 'four-angled cactus', Tamil *sadhurakkalli,* Kannada *chandara-galli*), which forms an important component of scrub jungles and rocky hills together with *E. tortilis* (spiral cactus, Tamil *thiruhukalli*) and the spiny *E. caducifolia.*

In dry deciduous forests one can find *Bridelia crenulata, Euphorbia nivulia, Givotia rottleriformis,* and the undershrub *Jatropha heynei. Trewia* spp. and *Homonoia* spp. (2 species each) are shrubs found mainly in moister vegetation zones and river banks.

Numerous tropical trees belong to this family and are mostly found in the wet evergreen or semi-evergreen zones. Saldanha (1996) lists some 23 genera comprising about 50 species from the Western Ghats in Karnataka. One of the more common genera is *Mallotus*, including 7 species, some of which extend into the dry deciduous zone (see below).

## Phyllanthus

A wide range of variation is encountered in this widespread genus. This has led to numerous proposals for segregating individual species and groups of species (see Samuel et al. 2005). There are some 350–400 species of *Phyllanthus* recognised in Asia, and Gamble (1935) lists 13 for South India. *Kirganelia reticulata*, found in hedges and scrub vegetation, is classified by some authors under *Phyllanthus.* As a result, wood anatomy varies substantially across this diverse genus.

Two fairly common species with edible fruits are the emblic myrobalan *(Phyllanthus emblica),* which is widely documented in the archaeobotanical record, and *Phyllanthus acidus* (syn. *Cicca disticha*).

**Ecological Notes** *Phyllanthus emblica* is a moderate-sized deciduous tree found in dry deciduous forests throughout India. It responds well to coppicing. *P. acidus* is widely cultivated for its fruits, the so-called country gooseberries.

**Ethnobotany** *P. emblica* wood makes good fuel. It is also used for the manufacture of agricultural implements, and as building and furniture timber (3). Its bark and leaves are used in tanning and traditional medicine (2, 3). It belongs to a group of five sacred trees (including *Ficus religiosa, F. benghalensis, Mangifera indica,* and *Saraca indica*) that are preferentially planted around villages (Simoons 1998:65).

*P. emblica* fruits (Hindi *aonla*, Tamil *nelli*) are rich in vitamin C. They are also used in traditional medicine, for procuring dyeing and tanning substances, and as a preservative. Emblic myrobalan is part of the *triphala* ('three fruits') associated with prosperity and the goddess Lakshmi (Achaya 1998:4) also including *Terminalia chebula* (chebulic myrobalan, Hindi *harra*) and *Terminalia bellerica* (belleric myrobalan, Hindi *bahera*).

Early uses of *P. emblica* are documented from a range of archaeobotanical finds across India. Finds from the peninsula include the Neolithic ashmound site of Budihal (2300–1700 B.C.E.) and the Jorwe phase sites of Navdatoli and Inamgaon (Kajale 1988, 1991). As these sites are located in the dry evergreen/savanna zone, these finds suggest that *P. emblica* fruits were gathered at some distance from them and were perhaps traded beyond the natural range of this species already from the late Neolithic/Chalcolithic. *P. emblica* has also been recovered from the Adam Cave (Iron Age layers). In northern India, *P. emblica* fruits have been identified from the last phase (2400–2200 B.C.E.) of Kunal in Haryana (Saraswat and Pokharia 2003).

*P. acidus* ('country goodberry' Hindi *harfarebari* or *hariphul,* Tamil *arunelli*) is widely cultivated and naturalised in the tropics, including South and Southeast Asia (thought to be native of Madagascar) (Verheij and Coronel 1991). Its earlier history in South Asia remains undocumented.

## Mallotus

**Ecological Notes** This genus consists largely of trees and shrubs found in the wet evergreen and moist deciduous zones. *Mallotus tetracoccus* ranges from the evergreen to the dry deciduous vegetation of the Western Ghats. *Mallotus philippensis* is a small evergreen tree found in forests and open scrublands throughout India, although it particularly favours river banks. It reproduces well from coppice.

**Ethnobotany** *Mallotus* wood is used mainly as fuel (3) but also for making small items (6). The bark is sometimes used in tanning. The fruit, especially of *Mallotus philippensis,* is also processed for extracting a red pigment (Chapter 4; 1, 2, 3, 6; Patnaik 1993). There are also a number of reported medicinal uses.

## Securinega (Fluggea)

This genus includes 2 climbing and/or straggling shrubs (*Securinega leucopyrus* and *S. virosa*) found in the dry deciduous forests and scrublands of inner Deccan. Of these, the spiny *S. leucopyrus* is more widespread and extends into the driest parts of the Bellary and Chitradurga districts (Saldanha 1984; Singh 1988).

**Ecological Notes** Large, straggling thorny shrub (dry areas).

**Ethnobotany** *Securinega leucopyrus* is noted for its edible, white fruits (2, 6), and its leaves may also be eaten (6). Its bark contains tannins and is also used as a fish poison (6). It has close-grained, hard wood (3).

# HERNANDIACEAE (FORM. INCLUDED IN COMBRETACEAE)

This is a relatively small tropical plant family (including the climbing shrubs of the genus *Illigera*) found in the moist tropics of Northeast India/ Southeast Asia. The evergreen *Hernandia* is distributed in Southeast Asia, the Andaman Islands, and Sri Lanka, whereas the deciduous *Gyrocarpus* is native to India.

## Gyrocarpus

This is a small genus, including only 3 species, of which *G. americanus* (syn. *G. jacquini,* syn. *G. asiatica*) is the only native to India.

**Ecological Notes** *G. americanus* is frequent in the dry deciduous woodlands of the Deccan plateau, especially in Karnataka.

**Ethnobotany** *Gyrocarpus* wood is very light and is preferred in the construction of catamaran boats, hence the English common name 'catamaran wood'. It is also used for fashioning small boxes and toys (1, 2, 6). Its seeds are used as beads in necklaces (2). The related species *Hernandia ovigera* yields timber that is preferred for canoe making (6).

# LAURACEAE

This family is prominently represented in the wet evergreen forests of the Western Ghats with 9 genera. The most diverse genera are *Cinnamomum* (11 species) and *Litsea* (11 species, some ranging into moist deciduous forests and in the northern Eastern Ghats).

A few species also occur in the southern Eastern Ghats, particularly at higher elevations in the Sirumalai and Kolli hills (Ellis 1987; Pallithanam 2001). All genera belonging to this family have disjunct distributions between South and Northeast India (Assam, Sikkim) (see Chapter 5).

## Cinnamomum

*Cinnamomum verum* (syn. *C. zeylanicum*) is the cinnamon of commerce. Numerous species have been exploited for their aromatic bark and leaves in the past in various parts of South and Southeast Asia, and South China.

**Ecological Notes** *Cinnamomum verum* is native to Sri Lanka and the southern Western Ghats (from southernmost Karnataka to Kerala). At present, it is widespread and cultivated over much of the Western Ghats. It is common as far north as Goa but occurs more sporadically in Maharashtra (Cooke 1908; Singh et al. 2001). It can grow almost on any soil type but establishes best on laterite. Other species that occur in the southern Western Ghats are *C. gracile, C. riparium, C. travancoricum, C. iners, C. litsaeaefolium, C. nitidum* (syn. *C. macrocarpum*), *C. sulphuratum.*

*C. wightii,* and *C. perrottetii* are found in montane *shola* forests. *C. caudatum* is reported from the northern Eastern Ghats

**Ethnobotany** The leaves, bark, wood, and roots of *Cinnamomum* are aromatic. The true cinnamon spice is produced primarily by the bark of *C. verum* (2, 3; Dalby 2000). No uses are reported for its wood. Under cultivation, *C. verum* is managed by coppicing. Older shoots with well developed bark are cut, and the bark is cleaned of its outer layers. The remaining is allowed to roll into quills, in which form it is collected and sold in the market. Historical sources suggest, however, that South Indian cinnamon was not widely traded in antiquity; most aromatic barks (for example, cinnamon, cassia) were associated with China and Northeast India (Miller 1968:74; but see Dalby 2000:39). By the tenth century, however, Sri Lankan cinnamon was traded to the Arabian peninsula (Dalby 2000:40). This is likely to have been cinnamon gathered from the wild, since at the start of the colonial era cinnamon from Ceylon derived entirely from wild sources; its cultivation began only in the seventeenth century (Boomgaard 1998). The Arab writer Ibn Batuta (fourteenth century) describes the collection of wild cinnamon in Sri Lanka by South Indian traders, and he also notes the presence of 'cinnamon' trees in the forests of southwest India (Dalby 2000:40). It is not clear when Western Ghats cinnamon began to be exploited or whether its commercial species (*C. verum*) was really native to South India and not introduced from Sri Lanka. Cinnamon bark of some kind had probably reached the Mediterranean world by the seventh century B.C.E., and there are also claims for its arrival at an earlier date based on the interpretation of an aromatic wood/bark mentioned in Egyptian New Kingdom texts as cinnamon (Dalby 2000). However, direct archaeobotanical evidence for the presence of cinnamon in ancient Egypt is lacking (see De Vartavan and Asensi Amoros 1997).

The bark of several other species (for example, *Cassia*) is also aromatic and has traditional medicinal uses. Species reported to be used as spices include *C. nitidum* (Saldanha 1984:61) and *C. iners*, which has numerous medicinal uses (1, 2, 6). *C. tamala* is cultivated in Northeast India, especially in Assam (7). Its leaves alongside those of *Cinnamomum* spp. are dried and are known by the Hindi vernacular name *tejpat*, the *malabathron* of ancient classical texts (since the first century C.E.), today known as the 'Indian bay-leaf'. It is also mentioned in Arabic and European *materia medica* (Casson 1989:241; Dalby 2000:41–42; Yule and Burnell 1886:543).

The camphor tree, *Cinnamomum camphora* is native to East Asia and widely cultivated in the Western Ghats.

The wood of *Litsea* has been widely used as tinder (Thurston 1907:464, 466).

## LEGUMINOSAE

The largest family of Indian trees and shrubs, it includes no less than 74 indigenous genera (further divided into the subfamilies of Caesalpiniaceae, Mimosaceae, and Papilionaceae).

## LEGUMINOSAE—CAESALPINIACEAE

Group of leguminous trees that includes *Bauhinia* (found in a range of vegetation zones), *Hardwickia* (dominant in some dry deciduous vegetation types), *Cassia,* and the important cultivar *Tamarindus. Caesalpinia* comprises shrubs and stragglers found across a range of habitats. *Pterolobium hexapetalum* is a spiny straggler of thorn forests in the Deccan. There is also a number of species occurring in the wet evergreen forests of the Western Ghats such as *Humboldtia, Kingiodendron pinnatum, Mezoneuron,* and *Moullava. Saraca asoca* is frequent in the moist deciduous forests and is widely regarded as a sacred tree (the *asoka* tree, Kannada *ashokada mara*). It is often planted.

### Bauhinia

**Ecological Notes** Saldanha (1984) lists 6 species in Karnataka, of which *B. foveolata, B. malabarica,* and *B. phoenicea* are the 'mountain ebonies' found in the wet evergreen vegetation of the Western Ghats. *B. malabarica* also occurs in the Nallamallai hills together with *B. vahlii* and *B. tomentosa. Bauhinia racemosa* is a small deciduous tree, frequent in dry and moist deciduous forests and occasionally found in thorn savanna woodlands as well. *B. variegata* is a species native to China. It is a moderate-sized deciduous tree, frequently cultivated, and is naturalised in South Indian dry deciduous forests.

**Ethnobotany** The inner bark of most *Bauhinia* species can provide a strong, coarse fibre used in rope making (3, 6; Dash 1998:228; Royle 1855:295–97;). The wood of *B. racemosa* is mostly used as fuel (3; Thurston 1907:466). *B. variegata* is used for manufacturing agricultural imple-ments (3). Its bark provides dyeing and tanning substances (3), and the leaves, pods, and flower buds are often consumed as a vegetable (3, 6), as are the leaves of *B. malabarica* (6). Various parts of *B. tomentosa* are used in traditional medicine (6).

## Cassia

This genus includes mostly shrubs as well as some herbs. In addition to the native species there is a number of introduced American taxa (*C. alata*, *C. hirsuta* and *C. floribunda*) which have been naturalized and are widespread in the subcontinent.

**Ecological Notes** *C. auriculata* (the eared *senna*) is a deciduous shrub growing on dry rocky hills and black cotton soils in central and South India (it is relatively more common in the dry interiors of Karnataka). *C. italica* occurs in similar settings. *C. tora* is a frequent undershrub growing as a weed in wastelands. *C. fistula* is a moderate-sized deciduous tree. *C. surattensis* occurs in the deciduous vegetation of the east-facing slopes of the Western Ghats and in the dry evergreen woodlands of southeastern India. *C. siamea*, a native of Southeast Asia, is now an established component of dry deciduous forests. *C. montana* occurs on exposed hills in southern Karnataka. *C. nigricans* occurs mainly along the west coast of India.

**Ethnobotany** The bark of many *Cassia* species is used in tanning, but *C. auriculata* is the preferred source of the bark used in South Indian tanneries (6). *C. auriculata* seeds, leaves, and flowers are widely used in traditional medicine (6). Its leaves are also used as a natural fertiliser in rice fields. *C. fistula* provides durable (albeit small-sized) timber (3). It makes a good fuel (both as wood and charcoal). Its leaves and fruits are edible, but it is not used as fodder (the leaves are avoided by cattle) (3).

## Hardwickia

*Hardwickia binata* is the only representative of this genus in South India.

**Ecological Notes** *Hardwickia binata* is a deciduous tree of dry deciduous woodlands, although its distribution is patchy and it forms gregarious isolated belts. It prefers sandstone substrates rather than trap or granite. Nowadays extensive logging and deforestation have made *Hardwickia binata* quite uncommon in dry deciduous vegetation.

**Ethnobotany** *H. binata* (Hindi *anjan*, Kannada *kammara*) produces an extremely hard, heavy wood, which does not split (2) and is used in ploughs, cartwheels, and pontoons (6). The bark yields a coarse fibre used for rope making and in tanning (2, 6). The leaves provide good fodder and green manure (6; Rangarajan 1998:587).

## Tamarindus

This is a monotypic genus represented by tamarind (*Tamarindus indica*).

**Ecological Notes** *T. indica* is a large evergreen tree extensively cultivated in India for its acidic to sweet fleshy pods. Most authors have accepted that it originates in central Africa, where it occurs naturally in dry savanna woodlands (equivalent to the dry evergreen vegetation of Central India). Within South Asia tamarind is considered to be commensal to human settlement, yet it is also reported from forests and woodlands in Karnataka and Kurnool (Singh N.P. 1988; Venkata Rajau and Pullaiah 1995; cf. Watt G. 1889–1893). It remains to be established whether tamarinds found in forests occur near or on the sites of old settlements, perhaps as the result of seed dispersal by humans (as argued by Talbot 1912; Gamble 1902), or whether tamarind might in fact have been part of the natural forest vegetation of India (see below).

**Ethnobotany** Its wood is not very durable when exposed, but is highly prized for internal house fittings (3). The fruit, rich in vitamin C, is used as flavouring in curries and in traditional medicine as a laxative (2, 6, 7).

**Excursus: Tamarind—Introduced or Native?** Most authors have presumed an African origin for tamarind, although a minority suggest and/or query the possibility of its Indian origin. Tamarind occurs as a wild component of the dry savannas of tropical Africa from Sudan, Ethiopia, Kenya, and Tanzania through sub-Sahelian Africa to Senegal (Brandis 1884). The belief in the African origin of tamarind is deeply rooted in the literature and has led to the assumption that this species was introduced to India as a cultivar (for example, Hooker 1875–1897; Roxburgh 1832).

Tamarind appears in the archaeobotanical record of South India relatively late, and this is compatible with its introduction from Africa. Seeds are reported from the early historic site of Ter in Maharashtra (Kajale 1991:176). Wood charcoal identifications of tamarind come from Narhan (c. 1300 B.C.E.) in the Ganges valley (Saraswat et al. 1994), a region where it is more likely to be planted rather than occur naturally. At the same time, however, there is circumstantial linguistic evidence for its greater antiquity in India. Zide and Zide (1976) have suggested a reconstruction for proto-Munda, which (conservatively dated) had been established in eastern India (Orissa) by the first half of the second millennium B.C.E. (Fuller 2003b). In addition, there is a widespread set of cognates including Maharati (*chinch, chicha*) and all the branches of the Dravidian subfamily with the exception of Brahui (DEDR 2529). This has been suggested to relate to proto-Dravidian *\*sint-* (Starostin 2003) or *\*cin-tta* (Fuller 2007:424; Southworth 2005:220) and is the source of the Sanskrit *chincha* (Achaya 1998:246). Even if the glosses for the northeast Dravidian languages (Malto 'sour taste' and Kurukh 'tamarind seed') are removed as being less clear, this relationship is comparable in antiquity to that of several endemic Indian fruits and the oldest indigenous crop plants (Fuller 2003b). Certainly, the Arabic name and its botanical and English derivatives imply that the inhabitants of the Near East and Egypt first encountered this species as an import from India; the Arabic name *tamr hindi* literally means the 'date of India'.

On presently available archaeobotanical and linguistic evidence, therefore, the story of tamarind's origins and its establishment in India remains unclear. While tamarind is certainly native to Africa, the assumption that there have never been disjunct wild populations in India, now or in the past, has been taken as an article of faith by botanists. Further archaeobotanical sampling and research may contribute in resolving this issue.

## LEGUMINOSAE—MIMOSACEAE

This is a vast group ranging from herbs to trees, and includes numerous species that are prominent in the drier savanna zones of the Deccan as well as species that find themselves at home in the wet evergreen forests. It comprises prickly shrubs such as *Acacia* spp., *Dichrostachys cinerea*, *Prosopis*, and *Mimosa* spp., smooth shrubs and trees such as *Albizia* spp., *Archidendron monadelphum*, and larger deciduous trees such as *Xylia xylocarpa*.

### Acacia

This is a large genus of spiny trees and shrubs. Saldanha (1984) includes 18 species for Karnataka, whereas Gamble (1935) recognised 23 native species in the region.

**Ecological Notes** *Acacia* species are well adapted to the environmental stresses and anthropogenic pressures of peninsular India. Most species are drought tolerant. Because they are spiny, they are also less prone to grazing. Furthermore, they tend to be fire-resistant and they re-sprout readily after light burning. They generally reproduce well from seed, although some taxa such as *A. nilotica* (see below) are adapted to animal seed dispersal. Most *Acacia* species respond very well to coppicing.

Among the species that form important components of peninsular vegetation are *Acacia chundra* (formerly included as a subspecies of *A. catechu*), prominent in the mixed dry deciduous forests and scrub vegetation of Karnataka (Singh 1988:57), and *A. catechu*, which also occurs in dry deciduous woodlands but is much more common to the north in Maharashtra. In the *Hardwickia binata – Anogeissus latifolia* woodlands, *A. chundra* and *A. leucophloea* are prominent understorey species and often intergrade with surrounding savanna scrub vegetation.

The predominant species in savannas and scrub are *Acacia leucophloea* and *A. horrida* (syn. *A. latronum*), although there is some geographical variation. For example, *A. caesia* is common on the quartzite and limestone hills of the Kurnool-Cuddapah region (Erramalais) together with *A. chundra* and *A. horrida* (Venkata Raju and Pullaiah 1995:10). On poor rocky soils, such as the granitic zone of Bellary and adjacent districts, it is *A. leucophloea* that accompanies *A. chundra* and *A. horrida*, with some *A. eburnea* in thickets dominated by other taxa. *A. horrida* and *A. caesia* become rarer as one moves north toward the Deccan Trap. *A. eburnea* is frequent along watercourses, including seasonal nallahs, in the dry deciduous zone (Singh 1988:67). It is also widely planted as a hedge plant (Singh et al. 2001:809).

*Acacia nilotica* (often mistakenly called *A. arabica*, Hindi *babul*) is also widespread along roadsides, field edges, and streams. It establishes well on black cotton soils, near old tank beds, and paddy fields and can tolerate saline/alkaline conditions. Under such conditions, it may dominate patches of scrub in which it grows to a moderate-sized or large tree. Such vegetation has been termed by some Indian botanists as 'babul savanna' (Singh 1988:66). *A. nilotica* reproduces primarily from seed; its seeds germinate best when passed through the digestive tract of sheep and goats, whereas free seeds may be destroyed by insects and birds. It coppices well and can also reproduce vegetatively from cuttings.

**Ethnobotany** The bark and the wood of several *Acacia* species are used in tanning. Most prominent are *A. catechu* and *A. chundra*, the sources of 'cutch', which is extracted from their heartwood and was traded in the past under the name of 'red ebony'. *A. nilotica*, *A. polycantha*, and *A. leucophloea* may be used in similar ways (2, 6).

*A. catechu* (Hindi *khair*) is a valued source of fuel and house building timber, owing to its extremely durable wood (3). It is also used for manufacturing bows, spears, sword handles, agricultural implements, etc. (3) Its gum is edible and has some medicinal properties (2). A refined form of the cutch, obtained by boiling the wood for an extended period, is called *kath* and used as an additive for betel leaf chewing (2). *A. chundra* has durable wood and produces gum with properties similar to that of *A. catechu* (2).

The wood of *A. leucophloea* (Hindi *rinj*) seasons well and provides an excellent fuel (3). The bark has been reported as a famine food and is also a source of fibre for nets and cordage (3, 6). Its young pods and seeds are edible, and the gum is used in traditional medicine (3, 6). The wood of *A. nilotica* (Hindi *babul*) is very durable when well seasoned (3). Its branches and boughs are commonly used for fencing fields. Its gum is used in traditional medicine while its pods and leaves are fed to cattle, sheep and goats (2, 3). The gum is consumed as a famine food (2). The bark and fruits are used to prepare a black dye (2). *A. horrida* has few reported uses, although it is said to procure quality fibre from its bark (2).

## Albizia

**Ecological Notes** *Albizia* spp. are deciduous trees without spines and thus prone to heavy damage by grazing livestock, in contrast to spiny *Acacia*. *A. amara* occurs in dry deciduous forests but is mostly found in evergreen savanna woodlands in association with *Acacia* spp., in the southern peninsula (south of the Deccan Traps) (Puri et al. 1989). *A. lebbeck* is another common component of dry deciduous woodlands but is also widely planted on roadsides. *A. procera* is a large deciduous tree found in lowland riverbanks throughout India and in moist deciduous woodlands. A fast-growing species, it is characterised by its tall straight or slightly curved bole and round canopy. *A. chinensis* is less common in moist deciduous vegetation. *A. odoratissima* may grow in a range of habitats including dry and moist deciduous woodlands.

**Ethnobotany** *A. amara* wood is strong, hard, and durable, being used in house building and plough-making (3, 6). It also makes a good fuel (3), and its gum is used for medicinal purposes (6). The timber of *A. procera* and *A. lebbeck* seasons well, is durable, and thus is favoured for quality furniture (6). Furthermore, it makes an excellent fuel both as dry wood and charcoal (3). Their leaves and seeds are used to treat eye problems (6). The gum of *A. odoratissima* and *A. lebbeck* is used as an adulterant for gum Arabic (6).

## Prosopis

**Ecological Notes** Both *Prosopis cineraria* (syn. *P. spicigera*) and *P. juliflora* occur in the dry deciduous forests of the inner peninsula. *P. juliflora* is often planted as part of reforestation programs, but in the wild it abounds on riverbanks. Its native status is dubious. *P. cineraria* is rare in this region (Saldanha 1984; Singh et al. 2001) but becomes more common toward the drier parts of northwestern South Asia. It is reported to favour heavy soils. These species are easily raised from seed and they propagate vegetatively through coppicing.

**Ethnobotany** The unripe pods of *P. cineraria* contain a sweet substance, and they have been traditionally consumed as a famine food (2). The pods and foliage are collected as fodder (2). Although widely used for carts and various implements, the wood is nevertheless prone to insect attacks and rotting (2). In Punjab, *P. cineraria* pods and galls have been used in traditional medicine (2). This species is regarded as sacred in many parts of India, its twigs and leaves being used as offerings in fire rituals (2).

## Xylia

**Ecological Notes** *Xylia xylocarpa* is a large, unarmed (that is, non-spiny) deciduous tree common in the moist deciduous forests of the Western Ghats (Saldanha 1984; Singh et al. 2001), and it also maintains a disjunct distribution in the northern Eastern Ghats (Gamble 1935). On good and suitable soil (gneiss), it can grow to large size. By contrast, on poor laterite soils it remains comparatively small. It is absent from the Deccan Traps (Meher-Homji 2001:115). *X. xylocarpa* reproduces from seed, and its germination is aided by fire. It is not eaten by cattle.

**Ethnobotany** *X. xylocarpa* is an important timber species, especially for building purposes (other local uses include boat-making, agricultural implements, carts, and tool handles). Its wood is very durable owing to its high resin content and is considered valuable for building purposes (3).

## LEGUMINOSAE—PAPILIONACEAE

This is a large group that includes many herbaceous plants and small shrubs but remains best known for its numerous cultivated species (pulses). It also includes some commercially important and ecologically prominent trees of the region, especially *Butea*, *Dalbergia*, and the less common *Pterocarpus santalinus*.

## Butea

*B. monosperma* (syn. *B. frondosa*) is a prominent tree throughout the Deccan, whereas *B. superba* is a woody creeper of dry and moist deciduous forests.

**Ecological Notes** *B. monosperma* is a moderate-sized deciduous tree, particularly common in dry deciduous woodlands, although it also occurs in open grasslands, marshes, and saline plains throughout India.

**Ethnobotany** *Butea monosperma* is sometimes called 'the flame of the forest' for its bright orange flowers that emerge during the dry season while it sheds its leaves. Its flowers, dried and powdered, produce an orange-yellow pigment used in the past for dying the robes of Buddhist monks (Patnaik 1993; Yule and Burnell 1886:312). The same pigment is also known as 'holi powder', referring to its use in the 'dye bombs' Indians throw during the Holi festival.

Its bark exudes from cuts and fissures a red substance that hardens into a ruby-coloured gum (*kino,* Bengal kino) and is used in medicine (2, 3, 4; see also *Pterocarpus* below). The bark gives a coarse fibre (3). *Butea* wood is not particularly durable (prone to fungal decay especially when cut), hence one of its English common names 'bastard teak'. Its seeds are consumed as a purgative and vermifuge (3). The leaves are used to make plates and wrap food, and occasionally as wrappers for local *beedi* cigarettes (4; 6; Saldanha 1984).

*Butea monosperma* (Hindi *dhak* or *palas*) is one of the hosts of the lac insect, *Laccifer* (*Coccus*) *lacca,* whose resinous secretion is gathered from the surface of the tree to make lacquer (2:409; 4: Chapter 4).

Cognate terms for *Butea monosperma* can be found in all the subfamilies of the Dravidian languages, from Tamil *murukku* to Malto *murko* (DEDR 4981), suggesting that this species may have been familiar to proto-Dravidian speakers (Fuller 2007:423; Southworth 2005:220).

## Dalbergia

With the exception of teak, *D. latifolia* is probably the most important timber species of the peninsula.

**Ecological Notes**  *D. latifolia* is a large deciduous tree common throughout India. It is a component of dry deciduous forests on both gneiss and laterite soils but finds optimal conditions on foothill laterite colluvium. It may also extend into moist deciduous vegetation. It propagates easily from seed and also responds well to coppicing. As its pods remain on the tree during the dry season and are shed only when the monsoon has started, its seeds remain protected from forest fires.

Other *Dalbergia* species of the dry deciduous vegetation of the Deccan are *D. lanceolata* (more common toward the northern parts of the peninsula in Maharashtra), *D. paniculata* (common), and *D. sissoo* (widespread in North India). In the moist deciduous and evergreen zones of the Western Ghats several other species of *Dalbergia* are reported, such as *D. acaciaefolia, D. candenatensis, D. horrida, D. malabarica, D. melanoxylon, D. pinnata, D. rubiginosa, D. sissoides,* and *D. volubilis*.

**Ethnobotany**  *Dalbergia* wood is very hard and close-grained, thus being highly appreciated as a furniture craft material (1, 2, 3, 5, 6). It may also provide a good fuel, although it is rarely used for this purpose. Sometimes it is planted in the fields to provide shade for cultivated crops (3). The timber of some *Dalbergia* species has been important in commerce. It is known as 'black wood' or Indian rosewood (especially *D. latifolia* and *D. sissoides*) on account of its dark heartwood described by Roxburgh (1832:III, 222) as 'greenish-black, with lighter coloured veins . . . which gives it that beautiful appearance'. This dark colour has led to confusion among some authors with ebony (Ebenaceae). The value ascribed to *Dalbergia* timber has led to extensive plantation production, at least since colonial times (2). The related species *D. sissoo* (Northwest and North India) has a lighter, greyish-brown wood with dark veins and is known as *sissoo* or *shisham* (see also Yule and Burnell 1886:842). The southern *D. latifolia* (and *D. sissoides*) is known in Hindi as *kala-shisham* (the 'black shisham'), which serves to indicate the importance attached to the colour distinction as well as the geographical separation between the geographical distributions of these species.

Ancient textual references to the trade in 'black wood' and sissoo need to be considered in the context of these geographical and colour distinctions. Sissoo is mentioned in the *Periplus Maris Erythraei* (Casson 1989:42) and was certainly exported from South Asia to Persia from as early as the sixth century B.C.E. (Maxwell-Hyslop 1983). There are probable textual references for its trade into Mesopotamia from Meluhha, the Harappan civilisation region, in the late third millennium B.C.E. (Ratnagar 2004:129, 133). *D. sissoo* occurs today in parts of Baluchistan and Afghanistan, and its charcoal is a recurrent find in Harappan and pre-Harappan Baluchistan (Tengberg and Thiébault 2003). A 'black wood of Meluhha' identified in Akkadian texts of the late third millennium B.C.E. (Ratnagar 2004:131) has generally been equated with ebony (*Diospyros* sp., see Ebenaceae), although its identification as *Dalbergia latifolia* cannot be ruled out.

## Pterocarpus

**Ecological Notes** This genus includes two species of dry deciduous forests with distinct geographical distributions. *P. marsupium* is a large tree (often crooked) widespread in the dry deciduous forests of South India in Karnataka, Andhra Pradesh, and the Nallamalai hills (Ellis 1987; Saldanha 1984; Singh 1988:52). *P. santalinus* characterises forest formations restricted to the southern Western Ghats (especially in the Cuddapah, northern Arcot, and Chingleput districts).

**Ethnobotany** *P. marsupium*, the 'Malabar kino tree' (Hindi *Bijasal*, Kannada *honne* or *bonge*) produces a gum-resin called *kino* (4), which is the principal kino of commerce (see also *Butea*, above). Its timber is highly valued after teak, dalbergias, and the ebonies (4). The leaves make excellent fodder (6). Dravidian names for this species are cognate in languages from the south, south-central, and central Dravidian subfamilies (DEDR 5520), suggesting that its antiquity is on par with that of numerous other dry deciduous trees (for example, *Terminalia*, *Diospyros melanoxylon*, *Gmelina arborea*, *Tectona grandis*, *Phyllanthus emblica*, *Pterocarpus marsupium*, *Syzygium cumini*).

*P. santalinus* (red sanders or red sandal wood, Hindi *rakta-chandana*) produces a red-coloured timber valued for house posts, tools, carts, and even musical instruments (6). Its wood is ground to produce reddish or orange dye for staining leather, cotton, wool, and wooden implements (6). As with true sandalwood, an emulsion made from this wood may be painted on the body of religious devotees after bathing (2). It is also widely used in traditional medicine (2, 6). At times it has been used as a substitute for sandalwood, especially in medieval times, although unlike true sandalwood it is not aromatic (Dalby 2000:96). Defunct timber may be used for charcoal making; the leaves are fed to domestic animals as fodder (6).

## LOGANIACEAE

This family is mainly represented by the genus *Strychnos* and a number of herbaceous plants. *Fagraea ceilanica* is a woody epiphyte in wet evergreen forests.

## Strychnos

Two species occur in South India.

**Ecological Notes** *S. nux-vomica* is a moderate-sized to large deciduous tree found in moist and dry deciduous forests of South India. *S. potatorum* is a moderate-sized deciduous tree (dry deciduous forests); it is less common than *S. nux-vomica* but ranges into the drier zones of the region, including the reserve forests of eastern Karnataka (Singh 1988).

**Ethnobotany** Several species of *Strychnos* contain alkaloids including the poisonous substances strychnine and brucine. The seeds of *S. nux-vomica* are used for extracting the poison strychnine (3). It is traditionally used in India as fish poison and, in small quantities, has a number of medicinal uses (1). For example, its root may be used to treat fevers and venomous snake bites (1). Almost all its parts (leaves, bark, fruit, and especially the seeds) are rich in these alkaloids. Its seeds are added to country spirits during distillation to make them more intoxicating (1). The young tender shoots of *S. nux-vomica* are eaten by goats, but otherwise the tree is untouched by browsing animals.

*S. nux-vomica* (Hindi *kuchla*) yields hard, durable, and close-grained wood that contains no heartwood or annual rings (3). There are no reported craft uses for it, although it has traditional magical associations (Thurston 1907:328). Its wood was used in sorcery (by carving an effigy of the enemy and then burying it in the embers of burnt rice husk. If hairs of the person involved could be obtained, these were enclosed in a coconut together with *Strychnos nux-vomica* wood).

*S. potatorum* is not poisonous. Its wood is used for ploughs, cartwheels, and as building timber (3). A Proto-South Dravidian name has been reconstructed as **cill*- (Southworth 2005: 221).

## LYTHRACEAE

This family includes the cultivated shrub from which the henna dye is derived (*Lawsonia*). *Woodfordia fruticosa* is a shrub of dry deciduous forests, more common toward the northern part of the peninsula. *Pemphis acidula* is a shrub of the west coast tidal zone.

### Lagerstroemia

A genus of tall deciduous trees, with 5 species reported in South India.

**Ecological Notes** *Lagerstroemia microcarpa* (syn. *L. lanceolata*) is a large deciduous tree of the moist deciduous vegetation of the Western Ghats and the dry deciduous forests of higher elevations (for example. the Sandur hills in Karnataka). *L. parviflora* occurs throughout the Eastern Ghats and the Nallamalai hills, and in deciduous forests along the east-facing slopes of the Western Ghats. It is rarer in the arid plains of the interior.

### Ethnobotany

Because of its large size, fast growth rate, and natural abundance *Lagerstroemia* is considered a valuable timber species used extensively in buildings, ships, coffee-cases, and furniture (1, 3).

### Lawsonia inermis

(syn. *L. alba*), the henna plant

**Ecological Notes** This deciduous shrub, often spiny, is cultivated throughout India as a hedge plant and is encountered along streams in more arid districts. It is usually considered a feral species, yet it is likely to be part of the native vegetation in these areas. Roxburgh (1832) and Gamble (1935) have suggested that it is wild in the southwest coast and perhaps parts of the Deccan as well (see Watt 1889–1893). De Candolle (1885:138–39) has argued for its origin in the Iranian plateau (see also Burkill 1966).

**Ethnobotany** Dried and powdered, its leaves are made into a paste that gives the henna dye (Hindi *mehndi,* Kannada *gorante,* Tamil *marutanri*) used for colouring hair, skin, and nails (1, 2, 3, 6, 7). The leaves and flowers are also used for medicinal purposes (1). The origins of the use of this plant for body ornamentation are unknown. It is generally regarded as having been in use in ancient Egypt, although it is not well documented before later periods, especially during Graeco-Roman times (after 300 B.C.E.) (de Vartavan and Asensi Amoros 1997:151). Although it has been suggested that the mummy of Ramses II has hair that may have been coloured with henna, this remains unconfirmed (ibid.). Henna is known in Sanskrit and thus has considerable antiquity in South Asia. Further east, it was introduced more recently. Chinese sources refer to its probable use by 'barbarians' from the sixth century; its cosmetic use by the Chinese dates much later (thirteenth century) (Laufer 1919:334–38). Wood charcoal from Harappan/late Harappan Rohira in Punjab confirms the antiquity of this species in the subcontinent. In addition, *Lawsonia* charcoal has been found in Sanghol (Kushana period, c. 50–250 C.E.), also in Punjab (Saraswat 2002).

## MELIACEAE

The most widespread member of this family is *Azadirachta indica.* Another important species is *Soymida.* Trees of the wet evergreen forests include *Aglaia* and a few other small genera. *Cipadessa baccifera* and *Melia dubia* are more widespread across different vegetation zones. In old floras, *Chloroxylon* has been often classified under Meliaceae. It is now recognised to belong to the Rutaceae.

### Aglaia

**Ecological Notes** There are six species of *Aglaia*, all confined to the wet evergreen and semi-evergreen forests of the Western Ghats (Saldanha 1996), of which *Aglaia elaeagnoidea* (syn. *A. roxburghiana*) is a representative. This tree abounds in ravines, near sources of water, and is a shade-loving species. *A. talbotii* occurs on sandy and laterite soils along the west coast.

**Ethnobotany** *Aglaia* wood is very heavy and useful for ornamental work, spokes of wheels, and axe-handles. The fruits are edible and have some traditional medicinal uses (6).

## Azadirachta

*Azadirachta indica* (syn. *Melia azadirachta*) is better known as the *neem* tree (Sanskrit *nimba*, Kannada *bevu*, Telegu/Tamil *vepa*). The neem tree is probably native to dry deciduous forests, although it is also widely planted. Its sole congeneric relative, *A. excelsa*, is a native of Malaya.

**Ecological Notes** *Azadirachta indica* is a large deciduous tree, widely planted in and around villages. It thrives in dry deciduous forests on black cotton soil but may represent a naturalised species. Its original wild distribution remains somewhat unclear, but it may trace its origins to Burma (Mabberley 1987) and/or the Himalayan foothills (Duthie 1903; Hooker 1875–1897). Its presence in Pleistocene pollen assemblages from the Indian Ocean (Prabhu et al. 2004) suggests that it is indigenous to peninsular India.

**Ethnobotany** The leaves of *Azadirachta indica* are edible. The tree is also used in traditional medicine and in religious ceremonies. It is generally associated with purification and protection from disease, in particular with the goddess Sitala, who provides protection against smallpox (Simoons 1998:308–09).

Almost all parts of the tree (bark, leaves, flowers, seeds and seed oil, its gum and wood) are used for medicinal purposes (1, 2, 3, 6) and as food (2, 3, 8). Its twigs are commonly used as toothbrushes (6). The wood is durable and beautifully mottled and is used for the construction of carts, ships, furniture, and agricultural implements (1, 3, 6). The bark produces a coarse fibre used for making rope (2). The gum is reported to be used for dyeing silk and as a mordant (2). The leaves have insect-repellent qualities (7).

An ancient name *wē-mpu* can be reconstructed for South Dravidian languages (Fuller 2007:424; Southworth 2005:221).

## Soymida

This is a monotypic genus: *Soymida febrifuga*.

**Ecological Notes** *S. febrifuga* is a large deciduous tree of dry deciduous vegetation throughout India. It favours low laterite hills and is often found in association with satin wood (*Chloroxylon swietenia*; see Rutaceae, below). It also occurs in dry deciduous teak forests and may be widespread in dry evergreen woodlands.

**Ethnobotany** *Soymida* wood is very durable and is used mainly for construction purposes (3, 6). Its bark is bitter and is used in traditional medicine as a febrifuge (3, 6). Other uses include tanning and the extraction of a strong red fibre used in cordage (3). When cut it exudes a beautiful clear gum in large pieces which is used as an adhesive (3, 6).

# MORACEAE

This family includes *Antiaris toxicaria*, a large tree found in wet evergreen forests. Wet evergreen and moist deciduous forests host *Artocarpus* spp. and several species of *Ficus*. Members of both genera are widely planted. *Plecospermum spinosum* is a shrub found in savanna scrub and dry deciduous woodlands. The latter are also the preferred habitat for *Streblus asper*.

## Artocarpus

**Ecological Notes** *Artocarpus heterophylla* (syn. *A. integrifolia*) is a large evergreen tree native to the Western Ghats forests. Elsewhere it is cultivated or feral. It is one of the most important fruit trees in India and requires deep moist rich soils and relatively high levels of rainfall. It coppices well and also reproduces from seed. *A. hirsuta* occurs wild in the Western Ghats, favouring stream edges in moist deciduous vegetation. *A. gomeziana* and *A. lakoocha* are less common species.

**Ethnobotany** *A. heterophylla* is also known by the common name 'jackfruit'. In addition to being a component of the native vegetation of the Western Ghats, it is widely cultivated throughout

India (1, 2) and Southeast Asia (Burkill 1966). All inner parts of its fruit are eaten, even the pulp and seeds, despite the fact that it has an unpleasant odour (2, 3). Its wood produces a yellow dye, and a gum is extracted from its bark (2, 3). A fast-growing species, its wood is widely used in carpentry especially for boxes and furniture (1, 2, 3). On the west coast, the wood of *A. hirsuta* is used in boat building (1, 6).

Other *Artocarpus* species also produce edible fruits. *A. hirsuta* has fruits (1, 2) that are considerably smaller (orange-sized) compared to the large fruits of *A. heterophylla*. The fruits of *A. gomeziana* and *A. lakoocha* are consumed as food in Malaya (Burkill 1966; 6). The flowers of *A. lakoocha* are also known to be pickled in India (Burkill 1966). The breadfruit (*A. communis*) is a native of Indonesia and is sometimes cultivated in South India (2).

Wood charcoal finds of *Artocarpus heterophylla* found in archaeological sites where it could not have formed part of the native vegetation imply that *Artocarpus* had begun to disperse through human activities by the end of the second millennium B.C.E. Wood charcoal has been identified in Bihar, in the central Ganges valley dating to Senuwar period II (1300–700 B.C.E.) (Saraswat 2004).

This species was known to early Dravidian speakers, indicated by cognates in South and Central Dravidian languages, from Tamil *palavu* to Parji *penac*, with a reconstructed proto-form such as \*pal-ac (Fuller 2007:425; Southworth 2005:214).

## Ficus

**Ecological Notes** There are numerous species of *Ficus* in South India. Their seeds are readily dispersed by birds, and most are strangler species that produce aerial roots. The status of *Ficus benghalensis* and *F. religiosa* as native to South India is doubtful. They are widely planted as ornamental trees, especially in or near temples, and have become feral in some forest environments. Both species are considered as native to the sub-Himalayan zone and perhaps Central India as well (2; Simoons 1998:42). They are likely to have dispersed across South India as cultivars associated with habitation sites.

Many other species of *Ficus* show fairly broad geographical distributions and environmental tolerances. Nevertheless, we can divide *Ficus* species into three groups with regard to their ecological preferences and distribution:

1. *Ficus* of dry deciduous forests: *Ficus amplissima, F. drupacea, F. heterophylla, F. microcarpa, F. mollis, F. tinctoria.*
2. *Ficus* of moist deciduous forests, crevices in the Western Ghats, along streams, and dense dry deciduous woodland on hilltops: *Ficus arnottiana, F. exasperata, F. hispida, F. microcarpa, F. nervosa, F. racemosa* (syn. *F. glomerata*), *F. tinctoria* (ranges to dry deciduous), *F. virens.*
3. *Ficus* of tropical moist evergreen (to semi-evergreen) forests: *F. albipila, F. beddomei, F. callosa, F. caulocarpa, F. geniculata, F. talboti, F. tsjakela.*

**Ethnobotany** The native *Ficus* species of India generally produce small fruits which are very sensitive to insect attacks and are eaten by birds. Therefore, they very rarely provide food suitable for human consumption except in times of food shortages. The common domestic fig (*Ficus carica*) has been also introduced from the Near East and is fairly widely cultivated. *Ficus* wood is generally regarded of little economic value (2), although the wood of *F. religiosa* is traditionally used as fuel in ritual fires (Thurston 1907:464).

Much more important are the sacred associations and uses of *Ficus religiosa* (Hindi *pipal*) and *F. benghalensis* (Hindi *banyan*). Both species are often regarded as the dwelling places of various deities (2; Simoons 1998:52–54; Yule and Burnell 1886:65, 691). The trees themselves are perceived as protective and wish-granting supernatural beings. Various parts of them are used in rituals, the twigs in sacred fires and the leaves for pouring libations. Cutting down of the trees proper, however, is discouraged. With the *pipal* regarded as female and the *banyan* as male they are sometimes planted in pairs followed by a symbolic tree marriage ceremony (Simoons 1998: 65–67). Occasionally, two *Ficus* trees of the same species may also be regarded as 'husband' and 'wife' or wedded to other significant trees, such as the neem (*Azadirachta indica*) or bananas (Dubois 1906:653). In other instances *Ficus* trees may also be regarded as wedded to deities and even humans (2; Simoons 1998:65–67).

Various parts of *F. religiosa* and *F. benghalensis* are used medicinally (2). Both species produce coarse fibres from their bark, which are used in rope making (2).

Numerous ancient names for several wild *Ficus* spp. can be reconstructed from early Dravidian, including cognates across South and Central Dravidian languages for the *papal, banyan,* and *Ficus glomerata* (Southworth 2005:209).

## MORINGACEAE

### Moringa

Two species are found in India, *M. oleifera* and *M. concanensis*.

**Ecological Notes** *Moringa oleifera* is a common tree near rivers and in the sub-Himalayan zone. Elsewhere it is widely cultivated.

**Ethnobotany** Its fruits, leaves, and flowers are edible, and its seeds are used in curries. The root has a strong flavour of horseradish and is also used in traditional medicine. Its branches are usually lopped for cattle fodder.

## MYRTACEAE

This family contains five genera indigenous to South India and a few introduced ones (for example, *Callistemon, Psidium,* and *Eucalyptus*). Among indigenous genera, *Syzygium* (= *Eugenia*) is perhaps the largest in India, numbering about 110 species. Other important Indian genera are *Barringtonia* and *Careya*. Most of these species, as well as *Jambosa* and *Meteoromyrtus,* occur in the wet evergreen zone, whereas *Rhodomyrtus tomentosa* is a shrub of montane *shola* forests of the Palni and Nilgiri hills.

### Barringtonia

There are about 9 species of *Barringtonia*, mainly from Burma. Native to India are *B. acutangula* and *B. racemosa* (both moderate-sized evergreen trees).

**Ecological Notes** *Barringtonia acutangula* is distributed from the sub-Himalayan zone southward to Bengal and Central and South India. It is a hygrophilous species, usually found in swamps and streamside habitats.

**Ethnobotany** *Barringtonia* wood is durable and has been used for cabinet-making, boat-building, carts, and rice pounders. Its bark is used to intoxicate fish and for tanning. The fruit, leaves, and bark are used in traditional medicine.

### Careya

**Ecological Notes** *Careya arborea* is a large deciduous tree found throughout India in moist deciduous forests (preferably in ravines and valley habitats) and in sal forests; it is rare in dry deciduous woodlands. Occasionally, isolated individuals (in stunted form) may be found in moist grasslands.

**Ethnobotany** *Careya* wood is durable and resistant to moisture. It is used for manufacturing agricultural implements. Its bark provides fibre used in cordage and is also used in traditional medicine as an astringent.

### Syzygium (Eugenia)

Thirty-three species of *Syzygium* are reported as native to South India. *Syzygium cumini* (= *Eugenia jambolana*) is the most widespread, found throughout India, Burma, and Ceylon.

**Ecological Notes** *Syzygium cumini* is an evergreen species found mainly along riverbanks and in wet evergreen and moist deciduous forests. It reproduces well from seed. *S. heyneanum* is a component of riverine forests in the Deccan.

**Ethnobotany** *Syzygium cumini* provides durable wood used as timber, fuel, and for manufacturing agricultural implements. A linguistic root for *Syzygium cumini*, Tamil *naval* (DEDR 2914), Telegu *nerudu* (DEDR 2917), is traced across all the Dravidian subfamilies except for the North Dravidian, for which no names are reported (Fuller 2003b:201, 2007:425).

## RHAMNACEAE

This family includes several genera of shrubs and trees. Many are spiny stragglers and climbers in dry deciduous forest thickets, such as *Sageretia parviflora* and *Scutia myrtina*. Others are climbers and shrubs of the moist deciduous to semi-evergreen woodlands, such as *Colubrina asiatica*, *Gouania microcarpa*, *Smythea bombaiensis*, *Ventilago* spp. (3 species), *Ziziphus* spp., and the rare *Rhamnus wightii*.

### Ziziphus

There are 9 species of *Ziziphus* in South India, which can be divided into those favouring moister environments (for instance, moist deciduous forests and coastal zones; *Z. rugosa*, *Z. xylopyrus*, *Z. glabrata*, *Z. williamii*) and those favouring dry deciduous habitats and scrub vegetation in arid plains (*Z. caracutta*, *Z. horrida*, *Z. nummularia*, and *Z. oenoplia*). Also present in dry deciduous and scrub vegetation is *Z. mauritiana*, which is widely cultivated.

**Ecological Notes** *Z. mauritiana* is a large deciduous thorny shrub of dry forests and scrubland. It is commonly maintained in and around settlements and cultivated fields and grows easily on poor soils. *Z. oenoplia* is a climber that prefers open scrubland, whereas *Z. nummularia* is a gregarious shrub growing preferentially on black cotton soils.

**Ethnobotany** *Ziziphus* provides leafy browse for camels, sheep, and goats (3, 6). Its wood procures excellent fuel (3), and its bark can be used in tanning (6). The fruits of many species are edible (*Z. rugosa*, *Z. oenoplia*, *Z. nummularia*, *Z. mauritiana*) (6, 7), and most are also used medicinally (1, 6). *Z. mauritiana* (the *ber* tree) is widely cultivated for its fruits. Its archaeobotanical remains have a wide distribution in Neolithic and later sites throughout South Asia (see Fuller 2002; Kajale 1991). In South India, it occurs at almost every site where archaeobotanical sampling has been carried out (see Fuller et al. 2001a, 2004). Its name is readily reconstructed to Proto-Dravidian, including cognates from Tamil *iratti* to the less documented North Dravidian language Malto *ilkru* (DEDR 475; Fuller 2007:424; Southworth 2005:198).

## RUBIACEAE

This family comprises genera occurring in wet evergreen and dry deciduous vegetation. The wet evergreen forests include more than 60 species corresponding to 14 genera.

The genus *Ixora* comprises shrubs commonly found in moist deciduous vegetation (see below). Trees abounding in dry deciduous forests are *Adina cordifolia*, *Canthium* spp., *Gardenia* spp., *Hamiltonia suaveolens*, *Hymenodictyon* (2 species), *Mitragyna* (2 species), *Morinda* (4 species, especially in the Eastern Ghats), *Randia* spp. (especially in the dry evergreen woodlands of the eastern peninsula and in the Western Ghats), *Tarenna asiatica* (occasionally present in the Eastern Ghats and along the Western Ghats), *Vangueria spinosa*, *Wendlandia notoniana*, and *W. tinctoria*. *Anthocephalus indicus* is a deciduous tree that is found throughout the Deccan at moist localities such as river banks. *Scyphiphora hydrophyllacea* is a mangrove species of the east coast.

### Canthium (syn. Plectronia in Gamble 1935)

A genus of small trees and shrubs, many of them spiny. Two species have been included here: *C. coromandelicum* and *C. dicoccum*.

**Ecological Notes** Several species of this genus occur in the dry scrub of the central Deccan. Further north (Karnataka, Andhra Pradesh) is found the ubiquitous spiny *C. coromandelicum* (syn. *C. parviflorum*) and the unarmed *C. dicoccum*, whereas in the south (inland Tamil Nadu) are found the spiny *C. rheedii* and *C. angustifolium* (in deciduous vegetation on the eastern side of the Western Ghats).

**Ethnobotany**   *Canthium* is used mainly in fencing/hedges (3). The fruits of *C. coromandelicum* (furrowed orange drupes) are edible (6; Singh et al. 2001).

## Gardenia

Shrubs in deciduous forests. *G. resinifera* is ubiquitous and widespread, whereas other species are less common.

**Ecological Notes**   *G. resinifera* is a small deciduous tree of dry deciduous forests in Central and South India, but it may also occur in dry scrubland.

**Ethnobotany**   Its wood is used for manufacturing small implements (3). The tree exudes a gum resin from cuttings on its bark and from its leaf buds; the resin is used for medicinal purposes and to ward off pests (3, 6).

## Ixora

This genus includes some 17 shrub species found in South India.

**Ecological Notes**   *Ixora* comprises evergreen shrubs found mainly in moist deciduous forests (Saldanha 1984:15). *I. pavetta* (syn. *I. parviflora*, *I. arborea*) is the most widespread in dry deciduous woods of the Indian peninsula. *I. notoniana* is a moist montane element of the shola forests (Matthew 1999), whereas *I. nigricans* occurs in the moist deciduous vegetation of the Sahyadris (northern Western Ghats).

**Ethnobotany**   *I. pavetta* is a shrub with conspicuous fragrant flowers. Its wood is used in turning, engraving, furniture, and for building purposes (although it is rarely of adequate size) (3, 4). It is also known as 'torchwood', because its wood is often used to make torches (2, 6, 7). Its small reddish drupes are edible (2, 6), and its bark is used in traditional medicine (2, 6).

## RUTACEAE

### Limonia acidissima, Aegle marmelos

**Taxonomic Notes**   The Rutaceae family includes many shrubs, climbers, and small trees, several of which produce aromatic essential oils, seasonings (for example, *Zanthoxylum* spp., *Murraya koenigii*), and edible fruits (*Limonia acidissima*, *Aegle marmelos*, *Citrus* spp., *Fortunella* spp., *Clausena lansium*). Although this family is widespread in the Old World tropics, its economic species are concentrated in India, Southeast Asia, and China. All the edible fruits and the curry leaf (*Murraya koenigii*) are included in the subfamily Aurantoideae, whereas *Zanthoxylum* spp., best known as the source of the Chinese or Sichuan pepper, belongs to the subfamily Rutoideae.

The taxonomy and nomenclature of *Citrus* is complex owing to extensive hybridisation, asexual reproduction, and human selection. Realistic taxonomies recognise 3 core species, each with many varieties and interspecific hybrids (Barrett and Rhodes 1976; Roose et al. 1995; Thomas et al. 1998). These are *Citrus medica* (the citron, including various limes and lemons), *Citrus aurantium* (the oranges), and *Citrus maxima* (the pommelo or shaddock). The widespread modern grapefruit (*C. paradisi*) derives from a Caribbean pommelo cultivar, possibly through hybridisation with orange trees.

**Ecological Notes**   Members of this family found in South India include *C. medica* (native to the Western Ghats), *C. aurantium*, and *C. decumana* (both cultivated). *Limonia acidissima* occurs on dry hills throughout India, including the inner Western Ghats (Hooker 1875–1897). *Aegle marmelos* is found wild and cultivated throughout India in 'dry hilly places' (Hooker 1875–1897:I, 517).

**Ethnobotany**   Most of the timber species of this family are commonly dense and yellow-coloured and are valued in craft production (see Gamble 1902; Watt 1889–1893). Yet *Citrus* spp. are best known for their edible fruits, rich in vitamin C, and the rinds of these fruits that are used as flavouring for pickles and candies.

Citron cultivation is likely to have begun in the second millennium B.C.E., probably in the Gangetic basin or the western part of the Himalayan foothills. The sole early archaeobotanical evidence of *Citrus* fruits in South Asia (reported as *C. lemon*, but the species identification remains problematic) derives from the late Harappan (Baran phase) site of Sanghol in Punjab (early second millennium B.C.E.) (Saraswat 1997). The citron reached the West by the mid-first millennium B.C.E.; it was cultivated by the Persians (Watson 1983:44; Zohary and Hopf 2001:184). A single archaeological find has been reported from late Bronze Age Cyprus (c. 1200 B.C.E.), but its antiquity has not been confirmed by direct radiocarbon dating (ibid.). Other *Citrus* cultivars probably did not arrive in the West until Islamic times, perhaps in the beginning of the eighth or ninth centuries (Watson 1983:45–50; Zohary and Hopf 2001). Clearly differentiated lemons and limes in the modern sense are probably a medieval introduction from Burma or Indochina, as can be inferred from linguistic data (Mahdi 1998). Although oranges are attested as medicinal plants in Sanskrit sources by the end of the first millennium B.C.E., their cultivation may not have begun until much later. Orange plantations are reported as part of agricultural expansion in medieval South India from the tenth to the thirteenth centuries (Nandi 2000:103).

The kumquats (*Fortunella* spp.), the wampee (*Clausena wampi*), and most *Zanthoxylum* spp. are cultivars indigenous to southern China and thus not particularly relevant to our region. *Clausena indica* occurs as a wild species in the Western Ghats (Hooker 1875–1897; Watt 1889–1893), and *C. dentata* has edible fruits. *Zanthoxylum rhetsa* (syn. *Fagara budrunga*) is reported from the Western Ghats as well as the eastern Himalayas and produces spicy fruits sometimes used in condiments. *Murraya koenigii* (syn. *Bergera koenigii*), the curry leaf, is native to the Himalayan foothills and is also reported from the western peninsula (Saldanha 1996:221). It is an essential traditional ingredient of all Indian curries and as such represents a common garden cultivar throughout India.

The bael fruit (*Aegle marmelos*) and the elephant apple (*Limonia acidissima* syn. *Feronia elephantum, Feronia limonia*) are both traditionally collected during the dry season in the Deccan and elsewhere in India. The elephant apple is a ubiquitous component of dry deciduous woodlands in peninsular and Central India. Bael is found only in association with the *Terminalia-Anogeissus-Tectona* variant, mainly on the northern peninsula (from the Tungabhadra basin northward) and through to eastern India in the moister varieties of sal forests (*Shorea—Terminalia—Adina* and *Shorea—Syzygium—Toona—Symplocos*). The bael is regarded as sacred and is often planted at temples. It produces sweet but acid edible fruits, and most plant parts have traditional medicinal uses. A yellow dye is procured from its rind. The elephant apple has a hard woody rind and a sour pulp, and is used in similar ways to the bael (Watt 1889–1893). Archaeobotanical evidence of bael wood charcoal has derived from late Neolithic/Chalcolithic contexts in the middle Ganges (1900–1300 B.C.E.) (Saraswat 2004:519).

Distinct etymological roots exist for the bael in south, south-central, and north Dravidian language subfamilies (Burrow and Emeneau 1984; DEDR 1910, 2072, 4821; Fuller 2007:427), whereas for elephant apples a root has been reported only from the south Dravidian languages with possible Central Dravidian cognates (DEDR 5509; Fuller 2007:423; Southworth 2005:221). For the citron (*Citrus medica*) a proto-South Dravidian reconstruction of *māt-al* is related to the Old Indo-Aryan *mātluga* (Fuller 2007:427; Southworth 2005:221).

## Chloroxylon

This is a monotypic genus endemic to South India: *Chloroxylon swietenia*.

**Ecological Notes** It is a moderate-sized deciduous tree abounding in the dry deciduous forests of the inner peninsula. It grows successfully even on poor sand and laterite soils and is found commonly on sandstone formations. It is shade-intolerant and colonises readily forest clearings.

**Ethnobotany** *Chloroxylon* wood, known as satin wood (Hindi *bhirra*, Kannada *mashula*, Telegu *billu*), is yellowish-brown, very hard, and is widely used as structural timber, for carts, agricultural implements, and in decorative furniture (1, 2, 3, 4, 6, 7). A yellow dye can be made from its resin (2, 4, 6). The bark is a rare medicinal astringent (2). It is not considered a good firewood because it smokes heavily (4).

## SANTALACEAE

Apart from sandal (*Santalum album*), which may not be native to South India, this family is also represented by *Osyris quadripartita*, a shrub occurring in drier scrub vegetation.

### Santalum album

**Ecological Notes** A small evergreen tree found mainly in South Indian dry deciduous forests. It prefers mostly open woodland habitats with patches of trees or scrub interspersed with grassland, on red stony soils. *Santalum* may also occur in hedgerows and is reported occasionally as a planted tree amid *Acacia* scrub vegetation (Singh 1988:71). Sandal seeds germinate in the shade and are dispersed by birds. It is a parasitic species drawing some of its nourishment by attaching to the roots of other trees and shrubs (Burkill 1966). This characteristic renders *Santalum* a species easy to transplant, hence facilitating its transference between different habitats. The tree itself is light-demanding and does not tolerate fire or overgrazing (Gamble 1902). Free-growing sandal is confined to the southern Deccan, although it is reported to be cultivable in the northern part of peninsular India (Burkill 1966; Gamble 1935; Haines 1921–1925; Hooker 1875–1897). Yet, this species is not widely accepted to be native to South India and is considered to have been naturalised owing to long-term cultivation (see below). Wild *S. album* occurs in the drier forests of Indonesia, certainly in Timor, and is widely distributed, from eastern Java through the Lesser Sunda Islands to Timor. Here it borders the distribution of other *Santalum* species found in New Guinea and Australia (Burkill 1966; Miller 1968:61).

**Ethnobotany** The heartwood of its yellow-white wood and its roots are scented (3). The wood is used in carving, yet its most known product is its scented oil used in perfumery, soaps, and as a medicinal substance. The paste is regarded as an effective treatment for sunburns (3; Dalby 2000:29), whereas an emulsion of it is spread on the body after bathing as part of religious observances (2). Sandalwood is also used in funeral pyres. Finally, Gamble (1902:588) recounts an interesting local story about the harvesting of sandalwood: 'the wood is brought out by parties of men who organise an expedition for this purpose in the cold weather. Only dead wood is extracted, and it is pretended that if the tree is artificially killed the scent of its wood is impaired'. The fragrance of sandalwood is probably affected by growing conditions as well, since trees growing on rocky soils in drier conditions are reported to produce a richer scent (Burkill 1966; Miller 1968:61).

**Excursus: Is Scented Sandalwood Introduced to India?** Sandal is known to have been imported via India to the Roman empire according to the *Periplus Maris Erythraei* (Miller 1968:86), yet many products introduced to the west from Indian ports had themselves been imported from further east. While some interpret the 'almug' wood mentioned in the Old Testament for the construction of Solomon's palace as sandalwood (for example, Miller 1968:62), this has not been convincingly argued (Burkill 1966), and aloes wood seems more likely (*Aquilaria*, which could have come from the eastern Himalayas in Bengal where *A. agallocha* occurs) (Dalby 2000). Sandal is reported as a trade commodity by the Egypt-based Kosmas Indicopleustes in the sixth century C.E. During this period, sandalwood along with silk, aloes wood (which at this period may include *Aquilaria malaccensis* from Indonesia), cloves, and clove-wood came by ship into Ceylon from further east (Miller 1968:25, 86). Sanskrit sources often mention the *chandana* wood, a name today ascribed to sandalwood and from which the word 'sandal' is etymologically derived (Achaya 1998; Fischer 1938). Although these sources make it clear that sandal was appreciated in India from the early historic period, none has convincingly described its native occurrence in India. Descriptions of its growth with betel-pepper and cardamom (as in the *Raghuvamsa* of Kalidasa, fifth century C.E.) seem unlikely, since these species could not co-occur on ecological grounds. In addition, the common name *chandana* was widely used for describing several scented or colourful woods including the Indian 'red sander' (*Pterocarpus santalinus*, Leguminosae-Papilionaceae) (Achaya 1998; Fischer 1938). When exactly sandal was transplanted to India remains to be established, with Dalby (2000:30) suggesting establishment by the first millennium B.C.E., whereas sources quoted in Fischer (1938), including Mughal and Portuguese texts, might imply the onset of its cultivation as late as the fifteenth century C.E. Be that as it may, it is suggested by historical sources of the early colonial period that the main supplier of sandalwood at that time was Timor (Boomgaard 1998:386).

In recent work, archaeobotanical evidence has confirmed the antiquity of sandalwood use and indicated its likely naturalised status in India. Charcoal has been identified among the charred remains recovered from a ritual fire altar context dating to the Kushana period (50–250 C.E.) at Sanghol in Punjab (Saraswat and Pokharia 1999). Since this is a region in which sandal could not have grown naturally, it was likely imported, either from South India (assuming it had already been established there) or from Indonesia. In the same assemblage there were also found fragments of black pepper (which must have been imported from South India) and nutmeg (which originated in Indonesia).

An ancient introduction to South India (in the late second millennium B.C.E.) is supported by archaeobotanical evidence from the authors' current project (Chapter 7). Wood charcoal from sandalwood has been found in the late Neolithic/Megalithic transition levels of Sanganakallu (Sannarachamma hill) dating between 1400 and 1000 B.C.E..Congruent with this archaeological horizon is historical linguistic evidence for proto-South Dravidian \**cāntu* (Fuller 2007:427; Southworth 2005:421).

## SAPINDACEAE

This is a widespread tropical family with some 11 genera found in South India (Gamble 1935). These are predominantly trees and shrubs of the wet evergreen vegetation of the Western Ghats and the west coast including *Allophyllus* spp., *Lepisanthes* spp., *Filicium decipiens*, *Sapindus* spp., *Thraulococcus erectus*, *Harpulia* sp., *Dodonaea viscosa*, and *Dimocarpus longan*, the wild variety of the edible fruit *longan* also known as a cultivar in South China. A few taxa extend to drier vegetation zones, including *Cardiospermum canescens* (a perennial climber of the Deccan), *Allophyllus* sp. and *Schleichera*. *Sapindus emarginatus* (the Indian soapnut) occurs in both moist and dry deciduous woodlands.

### Dodonaea viscosa

The only representative of this genus in South India, including tropical evergreen shrubs and trees.

**Ecological Notes** Dry evergreen shrub (hill scrub) planted throughout India as a hedge plant.

**Ethnobotany** The main uses of its wood include engraving, turning, and the manufacturing of tool-handles and walking sticks. Its branches are used in house building for the support of earthen flat roofs (3, 6). Its seeds are edible, and the fruits have been used in brewing, as a substitute for hops (*Humulus*) (6).

### Schleichera oleosa

**Ecological Notes** This monotypic genus represents a large deciduous tree of the dry and the moist deciduous forests of peninsular India, Sri Lanka, the Himalayan foothills, Burma, and the drier parts of Indonesia (Java and Timor) (Burkill 1966; Gamble 1935; Hooker 1875–1897).

**Ethnobotany** Its wood, known as 'Ceylon oak', is very strong and durable. It provides excellent firewood and charcoal (3). Its leaves and twigs are regularly lopped as cattle fodder (3). The leaves are edible, as are the fruits that are traditionally pickled while green. The seeds produce the edible *macassar* oil, which is also used in soap-making, as hair oil, and for lighting (1, 2, 5, 6). The wood of *Schleichera* has been traditionally selected for making pestles, at least in eastern India (Sivaramakrishnan 1999:187).

*Schleichera* is also a host for the lac insect, *Laccifer lacca* (family Coccidae), whose resinous secretion is collected in order to make lacquer, or red lac dye (2:409). Lac produced on this tree (Hindi *kusum*) is the true shellac of commerce and is regarded as the best material of this kind in India (2:411). It also has reported medicinal uses in China (Burkill 1966:1315). The red lac dye from this species is used on silk. Lac is produced twice a year, but the lac procured during the rainy season is reputed to be of higher quality (Burkill 1966:1313).

Dravidian linguistics suggest ancient familiarity with *Schleichera oleosa*, because a word root is known across all subbranches of the Dravidian family from Tamil *pûvam* to Kurux *pusra* (DEDR 4348; Fuller 2007:423).

## STERCULIACEAE

*Firmiana colorata*, *Pterygota alata,* and some species of *Sterculia* are found in moist deciduous forests. *Sterculia guttata* is reported from the Sandur hills and the Western Ghats. Other *Sterculia* species occur in drier localities, such as *S. urens*, which abounds on rocky hills in the dry deciduous forests of the inner peninsula. *Eriolaena* (3 species) has a similar distribution. The shrub *Helicteres ixora* is a common shrub in dry deciduous woodland openings. *Heritera littoralis* is an evergreen tree of the west coast, whereas *H. papilio* occurs in semi-evergreen woods. *Leptonychia moacurroides* is a southern Western Ghats wet evergreen forest species. *Pterospermum* (6 species) is largely confined to the wet evergreen zone, although it may be found occasionally in drier zones as well.

### Pterospermum

**Ecological Notes** The genus *Pterospermum* comprises understorey trees found in wet evergreen and moist deciduous forests. They become more common as one moves southward through the Western Ghats. Most widespread is *P. diversifolium*, a moderate-sized to large deciduous tree of moist deciduous and evergreen forests. *P. xylocarpum* tolerates drier conditions and occurs in the Nallamalais and the Eastern Ghats, on forest edges and stream banks. *P. suberifolium* is an evergreen species of the southeastern plains (Tamil Nadu).

**Ethnobotany** *Pterospermum* wood is used as fuel, for building, carts, and other purposes (3). *P. diversifolium* bark is used for dyeing fishnets; the root bark procures a fish poison (6). *Helicteres ixora* has fruits with medicinal properties (6; Singh et al. 2001). Its bark yields a coarse fibre used in cordage (6).

## TILIACEAE

This family includes the annual herbs of the genus *Corchorus* (jute), the subshrubs and herbs of the genus *Triumfetta*, as well as numerous trees and shrubs belonging to the genus *Grewia*. In addition, *Erinocarpus nimmonii* is a monotypic genus that is endemic in the moist deciduous and semi-evergreen forests of the Western Ghats in northern Karnataka (Saldanha 1984).

### Grewia sp.

South India hosts 26 species of *Grewia*.

**Ecological Notes** This genus can be divided ecologically into four main groups:

1. Moist deciduous to semi-evergreen vegetation-Western Ghats: *G. abutilifolia* (syn. *G. aspera*), *G. gamblei*, *G. glabra* (syn. *G. laevigata*), *G. heterotricha*, *G. lanceaefolia*, *G. lawsoniana*, *G. microcos*, *G. tiliaefolia*, *G. umbellifera*.
2. Dry deciduous forests of interior Deccan: *G. barberi* (extremely rare), *G. bracteata*, *G. hirsuta*, *G. orbiculata*, *G. oppositifolia* (syn. *G. emarginata*) (also in scrub), *G. orientalis* (rare), *G. rhamnifolia* (mainly towards east coast in Tamil Nadu and Andhra), *G. rothii* (extremely rare). *G. subinaequalis* (syn. *G. asiatica*), which is reported to occur wild in the Pune district of Maharashtra (Cooke 1903; Ingalhalikar 2001:58; Talbot 1907), might be considered to belong to this group. This species is mainly distributed in the Himalayan foothills from Sikkim

through Garhwal to the Siwaliks and the Salt Range in Pakistan. It is more widespread in India as a cultivated tree.

3. Scrub forests of the *Acacia—Albizia* zone: *G. damine*, extending into Pakistan (Baquar 1995), *G. serrulata* (syn. *G. disperma*), *G. pilosa* (syn. *G. flavescens*), *G. oppositifolia* (also in dry deciduous), *G. tenax* (syn. *G. betulaefolia*), *G. villosa*.
4. Northern Eastern Ghats in the *Terminalia—Anogeissus—Tectona* variant: *G. sapida*, *G. polygama* (*G. subinaequalis* may also occur wild here, or as an escaped cultivar; see Gamble 1935).

**Ethnobotany** The inner bark of *Grewia oppositifolia* is used as a fibre source for rope, rough cloth, and paper. Its bark is used in sandal making (1, 6). The inner bark of *G. tiliaefolia*, *G. rothii*, and *G. glabra* is used for cordage (2, 4, 6). The leaves of *G. oppositifolia* are reported to be good fodder that encourages milk production and are stored as winter animal feed (1, 2, 7). *G. sapida* and *G. tiliaefolia* are also lopped for fodder (2, 6). The wood of several species is used for manufacturing small items such as tool handles (1, 4, 6, 7). The branches of *G. pilosa* are used in basketry (6). *G. serrulata* is sometimes planted as a host for lac insects (6).

*Grewia subinaequalis* (Hindi *phalsa*) is cultivated through much of India, Pakistan, and parts of Southeast Asia for its edible fruits, which are produced toward the end of the dry season (Baquar 1995; Morton 1987; Singh 1992). Edible fruits are also reported from *G. abutilifolia* (8), *G. damine* (6), *G. hirsuta* (6, 8), *G. microcos* (2), *G. nervosa* (8), *G. pilosa* (6), *G. populifolia* (4), *G. rothii* (6), *G. sapida* (6), *G. tenax* (2, 7), *G. tiliaefolia* (2, 4, 7), and *G. villosa* (2, 4, 7). The young leaves of *G. tiliaefolia* are also known to be edible (8). Archaeobotanical evidence for the consumption of *Grewia* cf. *villosa* fruits has derived from pre-Harappan (4000–3500 B.C.E.) Miri Qalat in Makran (southwest Pakistan), where two different *Grewia* species have also been identified among wood charcoals (Tengberg and Thiébault 2003).

## VERBENACEAE

The most widespread trees in this family are *Tectona grandis* (teak), *Gmelina*, and *Vitex*. Three other genera of shrubs occur in the region: *Clerodendron* includes shrubs found mainly in dry deciduous forests (*C. viscosum* occurs in the moist deciduous to semi-evergreen zone). *Lantana* comprises small shrubs growing on sandy soils, woodland margins, and dry scrub vegetation, and *Premna* includes rare shrubs found on rocky slopes and riverbanks. In addition, several shrubs and climbers of the Verbenaceae have been introduced to peninsular India as cultivars in hedges and ornamental species in gardens (Singh et al. 2001:701–06).

## Gmelina

**Ecological Notes** *G. arborea* is a moderate-sized to large deciduous tree of dry deciduous woodlands. It coppices very well and is also reproduced from seed. *G. asiatica* is a spiny shrub found in dry deciduous woodland undergrowth.

**Ethnobotany** The wood of *G. arborea* is easily worked and is very durable under water (3). It is used in planking, furniture, door-panels, carriages, boats, toys, packing cases, and ornamental work (3). Its fruit is edible and is used together with the bark and root in traditional medicine (3). The local name for *Gmelina arborea* (Telugu *gummadi*) is cognate across the south, south-central, and central Dravidian language families (DEDR 1450; Fuller 2007:423; Southworth 2005:220), thus suggesting that it was a salient part of the cultural landscape of the Indian peninsula since ancient times, as is the case for several other dry deciduous tree species (for example, *Butea monosperma*, *Terminalia* spp., *Diospyros melanoxylon*, *Tectona grandis*, *Phyllanthus emblica*, *Pterocarpus marsupium*, *Schleichera oleosa*, *Syzygium cumini*).

## Tectona grandis

**Ecological Notes** A large deciduous tree, teak is regarded as a typically dominant species of South Indian moist deciduous forests, although it may extend to other vegetation zones as well, especially in the moister parts of the dry deciduous forests (Saldanha 1984; Meher-Homji 2001). Teak is found sporadically in forests throughout India but is particularly common on the peninsula. Thus Roxburgh (1832) regarded it as native to South India only (from the Godavari river in Maharashtra southward), although it is now generally accepted as native to the Narmada basin and parts of western and northern Madhya Pradesh, where its distribution overlaps with that of sal (*Shorea robusta*) (Verma, Balakrishnan, and Dixit 1993). The westernmost distribution of teak occurs in the Gir forests of southern Saurashtra in Gujarat. It is also a major element of the dry deciduous forests of mainland Southeast Asia. Two related species are found in Burma and the northern Philippines (Burkill 1966). It must be stressed, however, that *T. grandis* has been widely dispersed as a planted species.

Teak is a very resilient species. Even in the very dry, barren rocky hills of western Kurnool and Bellary, it may grow as patches of stunted gregarious trees. It can tolerate various soil types (including laterite and limestone) but establishes better on sandstone and metamorphic rocks. Pure teak forests are found on black cotton soils on the alluvial banks of the Godavari river. It is a light-demanding species, and its seedlings need open conditions in order to get established. It produces copious amounts of seeds, even when quite young, which germinate successfully if they receive sufficient warmth and moisture. It also coppices well. In general, plantations are considered to be much easier to manage than natural teak forests because they have higher productivity (that is, lower seedling mortality). By contrast, in forests teak tends to grow in patches instead of pure stands. In addition, growth in natural forests is considerably slower. It may take up to 10 years for a tree to get established. On the other hand, however, plantations do not produce as good timber as forests. Traditional management practices have often included the light burning of the understorey of teak plantations to clean up refuse, as a result of which colonial forest officers recognised for the first time that the heating of the seeds by burning promoted germination (Pyne 1997:419–21; see also Chapter 4).

**Ethnobotany** Teak wood is moderately hard and scented. It has high oil content, which preserves the wood from insect attacks. It provides very good timber, combining great durability with absence of warping under the most exacting conditions (2, 3), and forms the chief building timber in India. It is further used for shipbuilding, railway carriages, house carpentry, bridges, and carving. Indeed, teak was recognised as 'the most useful timber in Asia' (Roxburgh 1832:I, 602) by British administrators who set about introducing it from South India to the northern and eastern parts of the subcontinent (see Stebbing 1922)

The importance of teak as a planted species probably precedes European colonial presence in India. It is apparently illustrated as a garden tree on the Barhut stupa (second century B.C.E.) (Sitholey 1976:21). The disjunct distribution of teak in peninsular India and in mainland Southeast Asia may be due to climate influences, although some sources suggest that the occurrence of teak in Southeast Asia is due to human translocation. Teak was also apparently transported to Java prior to European contact, perhaps by c. 1000 C.E. (Chapter 4).

Its very large leaves provide a dyeing substance, and they are widely used as plates and for packing and thatching temporary huts (3). Various parts and products of teak are used in traditional medicine, including its oil, which is used to treat skin ailments such as eczema and ringworm (Burkill 1966; Singh et al. 2001:387). A likely proto-Dravidian name is reconstructed as *tenkk-*, although it lacks North Dravidian cognates (DEDR 3452; Fuller 2007:423; Southworth 2005:22).

## Vitex

**Ecological Notes** *Vitex altissima* is a large deciduous tree of the dry deciduous forests of the Deccan; *V. negundo* favours riverbanks throughout this zone and may also occur in hedges. *V. leucoxylon* is also found on riverbanks in moist deciduous vegetation.

**Ethnobotany** *Vitex* provides good-quality timber. Its wood is hard and close-grained and is widely used in building and for general construction purposes (3).

# CHAPTER 7

# WOOD IDENTIFICATION AND CHARCOAL ANALYSIS: THEIR CONTRIBUTION TO THE STUDY OF ANCIENT VEGETATION AND PAST ECONOMIES IN SOUTH INDIA

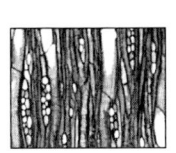

One of this book's purposes is to present the anatomical descriptions of selected South Indian trees and shrubs. By using these descriptions, together with the identification key and the microphotographs of individual species, a researcher can identify botanically the wood macro-remains found in archaeological excavations in this part of the world. Such remains may include pieces of wood preserved in various states (carbonised, desiccated, fossilised, or waterlogged). In most cases, however, they consist of charred wood macro-remains. Wood charcoals represent one of the most ubiquitous classes of plant remains found in archaeological sites. For this reason, they have been used for a variety of purposes in archaeological and archaeobotanical research, including the reconstruction of past woodland vegetation (for a general overview of the theory and methodology of archaeological wood charcoal analysis see Asouti and Austin 2005), dating (radiocarbon and dendrochronology; for example, Kuniholm and Newton 1996), the reconstruction of woodland management practices and deforestation processes (for instance, Kreuz 1992; Miller 1985), and for investigating the trade of valuable timber species in antiquity (for example, Asouti 2003a). Yet, the main objective of specialists working in this field from its inception has been the reconstruction of past vegetation. In this capacity, charcoal analysis has been particularly useful for palaeoecological investigations conducted in arid and tropical environments, where well-preserved pollen sequences are very often absent owing to the poor preservation of waterlogged sediments and the general rarity of suitable coring sites (lakes, marshes).

## A SHORT HISTORY OF CHARCOAL ANALYSIS

It was in 1864 that the idea was conceived for the first time to analyse prehistoric wood charcoal macro-remains by the Italian G. Passerini and, following him, the Swiss O. Heer, in the context of the then recent impressive discoveries of the Neolithic and Bronze Age 'Lake Dwellings' in Switzerland. At the beginning of the twentieth century, the French clergyman and prehistorian Henri Breuil was the first to take an active interest in the study of wood charcoals recovered from Palaeolithic sites in France. At these very early stages, only material deriving from prehistoric hearth structures was destined for analysis, and the interpretations sought by researchers were of limited palaeoecological interest. Instead, the focus was on the choice of combustibles by prehistoric groups (Badal Garcia 1992).

The first explicitly ecological interpretations based on charcoal evidence appeared in Britain with the publication in 1940 by E. J. Salisbury and F. W. Jane of their report on wood charcoals from the Maiden Castle excavations in Dorset. In this paper, Salisbury and Jane suggested that the observed frequencies of individual taxa are likely to correspond to their actual proportions in prehistoric woodland vegetation. They also used tree ring data in an attempt to reconstruct past climate patterns (Salisbury and Jane 1940).

Their interpretations were questioned by two of the most prominent ecologists of the time, H. Godwin and A. G. Tansley, who drew attention to the role of ecological variables (structure of plant communities and species physiology) and cultural parameters (wood selection) as important factors determining species availability. They also stressed the potential effects of differential wood combustion on taxon representation (Godwin and Tansley 1941). Hence, the debate was launched for the first time concerning the appropriateness of archaeological wood charcoals for reconstructing prehistoric vegetation. (For a more extensive discussion of the issues involved in this debate see Asouti and Austin 2005).

That such early developments should take place in Britain is not surprising given the long-standing tradition of prehistoric and ancient wood studies in the British Isles, from the seventeenth century onwards, dealing mainly with the remains of waterlogged artefacts and wood macrofossils (see Coles et al. 1978). These were matched later on by extensive and detailed studies on wood anatomy, initially addressed to botanists, foresters, and timber experts but later proven invaluable to archaeobotanists interested in wood charcoal identification, such as The Anatomy of the Dicotelydons by C. R. Metcalfe and L. Chalk (1950) and F. W. Jane's The Structure of Wood (1956).

Comparable events followed a little later in France, stimulated by an arguably stronger interest of French botanists and wood anatomists on archaeological charred wood macro-remains and their potential for palaeoecological interpretation. Momot (1955) used wood charcoals derived from late Palaeolithic hearths as a guide to reconstructing past climate patterns. In his treatise on the methodology of charcoal analysis, the French wood anatomist M. Couvert stressed the uniqueness of charcoal data in providing a picture of past vegetation that is contemporaneous to prehistoric settlement, a quality not always shared by pollen analytical investigations that usually offer a conflated picture of local and regional woodland composition (Couvert 1968). His studies of charcoal specimens from the cave sites of Khanguet Si Mohamed Tahar and Tamar Hat in Algeria provided the first direct evidence for the existence of vegetation types without modern analogues in this region during prehistoric times, which were interpreted as indicating different climate regimes in the past (Couvert 1969a, 1969b). Following a slightly different approach, in 1976 he published the results of his analysis of wood charcoals retrieved from the sixth millennium B.C.E. site of Relilaï in Algeria. In this paper, he attempted to reconstruct the spatial distribution of past vegetation based on modern rainfall values from wooded areas and topographic relief. His stated purpose was to reconstruct vegetation catchments, measure the distances people had to walk in order to collect wood and reconstitute their paths of movement (Couvert 1976).

A more qualitative approach to vegetation reconstruction was proposed by another French botanist, S. Santa, in his synthesis of charcoal data from North Africa. Basing his work on the axiom that 'the same floristic stock will generate identical vegetation groups' (that is, if vegetation communities are defined essentially as a group of species, then the same range of species will give rise to identical floristic associations, now and in the past), he used qualitative data (namely lists of taxa and their modern distributions in the area of study) in order to reconstruct past vegetation formations (Santa 1961). He was the first to introduce the concepts of the 'probability' of preservation and the 'possibility' of taxon recovery from the charcoal macro-remains. His answer to this problem was to exclude from his vegetation surveys species that were least likely to be collected by prehistoric groups (for example, those that have poor heat value) or those that, owing to their natural characteristics (for instance, small-sized woods), did not have a high chance of preservation in the archaeological record (Santa 1961:56). The remaining taxa were then classified into different vegetation types according to their ecological status in modern-day formations (as pioneer, dominant, climax, or secondary species), and these served as a comparative basis for the reconstruction of past vegetation.

After the Second World War, the widespread adoption of radiocarbon dating signalled a new focus on charred plant remains, particularly charcoal. However, the limitations of the then existing laboratory techniques hampered exploiting the full potential of wood charcoals. The preparation of charcoal for microscopic identification involved the impregnation of charred specimens with paraffin-based substances or polyester, in order to stabilise individual fragments, and then with a synthetic resin so as to obtain small, transparent blocks enclosing each specimen. These were then sectioned with the aid of a microtome in the three anatomical planes (transverse, radial, and tangential; see Figure 7.1). The upper surface of the resultant pieces was afterwards abraded to produce thin sections that could be examined under a transmitted light microscope (see Couvert 1968; Momot 1955; Santa and Vernet 1968). Predictably, this extremely time-consuming method of laboratory preparation resulted in few and in many cases even problematic identifications, owing to the distortion of anatomical characters. It also severely compromised the suitability of identified charcoal specimens for radiocarbon dating, owing to the contamination caused by their chemical treatment.

At the end of the 1960s, the adoption of reflected light microscopy by charcoal analysts was bound to revolutionise the state of affairs within the discipline (see Leney and Casteel 1975; Western 1969, 1971). In contrast to the impregnation methods, charcoal specimens are fractured either by hand or by using a razor blade in the three anatomical planes (Figure 7.1) and examined directly under the microscope. Simplifying preparation techniques and microscopy procedures meant that it was now possible to identify a high number of specimens in a relatively short time. Hence, it became realistic to undertake systematic studies of large wood charcoal assemblages, which could furthermore produce statistically meaningful results. These advances in laboratory procedures were in line with the widespread implementation in the field of various water flotation techniques (separating soil matrix from charred plant remains with the use of water; see Pearsall 2000:14–27) that enhanced dramatically the recovery and retrieval of charred plant macro-remains.

At the same time, the first major syntheses and systematic studies were produced in the western Mediterranean, particularly in France, under the influence of Jean-Louis Vernet, who was the founder of a strong research tradition centred on the University of Montpellier. During the 1980s, another generation of researchers laid

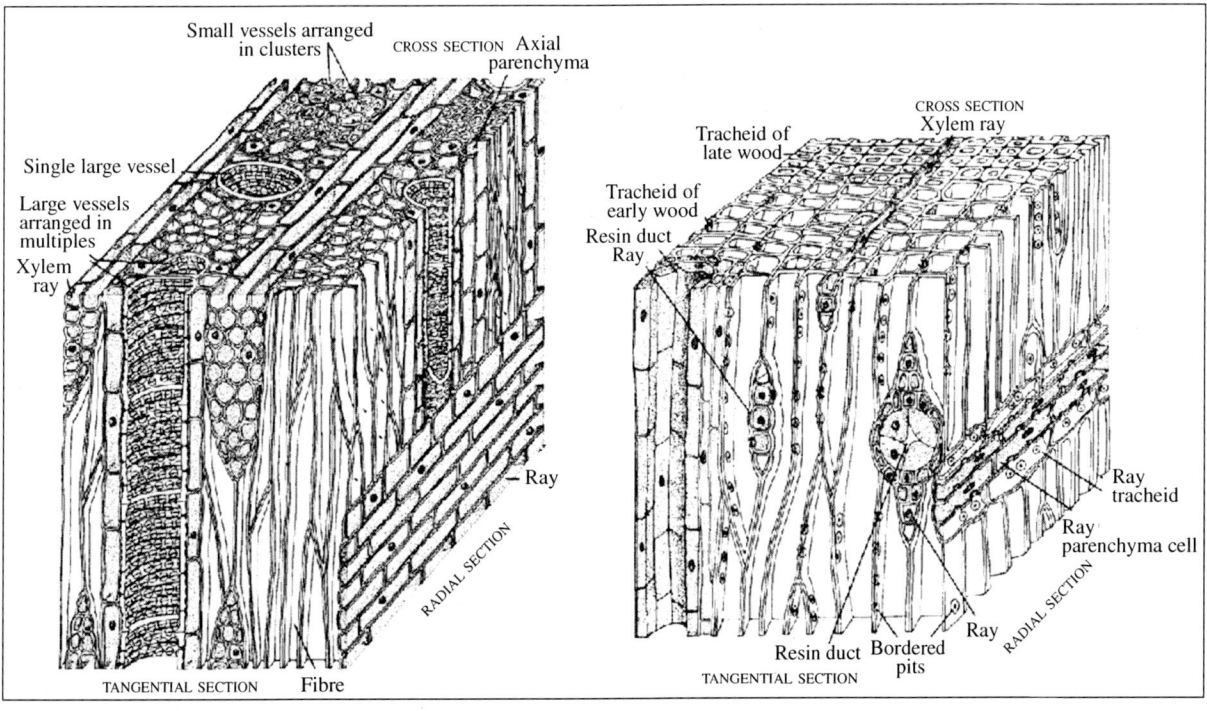

Figure 7.1. The structure of wood: schematic three-dimensional outline of the anatomy of conifers & dicotyledons

the foundations for the systematic application of charcoal analysis on archaeological sites, with a renewed emphasis on appropriate sampling strategies and the need for charcoal analysts to have an active role in excavating and sampling archaeological sites. Furthermore, new avenues were explored for the interpretation of charcoal data in relation to wood combustion experiments, ethno-graphic research, and wood eco-anatomy (see Chabal et al. 1999). Parallel to these developments was the expansion of the methodology in other Mediterranean countries as well, such as Portugal, Spain, and Italy, in the rest of Europe, in Africa, the Near East, North and South America, etc. (for example, Asouti 2003a, 2003b, 2005; Asouti and Austin 2005; Asouti and Hather 2001; Badal Garcia 1992; Chabal et al. 1999; Miller 1985; Neumann 1992; Smart and Hoffman 1988; Willcox 1992, 1999).

## WOOD AND CHARCOAL ANALYSIS IN SOUTH ASIA

In India, archaeological wood identification began in the 1940s. Indeed, the first detailed publications on archaeobotany in South Asia were devoted to wood identification work carried out in India by K. A. Chowdhury and S. S. Ghosh (see Fuller 2002). Chowdhury and Ghosh, who were based at the Indian Forest Research Institute (Dehra Dun), began working with archaeological wood remains from botanical assemblages recovered in Mortimer Wheeler's excavations at Arikamedu (Chowdhury and Ghosh 1946) and continued later with desiccated wood and charcoals from Harappa, Sisulpalgarh, Hastinapur, and Maski (Chowdhury 1955; Chowdhury and Ghosh 1951, 1952, 1957). As was the case with early wood identification work in Europe, they also relied on time-consuming embedding and thin-sectioning methods of charcoal preparation. Much of the more recent wood charcoal studies have continued to employ this technique (see Saraswat 2004; Saraswat et al. 1994).

Yet, despite this close chronological association between developments in India and Europe (Britain), there is no reason to infer that the onset of wood and charcoal analysis in the subcontinent had been affected in any substantial way from contemporaneous debates in Britain. Instead, it represented an independent development stemming from a strong preoccupation of Indian botanists with plant taxonomy studies as well as a long tradition in wood anatomical studies that had its roots in the early nineteenth and early twentieth century colonial and postcolonial scientific forestry. At that time, several manuals on the identification of Indian timbers were published addressing the needs of professional foresters, trainees, government officials, and timber traders, and they remain, to this day, the sole published compilations of information on the properties of Indian timbers (for example, Gamble 1902).

A comparison of the content and scope of these manuals with published Indian accounts of wood and charcoal finds from archaeological sites reveals a number of interesting similarities with regard to approaches to the interpretation of archaeobotanical data. The most prominent of these similarities relates to the clear preference of Indian palaeobotanists for interpretations of ethnobotanical nature, drawing from the information provided by the forestry manuals and ethnographic/historical accounts. Thus, most archaeobotanical reports consist of catalogues of identified wood species found in archaeological sites which are described by listing their properties as timbers, firewood and/or sources of medicinal substances with little if any mention of the potential palaeoenvironmental significance of their presence in the archaeological record. Indeed, the vast majority of Indian publications on wood and charcoal analysis, including more recent ones, have shunned more formal approaches to archaeobotanical analysis favouring instead interpretations based on direct ethnographic analogy (for instance, Chowdhury 1955; Chowdhury et al. 1977; Ghosh and Lal 1963; Rao and Lal 1985; Savithri 1977; Vishnu-Mittre and Savithri 1990). Such an approach has had the obvious benefit of maintaining at the forefront of research a very rich body of ethnographic evidence on the properties and uses of Indian trees and shrubs. On the other hand, however, it has suffered from analytical deficiencies, particularly regarding the systematic sampling of botanical remains from archaeological sediments and the description and interpretation of context-related variation in archaeobotanical assemblages. Furthermore, little use has been made of archaeobotanical results for addressing questions of particular interest for Indian prehistory such as palaeoenvironmental change and human impact on ancient landscapes.

One scholar whose work has addressed the questions of sample size and retrieval methodologies is K. S. Saraswat, a student of Chowdhury and an active member of the Birbal Sahni Institute of Palaeobotany in Lucknow (see Saraswat 1986, 2004; Saraswat et al. 1994). Saraswat was among a cohort of pioneer Indian botanists who promoted the use of water flotation for the separation of plant remains from archaeological sediments instead of examining solely hand-picked specimens (Fuller 2002:257). This practice resulted in the examination of large numbers of specimens per stratigraphic unit, and thus the retrieval of relatively reliable information on temporal patterns in sample composition and species representation. Yet, despite these analytical advances, interpretations remained strongly ethnobotanical in outlook with the emphasis being placed on the detailed description of botanical identifications and the listing of the properties of each species as reported in older timber manuals and related publications.

The lack of distinctly ecological arguments informing the interpretation of ancient plant remains might also be explained as the result of the different research agendas between botanists on the one hand and ecologists (including palaeoecologists) on the other. The potential of archaeobotanical data (seeds, charcoal) to contribute towards a better understanding of past environments was not immediately recognised, in clear contrast to the treatment of traditionally collected palaeobotanical datasets (for example, off-site pollen cores), which were used extensively for palaeoenvironmental reconstructions. This is evident, for example, in the work of Vishnu-Mittre, the renowned Indian palaeobotanist who was active in the analysis of all three major classes of botanical materials (seeds, charcoal, and pollen). While his pollen work maintained a strongly palaeoenvironmental outlook and dealt explicitly with the correlation of past vegetation, climate change, and human settlement, his archaeobotanical work remained largely confined in the realm of direct ethnographic analogy and ethnobotanical interpretation. (For a summary of Vishnu-Mittre's career with bibliography, see Gupta 1994; Fuller 2002:250–57.)

Most of the archaeological wood charcoal work undertaken in India has concentrated in the northern part of the country. A first synthesis was produced in the late 1970s, under the title Ancient Agriculture and Forestry in North India (Chowdhury et al. 1977) that highlighted possible shifts in the distribution of timber trade between the Himalayas and the Ganges basin in later prehistory/protohistory. This research continued to augment through the contributions of K. S. Saraswat, who succeeded Vishnu-Mittre at the Birbal Sahni Institute of Palaeobotany in Lucknow. Detailed studies were carried out on three sites in Kashmir in the 1980s, which included the first use in Indian archaeobotany of scanning electron microscopy (SEM) performed on non-paraffin-embedded wood charcoals (Lone, Khan, and Buth 1993). This study was also the first to consider likely ecological as well as ethnobotanical factors that might have affected the presence of wood species in the archaeological contexts. Special mention should also be made here to the pioneering efforts of Kashmiri researchers to quantify wood charcoal data and to consider whether any temporal trends observed in charcoal density, species diversity, and coefficients of similarity among samples belonging to different periods might relate to shifts in species availability and/or adjustments of wood procurement practices (Lone, Khan, and Buth 1993). At the same time, a number of wood charcoal studies were conducted by European researchers on assemblages derived from sites outside India, in northwest South Asia including French projects in Baluchistan (Tengberg and Thiébault 2003; Thiébault 1988) and Afghanistan (Willcox 1989), and Italian ones in the Thar desert (Casteletti, Madella, and Qayom Mahar 1994).

Of particular interest to Indian archaeobotanical research has been the potential offered by wood charcoal analysis for investigating the beginnings of arboriculture (the cultivation of fruit tree crops). For the middle Ganges region, Saraswat has suggested that during the late Chalcolithic (c. 1300 B.C.E.) arboriculture was being practiced in North India, as indicated by the presence of charcoal from mango (*Mangifera indica*) and bael fruit (*Aegle marmelos*) in sites that were probably located outside the natural distribution of these species (Saraswat 2004; Saraswat et al. 1994). The cultivation of fruit trees such as almonds, apricots, and perhaps peaches, too, is likely to have begun in Kashmir before 1700 B.C.E.—that is, in the late Neolithic (Lone, Khan, and Buth 1993). Arboriculture formed part of the Harappan agricultural systems, as indicated by the finds of charcoal from *Citrus* and pomegranate (*Punica granatum*) in the Mature Harappan phase at Banawali, that is, before 2000 B.C.E. (Saraswat 2002). Also interesting are the charcoal finds of white mulberry (*Morus alba*, likely to have been cultivated for its fruit and, more importantly perhaps, for feeding silk moths) from the same site, particularly if we consider that this species is unlikely to be native to the Indo-Gangetic plains. Later finds of mulberry charcoal have derived from the early centuries C.E. at Sanghol (Saraswat 2002), again in the northwest, and from Semthan in the Kashmir valley (Lone, Khan, and Buth 1993). The presence of charcoal identified as *Platanus orientalis* in Kashmir from the first millennium B.C.E. onward may attest to the deliberate planting of planes as ornamental shade trees (ibid.).

## A BRIEF OUTLINE OF SAMPLING METHODOLOGIES FOR CHARCOAL ANALYSIS

A detailed discussion (accompanied by the relevant bibliography) of the methodologies and the interpretative tools used in charcoal analysis is presented in Asouti and Austin (2005). The most important consideration relates to the types of contexts and assemblages that are likely to provide reliable results for reconstructing ancient wood exploitation practices, and the composition and structure of woodland vegetation in the past. To interpret the frequencies of individual species of trees and shrubs found in archaeobotanical samples, a researcher needs to understand in advance the provenance and function of the wood from which the charcoal macro-remains have originated. In other words, analysts should be able to tell whether wood charcoals represent the remains of fuel (domestic or otherwise) or structural wood, by exploring their location in the site matrix, and their associations with particular archaeological contexts and features. Do they derive from domestic fire installations, open hearths, cremation fires, and burnt timber, or were they found scattered in external (non-domestic) spaces? Naturally, not all deposits have the same potential for addressing questions about the uses of wood, the site environment, and prehistoric woodland management practices. Distinguishing these possibilities should be achieved through the detailed consideration of the excavation records and the features and finds inventory for each sampled location (also including other classes of bioarchaeological data such as animal bones, seeds, phytoliths, etc.

Once function and provenance have been established, attention must be paid to the duration of the activities represented in the archaeological record. We can isolate two categories of deposits for which such predictions are feasible:

1. Short-term: Typical examples are contexts holding primary refuse, such as hearths and fire installations. Wood charcoals found in them are likely to represent the remains of their last use prior to abandonment and may also contain a limited number of taxa. Even if substantial quantities of charcoal are retrieved and a high degree of taxonomic diversity is established, the probability that these relate to the specific circumstances of the last firing event and do not represent long-term trends cannot be eliminated. However, such assemblages may provide important information on the structure and function of particular hearth types. Furthermore, destruction levels can provide

evidence on other aspects of wood use (for example, choice of building materials and woodworking).

2. Long-term: These are archaeobotanical assemblages that represent mainly discarded secondary refuse (middens, fills, and so on). Such contexts are likely to contain the mixed residues of multiple firing episodes occurring in different hearths, ovens, or other fire installations found in an ancient habitation site. As such, they provide an averaged picture of fuel use over the lifetime of the site and are thus better suited to describe long-term patterns of firewood selection and consumption. They are also far more likely to produce a high diversity of wood species and thus maximise the potential of the analysis for palaeoenvironmental reconstruction.

## THE IDENTIFICATION OF ARCHAEOLOGICAL WOOD AND CHARCOAL MACRO-REMAINS

Wood identification (of modern and ancient specimens alike) is achieved through the observation of specific characters of their internal anatomy that usually vary between different families, genera, and (less often) individual species. According to the classic definition by A. Fahn, the most distinctive feature of wood tissue

> is the existence of two systems of elements which differ in the orientation of their longitudinal axes – one system is vertical and the other horizontal. (Fahn 1990:332)

The horizontal (radial) system (Figures 7.1, 7.2) consists of the rays (ranging from the simplest structure, that of uniseriate—that is, one-cell wide rays—to complex ones comprising many different types and sizes of ray cells) whose primary function is to transport water across the radius of the plant stem. The axial (vertical) system (Figures 7.1, 7.2) consists of a much wider variety of anatomical elements including vessels, various types of fibres, vascular tracheids, and axial parenchyma (for examples of the more common anatomical characters see Chapter 8 and references therein). Such diversity is the case for the dicotyledons (broadleaved trees and shrubs, also known as hardwoods) that have a much more complex anatomy compared to the gymnosperms (for instance, conifers), which

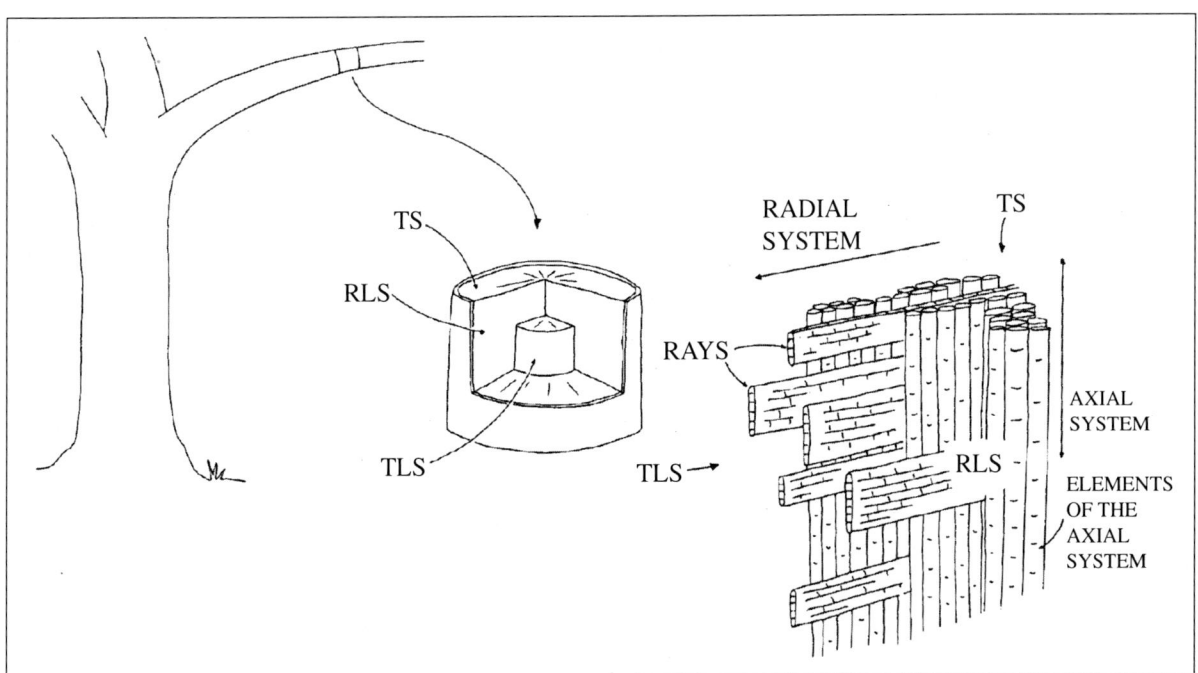

Figure 7.2. The axial and radial systems of wood tissue

are not dealt with in the present volume because they are very rare in the forests and woodlands of South India. (*Gnetum gnemon* (Gnetales) and *Podocarpus wallichiana* (Coniferales) are found in the wet evergreen rainforests, and the occasional *Cycas circinalis* (Cycadales) in dry deciduous woodland and scrub.)

The size and arrangement of vessels on the transverse section represent one of the most important characters for the identification of the dicotyledons. Other characters include the arrangement of the axial parenchyma in the transverse section and the structure of the rays (homogeneous versus heterogeneous, plus a range of special features such as the presence and shape of upright cells, tile cells, and so on), as well as their height and width (uni- or multiseriate, sometimes combined in the same species). Most of the ray-related features are best observed in the radial and tangential-longitudinal sections (see Figures 7.1, 7.2). As a general principle, based on the occurrence and diagnostic value of these anatomical characters, it is possible to group tree species into different anatomical categories and from these to separate wood specimens of unknown taxonomic status through the use of a wood identification key.

Several factors may inhibit the precise identification of archaeological wood charcoals. In many cases, it may prove very difficult to identify individual specimens to species level owing to the similarities in anatomical structure exhibited among members of the same family and/or genus (Hather 2000:11–12). In addition to this, variation in anatomical characters may occur even among specimens belonging to the same taxon (genus or even species) owing to differences in genetic stock, habitats, growing conditions, age, and part (bark, stem, twig, branch, and root) of individual plants and/or the exposure to occasional hazards such as fire, frost, and pest outbreaks that may distort anatomical features (Dimbleby 1967:107–08, Wilson and White 1986:198–99). For tropical species, the high floristic diversity usually encountered in their habitats may also obstruct precise botanical identifications owing to the lack of sufficient reference material.

One remedy to this situation is the use of wood anatomical descriptions and extensive comparative collections covering particular geographical regions. However, such collections and descriptions usually comprise only trunk wood specimens and are mostly assembled from thin sections of fresh wood. For the purpose of charcoal identification, this can be problematic. Characteristics such as the size and dimensions of pores, vessel elements, and rays that may be of diagnostic value in fresh specimens (see, for example, Fahn, Werker, and Baas 1986) in charred specimens are either seriously deformed, because of shrinkage and cracking, or missing altogether, as is the case with certain types of parenchyma and also septate fibres and crystals. Other features as well (for instance, spiral thickenings, intervascular pits) can be difficult to locate and describe with any precision, owing to variations of lighting on charcoal surfaces during microscopic examination, or if fragments are not studied under sufficiently high magnifications (Western 1969:112–13, 115).

Difficulties may also arise from the small size of individual fragments. The required size will vary among taxa, pending on the relative frequency of the diagnostic features preserved within the charred specimen and the uniqueness of these features among the woody plants of the region (Smart and Hoffman 1988). Some anatomical characters that occur infrequently may be absent from specimens <4 mm, whereas others can be quite distinctive even in smaller fragments if they are not shared between many taxa (for example, the size and structure of multiseriate rays in oak). For tropical taxa in particular, charcoal fragments <4 mm usually are very difficult to identify with any degree of certainty, owing to the overall lack of sufficient anatomical detail. The absence of annual growth rings and the variation found even among specimens belonging to the same taxon (for instance, vessel and axial parenchyma distribution in the Leguminosae) mean that for most of the tropical species usually only large fragments (>4 mm) can be reliably identified.

All these problems can be partly overcome by using modern specimens that include round wood as reference material, by examining in detail all three anatomical surfaces (transverse, radial, and tangential) at least for the more 'problematic' taxa, and through the appropriate adjustment of identification criteria. For floras that are anatomically well studied, the charring of modern specimens and their comparison with ancient ones may also prove useful. However, as it so often happens, specific identifications apart from ascribing to specimens a family or genus label are in most cases unattainable.

## REFERENCE MATERIAL FOR SOUTH INDIAN WOODS AND ITS UTILITY FOR ARCHAEOBOTANICAL AND PALAEOENVIRONMENTAL RESEARCH

The main precondition for any study of archaeological wood charcoals is to obtain a comparative collection of modern wood specimens. Given that the microscopic wood anatomy of South Indian trees is not adequately described in existing timber manuals (for example, Chowdhury and Gosh 1958; Gamble 1902) we have compiled a collection of wood specimens from several species found in different vegetation zones and environments in South India, covering a transect through the core area of the Southern Neolithic cultures in the Bellary district of Karnataka and extending into the moister woodland habitats of the Western Ghats (Dharwar and Belgaum districts). We have also received specimens from northern Tamil Nadu, more specifically the Madurai, Erode, and Coimbatore districts (for a detailed map of woodland vegetation in these areas see Figure 7.3). Given the enormous floristic diversity of the tropical vegetation of the peninsula (particularly in the south), it would be unrealistic to expect to cover all the tree and shrub species encountered in the region today. Species were thus selected taking into account the following criteria: their occurrence and indicator status in vegetation environments (that is, the savanna scrub, and the dry and moist deciduous zones) associated with prehistoric habitation, especially the Neolithic; the absence of detailed published anatomical descriptions; the economic and ethnobotanical status of individual species (reviewed in Chapter 6); and (last but not least) the availability of specimens for microscopic analysis. Despite the incomplete status of the collection, we are confident that it contains almost all the major species encountered in the region today, thus serving adequately the purpose of reconstructing the broad pattern of past vegetation and its transformations through time.

The description of the anatomy of the different tree species was done following the nomenclature established by the International Association of Wood Anatomists (IAWA Bulletin 1989). Additional information derived from published descriptions, especially the standard reference work of Metcalfe and Chalk (1950), was also taken into account when we compiled the anatomical descriptions presented in Chapter 9. Macroscopic features (colour of wood, density, and so forth) that are not of immediate interest or use to archaeobotanists dealing with the botanical identification of ancient wood remains have not been included in the descriptions. There is an extensive literature, addressed primarily to forestry experts, that describes the macroscopic features of Indian timbers and all such characteristics in exhaustive detail (for example, Chowdhury and Gosh 1958; Gamble 1902).

The assembled reference material was used for the identification of charcoal specimens retrieved through water flotation from several Southern Neolithic sites (ashmounds as well as hilltop sites) in Karnataka and Andhra Pradesh. Archaeological investigations of the Southern Neolithic in recent years have included systematic sampling and flotation for the recovery of charred archaeobotanical remains as a core component of field research (Fuller et al. 2001a, 2001b, 2004; Korisettar 2004; Korisettar et al. 2001b). Hitherto archaeobotanical research in South India has focused on the identification and the interpretation of carbonised seed and fruit remains for reconstructing early agricultural systems and plant gathering. One of the principal objectives has been to investigate the origins of agriculture in this part of the world (see Fuller 2003a). In this context, the main aim of charcoal analysis has been to provide a major source of data that can be used

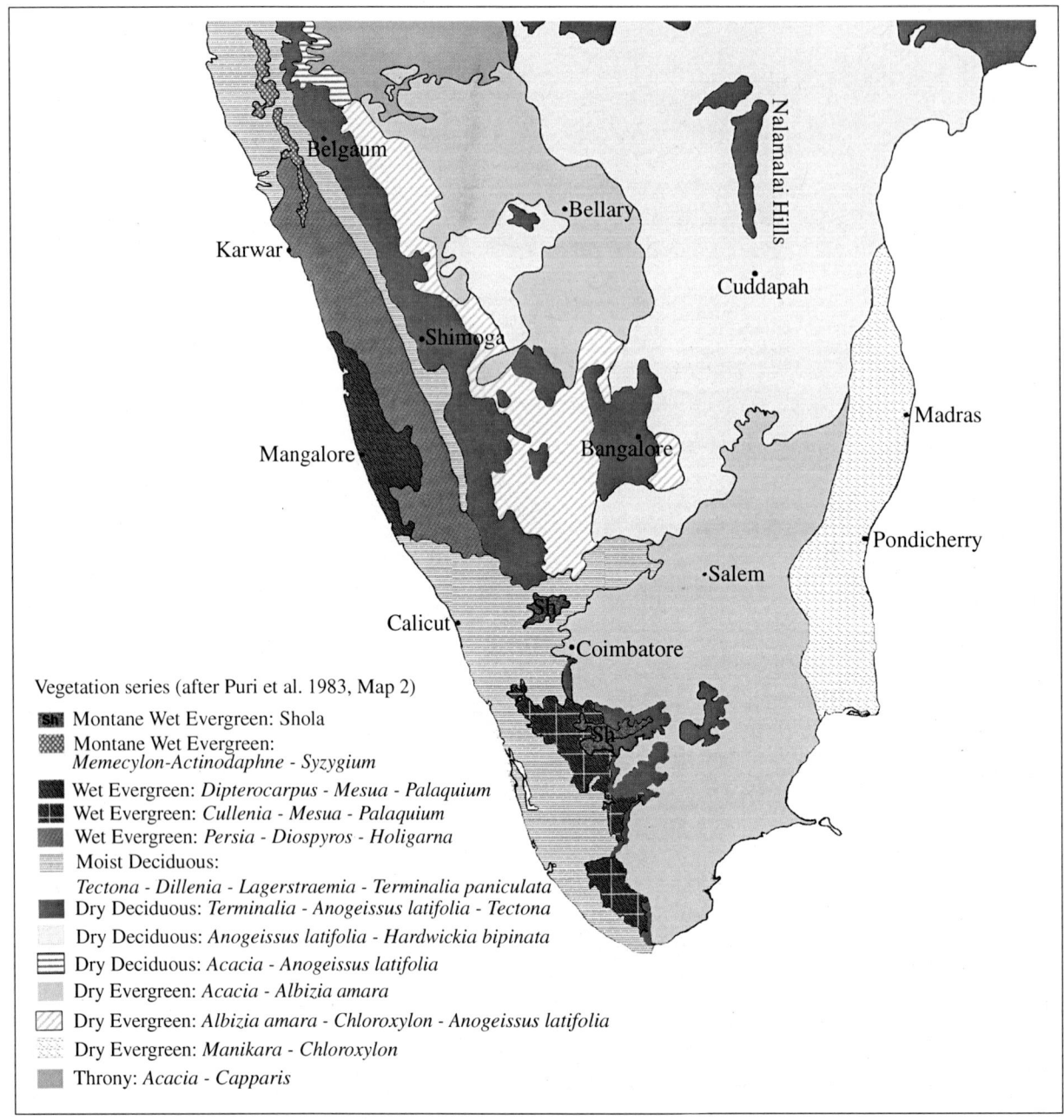

Figure 7.3. Detailed vegetation map of South India

for reconstructing the vegetation environment and the palaeoecology of Neolithic habitation in South India. More specifically:

1. The environmental context of the onset of the South Indian Neolithic. Was environmental change one of the factors instigating the beginnings of food production and agriculture in this region?
2. The likely impact of permanent settlement and agricultural activities on the vegetation environment and the landscapes inhabited by Southern Neolithic communities.

Human impact can be assessed in different ways. For example, at the ecological level, by identifying woodland clearance and changes in the representation of the dominant tree and shrub species that could be attributed to the effects of human activities such as fuel collection, grazing, and browsing by herds of domestic animals. At the anthropological level, tracing such changes can also provide useful information on the precise content and direction of human choices. By considering appropriate ethnographic data and anthropological/archaeological theory, the archaeologist can interpret such cultural choices as signifiers of settlement economy and the socioeconomic structures conditioning resource perception and use by prehistoric groups. Ultimately, when undertaken in a systematic manner, such a study of landscape use alongside that of crop and pastoral production (the objects of seed archaeobotany and archaeozoology respectively) may create the conditions for a more meaningful appreciation and understanding of the origins and development of agricultural production and sedentism in South India.

## RESEARCH CONTEXT: SOUTHERN NEOLITHIC AGRICULTURE

Earlier stages of field and laboratory work had focused on the systematic collection and analysis of archaeobotanical remains of cultivated crops. Our research has indicated the widespread importance of indigenous crops, such as small millets and pulses, in the agricultural systems of the Southern Neolithic. Definitive evidence for these crops dates from least 2000 B.C.E. (phase II in the traditional chronology of the Southern Neolithic; see Allchin and Allchin 1982; Korisettar et al. 2001a; also Tables 3.1, 3.2). Verified crop species found in all sites include browntop millet (*Brachiaria ramosa*), bristley foxtail (*Setaria verticillata*), mung bean (*Vigna radiata*), and horsegram (*Macrotyloma uniflorum*). These four species have been shown to represent a package of indigenous crops, probably domesticated locally in South India (Fuller and Korisettar 2004; Fuller et al. 2001a, 2004) There is also evidence for the use, at a smaller scale, possibly by selected communities, of introduced non-monsoonal crops such as wheat (*Triticum* spp.) and barley (*Hordeum vulgare*), by c. 1900 B.C.E., and the adoption of hyacinth bean and pearl millet of African origin as well as pigeon pea (*Cajanus cajan*) originating further north in eastern India by c. 1500 B.C.E. The earliest verified evidence of finger millet (*Eleusine coracana*) dates at c. 900 B.C.E. Fibre crops such as cotton (*Gossypium arboreum*) and flax (*Linum usitatissimum*) had been established earlier in the Indus valley region (before 2500 B.C.E.) and were probably incorporated in South Indian cultivation systems in the mid- or late-second millennium B.C.E. (although the earliest evidence currently available dates from c. 900 B.C.E.). The evidence for African millets, including pearl millet and finger millet is, however, extremely limited, suggesting that these crops were of minor significance when they were first introduced. By contrast, in recent times they have been major staples in the semi-arid Deccan and in the shifting cultivation systems of the Western Ghats, whereas indigenous cultivars such as *Brachiaria ramosa* represent only marginal relict crops.

Archaeobotanical sampling has included sites in the core region of the Ashmound Tradition in the Bellary district and Andhra Pradesh. Recent archaeobotanical study of material from the sites of Budihal and Watgal has confirmed the presence of the same range of crops in the Raichur and Shorapur districts, in the adjacent and broadly contemporaneous cultural traditions of the Kunderu river catchment (Kurnool and Cuddapah districts), and in the Hallur area on the upper Tungabhadra river (Fuller et al. 2004). Further research will hopefully clarify the timing of introduction and how widespread were these non-indigenous crops. It will also elucidate which tree fruit species were exploited by Neolithic communities and what kind of cultivation and field management practices were implemented through the detailed analysis of the field weed floras that accompanied the main crop species.

## MODELLING THE GEOGRAPHY OF PLANT DOMESTICATION

On the basis of published information about vegetation zones in the region and past climate change, it has been suggested (Fuller 2003a:365; Fuller and Korisettar 2004; Fuller et al. 2004; (Korisettar et al. 2001a:195–96) that the dry deciduous woodland zone and its transition into the moist deciduous vegetation to the west were probably the areas where the wild progenitors of the local crop species flourished in prehistoric times. However, more recent assessment of herbarium data on wild mung bean and urd has indicated extensive overlap of the distribution of these species in the

Western Ghats zone. The absence of urd from the Southern Neolithic crop package might therefore indicate that the wild progenitors of mung bean were not brought under cultivation in this zone. By contrast, wild mung bean stands without urd are widespread in the Eastern Ghats, thus suggesting this area as a likely locus of its early cultivation. With regard to their ecological preferences, the optimal habitats for pulses are woodland openings (natural and anthropogenic) and/or forest edges, with mung bean favouring moist deciduous and teak woodlands while horsegram flourishes in drier localities characterised by savanna vegetation. For the millets, suitable environments include streamside habitats and foothill slopes in dry deciduous woodlands and savannas.

Drawing from the results of modern botanical surveys, we have modelled the distribution of these vegetation zones (Chapter 4) by way of a potential vegetation map (Figures 4.2, 7.3). This map can be modified in the light of the results of charcoal analysis and independent evidence on past climate change. Of particular importance is the postulated mid-Holocene (fifth to fourth millennium B.C.E.) wet phase (Chapter 5), which could have favoured forest expansion and thus the spread of moist deciduous woodland outside its present geographical distribution around the Western Ghats and parts of the Eastern Ghats, where occasional relict populations of mung beans are found (the Nallamalai, Impaghat, Pochangat, and Kandenmari hills of western Andhra Pradesh). With the end of this wet phase and as forests gradually retreated (from the fourth millennium through the third millennium B.C.E.), it is likely that the availability of the wild progenitors of crop plants was severely reduced (Fuller and Korisettar 2004). This reduction would have affected the availability of mung bean, *Setaria* spp., and *Brachiaria ramosa*. The ecology of *Macrotyloma uniflorum* is too poorly understood at present to be modelled with any degree of confidence, but it seems inherently plausible that its distribution was locally affected as well. This reduction of wild plant food sources, together with other pressures on the subsistence base (such as changes in animal habitats and fruit tree distributions), might have encouraged some hunting-gathering groups to take up cultivation as a means of conserving key food species, in a process comparable (at least in the ecological sense) to that proposed by currently available models on the beginnings of cultivation in parts of Southwest Asia during the Younger Dryas cold episode at the very end of the Pleistocene (Hillman et al. 2001).

This model of vegetation change has important implications for conceptualising the geography of the origins and spread of the Southern Neolithic. Essentially, it predicts that the beginnings of agriculture took place in those environmental zones that were most affected by the reduction in the availability of edible wild species (that is, the Western Ghats and adjacent areas, or certain areas of the Eastern Ghats) and not necessarily in the arid central Deccan, the heartland of the pastoralist Ashmound Tradition. In turn, this would imply that agriculture in the territories of the Ashmound Tradition was introduced at a somewhat later date, either through the movement of groups from further west and east or via the adoption of crop species by pastoralist and hunter-gatherer groups living in drier areas.

Until now, a data-informed evaluation of any model on the origins of agriculture in South India has been impeded by a lack of direct evidence for the presence in archaeological sites of the progenitors of cultivated millets and pulses, their ancient distribution, and palaeoenvironmental data. Seed remains have been recovered so far from sedentary or semisedentary habitation sites that have better preserved charred plant remains compared to the ashmounds. Almost all sites from which we have obtained archaeobotanical samples are dated (based on their pottery) to Phase II of the Southern Neolithic, that is, from approximately 2200 B.C.E., and more likely (based on the latest radiocarbon dates) from as late as 2000 B.C.E. By that time, however, cultivation alongside cattle, sheep, and goat pastoralism had been already established (Table 2.2). Therefore, earlier periods, during which the transition to food production took place, remain to be elucidated. It would appear very likely that during Phase I habitation was probably more mobile and therefore archaeologically less visible. Although pastoralism during this period is indicated by the very occurrence of ashmound sites and the few studied bone assemblages (providing evidence for the presence of domesticated ungulates), the extent to which plant cultivation was an integral part of the local subsistence economy remains unclear. It is theoretically possible that cattle were domesticated locally, but there is as yet no evidence from animal bone remains supporting this hypothesis (Korisettar et al. 2001b). By contrast, it would seem very likely that cattle were introduced into the region, which is also the case with domestic sheep and goat. The timing of the importation of animal domesticates, around 3000 B.C.E., raises the possibility that domestic livestock and (more importantly perhaps) the knowledge of breeding techniques, spread among indigenous hunter-gatherers. Therefore, it is likely that a herder-forager phase preceded the beginnings of plant cultivation in central Deccan. This hypothesis, although in need of sound empirical demonstration, makes the most sense of the incomplete archaeological record currently available.

Returning to the palaeovegetation evidence, previous analyses of charcoals from Southern Neolithic sites are extremely limited. The most recently published by Vishnu-Mittre and Savithri (1990) dealt with material from the sites of Tekkalakota, Sanganakallu, and Hallur. Charcoal specimens were hand-picked from the charred remains that were visible during excavation, without systematic collection of material from floated sediment samples. As a result of this, their identifications have little quantitative value and can serve at best as indicators for the presence or absence of taxa in the environs of the site, with no reliable information available on the relative proportions of tree species and fuel types in prehistoric times. Charcoals are reported to belong to a number of taxa, including *Soymida febrifuga*, *Acacia*, *Albizia*, *Anogeissus*, *Holarrhena*, and *Polyalthia*. There is no way to verify these identifications, since neither the precise anatomical criteria used for botanical identification nor photographs or detailed descriptions of the microscopic characters of the taxa in question have been included in the published results. Nevertheless, all of them could have been collected from dry evergreen scrub and/or dry deciduous woodland.

The first results of the ongoing charcoal project have verified thus far the antiquity of the distinction between the vegetation zones of the plains and the Western Ghats. They have furthermore provided a much more precise picture of the vegetation on the plains. Materials from a number of sites associated with ashmounds (such as Kurogudu, Palavoy, and Choudammaguda) have all given evidence for the prevalence of the *Acacia – Albizia* savanna scrub vegetation characteristic of the area to this day. These finds have major implications for evaluating and reassessing established views of savanna woodland as an anthropogenic vegetation type (Chapter 4). They indicate that instead of being the result of degradation and the impoverishment of dry deciduous forest owing to intensive fuel extraction and pastoral activities, *Acacia—Albizia* savanna grasslands may indeed represent natural vegetation formations in the arid plains of South India ('natural' meaning that they were present locally at the time of the foundation of the first agro-pastoral communities in Karnataka). Charcoal assemblages from later sites (for example, Sanganakallu, Hiregguda, and Tekkalakota) located in similar ecological zones (that is, the savanna plains) present an almost identical picture of vegetation environments as the earlier assemblages. With regard to upland woodland vegetation, the charcoal evidence from the site of Hallur (Phase II and later) on the Western Ghats has provided more sensitive indicators of environmental change, evidenced in the prevalence (during the early levels of the site) of dry deciduous elements (most notably *Anogeissus*; Figure 7.4) and the gradual rise through time of moist deciduous woodland species (for example, *Tectona*, *Terminalia*, etc.). Such a pattern of vegetation change would appear to confirm our hypothesis that environmental conditions during the sedentary phase of the Ashmound Tradition (2200–2000 B.C.E.) were drier compared to later periods. Repetitive arid events between the fourth millennium and the beginning of the second millennium (the latest probably connected to the arid spell of 2200 B.C.E., see Chapter 5) are thus likely to have exerted a significant impact on regional subsistence practices. This pattern also indicates that (at least in theory) millets could have been brought under cultivation in South India in both the moister uplands and the dry lowland savannas (either vegetation habitat can support stands of wild millets). Perhaps the reduced availability of

Figure 7.4. Scanning Electron Microscope (SEM) microphotographs of charcoals from the Southern Neolithic sites of Hallur (*Anogeissus* - top row and bottom to the left) and Sanganakallu (*Strychnos* - bottom row to the right)

millet grasses after the mid-Holocene dry spell and through the third millennium B.C.E. instigated early attempts at their cultivation by mobile groups of itinerant cattle pastoralists. Sedentism occurred at a later date (most sites date from Phase II) and, to a certain degree, might have been the (unintended?) outcome of plant cultivation.

As regards Neolithic and later woodland management, the archaeobotanical evidence has been thus far minimal. Our best indications have come from two sites located in contrasting environmental zones, Hallur (on the Western Ghats) and Sanganakallu (on the arid plains zone), in the presence of charcoal specimens that appear to be remains of mango wood (*Mangifera indica*). Finds of mango fruit offer additional credence to this identification. For Hallur, the occurrence of mango is not surprising, since moist deciduous forest is home to abundant and dense stands of mango trees. For Sanganakallu, however, it is more difficult to interpret. It may indicate the occurrence of this species exceptionally in woodland stands growing around natural springs (since the area is otherwise too dry for this species to occur naturally). The cultivation of mango trees is another possibility. If the presence of this species is verified by further finds of wood and (more crucially) fruits, its implications may prove very important for the interpretation of Neolithic subsistence in South India. In effect, it would indicate the removal of mango from its natural habitat and its cultivation under conditions of irrigation in the Bellary district from as early as the Neolithic.

More exceptional charcoal finds from Sanganakallu have also enabled us to gain some rare insights into potential ritual and/or symbolic and medicinal uses of plants. The single finds of charcoals from sandalwood (*Santalum album*) and the strychnine tree (*Strychnos* sp./spp.) in association with prehistoric contexts are two such cases (Figures 7.4, 7.5; Chapter 6). Both species do not grow naturally in the arid plateaus away from dry deciduous woodland habitats. Therefore, their presence in the archaeobotanical assemblages of Sanganakallu may imply long-distance transport.

Research on the finds of charcoal analysis from Southern Neolithic sites is still ongoing, and its results are being processed for publication. (For some preliminary evidence, see Asouti et al. 2005). We anticipate that, as results from a larger number of sites are collated (including several likely Mesolithic-Neolithic cave sites in the Kurnool District), we will obtain a more precise picture of vegetation and palaeoenvironmental change and woodland exploitation practices in prehistoric South India.

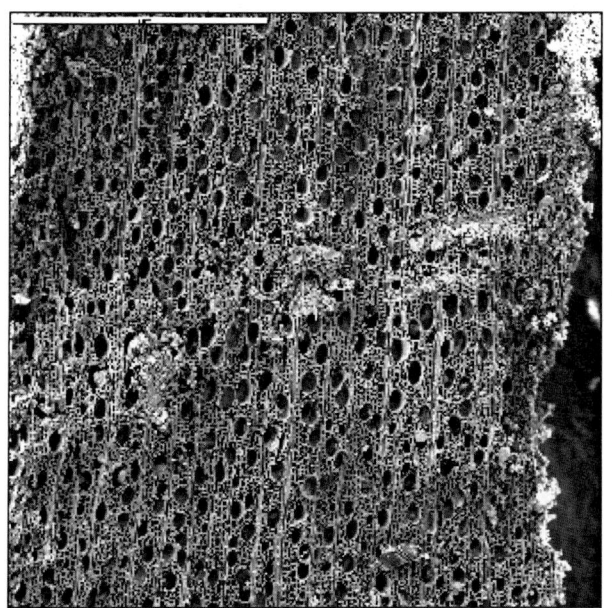
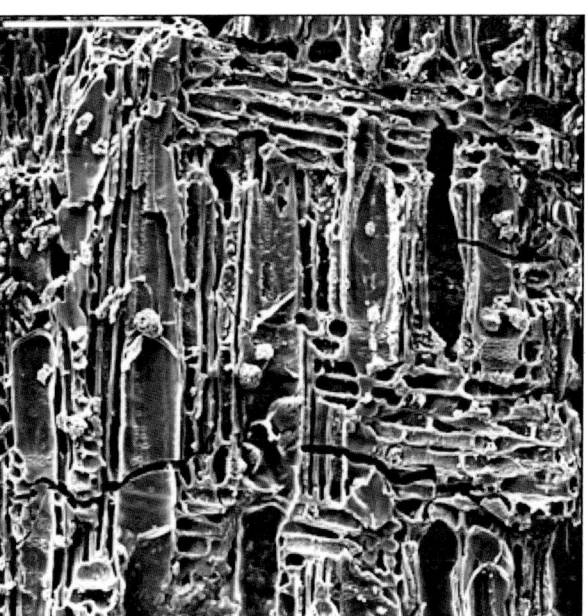

Figure 7.5. Scanning Electron Microscope (SEM) microphotographs of sandalwood charcoals from the site of Sanganakallu

# CHAPTER 8

# WOOD IDENTIFICATION KEY AND ANATOMICAL CHARACTERS

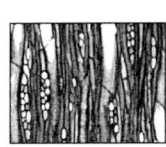

**Ring- to semi-ring porous** (asterisk denotes species that may occur under more than one anatomic description categories)

| Pores predominantly solitary and in radial multiples of 2 | Rays bi- to 3(4)seriate (homogeneous to heterogeneous) | Verbenaceae (*Tectona grandis*) | Usually semi-ring porous. Late-wood pores smaller, in radial multiples and/or irregular clusters |
|---|---|---|---|

**Diffuse to semi-ring porous** (asterisks denote taxa that fall under more than one category)

| Pores exclusively or predominantly solitary | Rays uni- to biseriate (homogeneous) | Hernandiaceae (*Gyrocarpus*)* | |
|---|---|---|---|
| | (heterogeneous) | Burseraceae (*Commiphora*), Rubiaceae (*Canthium, Gardenia*), Santalaceae (*Santalum*) Anacardiaceae (*Mangifera*)*, Leguminosae—Caesalpiniaceae (*Tamarindus*)* | <u>Santalum</u>: rays occasionally up to 4 cells wide <br> <u>Canthium</u>: may display simple and scalariform plates |
| | Rays bi- to 3seriate (heterogeneous) | Anacardiaceae (*Holigarna, Mangifera*)* (large pores) | |
| | Rays 3–4seriate | Verbenaceae (*Gmelina, Vitex*), Dipterocarpaceae (*Hopea*)* | |
| | Rays uni- and multiseriate (3–4 cells) (heterogeneous) | Tiliaceae (*Grewia*), Rubiaceae (*Adina, Ixora, Mitragyna*) | <u>Grewia</u>: tile cells <br> <u>Ixora</u>: pores in slight dendritic arrangement |
| | Rays uni- and multiseriate (4–10 cells) (heterogeneous) | Dilleniaceae (*Dillenia*), Tiliaceae (*Grewia tiliaefolia* type) | <u>Dillenia</u>: scalariform perforation plates <br> <u>Grewia tiliaefolia type</u>: semi-ring porous, tile cells |

**Diffuse to semi-ring porous** (continued)

| | | | |
|---|---|---|---|
| **Pores predominantly in radial multiples of 2–3(4)** | **Rays uni- to biseriate** (all cells procumbent) | Leguminosae—Mimosaceae (*Acacia catechu* type, *Albizia amara* type), Leguminosae—Papilionaceae (*Dalbergia*)*, Meliaceae (*Azadirachta*)*, Sapindaceae (*Schleichera*) | <u>*Azadirachta*</u>: rays mostly biseriate |
| | (homogeneous to heterogeneous) | Leguminosae—Caesalpiniaceae (*Bauhinia, Cassia, Tamarindus**), Leguminosae—Papilionaceae (*Dalbergia*, *Pterocarpus*), Lythraceae (*Lagerstroemia*), Rhamnaceae (*Ziziphus*) | <u>*Bauhinia, Tamarindus*</u>: biseriate rays rare |
| | (heterogeneous with 1(2) rows of enlarged marginal cells) | Meliaceae (*Aglaia*), Sapindaceae (*Dodonaea*)*, Combretaceae (*Terminalia*), Hernandiaceae (*Gyrocarpus*)*, Anacardiaceae (*Mangifera*)* | <u>*Terminalia*</u>: biseriate rays rare |
| | **Rays bi- to 3seriate** (all cells procumbent) | Leguminosae—Mimosaceae (*Acacia leucophloea* type), Meliaceae (*Azadirachta*)*, Moringaceae (*Moringa*)* | |
| | (heterogeneous) | Moringaceae (*Moringa*)*, Meliaceae (*Azadirachta*)*, Anacardiaceae (*Holigarna*)* | |
| | **Rays 3-4seriate** (all cells procumbent) | Leguminosae—Mimosaceae (*Albizia procera* type) | |
| | (heterogeneous) | Ehretiaceae (*Cordia*), Lauraceae (*Cinnamomum*), Meliaceae (*Soymida*), Dipterocarpaceae (*Hopea*)*, Clusiaceae (*Garcinia*)*, Moraceae (*Streblus*) | |
| | **Rays 4-6seriate** (all cells procumbent) | Leguminosae—Mimosaceae (*Acacia nilotica* type) | <u>*Acacia nilotica*</u>: up to 10seriate rays |
| | (heterogeneous) | Bombacaceae (*Bombax*), Moraceae (*Artocarpus, Ficus*) | <u>*Bombax*</u>: up to 10seriate rays, tile cells present |
| | **Rays uni- and multiseriate (3-4 cells)** (all cells procumbent) | Leguminosae—Mimosaceae (*Xylia*) | |
| | (heterogeneous) | Celastraceae (*Gymnosporia*), Myrtaceae (*Barringtonia*)* | |
| | **Rays 1(2) and multiseriate (6-8 cells)** (homogeneous to heterogeneous) | Leguminosae—Papilionaceae (*Butea*), Myrtaceae (*Barringtonia*)* | |

**Diffuse to semi-ring porous** (continued)

| | | | |
|---|---|---|---|
| **Pores predominantly in radial multiples of 2–4 or more** | **Rays uni- to biseriate** (heterogeneous) | Combretaceae (*Anogeissus*), Ebenaceae (*Diospyros*), Lythraceae (*Lawsonia*)*, Sapindaceae (*Dodonaea*)* | <u>Anogeissus</u>: tile cells <br> <u>Ebenaceae</u>: biseriate rays rare |
| | **Rays bi- to 3seriate:** (heterogeneous) | Rutaceae (*Chloroxylon, Limonia*) | |
| | **Rays 3–4seriate** (heterogeneous) | Clusiaceae (*Garcinia*)* | |
| | **Rays 4–6 (or more) seriate** (heterogeneous) | Annonaceae (*Annona*), Euphorbiaceae (*Phyllanthus emblica*) | |
| | **Rays uni- and multiseriate (3–4 cells)** (heterogeneous) | Annonaceae (*Polyalthia*), Apocynaceae (*Holarrhena, Wrightia*), Lythraceae (*Lawsonia*)*, Sterculiaceae (*Pterospermum*), Myrtaceae (*Careya, Syzygium*), Euphorbiaceae (*Cicca, Securinega, Mallotus*), Rubiaceae (*Morinda*) | <u>Polyalthia</u>: abundant uniseriate rays <br> <u>Pterospermum</u>: tile cells |
| **Pores predominantly in clusters and/or irregularly arranged** | **Rays uni- and multiseriate (4–6 or more cells)** | Capparaceae (*Capparis sepiaria*), Loganiaceae (*Strychnos*) | |

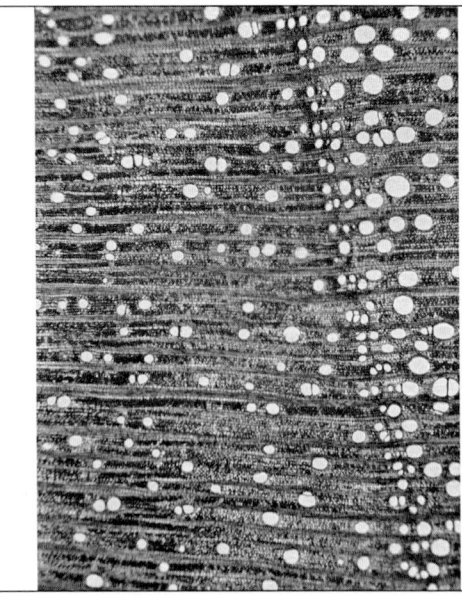

Wood ring porous: pores of two distinct sizes (*Tectona grandis* Tangential Section x100)

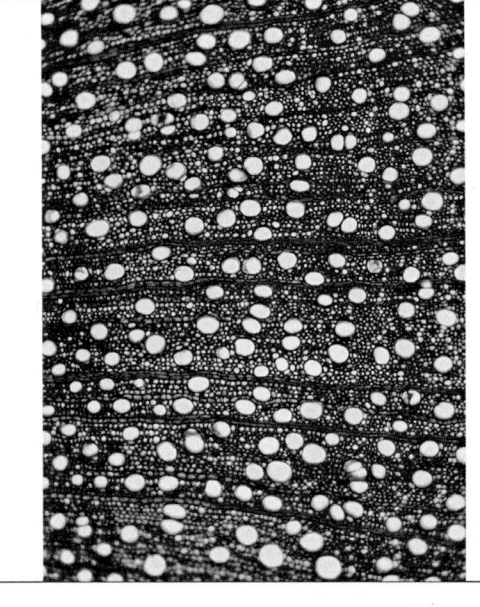

Wood diffuse porous: pores of the same size across the growth ring (*Santalum album* TS x40)

Wood diffuse to semi-ring porous (pores in the early wood are larger and more numerous (*Grewia tiliaefolia* TS x40)

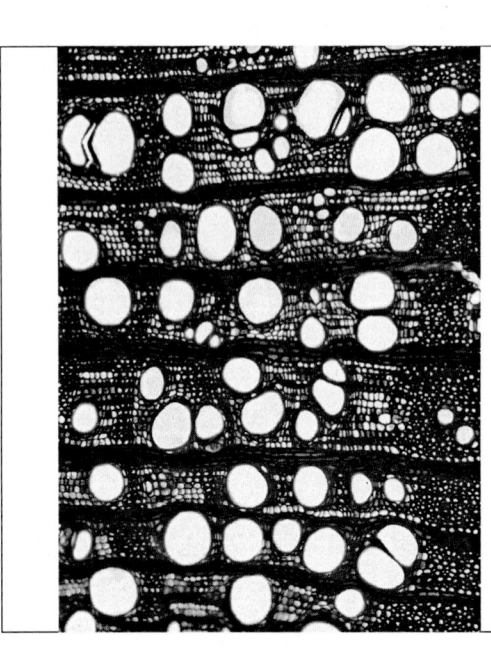

Pores solitary: predominantly not in contact with other pores (*Gardenia resinifera* TS x100)

Pores arranged in radial multiples (*Diospyros cordifolia* TS x40)

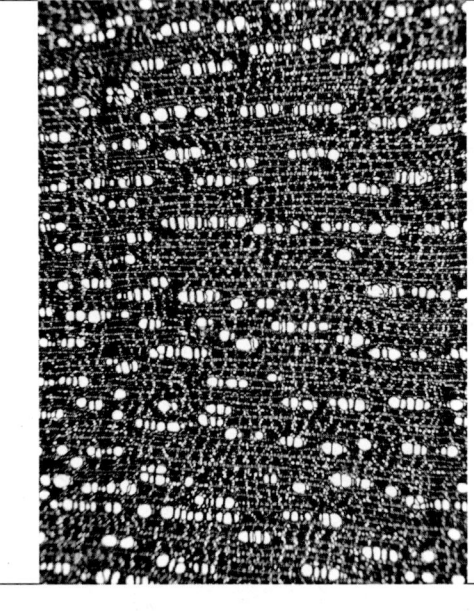

Pores irregularly distributed: dendritic pattern (*Strychnos nux-vomica* TS x40; larger openings: diffuse included phloem)

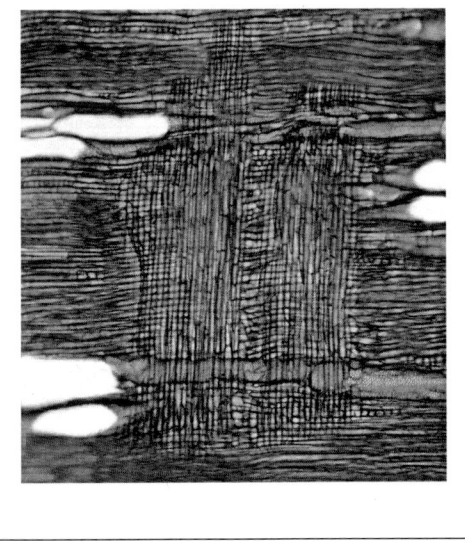

Perforation plates (the openings between 2 adjacent vessel elements) simple, i.e. round-oval (*Albizia procera* RLS x100)

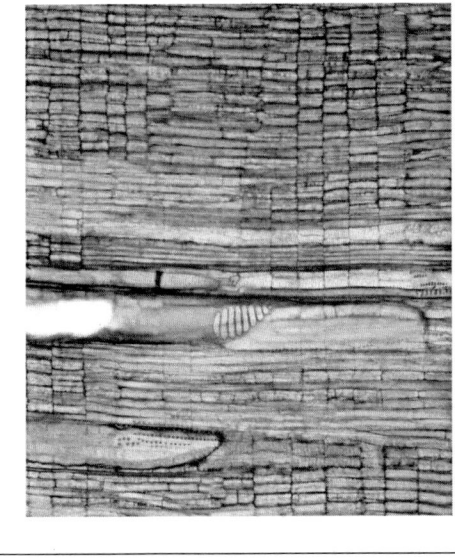

Perforation plates scalariform: vessel openings are subdivided by bars (*Dillenia pentagyna* RLS x100)

Rays homogeneous, all cells procumbent (rectangular and radially oriented in their long axis) (*Acacia nilotica* RLS x100)

Rays heterogeneous with tile cells (*Anogeissus latifolia* RLS x400)

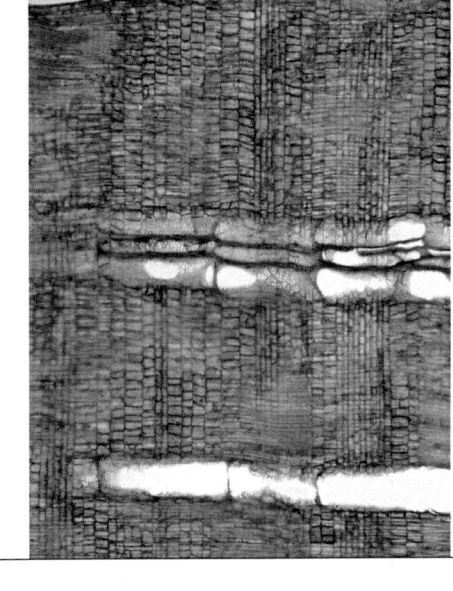

Rays heterogeneous with square, procumbent and upright cells (*Mallotus philippensis* RLS x100)

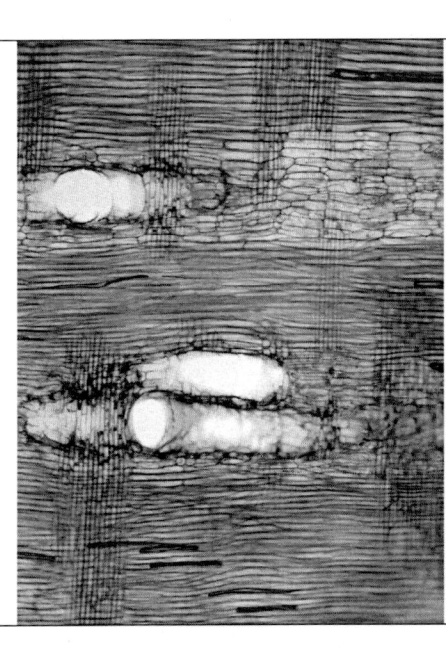

Rays homogeneous to heterogeneous with 1-2 rows of enlarged marginal cells (*Terminalia tomentosa* RLS x100)

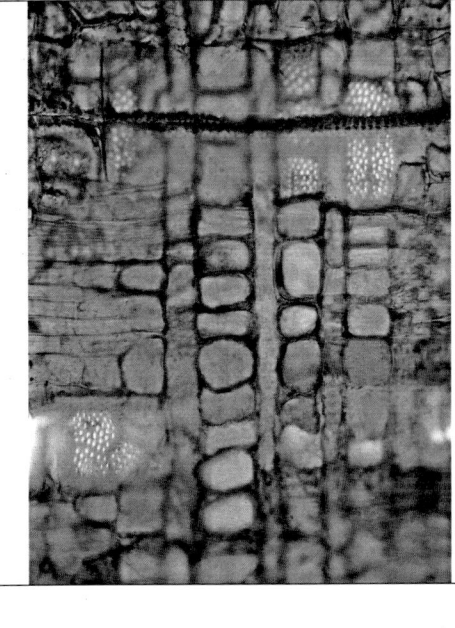

Rays uniseriate (*Terminalia tomentosa* TLS x100)

Rays bi- to 3seriate (*Holigarna arnottiana* TLS x100)

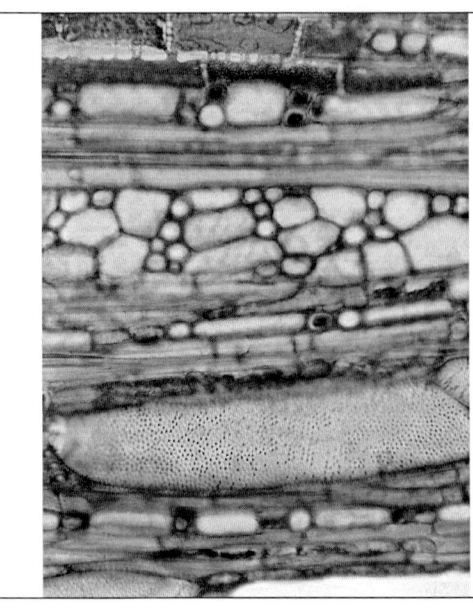

Rays 3-4seriate (*Soymida febrifuga* TLS x100)

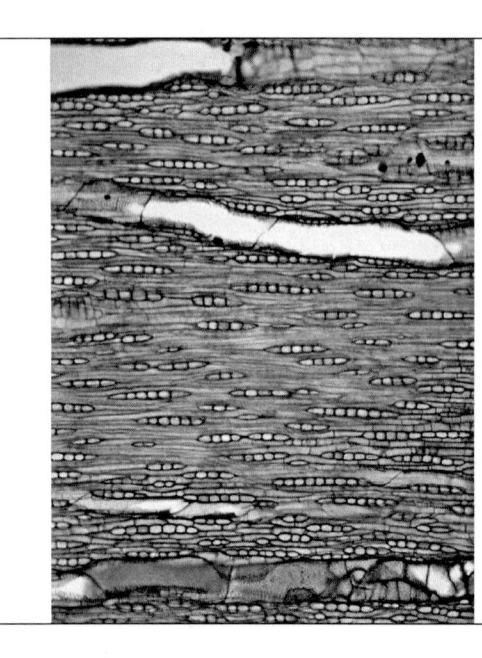

Rays uniseriate and multiseriate (multiseriates 8-10 cells wide) (*Dillenia pentagyna* TLS x100)

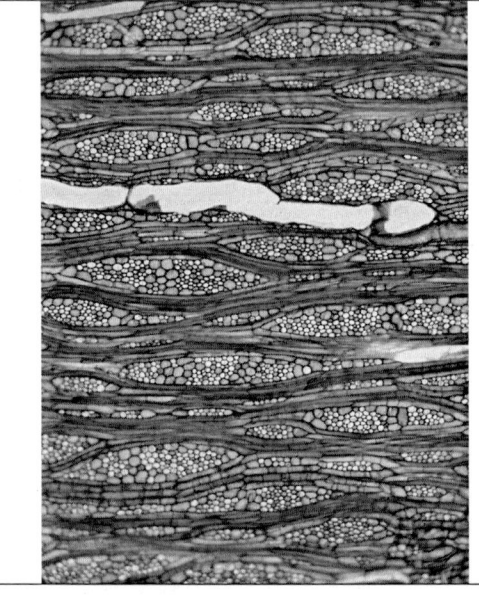

Rays with sheath cells (*Grewia tiliaefolia* TLS x100)

Rays with tile cells (*Pterospermum diversifolium* TLS x400)

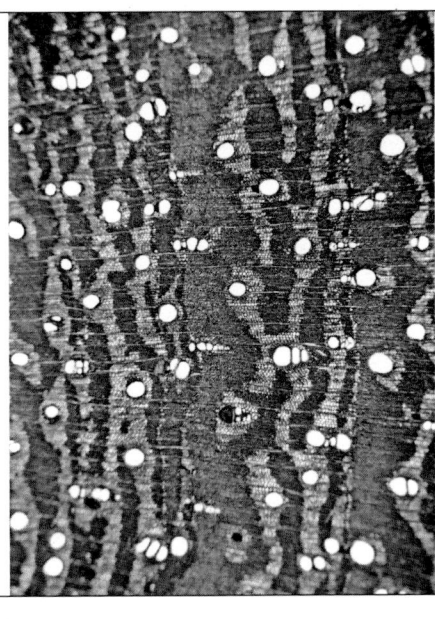

Parenchyma paratracheal, aliform, confluent (*Cassia fistula* TS x40)

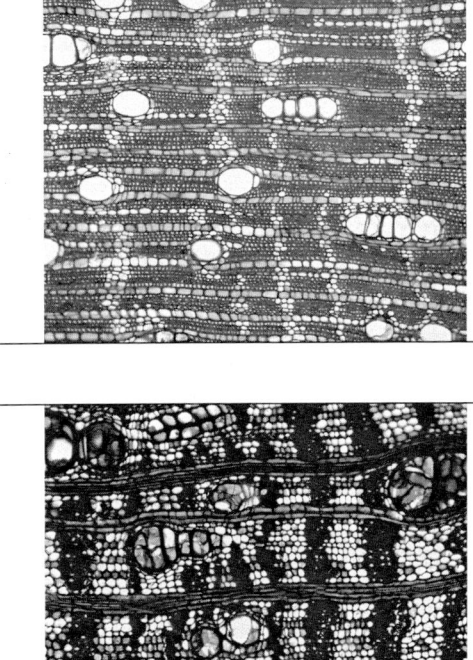

Parenchyma paratracheal, aliform, winged (*Polyalthia fragrans* TS x100)

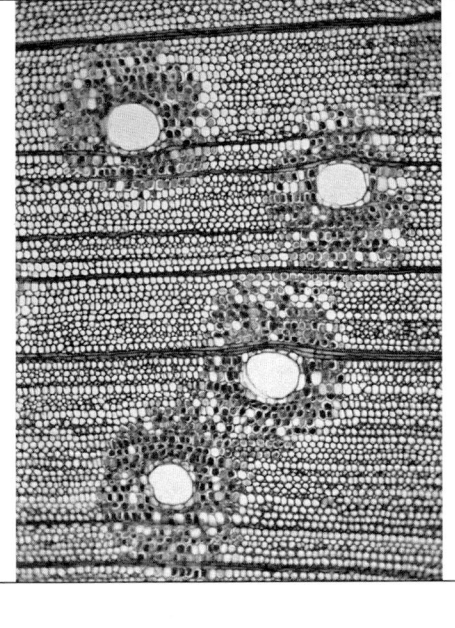

Parenchyma paratracheal, vasicentric (surrounding vessels) (*Albizia procera* TS x100)

Parenchyma banded (bands more than 3 cells wide) (*Ficus benghalensis* TS x100)

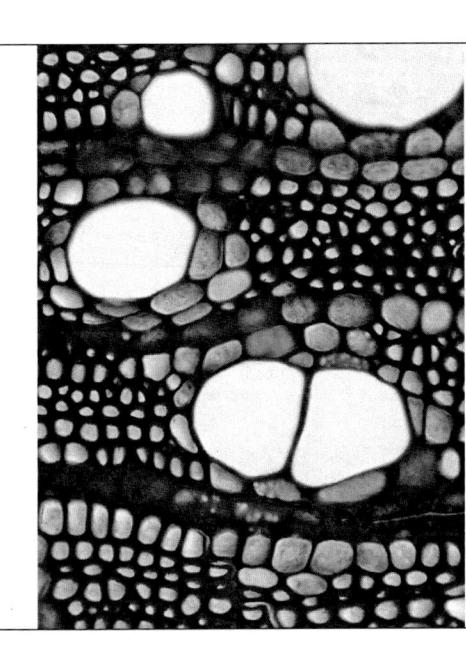

Parenchyma paratracheal (axial parenchyma associated with vessels) (*Cinnamomum zeylanicum* TS x400)

Rays and parenchyma storied (*Pterocarpus marsupium* TLS x400)

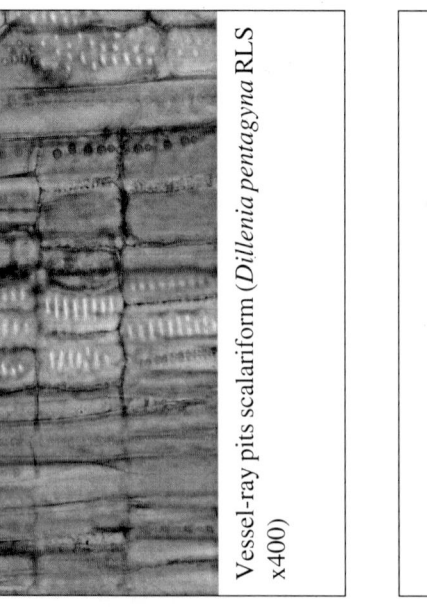

Vessel-ray pits scalariform (*Dillenia pentagyna* RLS x400)

Grond tissue of traumatic origin (*Mallotus philippensis* TS x100)

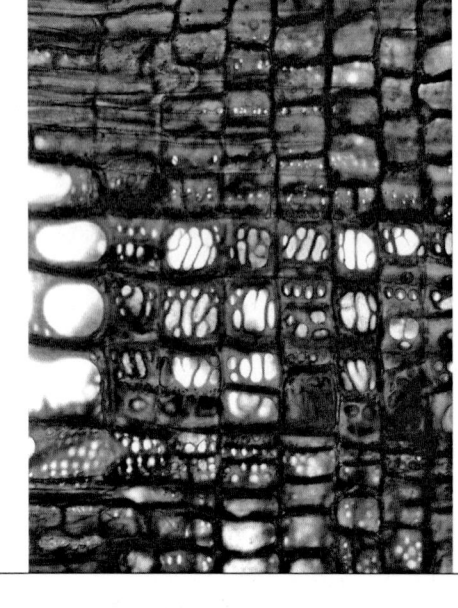

Vessel-ray pits horizontal (scalariform, gash-like) to vertical (palisade) (*Careya arborea* RLS x400)

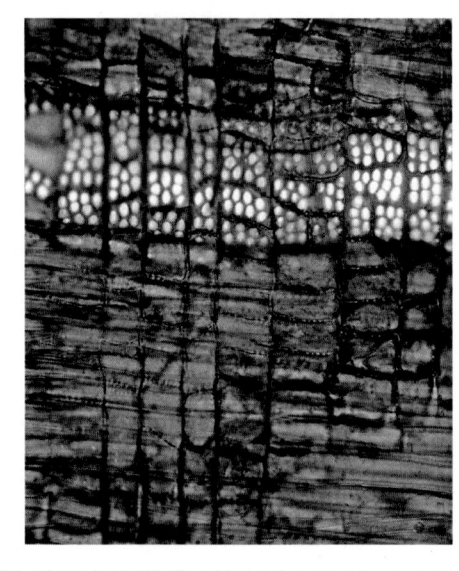

Vessel-ray pits rounded to angular (*Bauhinia racemosa* RLS x400)

Vessel-ray pits rounded/angular/scalariform (*Ficus bengalensis* RLS x630)

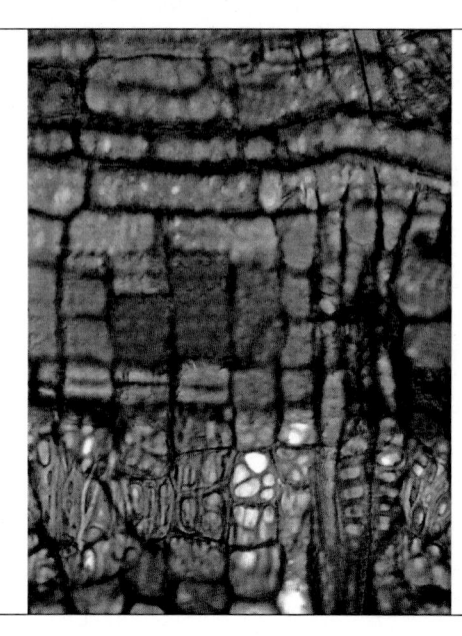

Vessel-ray pits similar in size, shape to intervessel pits (*Acacia catechu* RLS x400)

# CHAPTER 9
# WOOD ANATOMICAL DESCRIPTIONS

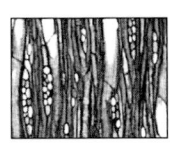

## ANACARDIACEAE

*Holigarna* sp.
(species examined: *H. arnottiana*)

Description:

Transverse section
Diffuse porous. Ring boundary indistinct. Pores medium to large, sparse, solitary (common), in radial multiples of 2–3 and in radial irregular multiples/clusters of smaller pores. Parenchyma apotracheal diffuse, paratracheal (aliform, occasionally confluent), and scanty paratracheal.

Radial section
Perforation plates simple. Intervessel pits alternate, medium to large. Vessel-ray pits with reduced to apparently simple borders, horizontal (scalariform, gashlike) to vertical (palisade). Ground tissue fibres with simple to minutely bordered pits, thin-walled. Rays heterogeneous, with a central portion of procumbent cells and 1–2 or more rows of square and upright marginal cells. Uniseriate rays composed of both square and upright cells.

Tangential section
Rays (1)2-3seriate.

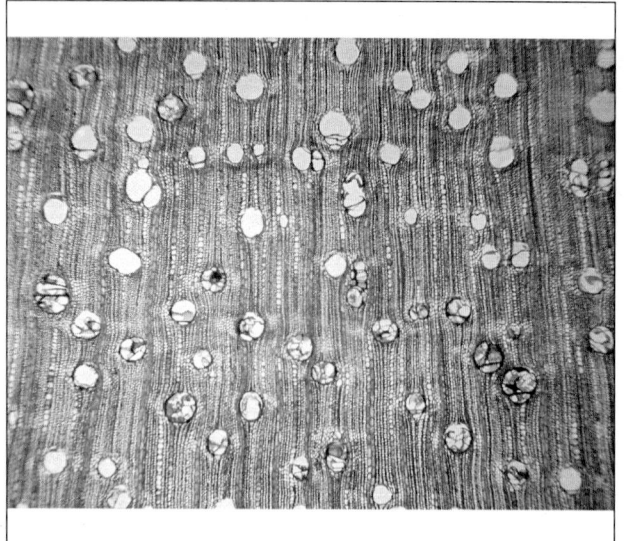
Holigarna arnottiana TS x40

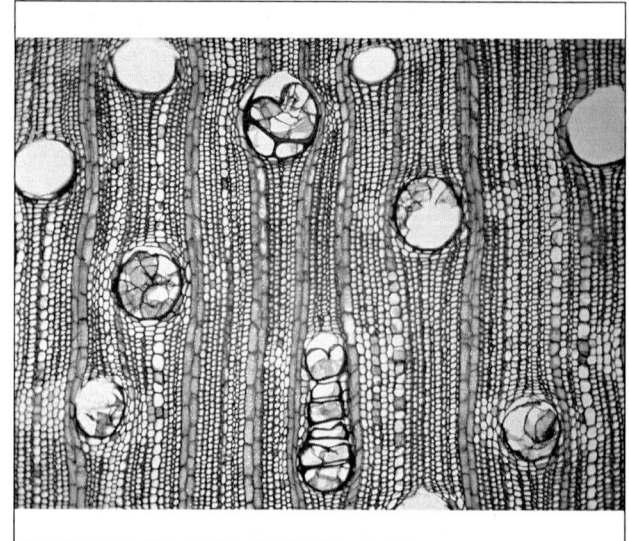
Holigarna arnottiana TS x100

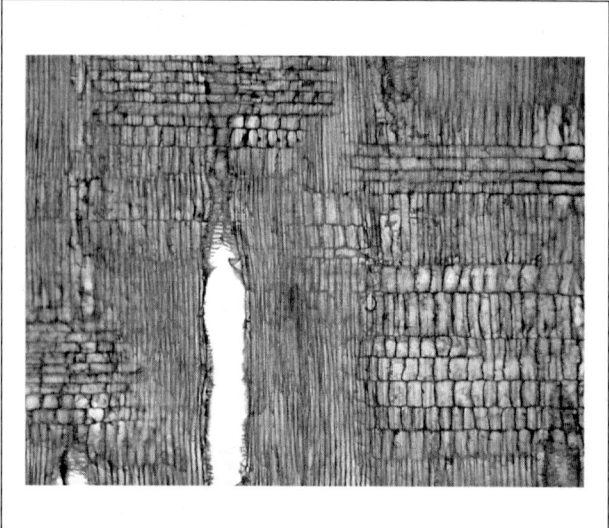
Holigarna arnottiana RLS x100

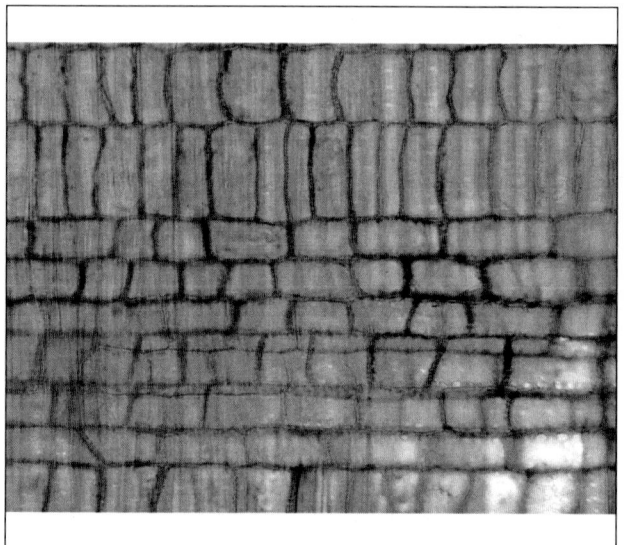
Holigarna arnottiana RLS x400

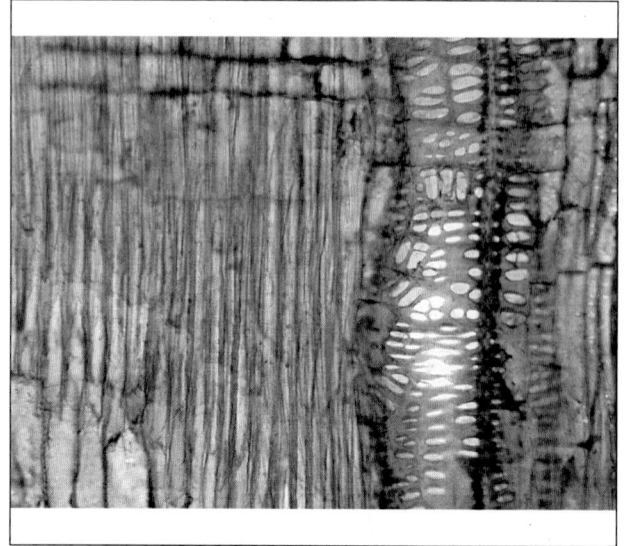
Holigarna arnottiana RLS x400

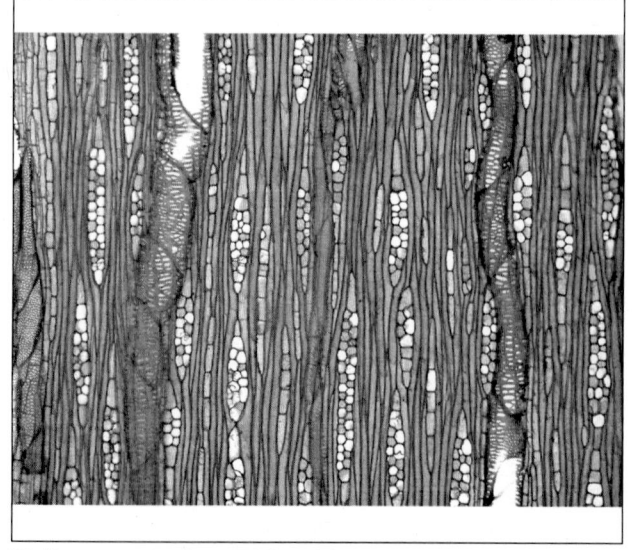
Holigarna arnottiana TLS x100

# ANACARDIACEAE

*Mangifera* sp.
(species examined: *M. indica*)

Description:

Transverse section
Diffuse porous. Ring boundary indistinct to distinct. Pores medium to large, solitary (common), in radial multiples of 2–3 and in radial irregular multiples/clusters of smaller pores. Parenchyma paratracheal (aliform with large sheath, confluent), banded (terminal bands 1-5 cells wide), and scanty paratracheal.

Radial section
Perforation plates simple. Intervessel pits alternate, medium to large. Vessel-ray pits with reduced to apparently simple borders, horizontal (scalariform, gashlike) to vertical (palisade). Ground tissue fibres with simple to minutely bordered pits, thin-walled. Septate fibres present occasionally. Rays heterogeneous, with a central portion of procumbent cells and 1–2 rows or more of upright and square marginal cells. Uniseriate rays composed of both square and upright cells.

Tangential section
Rays 1-2seriate (very rarely 3-seriate).

Note: Anatomically, *Mangifera* resembles closely *Comocladia*, *Gluta*, *Melanorrhoea*, and certain species of *Swintonia* and *Thyrsodium*, all of which have mostly uniseriate rays (Metcalfe and Chalk 1950:457–58).

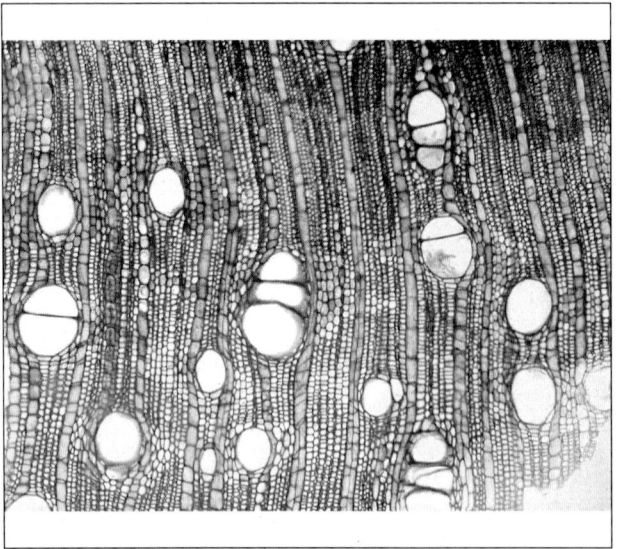

Mangifera indica TS x100

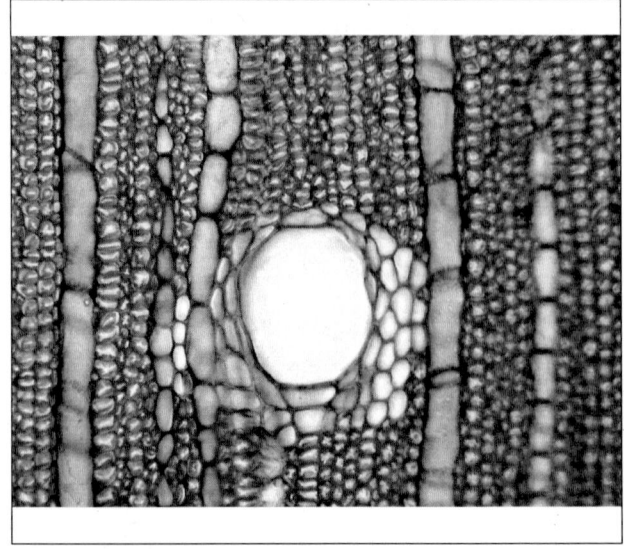

Mangifera indica TS x400

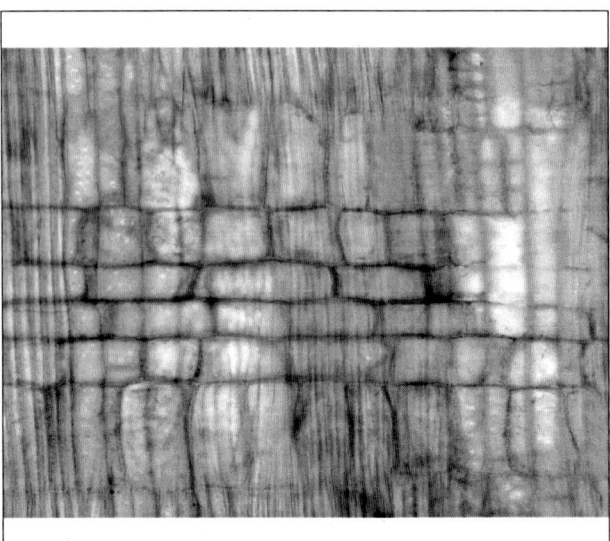

Mangifera indica RLS x400

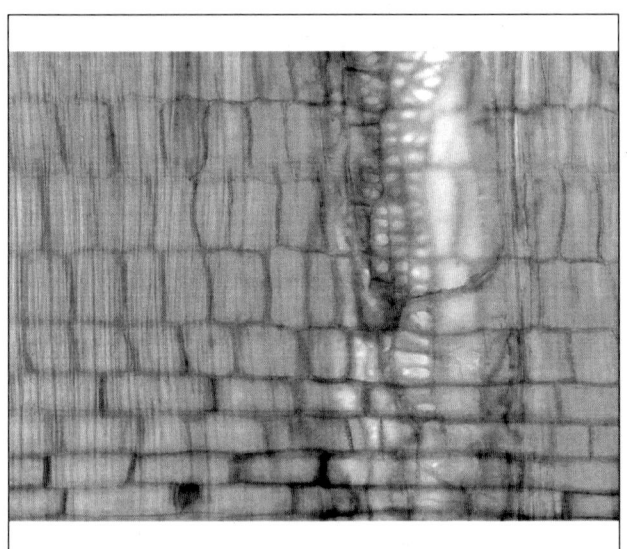

Mangifera indica RLS x400

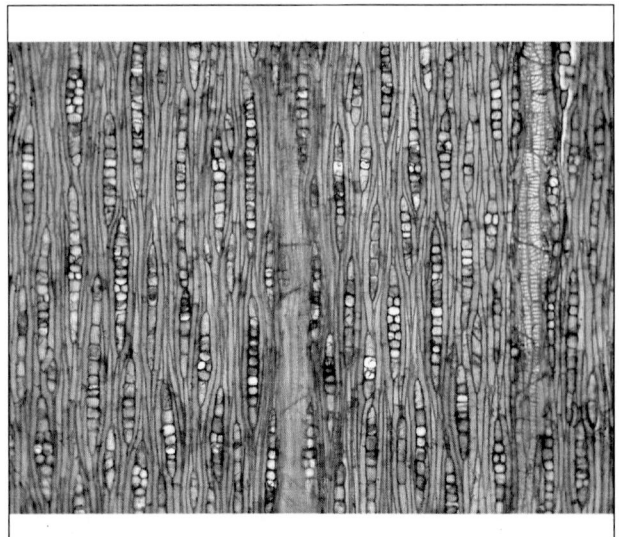

Mangifera indica TLS x100

# ANNONACEAE

*Annona* sp.
(species examined: *A. reticulata*)

Description:

Transverse section
Diffuse-porous. Ring boundary distinct to indistinct. Pores small to medium (occasionally very small), in radial multiples of 2–4 or more, solitary and occasionally in irregular clusters. Parenchyma apotracheal, banded (1-3seriate closely spaced bands), scalariform. Scanty paratracheal parenchyma present.

Radial section
Perforation plates simple. Intervessel pits alternate, medium. Vessel-ray pits with distinct borders, similar in shape and size to intervessel pits. Ground tissue fibres with simple to minutely bordered pits, thin to thick-walled. Rays heterogeneous, with a central portion of strongly procumbent cells and 1–2 rows of square marginal cells. Rows of large, almost square cells may also occur, interspersed amongst the smaller procumbent cells. Ray cells often irregular in size. Axial parenchyma storied.

Tangential section
Rays (3)4-6(8)seriate.

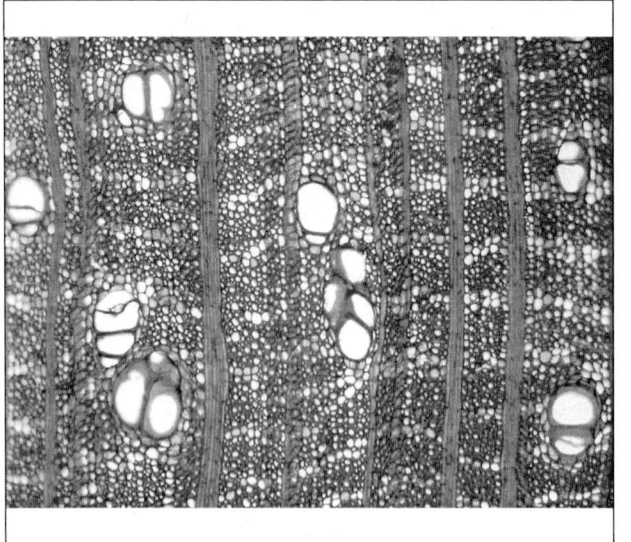
Annona reticulata TS x100

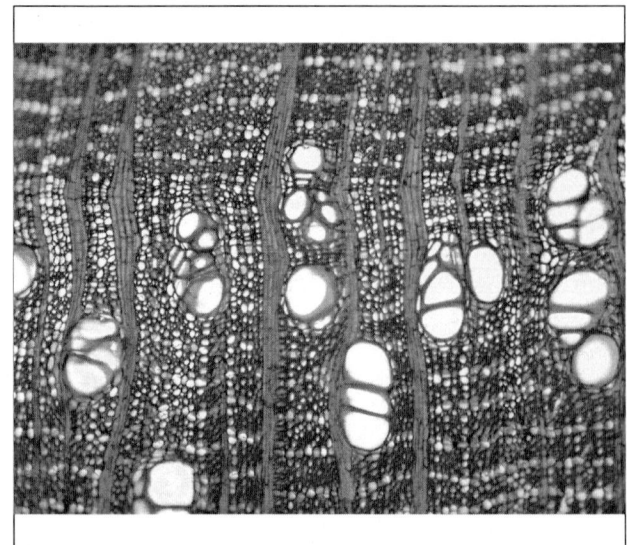
Annona reticulata TS x100

Annona reticulata RLS x100

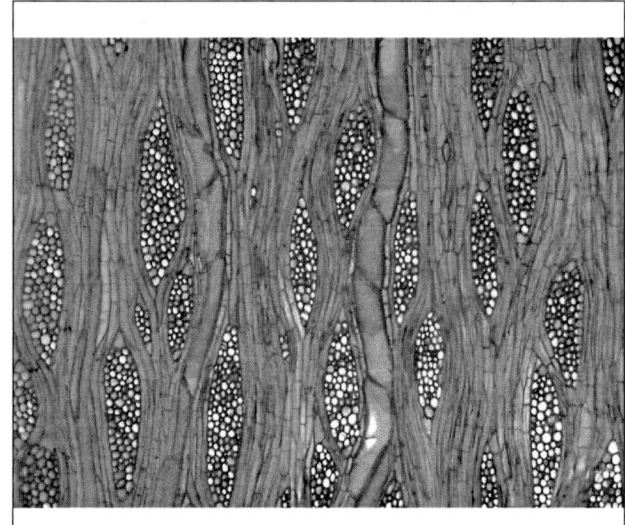
Annona reticulata TLS x100

# ANNONACEAE

*Polyalthia* sp.
(species examined: *P. fragrans*)

Description:

Transverse section
Diffuse-porous. Ring boundary indistinct. Pores small to medium, solitary and in radial multiples of (2-3)4 or more. Paratracheal parenchyma present (aliform-winged, occasionally confluent). Also apotracheal, diffuse-in-aggregates and banded (1–3 seriate bands).

Radial section
Perforation plates simple. Intervessel pits small to medium, alternate. Vessel-ray pits horizontal, scalariform. Ground tissue fibres with simple to minutely bordered pits, thin to thick-walled. Rays heterogeneous with 2–4 and sometimes over 4 rows of upright and/or square marginal cells. Uniseriate rays are composed of entirely upright and/or square cells. Vessel elements occasionally storied.

Tangential section
Rays in the observed specimen fine (1)2-3seriate, often with long uniseriate tails. Metcalfe and Chalk (1950:47), however, report most common ray width between 4–8 cells. Cells are irregular in size, with occasional rows of large, almost square cells interspersed amongst the smaller procumbent cells. A relative abundance of uniseriate rays in *Polyalthia* spp. has been also reported by Chowdhury and Ghosh (1958:24).

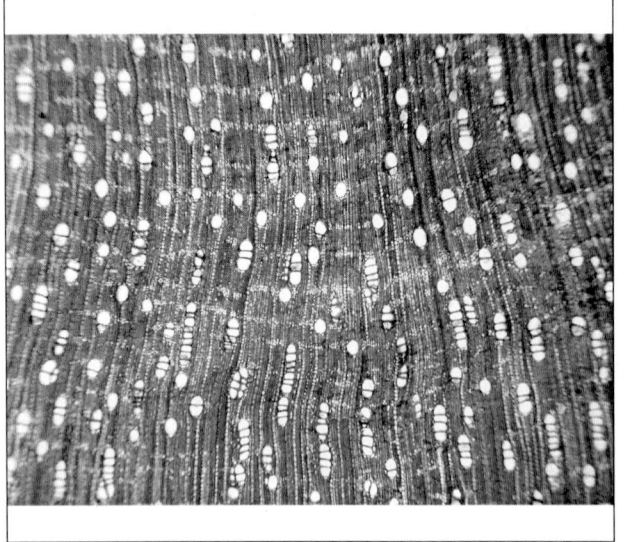
Polyalthia fragrans TS x40

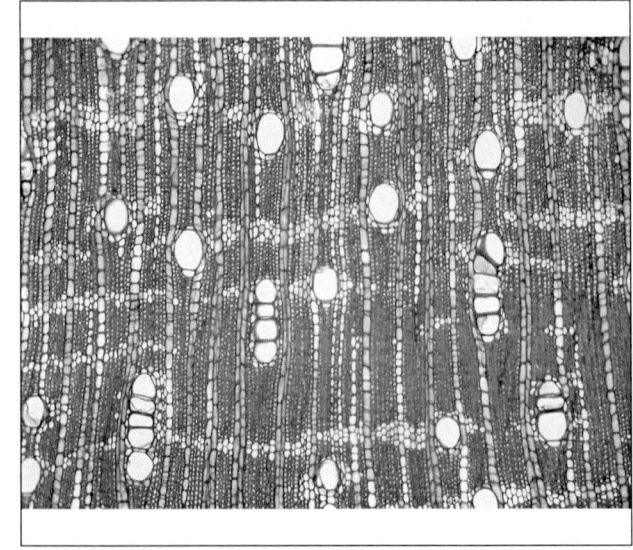
Polyalthia fragrans TS x100

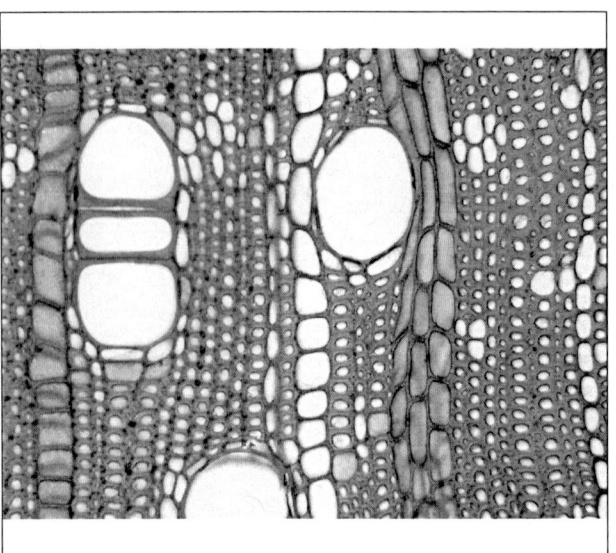
Polyalthia fragrans TS x400

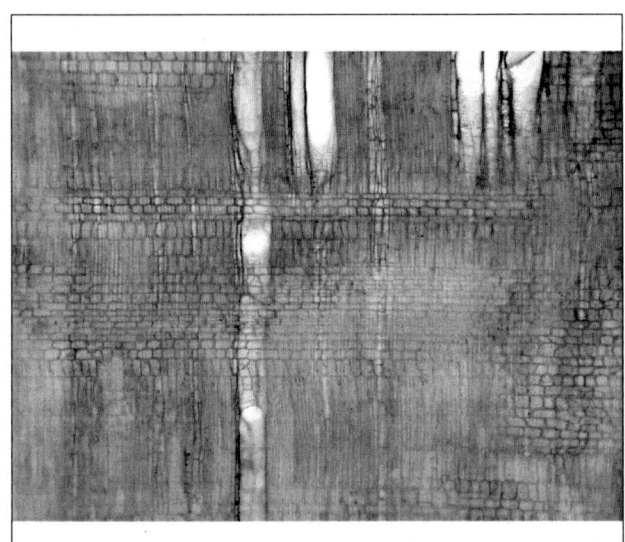
Polyalthia fragrans RLS x100

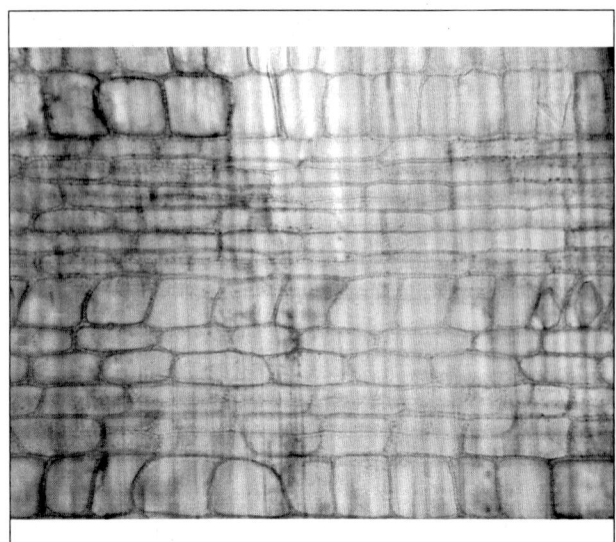
Polyalthia fragrans RLS x400

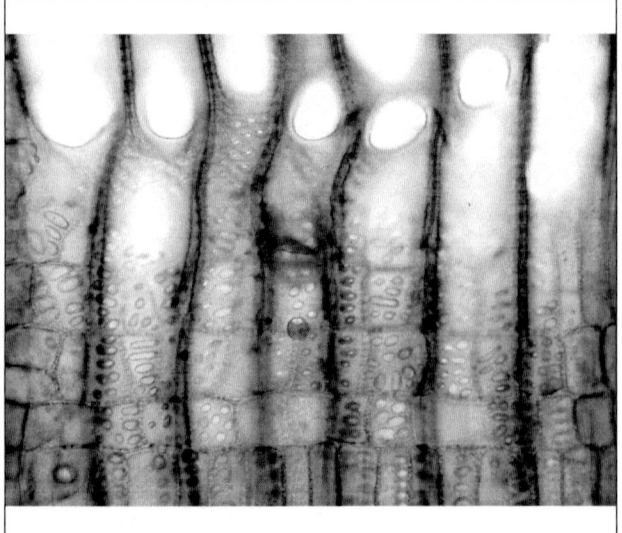
Polyalthia fragrans RLS x400

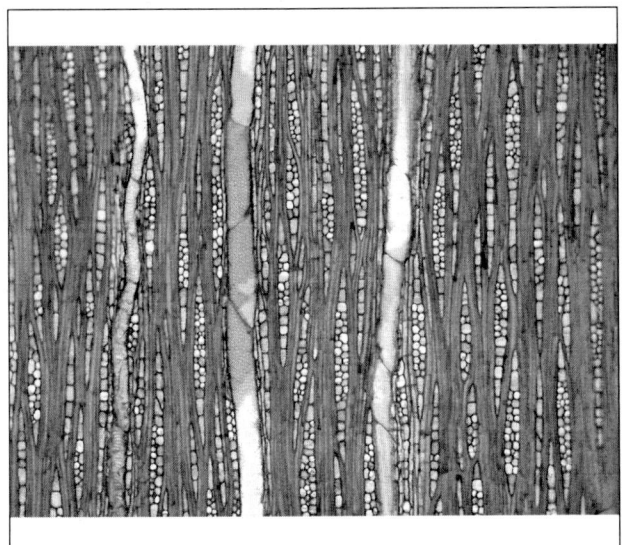

Polyalthia fragrans TLS x100

# APOCYNACEAE

*Holarrhena* sp.
(species examined: *H. antidysenterica*)

Description:

<u>Transverse section</u>
Diffuse-porous. Ring boundary indistinct. Pores small to medium, in radial multiples of 4 or more (common) and clusters, with a radial to oblique pattern. Parenchyma apotracheal banded (irregular narrow bands less than 3 cells wide, scalariform and diffuse-in-aggregates), and scanty paratracheal (rare).

<u>Radial section</u>
Perforation plates simple. Intervessel pits alternate, small to minute, with slitlike apertures. Vestured pits present. Vessel-ray pits vestured with distinct borders, similar in shape, size to intervessel pits. Ground tissue fibres with simple to minutely bordered pits, thick-walled. Rays heterogeneous with a small central portion of procumbent cells and 4 or more rows of square and upright marginal cells. Uniseriate rays composed entirely of upright cells.

<u>Tangential section</u>
1-3seriate (with uni- and multiseriate portions).

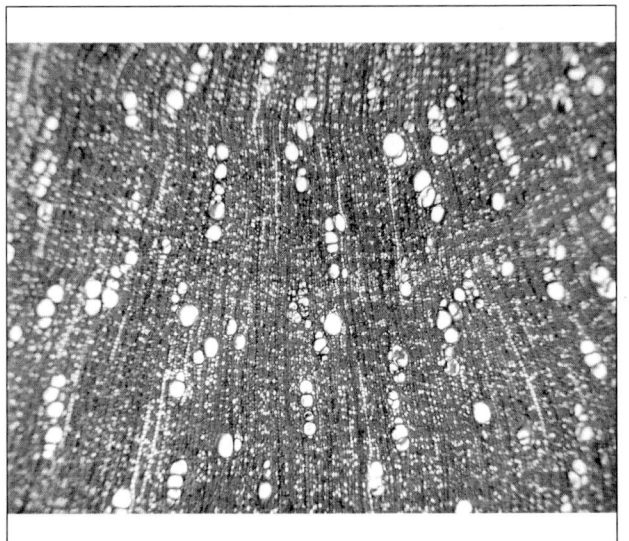

Holarrhena antidysenterica TS x40

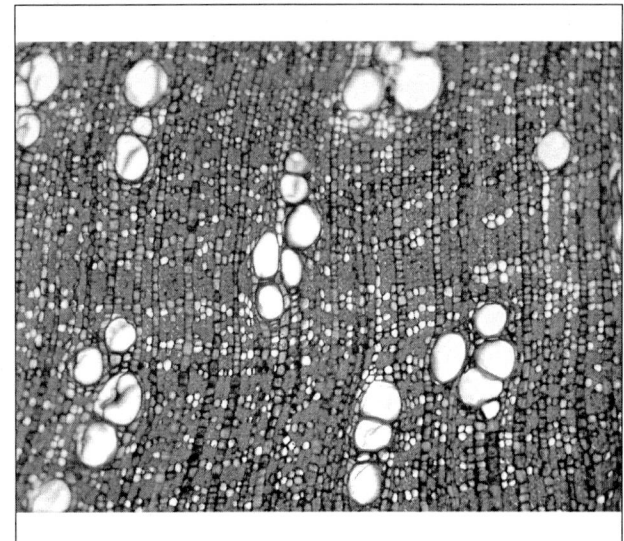

Holarrhena antidysenterica TS x100

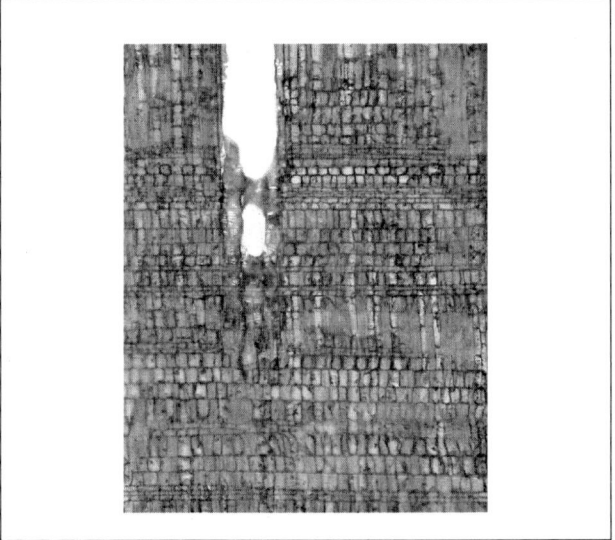

Holarrhena antidysenterica RLS x100

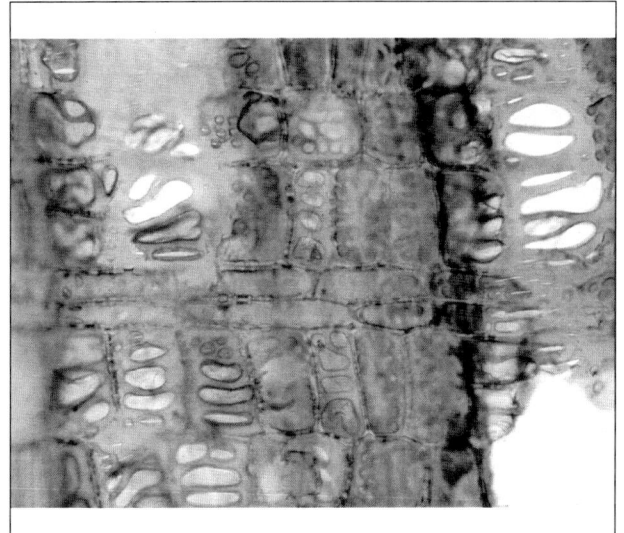

Holarrhena antidysenterica RLS x630

Holarrhena antidysenterica TLS x100

# APOCYNACEAE

*Wrightia* sp.
(species examined: *W. tinctoria*)

Description:

Transverse section
Diffuse-porous. Ring boundary distinct to indistinct. Pores small to medium, in radial multiples of (2-3) 4 or more (common). Parenchyma apotracheal, diffuse, occasionally banded (narrow bands less than 3 cells wide) and scanty paratracheal (rare).

Radial section
Perforation plates simple. Intervessel pits alternate, minute. Vestured pits present. Vessel-ray pits vestured with distinct borders, similar in shape, size to intervessel pits. Ground tissue fibres with simple to minutely bordered pits, thin- to thick-walled. Rays heterogeneous, with a small central portion of procumbent cells and over 4 rows of upright and square marginal cells. Uniseriate rays composed entirely of upright and square cells.

Tangential section
Rays 1-2seriate (with uni- and multiseriate portions).

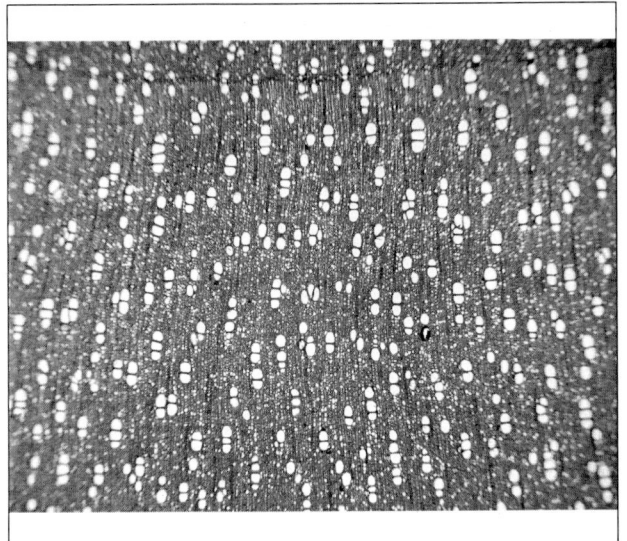
Wrightia tinctoria TS x40

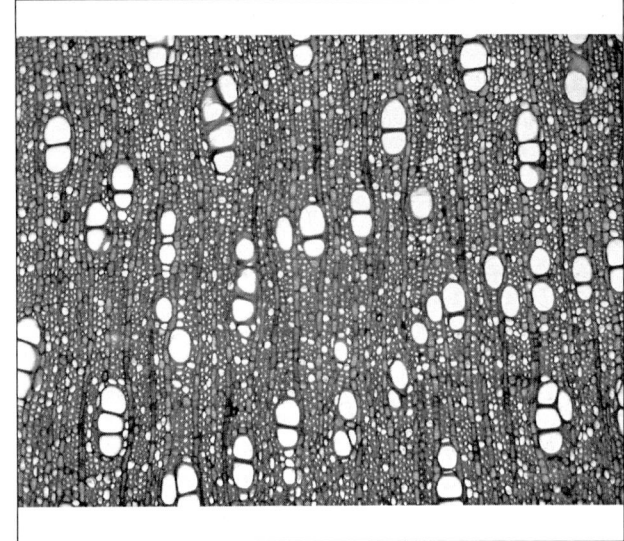
Wrightia tinctoria TS x100

Wrightia tinctoria RLS x100

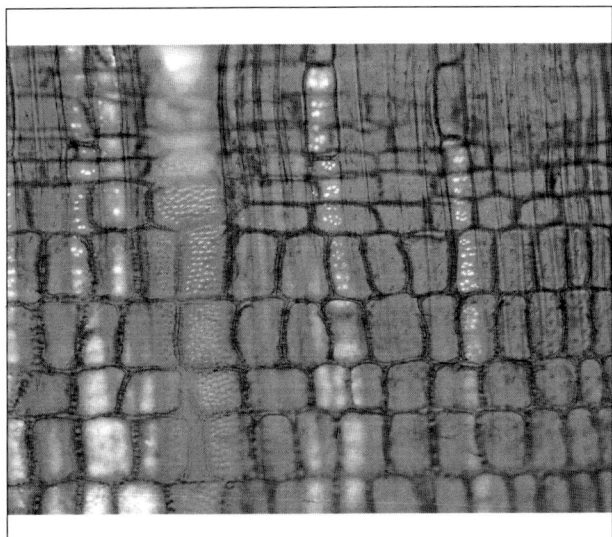
Wrightia tinctoria RLS x400

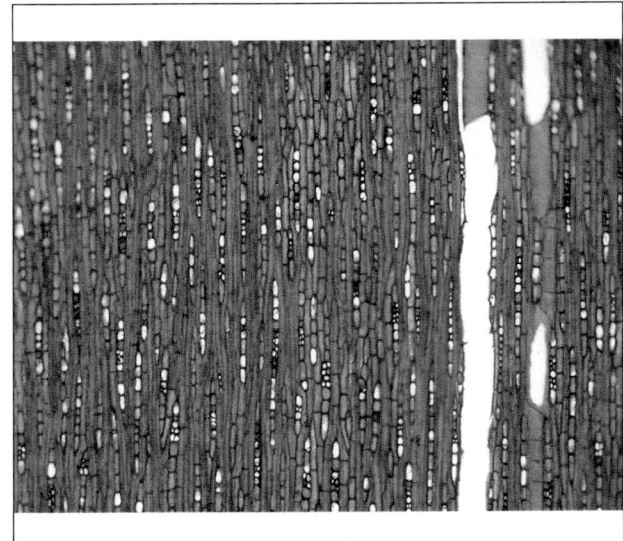
Wrightia tinctoria TLS x100

# BOMBACACEAE

*Bombax* sp.
(species examined: *Bombax malabaricum*)

Description:

Transverse section
Diffuse-porous. Ring boundary distinct to indistinct. Pores medium, solitary (angular), and in radial multiples of 2–3. Parenchyma apotracheal (diffuse) and paratracheal (vasicentric).

*Radial section*
Perforation plates simple. Intervessel pits alternate. Vessel-ray pits with reduced to apparently simple borders, horizontal (scalariform, gashlike) to vertical (palisade). Ground tissue fibres with simple to minutely bordered pits, thin-walled. Rays heterogeneous, with tile cells (*Durio* type). Uniseriate rays composed entirely of upright cells. Crystals and gum deposits present.

Tangential section
Rays (2)4-10seriate, tall. Uniseriate rays rare, short.

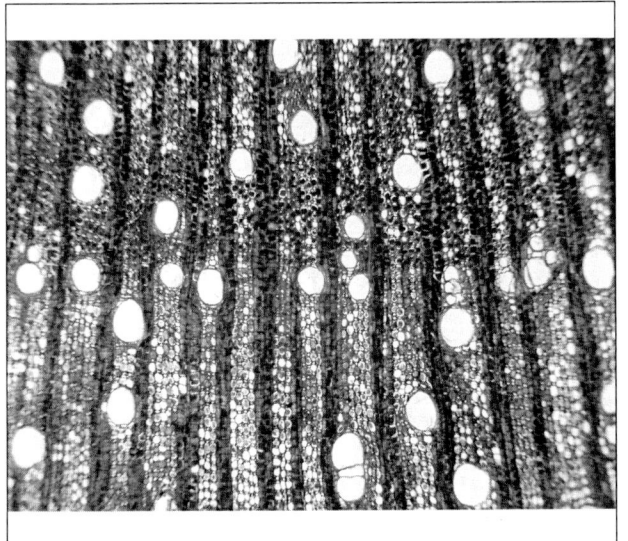

Bombax malabaricum TS x40

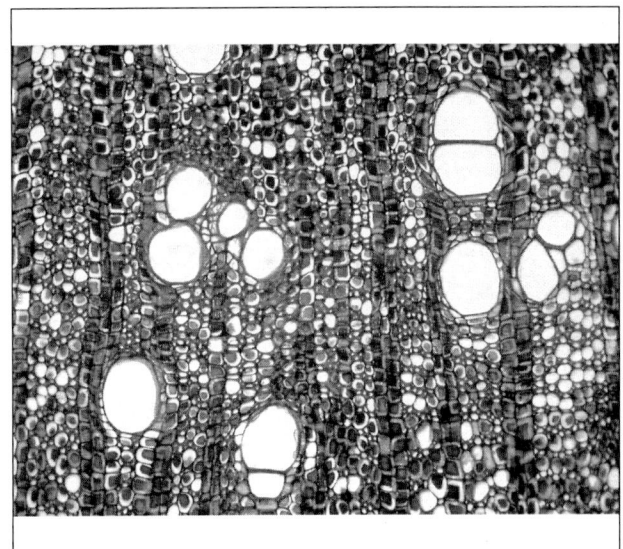

Bombax malabaricum TS x100

Bombax malabaricum RLS x100

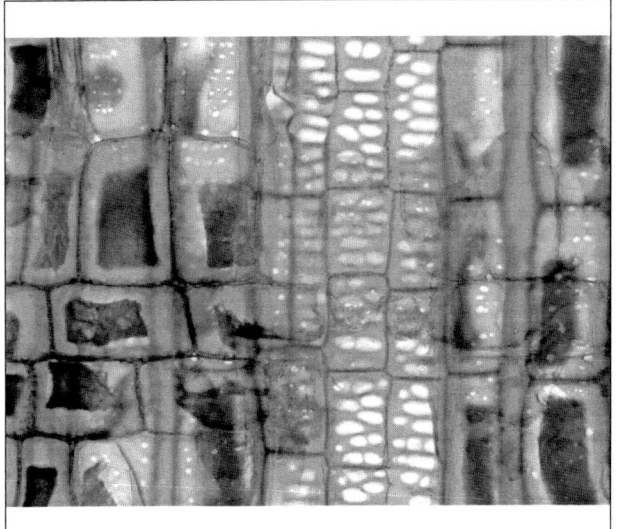

Bombax malabaricum RLS x400

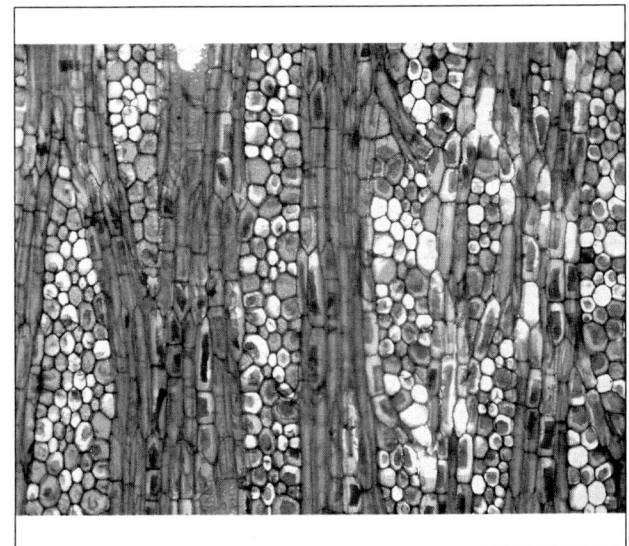

Bombax malabaricum TLS x100

# BURSERACEAE

*Commiphora* sp.
(species examined: *C. berryi, C. caudata*)

Description:

Transverse section
Diffuse-porous. Ring boundary distinct to indistinct. Pores medium, mostly solitary (angular), and in radial multiples of 2–3 or irregular clusters (rare). Parenchyma apotracheal (diffuse) and scanty paratracheal (rare).

Radial section
Perforation plates simple. Intervessel pits alternate to opposite, medium to large, with slitlike apertures. Vessel-ray pits with reduced to apparently simple borders-horizontal (scalariform, gashlike) to vertical (palisade). Ground tissue fibres with simple to minutely bordered pits, thin-walled. Septate fibres present. Rays heterogeneous, with procumbent, square, and upright cells mixed throughout and/or 1-3(4) rows of upright and/or square marginal cells. Radial intercellular canals present.

Tangential section
Rays 1-2(3) seriate. Radial canals present in larger rays.

Note: members of the Burseraceae family exhibit some anatomical similarities to members of the Anacardiaceae family (Metcalfe and Chalk 1950:348).

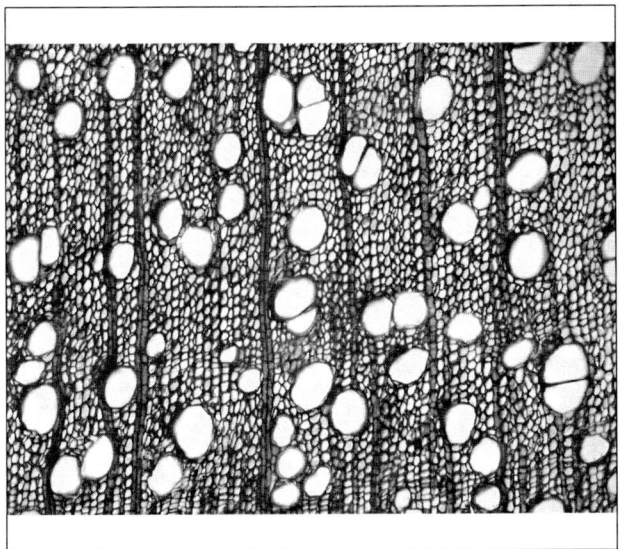

Commiphora berryi TS x100

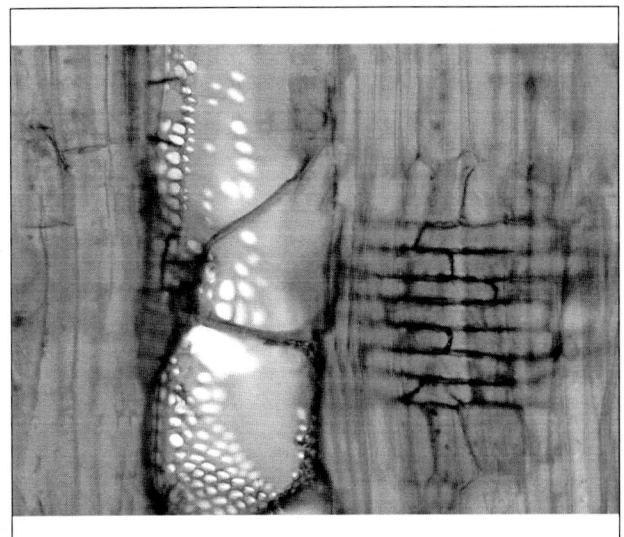

Commiphora berryi RLS x400

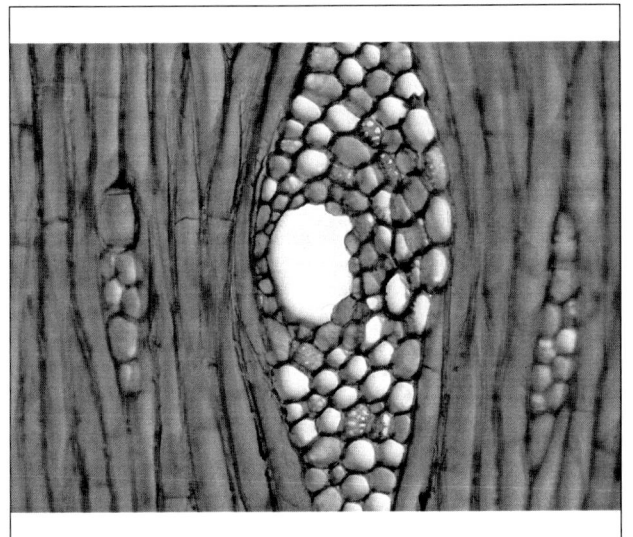

Commiphora berryi TLS x400

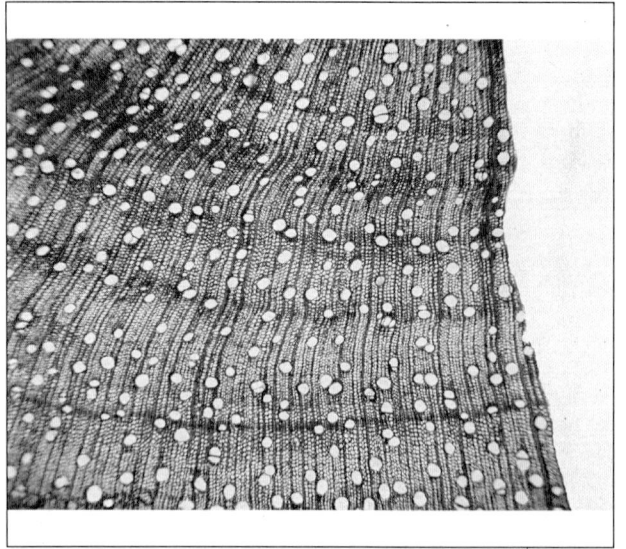
Commiphora caudata TS x40

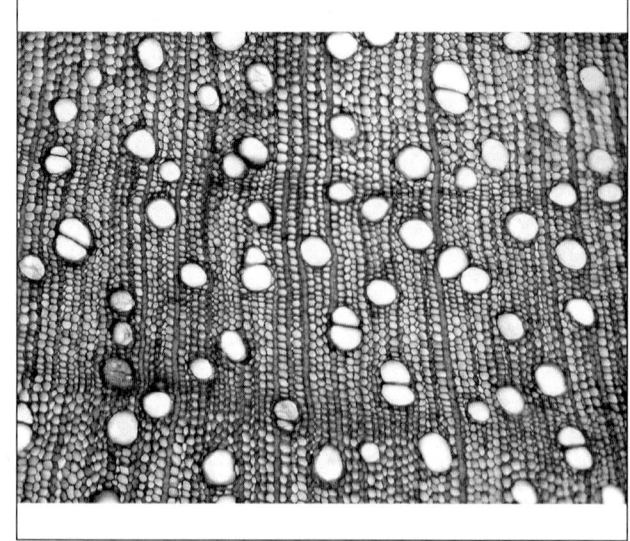
Commiphora caudata TS x100

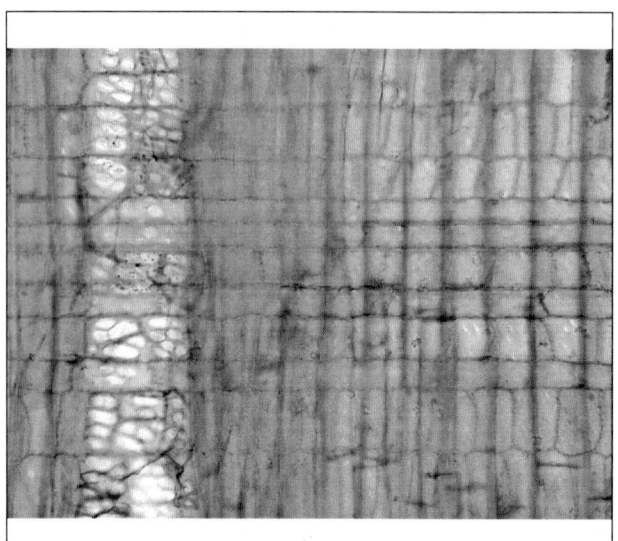
Commiphora caudata RLS x400

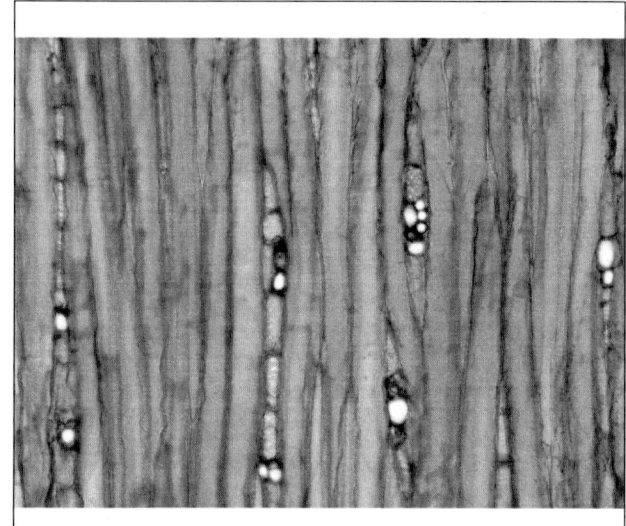
Commiphora caudata TLS x400

# CAPPARACEAE

*Capparis* sp.
(species examined: *C. sepiaria*)

Description:

Transverse section
Diffuse-porous. Ring boundary indistinct. Pores of two sizes: medium to large (in irregular clusters, solitary and in radial multiples of 2–6) and very small (in clusters or multiples with the large ones, solitary and in radial multiples). Parenchyma apotracheal (diffuse-in-aggregates) and scanty paratracheal.

Radial section
Perforation plates simple. Intervessel pits opposite to alternate, small to minute. Vessel-ray pits with distinct borders, similar in shape, size to intervessel pits. Ground tissue fibres with simple to minutely bordered pits, thick-walled. Rays heterogeneous with a central portion composed of procumbent cells and multiple rows of square and/or upright marginal cells (sometimes weakly procumbent).

Tangential section
(1)2-(3-4)5seriate, tall.

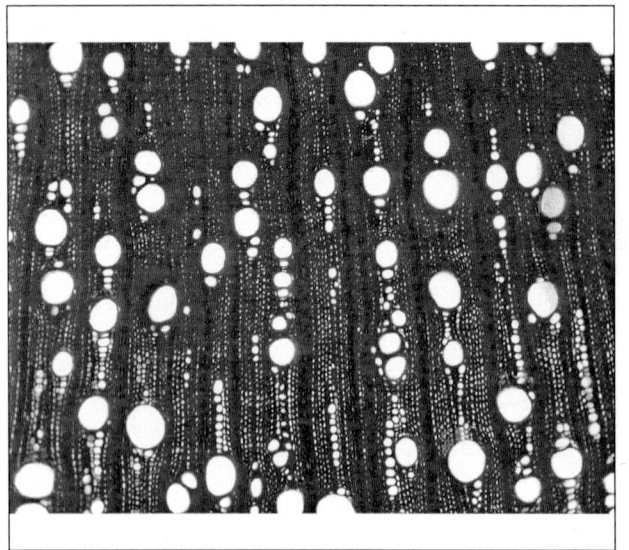

Capparis sepiaria TS x100

Capparis sepiaria RLS x400

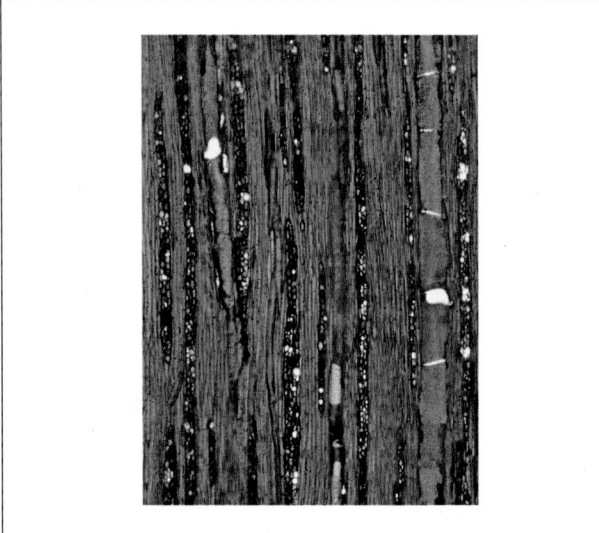

Capparis sepiaria TLS x100

# CELASTRACEAE

*Gymnosporia* sp.
(species examined: *G. montana*)

Description:

Transverse section
Diffuse porous. Ring boundary distinct. Pores small to medium, solitary, in radial multiples of 2–3 and occasionally in clusters. Parenchyma apotracheal diffuse and banded (in marginal or seemingly marginal bands; bands usually 6 cells wide).

Radial section
Perforation plates simple. Intervessel pits alternate, small. Vessel-ray pits with distinct borders, similar in size, shape to intervessel pits. Ground tissue fibres with distinctly bordered pits, thin to thick-walled. Rays heterogeneous, with a short central portion of procumbent cells and usually over 4 rows of upright marginal cells. Uniseriate rays are composed entirely of upright cells. Crystals present in upright ray cells.

Tangential section
Rays 1-3seriate (multiseriate rays with long uniseriate tails).

Note: members of the Celastraceae family are reported to be anatomically similar (Metcalfe and Chalk 1950:395).

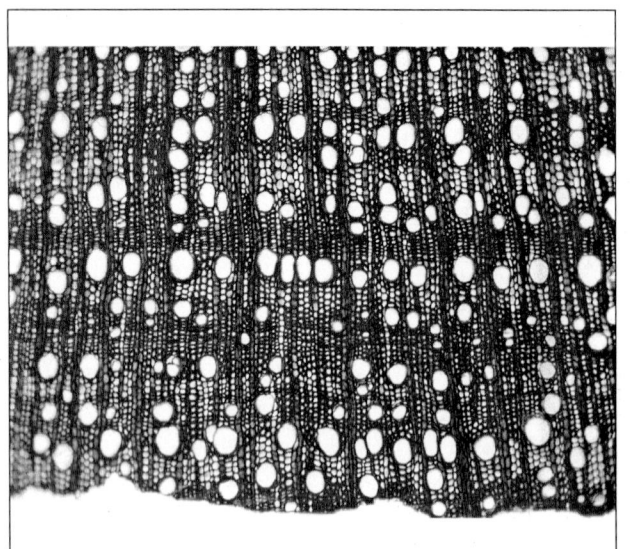
Gymnosporia montana TS x100

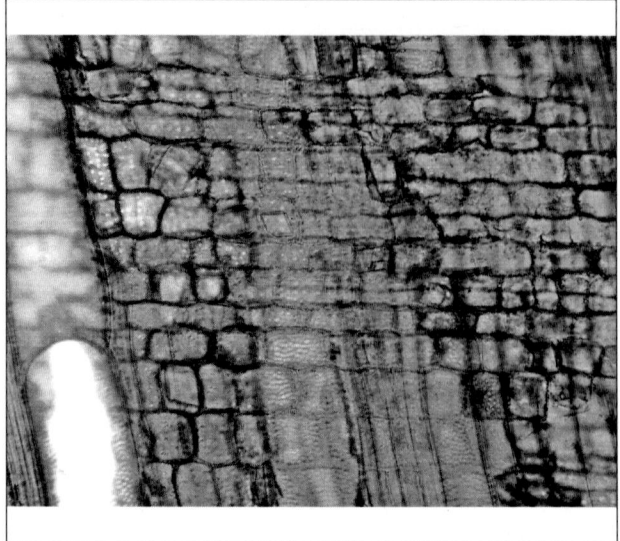
Gymnosporia montana RLS x400

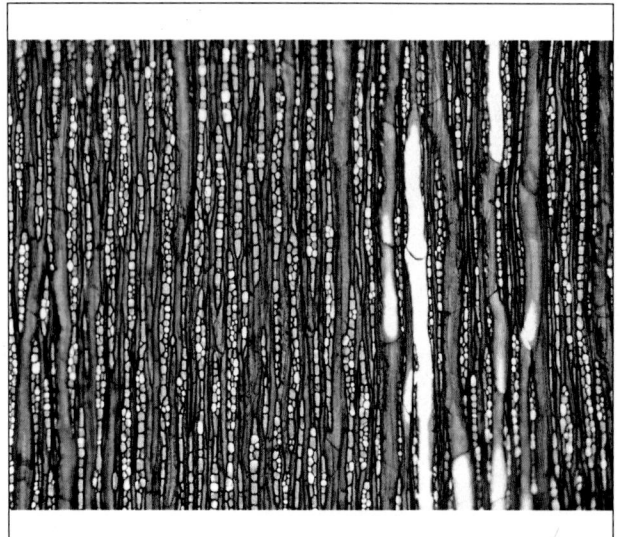
Gymnosporia montana TLS x100

# CLUSIACEAE
(form. Guttiferae)

*Garcinia* sp.
(species examined: *G. indica*)

Description:

<u>Transverse section</u>
Diffuse porous. Ring boundary indistinct. Pores medium, in radial multiples of (2-3)4 or more (common) and in clusters. Parenchyma predominantly apotracheal, banded (bands 3–5 cells wide) scalariform.

<u>Radial section</u>
Perforation plates simple. Intervessel pits alternate, small. Vessel-ray pits with distinct borders, similar in shape, size to intervessel pits. Ground tissue fibres with simple to minutely bordered pits, thick-walled. Rays with a central portion of procumbent cells and 1–4 or more rows of upright and square marginal cells. Uniseriate rays composed entirely of upright cells.

<u>Tangential section</u>
Rays (1)2-4seriate. Sheath cells present.

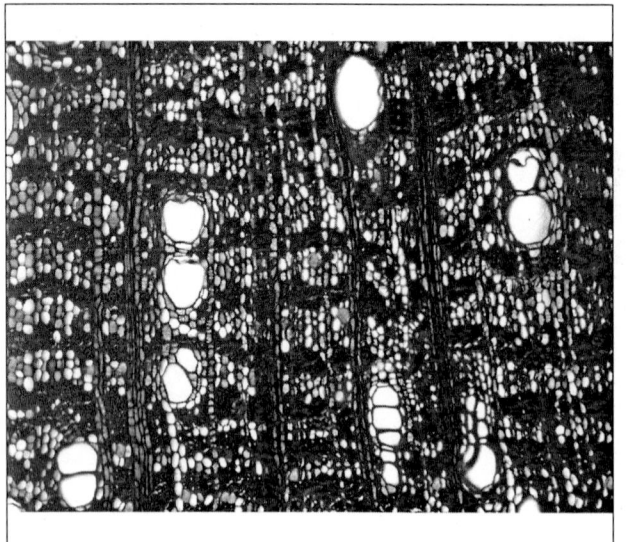
Garcinia indica TS x100

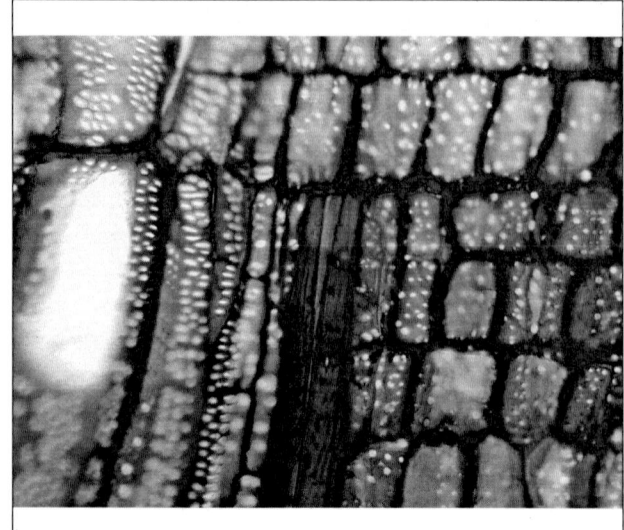
Garcinia indica RLS x400

Garcinia indica TLS x100

# COMBRETACEAE

*Anogeissus* sp.
(species examined: *A. latifolia* syn. *A. parviflora*)

Description:

Transverse section
Diffuse porous. Ring boundary indistinct. Pores medium, in radial multiples of 2–4 or more, sometimes in clusters. Parenchyma paratracheal (aliform winged with narrow sheath, confluent) and scanty paratracheal (common). Apotracheal parenchyma (few) are also present (diffuse, diffuse-in-aggregates).

Radial section
Perforation plates simple. Intervessel pits alternate, medium to small. Vestured pits present. Vessel-ray pits slightly enlarged, with much reduced borders, apparently simple. Ground tissue fibres with simple to minutely bordered pits, thin to thick-walled. Septate fibres rare. Tile cells (Pterospermum type, that is, higher than the procumbent cells) present. Crystals present in tile cells.

Tangential section
Rays 1-2seriate.

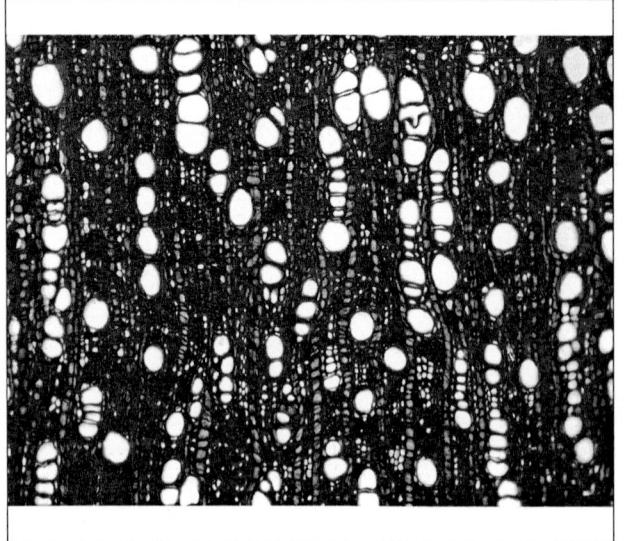

Anogeissus latifolia syn. parviflora TS x100

Anogeissus latifolia syn. parviflora RLS x400

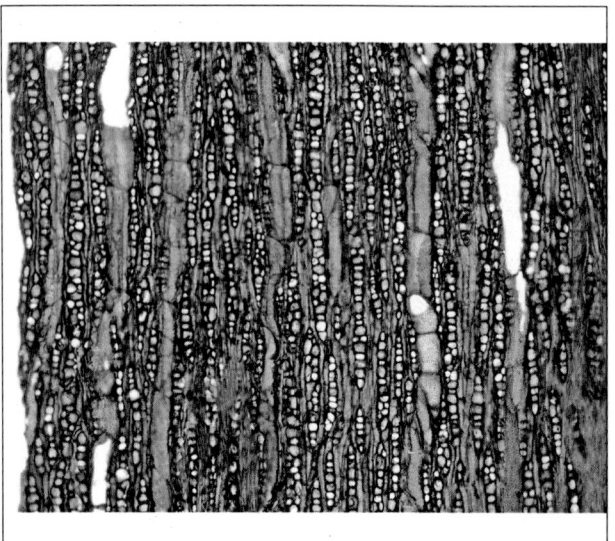

Anogeissus latifolia syn. parviflora TLS x100

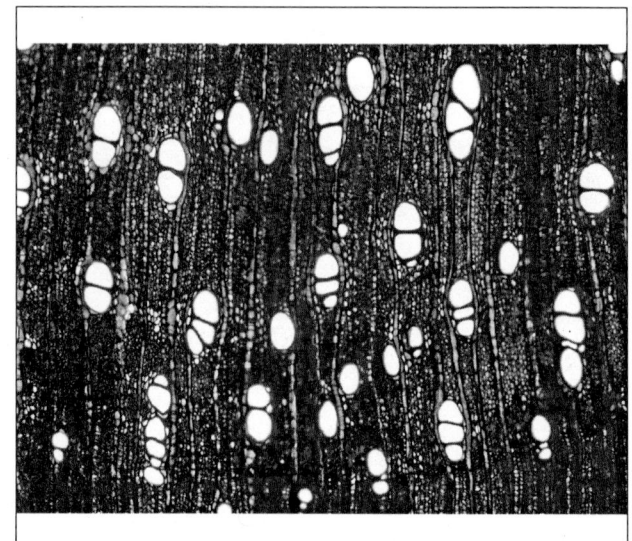

Anogeissus latifolia syn. parviflora TS x100

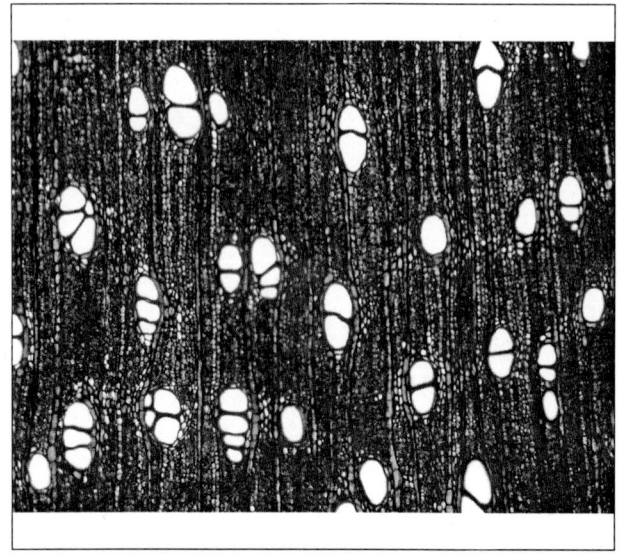

Anogeissus latifolia syn. parviflora TS x100

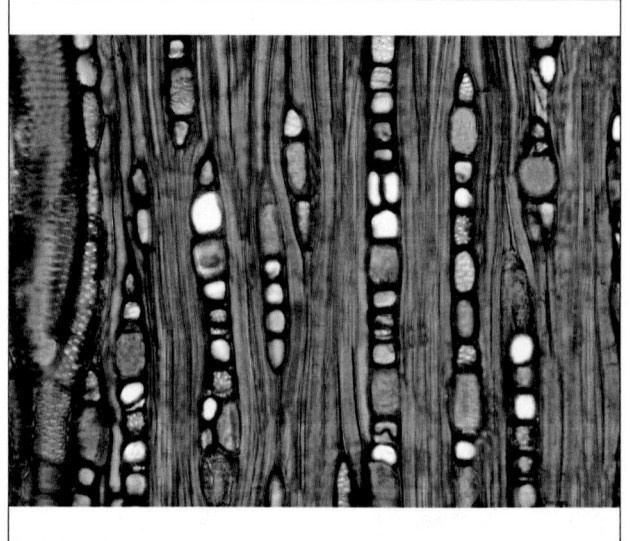

Anogeissus latifolia syn. parviflora TLS x400

# COMBRETACEAE

*Terminalia* sp.
(species examined: *T. arjuna, T. paniculata, T. tomentosa*)

Description:

Transverse section
Diffuse porous. Ring boundary indistinct. Pores mostly large, solitary, in radial multiples of 2–3 and in irregular clusters. Parenchyma paratracheal, aliform (winged-lozenge), confluent and banded (broad, irregular confluent bands and narrow terminal bands). Intercellular canals of traumatic origin present.

Radial section
Perforation plates simple. Intervessel pits medium, alternate, vestured. Vessel-ray pits with distinct borders, similar in shape and size to intervessel pits, slightly enlarged. Ground tissue fibres with simple to minutely bordered pits, thin to thick-walled. Rays homogeneous (all cells slightly procumbent).

Tangential section
Rays 1-2seriate.

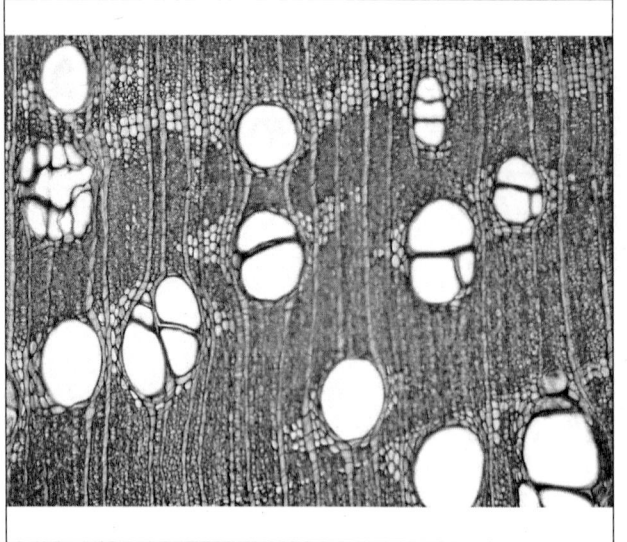
Terminalia arjuna TS x100

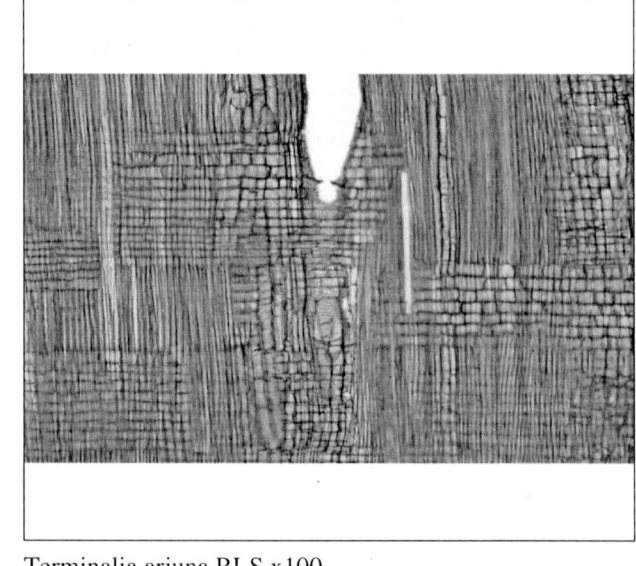
Terminalia arjuna RLS x100

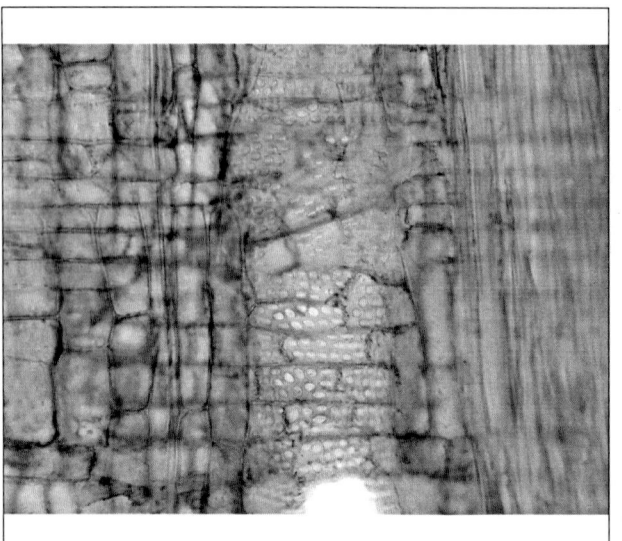
Terminalia arjuna RLS x400

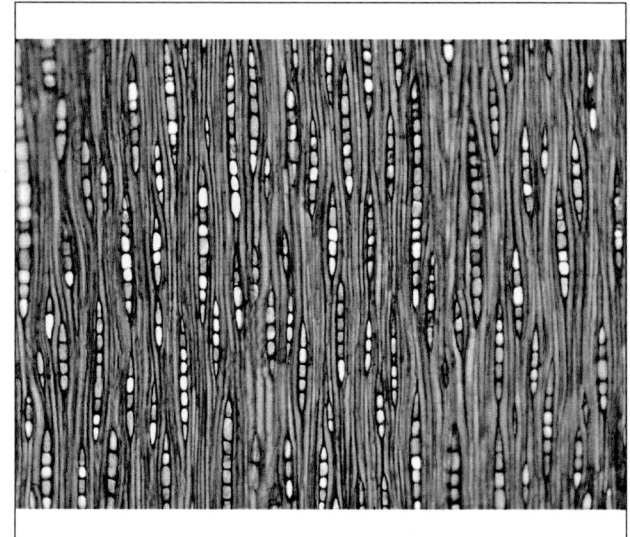
Terminalia arjuna RLS x400

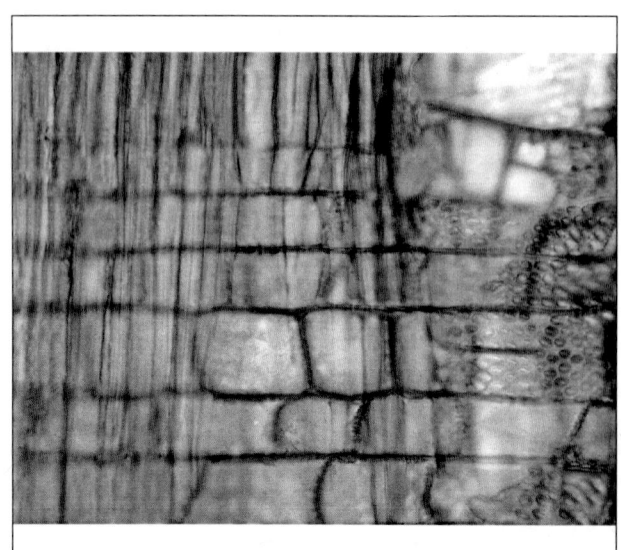
Terminalia paniculata RLS x400

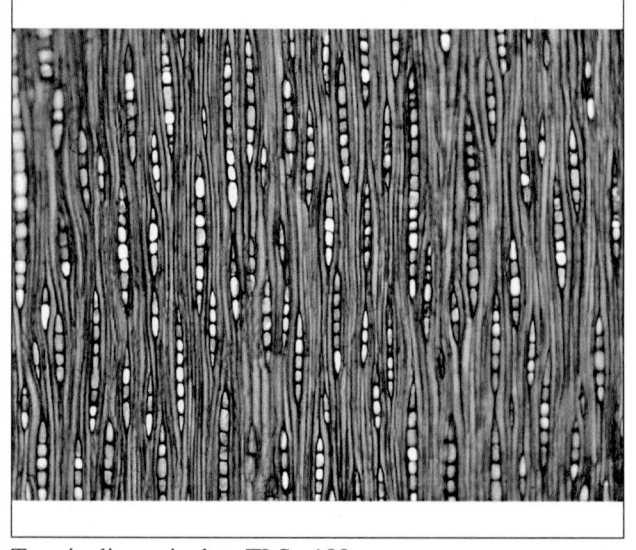
Terminalia paniculata TLS x100

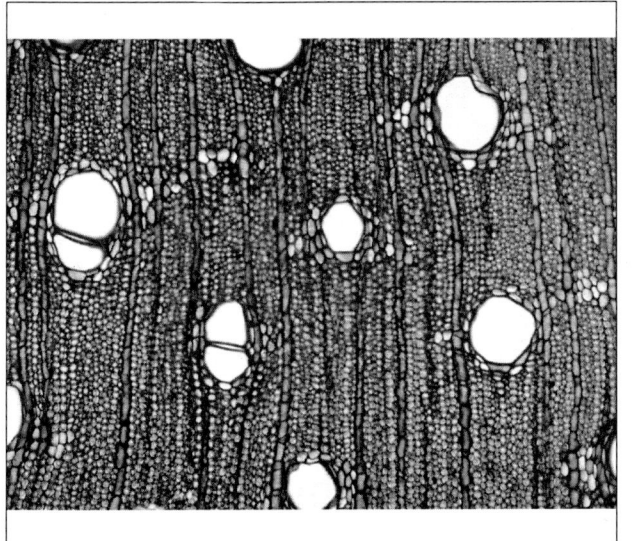

Terminalia paniculata TS x100

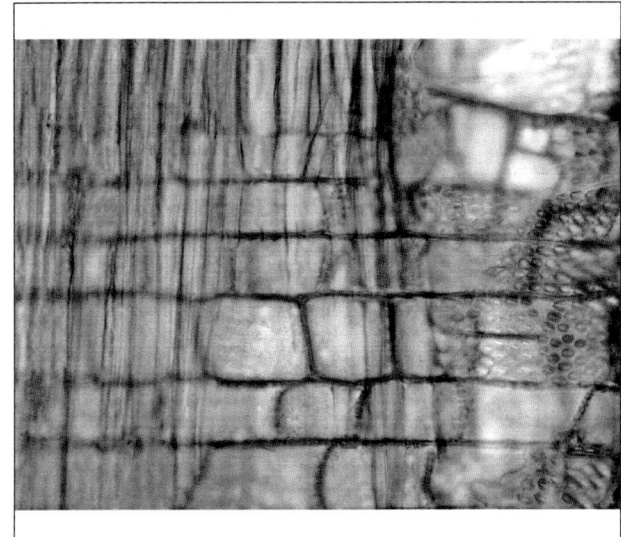

Terminalia paniculata RLS x400

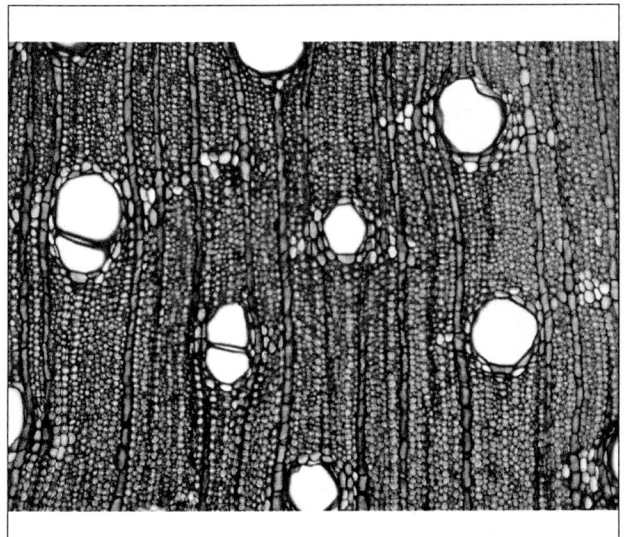

Terminalia paniculata TS x100

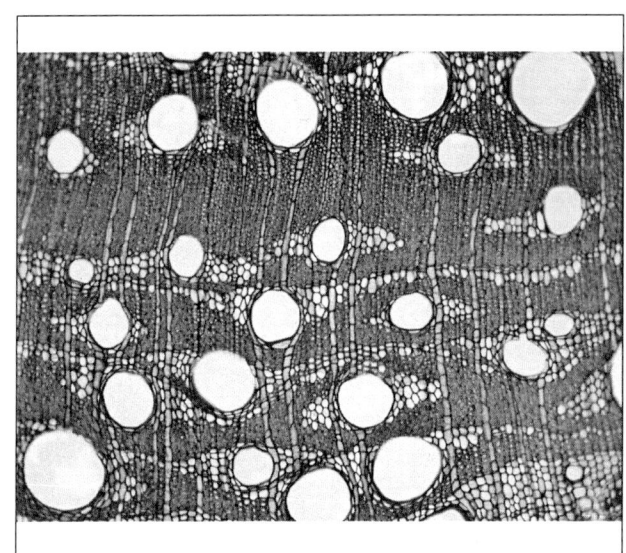

Terminalia tomentosa TS x100

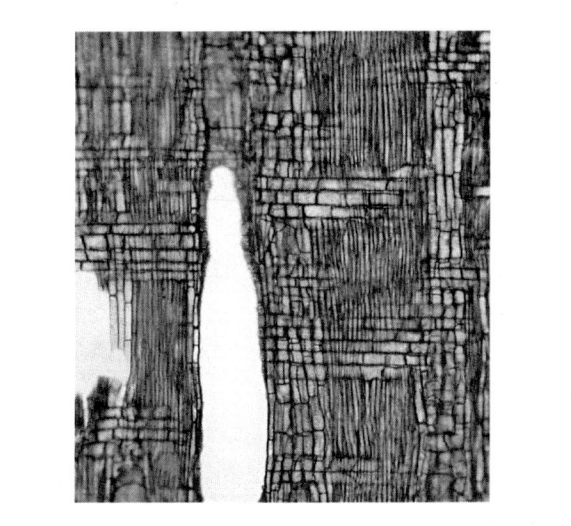

Terminalia tomentosa RLS x100

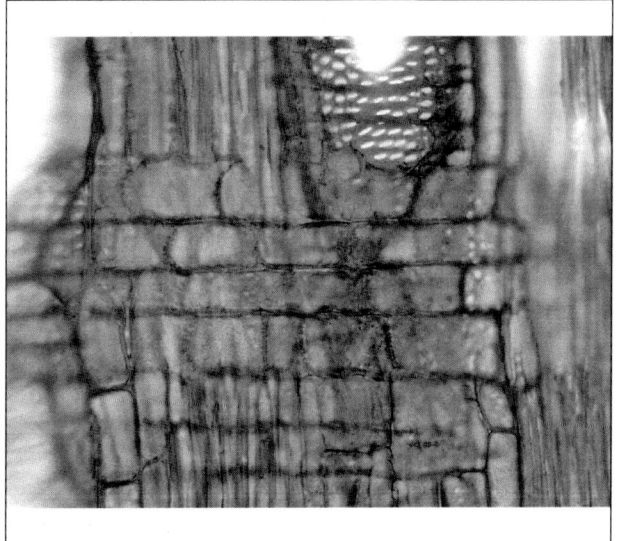

Terminalia tomentosa RLS x400

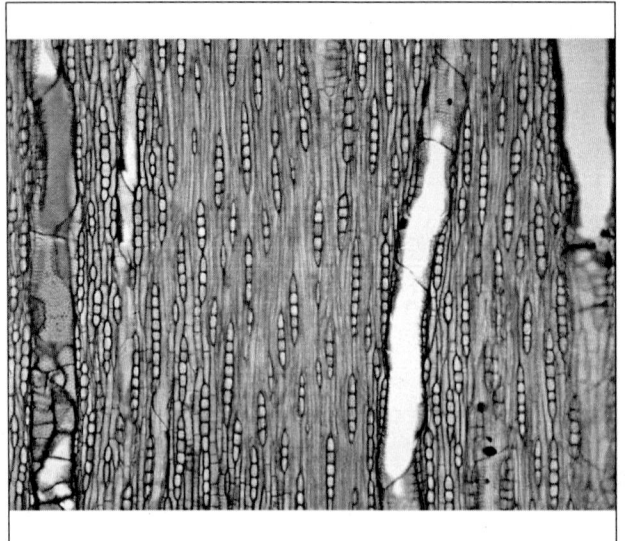
Terminalia tomentosa TLS x100

# DILLENIACEAE

*Dillenia* sp.
(species examined: *D. pentagyna*)

Description:

Transverse section
Diffuse-porous. Ring boundary distinct. Pores small to medium, solitary (normal to angular). Parenchyma apotracheal diffuse and scanty paratracheal.

Radial section
Perforation plates scalariform (c. 15–20 thin bars). Intervessel pits opposite to alternate (often scalariform), medium. Vessel-ray pits with reduced to apparently simple borders-rounded/angular/scalariform. Ground tissue fibres with distinctly bordered pits, thin to thick-walled. Rays homogeneous to heterogeneous (with over 4 rows of square and/or upright marginal cells). Uniseriate rays composed entirely of upright cells.

Tangential section
Rays uniseriate and 4-8(10)seriate, many higher than 1 mm.

Dillenia pentagyna TS x40

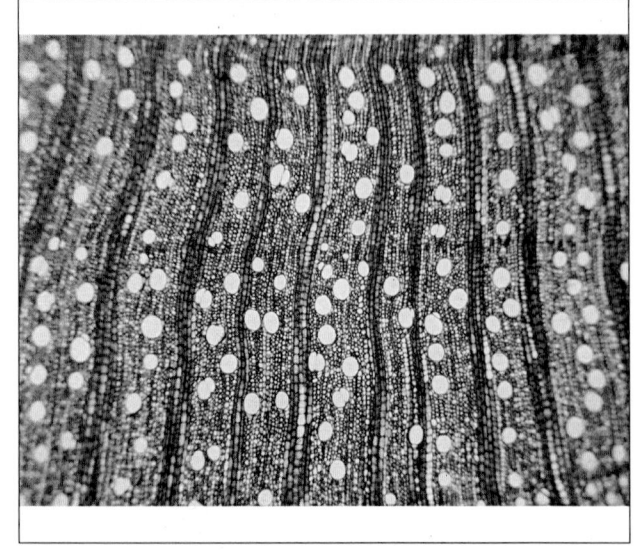
Dillenia pentagyna TS x40

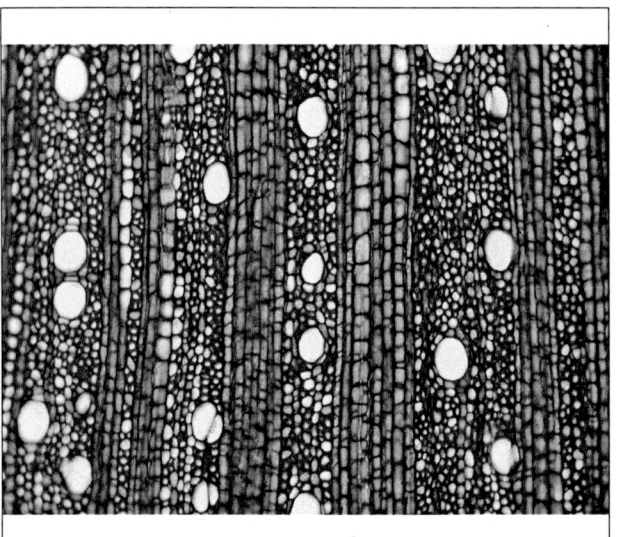
Dillenia pentagyna TS x100

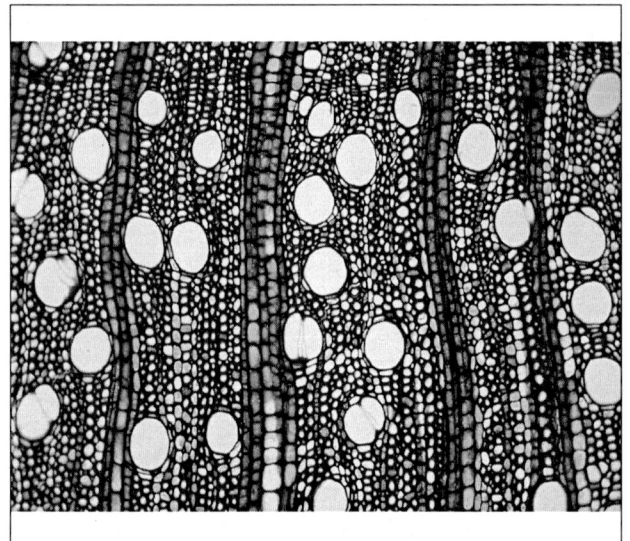
Dillenia pentagyna TS x100

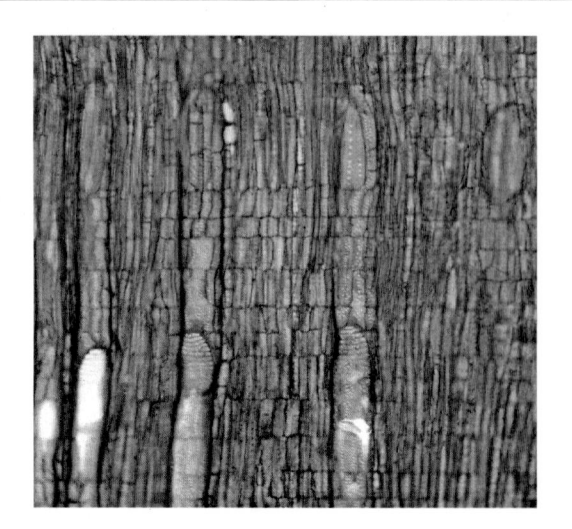
Dillenia pentagyna RLS x100

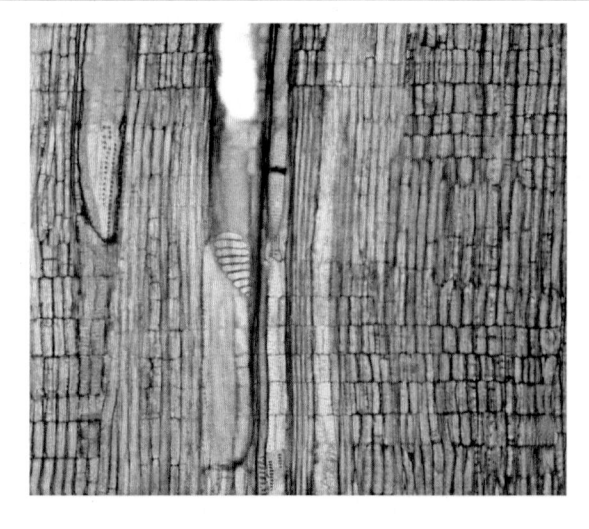
Dillenia pentagyna RLS x100

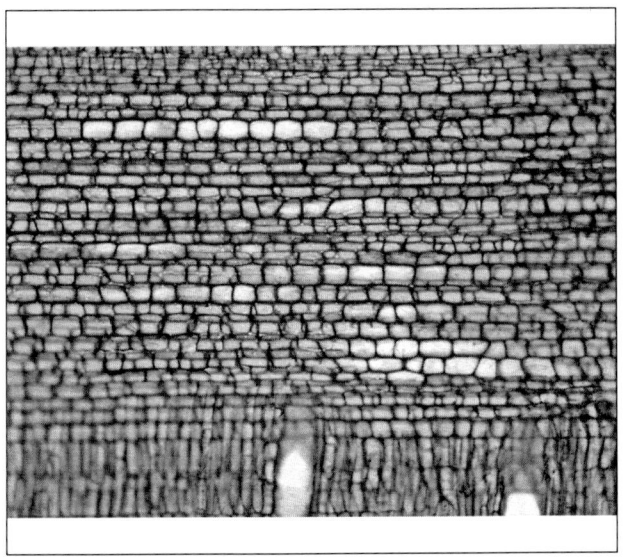

Dillenia pentagyna RLS x100

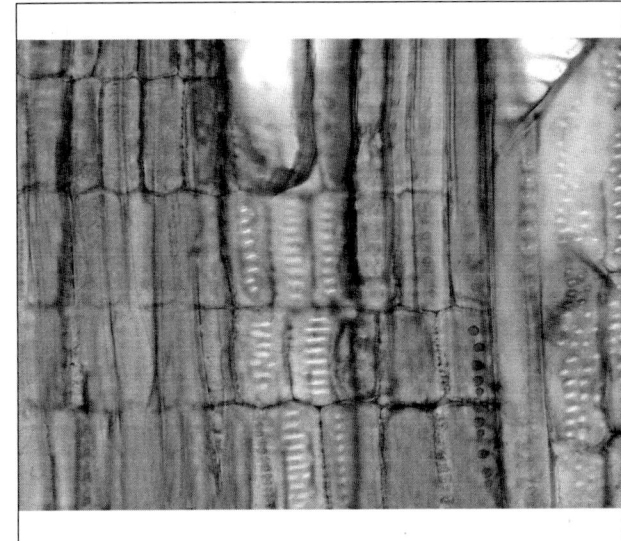

Dillenia pentagyna RLS x400

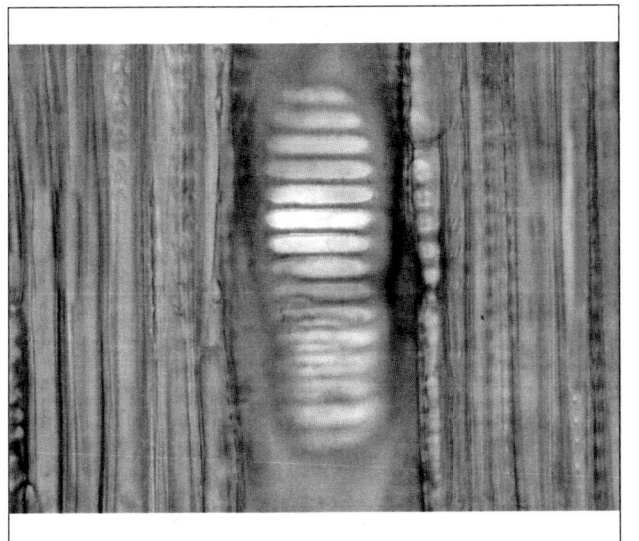

Dillenia pentagyna RLS x400

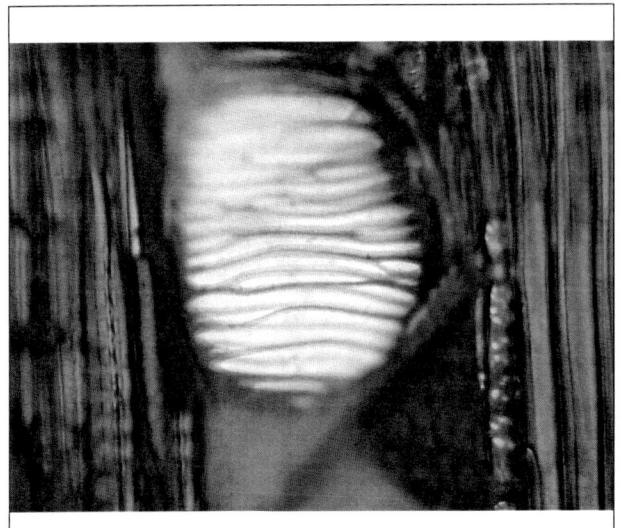

Dillenia pentagyna RLS x630

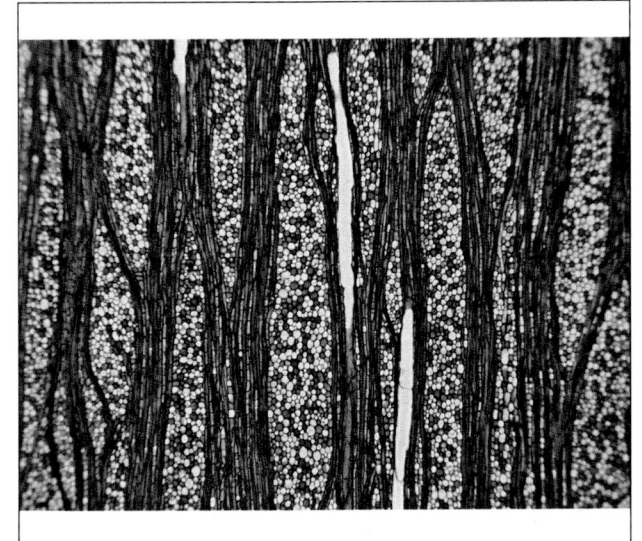

Dillenia pentagyna TLS x40

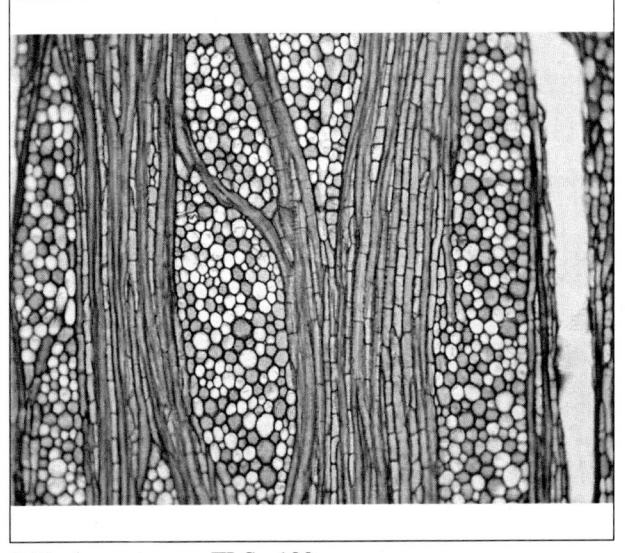

Dillenia pentagyna TLS x100

# DIPTEROCARPACEAE

*Hopea* sp.
(species examined: *H. parviflora*)

Description:

Transverse section
Diffuse-porous. Ring boundary indistinct. Pores small to medium, solitary, in radial multiples of 2(3) and in clusters. Parenchyma paratracheal (aliform, confluent). Axial intercellular canals present (scattered and in long tangential lines).

Radial section
Perforation plates simple. Intervessel pits alternate, small. Vessel-ray pits unilaterally compound and coarse, occasionally scalariform. Ground tissue fibres with simple to minutely bordered pits, thin to thick-walled. Rays heterogeneous. Sheath cells present (resembling tile cells). Crystals present in ray cells.

Tangential section
Rays 2-3(4)seriate.

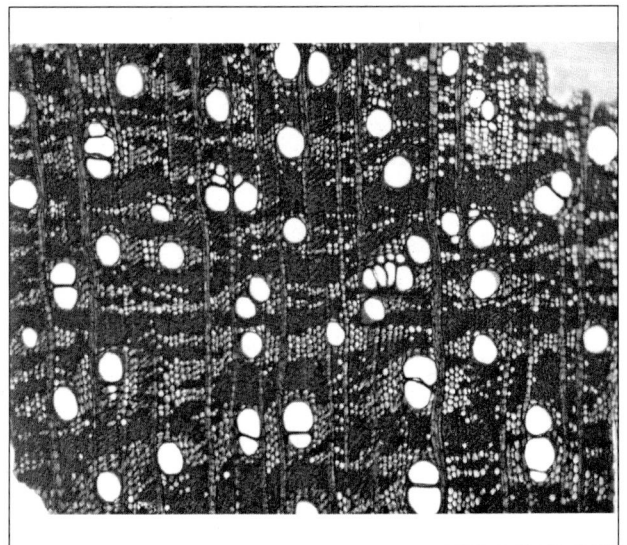
Hopea parviflora TS x100

Hopea parviflora RLS x400

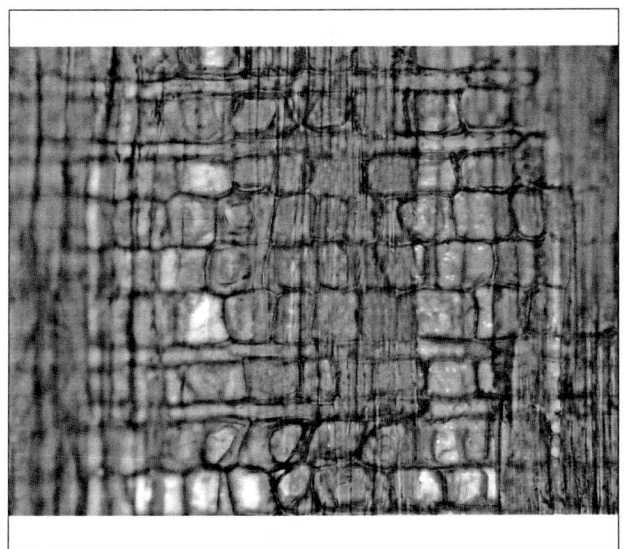
Hopea parviflora RLS x400

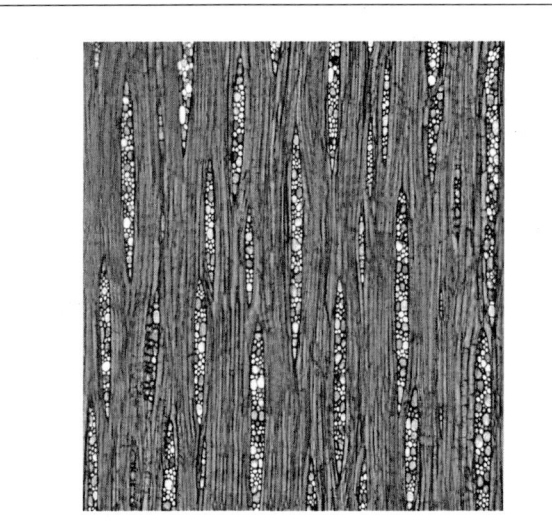
Hopea parviflora TLS x100

# EBENACEAE

*Diospyros* sp.
(species examined: *D. embryopteris*, *D. montana* syn. *D. cordifolia*)

Description:

<u>Transverse section</u>
Diffuse-porous. Ring boundary indistinct. Pores small, in radial multiples of 4 or more (common). Parenchyma apotracheal diffuse, scanty paratracheal and banded (narrow bands 1–2 cells wide).

<u>Radial section</u>
Perforation plates simple. Intervessel pits alternate, minute. Vessel-ray pits with distinct borders, similar in shape, size to intervessel pits. Ground tissue fibres with simple to minutely bordered pits, moderately thick-walled. Rays heterogeneous, with over 4 rows of square and/or upright marginal cells. Crystals present in ray cells.

<u>Tangential section</u>
Rays 1(2)seriate.

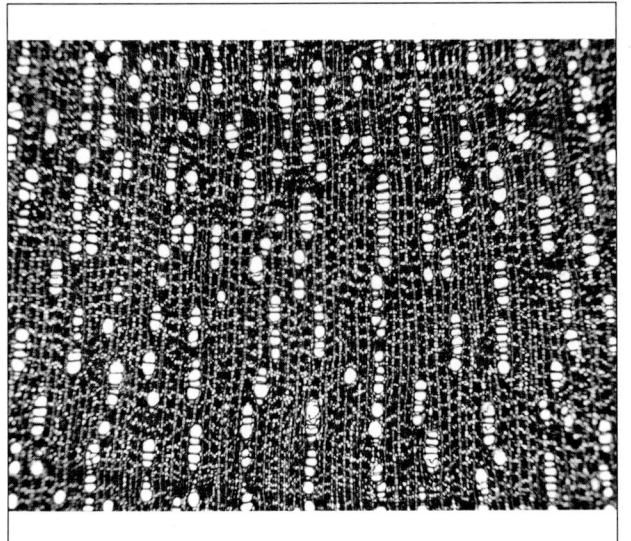
Diospyros cordifolia TS x40

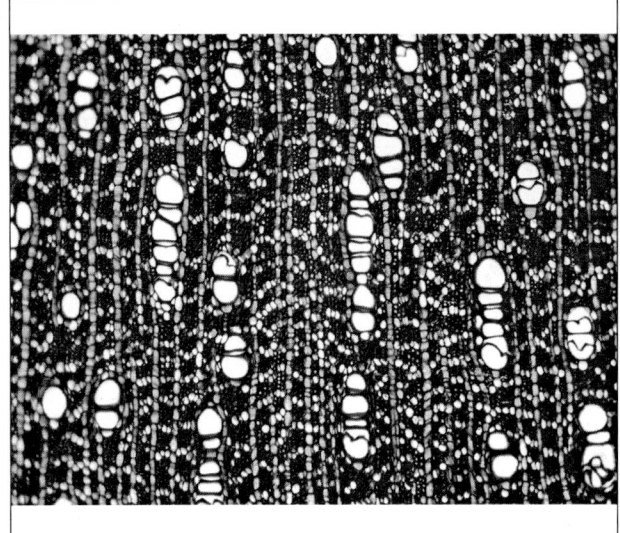
Diospyros cordifolia TS x100

Diospyros cordifolia RLS x100

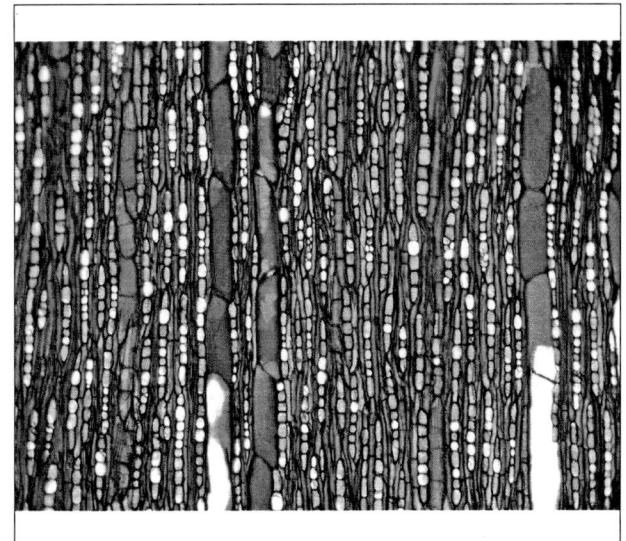
Diospyros cordifolia TLS x100

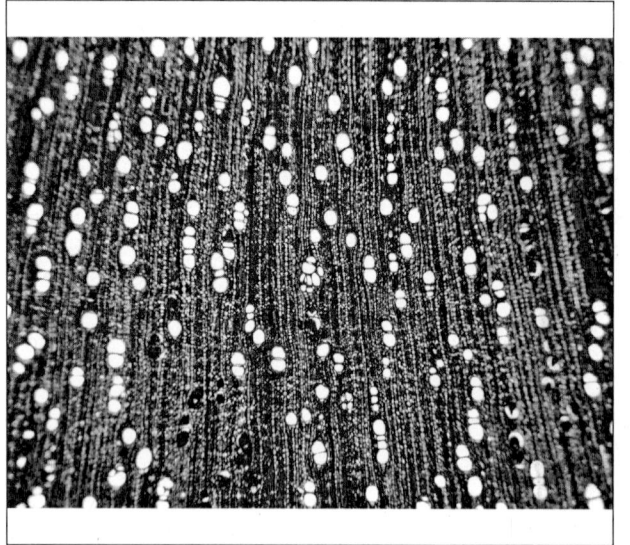

Diospyros embryopteris TS x40

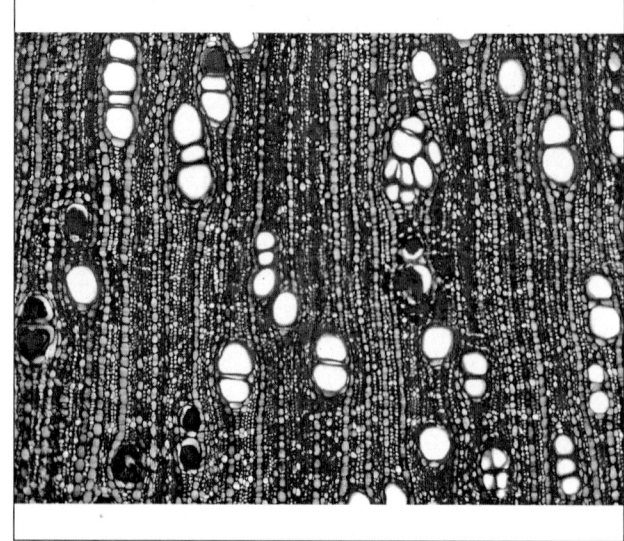

Diospyros embryopteris TS x100

Diospyros embryopteris RLS x100

Diospyros embryopteris RLS x400

Diospyros embryopteris RLS x400

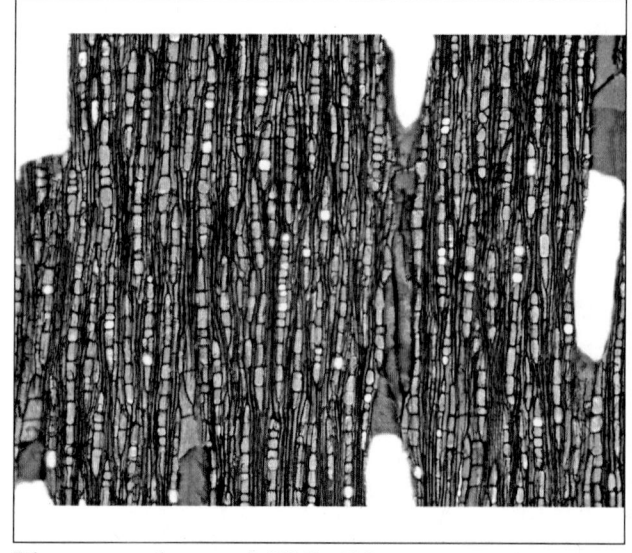

Diospyros embryopteris TLS x100

# EHRETIACEAE
(form. under Boraginaceae)

*Cordia* sp.
(species examined: *C. myxa*)

Description:

<u>Transverse section</u>
Diffuse-porous. Ring boundary indistinct. Pores medium to large, solitary, in radial multiples of 2 and in clusters. Parenchyma paratracheal (aliform, confluent) and apotracheal (banded; bands >3 cells wide).

<u>Radial section</u>
Perforation plates simple. Intervessel pits alternate, small, coalescent. Vessel-ray pits with distinct borders/similar in shape, size to intervessel pits (some elongated pits are occasionally present). Ground tissue fibres with simple to minutely bordered pits, thin to thick-walled. Septate fibres occasionally present. Rays heterogeneous with a central portion of procumbent cells and 2–4 (occasionally more) rows of upright and square marginal cells.

<u>Tangential section</u>
Rays 3-4seriate. Sheath cells present.

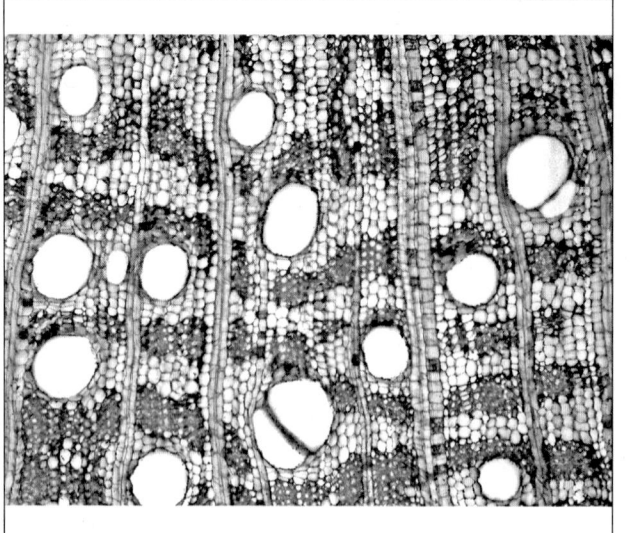

Cordia myxa TS x100

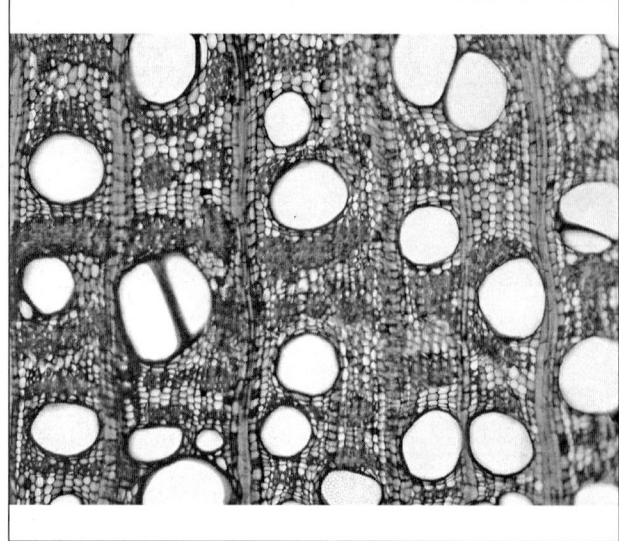

Cordia myxa TS x100

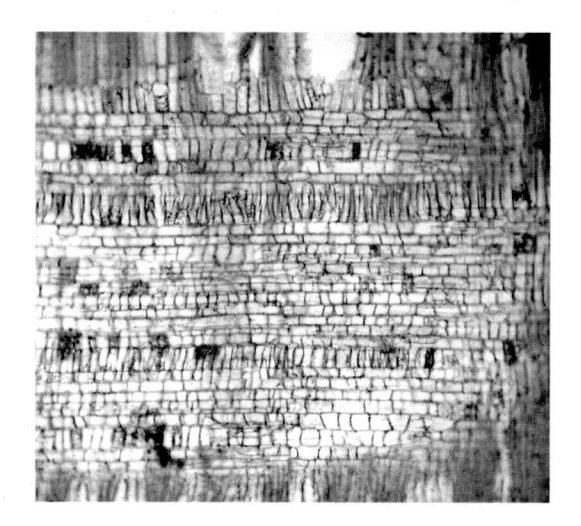

Cordia myxa TS x100

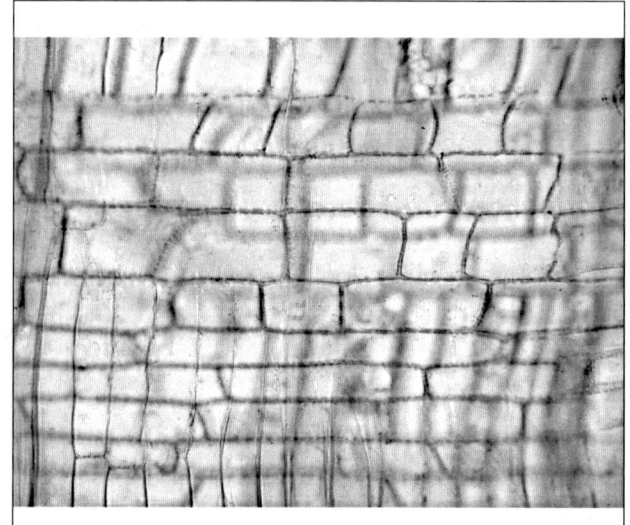

Cordia myxa RLS x400

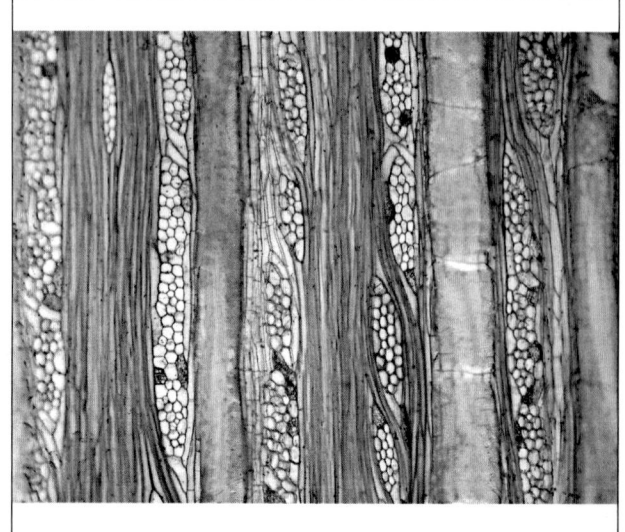

Cordia myxa TLS x100

# EUPHORBIACEAE

*Cicca* sp.
(species examined: *C. acida*)

Description:

Transverse section
Diffuse-porous. Ring boundary distinct to indistinct. Pores medium, in radial multiples of (2-3)4 or more (common) and in clusters (occasional). Parenchyma rare, apotracheal (diffuse) and scanty paratracheal (rare).

Radial section
Perforation plates scalariform (occasionally foraminate and reticulate). Intervessel pits alternate, minute. Vessel-ray pits with reduced to apparently simple borders-horizontal (scalariform, gashlike) to vertical (palisade). Ground tissue fibres with simple to minutely bordered pits. Rays heterogeneous, with over 4 rows of square and upright marginal cells. Uniseriate rays composed entirely of upright cells. Crystals present in ray cells.

Tangential section
Rays (1)2-(3)4seriate.

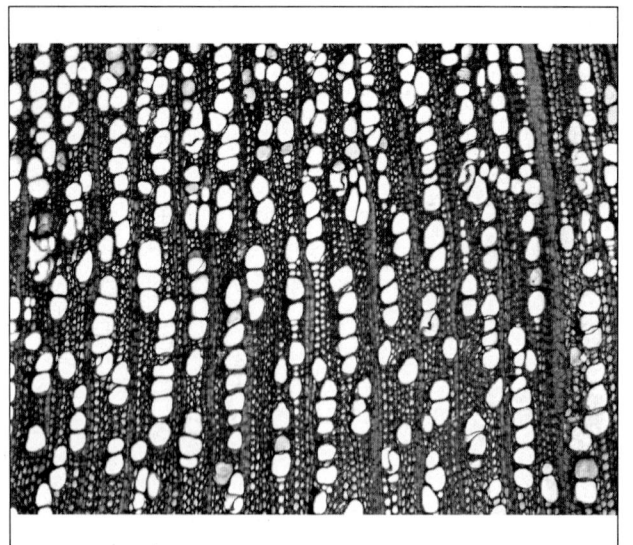
Cicca acida TS x100

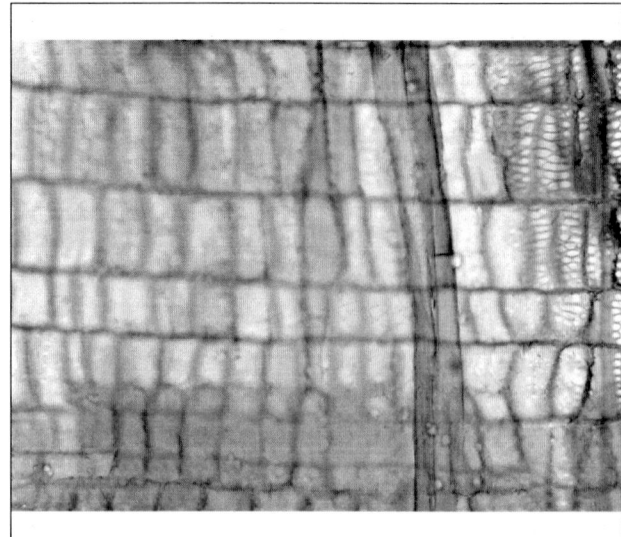
Cicca acida RLS x400

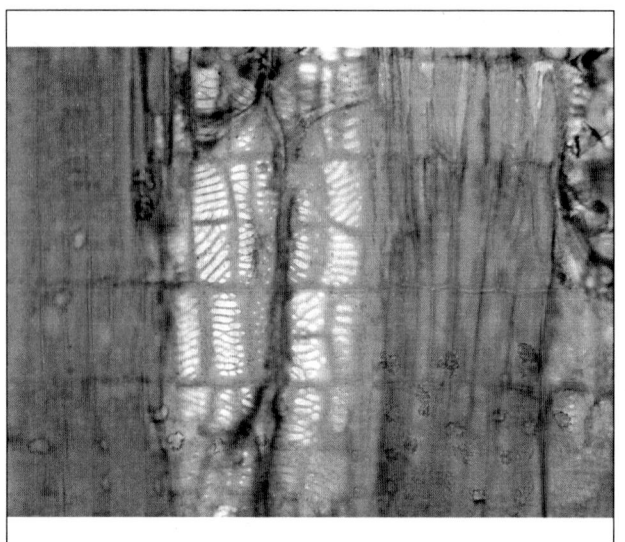
Cicca acida RLS x400

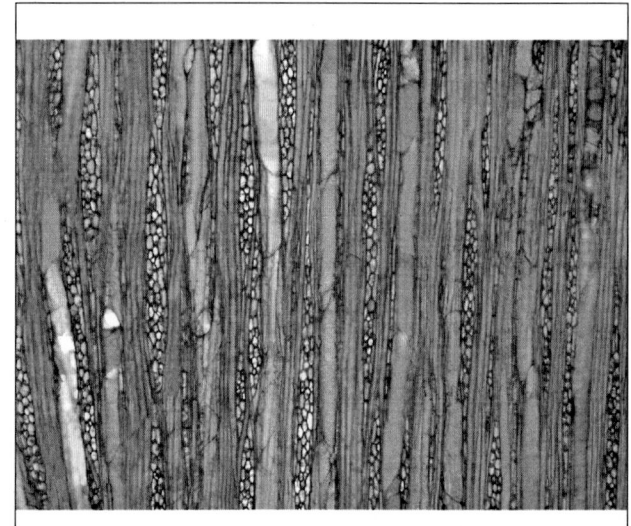
Cicca acida TLS x100

# EUPHORBIACEAE

*Mallotus* sp.
(species examined: *M. philippensis*)

Description:

Transverse section
Diffuse-porous. Ring boundary indistinct. Pores in radial multiples of 4 or more common, larger pores usually in radial multiples of 2–4. Parenchyma apotracheal (diffuse and banded in uni- to biseriate bands) and scanty paratracheal (rare).

Radial section
Perforation plates simple (foraminate plates rare). Intervessel pits alternate to opposite, medium to large. Vessel-ray pits with reduced to apparently simple borders, scalariform. Ground tissue fibres with simple to minutely bordered pits, thick-walled. Rays heterogeneous, with over 4 rows of upright and square marginal cells. Perforated ray cells present. Crystals present in ray cells. Intercellular canals of traumatic origin present.

Tangential section
Rays (1)2-3seriate (with uni- and multiseriate portions).

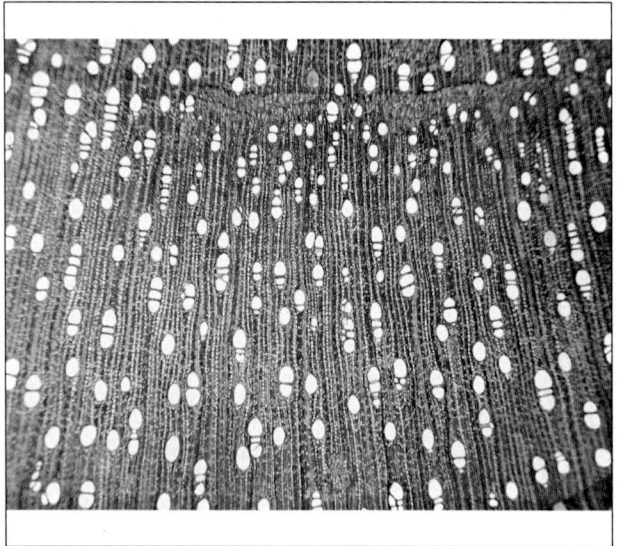

Mallotus philippensis TS x40

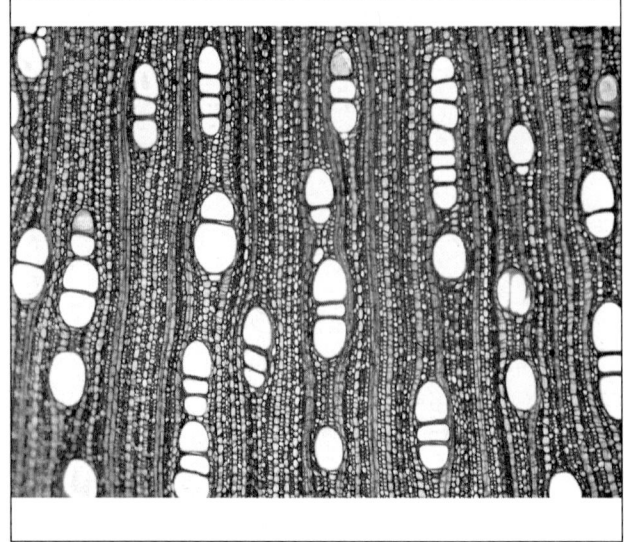

Mallotus philippensis TS x100

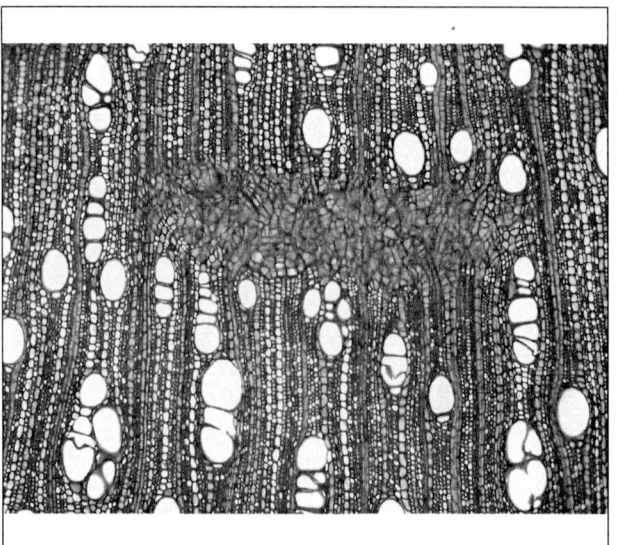

Mallotus philippensis TS x100

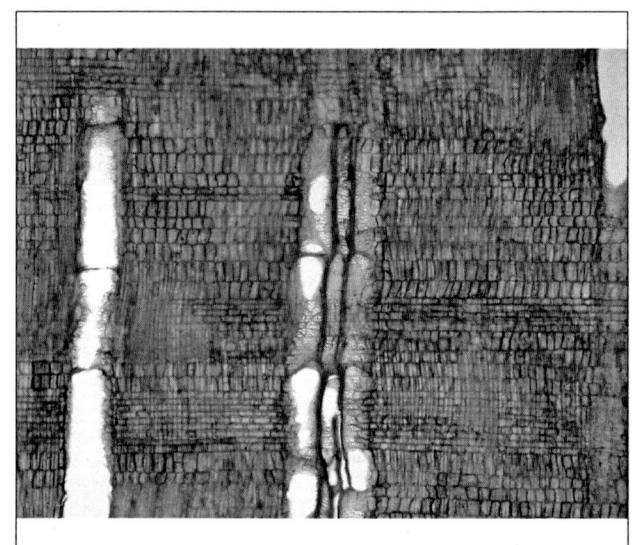

Mallotus philippensis RLS x100

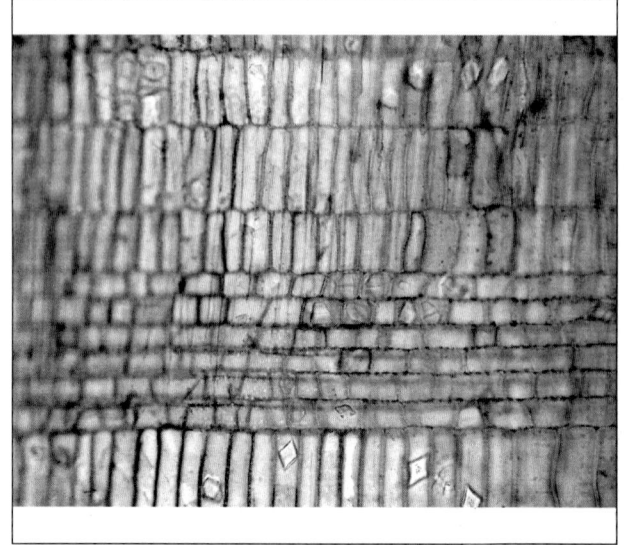

Mallotus philippensis RLS x400

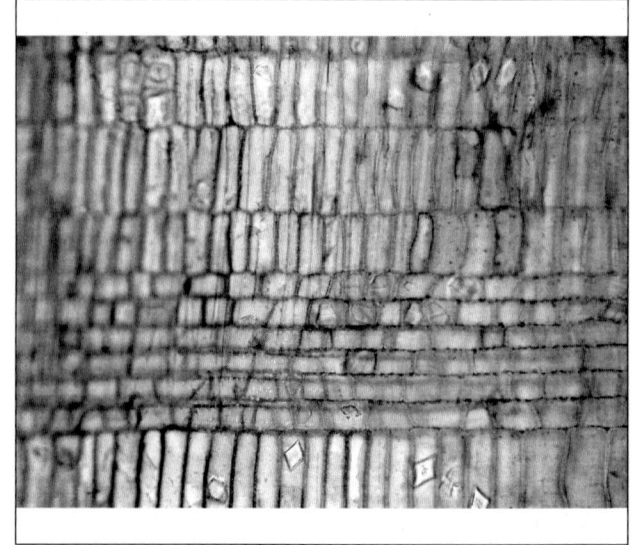

Mallotus philippensis RLS x400

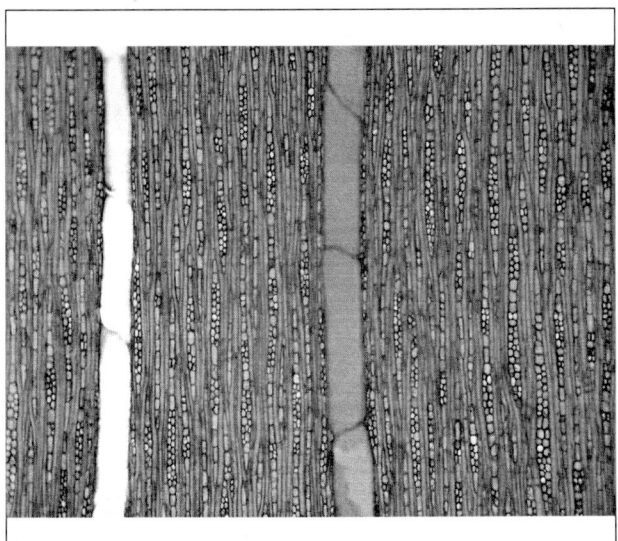

Mallotus philippensis TLS x100

# EUPHORBIACEAE

*Phyllanthus* sp.
(species examined: *P. emblica*)

Description:

Transverse section
Diffuse-porous. Ring boundary indistinct. Pores medium, in radial multiples of 2–4 or more, irregular clusters and solitary (angular, rare). Parenchyma rare, apotracheal (diffuse) and scanty paratracheal.

Radial section
Perforation plates simple and scalariform. Intervessel pits alternate, minute. Vessel-ray pits with reduced to apparently simple borders-horizontal (scalariform, gashlike) to vertical (palisade). Ground tissue fibres with simple to minutely bordered pits, moderately thick-walled. Rays heterogeneous, with procumbent, square and upright cells mixed throughout. Uniseriate rays composed entirely of upright cells. Perforated ray cells present. Crystals present in ray cells.

Tangential section
Rays (3)4-10seriate. Sheath cells present.

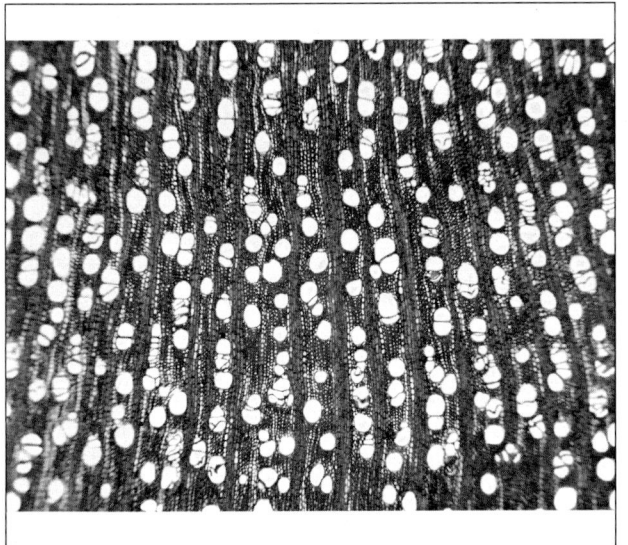
Phyllanthus emblica TS x40

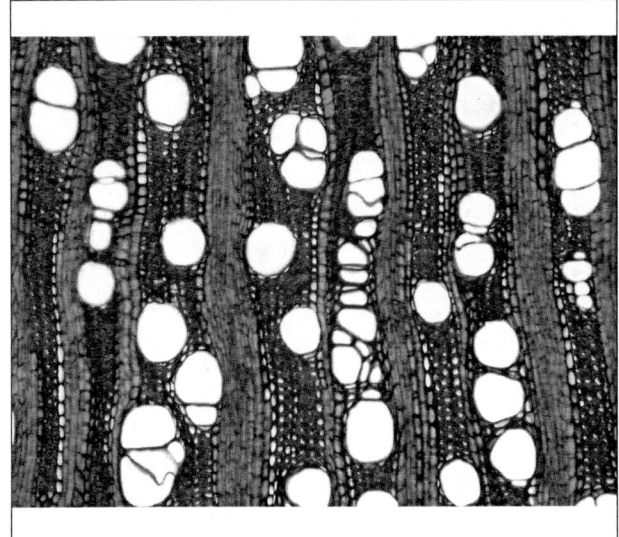
Phyllanthus emblica TS x100

Phyllanthus emblica RLS x100

Phyllanthus emblica RLS x400

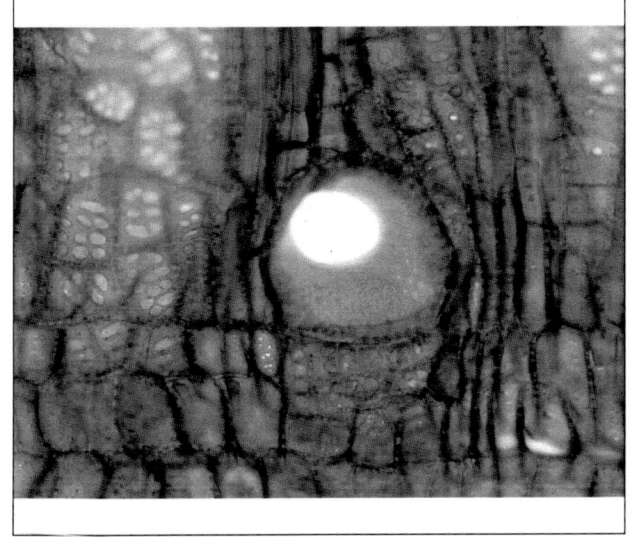
Phyllanthus emblica RLS x400

Phyllanthus emblica TLS x40

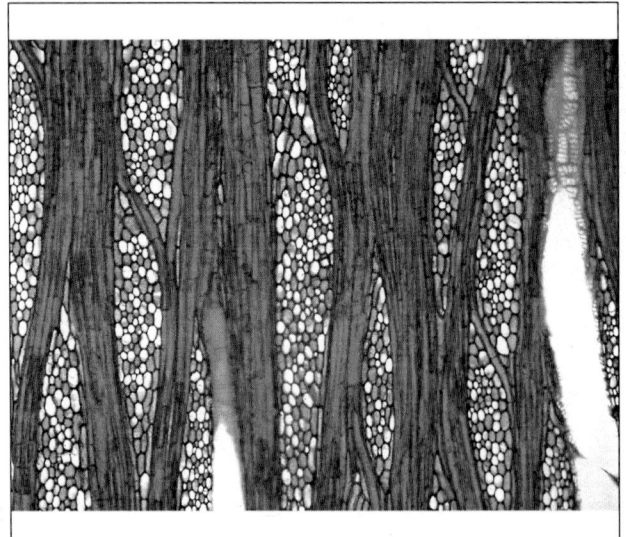
Phyllanthus emblica TLS x100

# EUPHORBIACEAE

*Securinega* (*Fluggea*) sp.
(species examined: *S. leucopyrus*)

Description:

Transverse section
Diffuse-porous. Ring boundary distinct to indistinct. Pores medium to small, in radial files of (2-3)4 or more (common) and in clusters. Parenchyma rare, apotracheal (diffuse), and scanty paratracheal (rare).

Radial section
Perforation plates simple. Intervessel pits alternate, minute. Vessel-ray pits with reduced to apparently simple borders, horizontal (scalariform, gashlike) to vertical (palisade). Ground tissue fibres with simple to minutely bordered pits, thin- to thick-walled. Rays heterogeneous, with few rows of procumbent cells and multiple rows of upright and square marginal cells. Uniseriate rays composed entirely of upright cells.

Tangential section
Rays 1(2)-3(4)seriate. Sheath cells present.

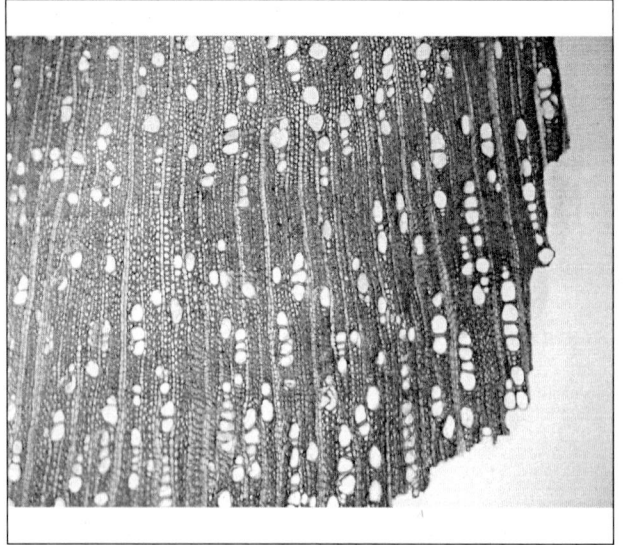
Securinega leucopyrus TS x100

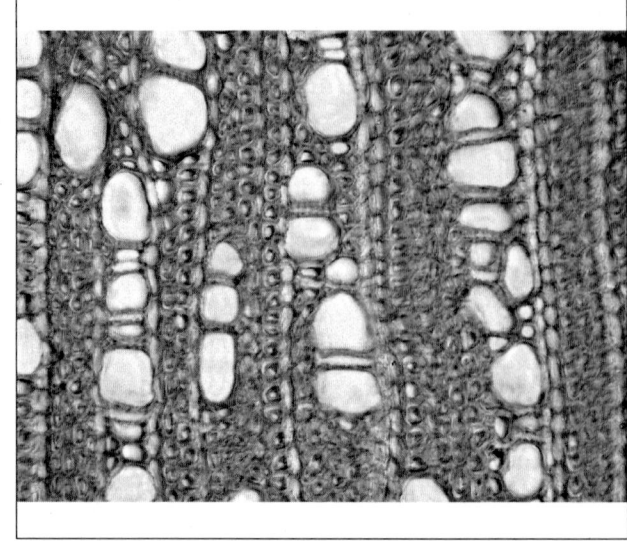
Securinega leucopyrus TS x400

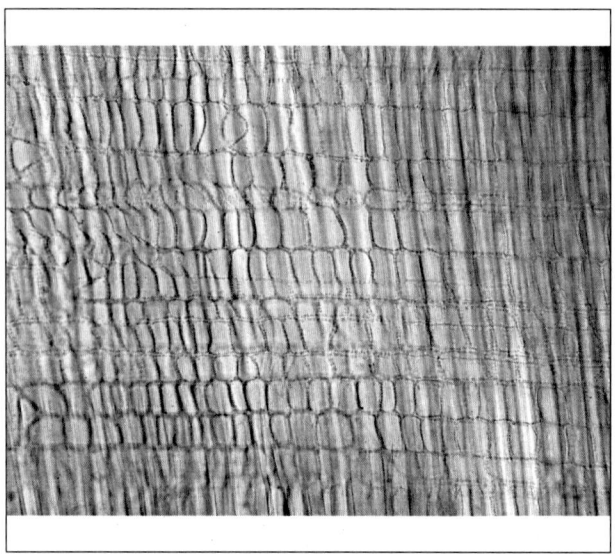
Securinega leucopyrus RLS x400

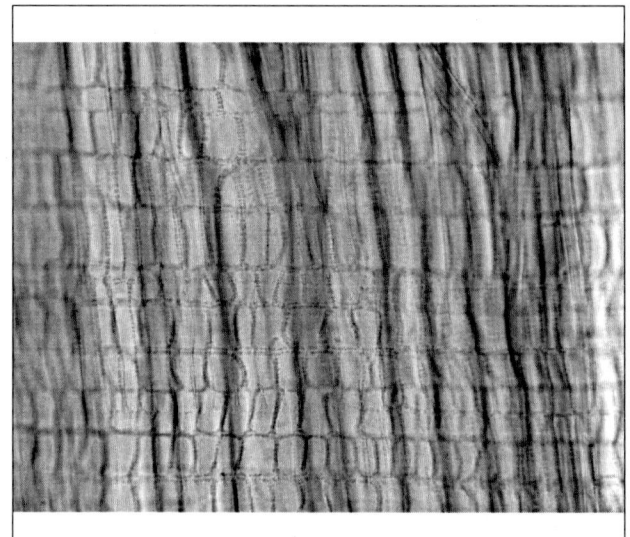
Securinega leucopyrus RLS x400

Securinega leucopyrus TLS x100

# HERNANDIACEAE
(form. under Combretaceae)

*Gyrocarpus* sp.
(species examined: *G. americanus*)

Description:

<u>Transverse section</u>
Diffuse porous. Ring boundary distinct. Pores medium, solitary (angular) and in radial multiples of 2–3. Parenchyma paratracheal (aliform winged with narrow sheath, confluent) and scanty paratracheal.

<u>Radial section</u>
Perforation plates simple. Intervessel pits medium alternate to opposite, occasionally coalescent. Vessel-ray pits with reduced to apparently simple borders, horizontal (scalariform, gashlike) to vertical (palisade), and of two distinct sizes in the same ray cell. Ground tissue fibres with simple to minutely bordered pits, thin-walled. Rays homogeneous.

<u>Tangential section</u>
Rays 1-2(3)seriate, short (uniseriate rays very short).

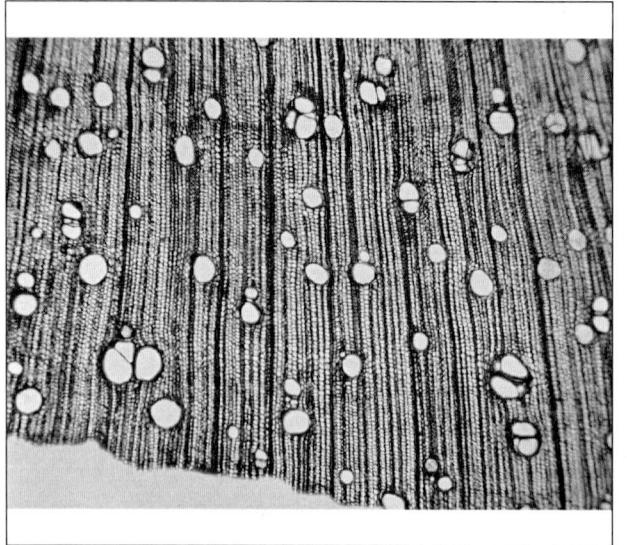
Gyrocarpus americanus TS x40

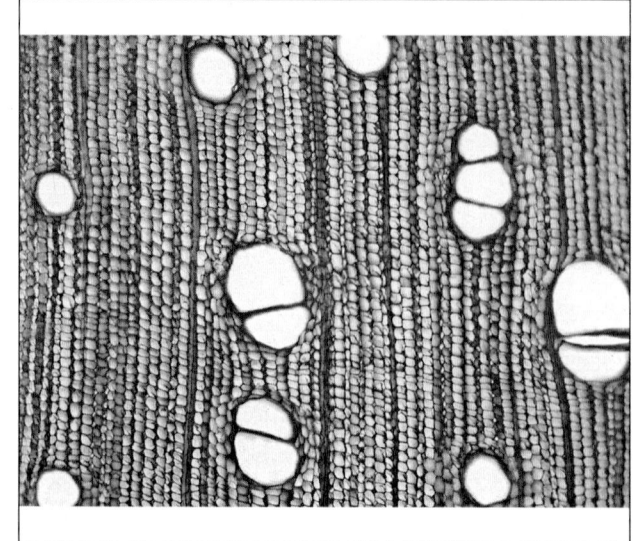
Gyrocarpus americanus TS x100

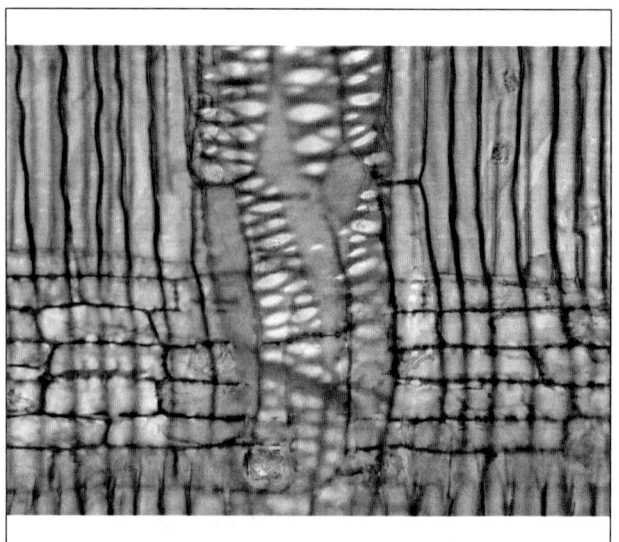
Gyrocarpus americanus RLS x400

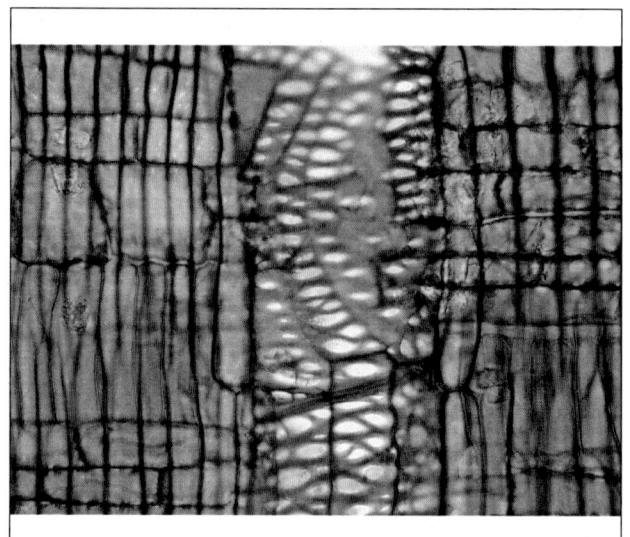
Gyrocarpus americanus RLS x400

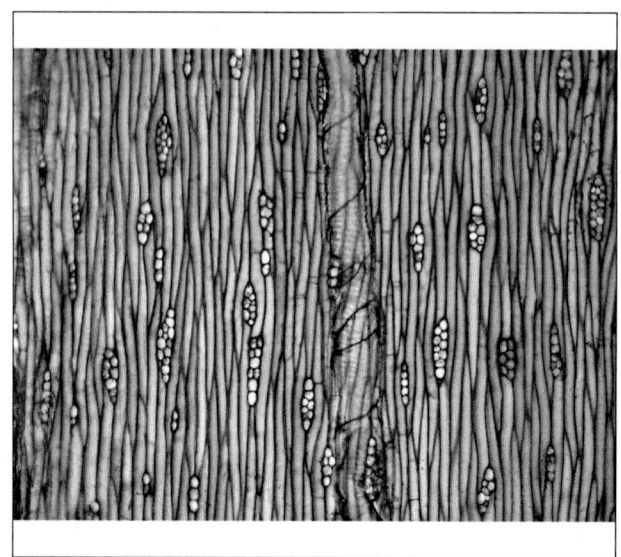
Gyrocarpus americanus TLS x100

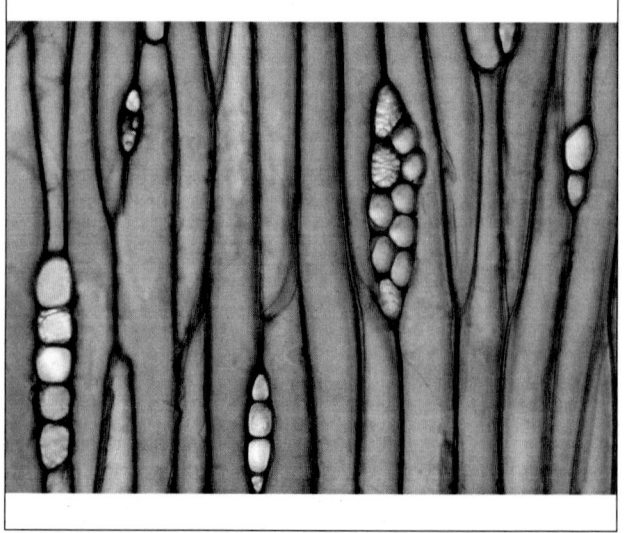
Gyrocarpus americanus TLS x400

# LAURACEAE

*Cinnamomum* sp.
(species examined: *C. zeylanicum*)

Description:

Transverse section
Diffuse porous. Ring boundary distinct. Pores medium, solitary (angular), in radial multiples of 2–3 (common) and in clusters. Parenchyma paratracheal and unilateral paratracheal.

Radial section
Perforation plates simple and scalariform. Intervessel pits alternate, medium. Vessel-ray pits with simple borders, scalariform. Ground tissue fibres with simple to minutely bordered pits, thin- to thick-walled. Septate fibres present. Rays with a central portion of procumbent cells and 1 or more rows of upright and/or square marginal cells. Perforated ray cells present.

Tangential section
Rays (2)3-4seriate.

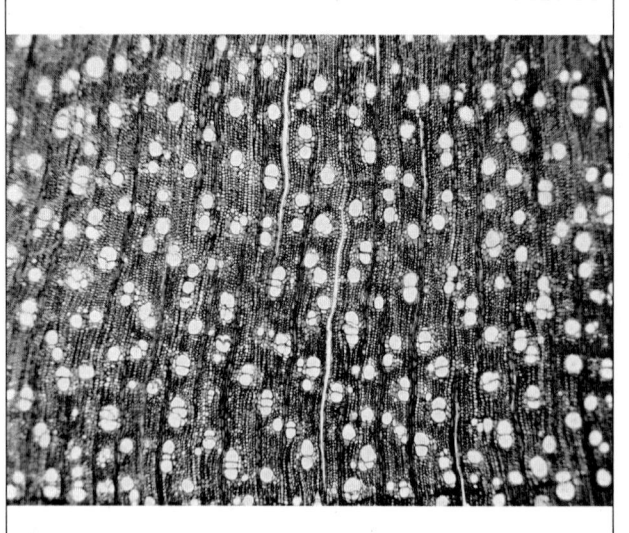
Cinnamomum zeylanicum TS x40

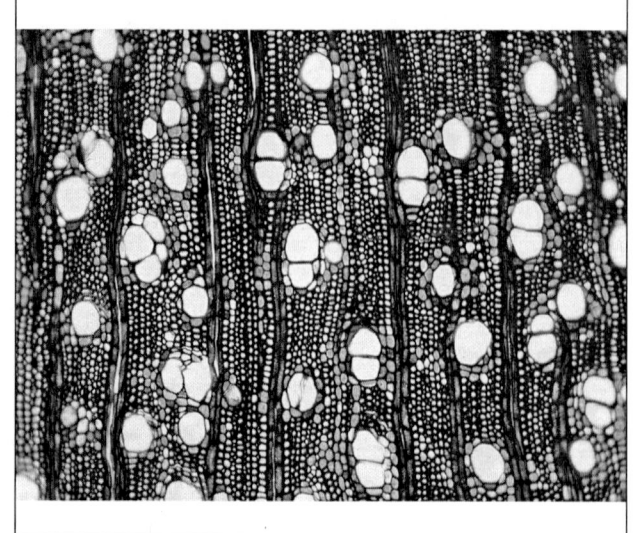
Cinnamomum zeylanicum TS x100

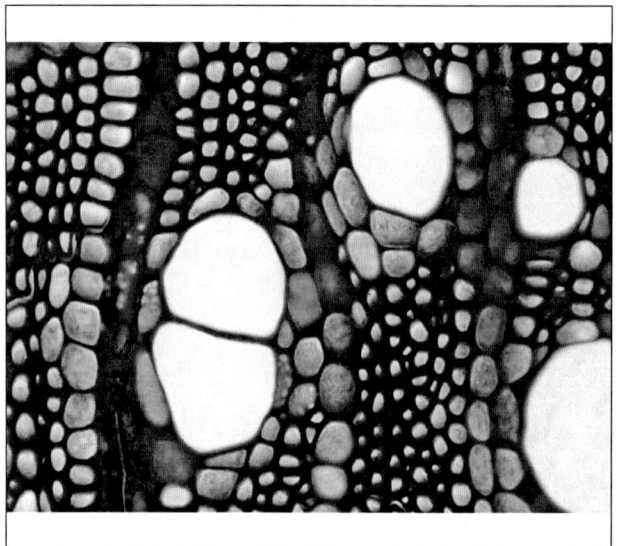
Cinnamomum zeylanicum TS x400

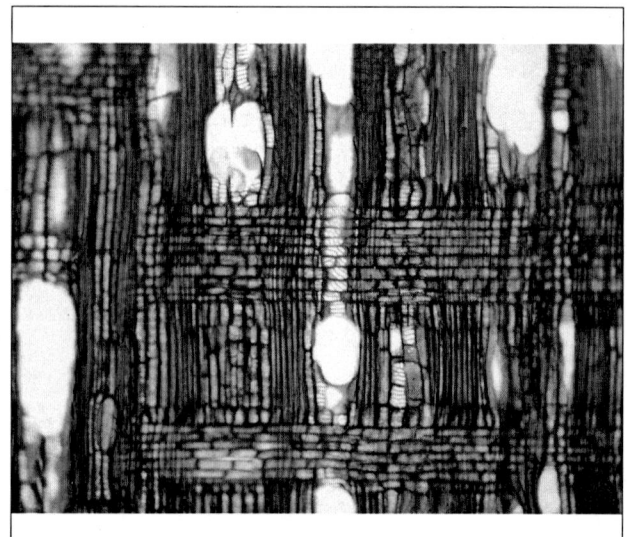
Cinnamomum zeylanicum RLS x100

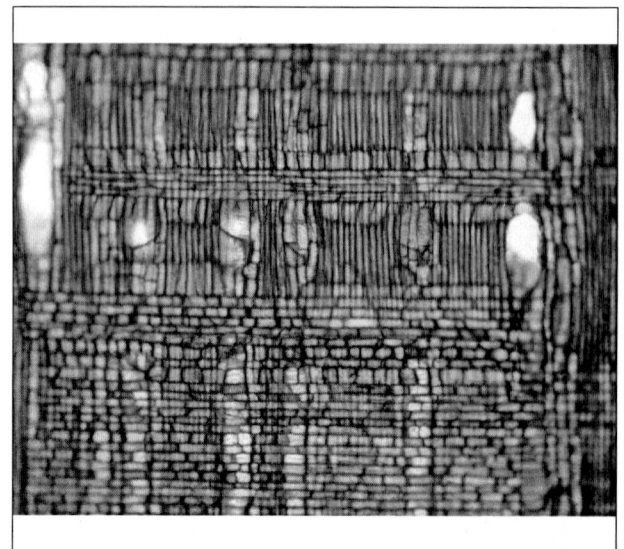
Cinnamomum zeylanicum RLS x100

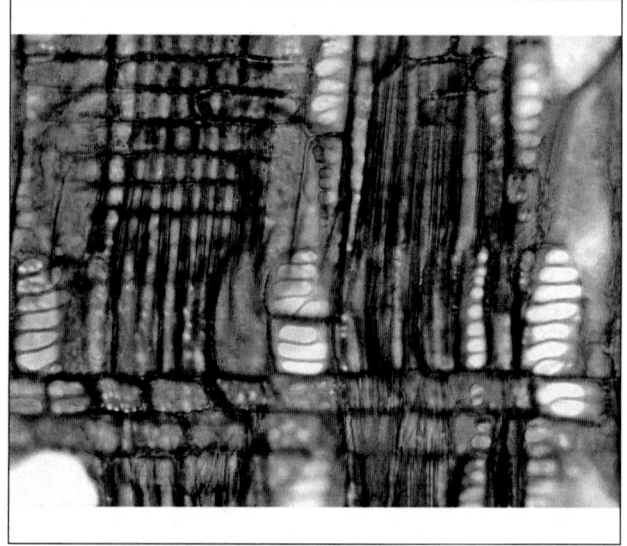
Cinnamomum zeylanicum RLS x400

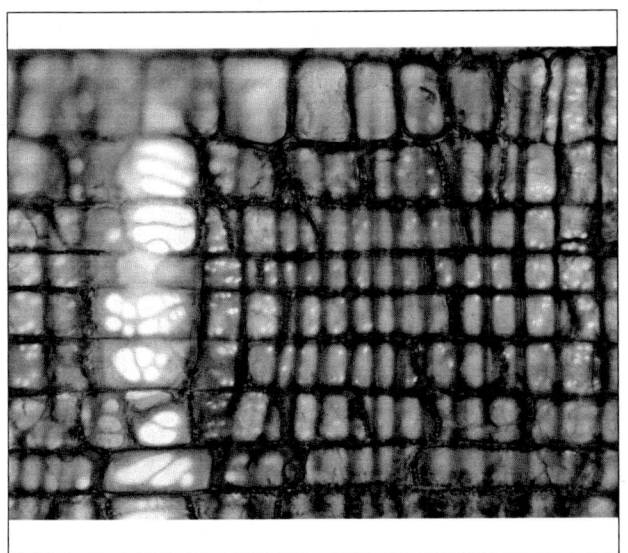
Cinnamomum zeylanicum RLS x400

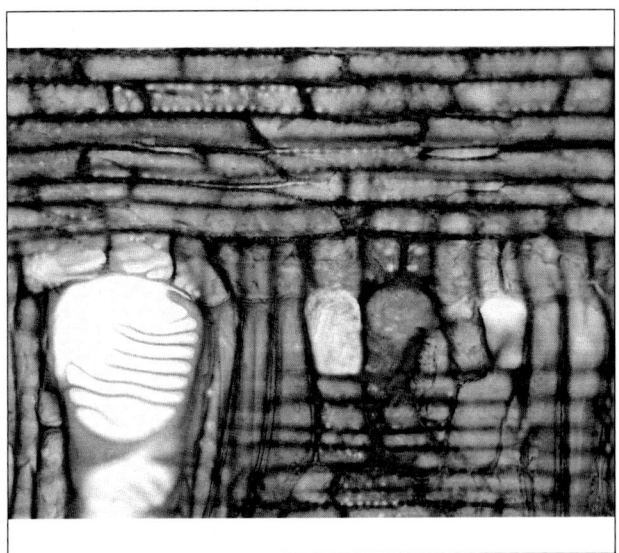
Cinnamomum zeylanicum RLS x400

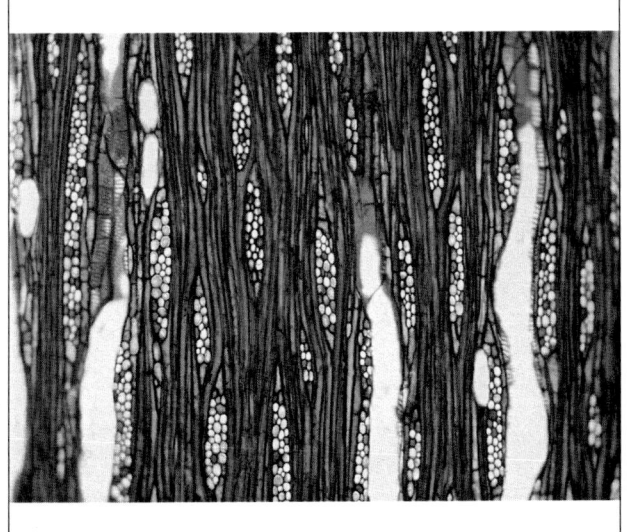
Cinnamomum zeylanicum TLS x100

# LEGUMINOSAE – CAESALPINIACEAE

*Bauhinia* sp.
(species examined: *B. racemosa*, *B. variegata*)

Description:

Transverse section
Diffuse-porous. Ring boundary indistinct. Pores medium to large, solitary, in radial multiples of 2–4 (sometimes more, as tails to larger pores), and clusters (together with smaller pores). Parenchyma banded (bands generally 3–5 cells wide, sometimes discontinuous, scalariform) and paratracheal (aliform-winged, confluent). Intercellular canals of traumatic origins occasionally present.

Radial section
Perforation plates simple. Intervessel pits alternate to opposite, medium. Vestured pits absent. Vessel-ray pits with reduced to apparently simple borders- rounded/angular. Fibres with simple to minutely bordered pits, thick-walled. Rays homogeneous to heterogeneous, with 1–4 or more rows of square marginal cells. Crystals present in ray cells, axial parenchyma and fibres (sometimes forming short chains).

Tangential section
Uniseriate rays. Aggregate rays may be present sometimes (irregularly shaped, short).

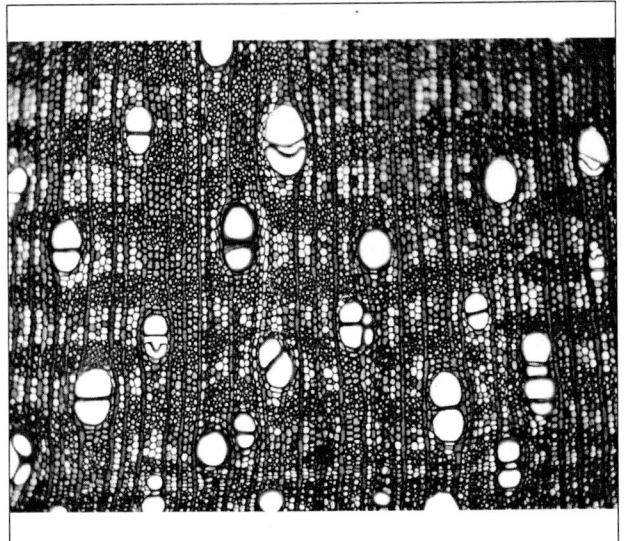
Bauhinia racemosa TS x100

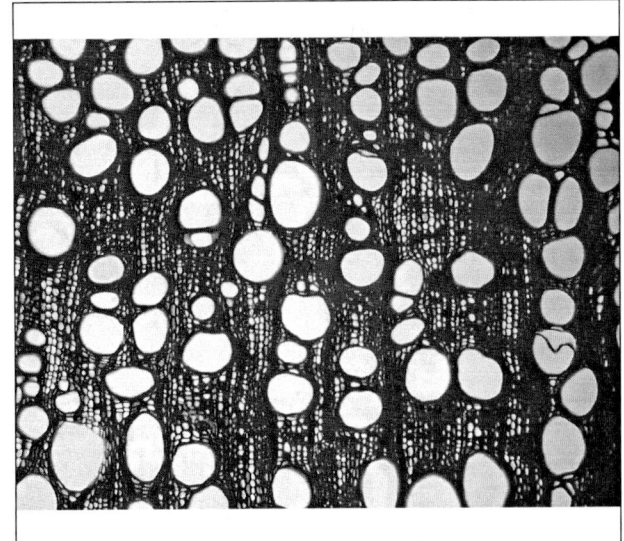
Bauhinia racemosa TS x100

Bauhinia racemosa RLS x100

Bauhinia racemosa RLS x400

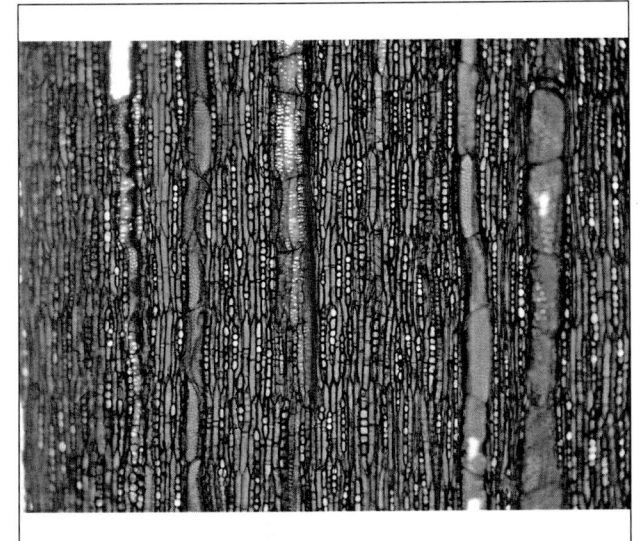
Bauhinia racemosa TLS x100

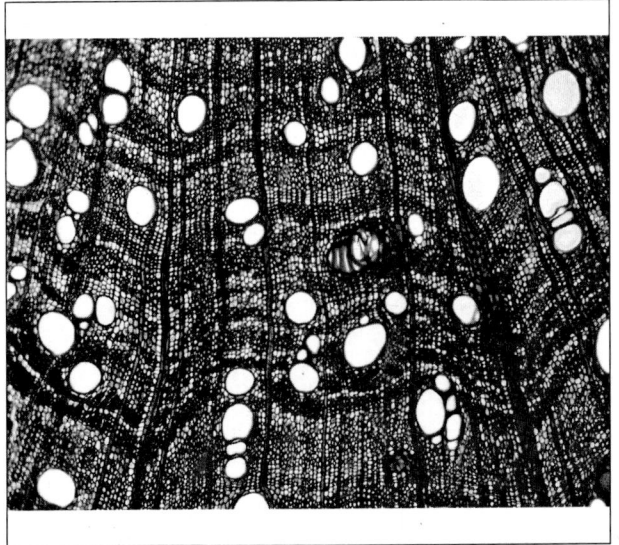
Bauhinia variegata TS x100

# LEGUMINOSAE – CAESALPINIACEAE

*Cassia* sp.
(species examined: *C. auriculata*)

Description:

Transverse section
Diffuse-porous. Ring boundary distinct to indistinct. Pores medium, in radial multiples of 2-3(4) (or more, sometimes as tails to larger pores), solitary and in clusters (relatively rare). Parenchyma banded (bands 3–5 cells wide) and paratracheal (aliform-winged, confluent).

Radial section
Perforation plates simple. Pits vestured. Intervessel pits alternate, coalescent, medium. Vessel-ray pits with reduced to apparently simple borders-rounded/angular. Ground tissue fibres with simple to minutely bordered pits, thin to thick-walled. Rays heterogeneous, with 1–4 or more rows of square marginal cells.

Tangential section
Rays 1(2)seriate.

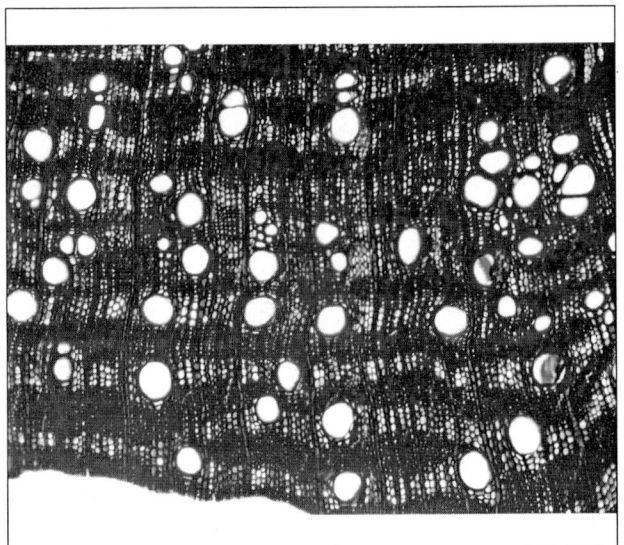
Cassia auriculata TS x100

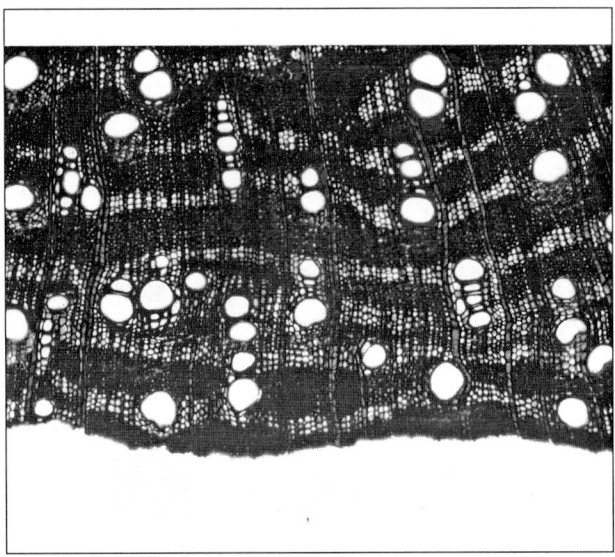
Cassia auriculata TS x100

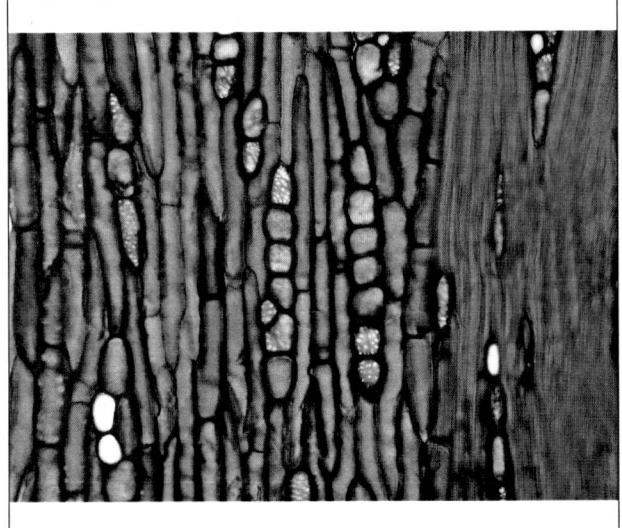
Cassia auriculata TLS x400

# LEGUMINOSAE – CAESALPINIACEAE

*Cassia* sp.
(species examined: *C. fistula*)

Description:

Transverse section
Diffuse-porous. Ring boundary indistinct. Pores medium to large, solitary, and in radial multiples of 2–3. Parenchyma paratracheal (aliform lozenge, confluent).

Radial section
Perforation plates simple. Pits vestured. Intervessel pits alternate, small to medium. Vessel-ray pits with distinct borders, similar in shape, size to intervessel pits (occasionally slightly enlarged and or/rounded). Ground tissue fibres with simple to minutely bordered pits, thin- to thick-walled. Rays homogeneous (all cells slightly procumbent). Crystals present in axial parenchyma and fibres (sometimes forming short chains).

Tangential section
Rays 1(2)seriate.

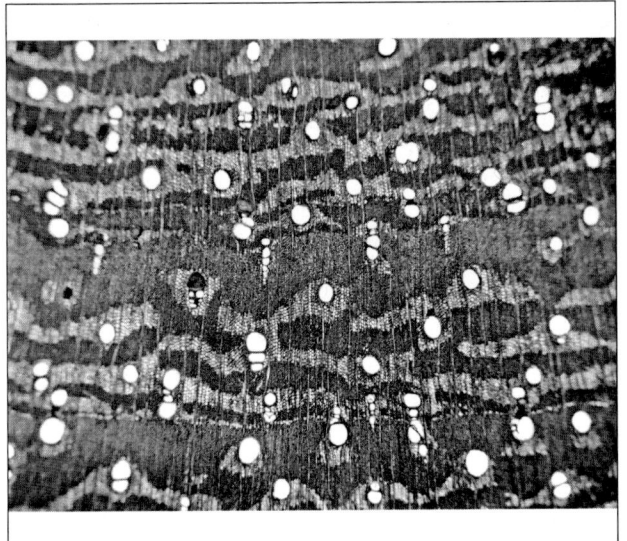

Cassia fistula TS x40

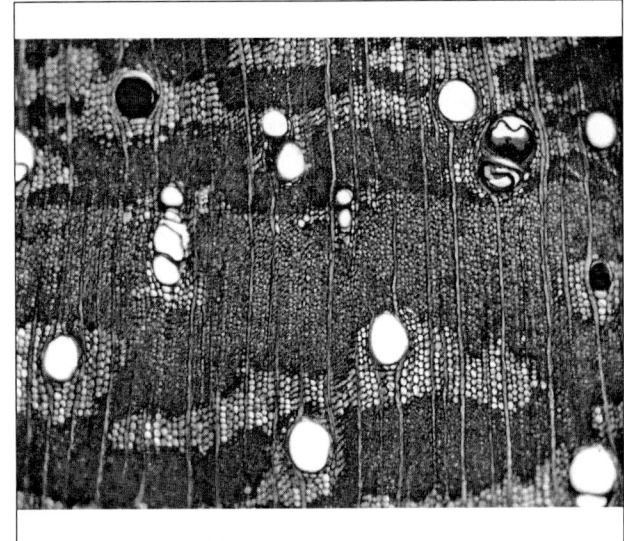

Cassia fistula TS x100

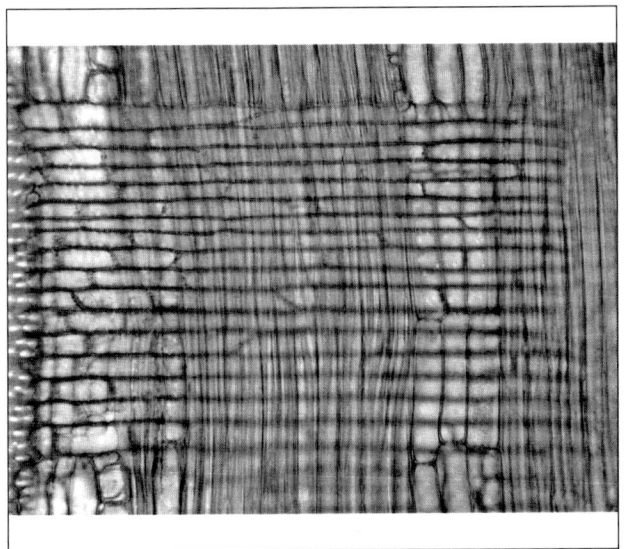

Cassia fistula RLS x400

Cassia fistula RLS x100

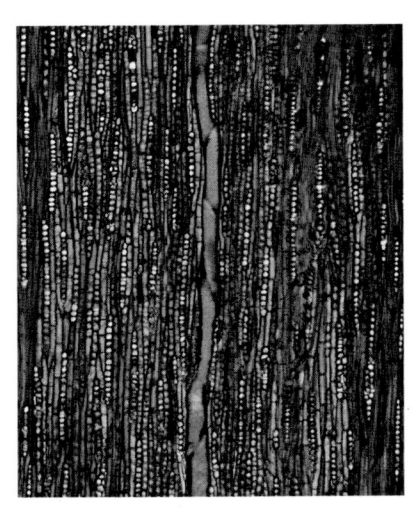

Cassia fistula TLS x100

# LEGUMINOSAE – CAESALPINIACEAE

*Tamarindus* sp.
(species examined: *T. indica*)

Description:

Transverse section
Diffuse-porous. Ring boundary distinct to indistinct. Pores medium to large, solitary and in radial multiples of 2-3(4). Parenchyma paratracheal (aliform lozenge, occasionally confluent).

Radial section
Perforation plates simple. Pits vestured. Intervessel pits alternate, medium. Vessel-ray pits with distinct borders, similar in shape/size to intervessel pits. Fibres with simple to minutely bordered pits, thin- to thick-walled. Rays homogeneous to heterogeneous (1 row of square and/or upright marginal cells). Crystals present in axial parenchyma.

Tangential section
Rays 1(2)seriate.

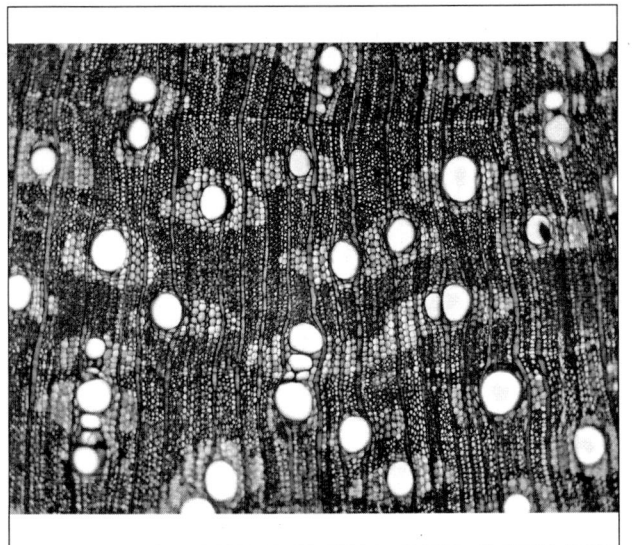
Tamarindus indica TS x100

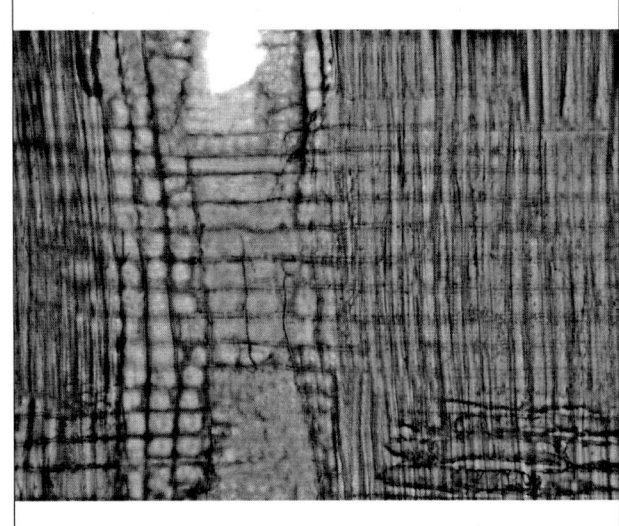
Tamarindus indica RLS x400

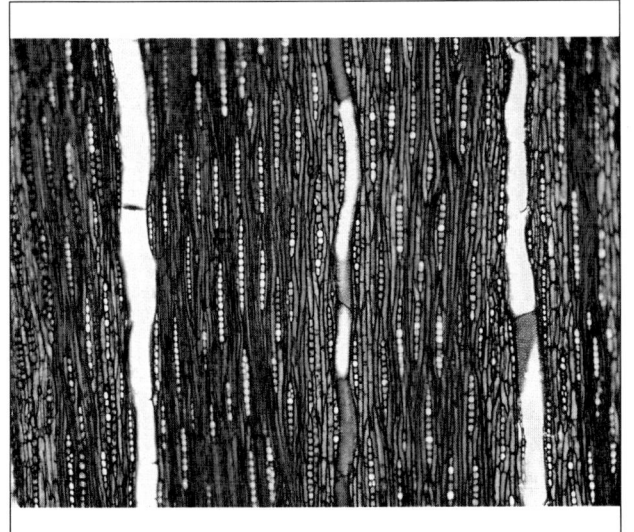
Tamarindus indica TLS x100

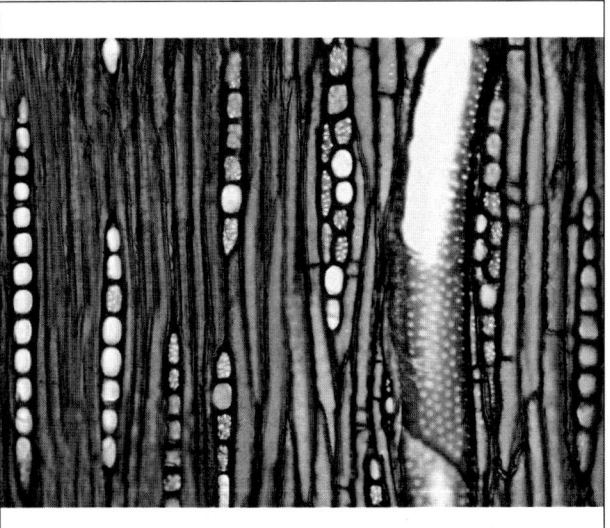
Tamarindus indica TLS x400

# LEGUMINOSAE – MIMOSACEAE

*Acacia* sp.
(species examined: *A. catechu*, *A. leucophloea*, *A. nilotica*)

Description:

Transverse section
Diffuse-porous. Ring boundary distinct to indistinct. Pores medium to large, solitary, in radial multiples of 2–3, tangential rows and irregular clusters (rare, usually accompanied by multiples consisting of 1 large and several small pores). Parenchyma paratracheal (large sheath) aliform, confluent.

Radial section
Perforation plates simple. Vestured pits present. Inter-vessel pits alternate, small to medium. Vessel-ray pits with distinct borders, similar in shape, size to intervessel pits. Fibres with simple to minutely bordered pits, thick-walled. Rays homogeneous (all cells strongly procumbent). Crystals present in axial parenchyma and fibres (forming short chains).

Tangential section
*A. catechu*: rays 1-2(3)seriate.
*A. leucophloea*: rays 2-3(4)seriate, storied. Uniseriate (rare) and biseriate rays short.
*A. nilotica*: rays (2-3)4-10seriate.

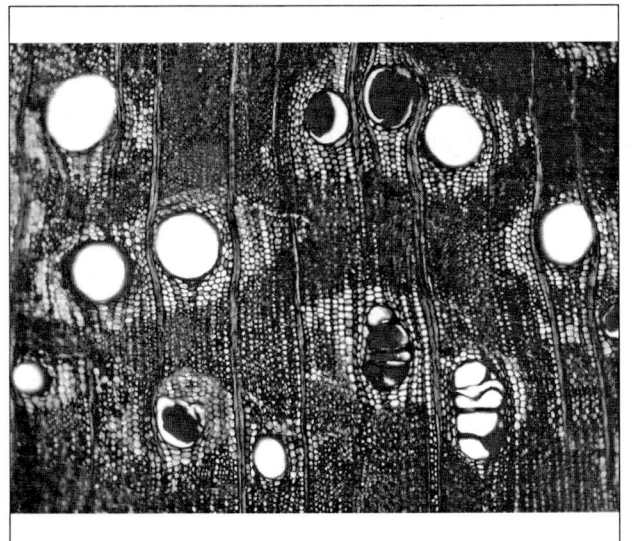
Acacia catechu TS x100

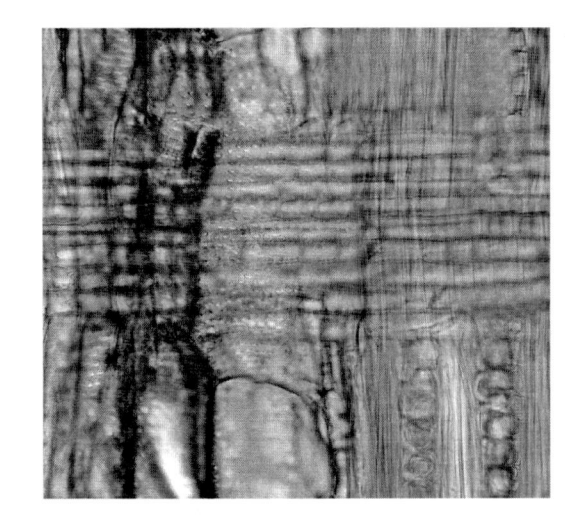
Acacia catechu RLS x400

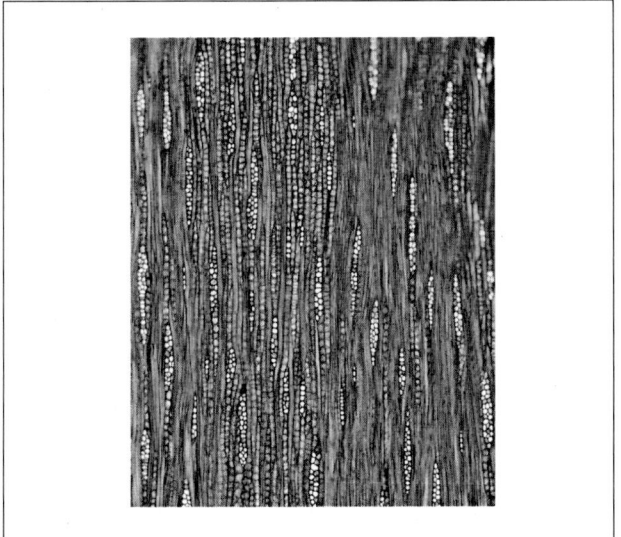
Acacia catechu TLS x100

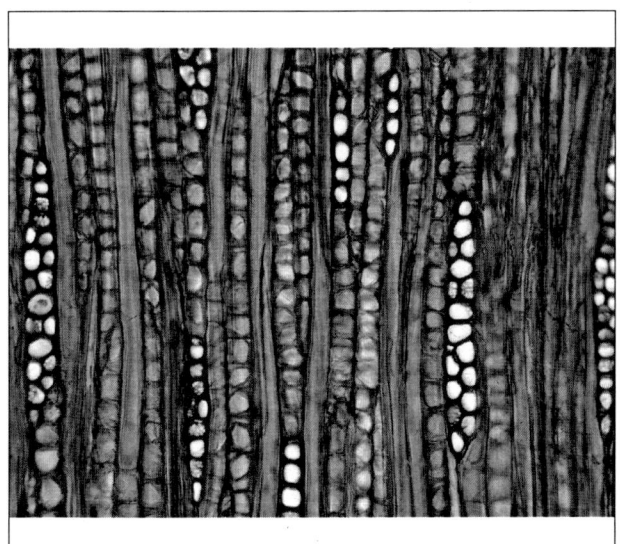
Acacia catechu TLS x400

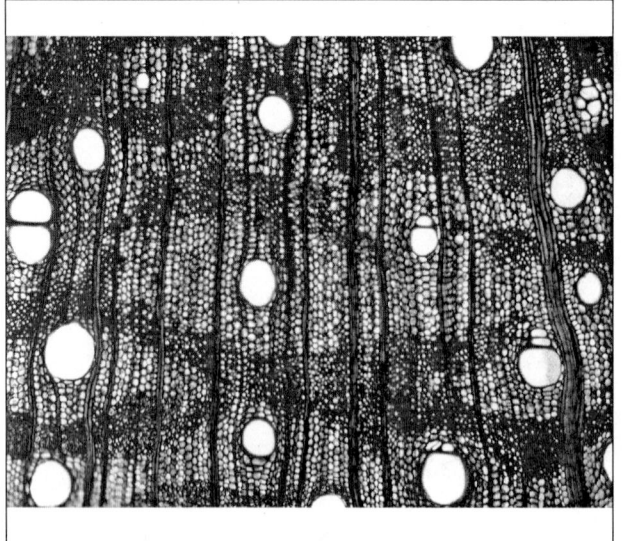

Acacia leucophloea TS x100

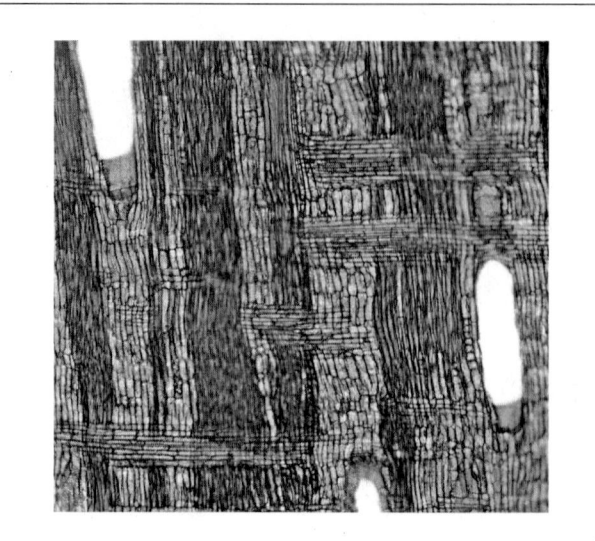

Acacia leucophloea RLS x100

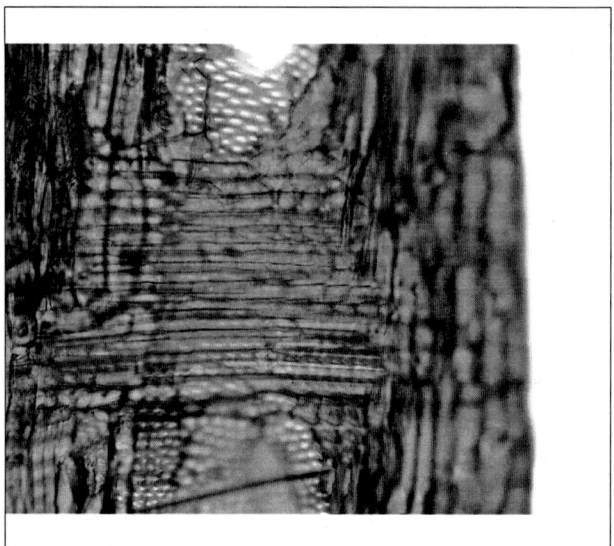

Acacia leucophloea RLS x400

Acacia leucophloea TLS x100

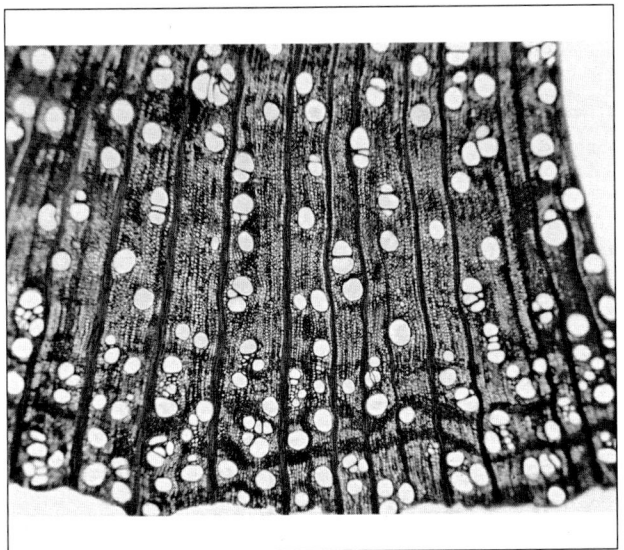

Acacia nilotica TS x40

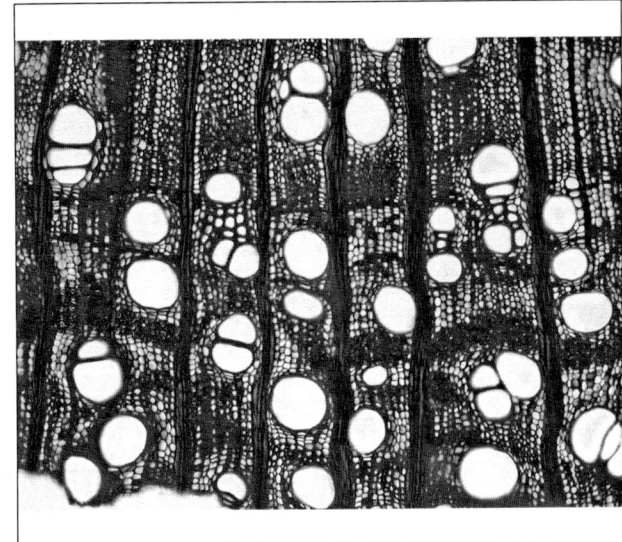

Acacia nilotica TSx100

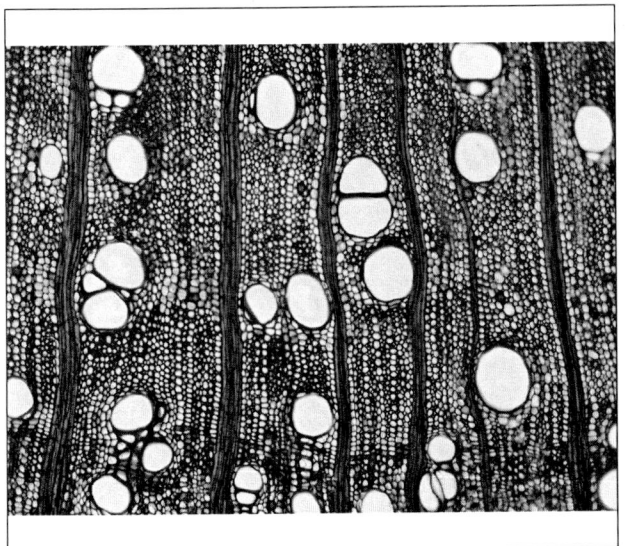

Acacia nilotica TS x100

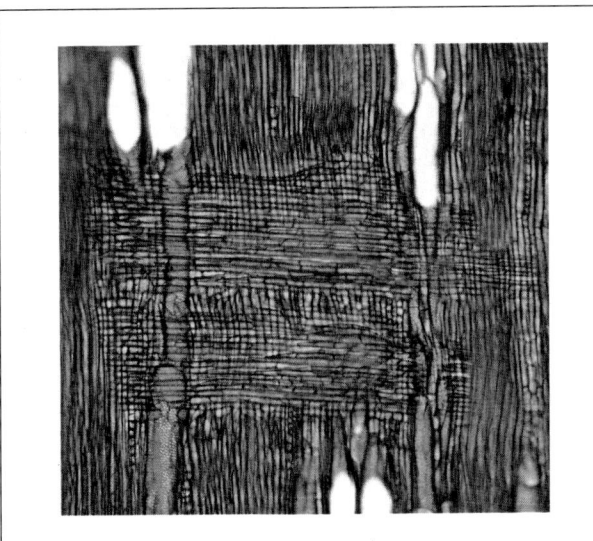

Acacia nilotica RLS x100

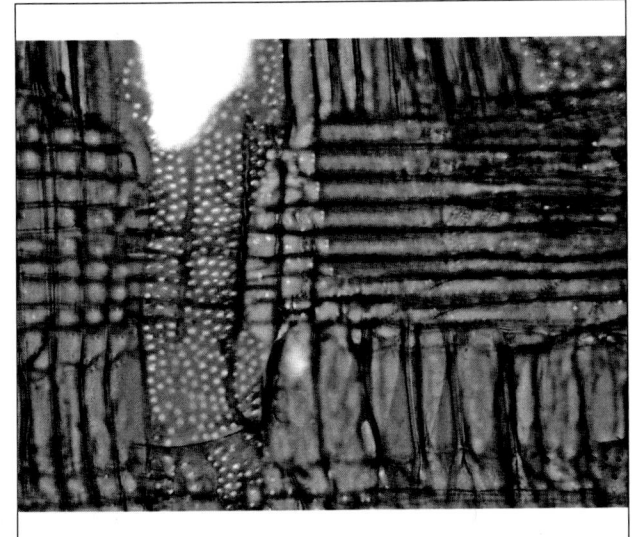

Acacia nilotica RLS x400

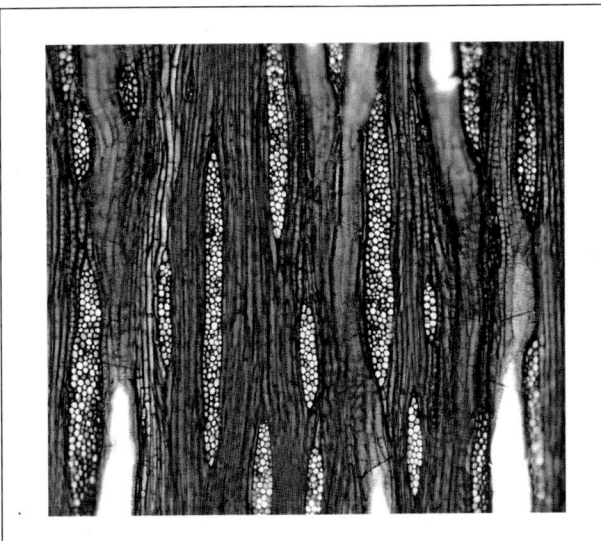

Acacia nilotica TLS x100

# LEGUMINOSAE – MIMOSACEAE

*Albizia* sp.
(species examined: *A. amara, A. procera*)

Description:

Transverse section
Diffuse-porous. Ring boundary indistinct. Pores medium to large, solitary, in radial multiples of 2–3, sometimes in tangential rows and clusters (rare). Parenchyma paratracheal, aliform-lozenge (with large sheath), sometimes confluent.

Radial section
Perforation plates simple. Pits vestured. Intervessel pits opposite to alternate, medium to small. Vessel-ray pits with distinct borders/similar to shape, size to intervessel pits Septate fibres present. Ground tissue fibres with simple to minutely bordered pits, thin- to thick-walled. Rays homogeneous (all cells strongly procumbent). Crystals present in axial parenchyma and fibres (sometimes forming short chains).

Tangential section
*A. amara*: rays 1(2)seriate.
*A. procera:* rays (2)3-4seriate.

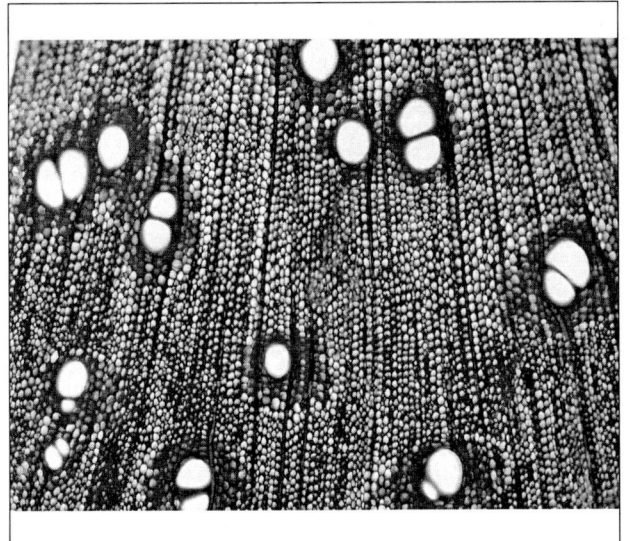

Albizia amara TS x100

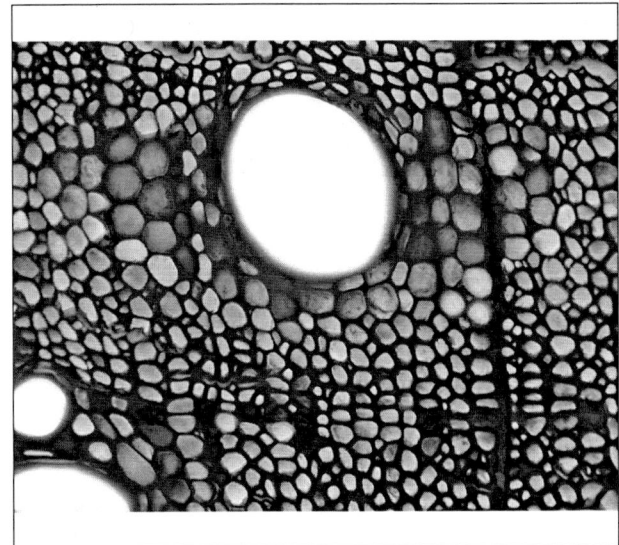

Albizia amara TS x400

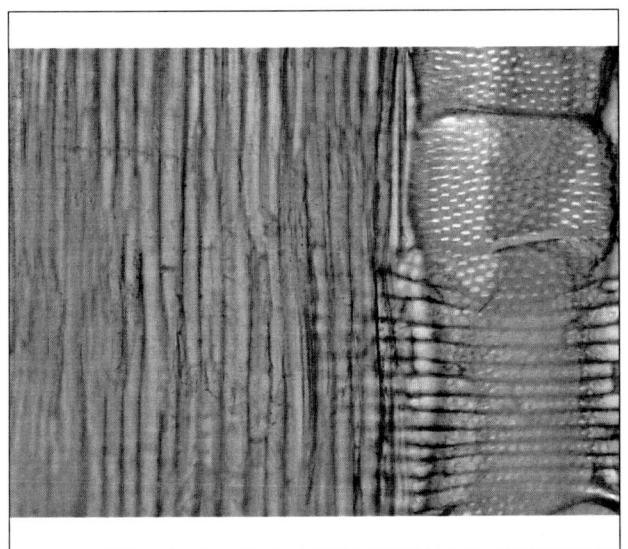

Albizia amara RLS x400

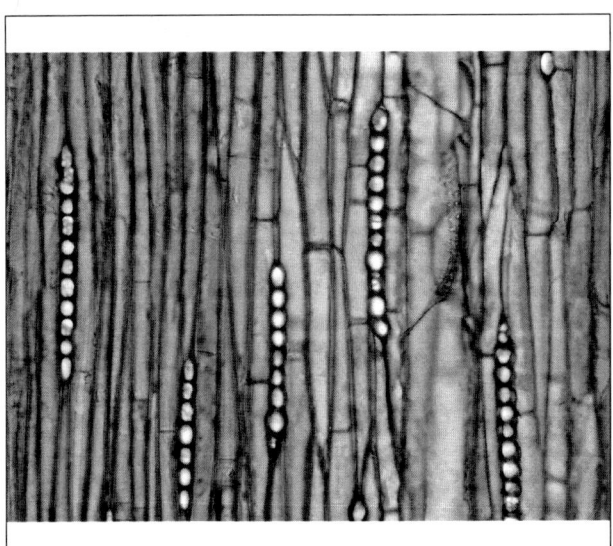

Albizia amara TLS x400

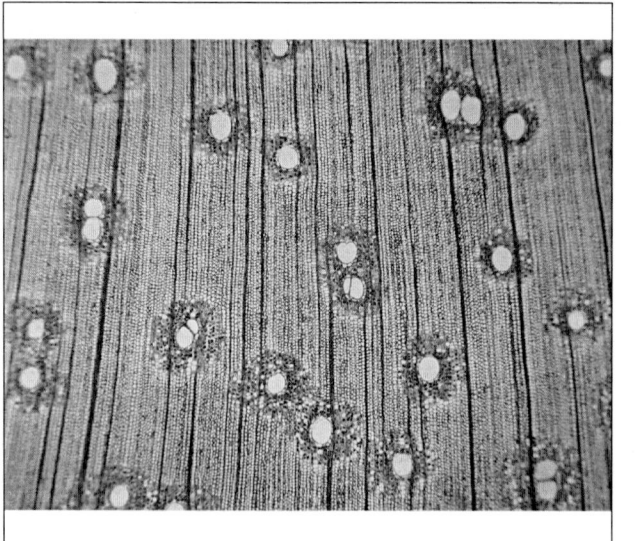

Albizia procera TS x40

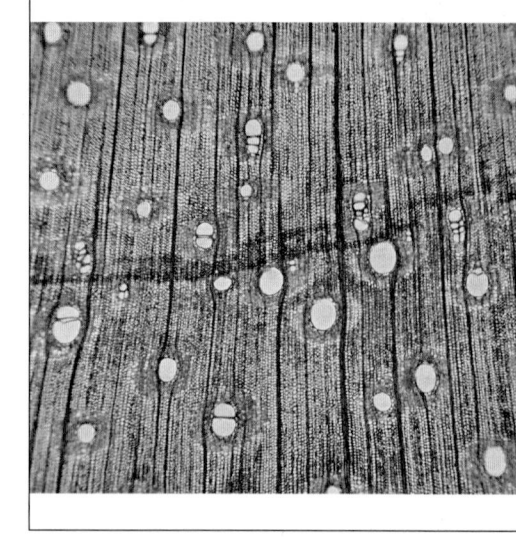

Albizia procera TS x40

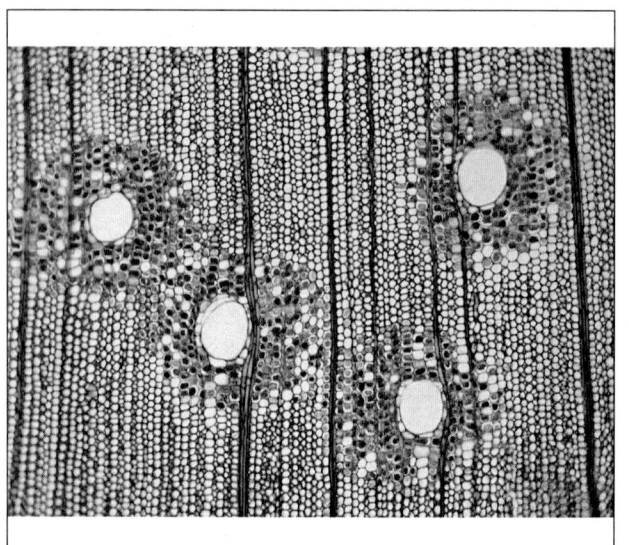

Albizia procera TS x100

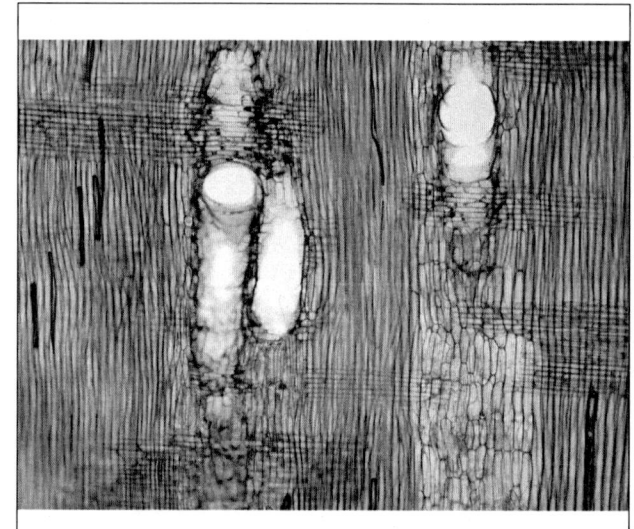

Albizia procera RLS x100

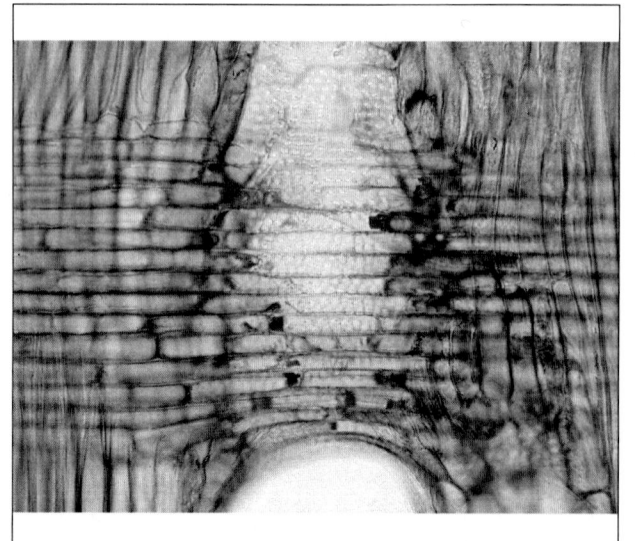

Albizia procera RLS x400

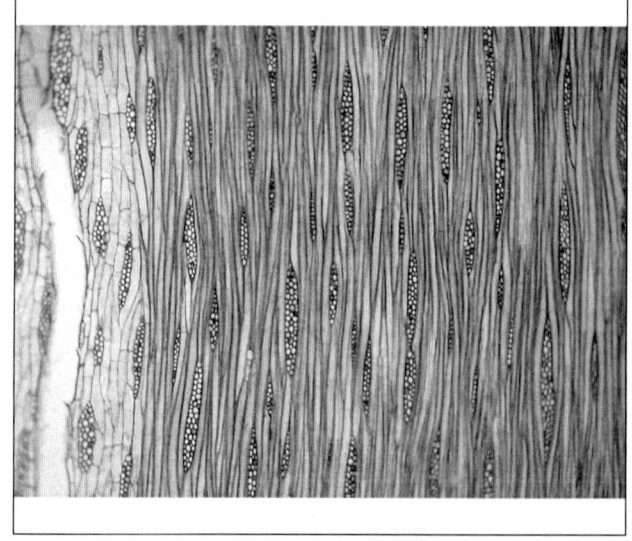

Albizia procera TLS x100

# LEGUMINOSAE – MIMOSACEAE

*Xylia* sp.
(species examined: *X. xylocarpa*)

Description:

Transverse section
Diffuse- to semi ring porous. Ring boundary distinct to indistinct. Pores medium to large, solitary and in radial multiples of 2–3. Parenchyma paratracheal (aliform-lozenge, confluent) and unilateral paratracheal (rare).

Radial section
Perforation plates simple. Intervessel pits alternate, small. Vessel-ray pits with distinct borders, similar in shape, size to intervessel pits. Ground tissue fibres with simple to minutely bordered pits, thin to thick-walled. Septate fibres present. Rays homogeneous (all cells weakly procumbent). Crystals present in ray cells and axial parenchyma.

Tangential section
Rays (1)2-3seriate, somewhat irregular in shape, tall.

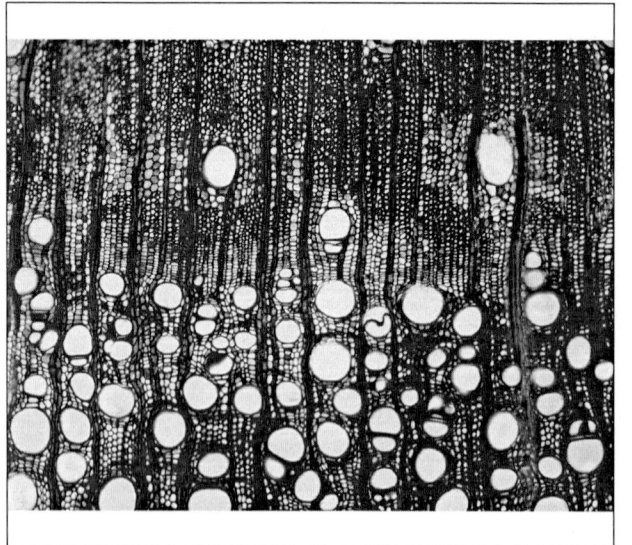
Xylia xylocarpa TS x100

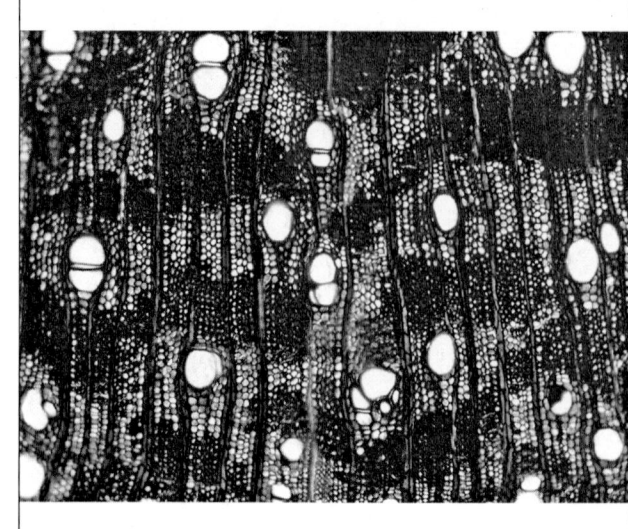
Xylia xylocarpa TS x100

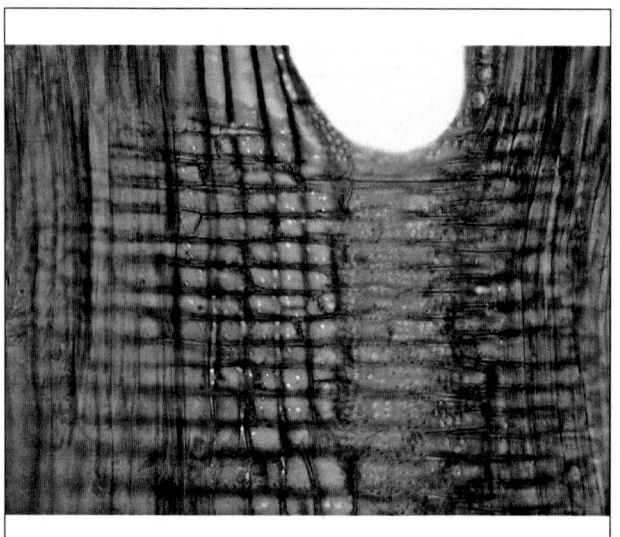
Xylia xylocarpa RLS x400

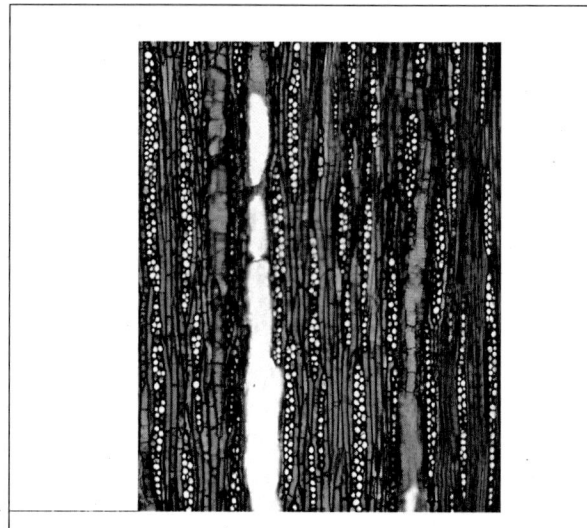
Xylia xylocarpa TLS x100

# LEGUMINOSAE – PAPILIONACEAE

*Butea* sp.
(species examined: *B. monosperma*)

Description:

Transverse section
Diffuse-porous. Ring boundary distinct. Pores in early wood solitary (large) or in radial multiples of 2, in late wood in short radial multiples of 2-3(4), and clusters. Parenchyma banded (bands more than 3 cells wide) and paratracheal vasicentric.

Radial section
Perforation plates simple. Pits vestured. Intervessel pits opposite to alternate, medium to large. Vessel-ray pits with distinct borders, similar in shape, size to intervessel pits, enlarged. Ground tissue fibres with simple to minutely bordered pits, thin- to thick-walled. Rays homogeneous to slightly heterogeneous (1–2 or more rows of square marginal cells). Crystals present in fibres and axial parenchyma.

Tangential section
Rays uni- and multiseriate 1(2) and 4-7(8)seriate.

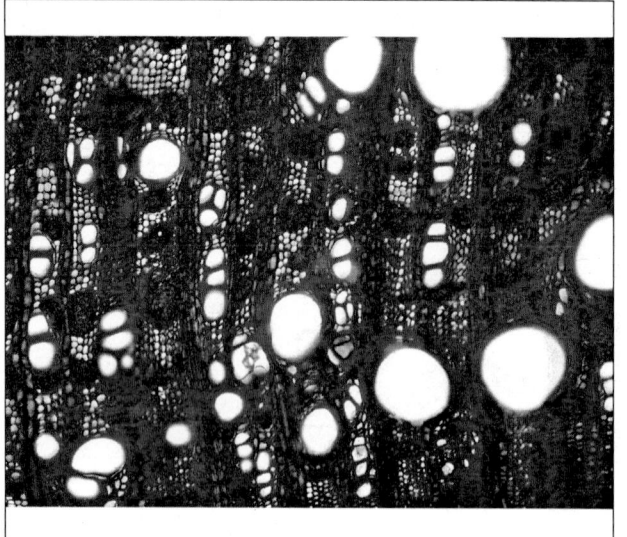
Butea monosperma TS x100

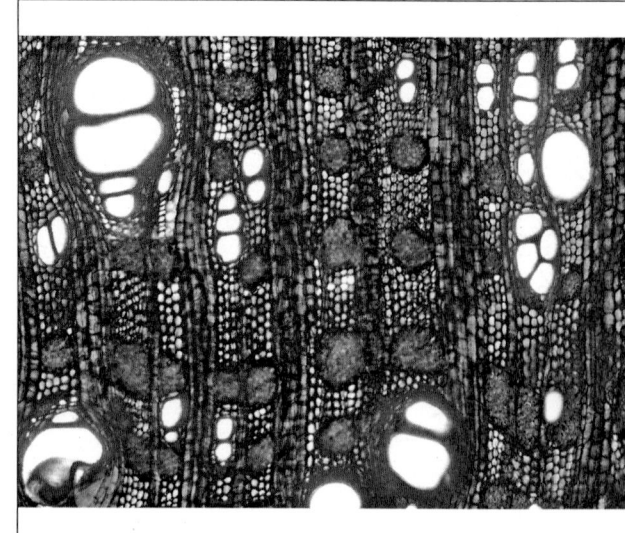
Butea monosperma TS x100

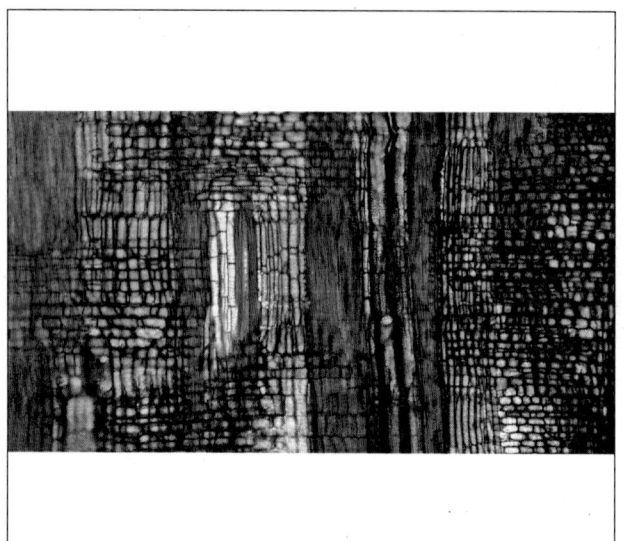
Butea monosperma RLS x100

Butea monosperma RLS x400

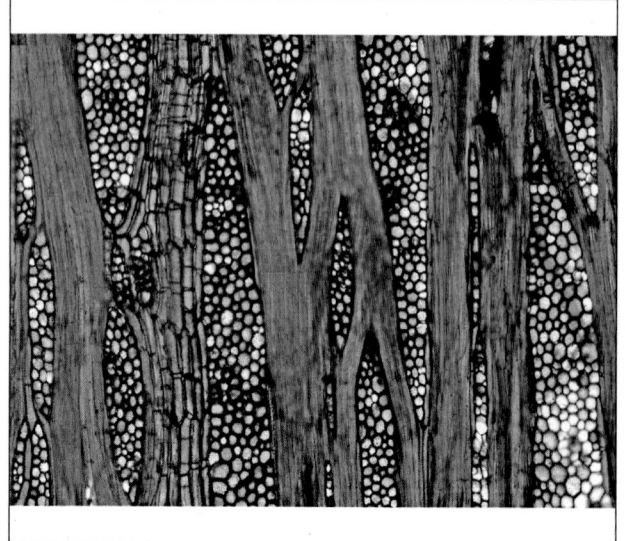
Butea monosperma TLS x100

# LEGUMINOSAE – PAPILIONACEAE

*Dalbergia* sp.
(species examined: *D. latifolia, D. paniculata*)

Description:

<u>Transverse section</u>
Diffuse-porous. Ring boundary indistinct. Pores sparse, medium to large, solitary (larger), in radial multiples of 2–4 (smaller), and some irregular clusters. Parenchyma banded (narrow to larger discontinuous bands) and paratracheal (vasicentric, aliform with narrow sheath). Intercellular canals of traumatic origin occasionally present.

<u>Radial section</u>
Perforation plates simple. Pits vestured. Intervessel pits alternate, medium to small. Vessel-ray pits with distinct borders, similar in shape, size to intervessel pits. Ground tissue fibres with simple to minutely bordered pits, thick-walled. Rays homogeneous (all cells slightly procumbent) to heterogeneous (one row of square marginal cells). Crystals present in ray cells.

<u>Tangential section</u>
Rays 1-2(3)seriate, short (especially in *D. latifolia*), storied.

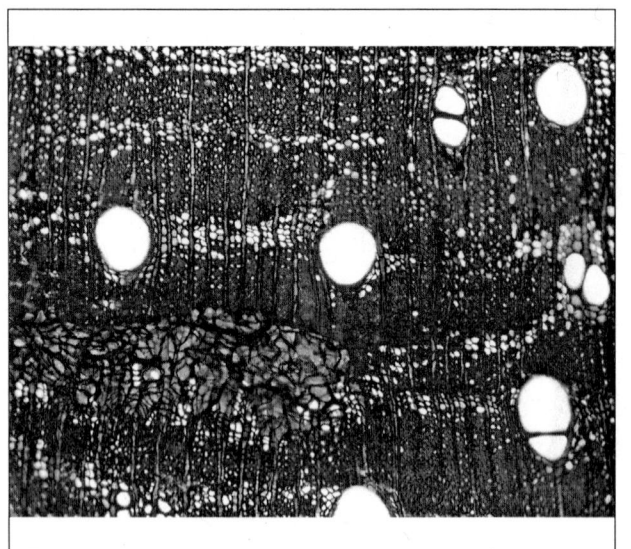
Dalbergia latifolia TS x100

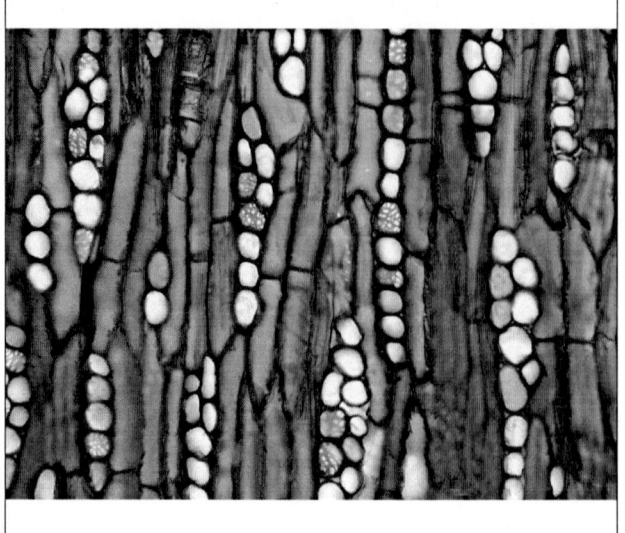
Dalbergia latifolia TLS x400

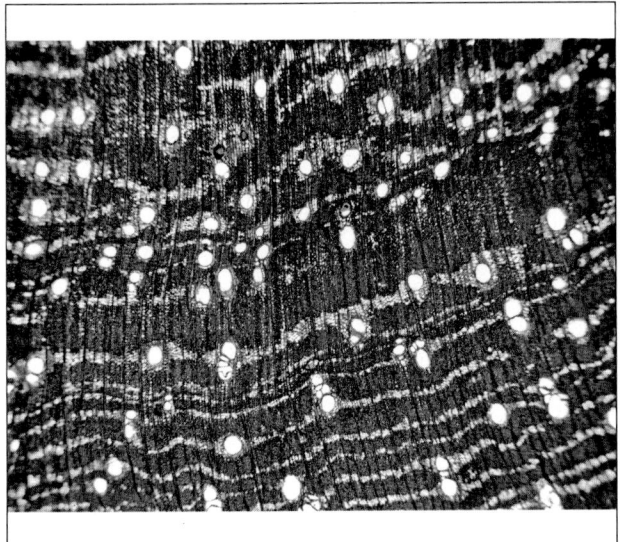

Dalbergia paniculata TS x40

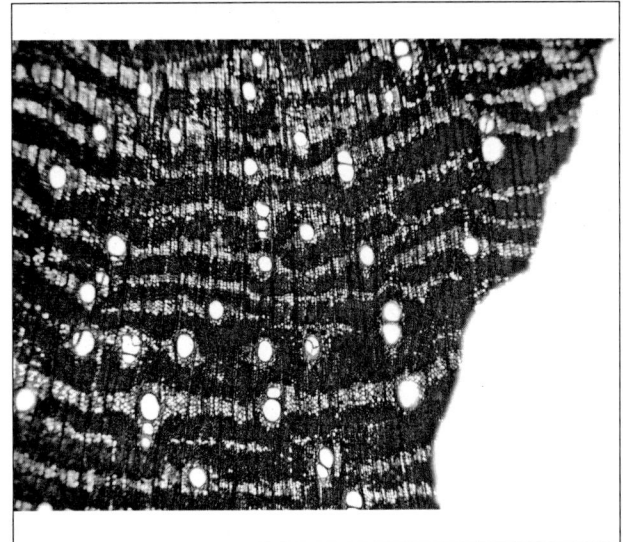

Dalbergia paniculata TS x40

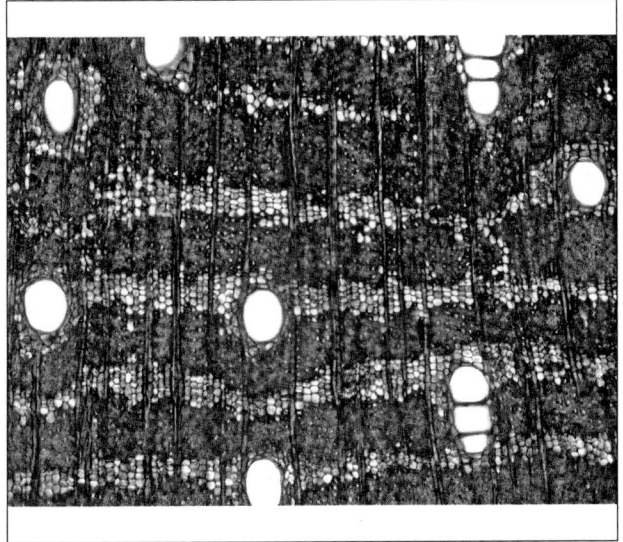

Dalbergia paniculata TS x100

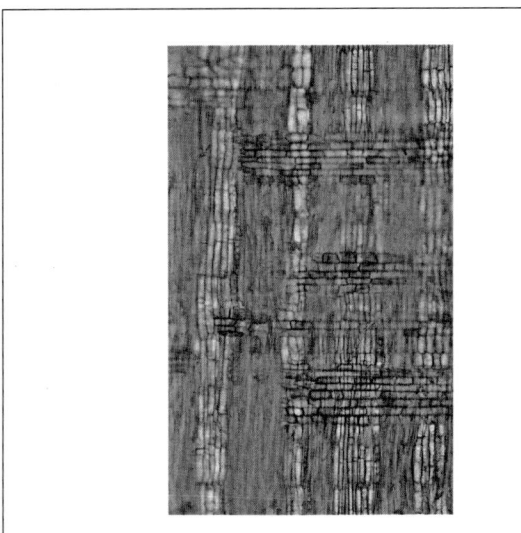

Dalbergia paniculata RLS x100

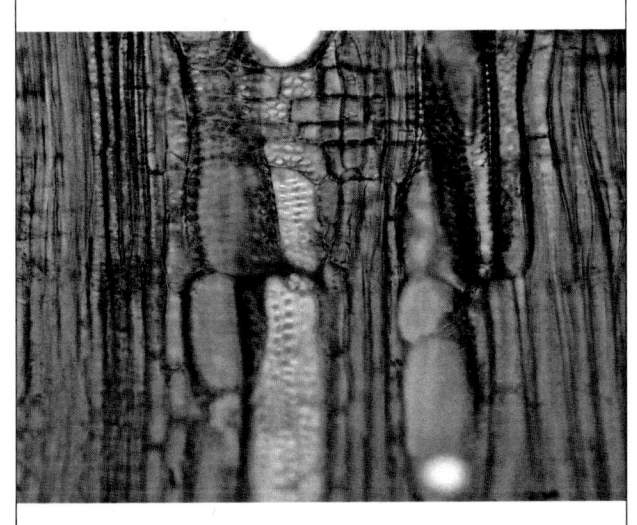

Dalbergia paniculata RLS x400

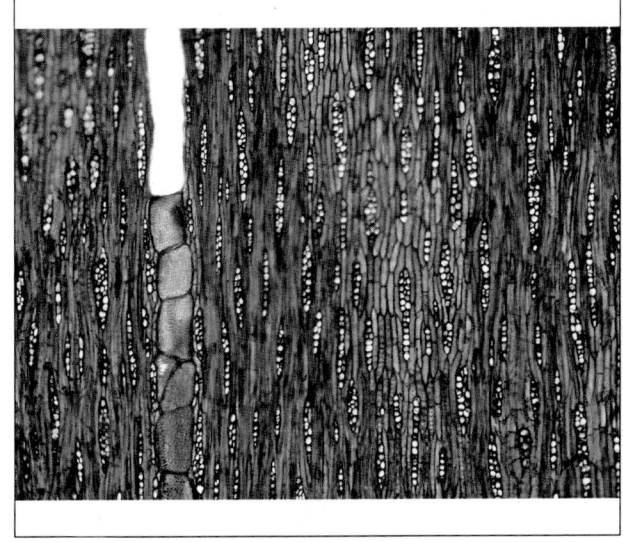

Dalbergia paniculata TLS x100

# LEGUMINOSAE – PAPILIONACEAE

*Pterocarpus* sp.
(species examined: *P. marsupium*)

Description:

Transverse section
Diffuse-porous. Ring boundary distinct to indistinct. Pores sparse, medium, solitary, in radial multiples of 2-3(4) (common), and some irregular clusters. Parenchyma banded (narrow to larger bands) and paratracheal (aliform with narrow sheath). Intercellular canals of traumatic origin occasionally present.

Radial section
Perforation plates simple. Pits vestured. Intervessel pits alternate, medium to small. Vessel-ray pits with distinct borders, similar in shape, size to intervessel pits. Ground tissue fibres with simple to minutely bordered pits, thin- to thick-walled. Rays homogeneous (slightly procumbent) to heterogeneous (1 row of square marginal cells). Crystals present in parenchyma and ray cells.

Tangential section
Rays 1(2)seriate, short, storied.

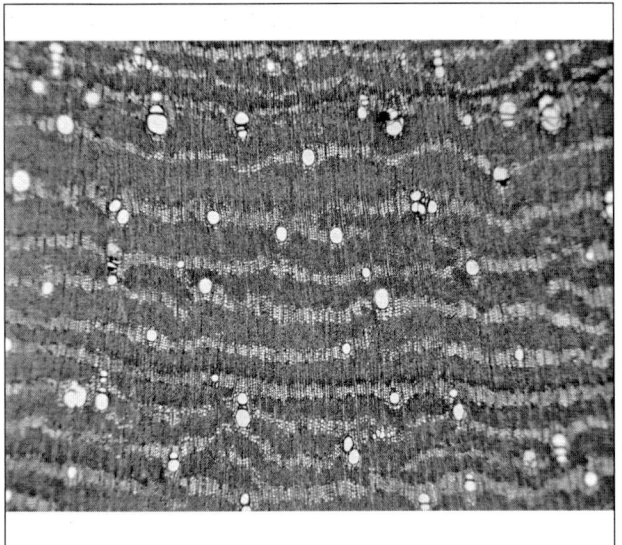
Pterocarpus marsupium TS x40

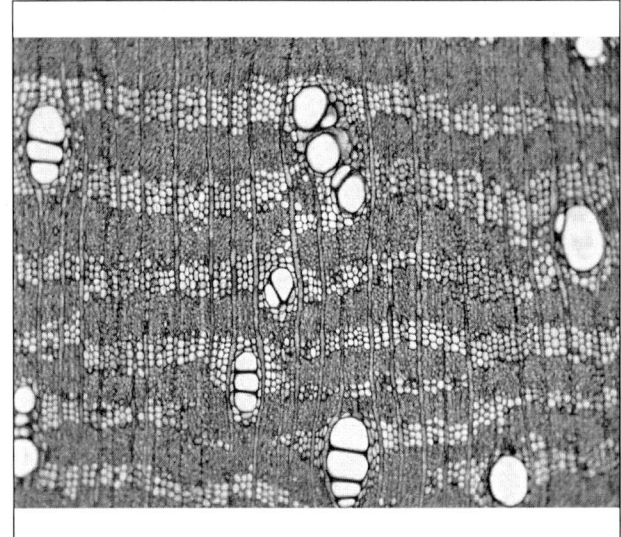
Pterocarpus marsupium TS x100

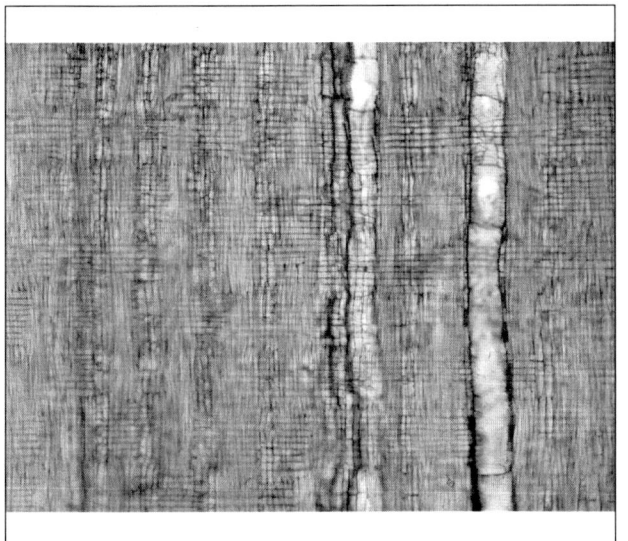
Pterocarpus marsupium RLS x100

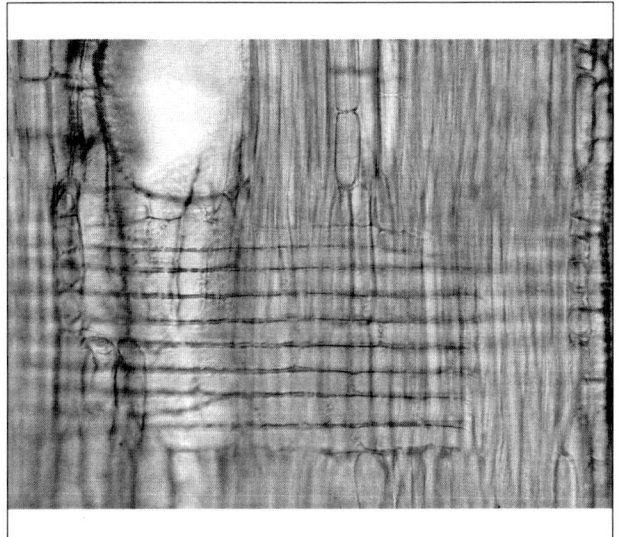
Pterocarpus marsupium RLS x400

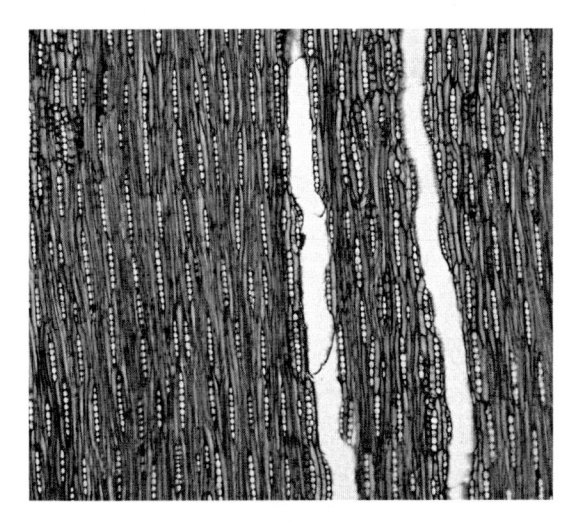
Pterocarpus marsupium TLS x100

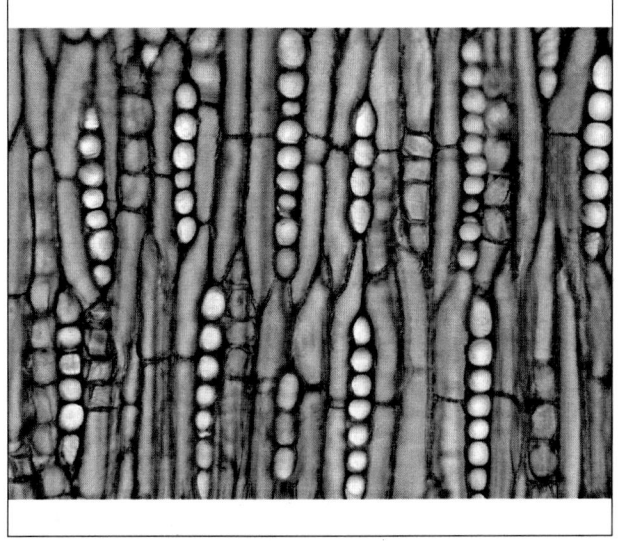
Pterocarpus marsupium TLS x400

# LOGANIACEAE

*Strychnos* spp.
(species examined: *S. nux-vomica, S. potatorum*)

Description:

Transverse section
Diffuse-porous. Ring boundary distinct. Pores small, numerous, in radial multiples of 4 or more and clusters (diagonal-dendritic). Parenchyma very variable, apotracheal (diffuse, diffuse-in-aggregates), paratracheal (vasicentric), and banded (terminal bands). Included phloem, diffuse (scattered, isolated phloem strands) present.

Radial section
Perforation plates simple. Intervessel pits alternate, small. Vessel-ray pits with distinct borders, similar in shape, size to intervessel pits. Ground tissue fibres with simple to minutely bordered pits, thin- to thick-walled. Rays heterogeneous, with over 4 rows of square and upright marginal cells. Uniseriate rays composed entirely of upright cells. Crystals sometimes present in ray cells.

Tangential section
Rays uni- and multiseriate (4, 5-6seriate, occasionally more), sometimes irregular in shape.

Strychnos nux-vomica TS x40

Strychnos nux-vomica TS x100

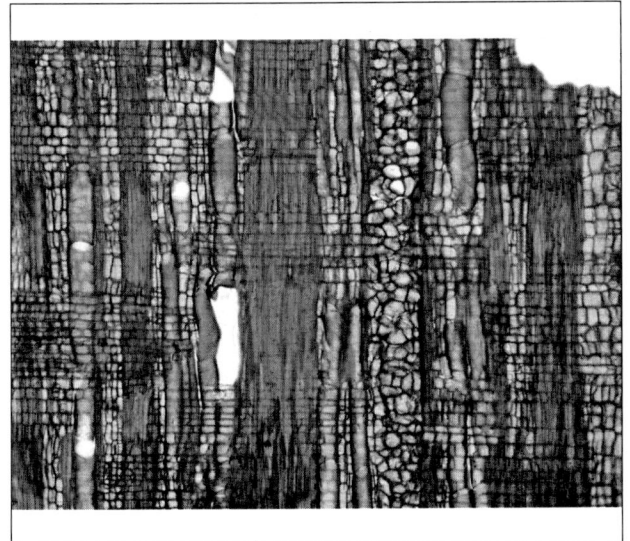
Strychnos nux-vomica RLS x100

Strychnos nux-vomica RLS x400

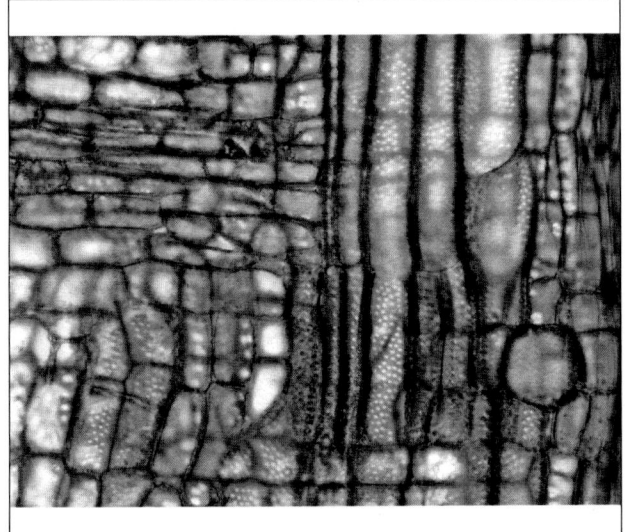
Strychnos nux-vomica RLS x400

Strychnos nux-vomica TLS x100

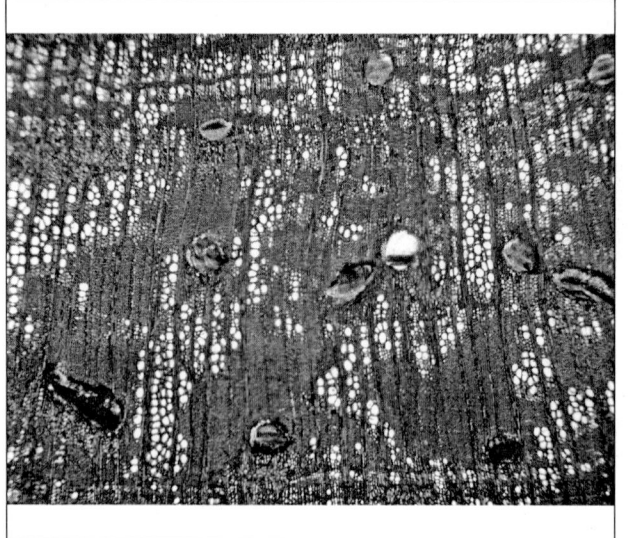
Strychnos potatorum TS x40

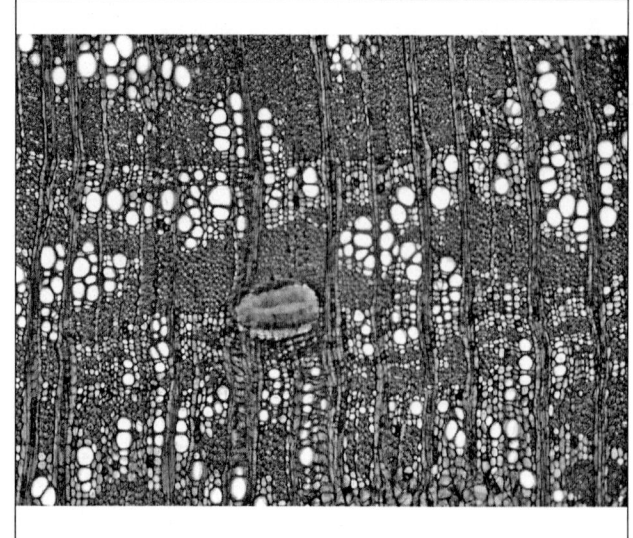
Strychnos potatorum TS x100

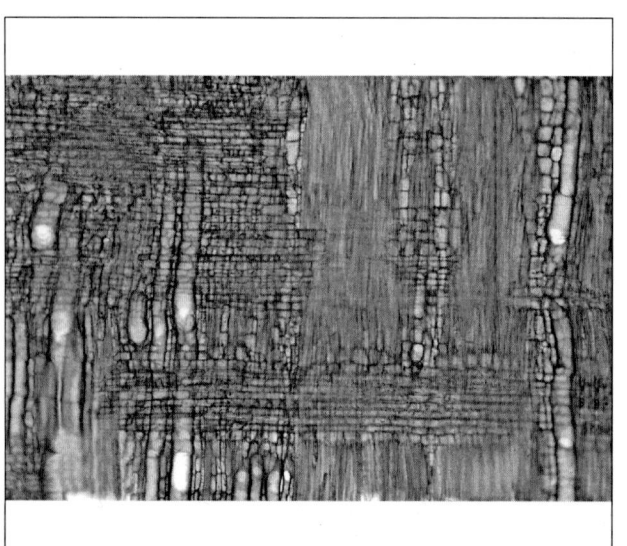
Strychnos potatorum RLS x100

Strychnos potatorum RLS x400

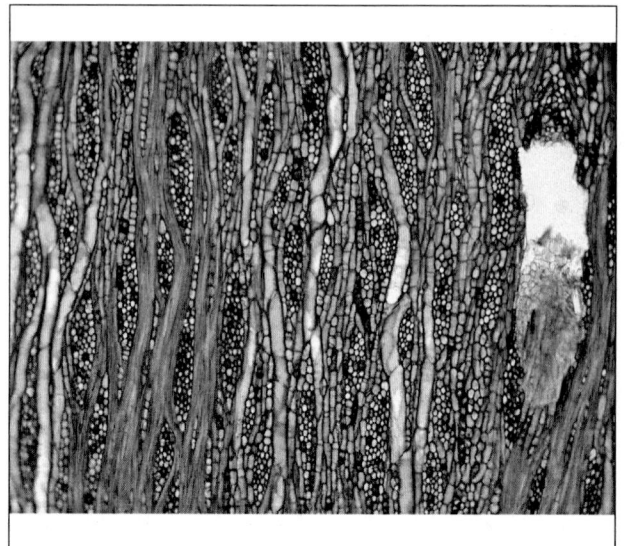
Strychnos potatorum TLS x100

# LYTHRACEAE

*Lagerstroemia* sp.
(species examined: *L. lanceolata*)

Description:

Transverse section
Diffuse porous. Ring boundary distinct to indistinct. Pores large, solitary, in radial multiples of 2–3 (sometimes irregular) and in clusters (both radial files and clusters occasionally consist of very small pores). Parenchyma apotracheal (diffuse-in-aggregates), paratracheal (vasicentric, aliform and scanty paratracheal) and in narrow bands (no more than 3 cells wide).

Radial section
Perforation plates simple. Pits vestured. Intervessel pits alternate, confluent, small to medium. Vessel-ray pits with reduced to apparently simple borders rounded/angular. Ground tissue fibres with simple to minutely bordered pits, thin- to thick-walled. Septate fibres present. Rays homogeneous to slightly heterogeneous (1–2 rows of square and/or upright cells). Crystals present in fibres and parenchyma.

Tangential section
Rays 1(2)seriate.

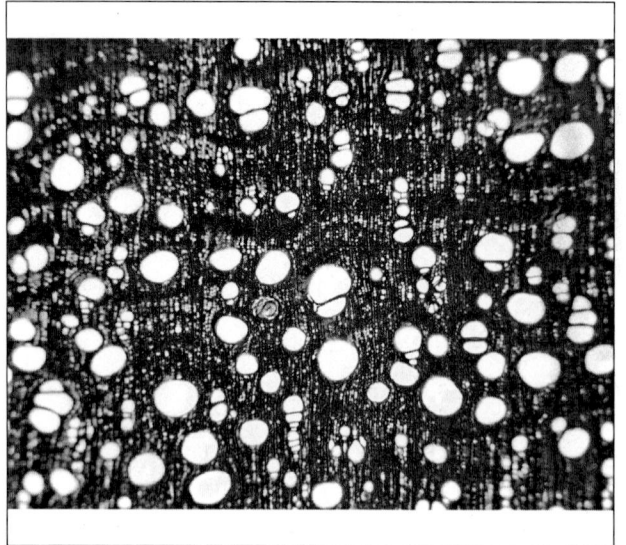
Lagerstroemia lanceolata TS x40

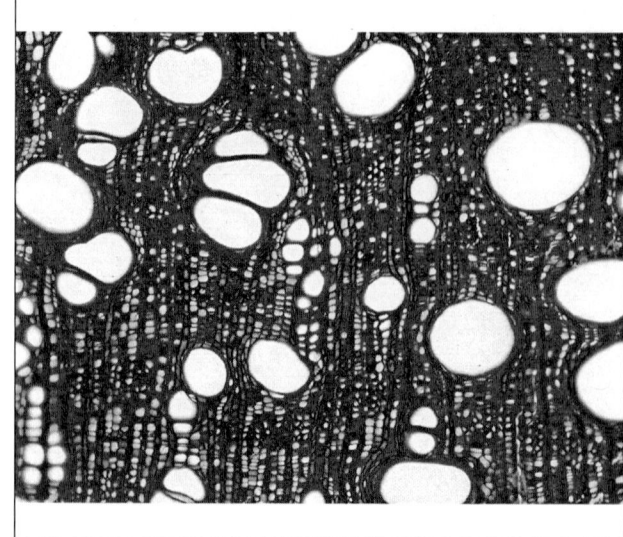
Lagerstroemia lanceolata TS x100

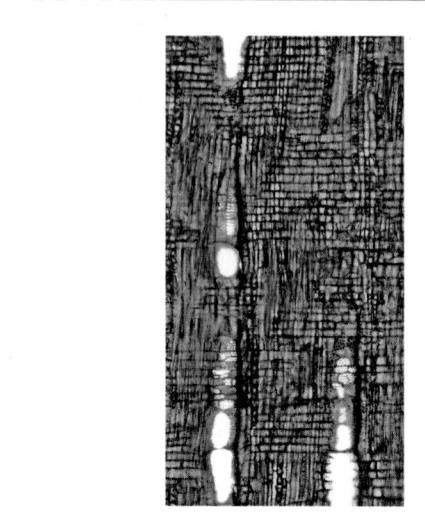
Lagerstroemia lanceolata RLS x100

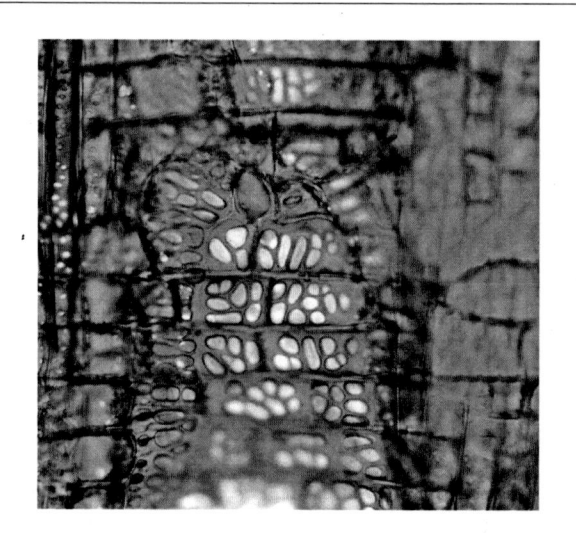
Lagerstroemia lanceolata RLS x400

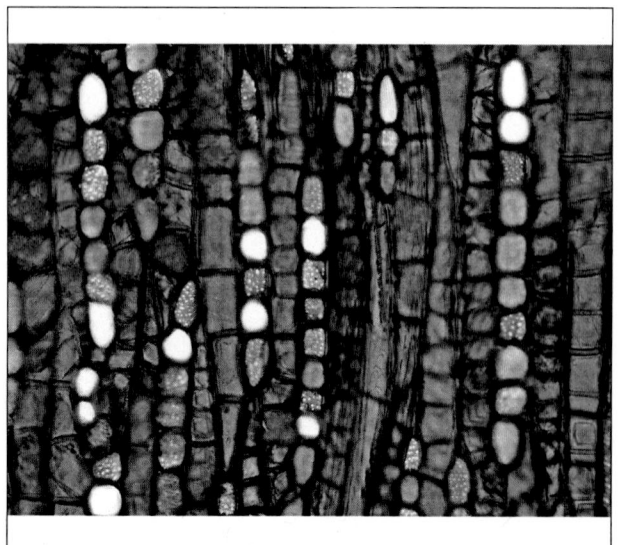
Lagerstroemia lanceolata TLS x400

# LYTHRACEAE

*Lawsonia* sp.
(species examined: *L. alba*)

Description:

Transverse section
Diffuse porous. Ring boundary distinct, wavy. Pores medium, in radial multiples of 4 or more (common), and in clusters. Parenchyma apotracheal (diffuse-in-aggregates), scanty paratracheal and banded (marginal bands).

Radial section
Perforation plates simple. Intervessel pits alternate, small. Pits vestured. Vessel-ray pits with distinct borders, similar in shape, size to inter-vessel pits. Ground tissue fibres with simple to minutely bordered pits, thin- to thick-walled. Rays heterogeneous, with a central part of strongly procumbent cells and 1–2 rows of upright and/or square marginal cells. Uniseriate rays composed entirely of upright cells. Crystals present in fibres and parenchyma.

Tangential section
Rays (1)2-3seriate.

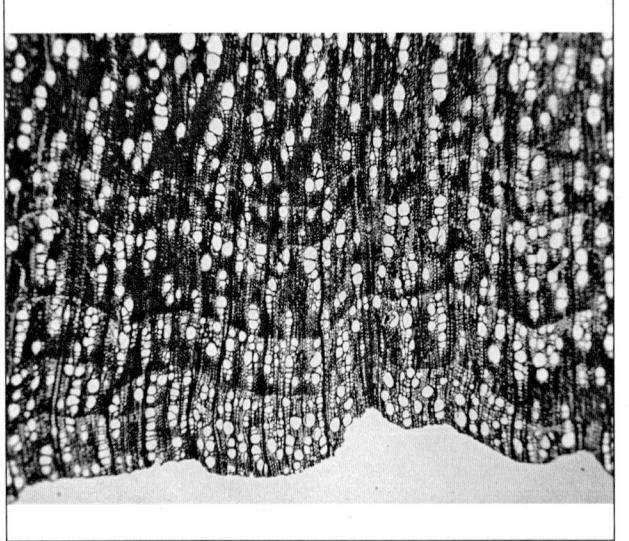

Lawsonia alba TS x40

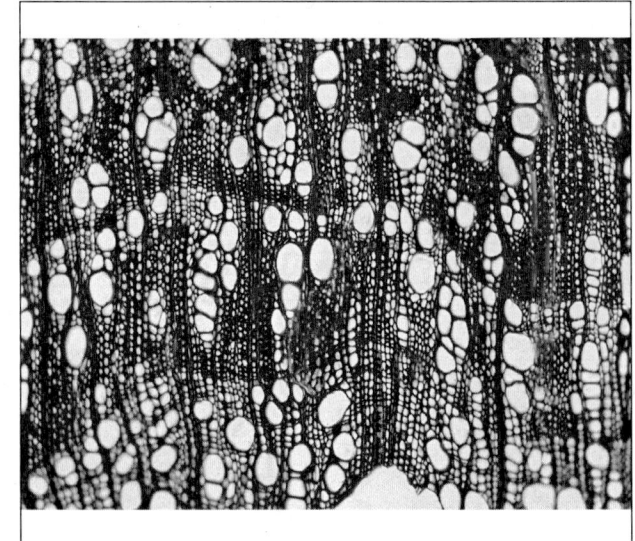

Lawsonia alba TS x100

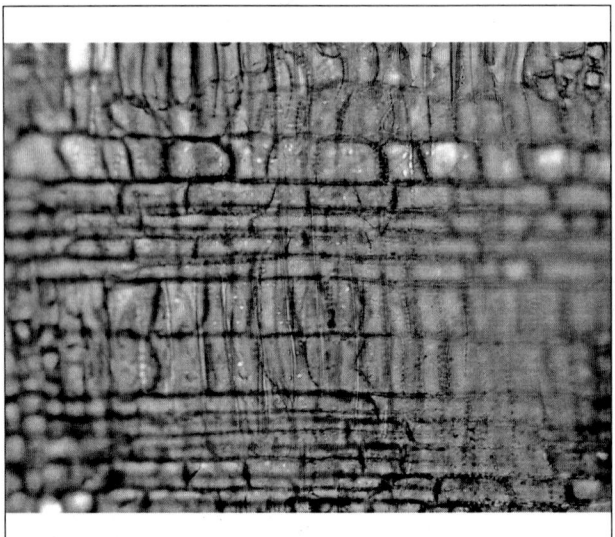

Lawsonia alba RLS x400

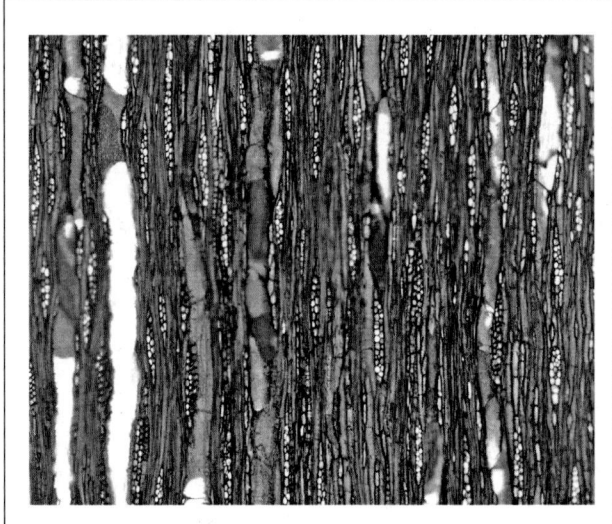

Lawsonia alba TLS x100

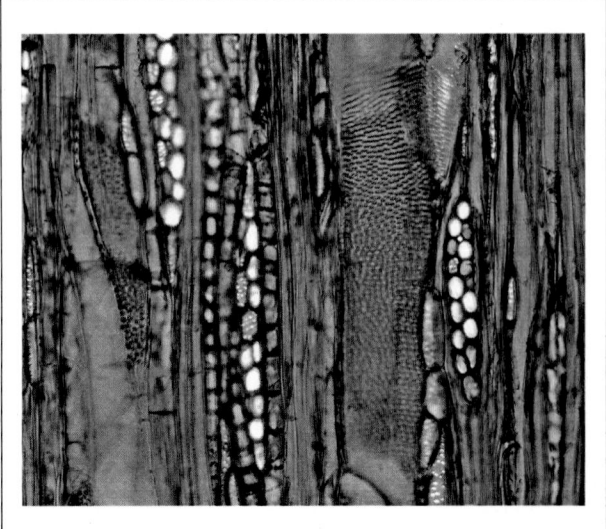

Lawsonia alba TLS x400

# MELIACEAE

*Aglaia* sp.
(species examined: *A. roxburgiana*)

Description:

Transverse section
Diffuse-porous. Ring boundary indistinct. Pores small to medium, solitary and in radial multiples of 2–3. Parenchyma paratracheal (aliform, confluent) and banded (3–5 cells wide).

Radial section
Perforation plates simple. Intervessel pits alternate to opposite, minute. Vessel-ray pits with distinct borders, similar in shape, size to intervessel pits. Ground tissue fibres with simple to minutely bordered pits, thin- to thick-walled. Rays heterogeneous composed of weakly procumbent cells with 1 row of square and/or upright marginal cells). Axial parenchyma storied.

Tangential section
Rays (1)2-3seriate (mostly biseriate).

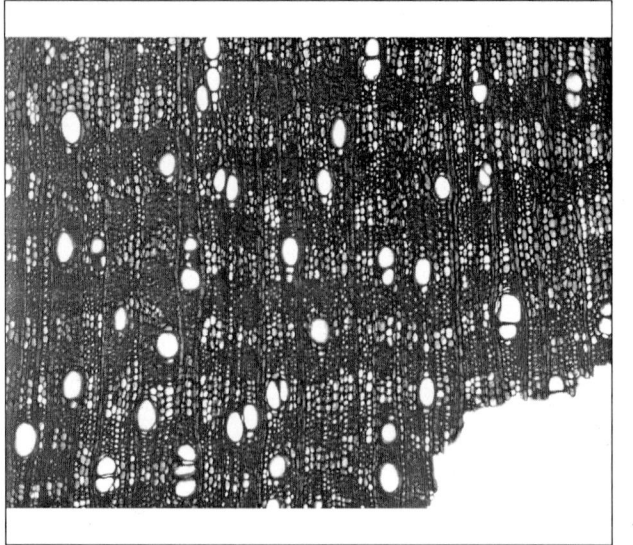

Aglaia roxburgiana TS x100

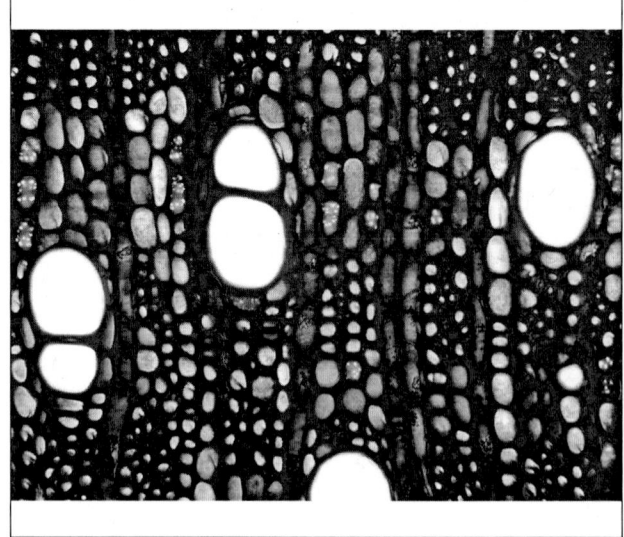

Aglaia roxburgiana TS x400

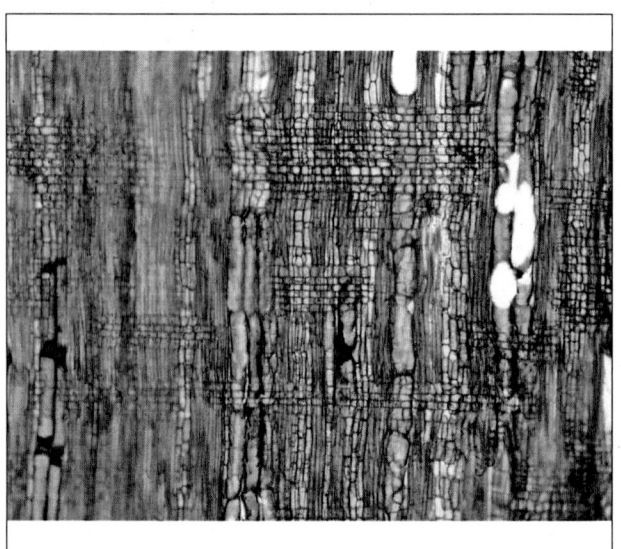

Aglaia roxburgiana RLS x100

Aglaia roxburgiana RLS x400

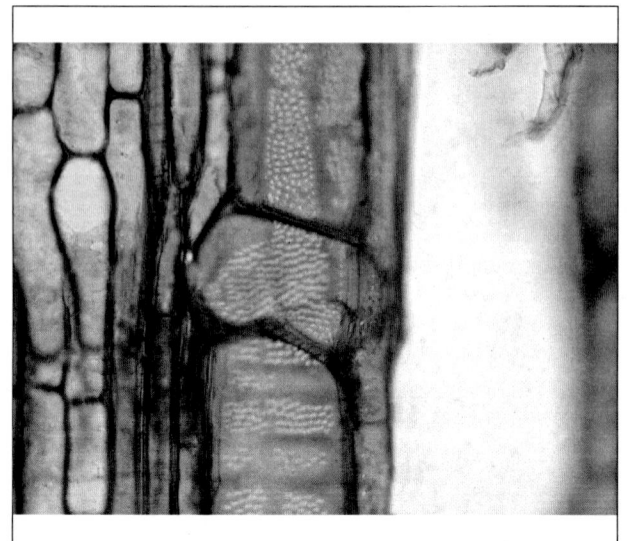

Aglaia roxburgiana RLS x630

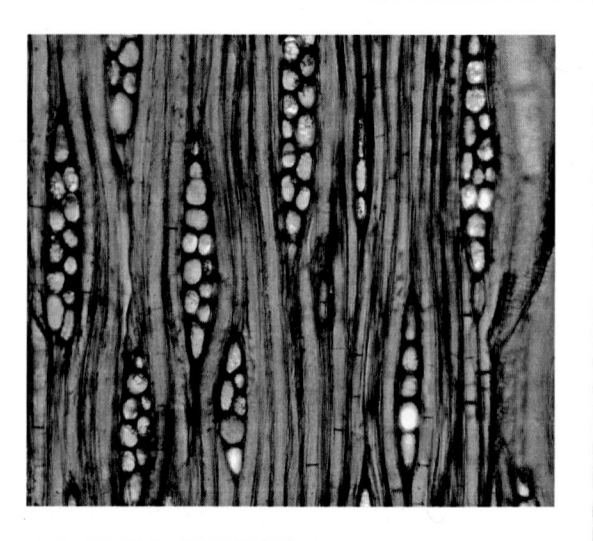

Aglaia roxburgiana TLS x400

# MELIACEAE

*Azadirachta* sp.
(species examined: *A. indica*, syn. *Melia azadirachta*)

Description:

<u>Transverse section</u>
Diffuse-porous. Ring boundary indistinct. Pores medium to large, partly solitary, mostly in radial multiples of 2–4 and irregular clusters. Parenchyma apotracheal (diffuse, diffuse-in-aggregates) scanty paratracheal and in terminal bands (4 or more cells wide).

<u>Radial section</u>
Perforation plates simple. Intervessel pits alternate, small, slitlike. Vessel-ray pits with distinct borders, similar in shape, size to intervessel pits. Ground tissue fibres with simple to minutely bordered pits, thin- to thick-walled. Septate fibres present. Rays homogeneous to slightly heterogeneous, with 1 row of square marginal cells. Crystals present in fibres.

<u>Tangential section</u>
Rays 1-2(3)seriate (mostly biseriate).

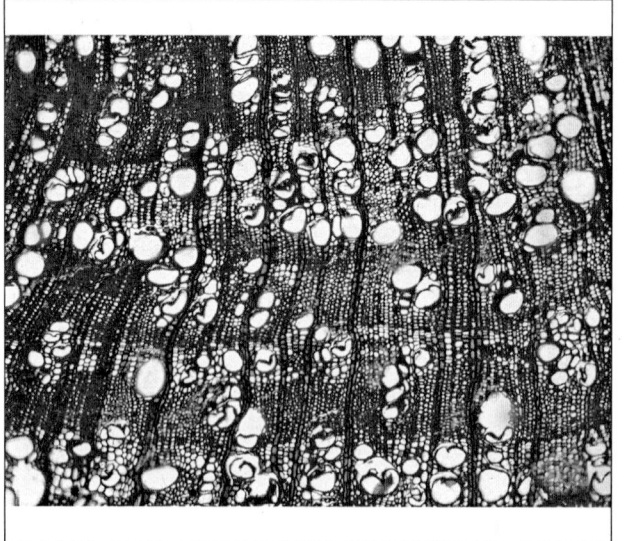

Azadirachta indica TS x100

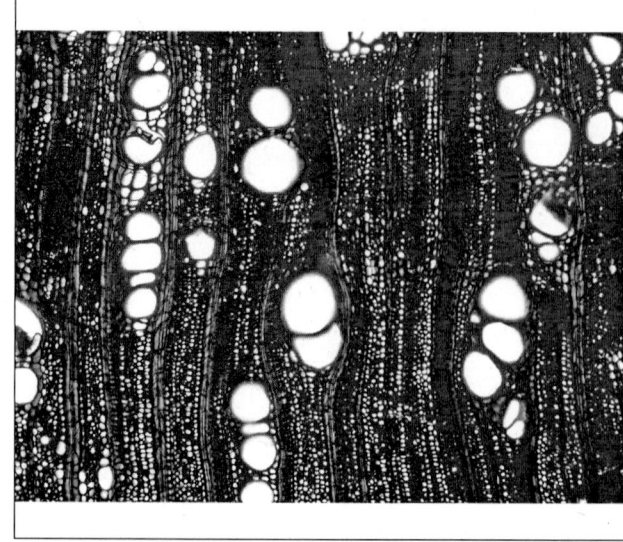

Azadirachta indica TS x100

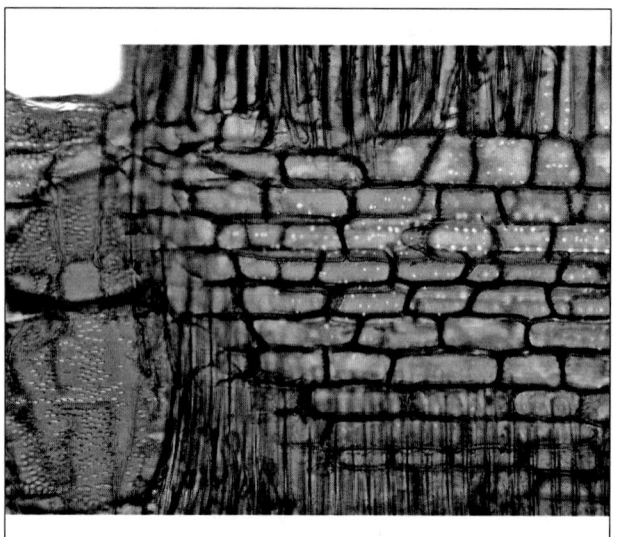

Azadirachta indica RLS x400

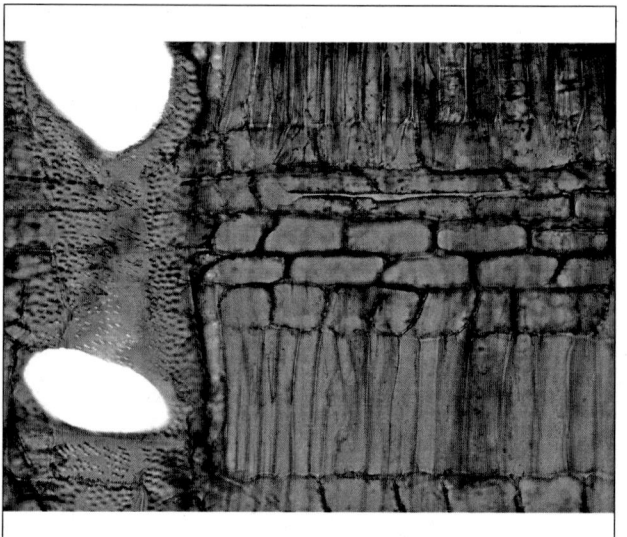

Azadirachta indica RLS x400

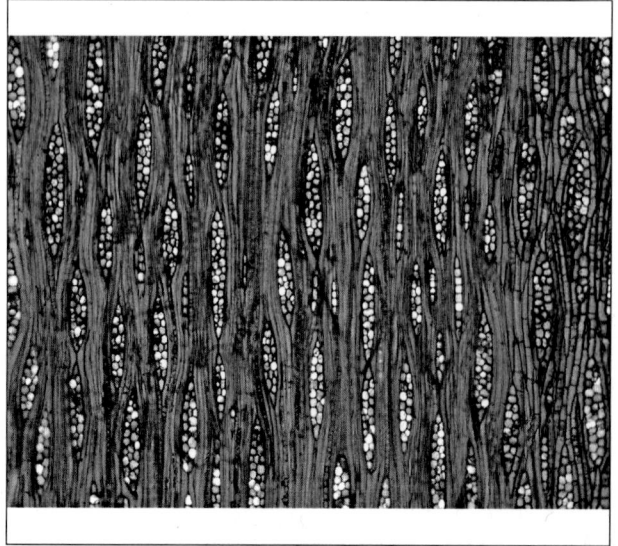

Azadirachta indica TLS x100

# MELIACEAE

*Soymida* sp.
(species examined: *S. febrifuga*)

Description:

Transverse section
Diffuse porous. Ring boundary distinct to indistinct. Pores medium, dense, in radial multiples of 2–3 and (irregular) clusters. Parenchyma paratracheal (aliform, occasionally confluent) and banded (terminal bands 3–5 cells wide and narrow bands).

Radial section
Perforation plates simple. Intervessel pits alternate, minute. Vessel-ray pits with distinct borders, similar in shape, size to intervessel pits. Ground tissue fibres with simple to minutely bordered pits, thick-walled. Rays homogeneous to heterogeneous (1 row of square marginal cells).

Tangential section
Rays 2(3)-5seriate.

Soymida febrifuga TS x40

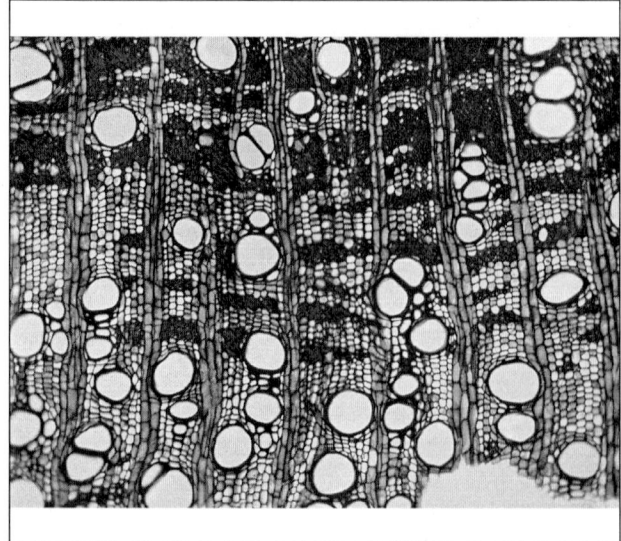
Soymida febrifuga TS x100

Soymida febrifuga RLS x100

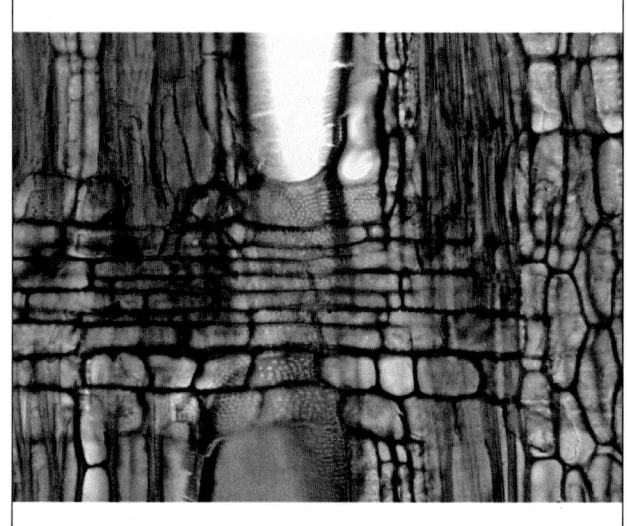
Soymida febrifuga RLS x400

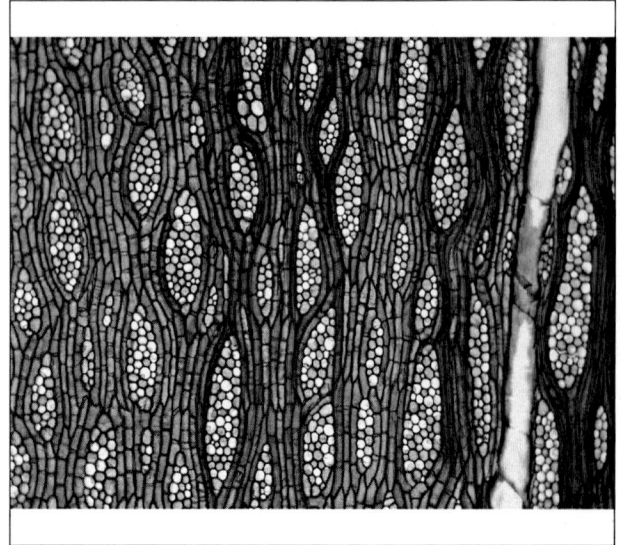
Soymida febrifuga TLS x100

# MORACEAE

*Artocarpus* sp.
(species examined: *A. heterophylla*, syn. *A. integrigolia*)

Description:

<u>Transverse section</u>
Diffuse-porous. Ring boundary indistinct. Pores medium to large, solitary, and in radial multiples of 2(3)-4, rarely in small clusters. Parenchyma paratracheal, scanty paratracheal, and apotracheal (diffuse, diffuse-in-aggregates).

<u>Radial section</u>
Perforation plates simple. Intervessel pits alternate, small. Vessel-ray pits with reduced to apparently simple borders, rounded/angular/scalariform. Ground tissue fibres with simple to minutely bordered pits, thin- to thick-walled. Rays heterogeneous (consisting of a central part of strongly procumbent cells and 1–4 rows of square and/or upright marginal cells). Parenchyma-like fibre bands present.

<u>Tangential section</u>
Rays (3)4-5(6)seriate. Sheath cells present. Latex tubes occasionally present.

Artocarpus heterophylla TS x40

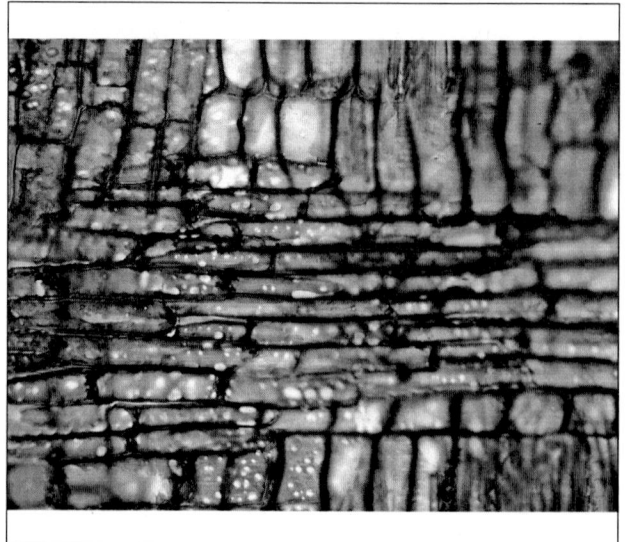

Artocarpus heterophylla RLS x400

Artocarpus heterophylla RLS x400

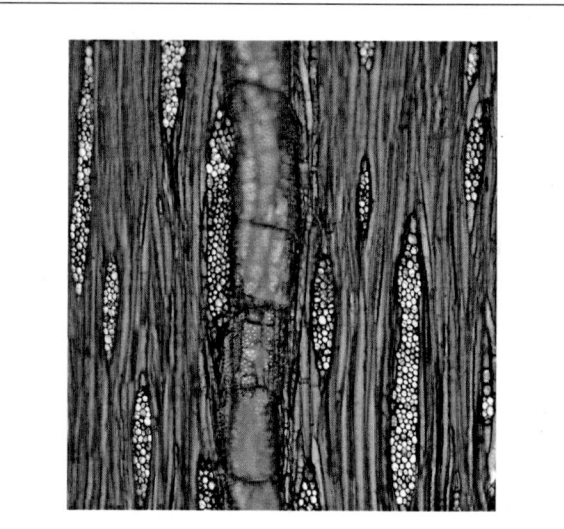

Artocarpus heterophylla TLS x100

Artocarpus heterophylla TS x100

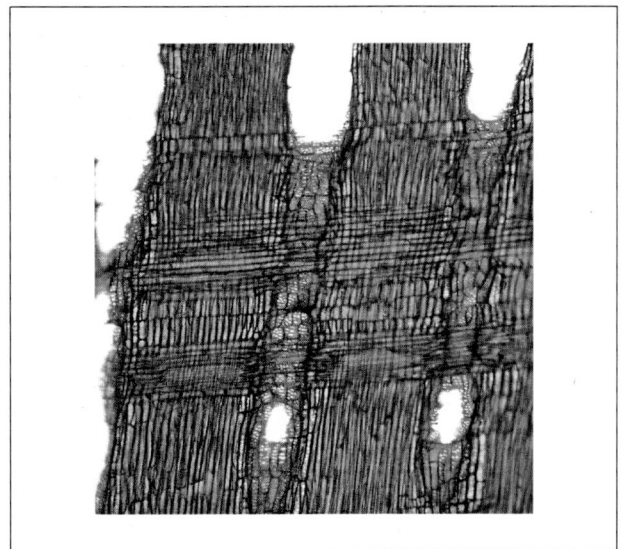

Artocarpus heterophylla RLS x100

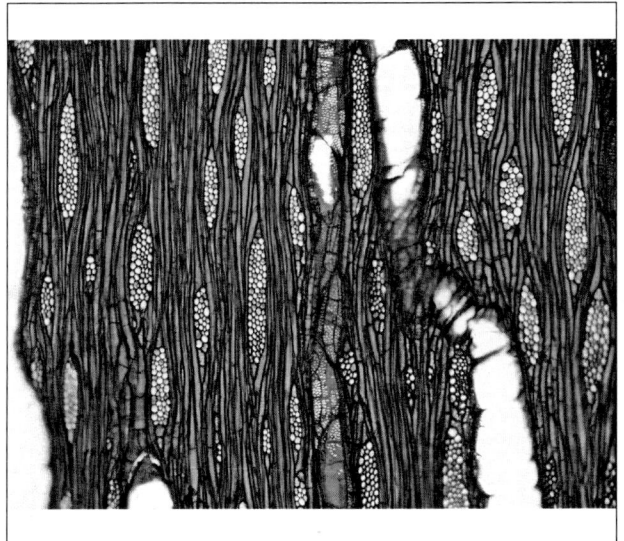

Artocarpus heterophylla TLS x100

# MORACEAE

*Ficus* sp.
(species examined: *F. benghalensis*)

Description:

Transverse section
Diffuse-porous. Ring boundary indistinct. Pores medium to large, solitary, in radial multiples of 2–4 (common) and clusters. Parenchyma banded (bands more than 3 cells wide).

Radial section
Perforation plates simple. Intervessel pits alternate, small. Vessel-ray pits with reduced to apparently simple borders, rounded/angular/scalariform. Ground tissue fibres with simple to minutely bordered pits, thin- to thick-walled. Rays heterogeneous (consisting of a central part of strongly procumbent cells and 2–4 rows of square and/or upright marginal cells). Parenchyma-like fibre bands present.

Tangential section
Rays (2-3)4-6seriate. Sheath cells present. Latex tubes occasionally present.

Ficus benghalensis TS x40

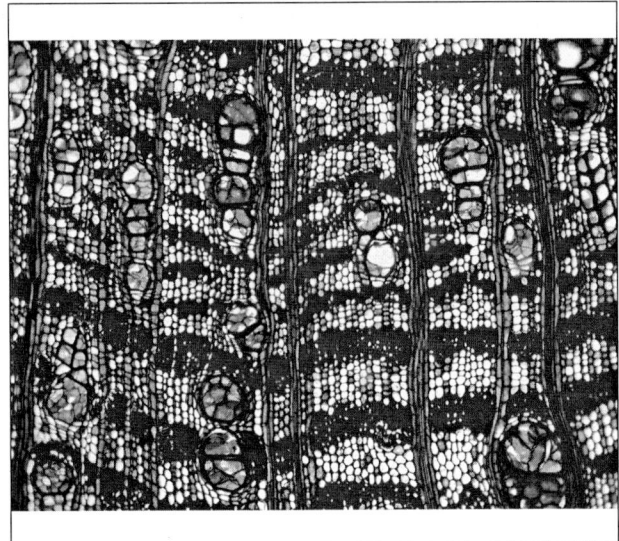
Ficus benghalensis TS x100

Ficus benghalensis RLS x100

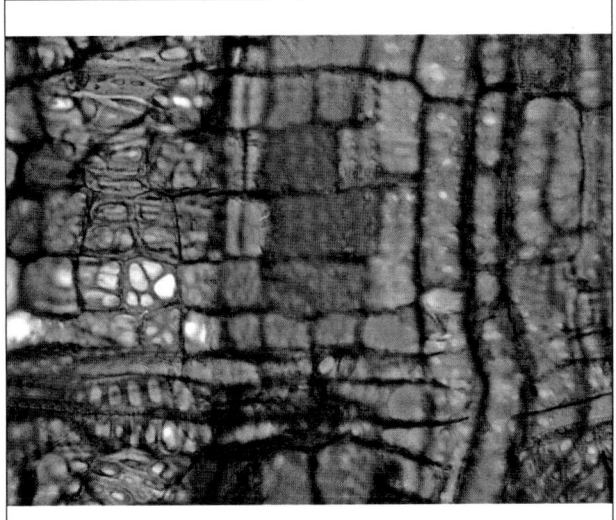
Ficus benghalensis RLS x630

Ficus benghalensis TLS x100

# MORACEAE

*Streblus* sp.

(species examined: *S. asper*)

Description:

Transverse section
Diffuse-porous. Ring boundary indistinct. Pores medium to large, solitary, in radial multiples of 2 (common) and clusters (rare). Parenchyma scanty paratracheal and diffuse, diffuse-in-aggregates.

Radial section
Perforation plates simple. Intervessel pits alternate. Vessel-ray pits with reduced to apparently simple borders, rounded/angular/scalariform. Ground tissue fibres with simple to minutely bordered pits, thin- to thick-walled. Rays heterogeneous (consisting of a central part of strongly procumbent cells and 2–4 or more rows of square and/or upright marginal cells).

Tangential section
Rays (1)2-3(4)seriate, tall. Sheath cells present.

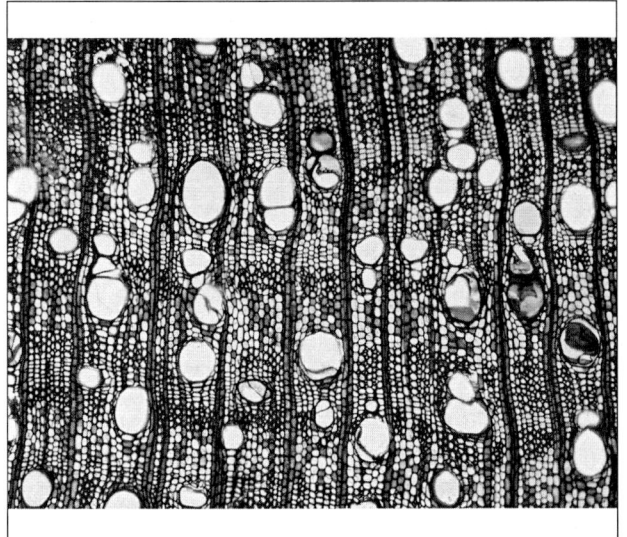

Streblus asper TS x100

Streblus asper RLS x400

Streblus asper RLS x400

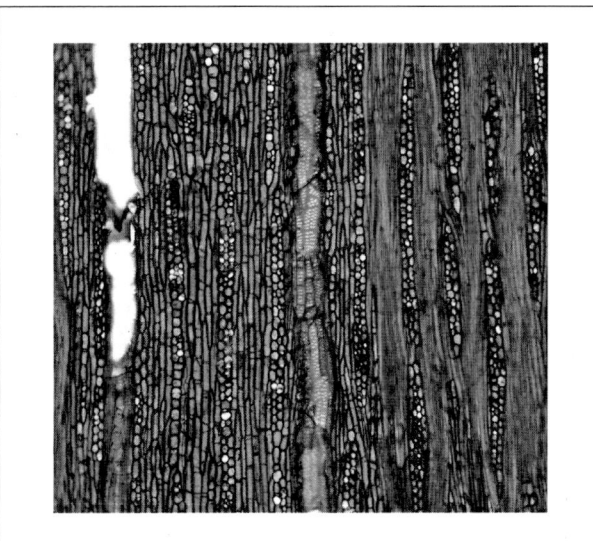

Streblus asper TLS x100

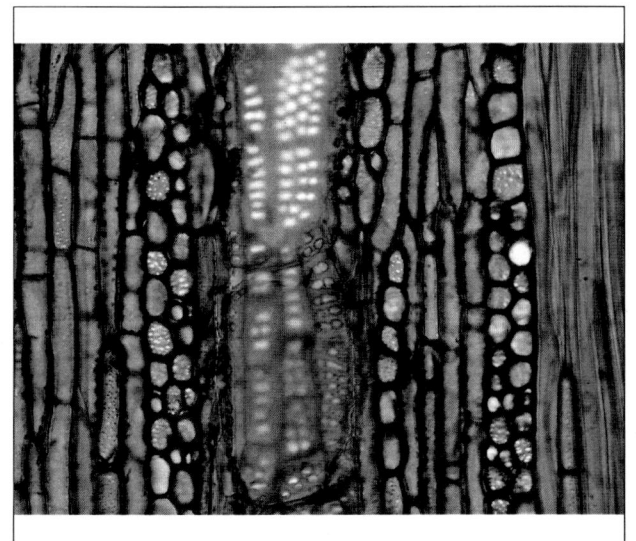

Streblus asper TLS x400

# MORINGACEAE

*Moringa* sp.
(species examined: *M. oleifera*)

Description:

Transverse section
Diffuse-porous. Ring boundary distinct to indistinct. Pores medium, in radial multiples of (2)3-4 and solitary, sparse. Parenchyma paratracheal, scanty paratracheal and vasicentric (sometimes slightly aliform).

Radial section
Perforation plates simple. Intervessel pits alternate, medium to large. Vessel-ray pits with reduced to apparently simple borders, rounded/angular. Ground tissue fibres with large pits on their radial walls, thin-walled. Rays homogeneous to heterogeneous (1 row of square and/or upright marginal cells).

Tangential section
Rays bi- to 3seriate, storied.

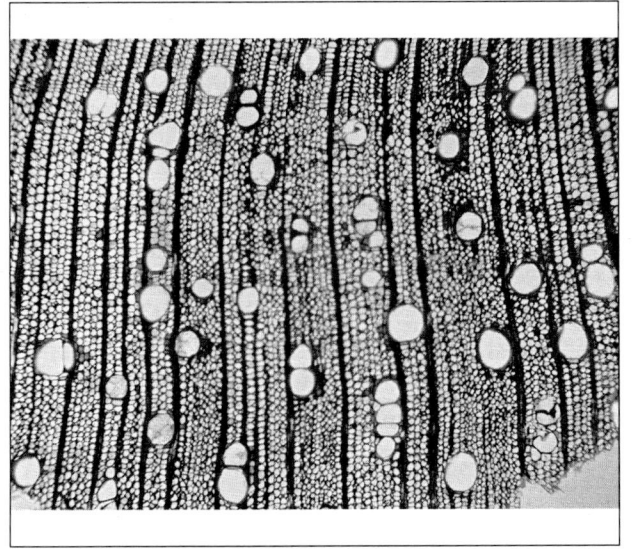
Moringa oleifera TS x100

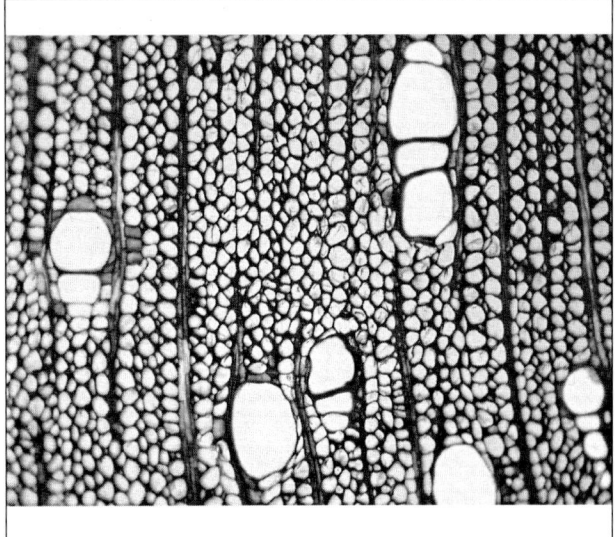
Moringa oleifera RLS x400

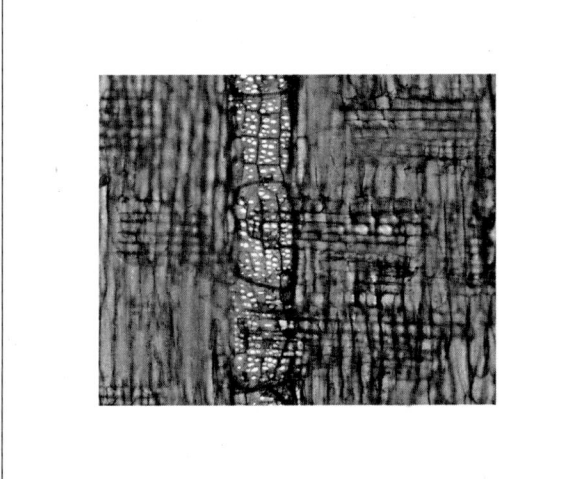
Moringa oleifera RLS x400

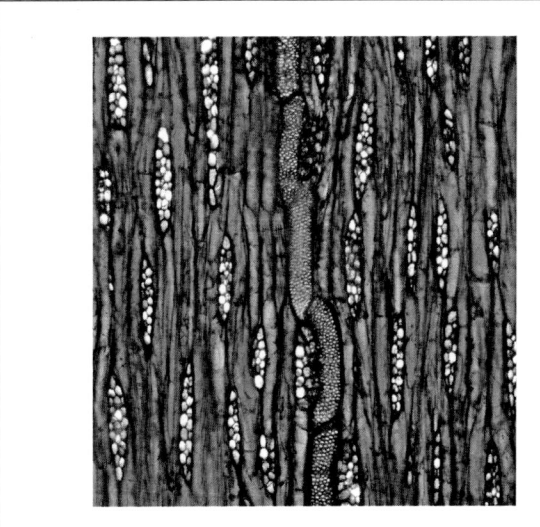
Moringa oleifera TLS x100

Wood Anatomical Descriptions

# MYRTACEAE

*Barringtonia* sp.
(species examined: *B. acutangula*)

Description:

Transverse section
Diffuse-porous. Ring boundary distinct to indistinct. Pores medium to large, in radial multiples of (2)3-4 or more and in clusters (the latter sometimes arranged in marginal rows). Parenchyma apotracheal (diffuse-in-aggregates) and scanty paratracheal.

Radial section
Perforation plates simple. Intervessel pits alternate, medium. Vessel-ray pits with reduced to apparently simple borders, rounded/angular/scalariform. Ground tissue fibres with simple to minutely bordered pits, thick-walled. Septate fibres present. Rays heterogeneous (2 to over 4 rows of square and/or upright marginal cells). Uniseriate rays composed entirely of upright cells. Axial parenchyma and vessels storied. Crystals present in ray cells.

Tangential section
Rays uni- and 3-4(5-6)seriate, tall.

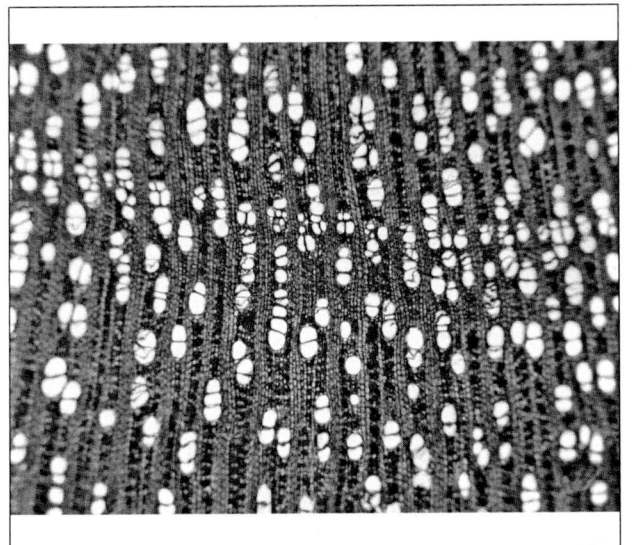

Barringtonia acutangula TS x40

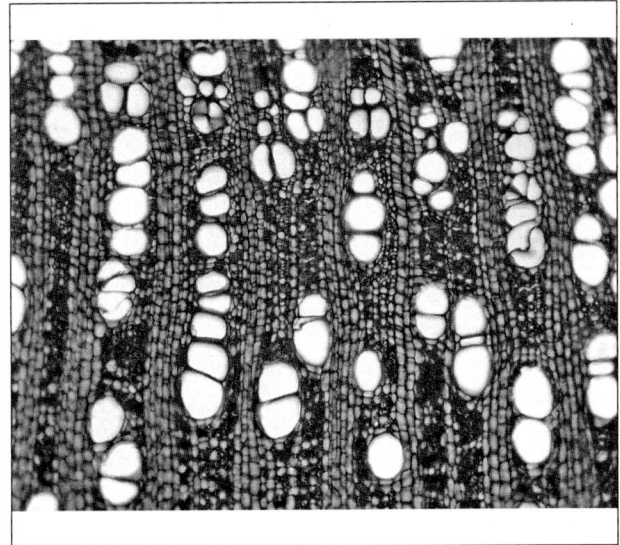

Barringtonia acutangula TS x100

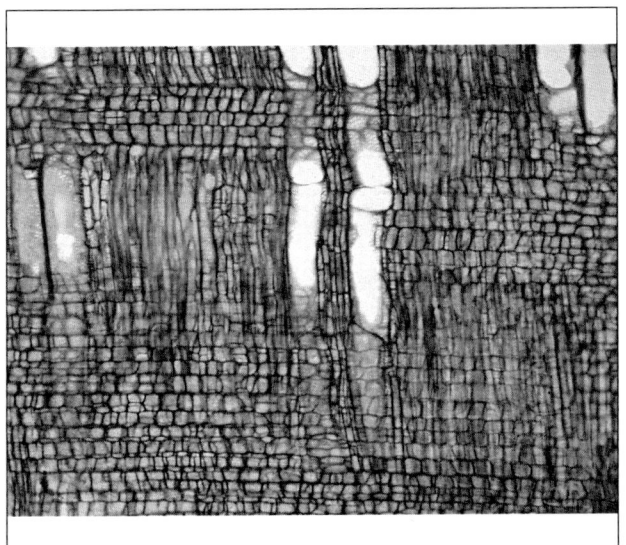

Barringtonia acutangula RLS x100

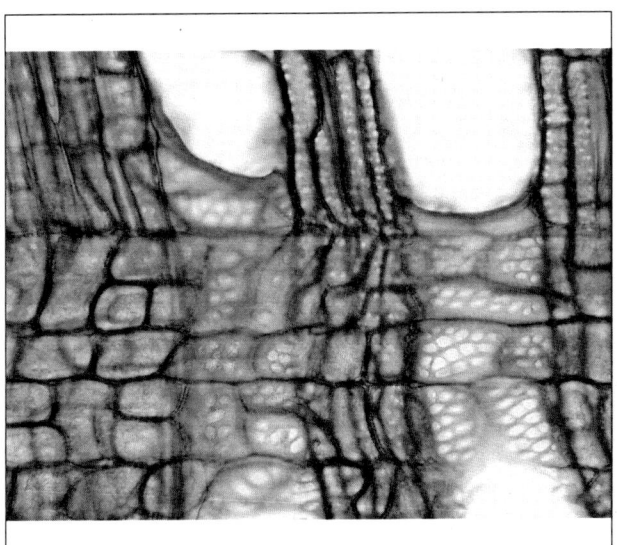

Barringtonia acutangula RLS x400

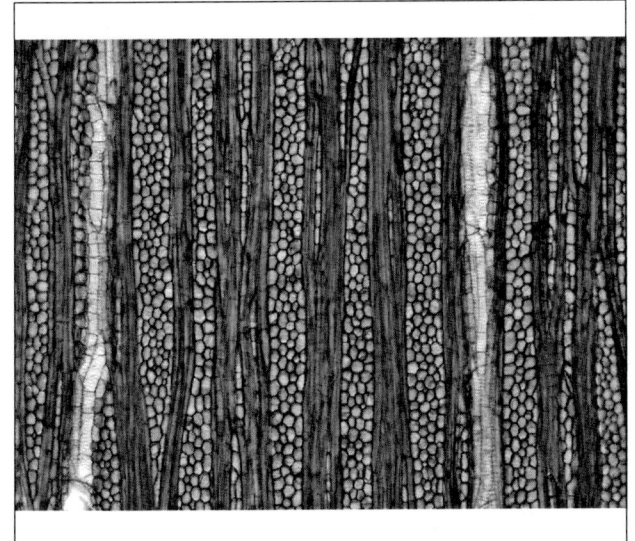

Barringtonia acutangula TLS x100

# MYRTACEAE

*Careya* sp.
(species examined: *C. arborea*)

Description:

Transverse section
Diffuse-porous. Ring boundary distinct to indistinct. Pores small to large, in radial multiples of 2-(3)4 or more (common) and clusters. Parenchyma apotracheal (diffuse), and scanty paratracheal.

Radial section
Perforation plates simple. Intervessel pits alternate, medium, polygonal. Vessel-ray pits with reduced to apparently simple borders, horizontal (scalariform, gashlike) to vertical (palisade). Ground tissue fibres with simple to minutely bordered pits, thick-walled. Rays heterogeneous (with over 4 rows of square and/or upright marginal cells). Uniseriate rays composed entirely of upright cells. Crystals present in fibres.

Tangential section
Rays uni- and (2-3)4-5seriate.

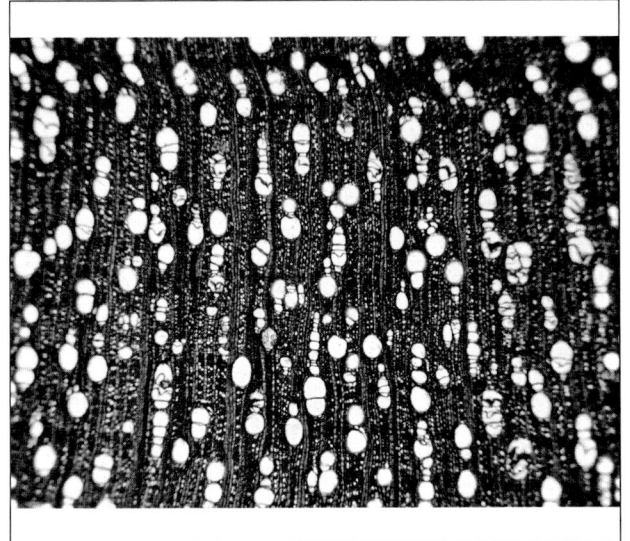
Careya arborea TS x40

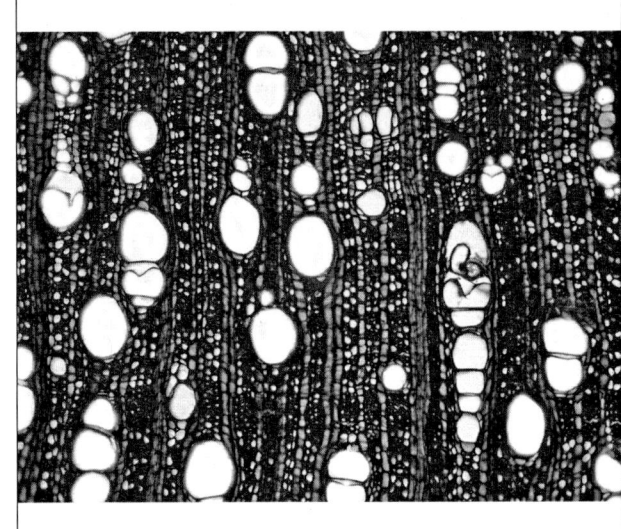
Careya arborea TS x100

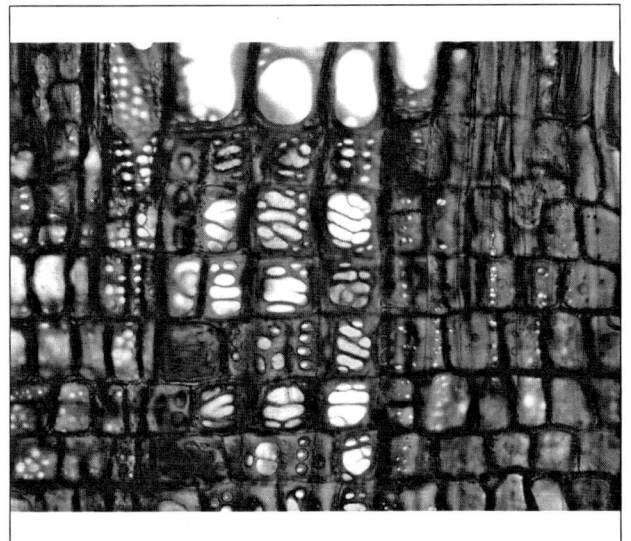
Careya arborea RLS x400

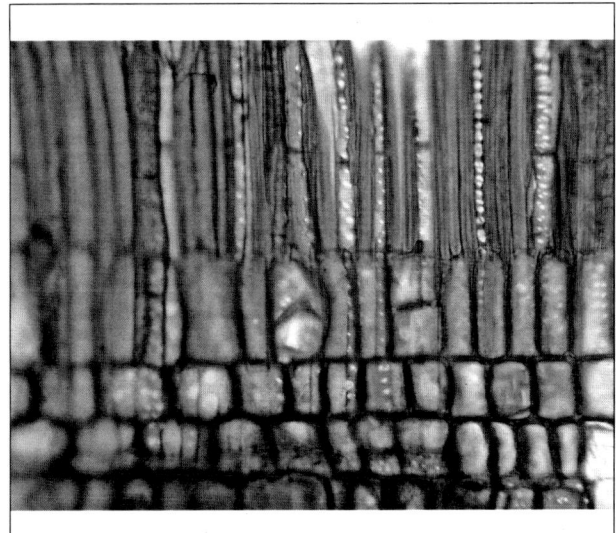
Careya arborea RLS x400

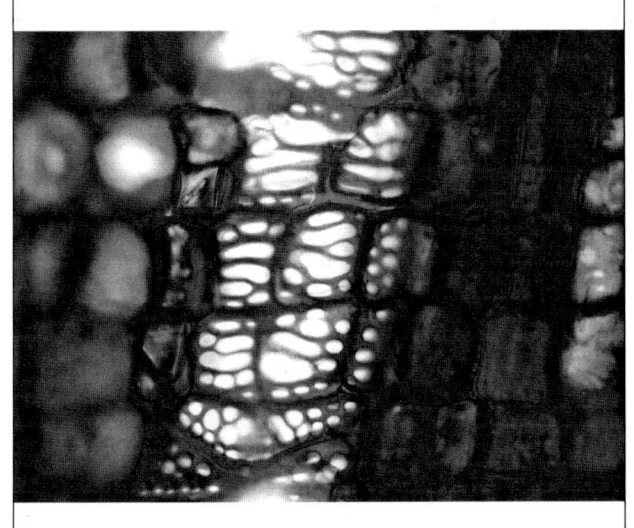
Careya arborea RLS x630

Careya arborea TLS x100

# MYRTACEAE

*Syzygium* sp.
(species examined: *Syzygium cumini*, syn. *Eugenia jambolana*)

Description:

### Transverse section
Diffuse-porous. Ring boundary distinct to indistinct. Pores medium to large, solitary, and in radial multiples of 2–4 or more. Parenchyma apotracheal diffuse, diffuse-in-aggregates and banded (common).

### Radial section
Perforation plates simple. Intervessel pits alternate, minute. Vessel-ray pits with reduced to apparently simple borders, horizontal (scalariform, gash-like) to vertical (palisade). Ground tissue fibres with simple to minutely bordered pits, thick-walled. Vascular tracheids present. Rays heterogeneous (with a central part of strongly procumbent cells and 2 to over 4 rows of square and/or upright marginal cells). Parenchyma-like fibre bands present. Uniseriate rays composed entirely of upright cells.

### Tangential section
Rays (1)2-3seriate (with uni- and multiseriate portions).

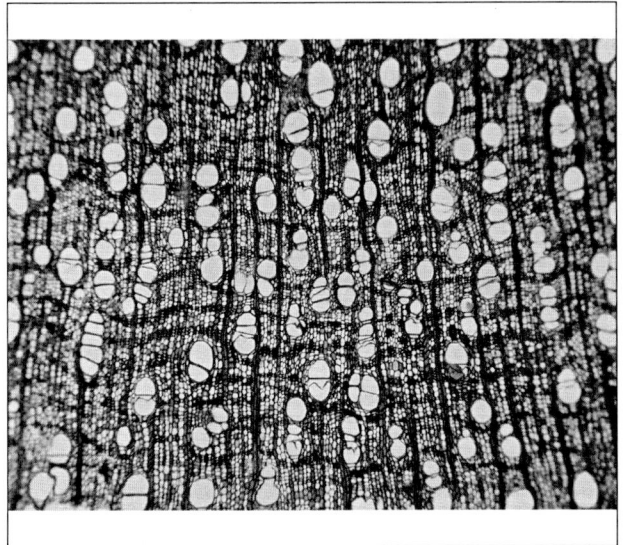
Syzygium cumini TS x40

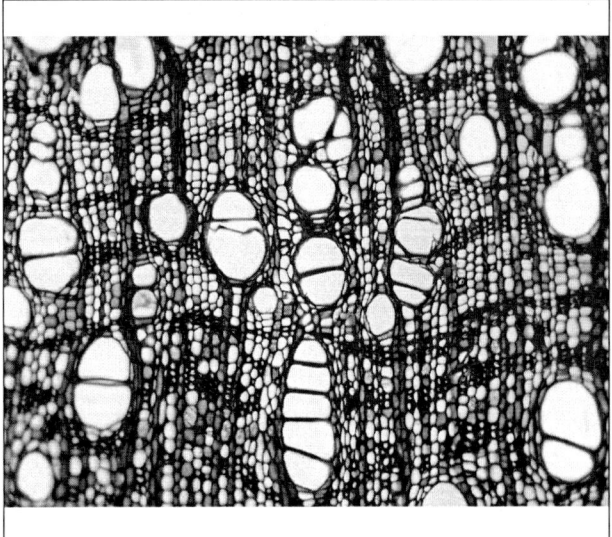
Syzygium cumini TS x100

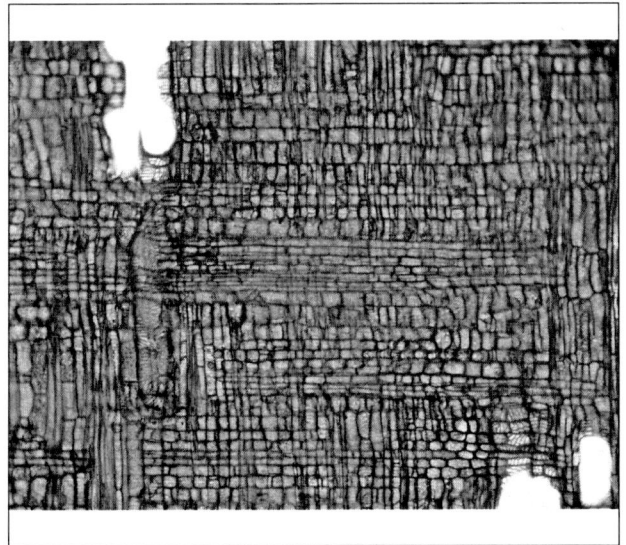
Syzygium cumini RLS x100

Syzygium cumini RLS x400

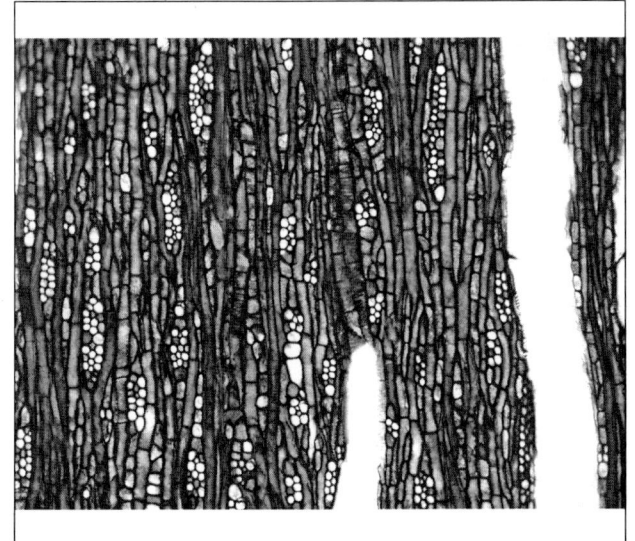
Syzygium cumini TLS x100

# RHAMNACEAE

*Ziziphus* sp.
(species examined: *Z. mauritiana*)

Description:

Transverse section
Diffuse-porous. Ring boundary indistinct. Pores medium to large, solitary, and in radial multiples of 2–3 (common). Parenchyma paratracheal (vasicentric and scanty paratracheal) and apotracheal (diffuse-in-aggregates).

Radial section
Perforation plates simple. Intervessel pits opposite to alternate, medium. Vessel-ray pits with distinct borders, similar in shape, size to intervessel pits. Ground tissue fibres with simple to minutely bordered pits, thick-walled. Rays homogeneous to heterogeneous (composed of square, upright and weakly procumbent cells).

Tangential section
Rays 1-2seriate.

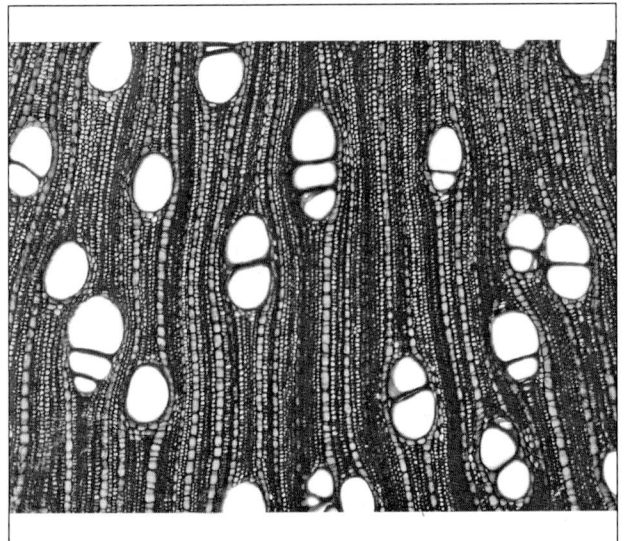

Ziziphus mauritiana TS x100

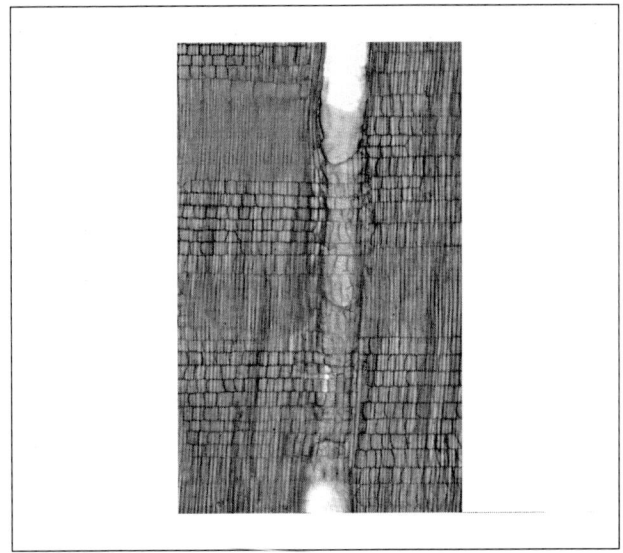

Ziziphus mauritiana RLS x100

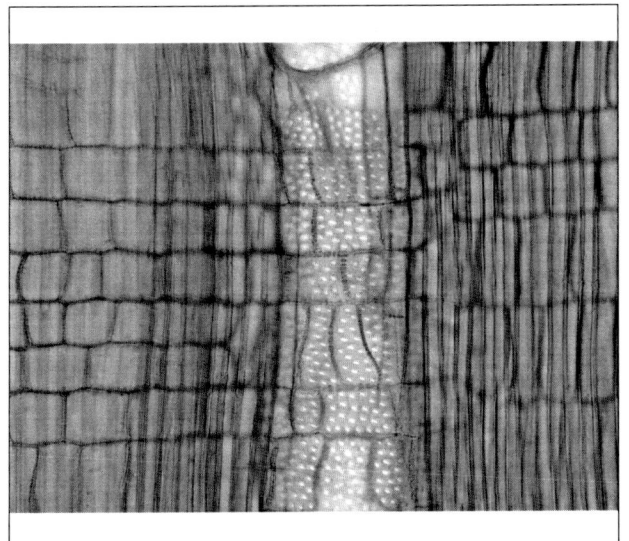

Ziziphus mauritiana RLS x400

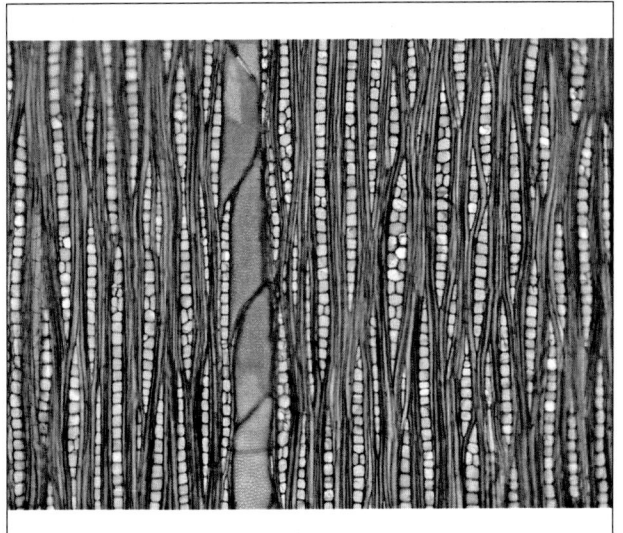

Ziziphus mauritiana TLS x100

# RUBIACEAE

*Adina* sp.
(species examined: *A. cordifolia*)

Description:

Transverse section
Diffuse-porous. Ring boundary distinct to indistinct. Pores small, solitary (common), and in radial multiples of 2(3) (rare). Parenchyma rare, scanty paratracheal and apotracheal (diffuse).

Radial section
Perforation plates simple. Intervessel pits alternate, minute. Vessel-ray pits with distinct borders, similar in shape, size to intervessel pits. Ground tissue fibres with distinctly bordered pits, thin to thick-walled. Rays heterogeneous, with a central part of procumbent cells and over 4 rows of square and/or upright marginal cells. Uniseriate rays composed entirely of upright cells.

Tangential section
Rays 1-2(3)seriate (with uni- and multiseriate portions).

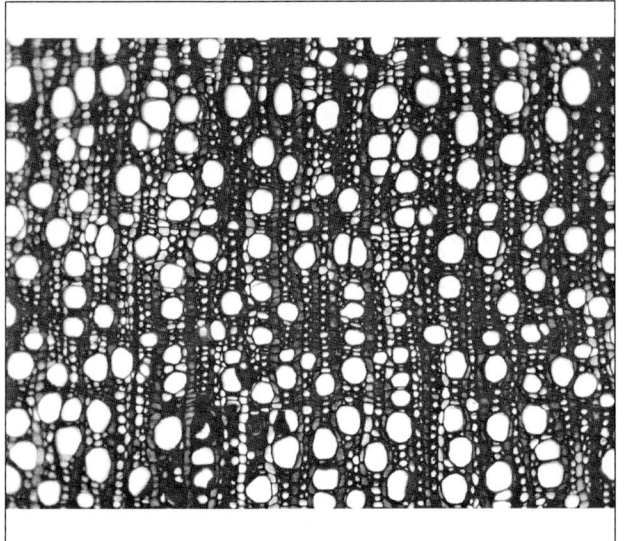
Adina cordifolia TS x100

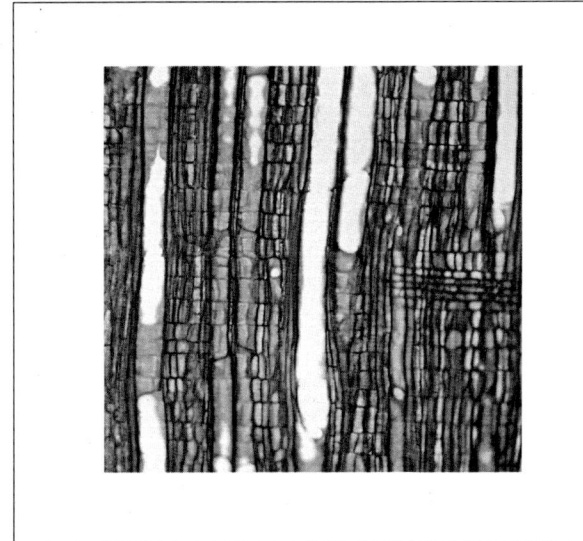
Adina cordifolia RLS x100

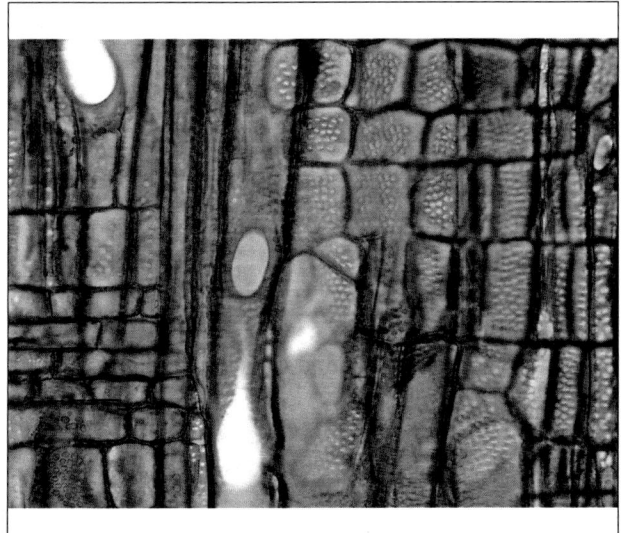
Adina cordifolia RLS x400

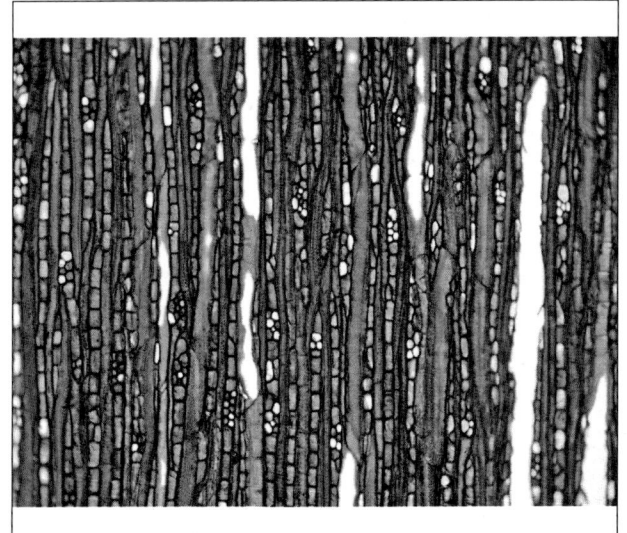
Adina cordifolia TLS x100

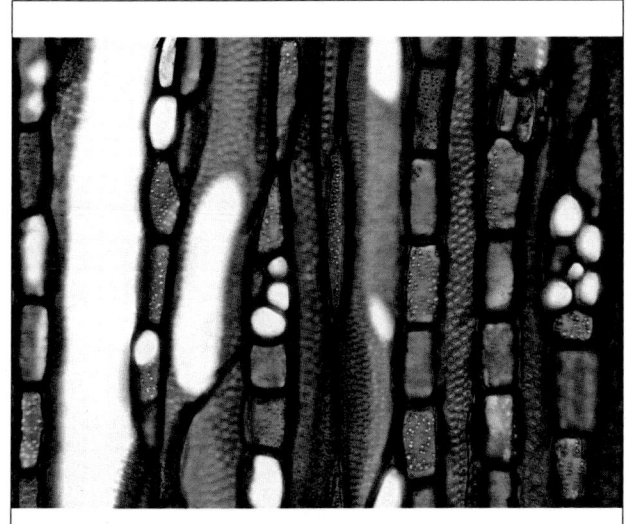
Adina cordifolia TLS x400

# RUBIACEAE

*Canthium* sp.
(species examined: *C. coromandelicum, C. dicoccum*)

Description:

<u>Transverse section</u>
Diffuse-porous. Ring boundary indistinct. Pores small, solitary (common), rarely in radial multiples of 2(3). Parenchyma apotracheal, diffuse.

<u>Radial section</u>
Perforation plates simple and scalariform (rare). Intervessel pits opposite to alternate, small to minute. Vessel-ray pits with distinct borders, similar in shape, size to intervessel pits. Ground tissue fibres with distinctly bordered pits, thin- to thick-walled. Rays heterogeneous, with a central part of procumbent cells and over 4 rows of square and/or upright marginal cells. Uniseriate rays composed entirely of upright cells.

<u>Tangential section</u>
Rays uni- to 2(3)seriate.

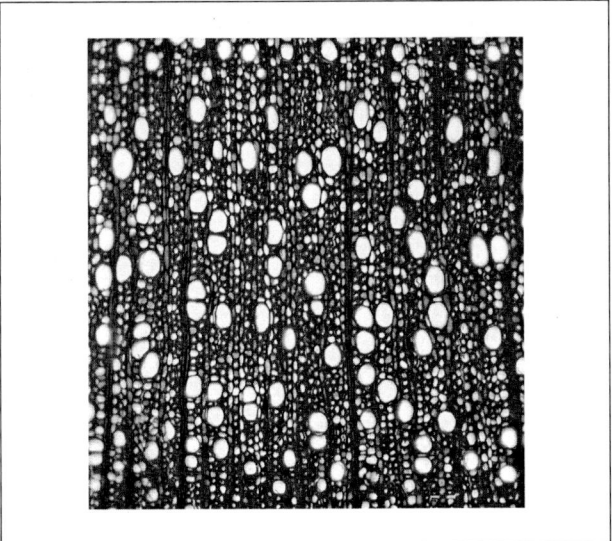
Canthium coromandelicum TS x100

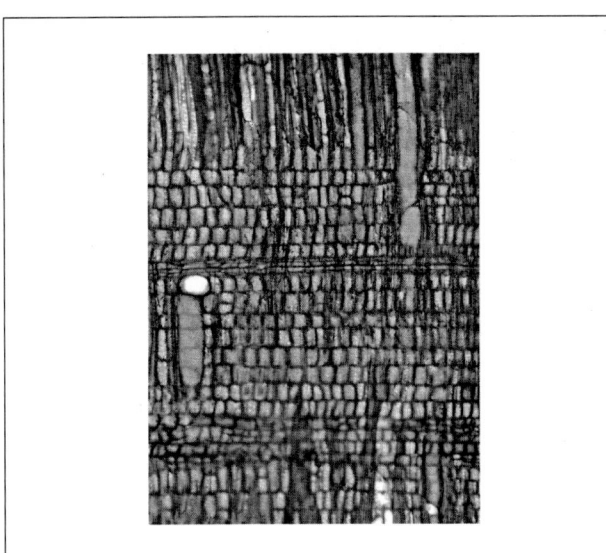
Canthium coromandelicum RLS x100

Canthium coromandelicum RLS x400

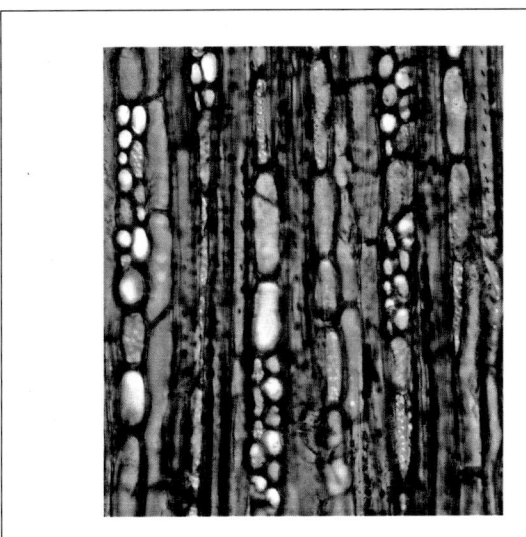
Canthium coromandelicum TLS x400

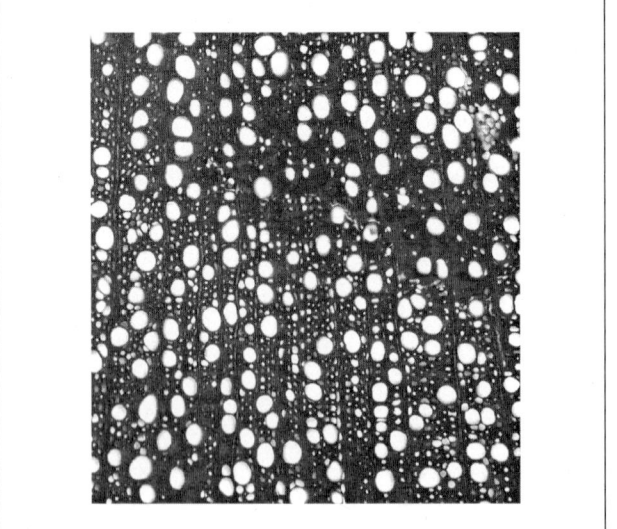

Canthium dicoccum TS x100

Canthium dicoccum RLS x100

Canthium dicoccum RLS x400

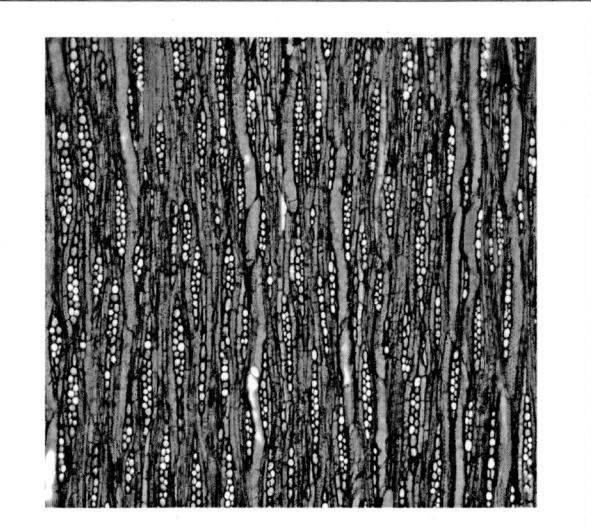

Canthium dicoccum TLS x100

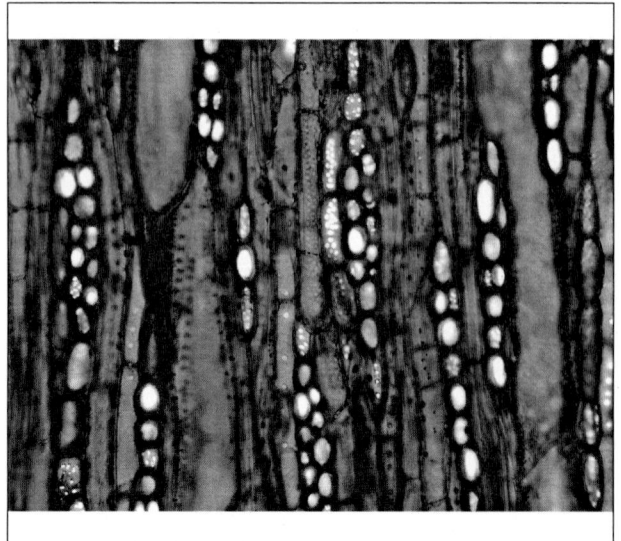

Canthium dicoccum TLS x400

# RUBIACEAE

*Gardenia* sp.
(species examined: *G. resinifera*)

Description:

Transverse section
Diffuse-porous. Ring boundary distinct to indistinct. Pores small, solitary (common) and in radial multiples of 2 (rare). Parenchyma apotracheal (diffuse) and scanty paratracheal.

Radial section
Perforation plates simple. Intervessel pits alternate, small to minute. Vessel-ray pits with distinct borders, similar in shape, size to intervessel pits. Ground tissue fibres with simple to minutely bordered pits, thin- to thick-walled. Rays heterogeneous with a central part of procumbent cells and over 4 rows of square and/or upright marginal cells.

Tangential section
Rays 1-2seriate.

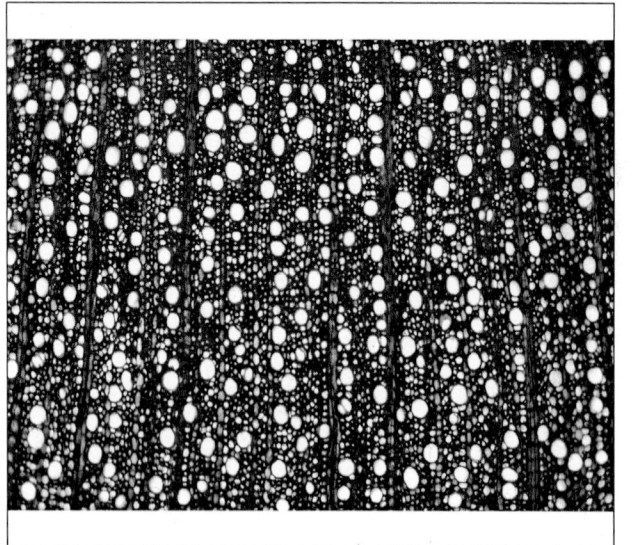

Gardenia resinifera TS x100

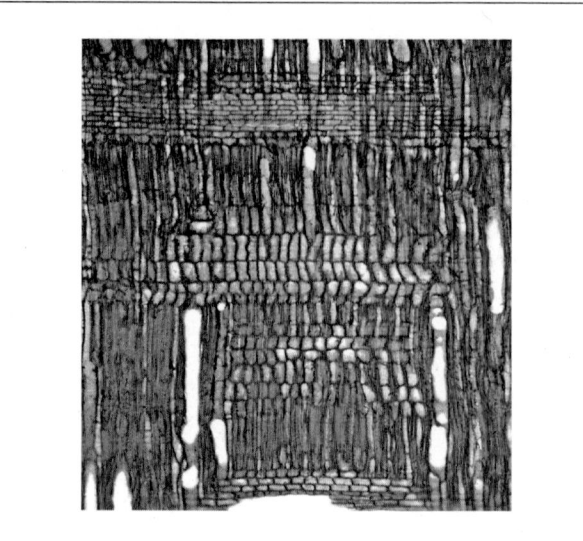

Gardenia resinifera RLS x100

Gardenia resinifera RLS x400

Gardenia resinifera TLS x400

# RUBIACEAE

*Ixora* sp.
(species examined: *I. parviflora*)

Description:

Transverse section
Diffuse to semi-ring porous. Ring boundary indistinct to distinct. Pores small to medium, solitary (common, in slightly dendritic arrangement), and in radial multiples of 2 (rare). Parenchyma apotracheal (diffuse) and scanty paratracheal (rare).

Radial section
Perforation plates simple. Intervessel pits alternate, small to minute. Vessel-ray pits with distinct borders, similar in shape, size to intervessel pits. Ground tissue fibres with distinctly bordered pits, thick-walled. Rays heterogeneous, with a narrow central part composed of procumbent cells and over 4 rows of square and/or upright marginal cells. Uniseriate rays composed entirely of upright cells. Crystals present in ray cells.

Tangential section
Rays 1-3seriate.

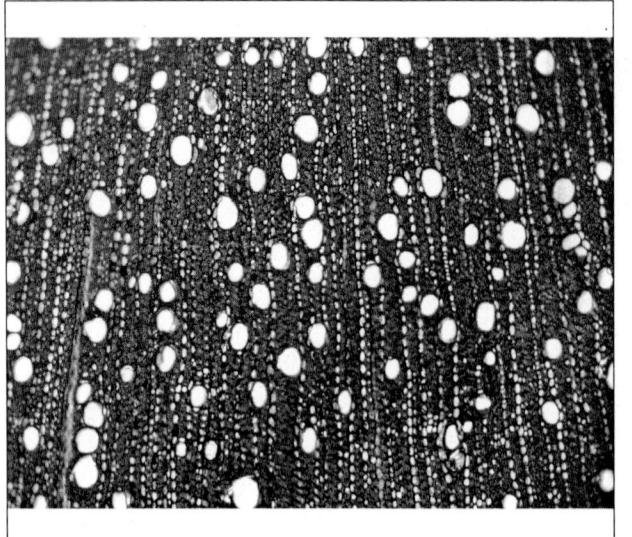
Ixora parviflora TS x100

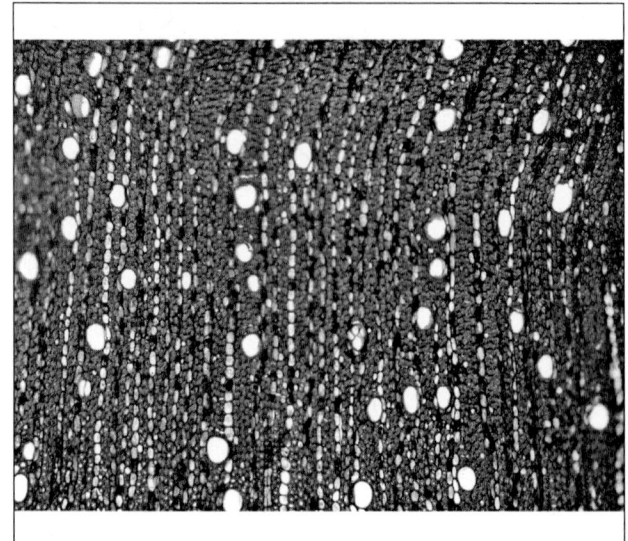
Ixora parviflora TS x100

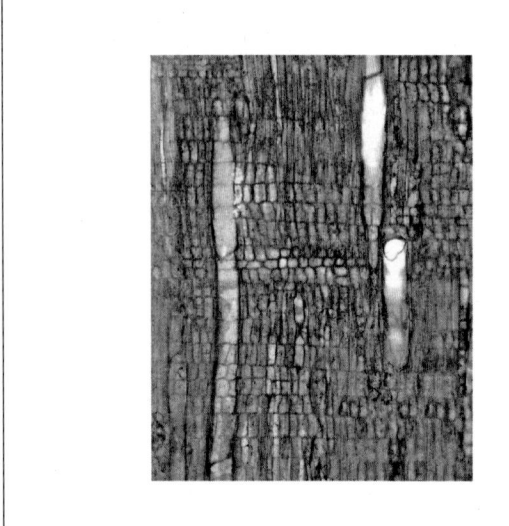
Ixora parviflora RLS x100

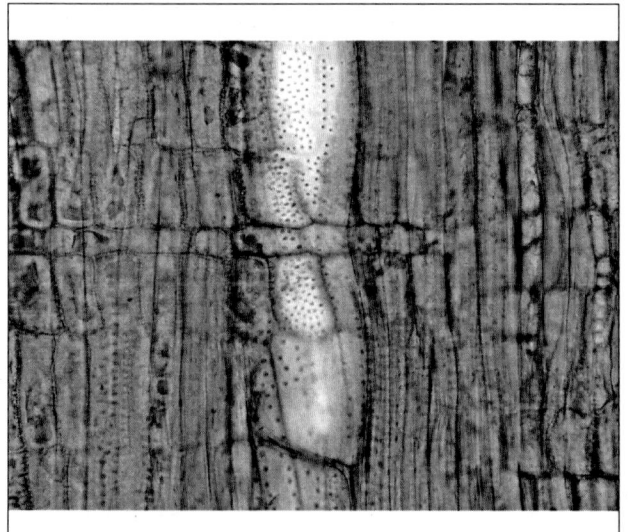
Ixora parviflora RLS x400

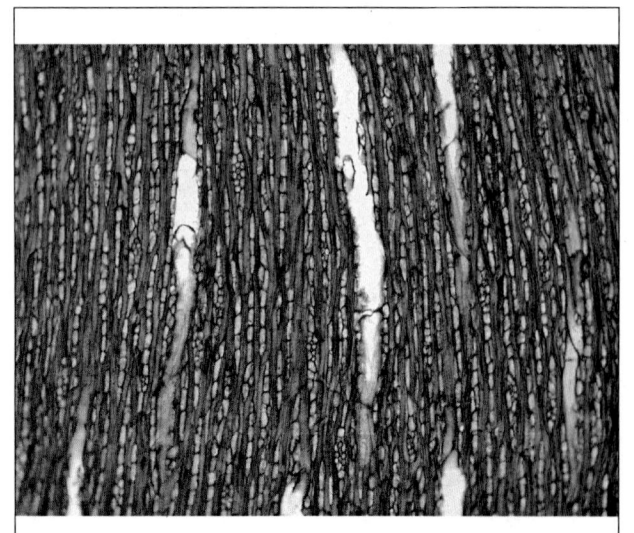
Ixora parviflora TLS x100

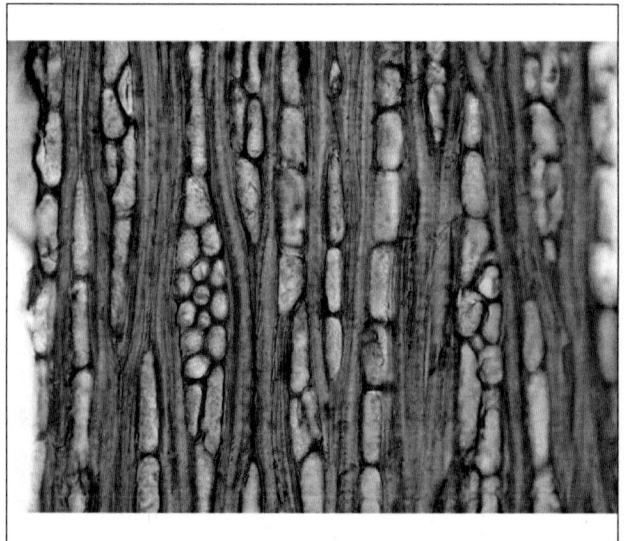
Ixora parviflora TLS x400

# RUBIACEAE

*Mitragyna* sp.
(species examined: *M. parvifolia*)

Description:

Transverse section
Diffuse porous. Ring boundary distinct to indistinct. Pores small, solitary (common), and in radial multiples of 2 (rare). Parenchyma apotracheal (diffuse and diffuse-in-aggregates).

Radial section
Perforation plates simple. Intervessel pits alternate, small to minute. Vessel-ray pits with distinct borders, similar in shape, size to intervessel pits. Ground tissue fibres with distinctly bordered pits, thin- to thick-walled. Rays heterogeneous, with a central part of strongly procumbent cells and over 4 rows of square and/or upright marginal cells. Uniseriate rays composed entirely of upright cells.

Tangential section
Rays uni- and 3-4seriate (with uni- and multiseriate portions).

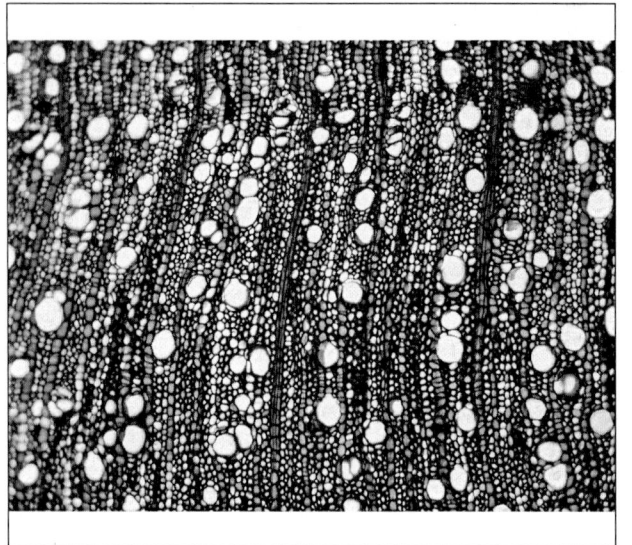
Mitragyna parvifolia TS x100

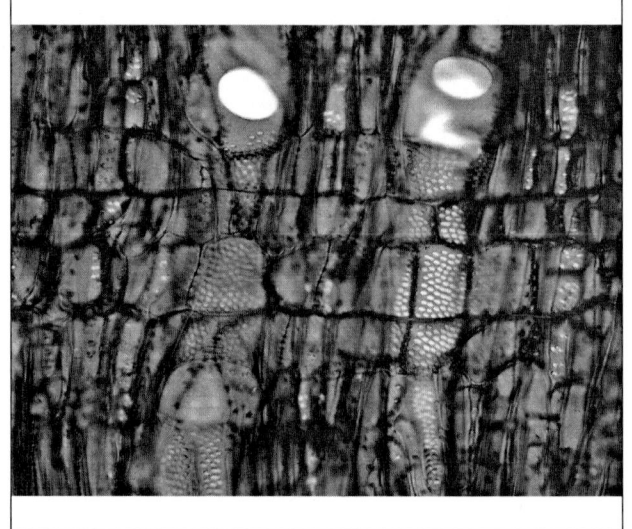
Mitragyna parvifolia RLS x400

Mitragyna parvifolia TLS x100

# RUBIACEAE

*Morinda* sp.
(species examined: *M. tinctoria*)

Description:

Transverse section
Diffuse porous. Ring boundary indistinct. Pores small to medium, in irregular clusters (common) and radial multiples of 3-4. Parenchyma apotracheal (diffuse).

Radial section
Perforation plates simple. Intervessel pits alternate, minute. Vessel-ray pits with distinct borders, similar in shape, size to intervessel pits. Ground tissue fibres with simple to minutely bordered pits, thin to thick-walled. Rays heterogeneous, with over 4 rows of square and/or upright marginal cells. Uniseriate rays composed entirely of upright cells. Crystals present in ray cells.

Tangential section
Rays 1(2)-4(5)seriate.

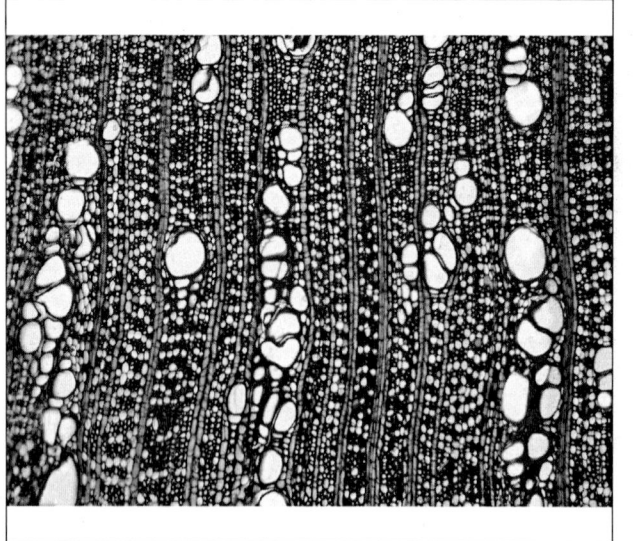
Morinda tinctoria TS x100

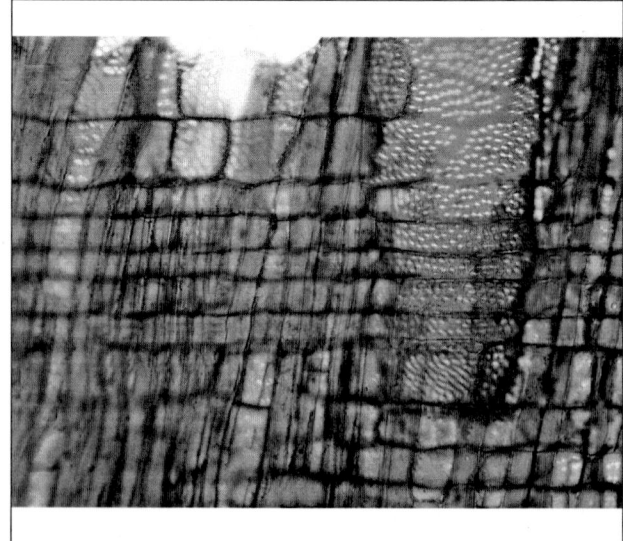
Morinda tinctoria RLS x400

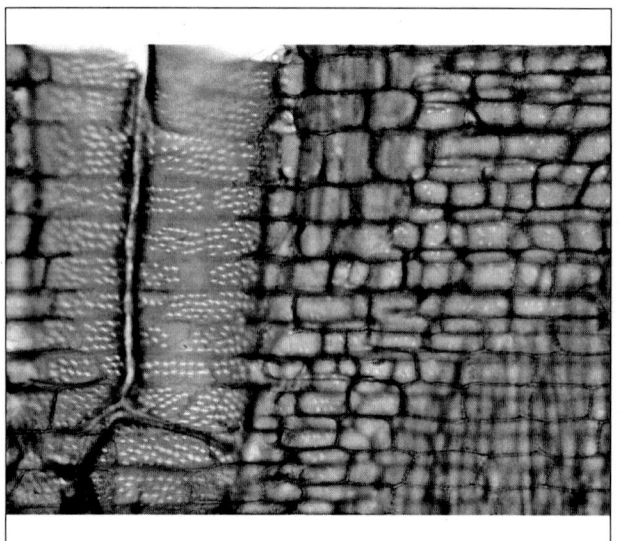
Morinda tinctoria RLS x400

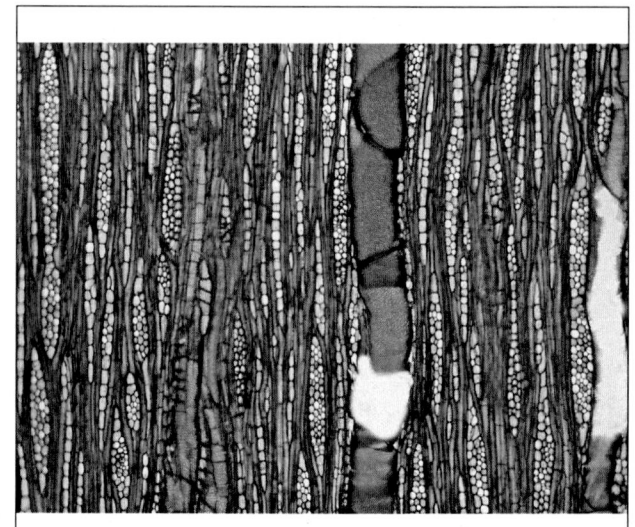
Morinda tinctoria TLS x100

# RUTACEAE

*Chloroxylon* sp.
(species examined: *C. swietenia*)

Description:

Transverse section
Diffuse to semi-ring porous. Ring boundary distinct. Pores medium to large, dense, in radial multiples of 4 or more (common), occasionally in clusters. Parenchyma paratracheal, vasicentric, scanty paratracheal and in marginal bands. Intercellular canals of traumatic origin present.

Radial section
Perforation plates simple. Intervessel pits alternate, minute. Vessel-ray pits with distinct borders, similar in shape, size to intervessel pits. Ground tissue fibres with simple to minutely bordered pits, thin- to thick-walled. Rays heterogeneous with a central part of procumbent cells and 1 row of square and/or upright marginal cells. Rays storied. Crystals present in fibres and parenchyma.

Tangential section
Rays (2)3-4seriate.

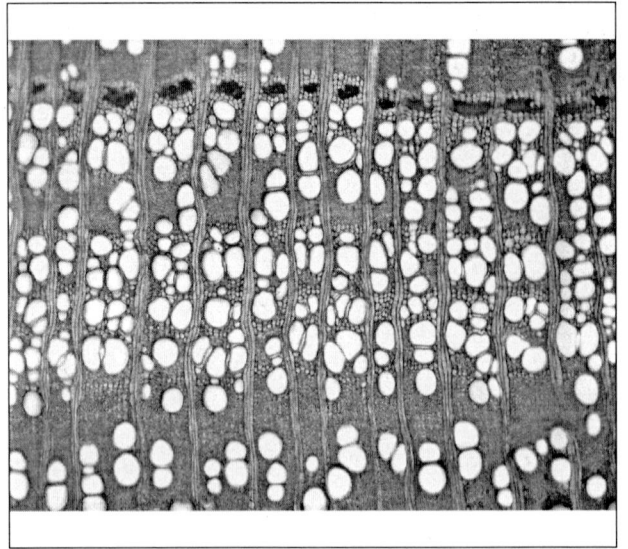
Chloroxylon swietenia TS x100

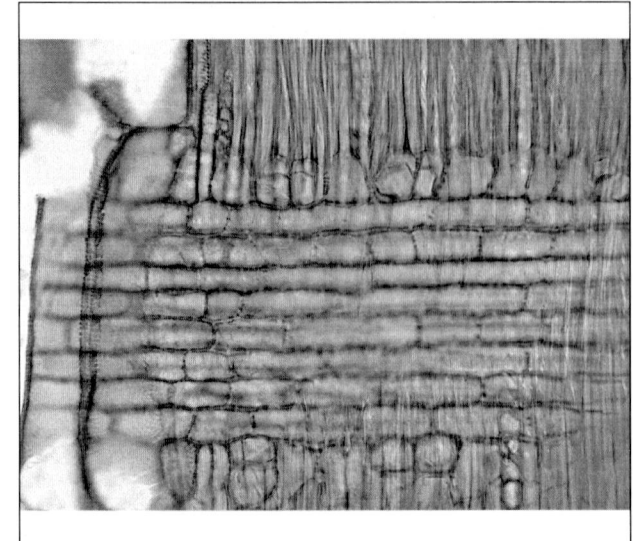
Chloroxylon swietenia RLS x400

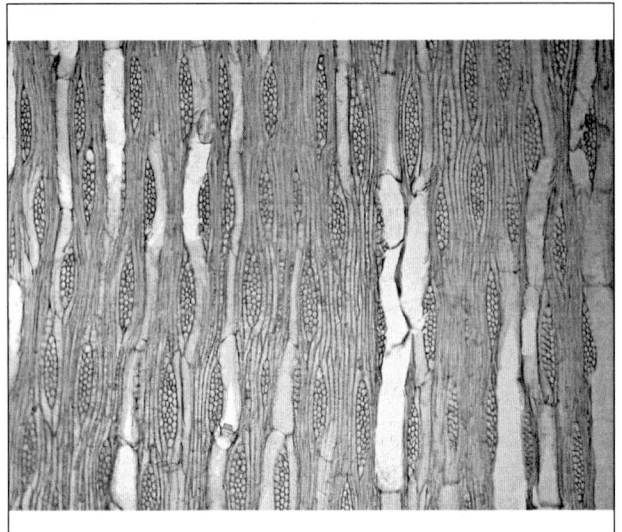
Chloroxylon swietenia TLS x100

# RUTACEAE

*Limonia* sp.
(species examined: *L. acidissima*)

Description:

Transverse section
Diffuse porous. Ring boundary distinct to indistinct. Pores small to medium, solitary, in radial multiples of 2–4 or more (common), and in clusters. Parenchyma apotracheal (diffuse-in-aggregates), paratracheal (scanty paratracheal, unilateral paratracheal), and banded (generally narrow discontinuous marginal bands).

Radial section
Perforation plates simple. Intervessel pits alternate, small. Vessel-ray pits with distinct borders, similar in shape, size to intervessel pits. Ground tissue fibres with simple to minutely bordered pits, thick-walled. Rays homogeneous (all cells procumbent).

Tangential section
Rays 2-3seriate.

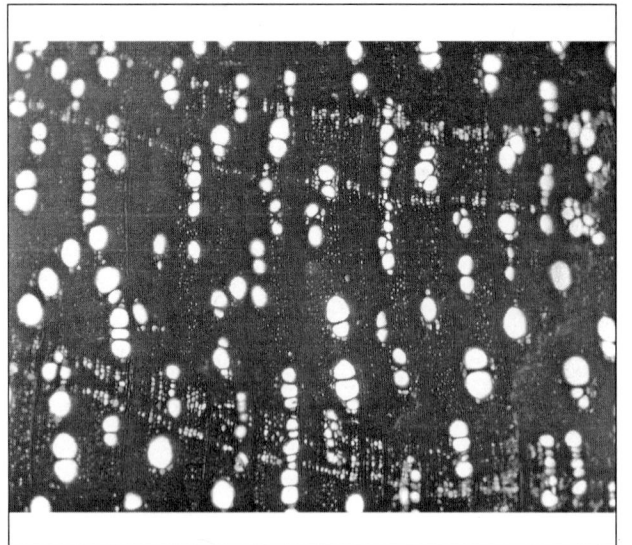
Limonia acidissima TS x100

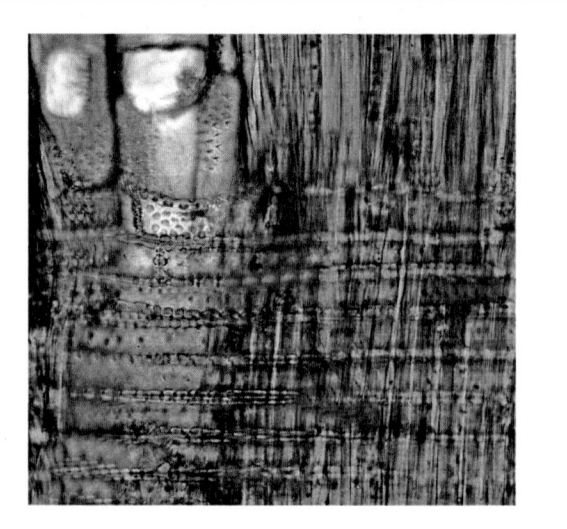
Limonia acidissima RLS x630

Limonia acidissima TLS x100

# SANTALACEAE

*Santalum* sp.
(species examined: *S. album*)

Description:

Transverse section
Diffuse-porous. Ring boundary distinct to indistinct. Pores small to medium, solitary. Parenchyma apotracheal (diffuse) and scanty paratracheal (rare).

Radial section
Perforation plates simple. Intervessel pits rare, alternate, medium to large. Vessel-ray pits with distinct borders, similar in size, shape to intervessel pits. Ground tissue fibres with distinctly bordered pits, thin- to thick-walled. Rays heterogeneous with a central part of procumbent cells and 1–2 rows of square and/or upright marginal cells. Vascular tracheids moderately common.

Tangential section
Rays 1-2(3)seriate (rays generally short).

Note: *Santalum* has less markedly heterogeneous rays compared to other species of this family, especially *Osyris* the rays of which consist of multiple rows of square and upright cells. The latter also has sparse pores, predominantly uni- and 3-4seriate rays and enlarged vessel-ray pit apertures (Schweingruber 1990:680–81).

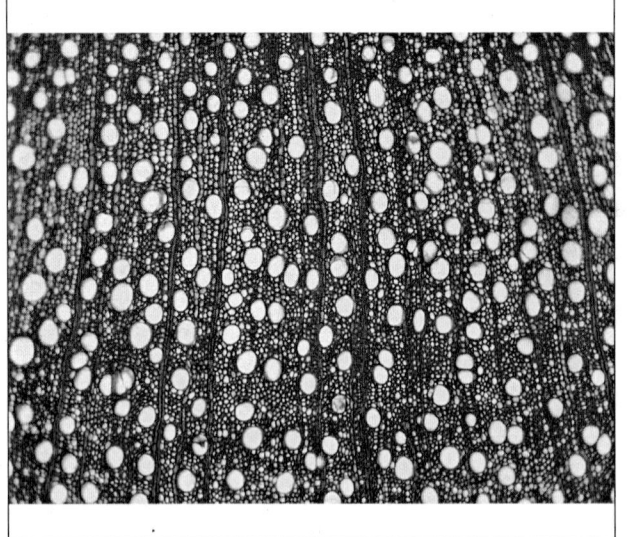
Santalum album TS x40

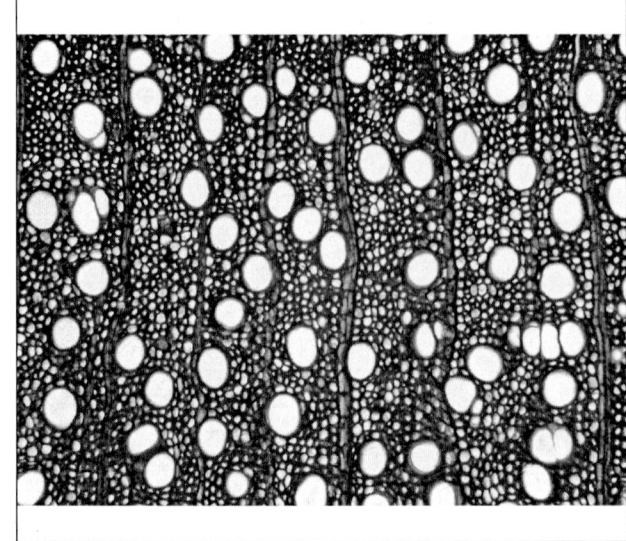
Santalum album TS x100

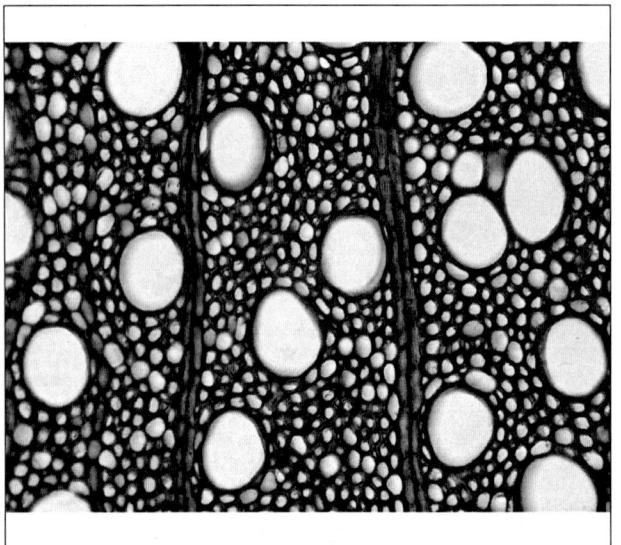
Santalum album TS x400

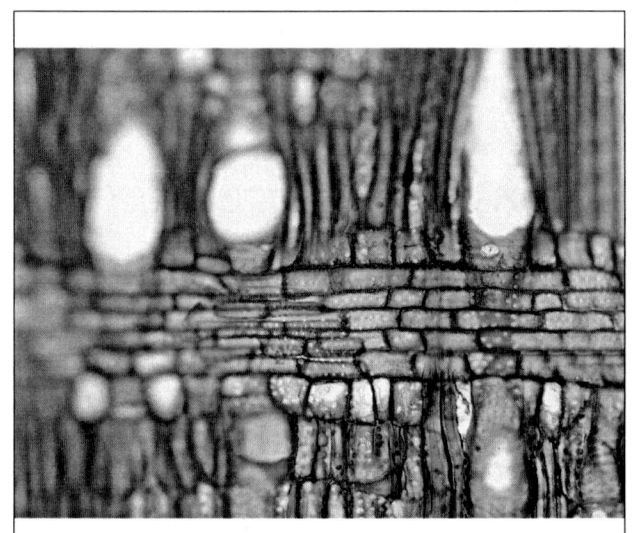
Santalum album RLS x400

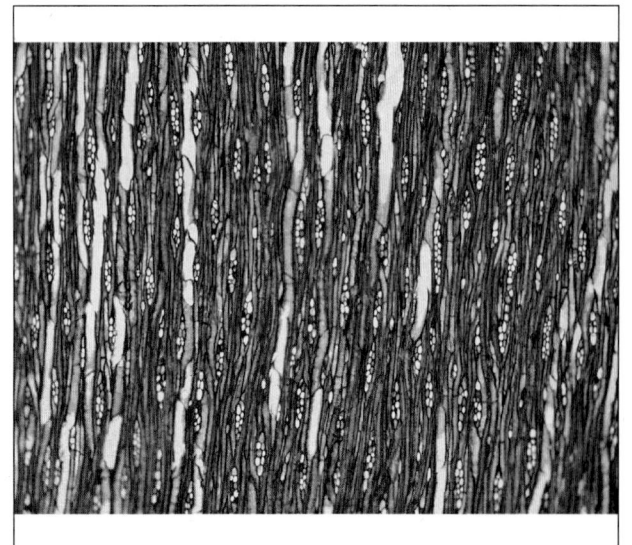
Santalum album TLS x100

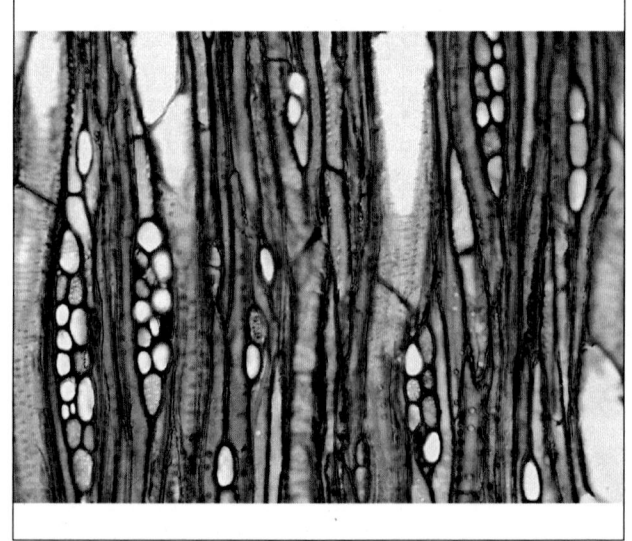
Santalum album TLS x400

# SAPINDACEAE

*Dodonaea* sp.
(species examined: *D. angustifolia*, *D. viscosa*)

Description:

<u>Transverse section</u>
Diffuse-porous. Ring boundary distinct. Pores medium to small, solitary, in radial multiples of 2(3)-4 or more (common) and in clusters. Parenchyma vasicentric, scanty paratracheal, sometimes apotracheal (diffuse) and in narrow, discontinuous, marginal bands.

<u>Radial section</u>
Perforation plates simple. Intervessel pits alternate to opposite, small to minute. Vessel-ray pits with distinct borders, similar in shape, size to intervessel pits. Ground tissue fibres with simple to minutely bordered pits, thin- to thick-walled. Rays homogeneous to heterogeneous composed mostly of weakly procumbent and square cells. Crystals present.

<u>Tangential section</u>
Rays 1-2seriate.

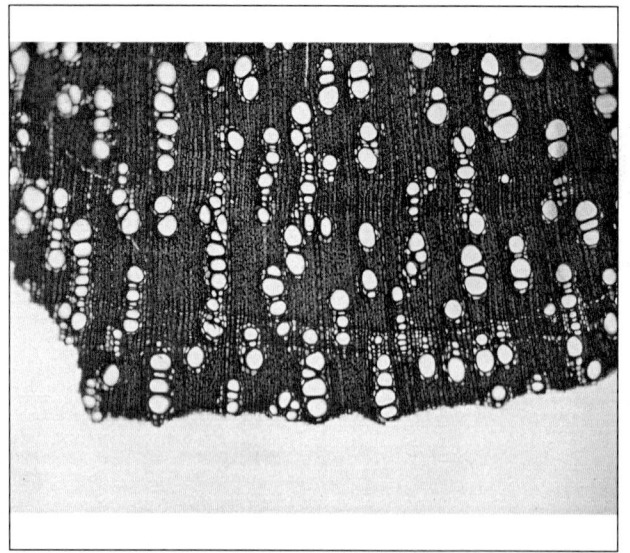
Dodonaea angustifolia TS x100

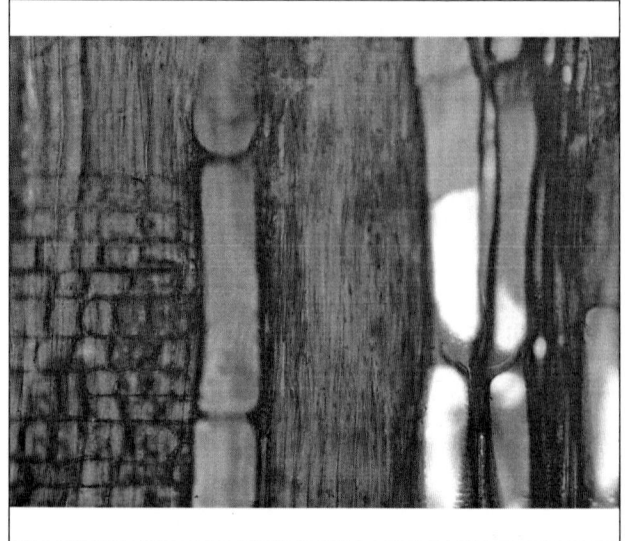
Dodonaea angustifolia TS x100 RLS x400

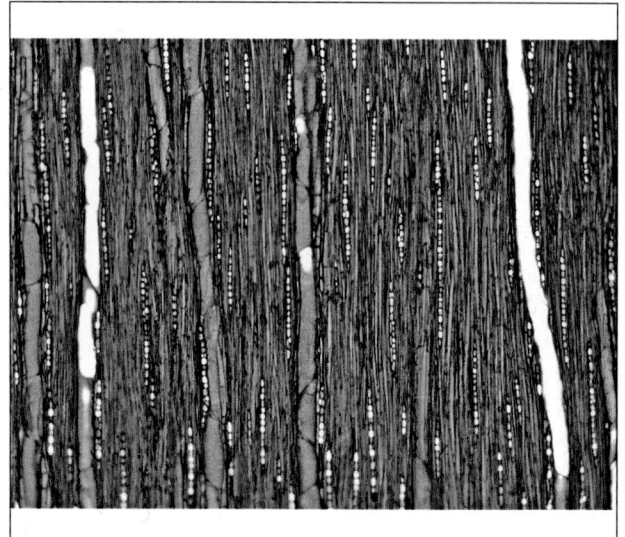
Dodonaea angustifolia TS x100 TLS x100

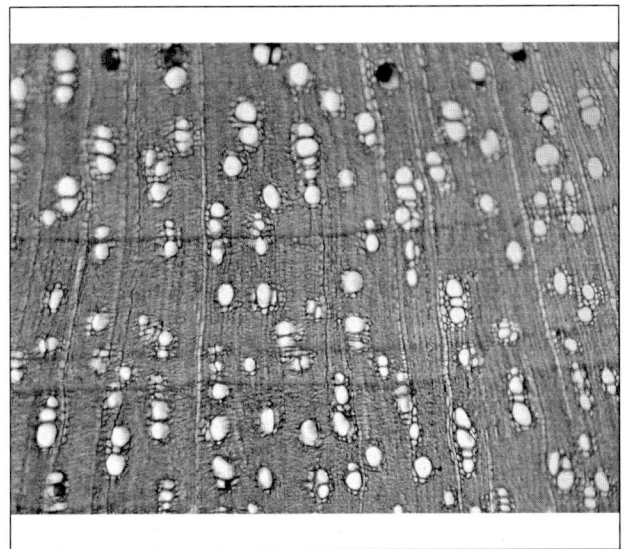

Dodonaea viscosa TS x100

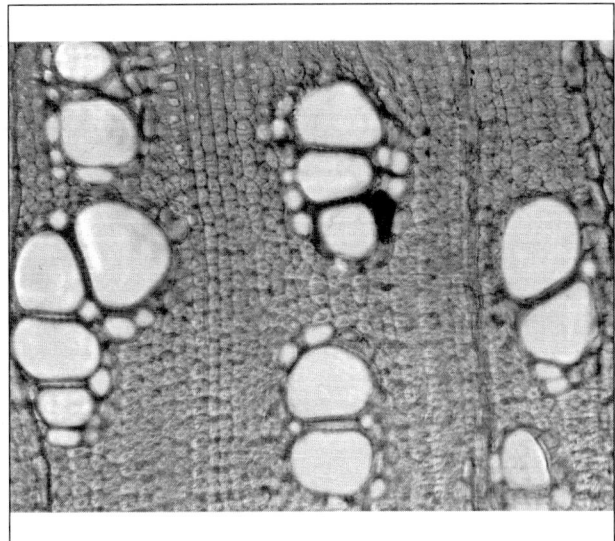

Dodonaea viscosa TS x400

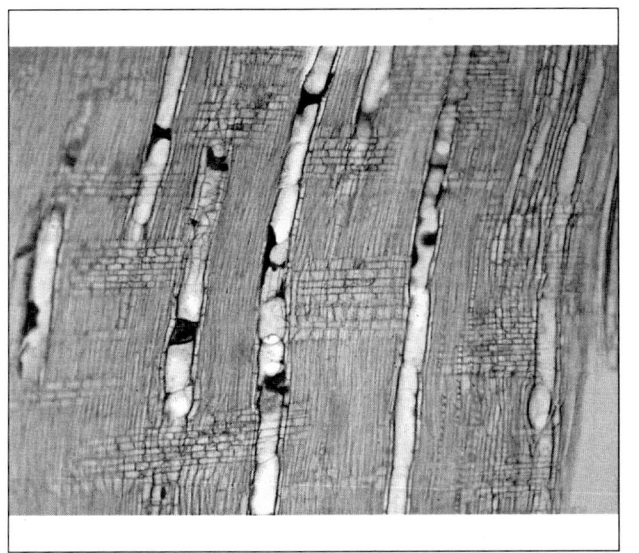

Dodonaea viscosa RLS x100

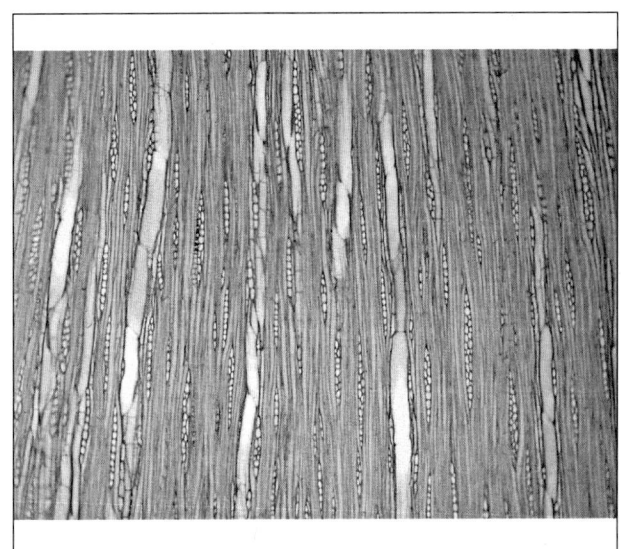

Dodonaea viscosa TLS x100

# SAPINDACEAE

*Schleichera* sp.
(species examined: *S. oleosa*)

Description:

Transverse section
Diffuse-porous. Ring boundary distinct to indistinct. Pores medium to large, solitary and in radial multiples of 2–3. Parenchyma apotracheal (diffuse, diffuse-in-aggregates), scanty paratracheal, vasicentric, and in narrow discontinuous bands (rare).

Radial section
Perforation plates simple. Intervessel pits alternate, medium. Vessel-ray pits with distinct borders, similar in shape, size to intervessel pits. Ground tissue fibres with simple to minutely bordered pits, thin- to thick-walled. Rays homogeneous (all cells procumbent).

Tangential section
Rays 1(2)seriate.

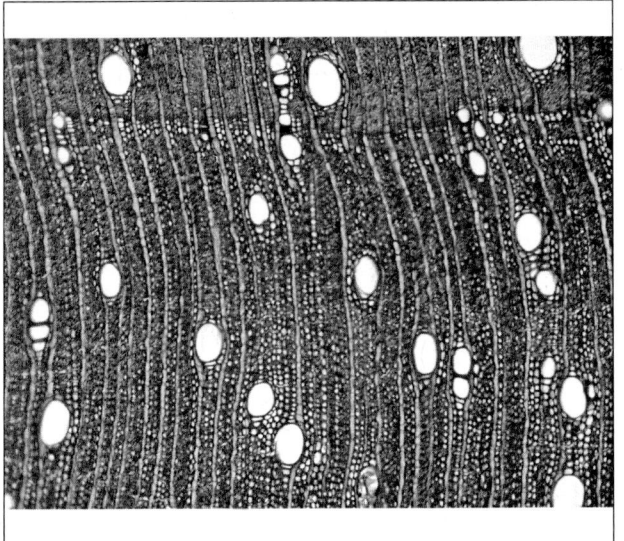

Schleichera oleosa TS x100

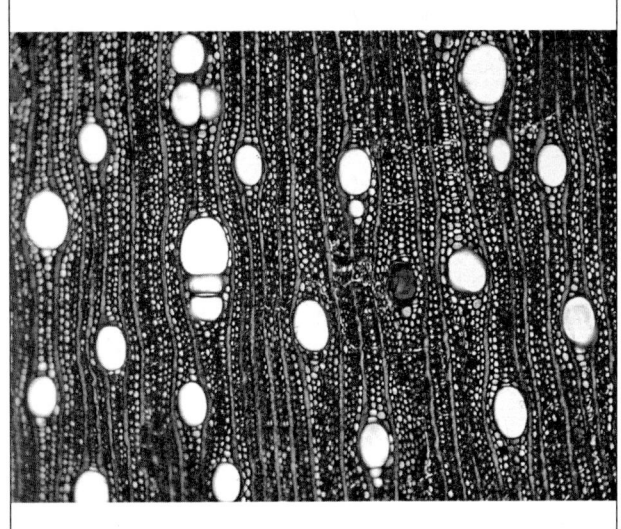

Schleichera oleosa TS x100

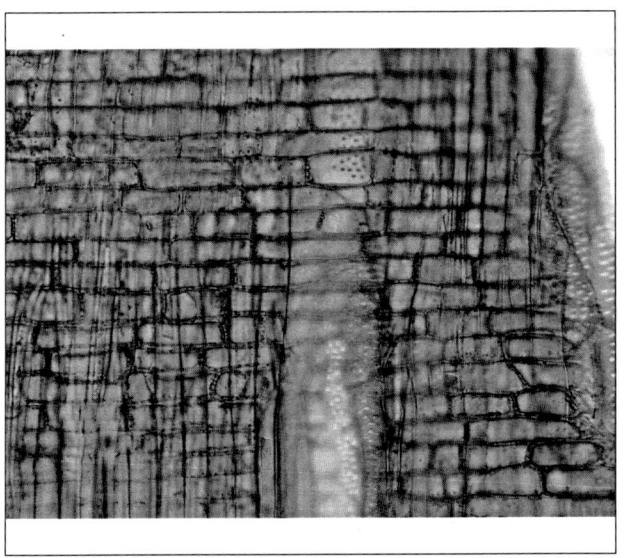

Schleichera oleosa RLS x400

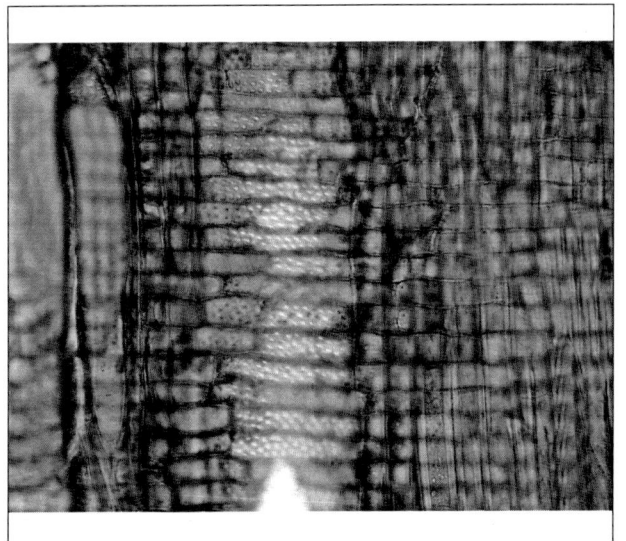

Schleichera oleosa RLS x400

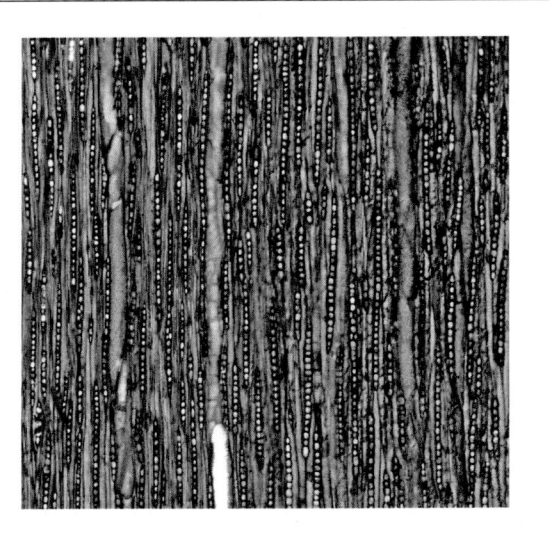

Schleichera oleosa TLS x100

# STERCULIACEAE

*Pterospermum* sp.
(species examined: *P. diversifolium*)

Description:

Transverse section
Diffuse-porous. Ring boundary distinct to indistinct. Pores medium to large, in radial multiples of (2-3)4 or more (common), solitary and in clusters. Parenchyma apotracheal (diffuse).

Radial section
Perforation plates simple. Intervessel pits alternate, minute, coalescent. Vessel-ray pits with distinct borders, similar in shape, size to intervessel pits. Ground tissue fibres with simple to minutely bordered pits, thin-walled. Rays heterogeneous with tile cells (Pterospermum type).

Tangential section
Rays uni- and multiseriate (2-4 cells).

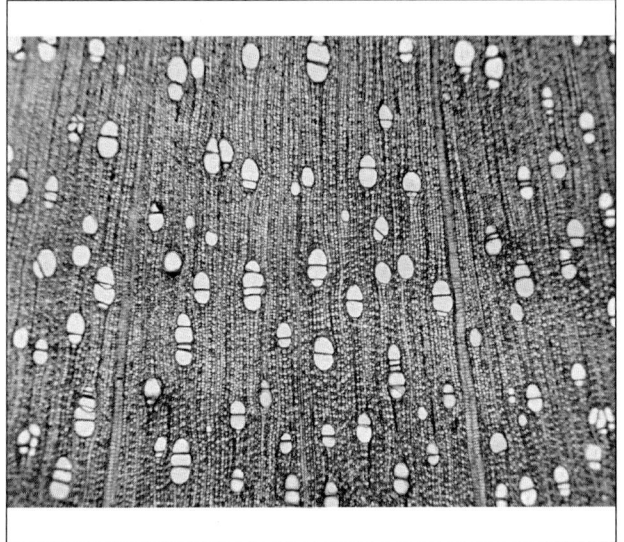
Pterospermum diversifolium TS x40

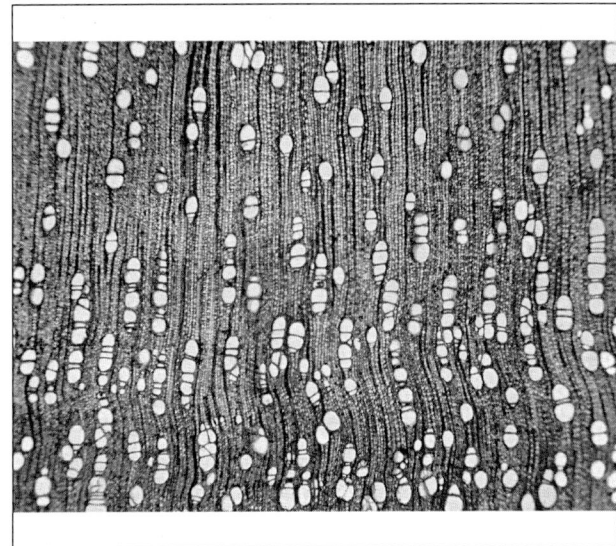
Pterospermum diversifolium TS x40

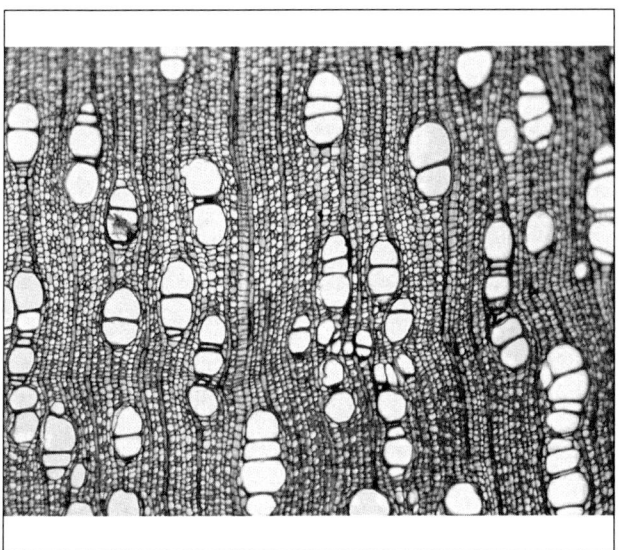
Pterospermum diversifolium TS x100

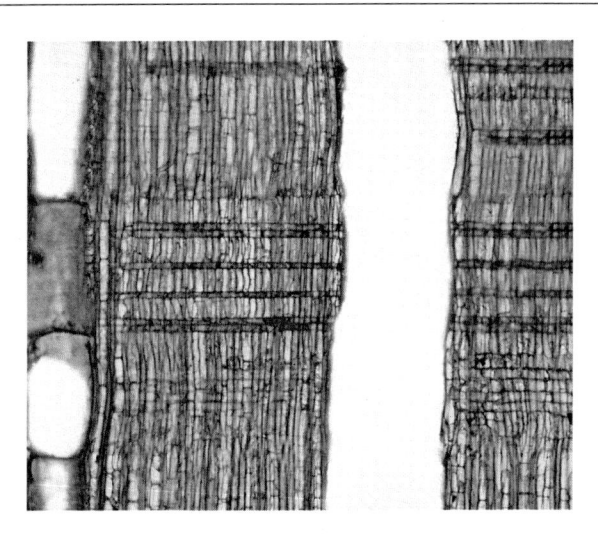
Pterospermum diversifolium RLS x100

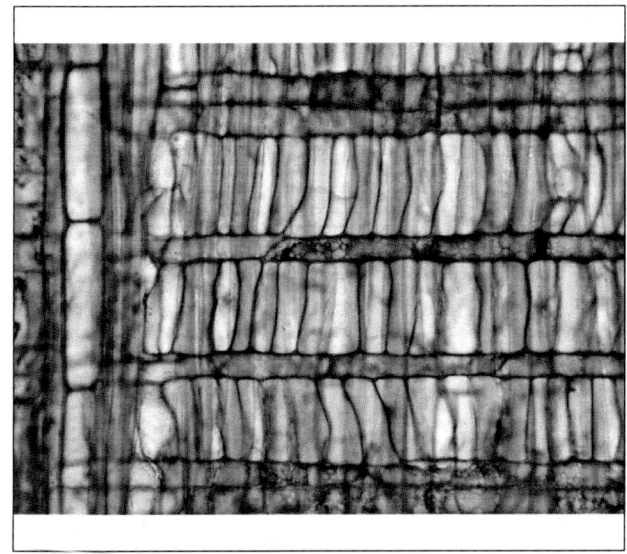
Pterospermum diversifolium RLS x400

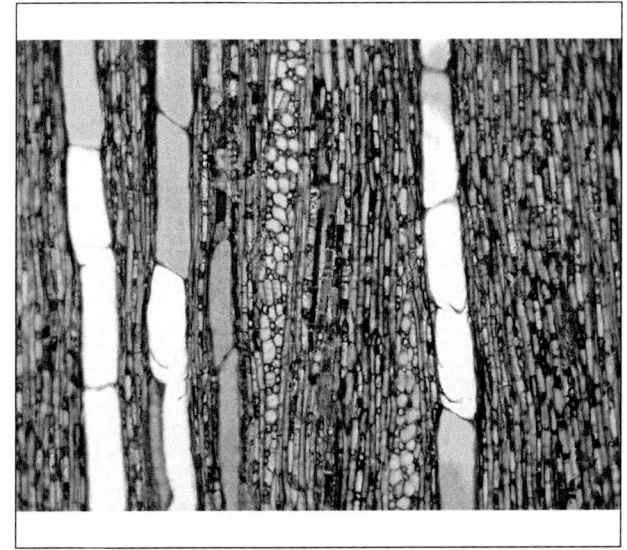
Pterospermum diversifolium TLS x100

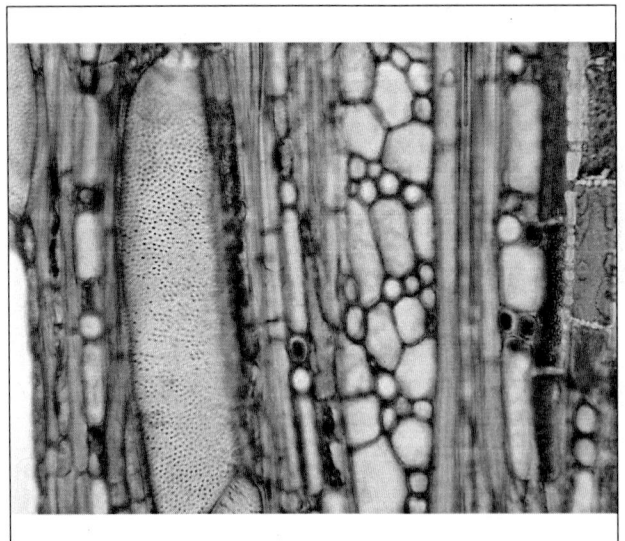

Pterospermum diversifolium TLS x400

# TILIACEAE

*Grewia* sp.
(species examined: *G. tenax*)

Description:

Transverse section
Diffuse porous. Ring boundary distinct. Pores small, solitary (common), in radial multiples of 2(3) (occasionally) and in clusters. Parenchyma apotracheal (diffuse) and scanty paratracheal.

Radial section
Perforation plates simple. Intervessel pits alternate, small to medium. Vessel-ray pits with distinct borders, similar in shape, size to intervessel pits. Ground tissue fibres with simple to minutely bordered pits, thin to thick-walled. Rays heterogeneous, with tile cells (*Pterospermum* type)

Tangential section
Rays 1-3(4)seriate.

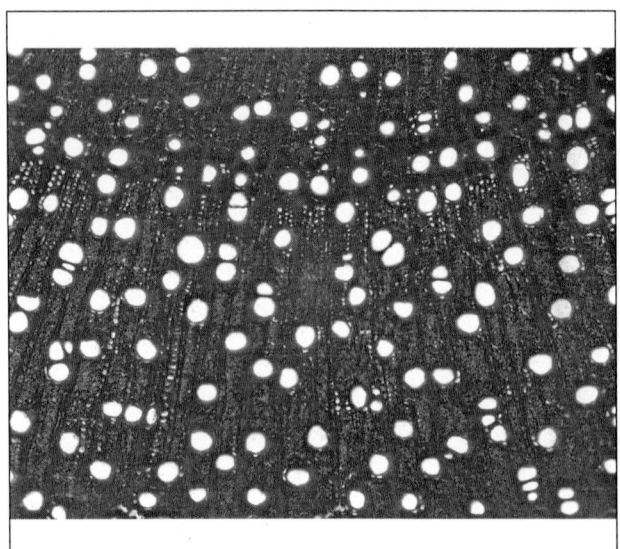

Grewia tenax TS x100

# TILIACEAE

*Grewia* sp.
(species examined: *G. tiliaefolia*)

Description:

Transverse section
Diffuse to semi-ring porous. Ring boundary distinct. Pores arranged in a single row (solitary, in radial multiples of 2, rarely in clusters) in early wood, and mostly solitary in latewood (relatively sparse in latewood). Parenchyma apotracheal (diffuse, diffuse-in-aggregates), paratracheal (vasicentric, scanty and unilaterally paratracheal), and occasionally banded (narrow, discontinuous scalariform bands).

Radial section
Perforation plates simple. Intervessel pits alternate to opposite, minute. Vessel-ray pits with distinct borders, similar in shape, size to intervessel pits. Ground tissue fibres with simple to minutely bordered pits, thick-walled. Rays heterogeneous (procumbent, square and upright cells mixed throughout) with tile cells present (*Pterospermum* type).

Tangential section
Rays 1(2)3seriate and 6-8(10)seriate. Sheath cells present.

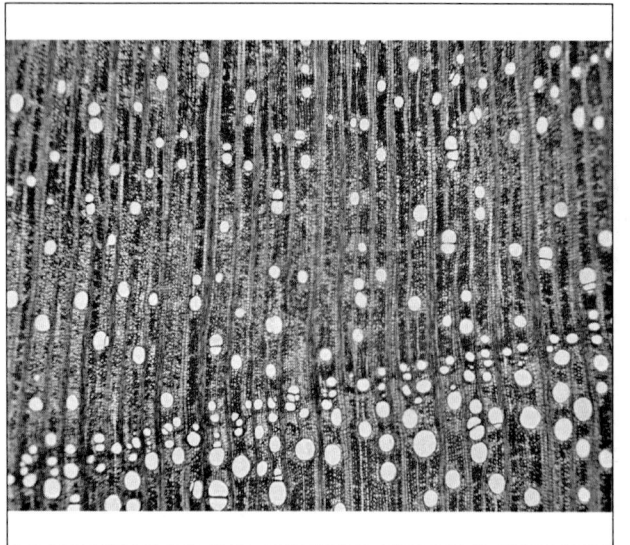
Grewia tiliaefolia TS x40

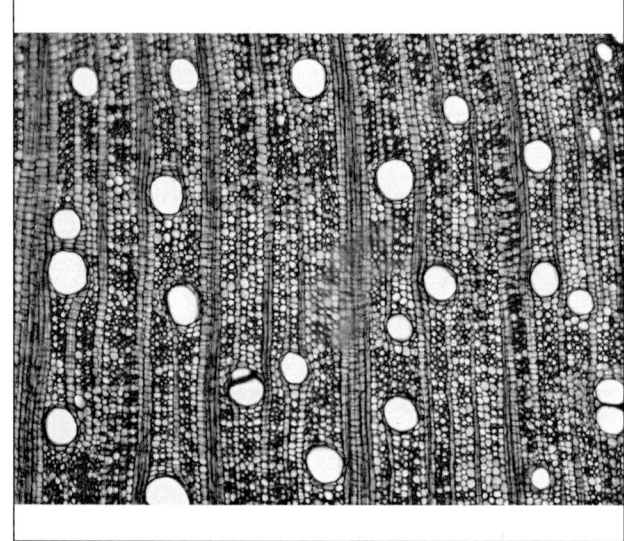
Grewia tiliaefolia TS x100

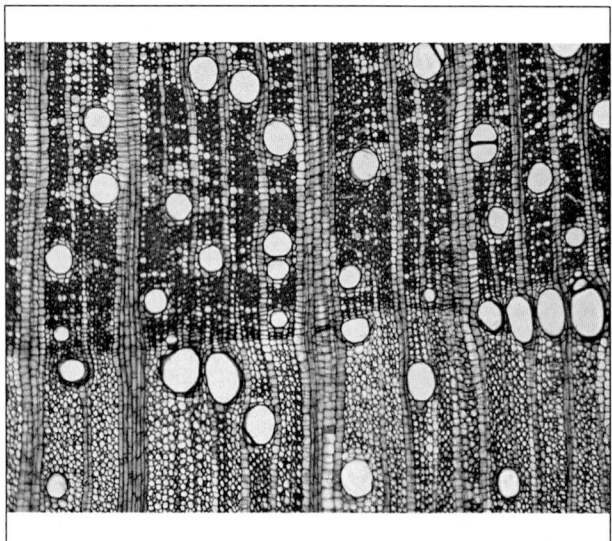
Grewia tiliaefolia TS x100

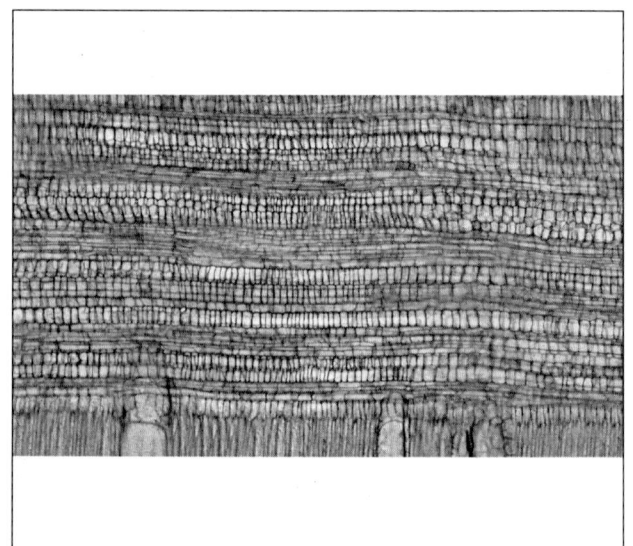
Grewia tiliaefolia RLS x100

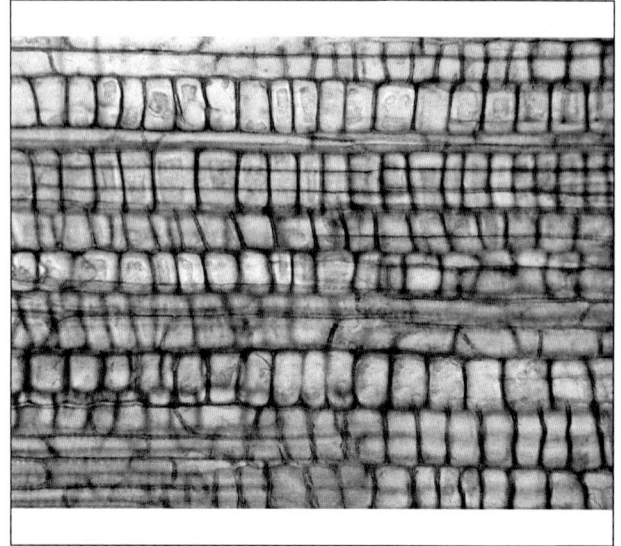
Grewia tiliaefolia RLS x400

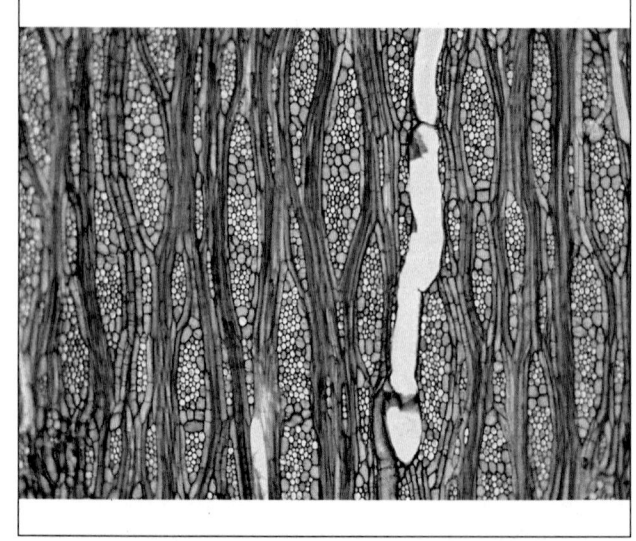
Grewia tiliaefolia TLS x100

# VERBENACEAE

*Gmelina* sp.
(species examined: *G. arborea*)

Description:

<u>Transverse section</u>
Diffuse to semi-ring porous. Ring boundary distinct to indistinct. Pores large, solitary (angular), in radial multiples of 2 and in clusters (rare). Parenchyma banded (bands more than 3 cells wide).

<u>Radial section</u>
Perforation plates simple. Intervessel pits alternate, medium. Vessel-ray pits with distinct borders, similar in shape, size to intervessel pits. Ground tissue fibres with simple to minutely bordered pits, thin- to thick-walled. Septate fibres present. Rays heterogeneous with a central part of procumbent cells and 2–4 rows of upright and/or square marginal cells. Crystals present in ray cells.

<u>Tangential section</u>
Rays 3-4(5)seriate. Sheath cells present.

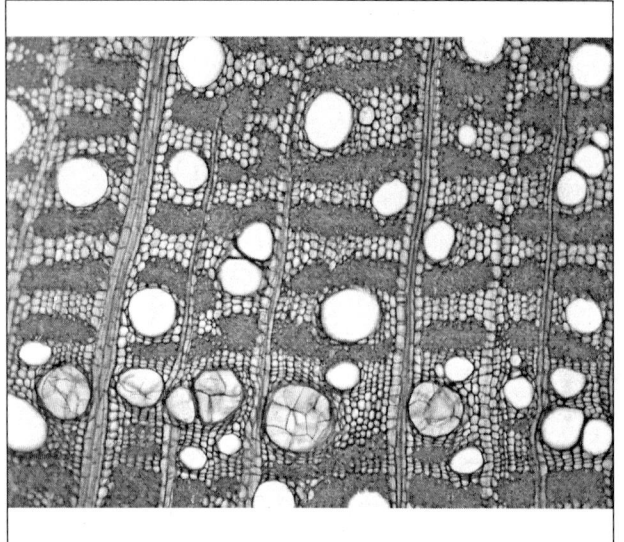
Gmelina arborea TS x100

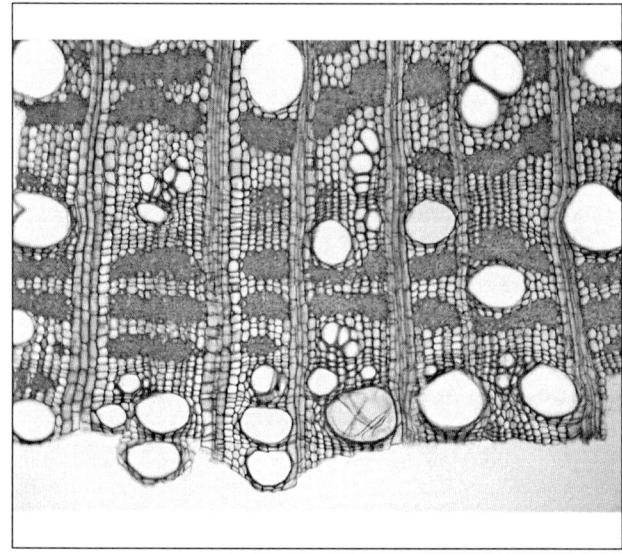
Gmelina arborea TS x100

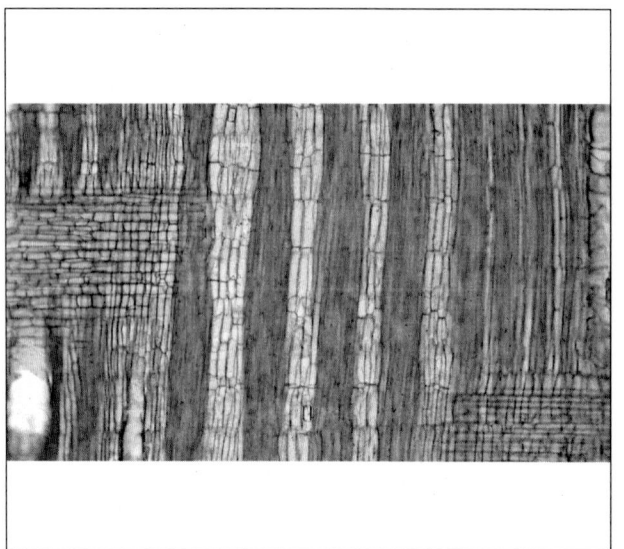
Gmelina arborea RLS x100

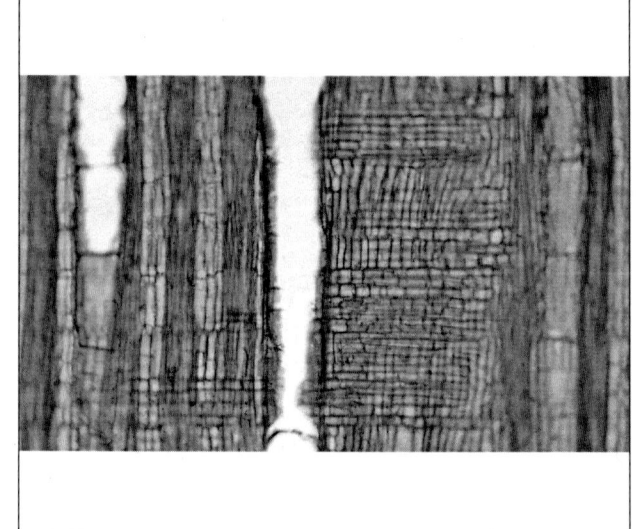
Gmelina arborea RLS x100

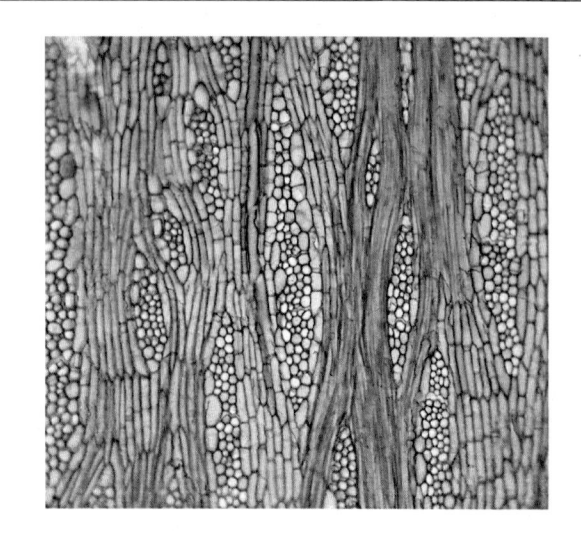
Gmelina arborea TLS x100

# VERBENACEAE

*Tectona* sp.
(species examined: *T. grandis*)

Description:

Transverse section
Ring to semi-ring porous. Ring boundary distinct. Pores in the early wood large (solitary and in radial multiples of 2) in the latewood smaller (solitary, in radial multiples and irregular clusters). Parenchyma paratracheal, in broad bands around pores.

Radial section
Perforation plates simple. Intervessel pits alternate, small, occasionally coalescent. Vessel-ray pits with distinct borders, similar in shape, size to intervessel pits (somewhat enlarged). Ground tissue fibres with simple to minutely bordered pits, thin- to thick-walled. Septate fibres present. Rays homogeneous to slightly heterogeneous, composed of weakly procumbent cells.

Tangential section
Rays 2-3(4)seriate.

Tectona grandis TS x40

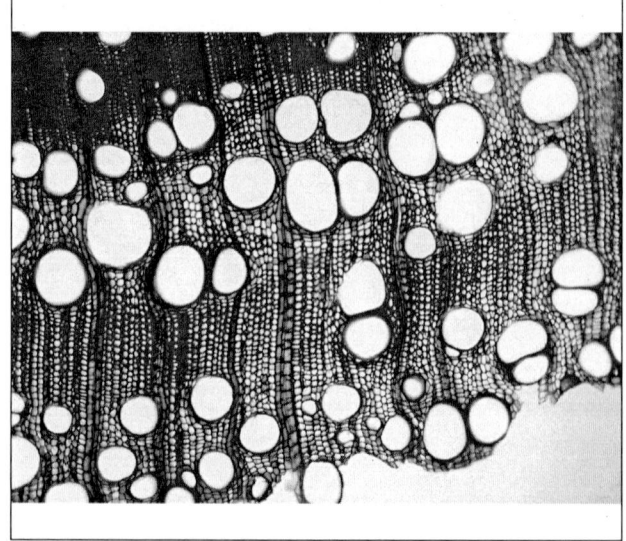
Tectona grandis TS x100

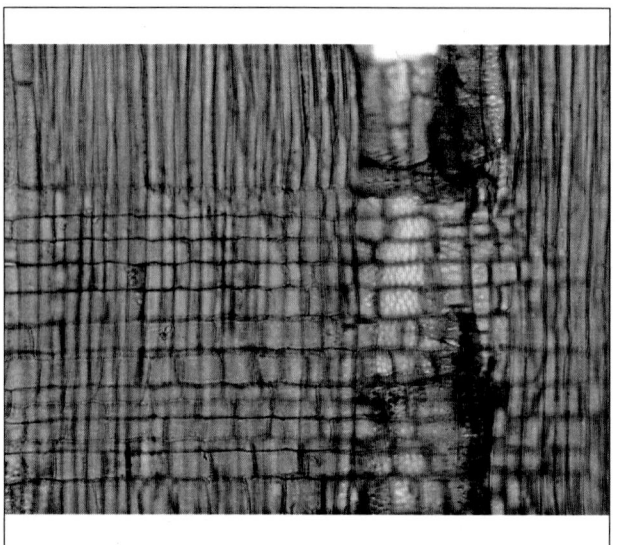
Tectona grandis RLS x400

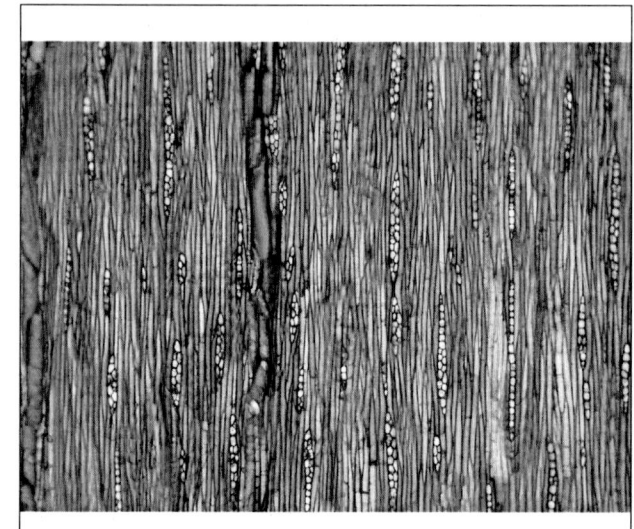
Tectona grandis TLS x100

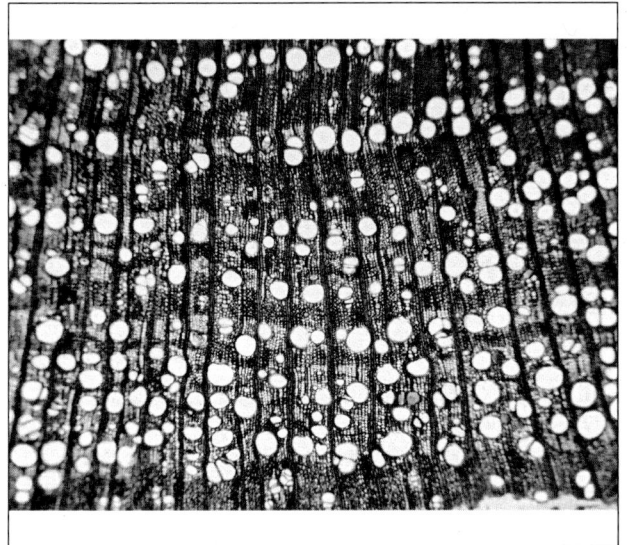

Tectona grandis TS x40

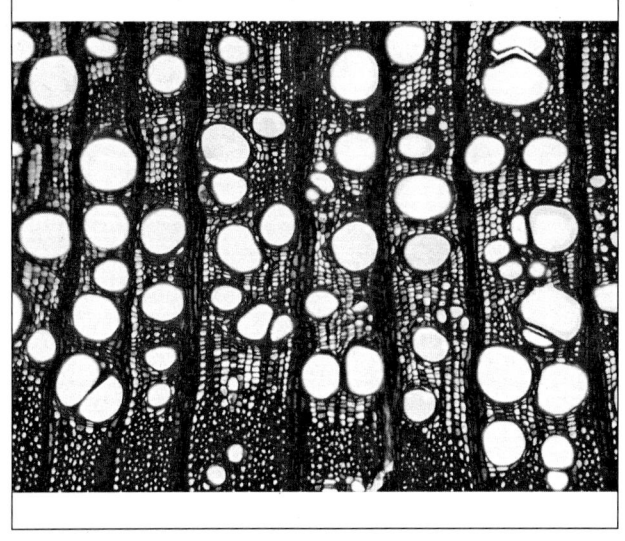

Tectona grandis TS x100

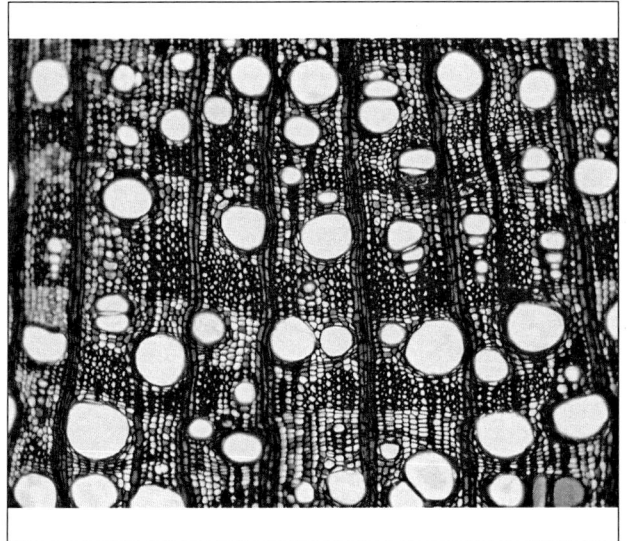

Tectona grandis TS x100

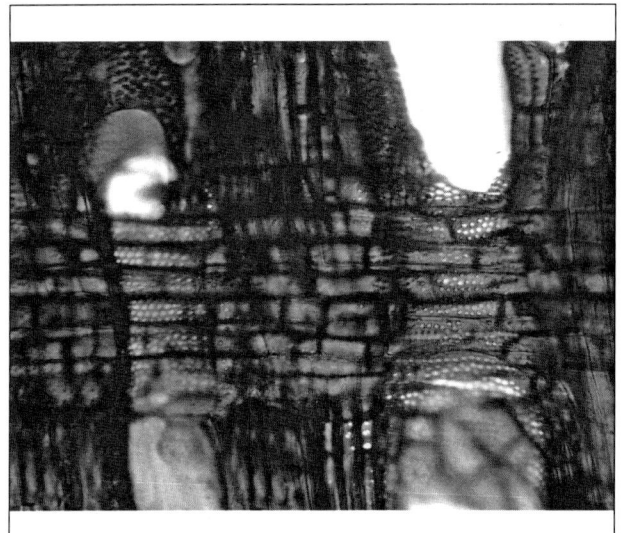

Tectona grandis RLS x400

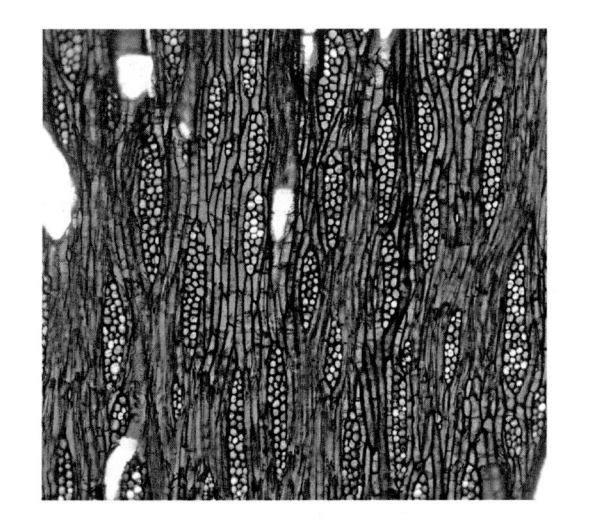

Tectona grandis TLS x100

# VERBENACEAE

*Vitex* sp.
(species examined: *V. altissima*)

Description:

Transverse section
Diffuse porous. Ring boundary distinct. Pores small to medium, solitary (common), in radial multiples of 2 or more and in clusters. Parenchyma paratracheal (scanty paratracheal) and apotracheal (diffuse, rare).

Radial section
Perforation plates simple and reticulate. Intervessel pits alternate, medium. Vessel-ray pits with reduced to apparently simple borders-rounded/angular. Ground tissue fibres with simple to minutely bordered pits, thin to thick-walled. Septate fibres present. Rays homogeneous to heterogeneous, with 1-2 rows of square and/or upright marginal cells.

Tangential section
Rays 2-3(4)seriate.

Vitex altissima TS x40

Vitex altissima TS x100

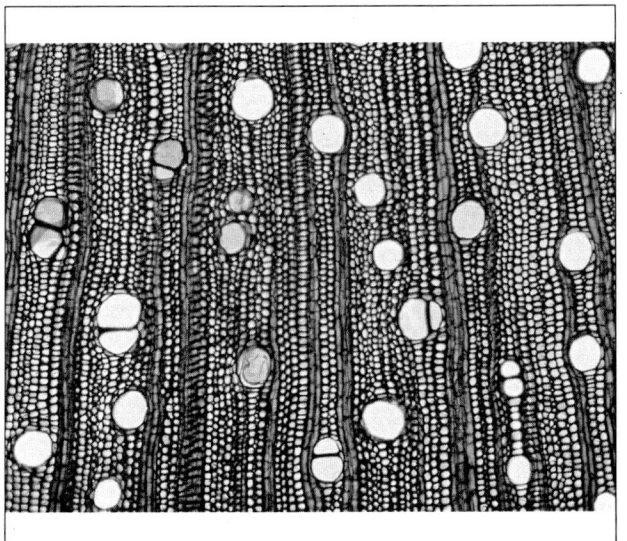
Vitex altissima TS x100

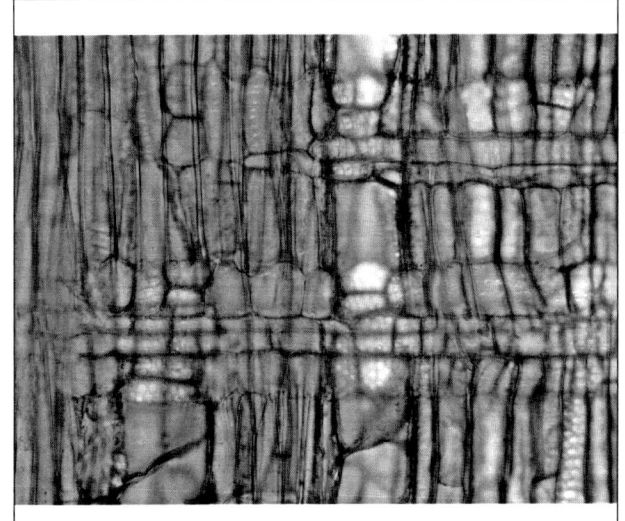
Vitex altissima RLS x400

Vitex altissima RLS x400

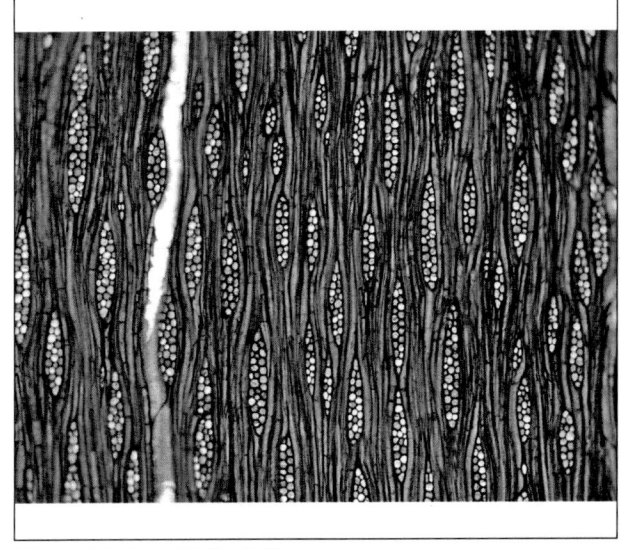
Vitex altissima TLS x100

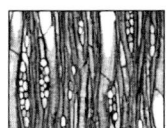

# BIBLIOGRAPHY

Abdulali, G. 1949. Some peculiarities of avifaunal distribution in peninsular India, *Proceedings of the National Institute of Science India* 15:387–93.

Achaya, K. T. 1994. *Indian food: A historical companion*. Oxford: Oxford University Press.

———. 1998. *A historical dictionary of Indian food*. New Delhi: Oxford University Press.

Agrawal, D. P. 1982. *The archaeology of India*. London: Curzon Press.

Ajithprasad, P. 2001. The pre-Harappan cultures of Gujarat. In Settar, S., and R. Korisettar (eds.), *Indian Archaeology in Retrospect, Volume II. Protohistory*, pp. 129–58. New Delhi: Manohar.

———. 2004. Holocene adaptations of the Mesolithic and Chalcolithic settlements in north Gujarat. In Yasuda, Y., and V. S. Shinde (eds.), *Monsoon and civilization*, pp. 115–32. New Delhi: Lustre Press/Roli Books.

Allchin, B., and F. R. Allchin. 1982. *The rise of civilisation in India and Pakistan*. Cambridge: Cambridge University Press.

Allchin, B., A. Goudie, and A. Hedge. 1978. *The prehistory and palaeogeography of the Great Indian Desert*. London: Academic Press.

Allchin, F. R. 1963. *Neolithic cattle keepers of South India: A case study of the Deccan ashmounds*. Cambridge: Cambridge University Press.

Allchin, F. R., and B. Allchin. 1997. *Origins of a civilisation: The prehistory and early archaeology of South Asia*. New Delhi: Penguin Books India.

Alley, R. B., P. A. Mayewski, T. Sowers, M. Stuiver, K. C. Taylor, and P. U Clark. 1997. Holocene climatic instability: A prominent, widespread event 8,200 yrs ago, *Geology* 25(6):483–86.

Ambasta, S. P., K. Ramachandran, K. Kashyapa, and R. Chand (eds.), 1986. *The useful plants of India*. New Delhi: Publications and Information Directorate.

Anker, P. 2001. *Imperial ecology: Environmental order in the British Empire, 1895–1945*. Cambridge, MA: Harvard University Press.

Arasaratnam, S. 1986. *Merchants, companies and commerce on the Coromandel coast 1650–1740*. New Delhi: Oxford University Press.

Arora, R. K. 1963. The forests of north Kanara District IV: Successional trends and synthesis of vegetation, *Journal of the Indian Botanical Society* 42:629–36.

———. 1966a. The vegetation of south Kanara district, Western Ghats, India II. *Xylia*-mixed type, *Journal of the Indian Botanical Society* 45:127–37.

———. 1966b. The vegetation of south Kanara district, Western Ghats, India III. Evergreen type, *Journal of the Indian Botanical Society* 45:304–16.

Asouti, E. 2003a. Wood charcoal from Santorini (Thera): New evidence for climate, vegetation and timber imports in the Aegean Bronze Age, *Antiquity* 77:471–84.

———. 2003b. Woodland vegetation and fuel exploitation at the prehistoric campsite of Pinarbasi, south-central Anatolia, Turkey: The evidence from the wood charcoal macro-remains, *Journal of Archaeological Science* 30(9):1185–201.

———. 2005. Woodland vegetation and the exploitation of fuel and timber at Neolithic Çatalhöyük. In Hodder, I. (ed.), *Inhabiting Çatalhöyük: Reports from the 1995–9 Seasons*, pp. 213–58. McDonald Institute Monographs/BIAA Monograph 40. McDonald Institute for Archaeological Research and British Institute at Ankara, Cambridge, and London.

Asouti, E., and P. Austin. 2005. Reconstructing woodland vegetation and its relation to human societies, based on the analysis and interpretation of archaeological wood charcoal macro-remains, *Environmental Archaeology* 10:1–18.

Asouti, E., D. Fuller, and R. Korisettar. 2005. Vegetation context and wood exploitation in the Southern Neolithic: Preliminary evidence from wood charcoals. In Franke-Vogt, U., and Weisshaar, H.-J. (eds.), *South Asian archaeology 2003. Proceedings of the 17th International Conference of the European Association of South Asian Archaeologists* (7–11 July 2003, Bonn), pp. 335-40. Linden Soft/Verlag, Aachen.

Asouti, E., and J. Hather. 2001. Charcoal analysis and the reconstruction of ancient woodland vegetation in the Konya basin, south-central Anatolia, Turkey: Results from the Neolithic site of Çatalhöyük East, *Vegetation History and Archaeobotany* 10:23–34.

Badal-Garcia, E. 1992. L' anthracologie préhistorique: à propos de certains problèmes méthodologiques, *Bulletin de la Société Botanique de France* 139: 167–89.

Badam, G. L. 1984. Holocene faunal material from India with special reference to domesticated animals. In Clutton-Brock, J. and C. Grigson (eds.), *Animals in archaeology III: Early herders and their flocks*, pp. 339–53. Oxford: British Archaeological Reports.

Badam, G. L., V. G. Sathe, and S. Salahuddin. 1989. Systematic study of fossil bovids from Nittur, Bellary district, Karnataka, *Bulletin of the Deccan College Post-Graduate and Research Institute* 47/48:1–8.

Baquar, S. R. 1995. *Trees of Pakistan: Their natural history, characteristics and utilisation*. Karachi: Royal Book Company.

Bellwood, P. 1997. *Prehistory of the Indo-Malaysian archipelago*. Honolulu: University of Hawaii Press.

Bentaleb, I., C. Caratini, M. Fontugne, M. T. Morzadec-Kerfourn, J. P. Pascal, and C. Tissot. 1997. Monsoon regime variation during the late Holocene in southwestern India. In Dalfes, H. N., G. Kukla, and H. Weiss (eds.), *Third millennium BC climate change and Old World collapse*, pp. 475–88. Berlin and Heidelberg: Springer Verlag.

Bera, S. K., H. P. Gupta, and A. Farooqui. 1996. Berijam Lake: 20,000 years sequence of palaeofloristics and palaeoenvironment in Palni Hills, South India, *Geophytology* 26(1):99–104.

Bera, S. K., A. Farooqui, and H. P. Gupta. 1997. Late Pleistocene/Holocene vegetation and environment in and around Marian shola, Palni Hills, Tamil Nadu, *The Palaeobotanist* 45:190–95.

Bews, J. W. 1935. *Human ecology*. Oxford: Oxford University Press.

Biagi, P., and M. Kazi. 1995. A Mesolithic site near Thari in the Thar Desert (Sindh, Pakistan), *Ancient Sindh* 2:7–12.

Biswas, K. 1949. Botanical notes on the Satpura theory, *Proceedings of the National Institute of Science India* 15:365–87.

Blumler, M. 1996. Ecology, evolutionary theory and agricultural origins. In Harris, D. R. (ed.), *The origins and spread of agriculture and pastoralism in Eurasia*, pp. 25–50. London: UCL Press.

Blunier, T., J. Chappellaz, J. Schwander, B. Stauffer, and D. Raynaud. 1995. Variations in atmospheric methane concentration during the Holocene epoch, *Nature* 374:46–49.

Bompard, J. M., and R. M. Schnell. 1997. Taxonomy and systematics. In Litz, R. E. (ed.), *The mango. Botany, production and uses*, pp. 21–48. Wallingford: CAB International.

Bonavia, D., C. M. Ochoa, O. Tovar, S. Cerrón Palomino, and R. Cerrón Palomino. 2004. Archaeological evidence of cherimoya (*Annona cherimolia* Mill.) and guanabana (*Annona muricata* L.) in ancient Peru, *Economic Botany* 58(4):509–22.

Boomgaard, P. 1998. The VOC trade in forest products in the seventeenth century. In Grove, R. H., V. Damodaran, and S. Sangwan (eds.), *Nature and the Orient: The environmental history of South and Southeast Asia*, pp. 375–95. New Delhi: Oxford University Press.

Bor, N. L. 1960. *The grasses of Burma, Ceylon, India and Pakistan (excluding Bambuseae)*. London: Pergamon Press.

Bose, T. K., and S. K. Mitra. 1990. *Fruits: Tropical and subtropical*. Calcutta: Naya Prokash.

Bossuyt, F., M. Meegaskumbura, N. Beenaerts, D. J. Gower, R. Pethiyagoda, K. Roelants, A. Manaert, M. Wilkinson, M. M. Bahir, K. Manamendra-Arachchi, K. L. Peter, C. J. Schneider, V. Oommen, and M. C. Milinkovitch. 2004. Local endemism within Western Ghats-Sri Lanka biodiversity hotspot, *Science* 306:479–81.

Botkin, D. B. 1990. *Discordant harmonies: A new ecology for the twenty-first century*. New York: Oxford University Press.

Bowler, P. J. 1992. *The Fontana history of the environmental sciences*. London: Fontana Press.

Bowman, D. M. J. S. 1998. The impact of Aboriginal landscape burning on the Australian biota, *New Phytologist* 140:385–410.

Bradnock, R. 1989. Physical Structure. In Robinson, F. (ed.), *The Cambridge encyclopedia of India, Pakistan, Bangladesh, Sri Lanka, Nepal, Bhutan and the Maldives*, pp. 12–15. Cambridge: Cambridge University Press.

Brandis, D. 1884. *Progress of forestry in India*. Edinburgh: McFarlane and Erskine.

Braun-Blanquet, J. 1932. *Plant sociology: The study of plant communities*. New York: McGraw-Hill.

Brubaker, R. 2001. Aspects of mortuary variability in the south Indian Iron Age, *Bulletin of the Deccan College Post-Graduate and Research Institute* 60/61:253–302.

Bryson, R. A., and A. M. Swain. 1981. Holocene variations of the monsoon rainfall in Rajasthan, *Quaternary Research* 16:135–45.

Buchy, M. 1998. British colonial forest policy in South India: An unscientific or unadapted policy? In Grove, R. H., V. Damodaran, and S. Sangwan (eds.), *Nature and the Orient: The environmental history of South and Southeast Asia*, pp. 636–73. New Delhi: Oxford University Press.

Burkill, I. H. 1966. *A dictionary of the economic products of the Malay peninsula.* Kuala Lumpur: Ministry of Agriculture and Co-operatives.

Burrow, T., and M. B. Emeneau. 1984. *A Dravidian etymological dictionary.* Oxford: Clarendon Press.

Caratini, C., I. Bentaleb, M. Fontugne, M. T. Morzadec-Kerfourn, J. P. Pascal, and C. Tissot. 1994. A less humid climate since ca. 3,500 yr B.P. from marine cores off Karwar, western India, *Palaeogeography, Palaeoclimatology, Palaeoecology* 109:371–84.

Casson, L. 1989. *The 'Periplus Maris Erythraei': Text with introduction, translation, and commentary.* Princeton, NJ: Princeton University Press.

Casteletti, L., M. Madella, and A. Qayom Mahar. 1994. Charcoal analysis at Kot Diji: A preliminary report, *Ancient Sindh* 1:37–41.

Chabal, L., L. Fabre, J.-Terral, and I. Théry-Parisot. 1999. L'anthracologie. In Bourquin-Mignot, C., J.-E. Brochier, L. Chabal, et al. (eds.), *La botanique*, pp. 43–104. Paris: Errance.

Chahuan, M. S. 1996. Origin and history of tropical deciduous Sal (*Shorea robusta* Gaertn.) forests in Madhya Pradesh, India, *Palaeobotanist* 43:89–101.

———. 2000. Pollen evidence of Late Quaternary vegetation and climate change in Northeastern Madhya Pradesh, India, *Palaeobotanist* 49:491–500.

———. 2002. Holocene vegetation and climatic changes in southeastern Madhya Pradesh, India, *Current Science* 83(12):1444–45.

Chauhan, O. S. 2003. Past 20,000-year history of Himalayan aridity: Evidence from oxygen isotope records in the Bay of Bengal, *Current Science* 84(1):90–93.

Champion, H. G. 1936. A preliminary survey of forest types of India and Burma, *Indian Forest Records (n.s.)* 1.

Champion, H. G., and F. C. Osmaston. 1962. *E. P. Stebbing's The Forests of India*, Volume 4. Oxford: Oxford University Press.

Chandra, V. 1997. *Edible plants of forestry origin.* Dehra Dun: Indian Council for Forestry Research and Education.

Chatterjee, R. 1991. The Tasar silk industry and its decline in Bengal and South Bihar: 1872–1921, *The Indian Historical Review* 17(1–2):174–92.

Chowdhury, K. A. 1955. Plant remains from Hastinapur, *Ancient India* 10–11:121–37.

Chowdhury, K. A., and S. S. Ghosh. 1946. Report on wood and fruit shells (from Arikamedu), *Ancient India* 2:104–08.

———. 1951. Plant remains from Harappa excavations in 1946, *Ancient India* 7:3–19.

———. 1952. Wood remains from Sisulpalgarh, *Ancient India* 8:28–32.

———. 1957. Charcoal remains, Maski Excavation, *Ancient India* 13:133–41.

———. 1958. *Indian Woods I.* Dehra Dun, Forest Research Institute.

Chowdhury, K. A., K. S. Saraswat, and G. M. Buth. 1977. *Ancient Agriculture and forestry in North India.* New Delhi: Asia Publishing House.

Clements, F. E. 1916. *Plant succession: An analysis of the development of vegetation.* Washington, D.C.: Carnegie Institute.

Clements, F. E. 1949. *Dynamics of vegetation.* New York: H. W. Wilson Company.

Coleman, M., and K. Hodges. 1995. Evidence for Tibetan plateau uplift before 14 Myr ago from a new minimum age for east-west extension, *Nature* 374:49–52.

Coles, J. M., S. V. E. Heal, and B. J. Orme. 1978. The use and character of wood in prehistoric Britain and Ireland, *Proceedings of the Prehistoric Society* 44:1–45.

Coningham, R. A. E., and F. R. Allchin. 1995. The rise of cities in Sri Lanka. In Allchin, F. R. (ed.), *The archaeology of early historic South Asia— The emergence of cities and states*, pp. 152–83. Cambridge: Cambridge University Press.

Connell, J. H., and R. O. Slayter. 1977. Mechanisms of succession in natural communities and their role in community stability and organisation, *American Naturalist* 111(982):1119–44.

Cooke, T. 1903–1908. *The flora of the Presidency of Bombay.* London: Taylor and Francis.

Corbett, G. E., and J. E. Hill. 1992. *The mammals of the Indomalayan region: A systematic review.* Oxford: Oxford University Press.

Couvert, M. 1968. Etude des charbons préhistoriques: méthodes de préparation et d'identification, *Libyca* 16:249–56.

Couvert, M. 1969a. Etude des quelques charbons préhistoriques de la grotte Capelleti, *Libyca* 17:213–18.

———. 1969b. Identification de charbons provenant du gisement de Tamar Hat, *Libyca* 17:49–52.

———. 1976. Traduction des éléments de la flore préhistorique en facteurs climatiques, *Libyca* 24:9–20.

Cunningham, A. 1879. *The stupa of Bharhut.* London: W. H. Allen and Co.

Dabadghao, P. M., and K. A. Shankarnarayan. 1973. *The grass cover of India.* New Delhi: Indian Council of Agricultural Research.

Dalby, A. 2000. *Dangerous tastes: The story of spices.* Berkeley and Los Angeles: University of California Press.

Das, D. 1969. *Economic history of the Deccan from the first to sixth century AD.* New Delhi: Munshiram Manoharlal.

Dash, J. 1998. *Human ecology of foragers: A study of Kharia (Savara), Ujia (Savara) and Birhor in Simlipal Hills.* New Delhi: Commonwealth.

De Candolle, A. 1885. *Origin of cultivated plants.* New York: Appleton and Co.

de Vartavan, C., and V. Asensi Amoros. 1997. *Codex of ancient Egyptian plant remains.* London: Triade Exploration.

De Wet, J. M. J., K. E. Prasada Rao, M. H. Mengesha, and D. E. Brink. 1983. Systematics and domestication of *Panicum sumatrense* (Graminae), *Journal d'Agriculture Traditionelle et de Botanique Appliquée* 30(2):159–68.

de Menocal, P. B. 2001. Cultural responses to climate change during the late Holocene, *Science* 292:667–73.

Deotare, B. C., M. D. Kajale, A. A. Kshirsagar, and S. N. Rajaguru. 1998. Geoarchaeological and palaeoenvironmental studies around Bap-Malar Playa, District Jodhpur, Rajasthan. *Current Science* 75(3):316–20.

Dhavalikar, M. K. 1984. Toward an ecological model for Chalcolithic cultures of central and western India, *Journal of Anthropological Archaeology* 3:133–58.

———. 1988. *The first farmers of the Deccan.* Pune: Ravish.

———. 2001a. Early farming cultures of central India: A recent perspective. In Settar, S., and R. Korisettar (eds.), *Indian archaeology in retrospect,* Volume 1, *Prehistory,* pp. 253–62. New Delhi: Manohar.

———. 2001b. Green imperialism: Monsoon in antiquity and human response, *Man and Environment* 26(2):17–28.

Dimbleby, G. W. 1967. *Plants and archaeology.* London: Duckworth.

———. 1977. *Ecology and archaeology.* London: Edward Arnold.

Drury, C. H. 1873. *The useful plants of India with notices of their chief value in commerce, medicine and the arts.* London: William Allan and Co.

Dubois, A. J. A. 1906. *Hindu manners, customs and ceremonies.* Oxford: Clarendon Press.

Ellis, J. L. 1987. *Flora of Nallamalais.* Calcutta: Botanical Survey of India.

Enzel, Y., L. Ely, et al. 1999. High resolution Holocene environmental changes in the Thar Desert, northwestern India, *Science* 284:125–27.

Erdosy, G. 1998. Deforestation in pre- and protohistoric South Asia. In Grove R. H., V. Damodaran, and S. Sangwan (eds.), *Nature and the Orient: The environmental history of South and Southeast Asia,* pp. 51–69. New Delhi: Oxford University Press.

Fahn, A. 1990. *Plant anatomy.* Oxford: Pergamon Press.

Fahn, A., E. Werker, and P. Baas. 1986. *Wood anatomy and identification of trees and shrubs from Israel and adjacent regions.* Jerusalem: The Israel Academy of Sciences.

Fairservis, W. 1971. *The roots of ancient India: The archaeology of early Indian civilisation.* New York: Macmillan.

Fischer, C. E. C. 1928. *Flora of the Presidency of Madras, Volume III.* London: Adlard and Son.

———. 1938. Where did the sandalwood tree (*Sanatalum album* Linn.) evolve? *Journal of the Bombat Natural History Society* 40:458–66.

Flenley, J. 1979. *The equatorial rain forest: A geological history.* London: Butterworth and Co.

Flint, E. P. 1998. Deforestation and land use in northern India with a focus on sal (*Shorea robusta*) forests from 1880–1980. In Grove, R. H., V. Damodaran, and S. Sangwan (eds.), *Nature and the Orient: The environmental history of South and Southeast Asia,* pp. 421–58. New Delhi, Oxford University Press.

Foote, R. B. 1887. Notes of some recent Neolithic and Palaeolithic finds in the south, *Journal of the Asiatic Society of Bengal* 56(2):259–82.

———. 1895. The geology of the Bellary district, Madras Presidency, *The Memoirs of the Geological Survey of India* 25(1):1–216.

Francis, P. J. 2002. Early historic South India and the international maritime trade, *Man and Environment* 27(1):153–60.

Fuller, D. Q. 1999. *The emergence of agricultural societies in South India: Sotanical and archaeological perspectives* (Unpublished Ph.D. Dissertation). Department of Archaeology, University of Cambridge.

———. 2001. Ashmounds and hilltop villages: The search for early agriculture in southern India, *Archaeology International* 4 (2000/2001):43–46.

———. 2002. Fifty years of archaeobotanical studies in India: Laying a solid foundation. In Settar, S., and R. Korisettar (eds.), *Indian archaeology in retrospect*, Volume III, *Archaeology and interactive disciplines*, pp. 247–363. Delhi: Manohar.

———. 2003a. Indus and non-Indus agricultural traditions: Local developments and crop adoptions on the Indian peninsula. In Weber, S. A., and W. R. Belcher (eds.), *Indus ethnobiology: New perspectives from the field*, pp. 343–96. Lanham: Lexington Books.

———. 2003b. African crops in prehistoric South Asia: A critical review. In Neumann, K., A. Butler, and S. Kahlheber (eds.), *Food, fuel and fields: Progress in African archaeobotany*, pp. 239–71. Köln: Heinrich-Barth Institut.

———. 2003c. An agricultural perspective on Dravidian historical linguistics: Archaeological crop packages, livestock and Dravidian crop vocabulary. In Bellwood, P., and C. Renfrew (eds.), *Examining the farming/language dispersal hypothesis*, pp. 191–213. Cambridge: McDonald Institute for Archaeological Research.

———. 2007. Non-human genetics, agricultural origins, and historical linguistics in South Asia. In Petraglia, M., and B. Allchin (eds.), *The Evolution and History of Human Populations in South Asia*, pp 393–443. Dordrecht: Springer Verlag.

Fuller, D. Q., N. Boivin, and R. Korisettar. In Press. Dating the Neolithic of South India: New radiometric evidence for key economic, social and ritual transformations. *Antiquity*.

Fuller, D. Q., and R. Korisettar. 2004. The vegetational context of early agriculture in South India, *Man and Environment* 29(1):7–27.

Fuller, D. Q., R. Korisettar, and P. C. Venkatasubbaiah. 2001. Southern Neolithic cultivation systems: A reconstruction based on archaeobotanical evidence, *South Asian Studies* 17:171–87.

Fuller, D. Q., R. Korisettar, P. C. Venkatasubbaiah, and M. K. Jones. 2004. Early plant domestications in southern India: Some preliminary archaeobotanical results, *Vegetation History and Archaeobotany* 13:115–29.

Fuller, D. Q., and M. Madella. 2001. Issues in Harappan Archaeobotany: Retrospect and Prospect. In Settar, S., and R. Korisettar (eds.), *Indian archaeology in retrospect, Volume II. Protohistory*, pp. 317–90. New Delhi: Manohar.

Fuller, D. Q., P. C. Venkatasubbaiah, and R. Korisettar. 2001. The beginnings of agriculture in the Kunderu river basin: Evidence from archaeological survey and archaeobotany, *Puratattva* 31:1–8.

Gadgil, M., and R. Guha. 1992. *This fissured land: An ecological history of India*. Delhi: Oxford University Press.

———. 1995. *Ecology and equity: The use and abuse of nature in contemporary India*. London: Routledge.

Gadgil, M., and V. D. Vartak. 1976. Sacred groves of Western Ghats of India, *Economic Botany* 30: 152–60.

Gamble, J. S. 1902. *A manual of Indian timbers: An account of the growth, distribution, and uses of the trees and shrubs of India and Ceylon with descriptions of their wood structure*. London: Sampson Low, Marston.

Gamble, J. S. 1921. *Flora of the Presidency of Madras*, Volume II. London: Adlard and Son.

———. 1935. *Flora of the Presidency of Madras*, Volume I. London: Adlard and Son.

Gasse, F. 2000. Hydrological changes in the African tropics since the last glacial maximum, *Quaternary Science Review* 19:189–211.

Ghosh, S. S., and K. Lal. 1963. Plant remains from Rangpur and other explorations in Gujarat, *Ancient India* 18/19:161–75.

Godwin, H. 1977. Sir Arthur Tansley—The man and the subject: The Tansley lecture, 1976, *The Journal of Ecology* 65(1):1–26.

Godwin, H., and A. G. Tansley. 1941. Prehistoric charcoals as evidence of former vegetation, soil, and climate, *Journal of Ecology* 19:117–26.

Gordon, S. 1994. *Maratha marauders and state formation in eighteenth century India*. New Delhi: Oxford University Press.

Gould, S. J. 1987. *Time's arrow, time's cycle: Myth and metaphor in the discovery of geological time*. London: Pelican.

Grigson, W. 1949. *The Maria Gonds of Bastar*. Oxford: Oxford University Press.

Grove, A. T. 1993. Africa's climate in the Holocene. In Shaw, T., P. Sinclair, B. Andah, and A. Okpoko (eds.), *The archaeology of Africa. Food, metals and towns*, pp. 32–42. London: Routledge.

Grove, A. T., and O. Rackham. 2001. *The nature of Mediterranean Europe: An ecological history*. New Haven, CT: Yale University Press.

Grove, R. H. 1995. *Green imperialism—Colonial expansion, tropical island Edens and the origins of environmentalism, 1600–1860*. Cambridge: Cambridge University Press.

———. 1998a. *Ecology, climate and empire—The Indian legacy in global environmental history, 1400–1940*. New Delhi: Oxford University Press.

———. 1998b. The East India Company, the Raj and the El Nino: The critical role played by colonial scientists in establishing the mechanisms of global climate teleconnections 1770–1930. In Grove, R. H., V. Damodaran, and S. Sangwan (eds.), *Nature and the Orient: The environmental history of South and Southeast Asia*, pp. 301–23. New Delhi: Oxford University Press.

Guha, R. 1989. *The unquiet woods: Ecological change and peasant resistance in the Himalayas*. New Delhi: Oxford University Press.

Guha, S. 1999. *Environment and ethnicity 1200–1991*. Cambridge: Cambridge University Press.

Gulati, A. N. 1961. *A note on the early history of silk in India*. Pune: Deccan College.

Gupta, H. P. 1971. Quaternary vegetational history of Ootacamund, Nilgiris, South India. 1. Kakathope and Rees Corner, *Palaeobotanist* 20:74–90.

———. 1994. A tribute to Vishnu-Mittre (1924–1991), *The Palaeobotanist* 42(2):241.

Gupta, S. 2002. The archaeo-historical idea of the Indian Ocean, *Man and Environment* 27(1):1–24.

Gururani, S. 2002. Forests of pleasure and pain: Gendered practices of labor and livelihood in the forests of the Kumaon Himalayas, India, *Gender, Place and Culture* 9(3):229–43.

Haberle, S. G., and B. David. 2004. Climates of change: Human dimensions of Holocene environmental change in low latitudes of the PEPII transect, *Quaternary International* 118/119:165–79.

Haberle, S. G., G. S. Hope, and W. A. Van der Kaars. 2001. Biomass burning in Indonesia and Papua New Guinea: Natural and human induced fire events in the fossil record, *Palaeogeography, Palaeoclimatology, Palaeoecology* 171:259–68.

Habib, I. 2001. *The economic history of medieval India: A survey*. New Delhi: Tulika.

Haines, H. H. 1921–1925. *Botany of Bihar and Orissa*. London: Adlard and Newmand.

Hajra, P. K., B. D. Sharma, M. Sanjappa, and A. R. K. Sastry (eds.). 1996. *Flora of India: Introductory Volume (Part I)*. Calcutta: Botanical Survey of India.

Hassan, F. A. 1997a. Holocenes palaeoclimates of Africa, *African Archaeological Review* 14(4): 213–30.

———. 1997b. Nile floods and political disorder in early Egypt. In Dalfes, H. N., G. Kukla, and H. Weiss (eds.), *Third millennium BC climate change and Old World collapse*, pp. 1–23. Berlin and Heidelberg: Springer Verlag.

Hather, J. 2000. *The identification of northern European woods*. London: Archetype.

Henry, A. C., N. C. Rathakrishnan, and T. Ravisankar. 1996. Deccan. In Hajra, P. K., B. D. Sharma, M. Sanjappa, and A. R. K. Sastry (eds.), *Flora of India: Introductory volume (part I)*, pp. 456–76. Calcutta: Botanical Survey of India.

Hillman, G. C., R. Hedges, A. Moore, S. Colledge, and P. Pettitt. 2001. New evidence of Late Glacial cereal cultivation at Abu Hureyra on the Euphrates, *The Holocene* 11(4):383–93.

Hooker, J. D. 1875–1897. *The flora of British India*. London: L. Reeve and Co.

———. 1904. *A sketch of the flora of British India*. London.

Hope, G., A. P. Kershaw, S. van der Kaars, S. Xiangjun, P.-M. Liew, L. E. Heusser, H. Takahara, M. McGlone, N. Miyoshi, and P. T. Moss. 2004. History of vegetation and habitat change in the Austral-Asian region, *Quaternary International* 118–19:103–26.

Hora, S. L. 1949. Satpura hypothesis of the distribution of the Malayan fauna and flora to peninsular India, *Proceedings of the National Institute of Science India* 15:309–14.

Huggett, R. J. 1995. *Geoecology: An evolutionary approach*. London: Routledge.

Huke, R. E. 1982. *Agroclimatic and dry-season maps of South, Southeast and East Asia*. Manila: International Rice Research Institute.

Ingalhalikar, S. 2001. *Flowers of the Sahyadris*. Pune: Corolloa Publications.

Jacobs, B. F., J. D. Kingston, and L. L. Jacobs. 1999. The origin of grass-dominated ecosystems, *Annals of the Missouri Botanical Garden* 86:590–643.

Jane, F. W. 1956. *The structure of wood*. London: A. & C. Black.

Jansen, P. C. M. 1989. *Macrotyloma uniflorum* (Lam.) Verdc. In van der Maeson, L. J. G., and S. Somaatmadji (eds.), *Plant resources of Southeast Asia 1. Pulses*, pp. 53–54. Wageningen: Pudoc.

Jodha, N. S. 2001. *Life on the edge—Sustaining agriculture and community resources in fragile environments.* Delhi: Oxford University Press.

Johnston, I. M. 1951. Studies in Boraginaceae XX. Representatives of three subfamilies in eastern Asia, *Journal of the Arnold Arboretum* 32:1—26.

Jolly, D., S. P. Harrison, B. Damnati, and R. Bonnefille. 1998. Simulated climate and biomes of Africa during the late Quaternary: Comparison with pollen and lake status data, *Quaternary Science Reviews* 17:629–57.

Jung, S. J. A., G. R. Davies, G. M. Ganssen, and D. Kroon. 2004. Synchronous Holocene sea surface temperature and rainfall variations in the Asian monsoon system, *Quaternary Science Reviews* 23:2207–18.

Kajale, M. D. 1988. Plant economy. In Dhavalikar, M. K., H. D. Sankalia, and Z. D. Ansari (eds.), *Excavations at Inamgaon*, pp. 727–821. Pune: Deccan College Postgraduate and Research Institute.

———. 1989. Archaeobotanical investigation on Megalithic Bhagimohari and its significance, *Man and Environment* 13:87–96.

———. 1990. Observations on the plant remains from excavation at Chalcolithic Kaothe, District Dhule, Maharashtra with cautionary remarks on their interpretations. In Dhavalikar, M. K., V. S. Shinde, and S. M. Atre (eds.), *Excavations at Kaothe*, pp. 265–80. Pune: Deccan College.

Kajale, M. D. 1991. Current status of Indian palaeoethnobotany: Introduced and indigenous food plants with a discussion of the historical and evolutionary development of Indian agriculture and agricultural systems in general. In Renfrew, J. M. (ed.), *New light on early farming: Recent developments in palaeoethnobotany*, pp. 155–89. Edinburgh: Edinburgh University Press.

Kajale, M. D., and B. C. Deotare. 1997. Late Quaternary environmental studies on salt lakes in Western Rajasthan, India: A summarized view, *Journal of Quaternary Science* 12(5):405–12.

Kajale, M. D., B. C. Deotare, and S. N. Rajaguru. 2004. Palaeomonsoon and palaeoclimatic background to the prehistoric cultures of western and central Thar Desert, Rajasthan, northwestern India. In Yasuda, Y., and V. S. Shinde (eds.), *Monsoon and civilisation*, pp. 83–98. New Delhi: Lustre Press/Roli Books.

Karanth, K. P. 2003. Evolution of disjunct distributions among wet-zone species of the Indian subcontinent: Testing various hypotheses using a phylogenetic approach, *Current Science* 85(9):1276–83.

Kellman, M., and R. Tackaberry. 1997. *Tropical environments: The functioning and management of tropical ecosystems.* London: Routledge.

Kennedy, K. A. R. 2000. *God-apes and fossil men: Paleoanthropology in South Asia.* Ann Arbor: The University of Michigan Press.

Kimata, M., E. G. Ashok, and A. Seetharam. 2000. Domestication, cultivation and utilisation of two small millets, *Brachiaria ramosa* and *Setaria glauca*, Poaceae in South India, *Economic Botany* 54:217–27.

Korisettar, R. 2001. The archaeology of the South Asian lower Palaeolithic: History and current status. In Settar, S., and R. Korisettar (eds.), *Indian archaeology in retrospect,* Volume I, *Prehistory*, pp. 1–66. New Delhi: Manohar.

———. 2004. *Geoarchaeology of the Purana and Gondwana basins of peninsular India: Peripheral or paramount—a suggested core-periphery model.* Presidential address, Archaeology Section, 65th session of the Indian History Congress. Bareilly: Mahatma Jyotiba Phule Rohilkhand University.

Korisettar, R., P. P. Joglekar, D. Q. Fuller, and P. C. Venkatasubbaiah. 2001. Archaeological re-investigation and archaeozoology of seven Southern Neolithic sites in Karnataka and Andhra Pradesh, *Man and Environment* 26(2):47–66.

Korisettar, R., P. C. Venkatasubbaiah, and D. Q. Fuller 2001. Brahmagiri and beyond: The archaeology of the Southern Neolithic. In Settar, S., and R. Korisettar (eds.), *Indian Archaeology in Retrospect,* Volume I, *Prehistory*, pp. 151–238. New Delhi: Manohar.

Kreuz, A. 1992. Charcoal from ten early Neolithic settlements in central Europe and its interpretation in terms of woodland management and wildwood resources, *Bulletin de la Société Botanique de France* 139:383–94.

Kuniholm, P. I., Kromer, B., Manning, S. W., Newton, M. W., Latini, C. E., and Bruce, M. J. 1996. Anatolian tree rings and the absolute chronology of the eastern mediterranean, 2220–718 BC, *Nature* 381:780–83.

Kutzbach, J. E. 1987. The changing pulse of the monsoon. In Fein, J. S., and P. L. Stephens (eds.), *Monsoons*, pp. 247–68. New York: John Wiley.

Laufer, B. 1919. *Sino-Iranica. Chinese contributions to the history of civilisation in ancient Iran.* Chicago: Field Museum of Natural History.

Legris, P., and V. M. Meher-Homji. 1977. Phytogeographic outlines of the hill ranges of peninsular India, *Tropical Ecology* 18:10–24.

Leney, L., and R. W. Casteel. 1975. Simplified procedure for examining charcoal specimens for identification, *Journal of Archaeological Science* 2:153–59.

Lézine, A.-M., J.-F. Saliège, C. Robert, F. Wertz, and M.-L. Inizian. 1998. Holocene lakes from Ramlat as-Sab'atayn (Yemen) illustrate the impact of monsoon activity in southern Arabia, *Quaternary Research* 50:290–99.

Lone, F. A., M. Khan, and G. M. Buth. 1993. *Palaeoethnobotany: Plants and ancient man in Kashmir.* Rotterdam: A. A. Balkema.

Ludden, D. 2002. *India and South Asia: A short history.* Oxford: Oneworld.

Mabberley, D. J. 1987. *The plant book: A portable dictionary of the higher plants.* Cambridge: Cambridge University Press.

Mackintosh-Smith, T. (ed.). 2002. *The travels of Ibn Battutah (abridged).* London, Picador.

Madella, M., and D. Q. Fuller. 2006. Palaeoecology and the Harappan civilisation of South Asia: A reconsideration, *Quaternary Science Reviews* 25:1283–1301.

Mann, M. 1999. *British rule on Indian soil: North India in the first half of the nineteenth century.* New Delhi: Manohar.

Matthew, K. M. 1995. *An excursion flora of central Tamil Nadu, India.* New Delhi: Oxford and IBH.

———. 1999. *The flora of Palni Hills.* Tiruchirapalli: The Rapinat Herbarium.

Maxwell-Hyslop, K. 1983. *Dalbergia Sissoo* Roxburgh. *Anatolian Studies* 33:67–72.

McClure, H. A. 1976. Radiocarbon chronology of the late Quaternary lakes in the Arabian Desert, *Nature* 263:755.

McIntosh, R. J., J. A. Tainter, and S. K. McIntosh (eds.), 2000. *The way the wind blows: Climate, history, and human action.* New York: Columbia University Press.

McIntosh, R. P. 1987. Pluralism in ecology, *Annual Review of Ecology and Systematics* 18:321–24.

Meher-Homji, V. M. 1967. On delimiting arid and semi-arid climates in India, *The Indian Geographical Journal* 42(1–2):1–6.

———. 1989. History of vegetation of peninsular India. *Man and Environment* 13:1–9.

———. 1994a. Climate changes over space and time: Their repercussion on the flora and vegetation, *Palaeobotanist* 42(2):225–40.

———. 1994b. Palynology: A tool to interpret past environments, climate change or human activity, *The Indian Geographical Journal* 69(1):36–38.

———. 1996a. Monsoon: A bioclimatologist's point of view, *Current Science* 71(5):327–57.

———. 1996b. Past environments though palynology: A short appraisal with reference to the Western Ghats, *Environment and History* 2:249–52.

———. 2001. *Bioclimatology and plant geography of peninsular India.* Jodhpur: Scientific Publishers.

———. 2002. Bioclimatology and quaternary palynology in India. In Settar, S., and R. Korisettar (eds.), *Indian Archaeology in Retrospect,* Volume III, *Archaeology and Interactive Disciplines,* pp. 61–86. New Delhi: Manohar.

Menon, V. 2003. *A field guide to Indian mammals.* Delhi: Dorling Kindersley India.

Metcalfe, C. R., and L. Chalk. 1950. *Anatomy of the dicotyledons* (2 volumes). Oxford: Clarendon Press.

Miller, J. I. 1968. *The spice trade of the Roman Empire.* Oxford: Oxford University Press.

Miller, N. F. 1985. Palaeoethnobotanical evidence for deforestation in ancient Iran: A case study of urban Malyan, *Journal of Ethnobiology* 5(1):1–19.

Misra, R. 1983. *Indian savannas.* Amsterdam: Elsevier.

Misra, V. N. 1989. Human adaptations to the changing landscape of the Indian arid zone during the Quaternary period. In Kenoyer, J. M. (ed.), *Old problems and new perspectives in the archaeology of South Asia,* pp. 3–20. Madison: Department of Anthropology, University of Wisconsin.

———. 2001. The Mesolithic age in India. In Settar, S., and R. Korisettar (eds.), *Indian archaeology in retrospect,* Volume I, *Prehistory,* pp. 111–26. New Delhi: Manohar.

Misra, V. N., and R. K. Mohanty. 2001. A rare Chalcolithic pottery cache from Balathal, Rajasthan, *Man and Environment* 26(2):67–74.

Mohanty, R. K., and V. Selvakumar. 2001. The archaeology of the Megaliths in India: 1947–1997. In Settar, S., and R. Korisettar (eds.), *Indian archaeology in retrospect,* Volume I, *Prehistory,* pp. 313–52. New Delhi: Manohar.

Momot, J. 1955. Méthode pour l'étude de charbons de bois, *Bulletin de la Société Préhistorique Française* 52:141–42.

Morgan, M. E., J. D. Kingston, and B. D. Marino. 1994. Carbon isotope evidence for the emergence of C4 plants in the Neogene of Pakistan and Kenya, *Nature* 367:162–65.

Morris, B. (1982) *Forest traders: A socio-economic study of the Hill Pandram*. London: Athlone Press.

Morrison, K. 1995. *Field of victory: Vijayanagara and the course of intensification*. Berkeley and Los Angeles: University of California Press.

———. 2002. Pepper in the hills: Upland-lowland exchange and the intensification of the spice trade. In Morrison, K., and L. J. Junker (eds.), *Forager-traders in South and Southeast Asia*, pp. 105–28. Cambridge: Cambridge University Press.

Morton, J. F. 1987. *Fruits of warm climates*. Miami: Julia F. Morton.

Mudgal, V., K. K. Khanna, and P. K. Hajra. 1997. *Flora of Madhya Pradesh*, Volume II, Calcutta: Botanical Survey of India.

Muzzolini, A. 1993. The emergence of a food-producing economy in the Sahara. In Shaw, T. A., P. Sinclair, B. Andah, and A. Okpoko (eds.), *The archaeology of Africa: Food, metals and towns*, pp. 227–39. London: Routledge.

Naidu, P. D. 1996. Onset of an arid climate at 3.5 ka in the ropics: Evidence from monsoon upswelling record, *Current Science* 71(9):715–18.

Nandi, R. N. 2000. *State formation, agrarian growth and social change in feudal South India c. AD 600–1200*. New Delhi: Manohar.

Nasir, Y. J. 1989. *Flora of Pakistan. No. 191. Boraginaceae*. Islamabad: National Herbarium, Pakistan Agricultural Research Council.

Netting, R. M. 1974. Agrarian ecology, *Annual Review of Anthropology* Longmans. 3:21–56.

Neumann, K. 1989. Holocene vegetation of the eastern Sahara: Charcoal from prehistoric sites, *African Archaeological Review* 7:97–116.

———. 1992. The contribution of anthracology to the study of the late Quaternary vegetation history of the Mediterranean region and Africa, *Bulletin de la Société Botanique de France* 139:421–40.

Paddaya, K. 1994. Investigation of man-environment relationships in Indian archaeology: Some theoretical considerations, *Man and Environment* 11(1–2):1–28.

———. 1998. Evidence of Neolithic cattle penning at Budihal, Gulbarga district, Karnataka, *South Asian Studies* 14:141–53.

Pal, J. N. 2001. The middle Palaeolithic cultures of South Asia. In Settar, S., and R. Korisettar (eds.), *Indian archaeology in retrospect, Volume I, Prehistory*, pp. 67–84. New Delhi: Manohar.

Pallithanam, J. M. 2001. *A pocket flora of the Sirumalai hills, South India*. Tiruchirapalli: The Rapinat Herbarium, St. Joseph's College.

Pandey, R. P. 1981. Significanc of animal fossils in the prehistoric studies of the upper Mahanadi valley, central India, *Puratattva* 12:37–46.

Pandey, R. P., and S. Chanda. 1996. *Economic botany*. New Delhi: Vikas Publishing House.

Panja, S. 1999. Mobility and subsistence strategies: A case study of Inamgaon, a Chalcolithic sites in western India, *Asian Perspectives* 38(2):154–85.

———. 2001. Research on the Deccan, Chalcolithic. In Settar, S., and R. Korisettar (eds.), *Indian archaeology in retrospect, Volume I, Prehistory*, pp. 263–76. New Delhi: Manohar.

Patnaik, N. 1993. *The garden of life: An introduction to the healing plants of India*. London: Aquarian.

Pearsall, D. .2000. *Paleoethnobotany*. New York: Academic Press.

Pemadasa, M. A. 1990. Tropical grasslands of Sri Lanka and India, *Journal of Biogeography* 17(4/5): 395–400.

Perry, C. A., and K. J. Hsu. 2000. Geophysical, archaeological, and historical evidence support a solar-output model for climate change, *Proceedings of the National Academy of Sciences USA* 97(23): 12433–38.

Pimpalapure, N. 1999. *Tendu* leaf and *bidis*, *Asian Agri-History* 3(2):111–16.

Piperno, D., and D. Pearsall. 1998. *The origins of agriculture in the lowland Neotropics*. New York: Academic Press.

Polunin, N. 1960. *Introduction to plant geography and some related sciences*. London: Longman.

Possehl, G. L. 1997a. Climate and the eclipse of the ancient cities of the Indus. In Dalfes H. N., G. Kukla, and H. Weiss (eds.), *Third millennium BC climate change and Old World collapse*, pp. 193–243. Berlin & Heidelberg: Springer Verlag.

———. 1997b. The transformation of the Indus civilisation, *Journal of World Prehistory* 11(4):425–72.

———. 1999. *Indus age: The beginnings*. Philadelphia, University of Pennsylvania Press.

Possehl, G. L., and P. Rissman. 1992. The chronology of prehistoric India from earliest times to the Iron Age. In Ehrich, R. W. (ed.), *Chronologies in Old World archaeology*, pp. 465–90 (Volume 1) and 447–74 (Volume 2). Chicago: University of Chicago Press.

Potts, R., and A. K. Behrensmeyer. 1992. Late Cenozoic terrestrial ecosystems. In Behrensmeyer, A. K., J. D. Damuth, W. A. DiMichele, R. Potts, H.-D. Sues, and

S. L. Wing (eds.), *Terrestrial ecosystems through time: Evolutionary paleoecology of terrestrial plants and animals*, pp. 419–514. Chicago: University of Chicago Press.

Prabhu, C. N., R. Shankar, A. Anupama, M. Taieb, R. Bonnefille, L. Vidal, and S. Prasad. 2004. A 200-ka pollen and oxygen-isotopic record from two sediment cores from the eastern Arabian Sea, *Palaeogeography, Palaeoclimatology, Palaeoecology* 214:309–21.

Pradhan, S. 2001. *Rock art in Orissa*. New Delhi: Aryan Books International.

Prasad, S., S. Kusumgar, and S. K. Gupta. 1997. A mid- to late Holocene record of palaeoclimatic changes from Nal Sarovar: A palaeodesert margin lake in western India, *Journal of Quaternary Science* 12:153–59.

Pruthi, J. S. 1993. *Major spices of India. Crop management and post-harvest technology*. New Delhi: Indian Council of Agricultural Research.

Puri, G. S. 1960. *Indian forest ecology*. New Delhi: Oxford Books.

Puri, G. S., V. M. Meher-Homji, R. K. Gupta, and S. Puri. 1983. *Forest ecology* (2nd edition), Volume I, *Phytogeography and forest conservation*. New Delhi: Oxford and IBH.

Puri, G. S., R. K. Gupta, V. M. Meher-Homji, and S. Puri. 1989. *Forest ecology* (2nd edition), Volume II, *Plant form, diversity, communities and succession*. New Delhi: Oxford and IBH.

Pyne, S. J. 1994. Nataraja: India's cycle of fire, *Environmental History Review* 18:1–20.

———. 1997. *Vestal fire: An environmental history told through fire of Europe and Europe's encounter with the world*. Seattle: University of Washington Press.

———. 2001. *Fire: A brief history*. London: The British Museum Press.

Rackham, O. 1986. *The history of the countryside*. London: Dent.

Radhakrishna, B. P., and R. Vaidyanadhan. 1994. *Geology of Karnataka*. Bangalore: Geological Society of India.

Raikes, R. L. 1984. *Water, weather and prehistory*. New Jersey: Humanities Press.

Rajan, K. 2002. Maritime trade in early Historic Tamil Nadu, *Man and Environment* 27(1):83–98.

Rajan, R. 1998. Imperial environmentalism or environmental imperialism? European forestry, colonial foresters and agendas of forest management in British India 1800–1900. In Grove, R. H., V. Damodaran, and S. Sangwan (eds.), *Nature and the Orient: The environmental history of South and Southeast Asia*, pp. 375–95. New Delhi: Oxford University Press.

Ramam, P. K.,l and V. N. Murty. 1997. *Geology of Andhra Pradesh*. Bangalore: Geological Society of India.

Rangarajan, M. 1996. *Fencing the forests: Conservation and ecological change in India's central provinces 1860–1914*. New Delhi: Oxford University Press.

———. 1998. Production, desiccation and forest management in the central provinces 1850–1930. In Grove, R. H., V. Damodaran, and S. Sangwan (eds.), *Nature and the Orient: The environmental history of South and Southeast Asia*, pp. 575–95. New Delhi: Oxford University Press.

———. 2001. *India's wildlife history*. New Delhi, Permanent Black.

Rao, D. P. 1997. Geomorphology and soils. In Ramam, P. K., and V. N. Murty (eds.), *Geology of Andhra Pradesh*, pp. 225–40. Bangalore: Geological Society of India.

Rao, R., and K. Lal. 1985. Plant remains. In Rao, S. R. (ed.), *Lothal*, pp. 667–84. Delhi: Archaeological Survey of India.

Ratnagar, S. 2004. *Trading encounters: From the Euphrates to the Indus in the Bronze Age*. New Delhi: Oxford University Press.

Ray, H. P. 1998. *The winds of change: Buddhism and the maritime links of early South Asia*. New Delhi: Oxford University Press.

Redman, C. L. 1999. *Human impact on ancient environments*. Tucson: University of Arizona Press

Research, I. C. f. A. 1980. *Handbook of agriculture*. New Delhi: Indian Council for Agricultural Research.

Roberts, N. 1992. Climate change in the past. In Jones, S., R. Martin, and D. Pilbeam (eds.), *The Cambridge Encyclopedia of human evolution*, pp. 174–78. Cambridge: Cambridge University Press.

———. 1998. *The Holocene: An environmental history*. Oxford: Blackwell.

Roberts, S. J. 2000. Tropical fire ecology, *Progress in Physical Geography* 24(2):281–88.

Roxburgh, W. 1832. *Flora Indica*. London: Carey.

Royle, J. F. 1855. *The fibrous plants of India*. London.

Saha, S. 2002. Anthropogenic fire regimes in the deciduous forests of central India, *Current Science* 82(9):1144–47.

Saldanha, C. J. 1984. *Flora of Karnataka, Volume 1*. New Delhi: Oxford and IBH.

———. 1996. *Flora of Karnataka, Volume II*. New Delhi: Oxford and IBH.

Saldanha, I. M. 1998. Colonial forest regulations and collective resistance: Nineteenth century Thana

District. In Grove, R. H., V. Damodaran, and S. Sangwan (eds.). *Nature and the Orient: The environmental history of South and Southeast Asia*, pp. 708–33. New Delhi: Oxford University Press.

Salisbury, K. J., and F. W. Jane. 1940. Charcoals from Maiden Castle and their significance in relation to the vegetation and climatic conditions in prehistoric times, *Journal of Ecology* 28:310–25.

Samuel, R., H. Kathriarachchi, P. Hoffman, M. H. J. Barfuss, K. J. Wurdack, C. C. Davis, and M. W. Chase. 2005. Molecular phylogenetics of Phyllanthaceae: Evidence from plastid *matK* and nuclear *PHYC* sequences, *American Journal of Botany* 92(1): 132–41.

Sant, H. R. 1964. Ecological studies with special reference to reproductive capacity in relation to grazing of *Panicum psilopodium* Trin., *Journal of the Indian Botanical Society* 43:476–86.

Santa, S. 1961. Essai de reconstitution de paysages végétaux Quaternaires d'Afrique de Nord, *Libyca* 6/7:37–77.

Santa, S., and J. L. Vernet. 1968. Une technique de préparation des charbons de bois préhistoriques en vue de leur étude anatomique—Application, *Naturalia Monspeliensia* 19:171–77.

Saraswat, K. S. 1986. Ancient crop economy of Harappans from Rohira, Punjab (c. 2000–1700 BC), *Palaeobotanist* 35:32–38.

———. 1997. Plant economy of Barans at ancient Sanghol (ca. 1900–1400 BC), Punjab, *Pragdhara (Journal of the U. P. State Archaeology Department)* 7:97–114.

———. 2002a. Balu (29o40' N; 76o22' E), District Kaithal, *Indian Archaeology 1996–1997: A Review*, pp. 198–203.

———. 2002b. Banawali (29o37'5"N; 75o23'6"E), District Hissar, *Indian Archaeology 1996–1997: A Review*, p. 203.

———. 2004. Plant economy of early farming communities. In Singh, B. P. (ed.), *Early farming communities of the Kaimur (excavations at Senuwar)*, pp. 416–535. Jaipur: Publication Scheme.

Sarawat, K. S., N. K. Sharma, and D. C. Saini. 1994. Plant economy at Ancient Narhan (ca. 1300 BC–300/400 AD). In Singh, P. (ed.), *Excavations at Narhan (1984–1989)*, pp. 255–346. Varanasi: Banaras Hindu University.

Saraswat, K. S., and A. K. Pokharia. 1998. On the remains of botanical material used in fire-sacrifice ritualized during Kushana Period at Sanghol (Punjab), *Pragdhara* 8:149–81.

———. 1999. Sanghol, Dist. Ludhiana, Punjab, *Pragdhara* 9.

———. 2003. Kunal (29o30' N; 75o41'E), District Hissar. *Indian Archaeology 1996–1997: A Review*, pp. 229–32.

Sastri, N. 1975. *A history of South India*. New Delhi: Oxford University Press.

Sauer, C. O. 1947. Early relations of man to plants, *Geographical Review* 37:1–25.

———. 1952. *Agricultural origins and dispersals*. New York: American Geographical Society.

Schaffer, J. G., and D. A. Liechtenstein. 1989. Ethnicity and change in the Indus valley cultural tradition. In Kenoyer, J. M. (ed.), *Old problems and new perspectives in South Asian archaeology*, pp. 117–26. Madison: Department of Anthropology, University of Wisconsin.

Schama, S. 1995. *Landscape and memory*. London: Harper Collins.

Schoff, W. H. 2002. *The Periplus of the Erythrean Sea: Travel and trade in the Indian Ocean by a merchant of the first century*. New Delhi: Munshiram Manoharlal.

Schott, F. A., and J. P. J. McCreary. 2001. Monsoon circulation of the Indian Ocean, *Progress in Oceanography* 51:1–123.

Sharma, B. D. 2000. Affinities: Palaeobotanical and geological evidences, relationship with adjacent regions, past and recent plant migration. In Singh, N. P., D. K. Singh, P. K. Hajra, and B. D. Sharma (eds.), *Flora of India: Introductory volume (part II)*, pp. 1–200. Calcutta: Botanical Survey of India.

Sharma, B. D., N. P. Singh, R. S. Raghavan, and U. R. Deshpande. 1984. *Flora of Karnataka analysis*. Calcutta: Botanical Survey of India.

Sharma, M., V. Prasad, A. Saxena, and I. B. Singh. 2004. Archaeological studies in Lahuradewa area, Ganga Plain: 8. Microscopic charcoal in lacustrine sediments of Lahuradewa as evidence of human activity [Abstract]. In *Joint Annual Conference of the Indian Archaeological Society, Indian Society for Prehistoric and Quaternary Studies, and the Indian History and Culture Society, 28–31 December, 2004. Abstracts*, pp. 48–49. D. o. t. U. P. S. Archaeology. Lucknow: Directorate of the Uttar Pradesh State Archaeology.

Sharma, R. K., and O. P. Misra. 2003. *Archaeological excavations in central India (Madhya Pradesh and Chattisgarh)*. New Delhi: Mittal.

Shinde, V. 1987. Farming in the Chalcolithic Deccan, India c. 2000–1000 BC, *Tools and Tillage* 5(4): 215–27.

Shinde, V. 1991. Craft specialisation and social organisation in the Chalcolithic Deccan, India, *Antiquity* 65:796–807.

———. 1994. The Deccan Chalcolithic: A recent perspective, *Man and Environment* 19(1–2):169–78.

———. 1998. *Early settlements in the central Tapi basin*. New Delhi: Munshiram Manoharlal.

———. 2002. The emergence, development and spread of agricultural communities in South Asia. In Yasuda, Y. (ed.), *The origins of pottery and agriculture*, pp. 89–115. New Delhi, Lustre Press/Roli Books.

Shinde, V. S., S. S. Deshpande, and Y. Yasuda. 2004. Human response to Holocene climate changes—A case study of Western India between 5th and 3rd millennia BC. In Yasuda, Y., and V. S. Shinde (eds.), *Monsoon and civilisation*, pp. 383–406. New Delhi, Lustre Press/Roli Books.

Simmons, I. G. 1996. *Changing the face of the earth*. Oxford: Blackwell.

———. 1998. *Plants of life, plants of death*. Madison: University of Wisconsin Press.

Singh, G. 1971. The Indus valley culture seen in the context of postglacial climatic and ecological studies in north-west India, *Archaeology and Physical Anthropology of Oceania* 6(2):177–89.

Singh, G., R. D. Joshi, S. K. Chopra, and A. B. Singh. 1974. Late Quaternary history of vegetation and climate in the Rajasthan Desert, India, *Philosophical Transactions of the Royal Society London* 267: 467–501.

Singh, G., R. J. Wasson, and D. P. Agrawal. 1990. Vegetational and seasonal climatic changes since the last full glacial in the Thar Desert, northwestern India, *Review of Palaeobotany and Palynology* 64:351–58.

Singh, J. S., and V. K. Singh. 1992. Phenology of seasonally dry tropical forests, *Current Science* 63(11):684–89.

Singh, N. P. 1988. *Flora of eastern Karnataka*. Delhi: Mittal Publishers.

Singh, N. P., P. Lakshminarasimhan, S. Kathikeyan, and P. V. Prasanna. 2001. *Flora of Maharashtra State. Dicotyledons*. Calcutta: Botanical Survey of India.

Singh, R. 1992. *Fruits*. New Delhi: National Book Trust, India.

Sinton, J. 1993. When Moscow looks Chicago: An essay on uniformity and diversity in landscapes and communities, *Environmental History Review* 17:23–41.

Sirocko, F. 1996. The evolution of the monsoon climate over the Arabian Sea during the last 24,000 years, *Palaeoecology of Africa* 24:53–69.

Sitholey, R. V. 1976. Plants represented in ancient Indian sculpture, *Geophytology* 6(1):15–26.

Sivaramakrishnan, K. 1999. *Modern forests: Statemaking and environmental change in colonial eastern India*. New Delhi: Oxford University Press.

Skaria, A. 1999. *Hybrid histories: Forests, frontiers and wildness in Western India*. New Delhi, Oxford University Press.

Smart, J. 1990. *Grain legumes: Evolution and genetic resources*. Cambridge: Cambridge University Press.

Smart, T. L., and E. S. Hoffman. 1988. Environmental interpretation of archaeological charcoal. In Hastorf, C. A., and V. S. Popper (eds.), *Current paleoethnobotany*, pp. 167–205. Chicago: University of Chicago Press:.

Smith, P. M. 1976. Minor crops. In Simmonds, N. W. (ed.), *Evolution of crop plants*, pp. 301–24. London, Longman.

Sopher, D. E. 1980. Indian civilisation and the tropical savanna environment. In Harris, D. R. (ed.), *Human ecology in savanna environments*, pp. 185–207. London: Academic Press.

Southworth, F. 1988. Ancient economic plants of South Asia: Linguistic archaeology and early agriculture. In Jazayery, M. A., and W. Winter (eds.), *Languages and cultures: Studies in honor of Edgar C. Polome*, pp. 649–88. Amsterdam: Mouton de Gruyter.

———. 2005. *Linguistic Archaeology of South Asia*. London: Routledge.

Spate, O. H. K., and A. T. A. Learmonth. 1967. *India and Pakistan: A general and regional geography*. London: Methuen.

Starostin, S. 2003. *The Tower of Babel: An international etymological database project*. The Russian State University of Humanities (Center of Comparative Linguistics).

Staubwasser, M., and F. Sirocko. 2001. On the formation of laminated sediments on the continental margin off Pakistan: The effects of sediment provenance and sediment redistribution, *Marine Geology* 172:43–56.

———. 2002. On the formation of laminated sediments on the continental margin off Pakistan: Reply to the comment by von Rad et al., *Marine Geology* 192:431–33.

Staubwasser, M., F. Sirocko, P. M. Grootes, and H. Erlenkeuser. 2002. South Asian monsoon climate change and radiocarbon in the Arabian Sea during the early and middle Holocene, *Paleoceanography* 17(4):1–12.

Staubwasser, M., F. Sirocko, P. M. Grootes, and M. Segl. 2003. Climate change at the 4.2 ka BP termination of the Indus valley civilisation and Holocene South Asian monsoon variability, *Geophysical Research Letters* 30(8):1425–29.

Staubwasser, M., and H. Weiss. 2006. Holocene climate and cultural evolution in late prehistoric-early historic West Asia, *Quaternary Research* 66: 373–87.

Stebbing, E. P. 1922. *The forests of India,* Volume I. London: John Lane.

———. 1923. *The forests of India,* Volume II. London: John Lane.

———. 1926. *The forests of India,* Volume III. London, John Lane.

Stein, B. 1980. *Peasant, state and society in medieval South India.* New Delhi: Oxford University Press.

Stone, L., and S. Ezrati. 1996. Chaos, cycles and spatiotemporal dynamics in plant communities, *Journal of Ecology* 84:279–91.

Stott, P. 2000. Combustion in tropical biomass fires: A critical review, *Progress in Physical Geography* 24(3):355–77.

Stuiver, M., P. J. Reimer, E. Bard, J. W. Beck, G. S. Burr, K. A. Hughen, B. Kromer, G. McCormac, J. van der Plicht, and M. Spurk. 1998. INTCAL98 Radiocarbon Age Calibration, 24000-0 cal BP, *Radiocarbon* 40(3):1041–83.

Stuiver, M., P. J. Reimer, and T. F. Braziunas. 1998. High-precision radiocarbon age calibration for terrestrial and marine samples, *Radiocarbon* 40(3):1127–51.

Subash Chandran, M. D. 1997. On the ecological history of the Western Ghats, *Current Science* 73(2): 146–55.

———. 1998. Shifting cultivation, sacred groves and conflicts in colonial forest policy in the Western Ghats. In Grove, R. H., V. Damodaran, and S. Sangwan (eds.), *Nature and the Orient: The environmental history of South and Southeast Asia,* pp. 674–707. New Delhi: Oxford University Press

Subrahmanyam, V. P., and A. A. L. N. Sarma. 1973. Studies in drought climatology, part II: Moist climates of South India, *Tropical Ecology* 14(2):129–37.

Subrahmanyam, V. P., and C. V. S. Sastry. 1971. Studies in drought climatology, part I: Dry climates of South India, *Tropical Ecology* 12(2):250–56.

Sukhija, B. S., D. Venkat Reddy, and P. Nagabhusanam. 1998. Isotopic fingerprints of paleoclimates during the last 30,000 years in deep confined groundwaters of southern India, *Quaternary Research* 50: 252–60.

Sukumar, R., R. Ramesh, R. K. Pant, and G. Rajagopalan. 1993. A $^{13}C$ record of late Quaternary change from tropical peats in southern India, *Nature* 364:703–05.

Sundar, N. 1997. *Subalterns and sovereigns: An anthropological history of Bastar 1854–1996.* New Delhi: Oxford University Press.

Sutra, J.-P., R. Bonnefille, and M. Fontugne. 1997. Étude palynologiue d'un nouveau sondage dans les marais de Sandynalah (massif des Nilgiris, sud-ouest de l'Inde), *Géographie physique et Quaternaire* 51(3):425–37.

Swain, A. M., J. E. Kutzbach, and S. Hastenrath. 1983. Estimates of Holocene precipitation for Rajasthan, India, based on pollen and lake-level data, *Quaternary Research* 19:1–17.

Talbot, W. A. 1909-1912. *Forest flora of the Bombay Presidency and Sind.* Pune: Poona Government Photozincographic Department.

Tansley, A. G. (ed.). 1911. *Types of British vegetation.* Cambridge: Cambridge University Press.

———. 1920. The classification of vegetation and the concept of development, *Journal of Ecology* 8:118–49.

———. 1946. *Introduction to plant ecology.* London: Allen and Unwin.

———. 1949. *Britain's green mantle: Past, present and future.* London: Allen and Unwin.

Tengberg, M., and S. Thiébault. 2003. Vegetation history and wood exploitation in Pakistani Baluchistan from the Neolithic to the Harappan period: The evidence from charcoal analysis. In Weber, S. A., and W. R. Belcher (eds.), *Indus ethnobiology: New perspectives from the field,* pp. 21–64. Lanham: Lexington Books.

Thevenon, F., E. Bard, D. Williamson, and L. Beaufort. 2004. A biomass burning record from the west equatorial Pacific over the last 360 ky: Methodological, climatic and anthropic implications, *Palaeogeography, Palaeoclimatology, Palaeoecology* 213:83–99.

Thiébault, S. 1988. Palaeoenvironment and ancient vegetation of Baluchistan based on charcoal analysis of archaeological sites, *Proceedings of the Indian National Science Academy* 54(A):501–09.

Thompson, L. G., T. Yao, M. E. Davis, K. A. Henderson, P.-N. Lin, J. Beer, H.-A. Synal, J. Cole-Dai, and J. F. Bolzan. 1997. Tropical climate instability: The

last glacial cycle from a Qinghai-Tibetan ice core, *Science* 276:1821–25.
Thurston, E. 1907 [1975 reprint]. *Ethnographic notes in southern India*. New Delhi: Cosmo Publications.
Troup, R. S. 1921. *Silviculture of Indian trees* (3 volumes). Oxford: Oxford University Press.
Uchiyamada, Y. 1998. 'The grove is our temple': Contested representations of *kaavu* in Kerala, South India. In Rival, L. (ed.), *The social life of trees: Anthropological perspectives on tree symbolism*, pp. 177–96. Oxford and New York: Berg.
Urban, D. L., R. V. O'Neill, and H. H. Shugart, Jr. 1987. Landscape ecology, *Bioscience* 37(2):119–27.
Vajravelu, E., and K. Vivekananthan. 1996. Southern Western Ghats—South of Goa. In Hajra, P. K., B. D. Sharma, M. Sanjappa, and A. R. K. Sastry (eds.), *Flora of India: Introductory volume (part I)*. Calcutta, Botanical Survey of India.
Valdiya, K. S. 1999. Rising Himalayas: advent and intensification of monsoon, *Current Science* 76(4): 514–24.
Van Balgooy, M. M. J. 1989. Java. In Campbell, D. G., and H. D. Hammond (eds.), *Floristic inventory of tropical countries: The status of plant systematic, collections and vegetation, plus recommendations for the future*, pp. 100–02. New York: New York Botanical Garden.
Van Campo, E., J. C. Duplessy, and M. Rossignol-Strick. 1982. Climatic conditions deduced from a 150-kyr oxygen isotope-pollen record from the Arabian Sea, *Nature* 296:56–59.
Van der Leeuw, S., and C. L. Redman. 2002. Placing archaeology at the center of socio-natural studies, *American Antiquity* 67(4):597–606.
Venkata Raju, R. R., and T. Pullaiah. 1995. *Flora of Kurnool (Andhra Pradesh)*. Dehra Dun: Bishen Singh Mahendra Pal Singh.
Verheij, E. W. M., and R. E. Coronel. 1991. Minor edible fruits and nuts. In Verheij, E. W. M., and R. E. Coronel (eds.), *Plant resources of Southeast Asia 2: Edible fruits and nuts*, pp. 313–70. Wageningen: Pudoc.
Verma, D. M., N. P. Balakrishnan, and R. D. Dixit. 1993. *Flora of Madhya Pradesh*, Volume I. Calcutta: Botanical Survey of India.
Vishnu-Mittre. 1979. Palaeobotanical evidence of the environment of early man in northwestern and western India, *Grana* 18:167-81.
Vishnu-Mittre and H. P. Gupta. 1970. The origin of shola forest in the Nilgiris, South India, *Palaeobotanist* 19:110–14.
Vishnu-Mittre and C. Sharma. 1973. Pollen analysis of the salt flat at Malwan, Gujarat, *Palaeobotanist* 22(2):118–23.
———. 1978. Pollen analysis of Nal Lake, Gujarat, *Palaeobotanist* 26:96–104.
———. 1979. Pollen analytical studies at the Nal Lake (Nalsarovar), Gujarat, *Palaeobotanist* 26(1): 95–104.
Vishnu-Mittre and R. Savithri. 1990. The environment and economy of the Neolithic cultures of South India: Palaeobotanical evidence. In Sundara, A., and K. G. Batsoori (eds.), *Archaeology in Karnataka*, pp. 100–12. Mysore: Directorate of Archaeology and Museums.
Von Rad, U., H. Schulz, V. Reich, M. den Dulk, U. Berner, and F. Sirocko. 1999a. Multiple monsoon-controlled breakdown of the oxygen-minimum conditions during the past 30,000 years documented in the laminated sediments off Pakistan, *Palaeogeography, Palaeoclimatology, Palaeoecology* 152:129–61.
Von Rad, U., M. Schaaf, K. H. Michels, H. Schulz, W. H. Berger, and F. Sirocko. 1999b. A 5,000-yr record of climate change in varved sediments from the oxygen minimum zone off Pakistan, Northeastern Arabian Sea, *Quaternary Research* 51:39–53.
Vrba, E. S. 1985. 'Environment and evolution: Alternative causes of temporal distribution of evolutionary events', *South African Journal of Science* 81: 229–36.
———. 1988. Late Pliocene climatic events and hominid evolution. In Grine, F. E. (ed.), *Evolutionary history of the 'Robust' Australopithecines*, pp. 405–26. New York: Aldine de Gruyter.
Walter, H. 1971. *Ecology of tropical and subtropical vegetation*. Edinburgh: Oliver and Boyd.
Warming, E. 1909. *Oecology of plants*. Oxford: Oxford University Press.
Wasson, R. J. 1995. The Asian monsoon during the late Quaternary: A test of orbital forcing and palaeo-analogue forecasting. In Wadia, S., R. Korisettar, and V. S. Kale (eds.), *Quaternary environments and geoarchaeology of India: Essays in honour of professor S. N. Rajaguru*, pp. 22–35. Bangalore: Geological Society of India.
Wasson, R. J., G. I. Smith, and D. P. Agrawal. 1984. Late Quaternary sediments, minerals and inferred geochemical history of Didwana Lake, Thar Desert, India, *Palaeogeography, Palaeoclimatology, Palaeoecology* 46:345–72.

Watson, A. M. 1983. *Agricultural innovation in the early Islamic world: The diffusion of crops and farming techniques, 700–1100*. Cambridge: Cambridge University Press.

Watt, A. S. 1947. Pattern and process in the plant community, *Journal of Ecology* 35:1–22.

Watt, G. 1889-1893. *A dictionary of the economic products of India*. London: Allen.

Weber, S. A. 1999. Seeds of urbanism: Paleoethnobotany and the Indus civilization, *Antiquity* 73:813–26.

———. 2001. Seeds of urbanism revisited, *Antiquity* 75:410–14.

———. 2003. Archaeobotany at Harappa: Indications for change. In Weber, S. A., and W. R. Belcher (eds.), *Indus ethnobiology: New perspectives from the field*, pp. 175–98. Lanham: Lexington Books.

Wei, K., and F. Gasse. 1999. Oxygen isotopes in lacustrine carbonates of west China revisited: Implications for the post glacial changes in summer monsoon circulation, *Quaternary Science Review* 18(12):1315–34.

Weiss, H., M. A. Courty, et al. 1993. The genesis and collapse of third millennium north Mesopotamian civilisation, *Science* 261:995–1004.

Wendorf, F., and R. Schild. 1994. Are the early Holocene cattle in the eastern Sahara domestic or wild? *Evolutionary Anthropology* 3:118–28.

Western, C. A. 1969. *An attempt at the ecological interpretation of charcoals with special reference to material from Jericho*. Unpublished B.Sc. dissertation, University of Oxford.

———. 1971. The ecological interpretation of ancient charcoals from Jericho, *Levant* 3:31–40.

Whyte, R. O. 1964. *The grassland and fodder resources of India*. New Delhi: Indian Council for Agricultural Research.

———. 1968) *Grasslands of the monsoon*. London: Faber and Faber.

Willcox, G. 1989. Etude archéobotanique. In Francfort, H.-P. (ed.), *Fouilles de Shortugai. Recherches sur l'Asie centrale protohistorique*, pp. 175–85. Paris: Mission Archéologique Française en Asie Centrale.

———. 1992) Bilan des données anthracologiques du Proche-Orient, *Bulletin de la Société Botanique de France* 139:539–51.

Wilson, K., and D. J. B. White. 1986. *The anatomy of wood: Its diversity and variability*. London: Stobart & Son.

Worster, D. 1985. *Nature's economy: A history of ecological ideas*. Cambridge: Cambridge University Press.

Yokoyama, Y., K. Lambeck, P. De Deckker, P. Johnston, and L. K Fifield. 2000. Timing of the Last Glacial Maximum from observed sea-level minima, *Nature* 406:713–16.

Yule, H., and A. C. Burnell. 1886 [1996 reprint]. *Hobson-Jobson. The Anglo-Indian dictionary*. Ware, Hertfordshire: Wordsworth Reference.

Zhu, G., H. Reidl, et al. 1995. Boraginaceae. *Flora of China*, Volume 16. Z. Wu, P. H. Raven, and D. Hong. St. Louis, Missouri Botanical Garden Press.

Zide, A. R. K., and N. H. Zide. 1976. Proto-Munda cultural vocabulary: Evidence for early agriculture. In Jenner, P. N., L. C. Thompson, and S. Starosta (eds.), *Austroasiatic studies, part II*, pp. 1295–334. Honolulu: University of Hawaii Press.

Zimmerer, K. S. 1994. Human geography and the 'new' ecology, *Annals of the Association of American Geographers* 84(1):108–25.

Zohary, D., and M. Hopf. 2001. *Domestication of plants in the Old World: The origin and spread of cultivated plants in West Asia, Europe, and the Nile Valley*. Oxford: Oxford University Press.

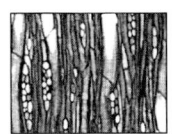

# LIST OF PLANT SPECIES WITH DETAILS ON BOTANICAL AUTHORITIES

This list presents the plant species included in the present volume alongside details of the botanical authorities on which the taxonomic descriptions and classifications are based. Abbreviations follow those which are in standard use by taxonomists. The first authority is that of the author who first published a valid description of the species. When species have been re-assigned to a different genus the original author's name is included in parentheses followed by the authority who first published the re-classification. In addition, a selection of common synonyms are indicated in parentheses by *syn.*, and preferred names are indicated after listed synonyms in parentheses by =.

*Acacia arabica* auct. pl. (=*Acacia nilotica* (L.) Willd. ex Del.)
*Acacia caesia* (L.) Willd. (syn. *A. intsia* (L.) Willd. var. *caesia*)
*Acacia catechu* (Roxb. ex Rottl.) Willd.
*Acacia chundra* (Roxb. ex Rottl.) Willd.
*Acacia eburnea* Willd.
*Acacia horrida* (L.) Willd. (syn. *A. latronum* (L.f.) Willd.)
*Acacia intsia* (L.) Willd. (problematic =*A. caesia* (L.) Willd., or =*A. pennata* (L.) Willd.)
*Acacia latronum* (L.f.) Willd. (=*Acacia horrida* (L.) Willd.)
*Acacia leucophloea* Roxb.
*Acacia nilotica* (L.) Willd. ex Del. (syn. *A. arabica* auct. pl.)
*Acacia pennata* (L.) Willd. (syn. *A. torta* (Roxb.) Craib, *A. intsia* auct. div.)
*Acacia torta* (Roxb.) Craib (=*A. pennata* (L.) Willd.)
*Adina cordifolia* Hook. f.
*Aegle marmelos* (L.) Correa
*Aglaia elaeagnoidea* (Juss.) Benth. (syn. *A. roxburgiana* Miq.)
*Aglaia roxburgiana* Miq. (=*Aglaia elaeagnoidea* (Juss.) Benth.)
*Aglaia talbotii* Sundrararaghavan
*Alangium lamarkii* Thw. (=*A. salvifolium* (L.f.) Wangerin)
*Alangium salvifolium* (L.f.) Wangerin (syn. *A. lamarkii* Thw.)
*Albizia amara* (Roxb.) Boivin
*Albizia chinensis* (Osb.) Merr.
*Albizia lebbeck* (L.) Bentham
*Albizia odoratissima* (Willd.) Bentham
*Albizia procera* (Roxb.) Bentham
*Allophyllus rheedii* Radlk.
*Alphonsea madraspatana* Bedd.
*Alstonia scholaris* (L.) R. Br.
*Annona cherimola* Miller
*Annona muricata* L.
*Annona reticulata* L.
*Annona squamosa* L.
*Anogeissus pendula* Edgw.
*Anogeissus acuminata* Wall.
*Anogeissus latifolia* (Roxb. ex DC) Wall.
*Anogeissus sericea* Brandis

*Anthocephalus indicus* A. Rich.
*Antiaris toxicaria* Lesch.
*Apluda mutica* L.
*Aquilaria agallocha* Roxb.
*Aquilaria malaccensis* Lam.
*Archidendron monadelphum* (Roxb.) Nielsen
*Aristida adscensionis* L.
*Aristida funiculata* Trin. & Rupr.
*Aristolochia indica* L.
*Artocarpus gomeziana* Wall. Ex Trecul
*Artocarpus heterophylla* Lam. (syn. *A. integrifolius* sensu Gamble)
*Artocarpus hirsutus* Lam.
*Artocarpus integrifolius* sensu Gamble (see *A. heterophylla* Lam.)
*Artocarpus lakoocha* Roxb.
*Atalantia floridunba* Wight. (=*A. monophylla* (L.) Correa)
*Atalantia monophylla* (L.) Correa (syn. *Atalantia floridunba* Wight.)
*Atalantia racemosa* Wight.
*Averrhoa acida* L. (=*Phyllanthus acidus* (L.) Skeels)
*Azadirachta excelsa* (Jack) Jacobs
*Azadirachta indica* A. Juss. (syn. *Melia azadirachta* L.)
*Balanites aegyptiaca* (L.) Delile
*Balsamodendron mukul* Hook. f. (=*Commiphora wightii* (Arn.) Bhand.)
*Bambusa arundinacea* Retz.
*Barringtonia acutangula* (L.) Gaertn.
*Bauhinia foveolata* Dalz. (syn. *B. lawii* Bentham ex Baker)
*Bauhinia lawii* Bentham ex Baker (=*B. foveolata* Dalz.)
*Bauhinia malabarica* Roxb.
*Bauhinia phoenicia* Heyne ex Wight. & Arn.
*Bauhinia racemosa* Lam.
*Bauhinia tomentosa* L.
*Bauhinia vahlii* Wight. & Arn.
*Bauhinia variegata* L.
*Bergera koenigii* Willd. (=*Murraya koenigii* Spreng.)
*Blumea obliqua* (L.) Druce
*Bombax ceiba* (syn. *B. malabaricum* DC)
*Borreria stricta* (Willd.) Mey (=*Spermacoce pusilla* Wall.)
*Boswellia glabra* Roxb. (=*Boswellia serrata* Roxb.)
*Boswellia ovalifoliolata* Balakr. & A.N.Henry
*Boswellia serrata* Roxb. (syn. *B. glabra* Roxb., *B. thurifera* Colebr.)
*Boswellia thurifera* Colebr. (=*Boswellia serrata* Roxb.)
*Bothriochloa pertusa* (L.) A. Camus
*Brachiaria eruciformis* (Sm.) Griseb.
*Brachiaria ramosa* (L.) Stapf.
*Bridelia crenulata* Roxb.
*Bridelia retusa* (L.) Sprengel
*Buchanania angustifolia* Roxb. (=*Buchanania axillaries* (Desr.) Ramamoorthy)
*Buchanania axillaries* (Desr.) Ramamoorthy (syn. *B. angustifolia* Roxb.)
*Buchanania lanzan* Sprengel (syn. *B. latifolia* Roxb.)
*Buchanania latifolia* Roxb. (=*Buchanania lanzan* Sprengel)
*Butea frondosa* Roxb. (=*Butea monosperma* (Lam.) Taub.)
*Butea monosperma* (Lam.) Taub. (syn. *B. frondosa* Roxb.)
*Butea superba* Roxb.

*Cadaba fruticosa* (L.) Druce
*Calycopteris floribunda* Lam.
*Canarium strictum* Roxb.
*Canthium parviflorum* Lamk. (=*C. coromandelicum* (Burm. F.) Alston)
*Canthium angustifolium* Roxb.
*Canthium coromandelicum* (Burm. F.) Alston (syn. *C. parviflorum* Lamk.)
*Canthium rheedii* DC
*Capparis aphylla* Roth. (=*Capparis decidua* (Forssk.) Edgw.)
*Capparis brevispina* DC (syn. *C. zeylenica* sensu Hook. f.)
*Capparis decidua* (Forssk.) Edgew. (syn. *Capparis aphylla* Roth.)
*Capparis divaricata* Lam. (syn. *C. stylosa* DC)
*Capparis grandis* L.
*Capparis sepiaria* L.
Capparis *zeylanica* L. (syn. *Capparis horrida* L.f.)
*Careya arborea* Roxb.
*Carissa carandas* L. (syn. *C. congesta* Wight.)
*Carissa congesta* Wight. (=*C. carandas* L.)
*Carissa spinarum* L.
*Carmona microphylla* (Lam.) G. Don. (=*C. retusa* (Vahl.) Masam.)
*Carmona retusa* (Vahl.) Masam. (syn. *Carmona microphylla* (Lam.) G. Don.)
*Cassia alata* L.
*Cassia auriculata* L.
*Cassia fistula* L.
*Cassia floribunda* Cavanilles
*Cassia hirsuta* L.
*Cassia italica* (Miller) Lam.
*Cassia montana* Heyne ex Roth.
*Cassia nigricans* Vahl.
*Cassia siamea* Lam.
*Cassia surattensis* Burm. f.
*Cassia tora* L.
*Cassine* (syn. *Elaeodendron*)
*Cassine glauca* (Rottboell) Kuntze
*Cassine paniculata* (Wight. & Arn.) Lobreau-Callen
*Catunaregam spinosa* (Thunb.) Tirveng. (syn. *Xeromphis spinosa* (Thunb.) Keay, *Gardenia spinosa* Thunb.)
*Celastrus emarginatus* Willd. (=*Maytenus emarginata* (Willd.) Ding Hou)
*Celastrus paniculatus* Willd.
*Celtis cinnamomea* Lindl. ex Planch.
*Chloris barbata* Sw.
*Chloris virgata* Sw.
*Chloroxylon swietenia* DC
*Chrysopogon fulvus* (Spreng.) Chiov.
*Cicca disticha* L. (=*Phyllanthus acidus* (L.) Skeels)
*Cinnamomum camphora* (L.) J. Presl.
*Cinnamomum caudatum* Nees
*Cinnamomum gracile* Hook. f.
*Cinnamomum iners* Reinw.
*Cinnamomum litsaefolium* Thw.
*Cinnamomum macrocarpum* Hook. f. (=*C. nitidum* (Roxb.) Hook.)
*Cinnamomum malabatrum* (N. Burman) Blume (=*C. nitidum* (Roxb.) Hook.)
*Cinnamomum perrottetii* Meissn.
*Cinnamomum riparium* Gamble

*Cinnamomum sulphuratum* Nees
*Cinnamomum tamala* (Buch.-Gham.) Nees et Eberm.
*Cinnamomum travancoricum* Gamble
*Cinnamomum verum* J. Presl. (syn. *Cinnamomum zeylanicum* Garc. ex Blume)
*Cinnamomum wightii* Meissn.
*Cinnamomum zeylanicum* Garc. Ex Blume (=*Cinnamomum verum* J. Presl.)
*Cipadessa baccifera* (Roth.) Miquel.
*Cipadessa fruticosa* Blume
*Cissus quadrangularis* L.
*Citrus aurantium* L.
*Citrus maxima* (Burm.) Merr. (syn. *C. decumana* nom. illeg., *C. grandis* Osbeck)
*Citrus medica* L.
*Clausena lansium* (Lour.) Skeels (syn. *C. wampi* (Blanco) Oliv.)
*Clausena indica* (Dalzell) Oliv.
*Clausena wampi* (Blanco) Oliv. (=*Clausena lansium* (Lour.) Skeels)
*Cleistanthus collinus* (Roxb.) Benth. & Hook. f.
*Cleistanthus patulus* Müll. Arg.
*Cocculus hirsutus* (L.) Diels
*Colubrina asiatica* (L.) Brongn.
*Combretum decandrum* Roxb.
*Combretum latifolium* Bl.
*Combretum ovalifolium* Roxb.
*Commiphora berryi* (Arn.) Engl.
*Commiphora caudata* (Wight. & Arn.) Engl.
*Commiphora mukul* Engl. (=*Commiphora wightii* (Arn.) Bhand.)
*Commiphora wightii* (Arn.) Bhand. (syn. *C. mukul* Engl.)
*Cordia dichotoma* Forst. f.
*Cordia domestica* Roth. and *C. wallchii* G. Don.
*Cordia evolutior* (Clarke) Gamble
*Cordia gharaf* (Forsk.) Ehrenb. ex Asch (syn. *C. rothii* Roem. and Sch.)
*Cordia macleodii* Hook. f.
*Cordia monoica* Roxb.
*Cordia myxa* auct. pl., misapplied name to *C. dichotoma* Forst. F.
*Cordia myxa* L. (syn. *Cordia obliqua* Willd.)
*Cordia obliqua* Willd. (=*C. myxa* L.)
*Cordia octandra* DC
*Cordia perrottetii* Wt.
*Cordia rothii* Roem. and Sch. (=*Cordia gharaf* (Forsk.) Ehrenb. ex Asch)
*Cordia wallchii* G. Don.
*Crataeva religiosa* Forst.
*Crinum defixum* Ker-Gawl.
*Crotalaria spectabilis* Roth.
*Cullenia exarillata* A. Robyns
*Cycas circinalis* L.
*Dactyloctenium aegyptium* L.
*Dalbergia acaciifolia* Dalz.
*Dalbergia candenatensis* (Dennst.) Prain
*Dalbergia horrida* (Dennst.) Mabberly
*Dalbergia lanceolata* Willd.
*Dalbergia malabarica* Prain
*Dalbergia melanoxylon* Guillemin et Perr.
*Dalbergia paniculata* Roxb. (=*D. lanceolata* ssp. *paniculata* (Roxb.) Thoth.)

*Dalbergia pinnata* (Lour.) Prain
*Dalbergia rubiginosa* Roxb.
*Dalbergia sissoides* Graham ex Wight. & Arn.
*Dalbergia sissoo* Roxb.
*Dalbergia volubilis* Roxb.
*Dalbergia latifolia* Roxb.
*Dendrocalamus strictus* (Roxb.) Nees
*Desmodium oojeinense* (Roxb.) H. Ohashi (syn. *Ougeinia dalbergioides* Benth.)
*Dichanthium annulatum* (Forssk.) Stapf
*Dichanthium caricosum* (L.) A. Camus
*Dichrostachys cinerea* (L.) Wight. & Arn.
*Dillenia bracteata* Wt.
*Dillenia indica* L.
*Dillenia pentagyna* Roxb.
*Dillenia retusa* Thunb.
*Dimocarpus longan* Lour.
*Diospyros affinis* Thw.
*Diospyros anguistifolia* (Miq.) Kostermans (syn. *Maba nigrescens* Dalz.)
*Diospyros assimilis* Bedd.
*Diospyros barberi* Ramas.
*Diospyros bourdilloni* Brandis.
*Diospyros buxifolia* (Blume) Hiern. (syn. *Diospyros microphylla* Bedd.)
*Diospyros candolleana* Wt.
*Diospyros chloroxylon* Roxb.
*Diospyros cordifolia* Roxb. (=*Diopsyros montana* Roxb.)
*Diospyros crumenata* Thw.
*Diospyros ebenum* Koenig.
*Diospyros embryopteris* Pers. (=*Diospyros malabarica* (Desr.) Kostel.)
*Diospyros exculpta* Buch. Ham. (=*D. tomentosa* Roxb.)
*Diospyros ferrea* (Willd.) Bakh. (=*Maba buxifolia* (Rottb.) A. L. Juss.)
*Diospyros foliosa* Wall.
*Diospyros humulis* Bourd.
*Diospyros insignis* Thw.
*Diospyros melanoxylon* Roxb.
*Diospyros microphylla* Bedd. (=*Diospyros buxifolia* (Blume) Hiern.)
*Diospyros montana* Roxb. (syn. *D. cordifolia* Roxb.)
*Diospyros nilagirica* Bedd.
*Diospyros oocarpa* Thw.
*Diospyros ovalifolia* Wt.
*Diospyros paniculata* Dalz.
*Diospyros pruriens* Dalz.
*Diospyros sulcata* Bourd.
*Diospyros sylvatica* Roxb.
*Diospyros tomentosa* Roxb. (=*D. exculpta* Buch.-Ham.)
*Diospyros toposia* Buch.-Ham.
*Dipterocarpus bourdilloni* Brandis
*Dipterocarpus indicus* Bedd.
*Dodonaea viscosa* L.
*Dolichandrone atrovirens* (B. Heyne ex Roth.) Sprague
*Dolichandrone falcata* (Wall. ex DC.) Seem.
*Drypetes sepiaria* Pax & K. Hoffm. (syn. *Putranjiva roxburghii* Wall.)
*Echinochloa colona* (L.) Link

*Elaeocarpus* spp.
*Eleusine indica* (L.) Gaertn.
*Eragrostis elongata* (Willd.) J. Jacq.
*Eragrostis interrupta* (Lam.) Doll (=*E. japonica* (Thunb.) Trin.)
*Eragrostis tenella* (L.) P. Beauv. ex Roem. & Schult.
*Eragrostis viscosa* (Retz.) Trin.
*Erythrina stricta* Roxb.
*Erythroxylum monogynum* Roxb.
*Euonymus crenulatus* Wall.
*Euphorbia antiquorum* L.
*Euphorbia caducifolia* Haines
*Euphorbia nivulea* Buch.-Ham.
*Euphorbia tortilis* Rottler ex Ainslie
*Fagara bundrunga* Roxb. (=*Zanthoxylum rhetsea* (Roxb.) DC)
*Fagraea ceilianica* Thunb.
*Ficus albipila* (Miq.) King
*Ficus amplissima* J. E. Smith
*Ficus arnottiana* (Miq.) Miq.
*Ficus beddomei* King
*Ficus benghalensis* L.
*Ficus callosa* Willd.
*Ficus caulocarpa* Miq.
*Ficus drupacea* Thunb.
*Ficus exasperata* Vahl.
*Ficus geniculata* Kurz.
*Ficus glomerata* Roxb. (=*Ficus racemosa* L.)
*Ficus heterophylla* L.f.
*Ficus hispida* L.f.
*Ficus microcarpa* Willd. Heyne ex Roth.
*Ficus mollis* Vahl.
*Ficus nervosa* B. Heyne ex Roth.
*Ficus racemosa* L. (syn. *F. glomerata* Roxb.)
*Ficus religiosa* L.
*Ficus talbotii* King
*Ficus tinctoria* Forst. f.
*Ficus tsahela* N. Burman
*Ficus virens* Aiton
*Filicium decipiens* (Wight. & Arn.) Thwaites ex Hook. f.
*Firmiana colorata* (Roxb.) R. Br.
*Flacourtia indica* (Burm. f.) Merr.
*Flacourtia jangomas* (Lour.) Raeusch.
*Garcinia indica* (Thouars) Choisy
*Garcinia spicata* (Wight. & Arn.) Hook. f.
*Gardenia resinifera* Roth.
*Gardenia spinosa* Thunb. (=*Catunaregam spinosa* (Thunb.) Tirveng.)
*Gardenia turgida* Roxb. (=*Ceriscoides turgida* (Roxb.) Tirveng.)
*Garuga gamblei* King
*Garuga pinnata* Roxb.
*Givotia rottleriformis* Griffith
*Gmelina arborea* Roxb.
*Gmelina asiatica* L.
*Gonothalamus cardiopetalus* Hook. F. & Thoms.

*Gouania microcarpa* DC
*Grewia abutifolia* Vent. ex A. Juss. (syn. *G. jacquini* Gaertn., syn. *G. asiatica* Willd.
*Grewia abutifolia* Vent. ex Juss. (syn. *G. aspera* Roxb.)
*Grewia asiatica* L. (syn. *G. subinaequalis* DC)
*Grewia asiatica* Willd. (=*G. abutifolia* Vent. ex A. Juss.)
*Grewia barberi* J. R. Drumm.
*Grewia bracteata* Heyne ex Roth.
*Grewia damine* Gaertner
*Grewia flavescens* A. Juss. (*G. pilosa* Wight. & Arn.)
*Grewia gamblei* J. R. Drumm.
*Grewia glabra* Blume (syn. *G. laevigata* Vahl.)
*Grewia heterotricha* Masters
*Grewia hirsuta* Vahl.
*Grewia jacquini* Gaertn. (=*G. abutifolia* Vent. Ex A. Juss.)
*Grewia lanceaefolia* Roxb. (=*G. polygama* Roxb.)
*Grewia lawsoniana* J. R. Drumm.
*Grewia microcos* L. (=*G. nervosa* (Lour.) Panigr.)
*Grewia nervosa* (Lour.) Panigr (syn. *G. microcos* L.)
*Grewia oppositifolia* Buch.-Ham. Ex DC (syn. *G. emarginata* Wi. & Arn.)
*Grewia orbiculata* Rottler
*Grewia orientalis* L.
*Grewia pilosa* Wight. & Arn. (=*G. flavescens* A. Juss.)
*Grewia polygama* Roxb. (syn. *G. lanceaefolia* Roxb.)
*Grewia rhamnifolia* Heyne ex Roth.
*Grewia rothii* DC
*Grewia sapida* Roxb.
*Grewia serrulata* DC (syn. *G. disperma* Rottl.)
*Grewia subinaequalis* DC (=*G. asiatica* L.)
*Grewia tenax* (Forsk.) Fiori (syn. *G. betulaefolia* Juss.)
*Grewia tiliaefolia* auct. div. (=*G. tiliifolia* Vahl.)
*Grewia tiliifolia* Vahl. (syn. *G. tiliaefolia* auct. div.)
*Grewia umbellifera* Bedd.
*Grewia villosa* Willd.
*Gyrocarpus americanus* Jacq.
*Gyrocarpus jacquini* Gaertner (=*G. americanus* Jacq.)
*Gyrocarpus jacquini* Roxb.
*Hamiltonia suaveolens* Roxb.
*Hardwickia binata* Roxb. (=*Kingiodendron pinnatum* (DC) Harms)
*Harpulia imbricata* Thw.
*Hedyotis puberula* (G. Don.) Arn. (=*Oldenlandia umbellata* L.)
*Helicteres ixora* L.
*Heritera littoralis* Dryand ex Wight.
*Heritera papilio* Bedd.
*Hernandia ovigera* L.
*Heteropogon contortus* (L.) P. Beauv. Ex Roemer & Schult.
*Holarrhena antidysenterica* Wall.
*Holigarna arnottiana* Hook. f.
*Holigarna beddomei* Hook. f.
*Holigarna ferruginea* Marchand
*Holigarna grahamii* (Wight.) Kurz.
*Holoptelea integrifolia* (Roxb.) Planch.
*Homonoia retusa* Müll. Arg.

*Homonoia riparia* Lour.
*Hopea parviflora* Bedd.
*Hopea racophloea* Dyer
*Hopea wightiana* Wall.
*Hugonia mystax* L.
*Illipe latifolia* (Roxb.) F. Muell. (=*Madhuca longifolia* (L.) J. F. Macbr.)
*Iseilema anthephoroides* Hack.
*Iseilema laxum* Hack.
*Ixora parviflora* Vahl. (=*Ixora pavetta* Andrews)
*Ixora arborea* Roxb. (=*Ixora pavetta* Andrews)
*Ixora nigricans* R. Br.
*Ixora notoniana* Wall. Ex G. Don.
*Ixora pavetta* Andrews (syn. *I. parviflora* Vahl., syn. *I. arborea* Roxb.)
*Jatropha heynei* Balakr.
*Kingiodendron pinnatum* (DC) Harms (syn. *Hardwickia binata* Roxb.)
*Kirganelia reticulata* (Poiret) Baillon
*Kurrimia indica* Gamble
*Kydia calycina* Roxb.
*Lagerstroemia lanceolata* Wall. (=*Lagerstroemia microcarpa* Wight.)
*Lagerstroemia microcarpa* Wight. (syn. *L. lanceolata* Wall.)
*Lagerstroemia parviflora* Roxb.
*Lannea coromandelica* (Houtt.) Merr. (syn. *Odina wodier* Roxb.)
*Lantana camara* L.
*Lawsonia alba* Lam. (=*Lawsonia inermis* L.)
*Lawsonia inermis* L. (syn. *L. alba* Lam.)
*Leptonychia moacurroides* Bedd.
*Limonia acidissima* L. (*Feronia elephantum* Correa, *Feronia limonia* Swingle)
*Litchi chinensis* Sonn.
*Lophopetalum wightianum* Arn.
*Maba buxifolia* (Rottb.) A. L. Juss. (=*Diospyros ferrea* (Willd.) Bakh.)
*Maba nigrescens* Dalz. (=*Diospyros anguistifolia* (Miq.) Kostermans)
*Madhuca indica* J. F. Gmel. (=*M. longifolia* (L.) J. F. Macbr.)
*Madhuca longifolia* (L.) J. F. Macbr. (syn. *M. indica* J. F. Gmel., syn. *Illipe latifolia* (Roxb.) F. Muell.)
*Maerua arenaria* Hook. f. & Thoms.
*Mallotus philippensis* (Lam.) Muell.-Arg.
*Mallotus tetracoccus* (Roxb.) Kurz.
*Mammea suriga* (Buch.-Ham. ex Roxb.) Kostermans
*Manilkara hexandra* (Roxb.) Dub.
*Maytenus heyneana* (Roth.) D.C.S. Raju & Babu
*Maytenus puberula* (Lawson) Loesener
*Maytenus rothiana* (Walpers) Lobreau-Callen
*Melia azadirachta* L. (=*Azadirachta indica* A. Juss.)
*Melia composita* Willd. (=*M. dubia* Cav.)
*Melia dubia* Cav. (syn. *M. composita* Willd.)
*Memecylon edule* Roxb. (=*M. umbellatum* Burm. f.)
*Memecylon umbellatum* Burm. f. (syn. *M. edule* Roxb.)
*Mesua ferrea* L.
*Microchloa indica* (Willd.) P. Beauv.
*Miliusa eriocarpa* Dunn.
*Millettia pinnata* (L.) Panigrahi (syn. *Pongamia pinnata* (L.) Pierre)
*Mimosa rubicaulis* Lam.
*Mitragyna parvifolia* (Roxb.) Korth.

*Mundulea sericea* (Willd.) A. Chev.
*Murraya koenigii* Spreng. (syn. *Bergera koenigii* Willd.)
*Niebuhria apetala* Dunn.
*Nyctanthes arbor-tristis* L.
*Odina wodier* Roxb. (=*Lannea coromandelica* (Houtt.) Merr.)
*Oldenlandia umbellata* L. (syn. *Hedyotis puberula* (G. Don.) Arn.)
*Oplismenus burmanii* (Retz.) P. Beauv.
*Oroxylum indicum* (L.) Vent.
*Osyris quadripartita* Salz. ex Decaisne (syn. *O. wightiana* Wall.)
*Osyris wightiana* Wall. (=*Osyris quadripartita* Salz. ex Decaisne)
*Ougeinia dalbergioides* Benth. (=*Desmodium oojeinense* (Roxb.) H. Ohashi)
*Palaquium ellipticum* Engl.
*Pandanus fascicularis* Lam.
*Panicum miliare* auct. pl. (=*Panicum sumatrense*)
*Panicum sumatrense* Roth.
*Parsonia spiralis* Wall.
*Paspalum scrobiculatum* L.
*Pemphis acidula* Forst.
*Petalidium barlerioides* Nees
*Phoenix humilis* Royle ex Becc. (=*Phoenix loureiroi* Kunth var. *pedunculata* (Griff.) Govaerts)
*Phoenix loureiroi* Kunth var. *pedunculata* (Griff.) Govaerts (syn. *Phoenix humilis* Royle ex Becc.)
*Phoenix sylvestris* (L.) Roxb.
*Phyllanthus acidus* (L.) Skeels (syn. *Cicca disticha* L., *Averrhoa acida* L.)
*Phyllanthus emblica* L.
*Plecospermum spinosum* (Wild) Trecul
*Pleurostylia opposita* (Wallich) Alston
*Poeciloneuron indicum* Bedd.
*Polyalthia cerasoides* (Roxb.) Bedd.
*Polyalthia coffeoides* (Thw.) Bentham & Hooker
*Polyalthia fragrans* (Dalzell) Bedd.
*Polyalthia korinthi* Hook. f. & Thoms.
*Polyalthia longifolia* Hook. f. & Thoms.
*Polyalthia suberosa* Hook. f. & Thoms.
*Polygala chinensis* L.
*Pongamia pinnata* (L.) Pierre (=*Millettia pinnata* (L.) Panigrahi)
*Prosopis cineraria* (L.) Druce (syn. *P. spicigera* L.)
*Prosopis juliflora* (SW) DC
*Prosopis spicigera* L. (=*Prosopis cineraria* (L.) Druce)
*Protium serratum* Engl.
*Pterocarpus marsupium* Roxb.
*Pterocarpus santalinus* L.
*Pterolobium hexapetalum* (Roxb.) Sant. & Wagh
*Pterospermum diversifolium* Bl.
*Pterospermum suberifolium* Lam.
*Pterospermum xylocarpum* (Gaertn.) Sant. & Wagh
*Pterygota alata* (Roxb.) R. Br.
*Putranjiva roxburghii* Wall. (=*Drypetes sepiaria* Pax & K. Hoffm.)
*Randia malabarica* Lam.
*Rhabdia lycioides* Mart. (=*Rotula aquatica* Lour.)
*Rhamnus wightii* Wight. & Arn.
*Rhus mysorensis* G. Don. (syn. *Rhus sinuata* Thunb.)
*Rivea hypocrateriformis* (Desr.) Choisy

*Rotula aquatica* Lour. (syn. *Rhabdia lycioides* Mart.)
*Rubia cordifolia* L.
*Sacrostemma acidum* (Roxb.) Voigt
*Sageretia parviflora* (Klein) G. Don.
*Santalum album* L.
*Sapindus emarginatus* Vahl.
*Saraca asoca* (Roxb.) de Wilde
*Schleichera oleosa* (Lour.) Oken (syn. *Schleichera trijuga* Willd.)
*Schleichera trijuga* Willd. (=*Schleichera oleosa* (Lour.) Oken)
*Scutia myrina* (N. Burman) Kurz.
*Scyphiphora hydrophyllacea* Gaertn.
*Securinega leucopyrus* (Willd.) Muell.-Arg.
*Securinega virosa* (Willd.) Baillon
*Securinega leucopyrus* (Willd.) Muell.-Arg.
*Sehima nervosum* (Rottler) Stapf
*Sehima sulcata* (Hack.) A. Camus
*Setaria glauca* auct. pl. (=*S. pumila* (Poir.) Roem. & Schult.)
*Setaria pallidefusca* (Schum.) Stapf ex C.E. Hubb. (=*S. pumila* (Poir.) Roem. & Schult.)
*Setaria pumila* (Poir.) Roem. & Schult. (syn. *S. glauca* auct. pl., syn. *S. pallidefusca* (Schum.) Stapf ex C. E. Hubb.*)*
*Setaria verticillata* (L.) P. Beauv.
*Shorea robusta* Gaertn.
*Shorea talura* Roxb.
*Shorea tumbuggaia* Roxb.
*Smilax zeylanica* L.
*Smythea bombaiensis* (Dalz.) Ban. & Mukh.
*Soymida febrifuga* (Roxb.) A. Juss.
*Spondias mangifera* Willd.
*Sporobolus diandrus* (Retz.) P. Beauv. (=*Sporobolus indicus* (L.) R. Br.)
*Sporobolus indicus* (L.) R. Br. (syn. *Sporobolus diandrus* (Retz.) P. Beauv.)
*Sterculia guttata* Roxb. ex DC
*Sterculia urens* Roxb.
*Streblus asper* Lour.
*Strychnos colubrina* L.
*Strychnos nux-vomica* L.
*Strychnos potatorum* Willd.
*Syzygium cumini* (L.) Skeels
*Syzygium gardneri* Thwaites
*Syzygium heyneanum* (Duthie) Wall. ex Gamble
*Tamarindus indica* L.
*Tamarix ericoides* Rottl.
*Tarenna asiatica* (L.) O. Kuntze
*Tectona grandis* L.
*Terminalia arjuna* (Roxb. ex DC) Wt. & Arn.
*Terminalia bellerica* (Gaertn.) Roxb.
*Terminalia catappa* L.
*Terminalia chebula* Bedd. (syn. *T. glabra* Thwaites)
*Terminalia coriacea* (Roxb.) Wight. & Arn. (=*T. elliptica* Willd.)
*Terminalia crenulata* Roth. (=*T. elliptica* Willd.)
*Terminalia glabra* Thwaites (=*T. chebula* Bedd.)
*Terminalia glabra* var. *tomentosa* Dalz. & Gibs. (=*T. elliptica* Willd.)
*Terminalia paniculata* Roth.

*Terminalia tomentosa* (Roxb. ex DC) Wight. & Arn. (=*T. elliptica* Willd.)
*Terminalia travancorensis* W. & A.
*Tetracera laevis* Vahl.
*Tetrameles nudiflora* R. Br.
*Themeda quadrivalvis* (L.) Kuntze
*Themeda triandra* Forssk.
*Thraulococcus erectus* Radlk.
*Trema orientalis* (L.) Blume
*Tylophora indica* (Burm. f.) Merr.
*Urochloa panicoides* P. Beauv.
*Vangueria spinosa* Roxb.
*Vateria indica* L.
*Vatica chinensis* L.
*Vitex altissima* Willd.
*Vitex negundo* L.
*Wendlandia notoniana* Wall.
*Wendlandia tinctoria* DC
*Woodfordia fruticosa* Kurz.
*Wrightia arborea* (Dennst.) Mabb. (syn. *W. tomentosa* Roem. & Sch.)
*Wrightia tinctoria* R. Br.
*Wrightia tomentosa* Roem. and Sch. (=*Wrightia arborea* (Dennst.) Mabb.)
*Xeromphis spinosa* (Thunb.) Keay (=*Catunaregam spinosa* (Thunb.) Tirveng.)
*Xylia xylocarpa* (Roxb.) Taub.
*Zanthoxylum rhetsea* (Roxb.) DC (syn. *Fagara bundrunga* Roxb.)
*Ziziphus caracutta* Roxb. (syn. *Z. glaberrima* (Sedgw.) Sant.)
*Ziziphus glaberrima* (Sedgw.) Sant. (=*Z. caracutta* Roxb.)
*Ziziphus glabrata* Heyne ex Roth.
*Ziziphus horrida* Roth.
*Ziziphus mauritiana* Lam.
*Ziziphus mummularia* (N. Burman) Wight. & Arn.
*Ziziphus oenoplia* (L.) Miller
*Ziziphus rugosa* Lam.
*Ziziphus williamani* Lam.
*Ziziphus xylopyrus* (Retz.) Willd.
*Zornia diphylla* (L.) Pers.

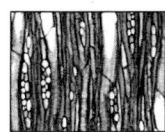

# TAXONOMIC INDEX

| | |
|---|---|
| *Acacia* | 46, 52, 54–6, 59, 60–7, 87, 91, 104–5, 116, 130, 133, 138, 141, 144, **208–11** |
| *Acacia caesia* | 63, 105 |
| *Acacia catechu* | 46, 54, 65, 67, 105, 138, 144, **208–9** |
| *Acacia chundra/catechu* | 54–6, 59, 60, 63–4, 67, 105 |
| *Acacia eburnea* | 60, 63, 105 |
| *Acacia feruginea* | 54 |
| *Acacia horrida* syn. *A. latronum* | 63–4, 67, 91, 105 |
| *Acacia intsia* | 64 |
| *Acacia leucophloea* | 56, 63–5, 67, 105, 138, **208, 210** |
| *Acacia nilotica* | 59, 64, 67, 104–5, 138, 141, **208, 211** |
| *Acacia pennata* | 54–5, 63–4 |
| *Acacia polycantha* | 105 |
| *Acacia senegal* | 46 |
| Acanthaceae | 48, 51, 63 |
| *Actinodaphne* | 46, 130 |
| *Adina* | 46, 51, 55, 59, 65, 113, 115, 137, **254–5** |
| *Adina cordifolia* | 51, 55, 59, 65, 113, **254–5** |
| *Aegle marmelos* | 54, 55, 57, 73, 92, 114–5, 126 |
| *Aerva* | 79–80 |
| *Aerva javanica* | 66 |
| *Aglaia* | 49, 109–10, 138, **231–2** |
| *Aglaia elaeagnoidea* (syn. *A. roxburghiana*) | 109, **231–2** |
| *Aglaia talbotii* | 109 |
| Alangiaceae | 60 |
| *Alangium salvifolium* | 60 |
| *Albizia* | 46, 51, 54–5, 59, 63–5, 87, 104–6, 130, 133, 138, 141, 143, **212–4** |
| *Albizia amara* | 46, 54–5, 63–4, 105–6, 130, 138, **212–3** |
| *Albizia chinensis* | 106 |
| *Albizia lebbek* | 63, 65, 105–6 |
| *Albizia odoratissima* | 54, 65, 106 |
| *Albizia procera* | 51, 54, 59, 65, 105–6, 138, 141, 143, **212, 214** |
| *Allophylus* | 117 |
| *Alphonsea* | 91 |
| *Alstonia* | 51, 93 |
| *Alstonia scholaris* | 51 |
| Amaranthaceae | 75–7, 79, 80 |
| Amaryllidaceae | 60 |
| Anacardiaceae | 49, 51, 54–5, 57, 59–60, 89, 137–8, **145, 147**, 160 |
| *Annona* | 55, 91–3, 139, **149–50** |
| *Annona cherimola, A. muricata* | 92 |
| *Annona reticulata* | 92, **149–50** |
| *Annona squamosa* | 55, 92 |
| Annonaceae | 48–9, 55, 91, 139, **149, 151** |

| | |
|---|---|
| *Anogeissus* | 46, 52–6, 65, 87, 94, 96, 99, 105, 115, 119, 130, 133–4, 139, 141, **169–70** |
| *Anogeissus acuminata* | 96 |
| *Anogeissus latifolia* (syn. *A. parviflora*) | 46, 52, 54–6, 65, 94, 96, 105, 130, 141, **169–70** |
| *Anogeissus pendula* | 46, 96 |
| *Anogeissus sericea* | 96 |
| *Anthocephalus* | 92 |
| *Anthocephalus indicus* | 113 |
| *Antiaris toxicaria* | 110 |
| *Apiaceae* | 77 |
| *Apluda mutica* | 66 |
| Apocynaceae | 51, 54–5, 63, 93, 139, **154**, **156**, |
| *Aquilaria agallocha*, *A. malaccensis* | 116 |
| *Archidendron monadelphum* | 104 |
| *Aristida* | 52, 66 |
| *Aristida adscensionis*, *A. funiculata* | 66 |
| *Aristolochia indica* | 63 |
| Aristolochiaceae | 63 |
| *Artemisia* | 75, 77, 79–81, 83–4 |
| *Artocarpus* | 48–9, 110–11, 138, **237–9** |
| *Artocarpus gomeziana*, *A. hirsuta*, *A. lakoocha* | 110–11 |
| *Artocarpus heterophylla* (syn. *A. integrifolia*) | 48, 110–11, **237–9** |
| Asclepiadaceae | 63–4 |
| *Atalantia monophylla* | 54, 63 |
| *Atalantia racemosa* | 63 |
| Aurantoideae | 114 |
| *Azadirachta excelsa* | 110 |
| *Azadirachta indica* (syn. *Melia azadirachta*) | 54–6, 64, 73, 91, 109–10, 112, 138, **233–4** |
| Balanitaceae | 54, 57, 64 |
| *Balanites aegyptiaca* | 54, 57, 64 |
| *Balanocarpus* | 97 |
| *Bambusa arundinacea* | 51, 59 |
| *Barleria buxifolia* | 66 |
| *Barringtonia* | 60, 112, 138, **246–7** |
| *Barringtonia acutangula* | 60, 112, **246–7** |
| *Barringtonia racemosa* | 112 |
| *Bassia latifolia* | 65 |
| *Bassia longifolia* | 51 |
| *Bauhinia* | 49, 51–2, 54–6, 64–5, 74, 102–3, 138, **200–1**, 244 |
| *Bauhinia foveolata* | 49, 102 |
| *Bauhinia lawil* | 65 |
| *Bauhinia malabarica* | 49, 51, 102–3 |
| *Bauhinia phoenicia* | 49 |
| *Bauhinia racemosa* | 54–5, 64–5, 102–3, 144, **200–1** |
| *Bauhinia tomentosa* | 51, 102–3 |
| *Bauhinia vahlii* | 51, 52, 56, 102 |
| *Bauhinia variegata* | 103, **200–1** |
| Bignoniaceae | 54–5, 59, 63–4 |
| *Blumea obliqua* | 63 |
| Bombacaceae | 49, 51, 54, 138, **158** |
| *Bombax* | 49–51, 54, 65, 73, 138, **158–9** |
| *Bombax ceiba*, syn. *B. malabaricum* | 51, 54, 65 |

| | |
|---|---|
| *Bombax malabaricum* | 49, 51, 65, 73, **158–9** |
| Boraginaceae (see also Ehretiaceae) | 51, 54–5, 60, 63, 94, 99 |
| *Borassus flabellifer* | 73 |
| *Borreria stricta* | 66 |
| *Boswellia* | 54–6, 65, 94 |
| *Boswellia ovalifoliolata* | 55 |
| *Boswellia sacra* | 94 |
| *Boswellia serrata* (syn. *B. glabra*, *B. thurifera*) | 54–5, 65, 94 |
| *Bothriochloa pertusa* | 66 |
| *Brachiaria* | 39–40, 58–9, 66, 131–2 |
| *Brachiaria eruciformis* | 66 |
| *Brachiaria ramosa* | 39–40, 58–9, 131–2 |
| Brassicaceae | 84 |
| *Bridelia crenulata* | 100 |
| *Bridelia retusa* | 48–9, 66 |
| *Buchanania* | 46, 56–57, 89–90 |
| *Buchanania axillaris* (syn. *B. angustifolia*) | 89–90 |
| *Buchanania lanzan* (syn. *B. latifolia*) | 57, 89, 90 |
| Burseraceae | 49, 51, 54–5, 63, 94, 137, **160** |
| *Butea* | 50, 54–6, 64–6, 91, 106–7, 119, 138, **217–8** |
| *Butea monosperma* (syn. *Butea frondosa*) | 50, 54, 56, 64–6, 91, 106–7, 119, **217–8** |
| *Butea superba* | 50, 55, 106 |
| *Cadaba fruticosa* | 94 |
| *Caesalpinia* | 102 |
| *Cajanus cajan* | 131 |
| *Calligonum* | 46, 79, 80–1 |
| *Callistemon* | 112 |
| *Calophyllum* | 49, 95 |
| *Calotropis gigantea* | 66 |
| *Calycopteris floribunda* | 54–5, 96 |
| *Canarium strictum* | 48–9, 50, 94 |
| *Canthium* | 63–4, 66, 113–4, 137, **256–8** |
| *Canthium angustifolium, C. rheedii* | 113 |
| *Canthium coromandelicum* (syn. *C. parviflorum*) | 63–4, 113–4, **256–7** |
| *Canthium dicoccum* | 66, 113, **256, 258** |
| *Canthium parvicoccum* | 66 |
| Capparaceae | 49, 54, 57, 63–4, 94, 139, **162** |
| *Capparis* | 23, 46, 49, 52, 54, 57, 63–4, 66, 73, 79, 82, 94–5, 130, 139, **163–4** |
| *Capparis brevispina* | 54, 95 |
| *Capparis decidua* (syn. *C. aphylla*) | 64, 73, 95 |
| *Capparis divaricata* | 54, 63–4, 66, 95 |
| *Capparis grandis* | 49, 63, 95 |
| *Capparis sepiaria* | 54, 63, 95, 139, **163–4** |
| *Capparis zeylanica* (syn. *C. horrida*) | 54, 63, 95 |
| *Cardiospermum canescens* | 117 |
| *Cardiospermum halicacabum* | 64 |
| *Careya* | 51, 65, 112, 139, 144, **248–9** |
| *Careya arborea* | 51, 65, 112, 144, **248–9** |
| *Carissa* | 54, 63, 65–6, 93 |
| *Carissa congesta* | 54, 66 |
| *Carissa spinarum* | 63, 65 |

| | |
|---|---|
| *Carmona microphylla* | 63 |
| *Carmona retusa* | 99 |
| Caryophyllaceae | 84 |
| *Cassia* | 50–1, 54–6, 63–7, 102–3, 138, 143, **202–5** |
| *Cassia alata, C. floribunda, C. hirsuta, C. italica, C. nigricans, C. siamea* | 103 |
| *Cassia auriculata* | 55–6, 63–4, 66, 103, **202–3** |
| *Cassia fistula* | 50, 51, 54–5, 65–6, 103, 143, **204–5** |
| *Cassia montana* | 63, 103 |
| *Cassia surattensis* | 54–5, 103 |
| *Cassia tora* | 66 |
| *Cassine* (syn. *Elaeodendron*) | 95 |
| *Cassine glauca, C. paniculata* | 95 |
| *Casuarina equisetifolia* | 65 |
| *Cedrela* | 50 |
| Celastraceae | 54–5, 63–4, 95, 138, **165** |
| *Celastrus emarginatus, C. paniculatus* | 95 |
| *Celtis cinnamomea* | 59 |
| *Cenchrus* | 67 |
| Chenopodiaceae | 74–5, 77, 79–80, 84 |
| *Chloris barbata, C. virgata* | 66 |
| *Chloroxylon* | 46, 54–6, 65, 94, 109–10, 115, 130, 139, **267–8** |
| *Chloroxylon swietenia* | 54–6, 65, 94, 110, 115, **267–8** |
| *Chrysopogon fulvus* | 66 |
| *Cicca* | 139, **185–6** |
| *Cicca acida* | **185–6** |
| *Cinnamomum* | 47, 49, 101–2, 138, 143, **197–9** |
| *Cinnamomum camphora, C. caudatum, C. perrottetii, C. tamala, C. wightii* | 102 |
| *Cinnamomum gracile, C. litsaeaefolium, C. riparium, C. sulphuratum, C. travancoricum* | 101 |
| *Cinnamomum iners* | 49, 101–2 |
| *Cinnamomum nitidum* (syn. *C. macrocarpum*) | 101–2 |
| *Cinnamomum verum* | 47, 49, 101–2 |
| *Cinnamomum zeylanicum* | 143, **197–9** |
| *Cipadessa baccifera* | 109 |
| *Cipadessa fruticosa* | 63 |
| *Cissus quadrangularis* | 63 |
| *Citrus* | 114–5, 126 |
| *Citrus aurantium, C. decumana, C. lemon, C. maxima, C. paradisi* | 114 |
| *Citrus medica* | 114–5 |
| *Clausena dentata, C. indica, C. A212wampi* | 115 |
| *Clausena lansium* | 114 |
| *Cleistanthus* | 46, 51, 54, 59 |
| *Cleistanthus collinus* | 51, 54 |
| *Cleistanthus patulus* | 59 |
| *Clerodendron viscosum* | 119 |
| Clusiaceae (syn. Guttiferae) | 49, 63, 95, 138–9, **167** |
| *Cocculus hirsutus* | 64 |
| *Colubrina asiatica* | 113 |

| | |
|---|---|
| Combretaceae | 51, 54–5, 59–60, 75–6, 96, 138–9, **169**, **171** |
| *Combretum decandrum* | 54 |
| *Combretum latifolium, C. ovalifolium* | 96 |
| *Commiphora* | 63, 67, 94, 137, **160–2** |
| *Commiphora berryi* | 63, 94, **160–1** |
| *Commiphora caudata* | 94, **160**, **162** |
| *Commiphora wightii* (syn. *C. mukul, Balsamodendron mukul*) | 67, 94 |
| *Comocladia* | 147 |
| Compositae | 63 |
| Coniferales | 128 |
| Convolvulaceae | 63 |
| *Corchorus* | 118 |
| *Cordia* | 51, 54–5, 57, 63–5, 67, 99, 138, **183–4** |
| *Cordia dichotoma* | 51, 99 |
| *Cordia domestica, C. evolutior, C. macleodii, C. monoica, C. obliqua, C. octandra, C. perrottetii, C. wallichii* | 99 |
| *Cordia gharaf* (syn. *Cordia rothii*) | 63, 99 |
| *Cordia myxa* | 57, 63–5, 73, 99, **183–4** |
| *Cosmarum* | 80 |
| *Cotoneaster* | 73 |
| *Crataeva religiosa* | 94 |
| *Crinum defixum* | 60 |
| *Crotalaria sericea* | 60 |
| *Cullenia* | 46, 48, 130 |
| *Cullenia exarillata* | 49 |
| *Curcuma longa* | 49 |
| Cycadaceae | 63, 128 |
| *Cycas circinalis* | 63, 128 |
| *Cymbopogon* | 52, 66 |
| Cyperaceae | 59, 75, 77, 80, 84–5 |
| *Dactyloctenium aegyptium* | 66 |
| *Dalbergia* | 49, 50–1, 54–5, 59, 65–6, 98, 106–8, 138, **219–21** |
| *Dalbergia acaciaefolia, D. candenatensis, D. horrida, D. malabarica, D. melanoxylon, D. pinnata, D. rubiginosa, D. sissoides, D. volubilis* | 107 |
| *Dalbergia lanceolata* | 54, 55, 107, 108 |
| *Dalbergia latifolia* | 51, 54, 65–6, 98, 107, **219–20** |
| *Dalbergia paniculata* | 51, 54–5, 65, 107, **219, 221** |
| *Dalbergia sissoo* | 54, 107 |
| Datiscaceae | 51 |
| *Dendrocalamus strictus* | 51, 54–5, 59 |
| *Dichanthium* | 57, 67 |
| *Dichanthium annulatum, D. caricosum* | 66 |
| *Dichrostachys cinerea* | 55, 64, 66, 104 |
| *Dillenia* | 46, 51, 72, 97, 130, 137, 141–2, 144, **175–7** |
| *Dillenia bracteata, D. indica* | 97 |
| *Dillenia pentagyna* | 51, 72, 97, 141–2, 144, **175–7** |
| *Dillenia retusa* | 97 |
| Dilleniaceae | 51, 97, 137, **175** |

| | |
|---|---|
| *Dimocarpus longan* | 48–9, 51, 117 |
| *Diospyros* | 46, 48–9, 54–5, 57, 59–60, 63–6, 91, 94, 98–9, 108, 119, 130, 139–40, **180–2** |
| *Diospyros affinis, D. assimilis, D. angustifolia* (syn. *Maba nigrescens*), *D. barberi, D. bourdilloni, D. buxifolia* (syn. *D. microphylla*), *D. candolleana, D. crumenata, D. foliosa, D. humilis, D. insignis, D. nilagirica, D. oocarpa, D. pruriens, D. paniculata, D. sulcata, D. sylvatica, D. toposia* | 98 |
| *Diospyros chloroxylon* | 55, 63, 98 |
| *Diospyros embryopteris* (syn. *D. malabarica, D. peregrina*) | 59–60, 98–9, **180**, **182** |
| *Diospyros melanoxylon* | 54–5, 57, 60, 63–6, 91, 94, 98–9, 108, 119 |
| *Diospyros montana* (syn. *D. cordifolia*) | 54, 98–9, 140, **180–1** |
| *Diospyros ovalifolia* | 54, 98 |
| *Diospyros tomentosa* (syn. *D. exsculpta*) | 54, 98–9 |
| *Diospyrus ebenum* | 98–9 |
| *Dipsacus* | 77 |
| *Dipterocarpaceae* | 49, 74, 97, 137–8, **178** |
| *Dipterocarpus* | 46, 48–9, 97, 130 |
| *Dipterocarpus bourdilloni* | 97 |
| *Dipterocarpus indicus* | 48–9, 97 |
| *Dodonaea* | 55, 63, 66, 117, 138–9, **273–5** |
| *Dodonaea angustifolia* | **273–4** |
| *Dodonaea viscosa* | 55, 63, 66, 117, **273**, **275** |
| *Dolichandrone atrovirens* | 54–5, 63 |
| *Dolichandrone falcata* | 54, 64 |
| *Drypetes sepiaria* | 63 |
| Ebenaceae | 49, 54–5, 57, 59–60, 63–4, 98, 139, **180** |
| *Echinochloa colonum* | 58–9 |
| *Ehretia aspera* | 99 |
| Ehretiaceae | 51, 55, 57, 63, 99, 138, **183** |
| Elaeagnaceae | 73 |
| *Elaeagnus* | 73 |
| *Elaeocarpus* | 49, 77 |
| *Elaeocarpus tuberculatus* | 50 |
| *Elettaria cardamomum* | 48 |
| *Eleusine indica* | 66 |
| *Elionurus* | 67 |
| *Ephedra* | 79–81 |
| *Eragrostis elongata, E. interrupta, E. tenella, E. viscosa* | 66 |
| *Erinocarpus nimmonii* | 118 |
| *Eriocaulon* | 77 |
| *Eriolaena* | 118 |
| *Erythrina stricta* | 51 |
| Erythroxylaceae | 55, 63 |
| *Erythroxylon* | 55, 63 |
| *Eucalyptus* | 112 |
| *Eulesine coracana* | 131 |
| *Euonymus* | 95 |
| *Euonymus crenulatus* | 95 |

| | |
|---|---|
| *Euphorbia* | 63–4, 66, 91, 100 |
| *Euphorbia antiquorum* | 63, 66, 91, 100 |
| *Euphorbia caducifolia* | 63, 100 |
| *Euphorbia neriifolia* | 64 |
| *Euphorbia nivulia* | 100 |
| *Euphorbia tirucali* | 66 |
| *Euphorbia tortilis* | 63, 100 |
| Euphorbiaceae | 49, 51, 54, 57, 59–60, 63–4, 77, 100, 139, **185**, **187**, **190**, **193** |
| Fabaceae | 84 |
| *Feronia limonia* | 54–5, 57 |
| *Ficus* | 47–8, 60, 51, 91, 100, 110–12, 138, 143, 144, **240–1** |
| *Ficus albipila, F. amplissima, F. arnottiana, F. beddomei, F. callosa, F. carica, F. caulocarpa, F. drupacea, F. geniculata, F. exasperata, F. heterophylla, F. mollis, F. nervosa, F. talboti, F. tinctoria, F. tsjakela, F. virens* | 111 |
| *Ficus benghalensis* | 47, 100, 111–12, 143, 144, **240–1** |
| *Ficus glomerata* (syn. *Ficus racemosa*) | 48, 60, 111–12 |
| *Ficus hispida, F. microcarpa* | 60, 111 |
| *Ficus religiosa* | 91, 100, 111, 112 |
| *Filicium decipiens* | 117 |
| *Firmiana colorata* | 118 |
| *Flacourtia* | 54–5, 59, 64, 66 |
| *Flacourtia indica* | 54–5, 64, 66 |
| *Flacourtia jangoma* | 54 |
| Flacourtiaceae | 54–5, 59, 64 |
| *Flemingia* syn. *Moghania* | 51 |
| *Fortunella* | 114–15 |
| *Garcinia* | 48–9, 63, 65, 95–6, 138–9, **167–8** |
| *Garcinia indica* | 48–9, 65, 95, **167–8** |
| *Garcinia morella* | 95 |
| *Garcinia spicata* | 63 |
| *Gardenia* | 54–5, 113–4, 137, 140, **259–60** |
| *Gardenia resinifera* | 54–5, 114, 140, **259–60** |
| *Gardenia turgida* | 54 |
| *Garuga* | 46, 49, 51, 94 |
| *Garuga gamblei* | 49, 94 |
| *Garuga pinnata* | 51, 94 |
| *Gentiana* | 77 |
| *Givotia rottleriformis* | 63, 100 |
| *Gliptopetalum* | 95 |
| *Gluta* | 147 |
| *Gmelina* | 54, 63, 65, 91, 108, 119, 137, **285–6** |
| *Gmelina arborea* | 54, 65, 91, 108, 119, **285–6** |
| *Gmelina asiatica* | 63 |
| Gnetales | 128 |
| *Gnetum gnemon* | 128 |
| *Gonothalamus* | 91 |
| *Gossypium arboreum* | 131 |
| *Gouania microcarpa* | 113 |
| *Grewia* | 51, 52, 54–7, 59, 63–5, 118–9, 137, 140, 142, **281–4** |

| | |
|---|---|
| *Grewia abutilifolia* (syn. *G. aspera*), *G. glabra* (syn. *G. laevigata*), *G. hirsuta, G. microcos, G. rothii* | 118–9 |
| *Grewia barberi, G. bracteata, G. gamblei, G. heterotricha, G. lanceaefolia, G. lawsoniana, G. oppositifolia* (syn. *G. emarginata*), *G. orbiculata, G. orientalis, G. rhamnifolia, G. subinaequalis* (syn. *G. asiatica*), *G. umbellifera* | 118 |
| *Grewia damine, G. nervosa, G. oppositifolia, G. pilosa (syn. G. flavescens), G. polygama, G. sapida, G. subinaequalis, G. villosa* | 119 |
| *Grewia serrulata* | 63–4, 119 |
| *Grewia tenax* (syn. *G. betulaefolia*) | 119, **281–2** |
| *Grewia tiliaefolia* | 51, 52, 54, 65, 118–9, 137, 140, 142, **283–4** |
| *Gymnosporia* | 95, 138, **165–6** |
| *Gymnosporia montana* | 95, **165–6** |
| *Gyrocarpus* | 54–5, 63, 96, 101, 137, 138, **195–6** |
| *Gyrocarpus americanus* | 54–5, 101, **195–6** |
| *Gyrocarpus jacquini* (syn. *G. asiatica*) | 63, 101 |
| *Hamiltonia suaveolens* | 113 |
| *Hardwickia* | 46, 52, 54–5, 65, 102–3, 105, 130 |
| *Hardwickia binata* | 46, 55, 65, 103, 105, 130 |
| *Harpulia* | 117 |
| *Helicteres ixora* | 118 |
| *Heracleum* | 77 |
| *Heritera littoralis, H. papilio* | 118 |
| *Hernandia, H. ovigera* | 101 |
| Hernandiaceae | 54–5, 63, 101, 137–8, **195** |
| *Heteropogon* | 52 |
| *Heteropogon contortus* | 66 |
| *Holarrhena* | 54, 65–6, 93–4, 133, 139, **154–5** |
| *Holarrhena antidysenterica* | 54, 65–6, 93–4, **154–5** |
| *Holigarna* | 46, 48–9, 89–90, 130, 137–8, 142, **145–6** |
| *Holigarna arnottiana* | 90, 142, **145–6** |
| *Holigarna beddomei, H. ferruginea, H. grahamii* | 90 |
| *Holoptelea* | 54–5, 60, 84 |
| *Holoptelea integrifolia* | 54–5, 60 |
| *Homonoia* | 100 |
| *Homonoia retusa* | 60 |
| *Homonoia riparia* | 59 |
| *Hopea* | 48–9, 97–8, 137–8, **178–9** |
| *Hopea parviflora* | 48, 97–8, **178–9** |
| *Hopea racophloea, H. wightiana* | 97 |
| *Hordeum vulgare* | 131 |
| *Hugonia mystax* | 63 |
| *Humboldtia* | 102 |
| *Humulus* | 117 |
| *Hymenodictyon* | 113 |
| *Hypericum* | 95 |
| *Illigera* | 101 |
| *Impatiens* | 77 |
| *Iseilema anthephoroides, I. laxum* | 66 |
| *Ixora* | 49, 51, 54–5, 59–60, 113–4, 137, **261–2** |

| | |
|---|---|
| *Ixora arborea* (syn. *I. parviflora, I. pavetta*) | 54–5, 59–60, 114, **261–2** |
| *Ixora nigricans, I. notoniana* | 114 |
| *Jambosa* | 112 |
| *Jasimum* | 77 |
| *Jatropha heynei* | 100 |
| *Justicia* | 84 |
| *Kingiodendron pinnatum* | 49, 102 |
| *Kirganelia reticulata* | 100 |
| *Kurrimia indica* | 95 |
| *Kydia calycina* | 51 |
| *Lagerstroemia* | 46, 51–2, 54, 58–9, 65, 84, 109, 130, 138, **227–8** |
| *Lagerstroemia microcarpa* (syn. *L. lanceolata*) | 51, 59, 65, 109, **227–8** |
| *Lagerstroemia parviflora* | 51, 54, 59, 65, 109 |
| *Lannea coromandelica* | 51, 54–5, 90 |
| *Lantana* | 51, 66, 119 |
| *Lantana camara* | 51, 66 |
| *Lasiurus indicus* | 46 |
| Lauraceae | 47, 49, 51, 101, 138, **197** |
| *Lawsonia* | 60, 67, 109, 139, **229–30** |
| *Lawsonia alba* | **229–30** |
| *Lawsonia inermis* | 60, 67, 109 |
| *Leea* | 51 |
| Leeaceae | 51 |
| Leguminosae | 49, 60, 63–4 |
| Leguminosae-Caesalpiniaceae | 49, 51, 54–5, 57, 60, 63–4, 102, 137–8, **200, 202, 204, 206** |
| Leguminosae-Mimosaceae | 51, 54–5, 57, 59–60, 63–4, 102, 104, 138, **208, 212, 215** |
| Leguminosae-Papilionaceae | 49, 51, 54–5, 59, 98, 102, 106, 117, 138, **217, 219, 222** |
| *Lejeunecysta* | 85 |
| *Lepisanthes* | 117 |
| *Leptonychia moacurroides* | 117 |
| *Limonia acidissima* (syn. *Feronia elephantum, F. limonia*) | 114–5, 139, **269–70** |
| Linaceae | 63 |
| *Linum usitatissimum* | 131 |
| *Litchi chinensis* | 92 |
| *Litsea* | 51, 102 |
| Loganiaceae | 54–5, 63, 108, 139, **224** |
| *Lophopetalum wightianum* | 95 |
| Lythraceae | 51, 54, 59–60, 67, 109, 138–9, **227, 229** |
| *Maba* | 98 |
| *Maba buxifolia* | 63–4, 98–9 |
| *Machilus* | 48 |
| *Machilus macrantha* (=*Persea macrantha*) | 49 |
| *Macrotyloma uniflorum* | 39, 57, 67, 131–2 |
| *Madhuca indica* | 23, 84 |
| *Madhuca longifolia* syn. *Bassia longifolia* | 51, 55 |
| *Maerua arenaria* | 94 |
| *Mallotus* | 48–9, 51, 59–60, 65, 100–1, 139, 141, 144, **187–9** |
| *Mallotus philippensis* | 48, 51, 59–60, 65, 101, 141, 144, **187–9** |

| | |
|---|---|
| *Mallotus tetracoccus* | 51, 100 |
| Malvaceae | 77 |
| *Mammea suriga* | 95 |
| *Mangifera* | 46, 48–9, 51, 59–60, 65, 89–91, 100, 126, 134, 137–8, **147–8** |
| *Mangifera indica* | 46, 48–9, 51, 59, 60, 65, 89–90, 100, 126, 134, **147–8** |
| *Manikara* | 46, 130 |
| *Manilkara hexandra* | 63 |
| *Maytenus* | 54–5, 63–4, 79, 81, 95 |
| *Maytenus (Gymnosporia) emarginata* | 54–5, 63–4 |
| *Maytenus heyneana* | 63, 95 |
| *Maytenus puberula, M. rothiana* | 95 |
| *Melanorrhoea* | 147 |
| Melastomataceae | 49, 63, 75–6 |
| *Melia composita* | 51 |
| *Melia dubia* | 109 |
| *Melia indica* | 65 |
| Meliaceae | 49, 54–5, 63–4, 109, 138, **231–3**, **235** |
| *Melochia coircorifolia* | 66 |
| *Memecylon* | 46, 49, 63, 130 |
| *Memecylon edule* | 49 |
| *Memecylon umbellatum* | 63 |
| Menispermaceae | 64 |
| *Mesua* | 46, 48–9, 95, 130 |
| *Mesua ferrea* | 49 |
| *Meteoromyrtus* | 112 |
| *Mezoneuron* | 102 |
| *Michelia* | 77 |
| *Microchloa indica* | 66 |
| *Microtropis* | 95 |
| *Miliusa* | 66, 91 |
| *Miliusa tomentosa* | 66 |
| *Mimosa* | 54, 104 |
| *Mimosa rubicaulis* | 54 |
| *Mitragyna* | 59–60, 65, 113, 137, **263–4** |
| *Mitragyna parvifolia* | 59–60, 65, **263–4** |
| Moraceae | 49, 51, 60, 75–6, 138, **237**, **240**, **242** |
| *Morinda* | 113, 139 |
| *Morinda tinctoria* | **265–6** |
| *Moringa* | 112, 138, **244–5** |
| *Moringa concanensis* | 112 |
| *Moringa oleifera* | 112, **244–5** |
| Moringaceae | 112, 138, **244** |
| *Morus alba* | 126 |
| *Moullava* | 102 |
| *Multispinula* | 85 |
| *Mundulea sericea* | 55 |
| *Murraya koenigii* (syn. *Bergera koenigii*) | 114–5 |
| Myrtaceae | 47, 49, 51, 55, 60, 112, 138–9, **246**, **248**, **250** |
| *Niebuhria apetala* | 94 |
| *Nyctanthes arbor-tristes* | 54 |

| | |
|---|---|
| *Oldenlandia* | 50, 64, 67, 77, 79–80, 81–3 |
| *Oldenlandia umbellata* | 50, 64, 67 |
| *Olea* | 77 |
| Oleaceae | 54, 77 |
| *Oplismenus burmanii* | 66 |
| *Oroxylum indicum* | 59 |
| *Osbeckia* | 77 |
| *Osyris quadripartita* | 54–5, 63, 116, 271 |
| *Ougeinia dalbergioides* | 51 |
| *Oxytenanthera monostigma* | 59 |
| *Palaquium* | 46, 48–9, 130 |
| *Palaquium ellipticum* | 49 |
| Palmae | 60, 63–4 |
| Pandanaceae | 60 |
| *Pandanus fascicularis* | 60 |
| *Panicum sumatrense* | 40, 58–9 |
| *Panicum turgidum* | 46 |
| *Paspalum scrobiculatum* | 58–9 |
| *Pemphis acidula* | 109 |
| *Pennisetum glaucum* | 40 |
| *Peperomia* | 77 |
| *Persia* | 46, 130 |
| *Petalidium barlerioides* | 51 |
| *Phoenix humilis* | 63, 66 |
| *Phoenix sylvestris* | 59, 60, 64, 66 |
| *Phragmites* | 67 |
| *Phyllanthus acidus* (syn. *Cicca disticha*) | 100 |
| *Phyllanthus emblica* | 51, 54, 57, 66, 84, 91, 96, 100, 108, 119, 139, **190–2** |
| *Piper betle* | 43 |
| *Piper nigrum* | 47, 49 |
| Piperaceae | 75–6 |
| *Platanus orientalis* | 126 |
| *Plecospermum spinosum* | 63, 110 |
| *Pleurostylia opposita* | 95 |
| Poaceae | 59, 75, 77, 80, 84–5 |
| Poaceae-Bambusoideae | 51, 54–5 |
| *Podocarpus wallichiana* | 128 |
| *Poeciloneuron indicum* | 48, 95 |
| *Polyalthia* | 49, 91, 93, 133, 139, 143, **151–3** |
| *Polyalthia cerasoides, P. korinthi, P. longifolia, P. suberosa* | 93 |
| *Polyalthia coffeoides, P. rufescens* | 49, 93 |
| *Polyalthia fragrans* | 49, 93, 143, **151–3** |
| *Polygala chinensis* | 66 |
| *Polygonum* | 84 |
| *Polykrikos swartzii* | 85 |
| *Polysphaeridium zoharyi* | 85 |
| *Pongamia pinnata* | 60 |
| *Portulaca* | 77 |
| *Potamogeton* | 84 |
| *Premna* | 119 |
| *Prosopis* | 23, 46, 54, 59–60, 63, 65, 80, 82, 104, 106 |

| | |
|---|---|
| *Prosopis cineraria* (syn. *P. spicigera*) | 54, 60, 63, 65, 106 |
| *Prosopis juliflora* | 60, 106 |
| *Protium serratum* | 94 |
| *Psidium* | 112 |
| *Pterocarpus* | 33, 50–2, 54–6, 65, 91, 106–8, 117, 119, 138, 143, **222–3** |
| *Pterocarpus marsupium* | 50–2, 54–6, 65, 91, 108, 119, 143, **222–3** |
| *Pterocarpus santalinus* | 33, 55, 106, 108, 117 |
| *Pterolobium hexapetalum* | 63, 66, 102 |
| *Pterospermum* | 46, 49, 51, 63, 118, 139, 142, **278–80** |
| *Pterospermum diversifolium* | 51, 118, 142, **278–80** |
| *Pterospermum suberifolium* | 63, 118 |
| *Pterospermum xylocarpum* | 51, 118 |
| *Pterygota alata* | 118 |
| *Punica granatum* | 126 |
| *Randia* | 63, 113 |
| *Randia malabarica* | 63 |
| Ranunculaceae | 77 |
| Rhamnaceae | 54–5, 57, 59, 63–4, 113, 138, **252** |
| *Rhamnus wightii* | 113 |
| *Rhododendron* | 77 |
| *Rhodomyrtus tomentosa* | 112 |
| *Rhus* | 57, 90–1 |
| *Rhus mysorensis* (syn. *R. sinuata*) | 57, 90–1 |
| *Rivea hypocrateriformis* | 63 |
| Rizophoraceae | 75 |
| Rosaceae | 73, 77 |
| *Rotula aquatica* | 60, 99 |
| *Rubia* | 50–1, 67 |
| *Rubia cordifolia* | 50, 67 |
| Rubiaceae | 49, 51, 54–5, 59–60, 63–4, 113, 137, 139, **254, 256, 259, 261, 263** |
| Rutaceae | 54–5, 57, 63, 94, 109–10, 114, 139, **267, 269** |
| Rutoideae | 114 |
| *Saccharum* | 67 |
| *Sageretia parviflora* | 113 |
| *Salvadora* | 46, 73 |
| *Salvadora persica* | 73 |
| Santalaceae | 54–5, 63, 116, 137, **271** |
| *Santalum album* | 54–6, 65, 73, 116, 135, 137, 140, **271–2** |
| Sapindaceae | 49, 51, 54–5, 63–4, 117, 138–9, **273, 276** |
| *Sapindus emarginatus* | 117 |
| Sapotaceae | 49, 51, 63 |
| *Saraca asoca* | 102 |
| *Saraca indica* | 100 |
| *Sarcostemma acidum* | 64 |
| *Schleichera* | 50–1, 54–5, 64, 84, 91, 117–9, 138, **276–7** |
| *Schleichera oleosa* | 50–1, 54–5, 64, 91, 117–9, **276–7** |
| *Scutia myrtina* | 113 |
| *Scyphiphora hydrophyllacea* | 113 |
| *Securinega* | 57, 63–4, 66, 101, 139, **193–4** |
| *Securinega leucopyrus* | 57, 63–4, 66, 101, **193–4** |

| | |
|---|---|
| *Securinega virosa* | 101 |
| *Sehima* | 57, 66–7 |
| *Sehima nervosum, S. sulcata* | 66 |
| *Selaginella* | 48 |
| *Senecio* | 77 |
| *Setaria* | 39–40, 58–9, 66, 131–2 |
| *Setaria pumila* | 58, 66 |
| *Setaria verticillata* | 39, 131 |
| *Shorea* | 23, 46, 56, 72, 84, 97, 115, 120 |
| *Shorea robusta* | 23, 72, 84, 97, 120 |
| *Shorea talura, S. tumbuggaia* | 97 |
| *Sida cordifolia* | 66 |
| *Smilacaceae* | 54 |
| *Smilax zeylanica* | 54 |
| *Smythea bombaiensis* | 113 |
| *Solanum* | 84 |
| *Soymida febrifuga* | 54–6, 65, 109–10, 133, 138, 142, **235–6** |
| *Spiniferites bentori, S. mirabilis, S. pachydermus, S. ramosus* | 85 |
| *Spondias mangifera* | 65, 89 |
| *Stenosiphonium* | 63 |
| *Sterculia* | 50, 94, 118 |
| *Sterculia guttata* | 118 |
| *Sterculia urens* | 94, 118 |
| Sterculiaceae | 49, 51, 63, 94, 118, 139, **278** |
| *Streblus asper* | 110, 138, **242–3** |
| *Strobilanthes* | 48, 77 |
| *Strychnos* | 54–6, 63, 65, 108–9, 134–5, 139, **224–6** |
| *Strychnos colubrina* | 55, 63 |
| *Strychnos nux-vomica* | 54, 56, 108, 140, **224–5** |
| *Strychnos potatorum* | 55, 108–9, **224, 226** |
| *Swintonia* | 147 |
| *Symplocos* | 46, 115 |
| *Syzygium* | 46, 48–9, 51, 57, 60, 65, 91, 108, 112–3, 115, 119, 130, 139, **250–1** |
| *Syzygium cumini* (=*Eugenia jambolana*) | 48, 49, 51, 57, 60, 65, 91, 108, 112–3, 119, **250–1** |
| *Syzygium gardneri* | 49 |
| *Syzygium heyneanum* | 60, 112 |
| Tamaricaceae | 60 |
| *Tamarindus indica* | 54–5, 57, 60, 63, 73, 102–3, 137–8, **206–7** |
| *Tamarix* | 59–60 |
| *Tamarix ericoides* | 60 |
| *Tarenna asiatica* | 63, 113 |
| *Tectona* | 23, 46, 51–2, 54–5, 65–6, 73, 87, 91, 94, 99, 108, 115, 119–20, 130–3, 137, 140, **287–9** |
| *Tectona grandis* | 23, 51–2, 54–5, 65–6, 73, 91, 94, 108, 119–20, 140, **287–9** |
| *Tephrosia purpurea* | 66 |
| *Terminalia* | 46, 51–2, 54–6, 58–60, 65, 74, 84, 87, 94, 96–7, 99–100, 108, 115, 119, 130, 133, 138, 141–2, **171–4** |
| *Terminalia arjuna* | 60, 96–7, **171–2** |
| *Terminalia bellerica* | 51, 65, 96–7, 100 |

| | |
|---|---|
| *Terminalia catappa* | 96 |
| *Terminalia chebula* | 54, 96–7, 100 |
| *Terminalia coriacea* | 96 |
| *Terminalia crenulata* | 51 |
| *Terminalia elliptica* | 54, 96 |
| *Terminalia paniculata* | 46, 51, 65, 130, **171–3** |
| *Terminalia tomentosa* | 51–2, 54, 56, 58–9, 65, 94, 96, 141–2, **171**, **173**, **174** |
| *Terminalia travancorensis* | 96 |
| *Tetracera laevis* | 97 |
| *Tetrameles nudiflora* | 49, 51 |
| *Themeda quadrivalvis, T. triandra* | 66 |
| *Thraulococcus erectus* | 117 |
| *Thyrsodium* | 147 |
| Tiliaceae | 49, 51, 54–5, 57, 59, 63, 118, 137, **281**, **283** |
| *Toona* | 46, 115 |
| *Trema* | 51, 59, 77 |
| *Trema orientalis* | 51, 59 |
| *Trewia* | 59, 100 |
| *Triticum* | 131 |
| *Triumfetta* | 66, 118 |
| *Triumfetta bartramia* | 66 |
| *Tuberculodium van campoe* | 85 |
| Tubuliflorae | 84 |
| *Tylophora indica* | 63 |
| *Typha* | 80, 84 |
| Ulmaceae | 51, 59 |
| *Urochloa panicoides* | 66 |
| Urticaceae | 54, 60, 63, 75–6, 84 |
| *Vangueria spinosa* | 113 |
| *Vateria indica* | 48–9, 97 |
| *Vatica chinensis* | 97 |
| *Ventilago* | 113 |
| Verbenaceae | 49, 51, 54–5, 59–60, 63, 119, 137, **285**, **287**, **290** |
| *Vigna* | 39–40, 52, 72, 87, 131 |
| *Vigna mungo* | 40, 52 |
| *Vigna radiata* | 39–40, 131 |
| *Vigna radiata* ssp. *sublobata* | 52 |
| Vitaceae | 63 |
| *Vitex* | 49, 51, 54–5, 59, 119–20, 137, **290–1** |
| *Vitex altissima* | 49, 51, 54–5, 120, **290–1** |
| *Vitex leucoxylon* | 59, 120 |
| *Vitex negundo* | 60, 120 |
| *Wendlandia notoniana, W. tinctoria* | 113 |
| *Woodfordia fruticosa* | 109 |
| *Wrightia* | 54–5, 56, 65–6, 93–4, 139, **156–7** |
| *Wrightia arborea* | 93–4 |
| *Wrightia tinctoria* | 54, 55–6, 65–6, 93–4, **156–7** |
| *Wrightia tomentosa* | 54, 65, 93 |
| *Xeromphis spinosa* | 54–5, 64, 66 |
| *Xylia* | 51–2, 66, 72, 104, 106, 138, **215–6** |
| *Xylia xylocarpa* | 51, 66, 72, 104, 106, **215–6** |
| *Zanthoxylum* | 114–5 |

| | |
|---|---|
| *Zanthoxylum rhetsa* (syn. *Fagara budrunga*) | 115 |
| *Zingiber officinale* | 49 |
| *Ziziphus* | 46, 54, 55–7, 59, 63–7, 113, 138, **252–3** |
| *Ziziphus caracutta*, *Z. horrida*, *Z. rugosa*, *Z. williamii* | 113 |
| *Ziziphus glaberrima* | 63 |
| *Ziziphus glabrata* | 63, 113 |
| *Ziziphus mauritiana* | 54, 57, 64–7, 113, **252–3** |
| *Ziziphus nummularia* | 63, 113 |
| *Ziziphus oenoplia* | 54–5, 63, 113 |
| *Ziziphus xylopyrus* | 54–5, 63–6, 113 |
| *Zornia diphylla* | 66 |

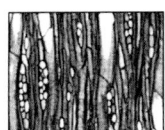

# SUBJECT INDEX

| | |
|---|---|
| Adam Cave | 100 |
| agriculture, origins of | 10, 12, 36–42, 63, 67, 79, 81, 84, 129–32 |
| alcohol, alcoholic beverages | 51 |
| Anamallai Hills | 90, 97 |
| anthropogenic vegetation (see also deforestation; ruined landscape; dry evergreen) | 10, 20, 21, 27, 35, 45, 49, 57, 64, 68–9, 73, 76, 79, 81, 82, 83, 85, 86, 87, 90, 104, 132, 133 |
| Aravalli Hills | 54 |
| Arikamedu | 124 |
| ashmounds | 12, 33, 35, 36, 39, 40, 41, 87, 100, 129, 131, 132, 133 |
| Baber | 92 |
| Balfour, Isaac | 19, 22 |
| Balu | 96 |
| Banawali | 98 |
| black wood | 49, 98, 107, 108 |
| Berijam Lake | 77 |
| Bews, John Williams | 22 |
| biotic forests, vegetation | 45, 59 |
| Brahmagiri | 36, 41 |
| Brandis, Dietrich | 23, 25, 104 |
| Breuil, Henri | 121 |
| Budihal | 41, 99, 100, 131 |
| burning, anthropogenic | 9, 12, 23, 25, 27, 35, 36, 40, 52, 57, 64, 68, 69, 76, 79, 81, 82, 84, 87, 104, 120 |
| Champion, Harry G. | 17, 18, 20, 25, 45, 59 |
| chickens (*Gallus gallus*) | 41, 91 |
| Chowdhury, K. A. | 124, 125 |
| cinnamon (see *Cinnamomum* in taxonomic index) | 101–2 |
| *Citrus* fruits | 114–15 |
| Cleghorn, Hugh | 18, 26 |
| Clements, Frederic | 17, 19, 22, 23, 25 |
| climate | 9, 10, 11, 17, 20, 22, 23, 29, 32–3, 45, 47, 59, 64, 68, 71, 73, 74, 77, 78, 83, 84, 85, 86, 92, 120, 121, 122, 125, 131, 132 |
| climatic proxies (see palaeoenvironment) | |
| climax | 10, 15, 17–20, 22, 23, 45, 52, 57, 84, 122 |
| collapse of cities (third millennium BC) | 83 |
| colonial period | 10, 16–20, 25, 26, 42–3, 49, 57, 92, 93, 98, 102, 107, 117, 120, 124 |
| colonial science, forestry | 15–20 |
| copper | 40, 41 |
| coppice | 51, 52, 57, 100, 101, 102, 105, 106, 107 |
| cordage (see fibres) | |
| Couvert, M. | 122 |

| | |
|---|---|
| cultivation (see agriculture) | |
| custard apple | 92 |
| Dangs, tribe | 26, 51 |
| Deccan Trap (geology) | 29, 33, 34, 39, 54, 64, 105, 106 |
| deforestation | 10, 16, 17, 20, 26, 103, 121 |
| Delhi Sultanate | 42 |
| Dhavalikar, M. K. | 42 |
| Didwana | 78, 79–83 |
| Dimbleby, Geoffrey | 9, 128 |
| disjunct distribution | 71–3, 95, 97, 101, 104, 106, 120 |
| domestication (see agriculture) | |
| Dravidian linguistics | 89, 90, 91, 97, 99, 104, 107, 108, 109, 110, 111, 112, 113, 115, 117, 118, 119, 120 |
| drought | 18, 33 |
| drought tolerant | 64, 65, 76, 79, 82, 83, 104 |
| dry deciduous | 10, 21, 45, 46, 50, 51, 52–7, 58, 59, 60, 64, 66, 67, 73, 76, 83, 84, 85, 87, 128, 131, 132, 133, 135 |
| dry evergreen | 9, 10, 33, 45, 46, 50, 58, 59–67, 81, 87, 133 |
| dry season | 33, 48, 49, 50, 52, 57, 59, 68, 73, 74, 107, 115, 119 |
| dung, cattle | 11, 12, 39, 40 |
| dye, dyestuffs | 50, 51, 56, 67, 94, 105, 107, 108, 109, 111, 115, 118 |
| ebony | 49, 98, 105, 107, 108 |
| ecology, origins of science of | 17–20 |
| edaphic vegetation | 45, 57 |
| ethnographic analogy (in wood charcoal studies) | 124 |
| environmental archaeology | 10, 11–3, 15, 86 |
| epiphytes | 50, 52 |
| Erramalai Hills | 35, 52, 64, 95, 105 |
| extinction | 16, 73 |
| fibres, sources of | 56, 105, 110, 112, 118, 119 |
| fire | 10, 52, 63, 66, 68, 69, 126, 127 |
| fish poisons | 101, 108, 118 |
| fodder | 11, 25, 68, 95, 103, 106, 108, 112, 117, 119 |
| Foote, Robert Bruce | 36 |
| forest, definition of | 16 |
| fruits, edible | 11, 12, 23, 51, 56, 57, 82, 90, 91, 93, 94, 95, 96, 97, 99, 100, 101, 103, 105, 110, 111, 112, 113, 114, 115, 117, 119 |
| geology | 29, 33–5 |
| Ghosh, S. S. | 124 |
| Godwin, Harry | 122 |
| Gond, tribes | 51, 56, 57, 69 |
| grasses, grasslands | 10, 12, 15, 20, 21, 32, 45, 46, 52, 54, 55, 57, 58, 59, 60, 61, 62, 63, 64, 66, 67, 68, 73, 74, 76, 77, 79, 81, 82, 83, 84, 85, 87, 129, 132, 133 |
| grazing (see also fodder; anthropogenic vegetation) | 9, 10, 11, 20, 23, 25, 27, 52, 55, 57, 63, 64, 66, 67, 68, 74, 84, 93, 104, 105, 116, 130 |
| Grove, A. T. | 16 |
| Grove, Richard | 17, 18 |
| Gujarat | 9, 51, 52, 58, 64, 76, 81, 83, 94, 95, 96, 98, 120 |
| gums (see also resins) | 50, 56, 90, 94, 105, 106, 107, 108, 110, 111, 114 |
| Hallur | 34, 36, 41, 91, 131, 133, 134 |

| | |
|---|---|
| Harappan cultures, Harappan civilization | 40, 58, 79, 83, 86, 96, 98, 99, 107, 108, 109, 115, 119, 126 |
| Heer, O. | 121 |
| Himalayas | 9, 73, 91, 98, 115, 116, 125 |
| Hiregudda | 41 |
| Holocene | 11, 23, 27, 36, 50, 71, 74, 76, 77, 79, 81, 82, 83, 132, 134 |
| honey | 12, 48, 49, 50 |
| Humbolt, Alexander von | 16, 17 |
| Ibn Batuta | 102 |
| Ibn Hawqal | 91 |
| Impaghat | 30, 132 |
| impregnation of charcoals | 123 |
| Inamgaon | 57, 90, 99, 100 |
| incense | 56, 67, 94 |
| Iron Age | 36, 41, 42, 58, 86, 96, 100 |
| isotopes, stable | 10 |
| jackfruit (see *Artocarpus heterophylla* in taxonomic index) | |
| Jane, F. W. | 121, 122 |
| Java | 73, 116, 117, 120 |
| jungle | 16–7, 42 |
| Kakathope Swamp | 76, 77 |
| Kandenmari Hills, or Kandrnmarai | 30, 132 |
| Kaothe | 40 |
| Kodekal | 36, 41 |
| Kunal | 99, 100 |
| kumri (see shifting cultivation) | |
| lac | 25, 42, 50, 55, 56, 64, 107, 117, 118, 119 |
| legume, crops (see pulses) | |
| light availability | 10, 65, 68–9 |
| lightening strikes | 68 |
| limiting factors | 68–70 |
| livestock (see also fodder) | 12, 16, 36, 39, 42, 57, 63, 67, 79, 82, 86, 87, 105, 132, 133 |
| longan (fruit) | 117 |
| Lunkaransar | 78, 79–83 |
| Madhya Pradesh, pollen data from | 81, 83–4 |
| Maiden Castle, Dorset | 121 |
| Malwan Lake, Gujarat | 83 |
| mangrove | 45, 85, 113 |
| mango (see *Mangifera indica* in taxonomic index) | |
| medicinal plants | 12, 25, 48, 51, 56, 57, 89, 94, 95, 96, 97, 99, 101, 102, 105, 106, 108, 109, 110, 114, 115, 116, 118, 124, 135 |
| Megalithic (see also Iron Age) | 36, 41, 42, 117 |
| Meluhha | 98, 107, 108 |
| Mesolithic | 76, 79, 135 |
| Milankovitch cycles | 74 |
| millet, crops | 40, 57, 58, 59, 67, 131, 134 |
| minor forest products | 43 |
| Miri Qalat | 119 |

| | |
|---|---|
| moist deciduous | 10, 20, 21, 45, 47, 48, 49, 50, 51, 52, 54, 55, 58, 59, 72, 85, 87, 90, 91, 93, 95, 96, 97, 98, 99, 100, 101, 102, 103, 106, 107, 109, 110, 111, 112, 113, 114, 117, 118, 119, 120, 129, 131, 132, 133, 134 |
| monsoon (see climate) | |
| Mughals, Mughal Empire | 16, 43, 117 |
| Nal Sarovar, Gujarat | 83 |
| Nallamalai Hills | 33, 35, 50, 52, 55, 59, 87, 102, 108, 109, 132 |
| Narsipur | 36, 41 |
| Navdatoli | 56, 100 |
| neem (see *Azadirachta indica* in taxonomic index) | |
| Neolithic | 10, 12, 32, 34, 35, 36, 37, 39, 40, 41, 42, 51, 57, 58, 59, 63, 67, 82, 86, 87, 91, 99, 100, 113, 115, 117, 121, 126, 129, 130, 131, 132, 133, 134, 135 |
| Neyveli Basin | 76 |
| Nilgiri Hills | 20, 29, 33, 35, 76, 77, 112 |
| oil, edible | 51, 95–6, 110, 117 |
| Palni Hills (see Nilgiri Hills) | |
| palaeoenvironment | 10, 11, 45, 71–86 |
| Palaeolithic | 35, 64, 121, 122 |
| Palavoy | 41, 133 |
| Passerini, G. | 121 |
| pastoralism (see livestock) | |
| Paiyampalli | 36, 41 |
| Periplus of the Erythraean Sea | 94, 98, 107, 116 |
| Piklihal | 36, 41 |
| Pleistocene | 21, 35, 36, 71, 73, 74, 76, 79, 110, 132 |
| pollen | 10, 11, 20, 23, 35, 69, 71, 74, 75, 76, 77, 78, 79, 80, 81, 82, 83, 84, 85, 86, 110, 121, 122, 125 |
| Pochangat | 30, 132 |
| potential vegetation (see climax) | |
| pulses, crops (see also *Macrotyloma uniflorum*; *Vigna* spp. in taxonomic index) | 39, 52, 57, 67, 72, 73, 87 |
| Rackham, Oliver | 16 |
| rainfall | 9, 29, 45, 46, 50, 52, 55, 59, 68 |
| rainforest (see wet evergreen) | |
| rainshadow | 32–3 |
| Rajasthan | 9, 23, 36, 39, 48, 58, 64, 67, 76, 79, 81, 82, 95, 96 |
| red sanders (see *Pterocarpus santalinus* in taxonomic index) | |
| Rees corner | 76, 77 |
| refugia | 74–5 |
| resins (see also gums) | 12, 48, 50, 56, 67, 94, 106, 108, 114, 116, 123 |
| rice, crop | 41, 58, 103, 108, 112 |
| riverine vegetation | 45, 57–9, 60, 83, 91, 96, 112 |
| rivers | 29 |
| Rohira | 109 |
| rosewood, Indian | 107 |
| Roxburgh, William | 17, 18, 20, 22, 89, 104, 107, 109, 120 |
| ruined landscape, theory of | 16 |
| sacred groves | 23, 25 |

| | |
|---|---|
| sal (see *Shorea robusta* in taxonomic index) | |
| sandalwood (see *Santalum album* in taxonomic index) | |
| Sandur Hills | 52, 53, 109, 118 |
| Sandynallah, pollen core | 76, 77 |
| Santa, S. | 122 |
| Sanganakallu | 36, 41, 51, 91, 117, 133, 134, 135 |
| Sanghol | 92, 97, 115, 117, 126 |
| Satpura Hills | 91 |
| Sauer, Carl | 11, 22 |
| savanna (see grasslands) | |
| scrub woodland (see also dry evergreen) | 10, 12, 15, 45 |
| sedentism | 10, 12, 17, 36, 41, 42, 82, 83, 86, 132, 133 |
| Semthan, Kashmir | 126 |
| shade (see light availability) | |
| Shevaroy Hills | 91 |
| shifting cultivation | 17, 25, 26, 131 |
| shola (see Nilgiri Hills) | |
| Siddapur Hills | 48, |
| silk | 25, 55, 56, 73, 110, 116, 118, 126 |
| Simlipal Hills | 49 |
| Sirumalai Hills | 50, 90, 95, 101 |
| sisso (see *Dalbergia sissoo* in taxonomic index) | |
| Smuts, General Jan Christian | 19, 22 |
| soapnut | 117 |
| soils | 10, 20, 45 |
| Southeast Asia | 9 |
| spices | 23, 26, 43, 47, 49, 102, 114, 117 |
| Sri Lanka | 33, 42, 72, 73, 74, 93, 97, 98, 101, 102, 117 |
| subsistence practices (see also livestock; agriculture) | 12, 17, 25, 26, 39, 40, 41, 42, 57, 86, 132, 133, 135 |
| succession, plant | 19 |
| tamarind (see also *Tamarindus indica* in taxonomic index) | 103–4 |
| Tansley, Arthur | 17–20, 122 |
| taphonomy, of archaeobotanical remains | 11, 122, 124, 126–27 |
| tasar (see silk) | |
| teak (see *Tectona grandis* in taxonomic index) | |
| Tekkalakota | 36, 41, 133, 134 |
| textiles (see also silk; dye) | 12, 41, 67 |
| Thoreau, Henry David | 16 |
| timber species | 15, 16, 19, 23, 25, 43, 48, 49, 51, 52, 55, 96, 97, 98, 100, 101, 103, 105, 106, 107, 108, 109, 112, 114, 115, 120, 121, 122, 124, 125, 126, 129 |
| time resolution (of charcoal assemblages) | 126–27 |
| trade | 12, 42, 49, 86, 87, 107, 116, 121, 125 |
| tribal communities (see also Dangs; Gond) | 12, 17 |
| triphala ('three fruits') | 96, 100 |
| Troup, Robert | 20 |
| turnover pulse hypothesis | 73 |
| Utnur | 36, 41 |
| Veerapuram | 41 |
| Velakonda Hills | 35 |

| | |
|---|---|
| Velpumagudu | 41 |
| Vijayanagar | 42 |
| villages (see sedentism) | |
| Vindyan plateau and hills | 54, 99 |
| Vishnu-Mittre | 125 |
| Watgal | 36, 41, 131 |
| weeds (of crops) | 58, 84, 131 |
| Western Ghats | 16, 23, 25, 26, 29, 32, 33, 35, 46, 47, 48, 49, 50, 51, 52, 55, 59, 71, 72, 74, 76, 87, 89, 90, 91, 93, 94, 95, 96, 97, 99, 100, 101, 102, 103, 106, 107, 108, 109, 110, 111, 113, 114, 115, 117, 118, 129, 131, 132, 133, 134 |
| wet evergreen | 10, 20, 23, 32, 45, 46, 47, 48, 49, 50, 52, 65, 72, 74, 76, 85, 87, 89, 90, 91, 93, 95, 96, 97, 98, 100, 101, 102, 104, 108, 109, 110, 112, 113, 117, 118, 128 |
| Wheeler, Mortimor | 124 |
| wild progenitors, of crops | 52, 57–9, 67, 72, 87, 131, 132 |
| wood anatomy | 127–29 |
| wood charcoal, methodology | 11, 121–29 |

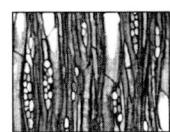

# ABOUT THE AUTHORS

**Eleni Asouti** is Lecturer in Environmental Archaeology at the School of Archaeology, Classics, and Egyptology, University of Liverpool. Her research and teaching interests include environmental and landscape archaeology, the prehistory and palaeoecology of the Eastern Mediterranean and South Asia, the prehistory and socioeconomics of ancient subsistence practices, and the Early Neolithic of Western Asia. She has previously held a Leverhulme Trust Research Fellowship at the Institute of Archaeology, University College London, and is currently involved in a number of research projects in Turkey, Jordan, Greece, and South India.

**Dorian Q. Fuller** is Lecturer in Archaeobotany at the Institute of Archaeology, University College London. His research focuses on human plant use in prehistory (with emphasis on food production and consumption), the prehistory and palaeoecology of South Asia and Africa, and the origins and spread of agriculture and crop domestication worldwide. He is currently undertaking research in Sudan, South Asia and China.